# ARCHAEOLOGY, ANTHROPOLOGY AND HERITAGE IN THE BALKANS AND ANATOLIA: THE LIFE AND TIMES OF F.W. HASLUCK, 1878-1920

Edited by

## David Shankland

Volume II

THE ISIS PRESS
ISTANBUL

Margaret Hardie (Mrs. F. W. Hasluck)

# ARCHAEOLOGY, ANTHROPOLOGY AND HERITAGE IN THE BALKANS AND ANATOLIA: THE LIFE AND TIMES OF F.W. HASLUCK, 1878-1920

© 2004 The Isis Press

*Published by*
The Isis Press
Şemsibey Sokak 10
Beylerbeyi, 34676 Istanbul
Tel.: (0216) 321 38 51
Fax.: (0216) 321 86 66
e-mail: isis@tnn.net
www.theisispress.org

First edition 2004

ISBN: 975-428-280-3
975-428-282-X

# CONTENTS OF VOLUME TWO

## PART FIVE:
## TRAVELLERS, EMPIRE AND NATION

## PART SIX:
## ARCHAEOLOGY, HERITAGE AND IDEOLOGY

*APPENDICES*

# PREFACE TO VOLUME TWO

This is the second volume of two devoted to the exploration of the life and works of Hasluck, the Assistant Director and Librarian of the British School at Athens in the years before the First World War. In the first was found an introductory account of his life, and diverse chapters on the schools and institutes abroad. It also covered his ethnographic work amongst the Alevi-Kızılbaş, and some account of their present situation.

This second volume extends the project's coverage by looking at other aspects of Hasluck's intellectual project, specificially questions of religious syncretism and conversion, the transition from empire to nation, and, finally, the relationship between archaeology, nationalism and heritage. Each contribution treats different chronological periods and epochs. For instance, in Part One Kamara and Stewart look at conversion to Christianity from Paganism; Hopwood, Shukurov and Simonian examine the gradual Turkification of Anatolia, whilst Baer describes the more direct religious influence of the Sultan after the establishment of the Ottomans in Istanbul. In total, the twelve chapters in this part provide detailed ethnographic insight into the phenomenon of religious and cultural interaction in different epochs.

The following section examines the incursion of the West into the Ottoman Empire, and the later emergence of nation state. For example, Wagstaff writes on Leake, and his uncertain relationship with the Ottomans, whilst Bakırer describes the many travellers in Istanbul who, in spite of their indisputable inadequacies, have left an invaluable accumulative record of Topkapı Palace. The emergence of nationalism, and its impact upon local populations, is covered in Hirschon's account of the *Rum* Greeks who came to Greece after the Great War, and, conversely by Tsibiridou's depiction of the *Pomak*s who were left behind in Komitini.

The third section looks specifically at the relationship between ideology, nationalism and archaeology in its modern setting. Özdoğan's comparative historical account is followed by a specific account of the use of archaeology and the past in Greek national history by Demetriou. Ergenekon describes the present-day place of archaeological remains with regard to Datcha, (the site that the British School at Athens were disappointed at not being able to dig at the beginning of the twentieth century). Nixon, in a most suggestive article, looks at the way encompassing visions of the past may impact on a society's interaction with archaeological remains. I offer the final chapter as an instance of the way I think anthropology could benefit enormously from taking more systematic notice of the work conducted by archaeologists. The reverse of course has already occurred, in that archaeology, and archaeologists, are increasingly learned with regard to social anthropology. It is surely time that we anthropologists return the compliment.

# PART FOUR

# SYNCRETISM AND CONVERSION

# 17. CHRISTIAN-MUSLIM SYMBIOSIS IN ANATOLIA

## Keith HOPWOOD

> At the first appearance of the Ottomans, towards the close of the thirteenth century, Christians and Turks had already been living for two centuries side by side in the interior of Asia Minor under the rule of Seljuks of Rum.[1]

So Hasluck, in one of the later chapters of his posthumously published work, *Christianity and Islam under the Sultans*, characterises the beginnings of Moslem-Christian symbiosis which that work so lovingly depicts. He cites as evidence shared shrines such as the old Greek monastery of St Chariton near Konya,[2] the possible representation or even burial of Eusebios (Efsepi) or St Chariton in the mausoleum of Mevlana himself,[3] the shrine of Shams-ed-Din of Tabriz (rumoured by the German Schiltberger to be a crypto-Christian) in Konya,[4] and the church of St Amphilochius of Konya, seen as the burial place of Plato as well as of its eponymous saint.[5]

Other than that, the periods of Konya's splendour are those of Ala'ud-Din Keykubad I (1219-34) and Jelal-ud-Din Rumi (Mevlana) (1207-1273/7). Most of the evidence he cites refers to the period after Jelal-ud-Din arrived in Konya (c.1233). The evidence consists of the Manâqib ul-'arifîn of Eflaki and some inscriptions from the church of the monastery of St Chariton.

Let us deal with these texts in turn. Eflaki[6] wrote a work consisting of a series of reminiscences concerning Jelal-ud-Din's predecessor, the great man himself, and some of his successors. The material does not seem to be grouped under any heading either by subject matter or by informants, yet its cumulative power is undeniable. It is a chronicle of a group of mystics who are attempting to find a spiritual path for their society that is in union with the will of God, based on a deep study of the philological and esoteric

---

[1] Hasluck (1929; 370).
[2] Hasluck (1929; 373-4).
[3] Hasluck (1929; 375).
[4] Hasluck (1929; 376).
[5] Hasluck (1929; 364-5).
[6] French tr. by Huart (1918-22).

meanings of the verses of the Koran, the *hadith*, and personal revelation. It is also aimed at encouraging faltering Muslims, oversecular Muslim rulers like the Mongol-appointed viceroy Mu'in-ud-Din himself, and outsiders, like the local Jewish and Christian communities, who are depicted going about their ordinary lives. It might be objected that this is a literary text of, in many cases, dubious historicity.[1] Nevertheless, such texts must still be convincing: the reality-effect of Roland Barthes[2] must apply even to such texts. The readers of the text cannot have found it odd that thirteenth century Konya was what we now call a 'multi-faith community'. This impression is strengthened in that it draws no attention to the everyday activities of non-Muslims. In nearly every case, the remark is a 'throw-away', not central to the narrative of the text. Even subconsciously, the text reinforces the picture.

That, however having been said, this is protreptic literature. The reader is encouraged to join the Mevlevi order, be they Jew, Christian or Muslim. Consequently, although the text gives ample evidence of Konya being a multi-faith community, the textual hermeneutic leads to conversion. This can be simple or complex. On one occasion, a dervish asks a Rabbi, 'Which of ours is the better faith?'. The Jew immediately gives in and becomes a Muslim.[3]

A more complex story has a Christian architect working on Jelal-ud-Din's house. Jocularly the associates of Jelal-ud-Din say 'Why don't you become a Muslim, as Islam is the better religion'. [4] The joke has a sour taste to modern ears. Richard Wagner taunted the Jewish conductor, Hermann Levi, whose skill he needed for the performance of his last work *Parsifal*, with pleas for his baptism and hoped to join him for his first communion.[5] However, Eflaki allows his Christian a dignified response: 'I have been a Christian for fifty years, and I would be ashamed to give up the religion of Jesus'. This view is surprisingly endorsed by the sudden appearance of Jelal-ud-Din who pronounces 'The mystery of faith is belief: whoever believes in God, even if he is Christian, is not irreligious, but pious'. At once, the architect converts to Islam. Other evidence suggests that Mevlana was not blind to the power of Christianity or Byzantine civilisation. His wife, Kyra Hatun (given her name), was almost certainly a Christian convert .

---

[1] Recently argued by Lewis (2000; 249-53).
[2] As discussed by Culler (1975; 193-4).
[3] 352; Huart (1918-22, Vol. 2; 9).
[4] 345; Huart (1918-22, Vol. 2; 3).
[5] Incident cited by Gutman (1968; 578-9).

The only Christian who does not convert to Islam is the abbot of the 'monks of the monastery of Plato'. Jelal-ud-Din visits him and stays in a cold water bath for seven days.[1] It is clear from the text that part of Jelal-ud-Din's appeal is his ability in asceticism and the mortification of the flesh. The abbot 'who had sought knowledge in Constantinople, in the land of the Franks, in Sis, and Trebizond[2] could compare Christian sages with Jelal-ud-Din. Here might be one reason for cultural change and cohabitation — the stories were the same.[3]

We shall return to Eflaki. A contemporary inscription was recorded on the walls of St Chariton and reproduced by Hasluck.[4] It dates the text 'in the patriarchy of the ecumenical patriarch his excellency Gregory, in the reign of the most pious king and emperor of the Romans his excellency Anronikos, in the days when the great Sultan of mighty family Mahsoud, son of Kaika us our lord (avthendis) in the anno mundi 6797, second indiction (AD 1289)'. For Hasluck, this attests that 'the relations between Christianity and Islam under the Seljuks of Konia were very friendly'. He is, of course, broadly right, but we can make the picture more subtle.

The reconstruction of the church was carried out by the hieromonk Matthew. As benefactor he would either compose, or at least, approve the draft of the dedicatory inscription. We have here the self-definition of a Christian after a century of Seljuk dominion. Firstly, as a Christian he cites the patriarch in Constantinople (Gregory II, 1283-89), as Christians 'in partibus infidelium' had since the conquest of Egypt by the Arabs in the seventh century. The placing of the doctrinal allegiance is paramount. Next follows the name of the Byzantine emperor who was the secular patron of Orthodox Christians overseas. Commerce between Constantinople and Konya was sufficient to allow knowledge of the proper titles of the Emperor to filter through to his faithful subjects under infidel rule. Then we have the local ruler, whose titles are preceded by the formula 'en tais hemerais' and suggest (possibly hopefully?) the ephemeral nature of his rule, and then the name with the Byzantine title of respect. That this was to become the major Turkish form of address attests to the survival of the Byzantine honorific tradition within the Turkish system. A contemporary survival of Byzantine life stands in the Turkish 'efendi'!

---

[1] 242; Huart (1918-22, Vol.1; 261).

[2] This is not impossible. Before the death of Jelal ud-Din in 1273,Byzantine embassies had travelled to Rome in 1263 and 1266, to Genoa in 1261, and to France in 1270. Geanakopolos (1959; passim).

[3] One can compare the recounts of strenuous ascetism in the *Tales of the Desert Fathers* or Palladius' *Lausiac History*. Just as Jelal ud-Din can move about miraculously, so could Orthodox holy men.

[4] Hasluck (1929; 381-2).

We then have the *anno mundi* date which the early Christians had used — not AD dates.[1] The Christians of Konya were tied to the Divine act of creation of the Universe.[2] The finite 'in the days of Sultan Mas'ud' contrasts with the eternity of the Judaeo-Christian tradition. The Hieromonk Matthew was hedging his bets in a rapidly changing world.

It is necessary now to consider the antecedents to this world: how had it become possible for such inter-faith acceptance to exist in Konya? More to the point, how could people, like the hieromonk Matthew, carry such a complex array of cultural and political loyalties? The answer lies in the nature of the Turkish conquest of Anatolia.

Türkmen had raided Anatolia before 1071,[3] but it was the defeat of the Byzantine field army and the capture of the Emperor by Alp Arslan in that year that opened Asia Minor to the Türkmen.[4] These were semi-nomads, the Turks who had refused to settle on the land of the Great Seljuks of Iran and had been extruded to the frontiers where they found a new way of life in pillaging the infidel and thereby carrying in the ghaza.[5] The early Turkish epics of the *Book of Dede Korkut* and the *Danişmendname* depict them as mounted. (There is also a rare Seljuk relief showing a mounted warrior fighting a heavily-armed Frankish knight).[6] This mobility enabled them to range widely across the Anatolian plateau, reappearing in many different places and so seeming to Byzantine observers to be more numerous than they were.

After the battle of Manzikert, a succession crisis meant that the Byzantines were involved in a civil war rather than restoring their frontier defences. The Türkmen could roam at leisure through central Anatolia, reaching the Western edge of the Anatolian plateau by 1077. By the 1090s, most of the plateau was in a state of transition towards a fully Turkish culture outside the towns.

The speed of the conquest needs explanation. A preliminary consideration is geographical. The Central Anatolian plateau drops gradually from East to West, with some hills and central features, and valleys where

---

[1] Herrin (1987; 3-5).

[2] Ever since the sixth century, the *anno mundi* dates were of particular importance in placing contemporary Christians in their place in God's design. On this, see Croke (1990; 11-12).

[3] Cahen (1948).

[4] On Manzikert and its consequences, see Vryonis (1971; 80-113), Cahen (1988; 11-13).

[5] See Hopwood (1991, 1993; 132-3, 2000; 97-8).

[6] Illustrated in Sözen (1987; 212-3).

agriculture can be easily carried out: mainly, however, it is best given over to livestock production, as seems to have been the case in Byzantine times.[1]

It was into this relatively empty landscape that the Türkmen came. The nature of warfare is geographically described in the *Danişmendname*:

> When morning came, Melik's army came to draw itself up on the field of battle. The army of Nestor followed suit and went to deploy on the opposite side. The warriors considered the lists: they say Mihriyanos came forward: he wheeled his horse and made a challenge. One of the Muslims entered the lists: The cursed one killed him. Another came on, he also was killed. In short, six Muslims found martyrdom. This time, Eyyub came in. The accursed one attacked Eyyub and struck him with his sword, but the blow was parried by Eyyub's shield. Even so, the sword broke through it and stuck three fingers' deep into the shoulder of Eyyub. On seeing this Melik Danişmend uttered a cry and prepared to enter the lists, when Efromiya came in. The accursed one levelled his lance to run her through, but she set an arrow to her bow, aimed at her opponent, and let fly: the arrow struck Mihriyanos in the eye, and came out by his nape. The accursed one fell from his horse and his soul flew off to Hell.[2]

The armies here are clearly cavalry forces: the mounted infidel challenges mounted *Danişmendids*. The infidels have heavier armour and weapons (e.g. the lance), and Efromiya, at least, has the typical central Asian light cavalry weapon: the bow.[3]

We must imagine many small-scale skirmishes such as these and raids on the villages which in the *Danişmendname* led to swift surrender and conversion. The Western observer, Ricoldus de Monte Crucis, claims that 'Greeks' would leave neither their cities nor farms without a horse to which they were tied for additional security.[4]

Protection on the plateau was breaking down.[5] This was exacerbated by the relative absence of clusters of cities where forces could be massed and from which the countryside could be protected. It is, I think, no accident that the major clusters of cities surviving into this period were to become the heartlands of Byzantium in its last years.[6] Those areas where there were few cities, particularly on the Anatolian Plateau itself, were to become zones of contestation between Seljuks and Byzantines.

---

[1] See Hendy (1985; map XXX).

[2] *Danişmendname Meclis* 4 (Mélikoff (1960; 249).

[3] Kaegi (1964).

[4] Cited in Vryonis (1971; 282).

[5] On this, for a later period, see Hopwood (1993; 134-5).

[6] These are the Pontus, Northern Aegean area, Central Aegean area. See Hendy (1985; maps 20-3).

So on the high plains, the Byzantine pastoralists met Türkmen in confrontation. They also sought protection from them by converting to Islam. After all, they also had vital knowledge to trade for protection: the route to the most serviceable wells, the best grazing — serious problems for pastoralists entering new territories. As the conception of Tepe-Göz in the *Book of Dede Korkut* testifies:

> One day the Oğuz migrated to their summer pasture. Now Uruz had a shepherd whom they called Konu Koja Saru Choban.Whenever the Oğuz migrated this man always went first There was a spring called Uzun Pınar which had become a haunt of the *peris* (fairies). Suddenly, something startled the sheep. The shepherd was angry with the goat which led the flocks.[1]

The Turks needed local help to find the water sources and the Byzantines needed the pastoral expertise of the Turks on land that was suitable for both arable and pastoral production.[2]

Also, the Byzantines had initially to face no state or religious authority to force their new found political and religious allegiance upon them and enforce an alien orthodoxy.[3] As members of a now decentralised society, they probably had considerably more personal liberty than they had had under the increasingly feudalising Byzantine state.

The transformation of the plateau was so complete that when Alexios Comnenos went in 1078 to Amaseia/Amasya on the Pontic coast, he found himself in hostile territory.[4] Forty years later, his son Manuel found himself in the same situation when he was leading an army against Konya itself. Passing Lake Pousegouse/Beyşehir he sought help from the local peasantry, but they refused him because as Nicetas Choniates puts it:

> Mingling with the Turks of Ikonion (Konya), not only strengthened the bonds of friendship between them, but also [they] had this way of life in common with them for the most past.[5]

The split loyalties of the Hieromonk Matthew are here foreshadowed by a century. These peasants were culturally and politically ambiguous: leaning both towards Byzantium and Konya. They communicate with the emperor as

---

[1] Section 8, tr. Lewis (1974; 140).

[2] Hopwood (1993; 131, 2000; 99).

[3] On the contrast between rural and centralised Islam, see Gellner (1972).

[4] Anna Comnena, *Alexiad*, I.2.

[5] (xv.3). Cf Cinnamus I.10.

if they were his subjects, but share the habits of the Turks. Loyalties on the plateau had become divided, and with loyalty, the sense of identity. These inhabitants of Lake Pusegouse/Beyşehir were neither Byzantines nor Turks: each day and each encounter forced a new accommodation on them. They were chameleons in a changing world, and matched their colour to the prevailing presence.

And so we must turn to the cities. Here there seems onomastically to have been the kind of gradual transition that allowed the pre-Turkish name to remain — Kayseri-Caesareia, Sivas-Sebaste, Konya-Iconion, Ankara-Ancyra. But note as an exception Aksaray, Kırşehir, Beyşehir and, right in the twelfth century war zone, Eskişehir for Dorylaeum. These attest to the speed of their conquest and conversion to Turkish ways.

This otherwise gradual transformation can again be explained by the circumstances following the battle of Manzikert. Many cities were, in fact, stormed by Turks. Vryonis gives a helpful table of these sites and indexes the level of destruction.[1] But that is not the only point. We have to ask whether the city recovered from its (in some cases) numerous sacks. Despite the horrific descriptions of destruction given by Vryonis, most seem to have done so.

The ability to reconstruct depends directly on the resources that can be marshalled from the city's hinterland. According to Neşri, Osman himself understood this. When his uncle Dundar suggested that he proceed against Nicaea by destroying its territory he is alleged to have replied that he wanted to take over cities that would benefit him. He therefore saw the essential relationship between the Mediterranean *polis* type community and its hinterland. Many cities even after a Turkish sack could find the means to survive, even if on a smaller, less ambitious scale.

But that is only a part of the picture. Many cities were handed over to the Turks. During the Byzantine civil wars that followed the Battle of Manzikert, both armies needed manpower. The closest supply was that of the Turks. We also hear of several men (of whom we shall hear more later) from this period who rose to extreme heights in Byzantine society. The contending

---

[1] Vryonis (1971; 166-7).

warlords needed to garrison the cities, and so Turkish forces were introduced into these cities. Another form of symbiosis developed here.[1]

By the late 1070s, the Grand Seljuks realised they had to do something about the province of Rûm that had so easily fallen to them. Süleyman-şah was sent out and established a capital at Nicaea/Iznik in 1078. His successor, Kılıç Arslan I was dislodged by the First Crusade in 1097. He set up a state based at Konya, which was to endure until the end of the thirteenth century.[2]

As the new lands attracted the attention of the dynasty of the Great Seljuks, so they attracted citizens from those states who, Islamised themselves, prepared to proselytise the local community while starting their new lives in the frontier zone. This gave rise to the culturally diverse society depicted in the Menâkib of Eflaki.

So much, then, for lower level exchanges. The sources prioritise elite interaction. I hope I may be pardoned now for turning to this also. Recent anthropological studies of inter-group interaction have stressed the importance of the elite in brokering deals. This is because the elite of one side is usually obvious to the elite of the other: few societies are so culturally diverse as to need to play the Martian game of saying 'take me to your leader!' The leader is usually obvious by his garb or position within the group, and as such, can be easily recognised.[3]

Some men may also gain exceptional status by being able to broker agreements between different groups. In the early days of the Turkish conquest of Anatolia, Turks who spoke Greek or Greeks who spoke Turkish were in great demand. The Seljuk sultanate quickly established a Greek chancery for correspondence with Byzantium or their Greek speaking subjects.[4] Greek defectors were very welcome and could rise to great heights: a Hasan ibn Gabras was Grand Vizier to a Seljuk sultan. A relative, also called Gabras, became a martyr when he was killed by the *Danişmendid*s in the Pontos. Families were split.

---

[1] Vryonis (1971; 113).
[2] Cahen (2001; chaps 2-3).
[3] Ahmed (1973).
[4] See Delilbaşı (1993).

Embassies were particularly dangerous. When the Great Seljuks were on the point of going to war with Tutuş of Antioch an embassy was sent to Constantinople seeking a marriage alliance between them and the Emperor, Alexios Comnenos. The prospective bride was to be Anna, the future historian. The leader of the embassy was a man whom Anna calls Siaous.[1] She is at great pains to describe him as a *mixobarbaros* as his mother was a Christian Iberian from the Caucasus. Intermarriage will figure strongly in this story, for it makes its descendants open to influence from both sides, so adding to the complexity of identity in Anatolia. Indeed, the very existence of *mixobarbaroi* attests to the speedy assimilation of Byzantines and turks within a generation of the first invasions.

However Siaus did good service for the Byzantines. For there he converted to Christianity and thereby effectvely became a Byzantine subject. having the Great Sultan's seal, he was able to play his previous rôle as a Seljuk officer and thereby bring Sinope over to Byzantium. For his services he was made Duke of Anchialos. All Orthodox Greeks must have a Christian name, based on a saint of the Orthodox Church. The name is not recorded, whether it was unobtainable at the time of Anna's writing (although she must have met him), or whether she deemed it beneath the dignity of her history we cannot tell.

We are on surer ground with John Axouch whose career is revealed in the pages of John Kinnamos and Nicetas Choniates.[2] Axouch was a Turk captured by Alexios and reared as a companion for his son John. Almost certainly Axouch was originally Ishak, a calque not of Ioannes but of Isaak. A later defector Ishak is given the name Isaakios. This was not to be the case of Axouch. Alexios Comnenus was his godfather, and he gave him the same name as his own son and Axouch's companion, John Comnenos. Axouch responded by giving his own son his godfather's name: Alexios. But why retain the name Axouch? It is possible that this is a creative misreading of Ishak, and so, by Hobson-Jobsonism (that is, rendering something meaningless in a foreign language into something meaningful by homophony) *axios exon* 'leader of worth'. That would fit his valued status during the reign of the first three Comneni. He seems to have married well: his son married the daughter of John II Comnenus and his daughter married Stephen Comnenus. They resisted the encroachments of the Latin states and

---

[1] *Alexiad* VI, 12, 3. See discussion in Hopwood (1997; 237).
[2] Kinnamos I.2; II.6-7; III.6. Choniates I.9-10; II.1.49;II.1.76-87; II.1.90.

favoured a pro-Seljuk policy. Alexios Axouch fell in the so-called AIMA conspiracy.[1]

Another course is that represented by Tzachas, or Çaka Beğ. [2] Like Axouch, he was captured in the wars after the battle of Manzikert. Unlike Axouch, who managed to be the servant of the Comnenoi, Tzachas/Çaka was allied to Nicephoros Botaneiates who had become Emperor in 1087, having been captured by him. Botaneiates was defeated by Alexios Comnenos. Tzachas' career was finished. He had promised *douleia* (slavery) to Botaneiates, according to Anna Comnena.[3] Presumably this reflects the increasing feudalisation of the Byzantine state during the reigns of the Comenenoi, and the institution was not sufficiently advanced as to become known by the Western loan-word *lizios*.[4] As *lizios* to Botaneiates he had become protonobelissimos — a post rarely open to Byzantines. Tzachas must therefore have converted and married into the elite: we know he had a daughter.

With Alexios' coup in 1081, all this came crashing down. He fled with his family to Smyrna/Izmir and negotiated with the Pechenegs in the Balkans and set himself up as rival Emperor in Izmir. He married his daughter to the Seljuk Sultan Kılıç Arslan I. He quickly gained control of the Bay of Izmir, capturing Phocaea (Foça) to the North and Clazomenae (Urla İskelesi) to the South. He closed the bay with his capture of Chios.

It is tempting (and I have fallen into this trap) to see Tzachas as an early uç-beğ — one of the maritime emirates so well discussed by Halil İnalcık.[5] However, we must pause. He was certainly a renegade Muslim: to build ships he needed Byzantine shipwrights and carpenters, and he needed skilled local oarsmen to man them. His aim was to unseat Alexios and so avenge his former lord, Nicetas Botaneiates. Yet his Turkish origins allowed him to negotiate with marauding Pechenegs in the Balkans and the Sultan in Nicaea. Here was a dangerous possibility: that a man with access to both Byzantine and Turkish avenues of power could manipulate them to create for himself a new power-base, and for the people he employed, a new identity. This cross-cultural traffic was most important in the formation of Turkish culture.

---

[1] See Magdalino (1993; 200).
[2] See Hopwood (forthcoming).
[3] *Alexiad* VII. 8.
[4] Magdalino (1993), 106-7.
[5] İnalcık (1985).

Ultimately, although his power-base emboldened him to ask for the daughter of Alexios in marriage (which would have re-instated him in Byzantine society), he fell to a complot between the Emperor and the Sultan, who had him assassinated at dinner.

Diplomatic and cultural exchanges continued. Manuel II Comnenos had a 'Persian Room', the Mouchloukos, decorated in Turkish fashion in the Great Palace.[1] Cultural interchange existed on a high level. These exchanges culminated in the state visit of the Sultan Kılıç Arslan II to Constantinople in 1162. Nicetas Choniates, brother of the bishop of Athens, disapproved of the splendours bestowed on an unbeliever, and relates only bad omens and incidents that shamed the Turkish delegation. Yet it is clear that both sides revelled in the triumphal procession (although it was interrupted by an earthquake) and enjoyed days of races in the Hippodrome which inspired one of the Turkish delegation to try to fly from the Column of the Porphyrogenitus.[2]

The end of the Comnenid dynasty saw more high-ranking exchanges. As Manuel II's reign drew to a close, his brother, Andronikos Comnenos, was accused of treason and headed by a complex route to the court of the emir of Coloneia. His guide was the retainer of John Axouch.[3] In time, he would return to be the hugely unpopular emperor Andronikos I, but for several years, he was the guest of the Seljuk state. Just before the fall of Constantinople to the Fourth Crusade in 1204, the Sultan, Kai-Khusraw I had sought refuge in Constantinople and been entertained by Theodore Lascaris and John Maurozomes. The latter managed to marry his daughter to the Sultan.[4]

After 1204, Lascaris and Maurozomes were trying to found states in Asia Minor. Lascaris carved out his successor state around Nicaea and Nymphaeion. Maurozomes was given lands around Laodiceia/Denizli and the holy city of Chonai/Honas from his son-in-law, the Seljuk Sultan. His state was peopled by Byzantines in the cities and Türkmen in the countryside. In this case, a Byzantine noble with Seljuk connections could lord it over the mixed populations of a fiefdom granted to him by the Seljuk Sultan. When Lascaris conquered him, Lascaris had himself crowned as Emperor of Nicaea: the threat was so strong that the victory legitimated the creation of the Nicene state. Kai-Khusraw himself was killed trying to reinstate Maurozomes whose

---

[1] Magdalino (1993; 118).
[2] Choniates III,118-20.
[3] Choniates VI.226.
[4] On this, see Hopwood (1999; 158).

descendants seem to have thrived in Konya, holding honour and retaining their faith until the end of the thirteenth century.[1] At an elite level, Jelal-ud-Din's Konya was strongly multicultural.

The Seljuk defeat by the Mongols at Köse Dağ in 1243 strengthened the multiculturalism, despite fatally weakening the Seljuk state. These invasions had already brought in refugees from Khorasan and Khwarezmenia, among them the mentors of Jelal-ud-Din and the man himself. Now Şeykhs set up Bektaşi movements in a mélange of Central Asian, Muslim and indigenous traditions.[2] Whence comes the tradition of tying cloth to trees or bushes? Turkologists assume that it is a Central Asian shamanist practice. However St Nicholas of Holy Sion preached and took action against this practice in Western Asia Minor in the sixth century AD.[3] Both Christians and pagans described the tree as holy. This practice seems to be getting more prevalent today: a recent visit to the shrine of the Seven Sleepers of Ephesus revealed cultic activity on the trees and fences around the shrine.

Paradoxically, these last years of the Seljuks under the supervision of Mongol overlords were to be culturally the richest Konya was to see. The İnce Minare Medresesi dates from 1258 (its architect, Keluk son of Abdullah, might be the descendant of a convert), the Karatay Medresesi dates from 1251, the Salip Ata (İnce Minare Medresesi) from 1258.[4] All these are contemporary with Jelal-ud-Din and the writing of the *Mesnevi*. Mongol controlled Konya was a cultural centre that attracted travellers from the entire Islamic world.

Dissentions furthered cross-border exchange. Izz-ud-Din Kai'Ka'us, the son of the daughter of an Orthodox priest, upon the failure of his anti-Mongol policy in 1256 fled to the Empire of Nicaea. He was quickly reinstated with Nicene support, and ceded Laodiceia/Denizli to the Empire. One of his hosts in Nicaea, Michael Palaeologos, joined him in exile a year later. In the Seljuk skirmishes with the Mongols, he held the rank of 'kondestabl'.[5] Cultural exchange was enhanced a few years later when in 1261 Izz-ud-Din Kai'Kaus fled again to Constantinople, with a considerable following. Despite rumours to the contrary, he did not convert to Christianity, but many of his followers did, who are now the Gaga'uz Turkish-speaking minority in Rumania.[6]

---

[1] Wittek (1935).
[2] See now Mélikoff (1998)
[3] Life of St Nicolas of Holy Sion 15-19.
[4] Cahen (1988; 223).
[5] Hopwood (1999; 158).
[6] Wittek (1952).

Hasluck did point to Kai'Khosraw I's exile in Constantinople,[1] but seems to have known nothing of this mutual chain of exiles and legitimations during the thirteenth century. The impact on the Byzantine side is very strong: the church historian Pachymeres can pun bilingually on Turkish and Byzantine words.[2]

The interaction does not stop at the verbal level. Jelal-ud-Din impressed the abbot of St Chariton's by his prolonged immersion in cold water.[3] Much of the Menâkib-ul-arifin is taken up with stories of this sort. The narratives of Hacı Bayram and Hacı Bektaş do also.

These stories of extreme mortification of the flesh would meet a sympathetic Byzantine response. Ever since the fourth century, stories of extreme mortification, particularly among the monks of Egypt and the Syrian deserts, were a central part of the 'mindset' of Eastern Christianity. Narratives of the feats of Jelal-ud-Din fit into a similar pattern and emphasise the 'sameness' of the world into which Byzantium was changing and facilitate the change.

The elite interaction stimulated an interest in the adjacent 'other'. During the Comnenian period the Byzantines set out the epic of *Digenes Akritas* who allegedly fought in the Byzantine-Arab wars of the eighth century. However certain features of the narrative (both the Grottaferrata and Escorial texts) are devoted to picking out the details in the life of a border warrior, *Akrites* Digenes himself is the son of a converted Arab emir and a Byzantine noblewoman. In that he is truly di-genes — doubly-born. However he is also an *Akrites*, who defends the border from much adulteration. His name therefore encapsulates the paradox of the border warrior who must both associate with his enemy and yet be distinct. At the same time as the Digenes Akrites text was being compiled,[4] in Central Asia the *Danişmendname* was being drafted. Again the mutability of frontier society is stressed. Artuki, the Byzantine convert to Islam, describes his birth:

> My father was a nomad, he lived in the mountains and had power over 12,000 tents.[5]

---

[1] Hasluck (1929; 370).

[2] Balivet (1993; 112ff).

[3] Eflaki 242.

[4] Magdalino (1993).

[5] II.22 Mélikoff.

Like Digenes, he is a *mixobarbaros*, for he is the son of a Greek nobleman and the shepherd-daughter of a Greek holy-man.

The two societies are telling themselves and each other the same stories. This trend was to continue later with the narratives of Alexios Philanthropenos' unsuccessful wooing of the widow of Menteşe Beğ in the 1290s,[1] and the contemporaneous account in Neşri and Aşıkpaşazade of the fall of Aydos castle and the infatuation of its castellan's daughter for Osman's son, Orhan.[2]

The outstanding frontier legend on the Seljuk side was that of Seyid Battal Gazi, now so notably edited by George Dedes. All the narrative patterns are there: he lays siege to Amorion, its castellan's daughter falls in love with him, and she tries to warn him of the approach of a Byzantine relief column. She wraps the message around a stone, throws it at him — and kills him. The two are buried together in a türbe.

But what a türbe! The shrine of Seyyid Battal Gazi was considerably augmented in the Ottoman period. However its Seljuk east wing is noticeable: There is the mausoleum of the Seyyid and his lover, but also the tomb of a Seljuk Valide Hatun. Earlier travellers to the state thought that these buildings had been a Byzantine ecclesiastic complex. It is now thought that the buildings are Seljuk, deeply influenced by Byzantine ecclesiastical (and therefore monumental) architecture.[3] Perhaps Byzantine architects contributed to the design of the building.

In any case, we know that many characteristic buildings of the Seljuk period owe much to Byzantine architects and builders. Madrasas in Sivas and Erzincan bear their signatures, and countless caravanserays throughout the Seljuk state bear masons' marks in Greek script. The architectual styles were merging.

It is necessary to direct attention to where the buildings are. Seyyid Battal Gazi is right in the Phrygian frontier zone The monument at once appropriates the area, yet invites in those who appreciate the story. It is, therefore, at once statement of the Islamisation of the area and, at the same time, an invitation for anyone to join in. As such it reflects in stone the

---

[1] Guilland (1923).

[2] Hickman (1979); Wittek (1965).

[3] Haspels (1971; 259-64).

activities of Jelal-ud-Din, who is staunchly Moslem, yet welcoming to strangers. And a monument in the frontier zone itself was a rallying point for the converted.

The converts are represented by a poorly-known monument not far from Seyyit-Gazi/Nacoleia. It is a kümbet of an unknown person but it incorporates classical and Byzantine sculptures in its façade. The very nature of the east wing of the complex hints at an architectural as well as a narrative synthesis. The türbes have been considered Byzantine work converted to Seljuk purposes, Seljuk copies of Byzantine buildings or buildings commissioned from Byzantine builders by Seljuk rulers. There seems in terms of non-decorated buildings to be a sort of Seljuk-Byzantine architectural *koine* developing: witness the Sultan Han near Kayseri.

The architectural *koine* is embodied in the church of Agia Sophia in Trebizond. The late Byzantine Church is enhanced with well-developed porches. As in Kümbet, many of the mouldings are re-used classical or early Byzantine pieces. However, the columns of the west porch have Seljuk style stalactite capitals. The roundels in the porches reminded the first publisher of this monument of Seljuk carvings.[1] If, as seems likely, this building is after 1243 (the date of Köse Dağ), the presence of Seljuk workmen need not be surprising.

Utilisation of earlier material might imply continuity or convey a notion that the new culture has supplanted the old. The classic example of the latter is the complete appropriation of Agia Sophia in Constantinople, with the removal of the cross bar of the crosses. However, the removal is always of a nature so that the observer can see what has been removed: the trace of the cross bar announces to the faithful exactly what has been removed and so emphasises the conversion of Constantinople into Islambol.

However, elsewhere such re-use might be more subtle, or reverential. I want to conclude with a rather later monument which epitomises much of what I have been saying: the Hüdavendigar Mosque at Behram Kale/Assos. The main door to the mosque is composed of a frame taken from an unknown sixth century church. The donor inscription is still in place, with only slightly damaged crosses and an intact Chi-Rho over the centre of the portal. The builders of this mosque felt no need to remove the previous Christian 'magic'.

---

[1] Talbot-Rice (1968).

This is the 'syncretism' or 'synthesis' so much a part of Hasluck's work. The continuity of these overlapping practices into the 1920s inspired his work, yet are now things of the past. Yet, the many by-ways and minor sites he explored attest to the continuity of practices within ever-changing matrices of meaning.

*References*

Balivet, M. 1993 ''Menteşe dit Sağlâm Bey' et Germian alias 'Mârpûç': deux surnoms turcs dans la chronique byzantine de Georges Pachymère', *Turcica* XXV.

Bryer, A. 1970 'A Byzantine Family: The Gabrades, c.979-c.1653', University of *Birmingham Historical Journal* XII, 164-87.

Bryer, A 1975 'A Byzantine Family: The Gabrades. An Additional Note', *Byzantinoslavica* XXXVI, 38-45.

Cahen, C. 1948 'La première pénétration turque en Asie Mineure', *Byzantion* 1948, 12-3

Cahen, C. 1988 *La Turquie Pré-Ottomane*, Istanbul; Institut français d'études anatoliennes d'Istanbul.

Comnène, A. 1989 *Alexiade, règne de l'empereur Alexis I Comnène, 1081-1118; livres (I-XV)*, Paris; Les Belles Lettres.

Croke B. 1990 'The Early Development of Byzantine Chronology', in E. Jeffreys (ed.) *Studies in John Malalas,* Sydney; Austrian Association for Byzantine Studies, 27-38.

Culler, J. 1975 *Structuralist Poetics*, London; Routledge and Kegan Paul.

Delilbaşı, M.1993 'Greek as a Diplomatic Language in the Turkish Chancery', in N. Moschonas ed. *E Epikoinonia sto Vyzantio* Athens, Kentro Vyzantinon Ereunon, 145-53.

Geanakoplos, D. 1959 *Emperor Michael Paleologus and the West*, Cambridge, Mass; Harvard University Press.

Gellner, E. 1972 'Doctor and Saint', in N. Keddie (ed.), *Scholars, Saints and Sufis*, Berkeley; University of California Press, 307-26.

Guilland. R. 1923 'Études de civilisation et literature byzantines: Alexios Philanthropène', *Revue du Lyonnais*, 47-59.

Gutman, R. 1968 *Richard Wagner: The Man, his Mind and his Music*, London; Harmondsworth; Penguin.

Hasluck, F. 1929 *Christianity and Islam under the Sultans*, Two vols, edited by M. Hasluck, Oxford: Clarendon.

Haspels, C. 1971 *The Highlands of Phrygia: Sites and Monuments*, Princeton, NJ; Princeton University Press.

Hendy, M.F. 1985 *Studies in the Byzantine Monetary Economy 300-1450*, Cambridge; CUP.

Herrin, J. 1987 *The Formation of Christendom*, Princeton, NJ; Princeton University Press.

Hickman, W. 1979 'The Taking of Aydos Castle: Further Considerations on a Chapter from Aşıkpaşazade', *Journal of the American Oriental Society* 99/3, 399-407

Hopwood, K. 1991 'Nomads or Bandits? The Pastoralist/Sedentarist Interface in Anatolia', *Byzantinische Forschungen* XVI, 179-94.

Hopwood, K 1993 'Peoples, Territories and States: The Formation of the Beğliks of Pre-Ottoman Turkey', in C. Farah (ed.), *Decision Making and Change in the Ottoman Empire*, Kirkswood, Mo., 129-38.

Hopwood, K. 1997 'Byzantine Princesses and Lustful Turks', in S. Deacy and K. Pierce eds, *Rape in Antiquity*, London; Duckworth, 231-42.

Hopwood, K. 2000 'Living on the Margin: Byzantine Farmers and Turkish Herders', *Journal of Mediterranean Studies* 10, 1-2, 93-106.

Hopwood, K. forthcoming 'Çaka Beğ'.

Huart, C. 1918-22 *Aflâkî: Les Saints des Derviches Tourneurs*, 2 vols, Paris; E. Leroux.

İnalcık, H 1985 'The Rise of the Turkish Maritime Principalities in Anatolia, Byzantium and the Crusades', *Byzantinische Forschungen* IX, 179-217.

Kaegi, W. 1964 'The Contribution of Archery to the Turkish Conquest of Anatolia', *Speculum* 39, 96-108.

Lewis, G. 1974 tr. *The Book of Dede Korkut*, Harmondsworth; Penguin.

Magdalino, P. 1993 *The Empire of Manuel I Komnenos 1143-1180*, Cambridge; CUP.

Mélikoff, I. 1960 *La Geste de Melik Danişmend*, Paris; Librairie Adrien Maisonneuve.

Mélikoff, I. 1998 *Hadji Bektach: un Mythe et ses Avatars: Genèse et Évolution du Soufisme Populaire en Tourkie*, Leiden; Brill.

Sözen, M. 1987 *The Evolution of Turkish Art and Architecture*, Istanbul; Haset Kitapevi.

Talbot-Rice, T. 1965 'An Analysis of the Decoration in the Seljukid Style', in D. Talbot-Rice ed., *The Church of Haghia Sophia at Trebizond*, Edinburgh; EUP, 55-82.

Vryonis, Sp. 1971 *The Decline of Medieval Hellenism in Asia Minor and the Process of Islamization from the Eleventh through the Fifteenth Century*, Berkeley, Ca; University of California Press.

Wittek, P. 1923 'L' Épitaphe d' un Comnène à Qunya', *Byzantion* X, 505-15.

Wittek, P. 1952 'Yazijioghlu Ali on the Christian Turks of the Dobrudja', *Bulletin of the School of Oriental and African Studies* 14, 639-62.

Wittek, P. 1965 'The Taking Of Aydos Castle: A Ghazi Legend transformed', in G. Makdisi ed., *Arabic and Islamic Studies in Honour of A.R. Gibb*, Leiden; Brill, 662-72.

# 18. RITUAL DREAMS AND HISTORICAL ORDERS: INCUBATION BETWEEN PAGANISM AND CHRISTIANITY

Charles STEWART

The practice of 'incubation', which involves a person sleeping at a temple or church in order to have dreams of a god or a saint, has been documented in the eastern Mediterranean at every historical stage from classical antiquity to the present.[1] That the Turkish Directorate of Religious Affairs should recently have sent a directive to be posted at all saints' tombs in the country within which is found the instruction that no one should sleep at these shrines indicates that the practice continues among Muslims in the region.[2] In Greece many Orthodox Christian saints' day pilgrimages entail sleeping overnight at churches thereby creating a situation where incubation dreams may occur. Outside of ritual contexts, and beyond church precincts, dreams of saints are entirely common throughout Greece. I have collected numerous cases from the island of Naxos where saints appear to people in dreams and heal them, or tell them where to find buried icons or treasures.[3]

Alongside ritual funeral lamentation, incubation presents one of the clearest examples of a cultural continuity from ancient to modern Greece. Our understanding of such continuities has been expanded by comprehensive studies such as Margaret Alexiou's *The Ritual Lament in Greek Tradition*, which pays careful attention to Byzantine and modern variations of the ancient tradition. The majority of continuity studies, however, demonstrate little interest in the changes and transformations that inevitably accompany continuity. A symptom of this is the rapidity with which they pass over the early Christian period.

---

[1] Deubner (1900), Hamilton (1906).
[2] David Shankland, personal communication.
[3] Stewart (1997, 2001).

Below I shall focus my attention entirely on the transition from pagan to Christian proprietorship of the practice of incubation in order to consider more closely the challenges which conversion posed to the continuity of incubation. Neither the early Christians nor the pagans thought of their incubation practices as continuous with one another. Christian rejections of continuity, and the alterations to incubation practice that they directed, remind us that Hellenic cultural practices carried over into later historical periods haphazardly, often only after undergoing modification. No transcendental *Volksgeist* guarded the rite of incubation to ensure its intact transmission. On the contrary, the practice of cultivating dreams was re-crafted by the Christians precisely in order to engineer changes in the religious imagination. Beneath the superficial continuity of incubation in late antiquity — and the practice of soliciting therapeutic dreams from holy figures by sleeping at their shrines did continue — there raged a struggle for possession of the 'sign'.[1] That sign was a ritual of healing that acted upon the unconscious producing powerful effects upon popular consciousness.

As Aline Rousselle has contended, and as will be seen in examples below, healing was a metaphor for conversion.[2] Healing rituals such as those formulated by Zulu Zionist Christians in South Africa, or by the Native American Church in the U.S.A., often come to the fore precisely during moments of cultural change. Such rituals offer a means of making sense in the face of changing circumstances; they articulate assured identities at moments when traditional assumptions have become destabilized.[3] Although the practice of incubation continued over the *longue durée*, this did not happen because it occupied a remote corner of social life insulated from the effect of events. Incubation was, rather, in a front line position in the mediation of social change. In this respect it differed from ritual lamentation which Christianity absorbed less problematically.[4] Late antiquity represented a period of conjuncture during which the meaning of ritual incubation underwent transformations while still retaining structural continuity with its past.[5]

---

[1] Comaroff (1985; 196ff).

[2] Rousselle (1990).

[3] Kiernan (1994), Csordas (1999), Colombo (1975; 97).

[4] Alexiou (1974).

[5] In his *Islands of History*, Marshall Sahlins (1995; xiv, 152) has adapted the idea of the 'conjuncture' from Braudel to capture the way in which Hawaiian rituals both continued and underwent transformation in the wake of Cook's visit.

Dreaming for cures was a prophetic enterprise and the intention to pronounce on temporal issues — the way things have been, are now, and will be — lent such dreams a synoptic, historicizing form. The people dreaming, or those writing on their behalf, often constructed scenarios, unconsciously and consciously, in which their religion would be maintained in the future. According to Patricia Cox Miller, dreams in late antiquity 'formed a distinctive pattern of imagination which brought visual presence and tangibility to such abstract concepts as time, cosmic history, the soul, and the identity of one's self. Dreams were tropes that allowed the world ... to be represented.'[1]

Consider, for example, the dream vision described by the Alexandrian poet Palladas after the destruction of the Sarapeion in 391 CE:

> I was amazed to see Zeus' bronze son [Herakles] who was once called upon in prayers but now cast aside. I said: "Averter of evils, offspring of three moons, you were never defeated but are today prostrate." But the god stood by me in the night and said: "Even though a god, I have learned to serve the times."[2]

Below I will consider similar dreams that formulated historical orderings, and influenced the social understanding of these orders, much as standard historiography does. Particular images in the dreams, such as statues, served as 'chronotropes' — images that enabled thinking about historical periodization. This study thus amplifies Leach's observation that rituals modulate the social perception of time by suggesting that rituals may also influence, and even induce, social perceptions of history.[3]

*The Last Pagan Dream?*

I begin by considering a dream from the waning days of pagan Hellenism. The year is 484 CE. The Goths had already destroyed numerous Greek temples during their invasion in 396. Meanwhile Theodosius II's decree (435 CE) that any still intact pagan temples should be destroyed and purified by the erection of a cross was slowly converting any remaining structures to Christian churches.[4] Proclus, the Head of the Academy of Athens, Plato's *diadokhos* (successor), was 72 years old. He would die in the following year, having devoted his life to resisting Christianity, and to serving the goddess Athena.

---

[1] Miller (1994; 3).

[2] *Greek Anthology*, 9.41, trans. Frank Trombley (2000; 35).

[3] Leach (1961). On ritual and history, see Lambek (1998).

[4] Frantz (1965; 187).

From the moment of his arrival in Athens Proclus had lived near Athena's shrine at the Parthenon. According to his disciple Marinus:

> The goddess herself acknowledged his devotion just after her statue — the one earlier erected in the Parthenon — was removed by those who even move immovables (*kai ta akinita kinounton*). The philosopher had a dream in which an attractive (*evskimon*) lady appeared to him and told him that he should prepare his house quickly. "Because the Mistress of Athens (*kyria Athinaïs*)", she said, "wishes to live with you." [1]

No more is said about this event. Marinus moves on immediately to another dream in which Asclepius heals Proclus, and which I shall consider below.

The disappearance of the statue of Athena from the Parthenon spelled the end of ancient Greek religion on the Acropolis, but the statue promptly resurfaced in the dream of the last great pagan philosopher. Paganism thus did not definitively disappear; rather, it went into symbolic suspension pending definitive interpretation. Ancient Greek religion was interrupted, but the possibility remained that it might resume, much as contemporary Greek folk traditions hold that the liturgy being sung in Hagia Sophia when the Ottomans overran Constantinople will one day be completed. Similarly, after the Christians defiled the sacra of the Serapeion of Alexandria by exposing them to public view, the stalwart Olympius rallied his dejected fellow pagans. He assured them that the statues themselves were just material objects destined to vanish, but that the powers that had infused them had flown to heaven where they still existed.[2]

This example begins to reveal how dreams of gods can offer an historicizing representation of events. Proclus's dream reacted to the removal of the chryselephantine statue of Athena during the Christianization of Athens. The removal or destruction of the cult statues of an ancient city marked the end of a civic order. A civic statue of Athena known as the Palladium, for example, protected Troy until its removal by Odysseus permitted the sack of the city. Statues of the domestic gods could play a similar foundational role. After the fall of Troy, Aeneas transferred figurines of the hearth gods, the *Penates*, to Rome as part of the process of establishing a new order.[3] During Alexander's siege of Tyre some people in the city experienced panic dreams that their god Apollo would betray them and go over

---

[1] Marinus, *Life of Proclus*, chap. 30, R. Masullo (1985), Trombley (2000; 34).

[2] Sozomen, *Ecclesiastical History*, 7.15, *MPG*, vol. 67, col. 1455.

[3] Virgil, *Aeneid*, 3.12 (*Penates*), 2.166 (Palladium). See also Faraone (1992; 4, 7).

to Alexander's side. To prevent this they strapped down the civic statue of Apollo with ropes and nailed the sculpture to its pedestal so that the god could not desert them.[1]

The removal of cult statues was like lowering the flag. Images of statues of Marx and Lenin being removed from central squares in eastern Europe, or the destruction of the enormous stone Buddhas of Bamiyan (Afghanistan) in 2001, provide more contemporary illustrations of the linkage between monumental sculpture and political change. The demolition and erection of statues after a change in political or religious regimes reflect new views of history governed by emerging 'chronologies of desire'.[2]

Once the statues of the ancient gods were removed there were unlikely to be very many more incubation dreams involving the ancient gods. Alterations to the architectural and artistic environment affected interior imagination. The Parthenon, for example, would eventually become a church of the Panagia. Granted this changing context, Proclus's dream was potentially the dream to end all pagan dreams.

In picturing the transfer of Athena's image from a public to a personal space, Proclus's dream represented a reversal of the process of religious development as conceptualized by Fustel de Coulanges. In Fustel's view, ancient religion began as a domestic religion of the hearth and then expanded until it encompassed the entire sphere of the polis. In this example religion proceeds in the opposite direction.[3] From a psychoanalytical perspective, Proclus's dream would be classed as a dream of mourning. Freud applied mourning to the loss of one's country, or the loss of an ideal, as well as to the loss of a beloved person.[4] The signal feature of mourning, in his view, was the attempt by the ego to incorporate the lost figure. In taking the statue of Athena into his private sphere Proclus was engaging in the most characteristic mourning practice, which involved, in the words of Melanie Klein: 'the individual's setting up [of] the lost loved object inside himself.'[5] In difficult cases of mourning, according to the psychoanalysts Abraham and Torok, individuals transferred painful realities into inner psychic enclaves, or

---

[1] Plutarch, *Life of Alexander*, 24.3. See also Diodorus Siculus, 17.41.8; cp. Herodotus, 8. 64, where images of the gods are brought to the encampment at Salamis to protect the Greek forces.
[2] See Nixon in this volume.
[3] Coulanges (nd; 132).
[4] Freud (1991; 252), 'Mourning and Melancholia'.
[5] Klein (1975; 362).

'crypts', where they were both entombed and encoded within the self.[1] Christianity had begun as a crypto-religion and now paganism entered its own crypt in the minds of those unwilling to relinquish it.

## The Limits of Incubation

It could be objected that the dream of Proclus was not an incubation dream because it occurred in his own home, but I don't think it necessary to be so strict in our appreciation of incubation. Incubation literally means sleeping in/at a shrine with the intention of cultivating a dream, but a number of intermediate possibilities such as dreaming of a god/saint while travelling as a pilgrim to or from the shrine need to be considered as part of the same concept. The magical papyri and theurgical texts circulating in the Roman Imperial period provided instructions on how to cultivate dreams at home, even how to fashion personal devotional statues of Hecate from rue.[2] It may, therefore, be inaccurate to draw too sharp a distinction between a house and a temple.

Proclus had devoted his entire life to serving the pagan gods. As a child the patron goddess of Byzantium[3] appeared to him in a dream and exhorted him to study philosophy, and when he became dissatisfied with his studies in Egypt he remembered this advice and moved to Athens, 'in order that the succession from Plato might be preserved without adulteration'.[4] At Athens he lived near the foot of the Acropolis, close to the Parthenon. He followed strict Neo-Platonic precepts, abstaining from eating living things, and performing sacrifices regularly. This exemplary level of devotion meant that dreams of gods might easily occur to him almost anytime, inside or outside of temples. In any case, Proclus did have healing dreams of the classic incubation variety.

Proclus's dream of Athena considered above, followed another story relating how he had prayed at Asclepius' temple on behalf of a sick girl, Asclepigeneia, who immediately recovered her health. The temple of Asclepius, located at the southern foot of the Acropolis, was even closer to Proclus's home than the Parthenon. This healing event occurred slightly

---

[1] Abraham and Torok (1994; 135), Gross (1992; 36).

[2] Eitrem, S. (1991; 179).

[3] Festugière identifies her as Athena (1966; 1584).

[4] *Life of Proclus*, trans. Edwards (2000; 6, 9).

earlier than the dream of Athena and Marinus makes the contrastive remark that 'at that time the whole city was fortunate in having the shrine of the Saviour [Asclepius] still unvandalized (*aporthiton*).'[1] In other words, divine care could be expected when temples still housed their statues, and particularly if one had a temple nearby (*geitona*).[2] Another time Proclus suffered a sudden paralysis that his 'neighbour', Asclepius, cured. According to Marinus, 'In a state between sleeping and waking he saw a snake entwining around his head. Then the paralysis began to disappear starting from his head downwards'.[3] On yet another occasion he was cured of arthritis of the foot when a sparrow[4] flew down and snatched away his bandage. Subsequently when he dreamt that 'someone from Epidaurus' kissed his knees he knew that he would not be further troubled by arthritis, which was congenital in his family.[5]

At the height of the Roman Empire there were hundreds of temples of Asclepius scattered throughout the Greco-Roman world. Asclepius was a compassionate healer of the sick, a miracle worker, child of a divine father and a mortal mother. Like Christ, he was often called simply *Soter* — Saviour. Even the early iconography of Christ seemed to draw on representations of Asclepius.[6]

Neo-Platonists like Proclus and his predecessors incorporated Asclepius into their theology as a transcendental deity located in the sun, holding the cosmos in balance.[7] These Platonic formulations had the effect of creating an abstract, celestial conception of the god which converged on conceptions of God that developed within Christian theology (also under the influence of Platonism). In his *Sacred Tales* (Second Century CE) the rhetorician Aelius Aristides dreamt that he was walking late at night with a Platonist friend who directed Aristides, who was sceptical about Platonism, to look at the night sky, perhaps at the dawn star. He instructed, 'This, as far as you are concerned,

---

[1] *Life of Proclus* (Edwards 2000; 29). See also Frantz (1965; 195).

[2] In a contemporary dream narrative that I collected on Naxos the Panagia appeared to a woman and proclaimed that she was her 'neighbour' (*geitonissa*), meaning that she was the manifestation of the Panagia from the main icon of the neighbourhood chapel. See Stewart (1997; 884). For similar ideas about neighbouring heroes in classical antiquity see, Rusten (1983), Brillante (1991; 95).

[3] *Life of Proclus* (Edwards 2000; 30).

[4] Sparrows could be sacred to Asclepius. See Aelian, *Varia Historia*, 5.17 collected in Emma and Ludwig Edelstein (1998, Vol. 1; 378).

[5] *Life of Proclus* (Edwards 2000; 31).

[6] For a comparison of Asclepius and Christ in iconography see Mathews (1999, 69ff).

[7] Edelstein and Edelstein (1998; Vol. 2; 107).

is what Plato calls the soul of the Universe.' Aristides gazed up and claimed to
see 'Asclepius of Pergamum established in heaven.' [1]

For the most part Aristides' *Sacred Tales* chronicled his illnesses,
sufferings and the therapies recommended by Asclepius in dreams. This pagan
text thus arrived at a correlation between physical suffering and divine
redemption very similar to the rising Christian genre of martyrs' stories.[2]
There was only one major difference between Christ and Asclepius. Christ
could raise the dead, but Asclepius could not. According to legend, he
accomplished this feat once but it so outraged Zeus that he slew Asclepius and
his resurrected patient with a thunderbolt.[3]

Despite this minor inadequacy the cult of Asclepius still represented
one of the greatest challenges to the spread of Christianity, and Asclepius was
one of the last pagan gods to lose currency.[4] The Christians attacked the
institution of incubation head on. Tatian, a contemporary of Aristides, declared
incubation cures to be cynical public relations exercises carried out by
demons. These demons first made people ill and then disclosed their identities
through dreams in order to receive praise before departing and terminating the
illness.[5] A couple of generations later Tertullian also attributed incubation to
demonic manipulation, adding the radical assertion that no one really dreamt at
incubation shrines. It was, all, he said, just a demonic ploy to mislead people
who were, by the way, just as vulnerable at home in their bedrooms as they
were at incubation shrines.[6] These objections did not, of course, stop
incubation practice at the grassroots level but it is worth bearing in mind that
the early Christians would have liked to do just that. Ultimately they
grudgingly contented themselves with modifying the external architecture and
the theological underpinnings of incubation.

*Dreams and Materiality*

In the Introduction to his impressive study of local religious cults shared
between Christianity and Islam, F.W. Hasluck, speculated that there would
probably have been more continuity from paganism to early Christianity  than

---

[1] Aelius Aristides, *The Sacred Tales*, 4.56, trans. Behr (1968; 266).

[2] Behr (1968; 46), Perkins (1995; 189).

[3] Pindar, *Pythian*, 3.56ff.

[4] Edelstein and Edelstein (1988, Vol; 2, 257).

[5] Tatian, *Oratio ad Graecos*, 18. Whittaker (1982).

[6] Tertullian, *De Anima*, 46, Waszink (ed. 1947).

from Christian Byzantium into the Islamic Ottoman period.[1] He plausibly contended that beliefs are more likely to be maintained in circumstances when a population remains largely the same and converts, as opposed to situations where invaders espousing a new/different religion populate an area. Hasluck further advocated a distinction between 'material' as opposed to 'spiritual' continuity. Was a later religion just using the buildings of the former religion, or was it also appropriating spiritual ideas?[2] In the case of incubation, however, such a distinction may be misleading. The material and the spiritual dimensions were not independent, but integrally related to one another.

As we have seen in the case of Proclus, the removal of the cult statues of ancient deities directly affected the imaginary world of dreamers. Gods often appeared in dreams as statues of themselves. Aristides, for example, frequently dreamt of the various gods as statues (Asclepius, Zeus, Athena) and in other dreams he found it significant to report that he saw himself standing beside statues of the gods even though these were just background props.[3] In one dream a statue apparently crossed the divide between inanimate and animate right before his eyes: 'Next we worshippers stood by it [a statue of Asclepius] just as when the paean is sung, I almost among the first. At this point, the God, now in the posture in which he is represented in statues, signaled our departure ... [a]nd the God, with his hand, indicated for me to stay. And I was delighted by the honor and the extent to which I was preferred to the others, and I shouted out, "The One," meaning the God. But he said, "It is you." [4] Aristides' close relation to Asclepius — some would say his own megalomania — gave rise to another dream in which he saw a statue of himself morph into a statue of Asclepius. He considered this dream 'very honorable'.[5]

As Artemidorus wrote: 'It makes no difference whether we see the goddess herself as we have imagined her to be or a statue of her. For whether the gods appear in the flesh or as statues fashioned out of some material, they have the same meaning.' Except for the fact, he goes on to add, that 'when the gods have been seen in person, it signifies that the good and bad fulfillments will take place more quickly than they would have if statues of them had been

---

[1] Hasluck (1929, Vol 1; 4).

[2] Hasluck (1929, Vol 1; 5).

[3] Aristides, *The Sacred Tales*, (Behr 1968), 2.41, 3.47, 4.46f., 1.11.

[4] Aristides, *The Sacred Tales*, (Behr 1968), 4.50.

[5] Aristides, *The Sacred Tales*, (Behr 1968), 1.17; see also 4.49.

seen.'[1] Brillante has contended that as dreams were themselves images, the gods appearing in them ultimately also became images — representations of gods, but not the actual gods. Whether the gods appeared as statues or directly in dreams was thus a moot point since either way they would be flattened into images.[2] The latter part of the passage from Artemidorus suggests, on the contrary, that the ancients made a subtle distinction here.

In any case, the important question of whether a god had really appeared or not, did not depend on whether the god appeared unmediated by symbolic representations (images) such as statues or dreams. *Epiphaneiai*, 'divine manifestations', could occur in mental states, or via images, that we would today variously classify as phantoms, illusions, hallucinations or dreams.[3] Artemidorus considered that some gods such as Pan and Ephialtes (nightmare) mainly manifested as emotional states in dreams, such as excitement, fear or panic. They did not assume visual (or cognizable) form as did the majority of gods. Asclepius exceptionally bridged both possibilities. He could manifest himself to the senses and to the intellect.[4]

Artemidorus's opinion that dreams of statues fashioned from precious materials such as gold, silver or amber were more auspicious than dreams of terra cotta, plaster or wax statues returns our attention to the conditioning effects that the aesthetic environment exerted upon dreams.[5] Statues and effigies of Asclepius were fashioned in all these media but the principal public statue at Epidaurus, as at many other major temples, was of ivory and gold and thus very good to dream. According to Pausanias, the god was depicted 'seated on a throne, grasping a staff, while holding the other hand over the head of a serpent; and a dog, lying by his side, is also represented'.[6] Pilgrims would encounter this statue as they entered the shrine, perhaps some would stop to meditate upon it at length, and its iconography evidently conditioned the subsequent dream narratives.[7]

---

[1] Artemidorus, *Oneirocritica*, 2.35, (see also 1.5, 2.44) trans. White (1975). See also Scholia Pindar, *Pythian*, 3.137b cited in Van Straten (1976; 15), also Gordon (1996).

[2] Brillante (1991; 97).

[3] Versnel (1987; 48), Pfister (1924; 284).

[4] Artemidorus (1975) 2.34.

[5] Artemidorus (1975) 2.39.

[6] Pausanias, *Description of Greece*, 2.27.2, in Edelstein and Edelstein (1998; 345); Lapatin (2001; 109ff).

[7] Edelstein and Edelstein (1998, Vol. 2; 151).

Contemporary psychological studies help to clarify how effective incubation might have been for fostering particular types of dreams. In one study, a sample of American college students were asked to set themselves the mental task of solving a problem of their own choosing in their dreams. Approximately 50 per cent of the students reported having dreams related to the topic. Of these subjects 50 per cent (i.e. 25 per cent of the original sample) felt that they had been able to solve their problem in the dream. Unrelated judges evaluated the dream transcripts and largely corroborated the dreamers' assessments of success in problem solving. These results were obtained in a secular society after only briefly exposing the subjects to the concept of incubation.[1] The percentage of successful incubation dreams would surely have been much higher in antiquity amongst faithful pilgrims conditioned by more elaborate, socially sanctioned preparations and exposed through ritual performance to impressive religious imagery.

The Christians' removal of these images and the prohibition of pagan public rituals would have interrupted the imaginary circuit between dream and artistic representation. Granted that artists often sculpted statues of gods after dream visions, or were commissioned to do so by patrons who had had such visions,[2] the destruction of material iconography instigated a vicious circle. Fewer images meant fewer dreams and thus the probability that still fewer images would creatively be produced in the future. Proclus's dream can thus be seen as a desperate cry against a vanishing world of ancient iconography; a last expression of the ancient religious imagination.

*New World Orders*

Around the same time as the statue of Athena was removed from the Parthenon the temple of Asclepius, where Proclus had prayed for Asclipigeneia, was also pillaged and soon destroyed — whether by Christians, earthquake or natural decay we can not be certain. Not long afterwards, a church dedicated to Saint Andrew, a healing saint, was constructed over the site of the former Asclepieion. Incubation continued at this church, which contained an additional aisle, perhaps a porch, such as was found in the earlier

---

[1] Barrett (1993). Within the discipline of psychology the term 'incubation' primarily means the activity of intentionally solving a particular problem in one's dreams. Work on this subject generally falls under the broader category of 'creativity'. For reports on current incubation exercises visit the website set up by Henry Reed, one of the foremost contemporary proponents of incubation: www.creativespirit.net/healingdreams.

[2] Van Straten (1976; 15).

temple and at other churches designed for incubation. Indications are that at least some of St Andrew's congregation had been born into pagan families devoted to Asclepius. Tombstones in the precinct of the church bear names such as Asklepiarion, and Asklepia.[1] In other words, the gap between the destruction of the temple and the building of the church was not so long that people would have been oblivious to the earlier god and form of worship.

The surprising thing is that these events occurred so late in Athens. Perhaps we may put this down to the conservative presence of the Academy in Athens, which did not close until well into the sixth century. At Aigai in Cilicia, on the other hand, the temple of Asclepius was torn down in the early fourth century at the order of Constantine the Great to prevent people being deflected from recognition of the true Saviour. In Eusebius' view, '[w]ith it (fell) the one lurking there, not a demon or a god, but a kind of deceiver of souls.'[2] According to the Byzantine commentator Zonaras, this was not the end of the story. When Julian the Apostate passed through Cilicia (363 CE) the priest of Asclepius from Aigai prevailed upon him to restore the temple. Julian agreed to retrieve the pillars of the original structure, which had been incorporated into a nearby church. Ultimately the task proved too difficult. After extracting the pillars the workers were unable to transport them to the site of the Asclepius temple. When Julian departed these pillars were left lying close to the church and the bishop easily reincorporated them into his building.[3]

Recognizing the pagan conviction in the animate power of their statues and temple structures the Christians frequently incised crosses on these to neutralize them. Some contemplated a policy of totally obliterating ancient temples so that no index of pagan worship would be left.[4] The precedent of events at the temple of Zeus Marnas in Gaza would have supported the case for such a policy. With the backing of Empress Eudoxia the local bishop, Porphyry, razed this temple to the ground in 402 CE. Some of the sacred marble stones from the Marneion were then used to construct a paved walkway (*plateian*) around the Christian basilica subsequently erected on the site. The fact that humans and animals alike were now treading on these sacred stones, '[c]aused greater grief to the idol-worshippers than the burning of the temple. Hence, the majority of them, especially the women, do not step on these

---

[1] Gregory (1986; 239).

[2] Eusebius, *Life of Constantine*, 3.56 in Edelstein and Edelstein (1998, Vol. 1; 420).

[3] Zonaras, *Epitome Historiarum*, 12c-d in Edelstein and Edelstein, (1998, Vol. 1; 421).

[4] Zacharias, *Life of Severus*, 18f, cited in Trombley (1994, Vol 2; 7).

marbles to the present day,'[1] It was difficult to be certain what recently converted Christians would revere in putatively Christian contexts. A similar situation was observed in highland Guatemala. There, Christian catechists, some of whom were also shamans in the traditional religion, came to church willingly. Their devotional attention did not, however, focus on the figure of Christ crucified set in raised position before the faithful, but rather on the spirits of the dead buried beneath the floor of the church.[2]

Granted the continued practice of incubation by Christians, the best that could be done was to try to make certain that people were contacting the right God in their dreams, and that they understood the basic theological principles behind incubation. In the latter part of the fourth century Athanasius, Bishop of Alexandria, perceived the need to correct local Christians who apparently held that Christian martyrs (saints) healed people by marshalling power over the demons of the lower air.[3] The idea that saints needed to resort to demons in order to be effective obviously allotted a theologically unacceptable role to pagan cosmology. In an Easter letter to his local priests, Athanasius declared: '[I]f they [the Christian populace] understood, they would believe that the martyrs are in Christ, not in the demons, and they would call upon Christ who is in them and wait until he reveals to them what they are seeking, either in a dream or by speaking in their heart, and they would not run to demons.'[4]

Theological suspicions about the role of dreams in the popular devotion to martyrs can also be seen in Canon 83 of the Council of Carthage, which opposed the construction of *martyria* (martyrs'/saints' shrines) founded on the basis of revelations in dreams.[5] There were, of course, legitimate dreams of martyrs. On his way to visit his sister, Macrina, Gregory of Nyssa dreamt three times in succession that he seemed to hold the 'relics of the martyrs' in his hands and that a light shone from them as from a mirror held up to the sun. This dream predicted the impending death of Macrina.[6]

---

[1] Mark the Deacon, *Life of Porphyry, Bishop of Gaza*, Grégoire and Kugener (1930; 76). English translation Rapp (2000). See also Trombley (1993; 166).

[2] Tedlock (1983). Visitors to the University of Thessaloniki in northern Greece might also find themselves worshipping a pavement. The University is located on the site of the old Jewish cemetery and some of the tombstones were incorporated as flagstones in campus walkways. The inscriptions on some of these gravestones may still be read.

[3] Brown (1995; 74).

[4] Athanasius, *Festal Letters*, 42 (A.D. 370), trans. in Brakke (1998; 480).

[5] Dagron (1985; 40).

[6] Gregory of Nyssa, *Life of Macrina*, 15, trans. P. Maraval (1971).

Shrines to the Christian martyrs where people came to be healed represented a counter balance to the old incubation temples of the pagans. Faced with the continuing success of the cult of Isis at Menouthis (near Alexandria), Cyril, Patriarch of Alexandria, had the relics of Saints John and Cyrus translated there to establish a Christian healing centre. Perhaps the political need for such sites explains his defence of Christian incubation against Julian's charge that Christians 'slept on tombs in order to have dreams'.[1] Cyril did not fully approve of the cultivation of prophetic dreams. When the shrine of John and Cyrus was founded he asserted that people could now come to the 'true and uncommercialized infirmary where no one has false dreams' (alithinon kai akapilefton iatreion· oudeis gar imin oneirata plattetai).[2] Accounts of dream visions of Saints John and Cyrus nonetheless figured prominently in the stories of cures that occurred at the shrine in Menouthis, and which were eventually recorded in the collection of miracles of Saints John and Cyrus.[3]

Julian's objection to Christian practice expressed revulsion at the idea of sleeping at a gravesite. To the pagan mind this must have seemed a singularly polluting and thus demented thing to want to do.[4] Pagans excluded birth and death from incubation temple precincts such as those of Asclepius at Epidaurus or Amphiaraus at Oropus, but often performed animal sacrifice before and/or after incubation. The Christians forbade blood sacrifice, but preferred to cultivate dreams in proximity to the tombs or relics of deceased saints. Pagan incubation involved expenditure on offerings, while Christian healing was advertized as free of charge — hence Cyril's quip that the shrine of John and Cyrus was 'uncommercialized', or the epithet 'anargyroi' (penny-less) for the healing saints Cosmas and Damian. The basic action of receiving a healing dream from a deity or saint was the same, but the ritual contexts and assumptions underlying pagan and Christian incubation were quite different.

Although they had begun by branding pagan incubation as demonic, the Christians ultimately settled into their own correlation of demons with healing. Demons went from cosmological principles mediating the transmission of dreams, to evil forces involved in the causation of illness. The

---

[1] Cyril of Alexandria, Against Julian, 10, MPG, 76, c. 1024, cited in Dagron (1985; 41). For an account of Cyril's politico-religious position see Takács (1994).

[2] Cyril of Alexandria, Collected Sermons, 18, MPG, 77, c. 1105; Athanassiadi (1993; 125). Another example of direct competition between pagan and Christian healing cults during this period would be the shrine of St Thecla, which displaced the cult of Apollo Sarpedonios in Cilicia. See Dagron (1978; 87).

[3] Marcos (1975).

[4] See Brown (1981; 7).

pagans' refusal to reject their demons (gods) and embrace Christ could provoke illness, likewise lapses and sins on the part of Christians could invite in demons, momentarily breaking the protective seal of the Holy Spirit imparted at baptism. The way to heal such pathogenic demonic infestation was by exorcism, or baptism (a rite that included several exorcisms). The Church Fathers, and especially ascetic writers like Evagrius and Cassian, promoted the view of dreams as windows onto the true condition of the self. Whereas Aristides' dreams revealed the protection of Asclepius, and a set of physical therapies to undertake, Augustine's dreams two centuries later provoked reflection on the purity of his soul.[1] The Christian suppression of dreams as prophetic encouraged a compensatory shift to seeing them as expressions of the inner self for which one was responsible.[2] To be healed as a Christian thus potentially involved embracing a new structure of 'self' where individual will-power contributed to the success of the cure.[3]

At first Christians did not produce very extensive public iconography or architecture. Not only did they face periodic state persecution, but they also initially adhered to the Jewish precept that one should not worship graven images.[4] By the time of Proclus, however, the average Christian shrine would very likely have been adorned with images, and this new iconography supplanted the religious imagery of the pagans.[5] The new churches could be likened to theatres where images told the life of Christ, or the saints, and architecture placed one in a Christian microcosm suspended between the present and the world to come. Visits to these places conditioned the dreams of the faithful just as surely as images of Asclepius had influenced pagan dreams in the preceding centuries. At Menouthis, St John appeared to a paralytic pilgrim 'in the form of a monk, not in a dream but in a waking vision just as he was, and as he is represented in paintings (*graphetai*).'[6] In a seventh-century account, St Artemios appeared in a vision to a girl stricken with a bubonic tumor and healed her. She related that, 'He resembled the icon standing on the left side of the ... church [where she was cured].'[7] The growing popularity of portable icons — and their effectiveness in colonizing the imagination — can be seen in the case of a soldier who carried an image of

---

[1] Dulaey (1973).

[2] Stroumsa (1999; 204).

[3] Rouselle (1990; 255).

[4] Bevan (1940; 47, 86).

[5] Fox (1987; 676).

[6] *Miracles of SS. John and Cyrus*, 52, in Marcos (1975; 365). See also miracle 70, where the author of the collection, Sophronios, sees both saints, 'in the forms which they had and in which they are represented in paintings,' Marcos (1975; 397).

[7] *Miracles of St Artemios*, 34 in Crisafulli and Nesbitt (1997; 181).

Cosmas and Damian painted on a special cloth while stationed far away from the saints' church. His local-born wife became familiar with the saints strictly through this image and then had a healing dream where the saints appeared to her 'in the form in which they are represented' (*en o ektupountai skhimati*).[1] The circular relationship that held between pagan statues and dreams now seems to have transferred to a circular relationship between dreams and Christian iconography. This relationship would be further cultivated and disseminated by icon painters who painted their personal dream visions of the saints, thereby giving the collective a fund of images which they, in turn, could dream.[2]

Some of the first representations of Christ already in the third century depicted him performing healing miracles such as curing the woman with an issue of blood, or healing the leper. Healing was clearly destined to become a point of competition between paganism and Christianity; it was an issue across which converts would either be won or lost. Two accounts from the *Miracles of Cosmas and Damian* further illustrate how incubation narratives expressed the relationship between healing and conversion.

Renowned Christian healers (from Cilicia), Cosmas and Damian were martyred under Diocletian (287CE). Churches dedicated to them had sprouted throughout the eastern Mediterranean by the mid-sixth century. During this period a set of stories reporting their miracles also accumulated.[3] One of these accounts related that the pagans habitually referred to Cosmas and Damian as Castor and Pollux. In one instance, a pagan man fell gravely ill and his friends counselled him to attend the clinic of Cosmas and Damian. Each day when they made their rounds among the sick he would call out for Castor and Pollux to attend to him, but they avoided him. Finally, stricken with pain he cornered the two doctors and they explained that they only answered to the names Cosmas and Damian and that their power came from Christ. If the man would recognize Christ then he could be healed. The pagan man accepted, was healed, and then, after being baptized a Christian, he returned to the pagan community to spread the good news. None of this is said to happen in a dream, but it sets the stage for the next miracle story.

---

[1] *Miracles of Cosmas and Damian*, 13, in Deubner (1907; 133). On the three-ply cloth 'icon', called *trimataria*, see Festugière (1971; 125, n. 52).

[2] Dagron (1991; 31).

[3] The stories of the miracles of Cosmas and Damian were certainly in circulation before 630 CE when Sophronios shows an awareness of them. See Festugière (1971; *Saint Thécle* 88).

A pagan man accompanied a Christian friend to a church of Cosmas and Damian. He was contemplating converting to Christianity and he thought that he might have a dream that would guide him. He spent a long time in the narthex of the church praying to Christ to give him a 'vision' (*optasia*) or 'divine illumination' (*theia ellampsi*).[1] He then has a dream of three children eating morsels of bread dipped into wine. He experiences a great desire to partake of this food, but the children refuse his request and he is overcome with fear that he will be killed. He realizes, even in his dream, that he has discovered the secret of the Eucharist and he also knows that Christians kill non-Christians who violate their mysteries. But Cosmas and Damian appear and give him bread to eat and he awakens confirmed in his intention to convert to Christianity.[2]

*Conclusion: Dreams and the Desire for Chronology*

Taken together these last two accounts narrate the final dissolution of pagan incubation, indeed of paganism itself. Just as Proclus's dream of Athena scripted a possible continuation of paganism, the Cosmas and Damian accounts narrated its impending absorption into Christianity. In this respect both of these dreams could be called historicizing — they are not just the reports of rituals or dreams but of historical orderings. The appearance of the statue of Athena in Proclus's dream no doubt reflected a response to changing times but I think we can also read it as a periodizing device; it offered a way of thinking about history, rather than solely a reaction to events.

The example of Nebuchadnezzar's dream in the Old Testament Book of Daniel (chap. 2) helps to clarify how a statue might offer a chronology. In this episode, Nebuchadnezzar, in fact, forgets his dream, and Daniel reminds him that he dreamt of a huge statue with a head of gold, chest of silver, midriff of bronze, legs of iron, and feet partly of iron and partly of clay. As he looked upon the statue a stone was thrown against it and toppled it. This stone remained and filled the whole earth. Daniel suggested that the head represented Nebuchadnezzar's current Babylonian kingdom, which would be replaced by inferior and still more inferior kingdoms until a final collapse.

---

[1] Although it is not said explicitly, he is quite probably contemplating an image of Christ. Compare Miracle 30 (in Deubner 1907; 174) where a sick man contemplates images of the Virgin, Christ and Cosmas and Damian before having a dream of the last two.

[2] These two stories follow each other as Miracles 9 and 10 in Deubner (1907; 113-121), French trans. in Festugière (1971; 110ff).

At the point of its delivery to Nebuchadnezzar this dream was prophetic, but for subsequent centuries it presented a ready-made periodizing framework within which ancient peoples could locate themselves.[1] The Jewish historian Josephus (First Century CE), retold the story of Nebuchadnezzar's dream reducing it to four kingdoms. The belly and thighs of bronze were clearly Alexander's empire, and the legs and feet of iron (no mention of clay) apparently represented Rome. He shied away from giving a meaning to the boulder — 'I am expected to write of what is past and done,' he wrote, 'not of what is to be.' -- because he probably thought it signified the Jewish messiah but did not wish to risk offending his Roman readers.[2] The Christian theologian Hippolytus (Third Century CE), interpreted the iron legs as the Romans and the mixed toes of the statue as representing ten future democracies. These democracies would disagree with one another and ultimately Christ would descend from heaven, like the boulder in the prophecy, and install 'the heavenly kingdom of the saints.'[3] The identification of the boulder with the Second Coming remained standard for most Christian writers.

The neo-Platonist, anti-Christian philosopher Porphyry contended that the Book of Daniel was not actually composed around the time of the Babylonian captivity, but rather four centuries later (ca. 165 BCE).[4] At this time the Seleucid king Anitochus Epiphanes ruled Judaea and pursued a harsh policy of Hellenizing the Jews. At the time of its composition then, the dream of Nebuchadnezzar was already largely history — the Babylonians, Medes, and Persians had all come and gone. The purpose of this history/dream was to give hope to a second century Jewish audience that the Seleucid rule would soon give way and the period of suffering would be over. No messianic reading of the boulder seems to have figured, simply a welcome change of rule. Eusebius and Jerome poured scorn on this offensive reading of the dream of Nebuchadnezzar and it is perhaps unsurprising that the volume in which Porphyry wrote these ideas, *Against the Christians*, survives only in fragments, mainly the citations of its critics.[5] Today, however, most scholars accept Porphyry's dating of the Book of Daniel. H. H. Rowley has argued that an earlier writer would not have made so many historical mistakes, such as

---

[1] Pomian (1981; 607).

[2] Josephus, *Jewish Antiquities*, 10.210.

[3] Hippolytus, *Commentary on Daniel*, 2.13, Bonwetsch (2000).

[4] Cited in Jerome, *Commentary on Daniel*, Prologue, *MPL*, 25; 491.

[5] Harnack (1916).

considering Darius to be a Mede rather than a Persian. Nebuchadnezzar's dream, then, was historically erroneous rather than prophetically accurate.[1]

This example relates to the present study of incubation not only because it suggests that Proclus and his contemporaries may well have been familiar with the figure of the statue as a chronotrope. It also helps to address the question of the relationship between 'real' dreams and their narration in texts. For a dream to be known publicly it must be represented by the person who experienced it. In the transition from experience to narration there is plenty of room for fabrication and in the case of important dreams such as those of Proclus, or the faithful at healing shrines, we might concede that we do not have accurate transcriptions of the original phenomenological dreams. What we do have, rather, are narratives that have themselves been 'incubated' over generations, even centuries, in the imaginations of those re-telling the stories. These dreams thus come to look more like the Book of Daniel — tales composed at a later date specifically for political purposes such as offering hope to those in straitened circumstances, or to wage triumphalist polemic. The temporality of these narratives is consequently highly convoluted. As prophecies these dreams involve looking into the future from a point in the past, while from the perspective of the telling everything that they relate is already historical.

Certainly the practice of incubation provoked contest between pagans and Christians in late antiquity and this imbued the dream accounts with, perhaps, more polemical overtones than are found in the dream cures of Asclepius recorded in the fourth century BCE.[2] The idea of dreaming to gain (healing) visions continued, yet few agreed on how and why it should carry on. This study has compiled evidence that would allow one to argue for either the continuity or discontinuity of incubation. Rather than treat the two as alternatives, it might be more productive, and realistic, to consider both to occur simultaneously.

This study also alerts present-day scholars interested in writing the history of incubation that some of the data which they seek to use also attempts the very same project of presenting a 'history'. Those who told stories of incubation often interpolated their partisan historical assessments right into the dreams themselves. The right dream might decide the struggle and change the course of events. In this respect, incubation in late antiquity can be viewed as a form of history in the guise of ritually induced dream.

---

[1] Rowley (1959; 175ff).

[2] Edelstein and Edelstein (1998, Vol. 1; 221ff). Also LiDonnici (1995).

*REFERENCES*

Abraham, N. and Torok, M. 1994 'Mourning or Melancholia: Introjection *versus* Incorporation,' in *The Shell and the Kernel: Renewals of Psychoanalysis*, (ed. and trans. N. Rand), Chicago; University of Chicago Press, 125-138.

Alexiou, M. 1974 *The Ritual Lament in Greek Tradition*, Cambridge; Cambridge University Press.

Artemidorus 1975 *Oneirocritica*, trans. R. J. White, *The Interpretation of Dreams*, Park Ridge, NJ; Noyes Press.

Athanassiadi, P. 1993 'Dreams, Theurgy and Freelance Divination,' *Journal of Roman Studies*, 83; 115-130.

Barrett, D. 1993 'The "Committee of Sleep": A Study of Dream Incubation for Problem Solving,' *Journal of the Association for the Study of Dreams*, Vol 3; 115-122.

Behr, C. 1968 *Aelius Aristides and the Sacred Tales*, Amsterdam; Hakkert.

Bevan, E. 1940 *Holy Images: An Inquiry into Idolatry and Image-Worship in Ancient Paganism and Christianity*, London; George Allen and Unwin.

Brakke, D. 1998 ' 'Outside the Places, Within the Truth': Athanasius of Alexandriaand the Localization of the Holy,' in *Pilgrimage and Holy Space in Late Antique Egypt*, ed. D. Frankfurter, Leiden; Brill, 445-481.

Brown, P. 1981 *The Cult of Saints: Its Rise and Function in Latin Christianity*, Chicago; University of Chicago Press.

Brown, P. 1995 *Authority and the Sacred: Aspects of the Christianization of the Roman World*, Cambridge; Cambridge University Press.

Brillante, C. 1991 'Metamorphosi di un'immagine: le statue animate e il sogno,' in his *Studi sulla rappresentazione del sogno nella Grecia Antica*, Palermo; Sellerio, 96-111.

Coulanges, Fustel de. (nd) *The Ancient City*, Garden City, New York; Doubleday.

Colombo, I. 1975 'Acculturation et cultes thérapeutiques,' in eds. F. Durand and P. Lévêque, *Les syncrétismes dans les religions de l'antiquité*, Leiden; Brill.

Comaroff, J. 1985 *Body of Power, Spirit of Resistance: The Culture and History of a South African People*, Chicago; University of Chicago Press.

Crisafulli V. and Nesbitt, J. (eds.) 1997 *The Miracles of St Artemios*, Leiden; Brill.

Csordas, T. 1999 'Ritual Healing and the Politics of Identity in Contemporary Navajo Society,' *American Ethnologist*, 26; 3-23.

Dagron G. 1978 *Vie et miracles de Saint Thècle*, Brussels; Société des Bollandistes.

Dagron, G. 1985 'Rêver de Dieu et parler de soi,' in *I sogni nel medioevo*, ed. T. Gregory, Rome; Edizione dell'Ateneo, 37-55.

Dagron, G. 1991 'Image and Likeness,' *Dumbarton Oaks Papers*, 45; 22-23

Deubner, L. 1900 *De incubatione,* Leipzig; Teubner.

Deubner, L. 1907 *Kosmas und Damian,* Leipzig; Teubner.

Dulaey, M. 1973 *Les rêves dans la vie et la pensée de saint Augustin,* Paris; Études Augustinniennes.

Edelstein, E. and L. 1998 *Asclepius: Collection and Interpretation of the Testimonies,* Baltimore; Johns Hopkins.

Edwards, M. 2000 *Neoplatonic Saints,* Liverpool; Liverpool University Press.

Eitrem, S. 1991 'Dreams and Divination in Magical Ritual,' in *Magika Hiera,* eds. C. Faraone, and D. Obbink, Oxford; Oxford University Press; 175-187.

Faraone, C. 1992 *Talismans and Trojan Horses,* Oxford; Oxford University Press.

Festugière, A. 1966 'Proclus et la religion traditionnelle,' in *Mélanges d'archéologie et d'histoire offerts à André Piganiol,* vol. 3, ed. R. Chevallier, Paris; SEVPEN; 1581-1590

Festugière, A. 1971 *Sainte Thècle, Saints Côme et Damien, Saints Cyr et Jean(Extraits), Saint Georges,* Paris; A. et J. Picard.

Fox, R. 1987 *Pagans and Christians,* San Francisco; Harper and Row.

Frantz, A. 1965 'From Paganism to Christianity in the Temples of Athens', *Dumbarton Oaks Papers,* 19; 187-205.

Freud, S. 1991 *On Metapsychology,* London; Penguin.

Gordon, R. 1996 'The Real and the Imaginary: Production and Religion in the Graeco-Roman World,' in his *Image and Value in the Graeco-Roman World: Studies in Mithraism and Religious Art,* London; Variorum, 5-34.

Grégoire, H. and Kugener, M. (eds.) 1930 *Vie de Porphyre,* Paris; Les Belles Lettres.

[Gregory of Nyssa] 1971 *Vie de Sainte Macrine,* trans. and ed. P. Maraval, Paris; Cerf (SC 178).

Gregory, T. 1986 'The Survival of Paganism in Christian Greece: A Critical Essay,' *American Journal of Philology,* 107; 229-242.

Gross, K. 1992 *The Dream of the Moving Statue,* Ithaca; Cornell.

Hamilton, M. 1906 *Incubation, or, the Cure of Disease in Pagan Temples and Christian Churches,* St Andrews; W.C. Henderson.

Harnack, A. 1916 *Porphyrius 'Gegen die Christen',* Berlin; Abhandlungen der Königl. Preuss. Akademie der Wissenschaften.

Hasluck, F. 1929 *Christianity and Islam Under the Sultans,* 2 Vols., Oxford; Clarendon Press.

Hippolytus 2000 *Kommentar zu Daniel* ed. G.N. Bonwetsch (revised second ed. M. Richard), Berlin; Akademie Verlag.

Kiernan, J. 1994 'Variation on a Christian Theme: The Healing Synthesis of Zulu Zionism,' in *Syncretism/Anti-Syncretism: The Politics of Religious Synthesis,* eds. C. Stewart and R. Shaw, London; Routledge, 69-84.

Klein, M. 1975 'Mourning and Its Relation to Manic-Depressive States,' in her *Love, Guilt and Reparation and Other Works (1921-1945)*, London; Hogarth, 344-369.

Lambek, M. 1998 'The Sakalava Poiesis of History: Realizing the Past Through Spirit Possession in Madagascar', *American Ethnologist*, 25, 106-27.

Lapatin, K. 2001 *Chryselephantine Statuary in the Ancient World*, Oxford; Oxford University Press.

Leach, E. 1961 'Two Essays Concerning the Symbolic Representation of Time,' in his *Rethinking Anthropology*, London; Athlone, 124-136.

LiDonnici, L. 1995 *The Epidaurian Miracle Inscriptions: Text, Translation and Commentary*, Atlanta; Scholars Press.

Marcos, N. 1975 *Los Thaumata de Sofronio: Contribución al Estudio de la Incubación Cristiana*, Madrid; Instituto Antonio Nebrija.

Masullo, R. 1985 *Vita di Proclo*, Napoli; M. D'Auria.

Mathews, T. 1999 *The Clash of the Gods: A Reinterpretation of Early Christian Art*, rev. and expanded ed., Princeton; Princeton University Press.

Miller, P. 1994 *Dreams in Late Antiquity: Studies in the Imagination of a Culture*, Princeton; Princeton University Press.

Perkins, J. 1995 *The Suffering Self*, London; Routledge.

Pfister, F. 1924 'Epiphanie,' in Pauly-Wissowa, *Realencyclopädie der classischen Altertumswissenchaft*, Supplementband, 4, Stuttgart; J.B. Metzlersche, columns 277-323.

Pomian, K. 1981 'Periodizzazione,' in *Enciclopedia: Opinione — Probabilitá*, vol. 10, Torino; Einaudi, 603-650.

Rapp, C. 2000 'Mark the Deacon, *The Life of Porphyry of Gaza*,' in *Medieval Hagiography: An Anthology*, T. Head, ed., New York; Garland, 53-75.

Rousselle, A. 1990 *Croire et guérir: La foi en Gaule dan l'antiquité tardive*, Paris; Fayard.

Rowley, H. 1959 *Darius the Mede and the Four World Empires in the Book of Daniel: A Historical Study of Contemporary Theories*, Cardiff; University of Wales Press.

Rusten, J. 1983 '*Geiton Heros:* Pindar's Prayer to Heracles (N. 7.86-101) and Greek Popular Religion,' *Harvard Studies in Classical Philology*, Vol. 87; 289-97.

Sahlins, M. 1985 *Islands of History*, Chicago; University of Chicago Press.

Stewart, C. 1997 'Fields in Dreams: Anxiety, Experience and the Limits of Social Constructionism in Modern Greek Dream Narratives', *American Ethnologist*, 24 (1997), 877-894.

Stewart, C. 2001 '*Oi oneirevamenoi: ta gegonota tou 1930 stin Korono* [The Religious Dreamers: The events of 1930 in Koronos],' *Arkhaiologiakai tekhnes*, 80 (2001), 8-14.

Stroumsa, G. 1999 'Dreams and Visions in Early Christian Discourse', in *Dream Cultures: Explorations in the Comparative History of Dreaming*, D. Shulman and G. Stroumsa (eds.), Oxford; Oxford University Press. 189-212.

Takács, S. 1994 'The Magic of Isis Replaced, or, Cyril of Alexandria's Attempt at Redirecting Religious Devotion,' *Poikila Byzantina*, 13 (1994), 491-507.

Tatian 1982 *Oratio ad Graecos*, trans. and edited M. Whittaker, Oxford; Clarendon.

Tedlock, B. 1983 'A Phenomenological Approach to Religious Change in Highland Guatemala,' in *Heritage of Conquest, Thirty Years Later*, eds. C. Kendall et. al., University of New Mexico Press; Albuquerque.

Tertullian 1947 *De Animai* ed. J. Waszink, Amsterdam; J.M. Meulenhoff.

Trombley, F. 1993/1994 *Hellenic Religion and Christianization, c. 370-529*, 2 *Vols.*, Leiden; Brill.

Trombley, F. 2000 'Religious Experience in Late Antiquity: Theological Ambivalence and Christianization,' *Byzantine and Modern Greek Studies*, 24; 2-60.

Van Straten, F. 1976 'Daikrates' Dream: a votive relief from Kos, and some other *Kat'onar* dedications,' *Bulletin Antieke Beschaving*, 51.

Versnel, H. 1987 'What Did Ancient Man See When He Saw a God? Some Reflections on Greco-Roman Epiphany,' in *Effigies Dei: Essays on the History of Religions*, ed. D. van der Plas, Leiden; Brill, 42-55.

# 19. THE CHRISTIANISATION OF RITE IN BYZANTINE ANATOLIA: F. W. HASLUCK AND RELIGIOUS CONTINUITY

Frank TROMBLEY

William Mitchell Ramsay was one of the first scholars to write about the complex religious phenomena in the cultural transitions that affected Anatolia since the Late Roman and Byzantine periods.[1] In a series of papers he put forward a series of radical theses, arguing that structures of religious ritual and belief could be identified that had persisted through all periods of transformation, from Hellenistic times into the epoch of Christianisation, and from Byzantine times into the Islamic period under the Seljuk and Ottoman Turks.[2] Ramsay's observations were significant, but he lacked the critical skills of an anthropologist and knowledge of Greek Patristic and Byzantine writers whose reports about Anatolian religious life clarify the lines of transition that he sought to demonstrate. One of his early critics was F. W. Hasluck, whose monumental but sadly posthumous work, *Christianity and Islam under the Sultans* marked a considerable step forward in understanding the peculiarities that Ramsay first identified. Hasluck was himself a keen observer of religious life whose approach to Greek and Turkish society was substantially empirical, whether he collected his data from reports by eyewitness travellers' accounts or from personal observation. His untimely death prevented him from systematising his analysis of the culturally mixed societies that were becoming more individuated and forming national states after the break-up of the Ottoman empire following the First World War.[3]

---

[1] On Ramsay's career, see Frend (1996; 93-104, 130-34, 193-95, etc.).

[2] e.g. 'The orthodox church in the Byzantine empire' (Ramsay 1908), 'The permanence of religion at the holy places in western Asia' (1906).

[3] See the note of Margaret M. Hasluck, in Hasluck, *Christianity and Islam* (1929). There is no biographical treatment of Hasluck comparable to what has been written about Ramsay by Frend (though see the chapter on Hasluck's life by Shankland in this volume).

Hasluck's work on these questions was original and significant, but requires updating in light of some Byzantine texts that he was not able to consider.[1] In what follows, I will consider Hasluck's approach to the phenomenology of religion. Before doing so, however, I would like to make some observations about methods of looking at early Christianity as a proselytising world religion. It is important to recognise that, even in its earliest expansion, the new religion made extensive use of the cultural tools available to it.[2] Werner Jaeger identifies the ways in which the Greek *paideia* was adapted to the Christian scriptures, tracing the fundamental ideas of Platonism and the late Stoa through its earliest writers, until a distinctively Christian sophistic had emerged by the beginning of the fourth century.[3]

The adaptive talents of Christian sophists like Eusebius of Caesarea had parallels in the way the new monotheism was presented to agriculturalists in the territories of the Greek cities of Asia Minor and Syria: but here the κοινή of everyday religious life, not the Greek *paideia*, was the norm to be imitated. When the Christian monks, *chorepiskopoi* and *periodeutai* first penetrated the countryside, to be followed later by the presbyters and deacons who staffed the rural churches, they discovered a synthetic language of ritual and belief that combined the ideas of Hellenistic religion with regional substrates. In the third to seventh centuries, this κοινή was subjected to a series of modifications that has at times been called *Ritenchristianisierung* ('Christianisation of rite'):[4] the older rituals, concepts and iconographies persisted but monotheistic formulae displaced those of the pre-Christian cults. The sacramental rites of the new religion were taken up, but the older liturgies coexisted with them, just as Christian and traditional pagan cults coexisted in peculiar synoikisms at rural sites associated with numinous springs, trees, stones and caves.[5] Pre-Christian ideas of the natural world, as also of the divine and daemonic, persisted in the rustic consciousness long after the admission of villagers to the status of catechumens, those being instructed in the basics of the Christian scriptures and the canons.

---

[1] Hasluck seems to have profited from Lawson's *Modern Greek Folklore and Ancient Greek Religion* (1910; repr. 1964). The latter is a seminal work that nevertheless has questions of approach analogous to those found in Hasluck's thinking on the subject.

[2] On the period down to 325, see von Harnack (1924). On the post-Nicaean period, see Trombley (1993-94). For updated discussion see Trombley (2000). The present paper should be read in light of an earlier study, Trombley (1985b).

[3] This subject still awaits definitive study, though see Jaeger (1961). Cf. Chadwick (1966).

[4] Kirsten (1978; 465).

[5] On this, see Trombley (1993-4; i, 98-122, 147-86; ii, 52-133).

It is easy to be dismissive of the questions raised by Ramsay and Hasluck: in essence, does it matter that identifiable structures of belief and ritual closely resemble those of the early Byzantine period in Anatolia? My own reply tends to be in the affirmative, inasmuch as the analysis of similar structures is a basic feature of comparative religion. The central question is not this, but whether cultural structures of Byzantine, Seljuk and early Ottoman Society had a sufficiently inherent importance to keep these imagined continuities in existence over a period of some thirteen centuries.[1] Diachronic analysis requires data of an intermediate date whose structures are clearly visible in the reports of observers. There is textual evidence of this kind in the Byzantine period which, as with epigraphy and archaeological data, owes its continued existence to random survival. The raw materials left over from early societies necessarily deliver only an imperfect and fragmentary picture of cultural structures. At this stage, I can only offer certain modifications to Hasluck's analysis of phenomena from the late Ottoman period, but am convinced that some structures, particularly the adaptations of pre-Christian cult to the new monotheism, can in fact be traced diachronically.

It is important to reject the proposition that Greek Christianity was monolithic from the standpoint of ritual and belief right from the start. On this point R. W. Hefner has observed:[2]

> Recent anthropological research has emphasized that Christianity in a cross-cultural context is far less socially and ideologically monolithic than the 'salvationist orthodoxy' ... often attributed to it. Contrary to essentialist characterisations of its meaning, Christianity has demonstrated a remarkable ability to take on different cultural shadings in local settings ... The Christian message of individual salvation, for example, has often been marginalized or recast to meet communal needs ... [However], we must not fall into the converse error of extreme cultural particularism, so thoroughly deconstructing Christianity as to conclude that it is really no more than a congeries of local traditions.

It is the object of my paper to suggest a middle path similar to this through a closer look at the Byzantine materials. In what follows, Hasluck's arguments on particular points will be tested against the Byzantine evidence.

---

[1] The late medieval religious synthesis in Anatolia is outlined in exceptional detail by Vryonis in his *The Decline of Medieval Hellenism in Asia Minor* (1971; 143-286, 351-402, etc). This work is a fundamental starting point for thinking about the phenomenology of the continuity question.

[2] Hefner (1993; 5).

*Sacrifice*

Sacrifice was a fundamental feature of pre-Christian Mediterranean religion, and is too well-known to require comment here.[1] The origin of the specifically Christian sacrifice in late Ottoman Anatolia is a much vexed question, but it appears to go all the way back to Late Antiquity. In discussing the *kurban* or Christian liturgical sacrifice in his chapter on the cult of the dead, Hasluck suggests it entered Anatolian Christianity for the most part through Turkish Islam:[2]

> From the Mohammedans this practice of *kurban* [in honour of a saint] has spread to the Christian races with whom they came in contact; this was aided by the Easter usages, derived at an earlier period by the Christians from the Semites, and on the other hand by the pagan elements surviving, especially on the folk-lore side, among Christians as well as Mohammedams. Both Armenian and Greek Orthodox Christians are familiar with the idea of apotropaic bloodshed and the half religious consumption of the victim.

However, *pace* Hasluck, the Christian sacrifice has an early origin, having been accepted into rural ritual not later than the sixth century. It seems initially to have been forbidden by the Twenty-eighth Canon of the fourth-century Council of Laodikea in the proscription of agape celebrations: 'It is not permitted on Sundays or in the churches to perform the so-called agapes and to eat them in the church of God and to spread couches' (ὅτι οὐ δεῖ" ... τὰς λεγομένας ἀγάπας ποιεῖ'ν καὶ ἐν οἴκῳ του" θεου" ἐσθίειν καὶ ἀκούβιτα στρωννύειν).[3]

This rule was not universally obeyed. For example, in sixth-century Lycia, St Nikolaos bishop and hegumen of the Hagia Sion monastery performed a series of sacrifices outside the rural chapels, but was careful to substitute Christian symbols and cite the Old Testament as the exemplar:[4]

> The clerics of Plenion with the Christ-loving people came with a procession and crosses and met the servant of God at the [chapel of the] famous saint. From there [Nikolaos] followed them with seven calves. When they had gone into the chapel of St George, he sacrificed (ἔθυσεν) the seven cattle. The crowds assembled, so 200 couches were made. The servant of God brought for expenditure 100 *metra* of wine and 40 *modii* of bread. All ate and were filled ... There were left over 60 *metra* of wine, 100 loaves of bread and four *metra* of oil.

---

[1] e.g. Trombley (1993-4; 3-35).

[2] Hasluck (1929; 259-61).

[3] Rhalles and Potles (1992; 195).

[4] Anrich (1913; 42f). Cf. the improved text of Sevcenko and. Sevcenko (1984; 86).

The terminology of the hagiographer is striking: there is no difference in ritual between this and the pagan except the use of processional crosses and the use of a Christian building as the focal point of the ritual. The story, and others like it, survived in the traditions about St Nikolaos, probably because the practice was not considered unusual. Two year later, Nikolaos made a circuit tour of ten rural chapels near the monastery at Hagia Sion and performed Christiansed sacrifices once again: the tour lasted twenty five days, and he visited the villages and hamlets of Karkabo, Kausai, Nea Kome, Partaessos, Symbolon, Naute, Serine, Trebendai, Kastellon and Hemalissoi.[1] The pre-Christian sacrifice had currency for a long time after this as well. For example, a letter of Photius patriarch of Constantinople (ninth century) mentions a group of men who performed the divinatory sacrifice of a dog to the goddess Ge to help them find buried treasure. When the divination failed, they confessed the offence to their bishop, who passed on the story to the patriarch.[2] Civil law continued to prohibit pagan sacrifice, keeping it as a capital offence, right through until the publication of the *Basilika* in the tenth century, but references to its practice disappear from hagiographic texts, probably because of the rhetorical tradition that invaded this genre of literature, destroying the precision of description seen in the early Byzantine period.[3] There is a report about a quasi-Greek *kurban* in 1570 in which the *dermatikon* or priest's share was retained.[4]

This practice did in fact survive until the early twentieth century when Hasluck was writing, as we learn from early twentieth-century Greek folkloric practice.[5] The configuration of pre-Christian sacrificial ritual underwent diachronic modification in Christian and Muslim folklore. This is seen in the instance of the shallow, circular recessed libation 'dishes' carved into the tops of pre-Christian Greek funerary and, it would seem, votive altars. Hasluck cites a particularly apposite case that was first noticed by William Mitchell Ramsay, but goes to the opposite extreme in trying to refute the latter's continuity argument. It is instructive to quote both accounts, as they illustrate the differences of phenomenological interpretation that separated these two pioneering scholars. Ramsay observes (my italics):[6]

---

[1] *Vita S. Nicolai* §§56-57 (Anrich 1, 43ff.; Sevcenko, 88-91).

[2] Photius, *Epistula* 1.20, *Patrologia Graeca* 102, col. 788.

[3] *Codex Iustinianus* 1.11.9-10, notes 16-17, in *Corpus Iuris Civilis II.* (1954; 63f).

[4] Vryonis (1972; 174).

[5] Lawson (1910; 262-68).

[6] Ramsay (1906; 156ff), cited by Hasluck (1929; 209).

> Three or four miles south of Pisidian Antioch we found in a village cemetery
> an altar dedicated to the god Hermes. On the top of the altar there is a
> shallow semicircular depression, which must probably have been intended
> to hold liquid offerings poured on the altar, and *which was evidently made*
> *when the altar was constructed and dedicated.* A native of the village ... told
> us that the stone was possessed of power, and that if any one who was sick
> came to it and drank, he was cured forthwith of his sickness. *This belief has*
> *lasted through the centuries; it has withstood the teaching and denunciation*
> *of Christians and Mohammedans alike.*

There can be little argument with Ramsay's interpretation of the function of
this libation dish. The ritual must date from long after the epoch of
Christianisation, however, because it does not entail any real species of
sacrifice; it is instead a folkloric adaptation, because in sacrifical ritual the
fluids poured out are for the divinity of the altar, not the dedicant. The
behavioural structure described by Ramsay could have arisen in the Byzantine,
Seljuk or Ottoman periods. Hasluck expresses vigorous dissent from
Ramsay's opinion:[1]

> The fact of the cultus of folk-lore practice attached to this stone is clear
> enough, but some of Ramsay's inferences are more than disputable. If, as
> seems beyond doubt, this inscribed stone is Sterret's No. 349, a
> quadrangular *cippus* with inscription recording the dedication of a *Hermes*,
> *i.e.* a statue of Hermes, the stone was never an altar except in form. There
> is, therefore, no reason to refer the beginnings of its cultus-use to ancient
> times. It was most probably selected as a suitable stone for a grave and
> transported in recent times to the Turkish cemetery. The hollow on the top
> of the 'altar' probably dates in its present form only from the adaptation of
> the stone to its use as a tombstone ... Circular sinkings are commonly
> madeon Turkish tombstones; the reason usually given is that birds are
> enabled to drink of the rain and dew that collects in them ... It will be seen
> that this reduces the fact that the stone is inscribed with the name of a god
> to a mere accident.

The difficulty with Hasluck's counter-argument is that there are no real
archaeological criteria for dating stone cuttings of this type. At the
archaeological museum at Beroia in Macedonia, libation dishes of this type are
found on many of the funerary altars, most of them of late Hellenistic and
Roman imperial date. The frequency of the practice and its occurrence in what
was a predominantly Greek town suggests that these features are original.[2]

---

[1] Hasluck (1929; 209f).

[2] Personal observation, September 2001.

This brings us to another question, the performance of cult beside sacred stones of different types. In the chapter on 'natural cults', Hasluck brings together some important data, but his system of classification may be in need of updating.[1] The first category is what Hasluck calls an 'aerolith' or meteorite stone; such an object is more commonly called a *baitylos*, from the Aramaic *bait-'el* of 'house of a god'. He produces no examples from Anatolia, but repeats the consensus that the black stone of Ka'ba in Makka is a meteorite.[2] The fragments of Damascius' sixth-century *Life of Isidore* provide us with precise information about how the cult worked: *baityloi* fallen from the sky were considered numinous because of their unusual fabric and appearance. Devotees retrieved them, dedicating them at the temples of sky gods and using them for oracular purposes. Damascius observes about a *baitylos* found by one of Isidore's fellow philosophers:[3]

> The sphere was round and its colour whitish, and sometimes purplish. It was a span in size, but it was here and there greater or smaller [in diameter]. He showed us letters coloured vermillon written on the stone. He hammered on it, through which it gave the oracle sought by the inquirer, giving forth the sound of a delicate Pan-pipe which Eusebius interpreted.

The stone's surface had markings on it that were perhaps understood in accordance with a practice later mentioned by Hasluck, that of Greeks and Turks using ancient inscribed stones for the divination of buried treasure.[4] Photius mentions that the indigenous population of ninth-century Greece in Boeotia and Phokida still collected *baityloi* and honoured them in this manner around Mt. Parnassos. The numinous quality of inscribed stones will detain us later when we return to the subject of excavating for buried treasure.

The rites surrounding the cults of natural stones were at times thoroughly Christianised, to the extent of imposing peculiar aetiologies, a practice that Hasluck frequently observed in the late Ottoman period. So, for example, there was peculiarly shaped stone bridge at a numinous hot spring near Tarsus in Cilicia that acquired a folkloric Christian aetiology sometime before the twentieth century: it was said to be the remnant of a shepherd petrified by a curse of St Helena, mother of Constantine the first Christian

---

[1] Hasluck (1929; 175-225).

[2] Hasluck (1929; 179-81).

[3] Damascius, *Epitome Photiana 203*, in *Vitae Isidori R eliquiae* (1967; 276).

[4] This is quite different from the stones cited by Hasluck that were thought to be marked with the footprints of Christian and Muslim holy men. Hasluck (1929; 185-87).

emperor and, to judge from Hasluck's description, apparently became the new focus of the local healing ritual.[1]

The medieval aetiologies established with ecclesiatical consent were more sophisticated. An example is found in the tenth-century life of St Paul the Younger, hegumen of the Stylos monastery at Latros in Caria (*ob*. 956) where it can be seen that public opinion was at times a factor in the persistence of stone cults:[2]

> A drought and generally extreme shortage of water gripped (αὐχμός...καὶ ἀπορία ὕδατος ἐπιεικω"ς ἐσχάτη) Miletus. Certain like-minded men, not less than forty of them, assembled from different villages, formed a procession and went up to the peak of the mountain with hymns beloved to God. The peak was not only very high and above the clouds, but very difficult to climb. An extremely large stone (λίθος) lies on the peak (ἀκρωρεία). This stone was called sacred from of old. The cause of its being called thus among the indigenous people (οἱ ἐγχώριοι) was twofold. [Here the hagiographer notes the widely circulated story that the stone came from a mountain peak in Palestine connected with the Old Testament traditions.] But others and I think this happened in truth because perfect gifts were given to many of the fathers [hermits of associated with the Latros monasteries]. As many of them as showed something notable or renowned, perfect gifts were given to them by the stone such as the gift of remedies, illuminations and the visitations of the good spirit.

The hagiographer adds that an ancient iron cross stood beside the stone (σταυρὸς ἐκ μακρω"ν τω"ν χρόνων ἐκει" πάρεστι σιδηρου"ς), being perhaps a token from the time when the site and its litugies were first Christianised. The site of the sacred stone was a pre-Christian 'high place'.

Hermann Usener who first noticed this text was inclined to assign a pre-Greek origin to the cult.[3] Hasluck did not notice this text, which provides an important intermediate link for any theory of structural continuity. In his discussion of more recent examples Hasluck expresses doubt as to the continuity of such cults from the ancient period, but nevertheless recognises that such a temenos was normally dedicated to the local sky god who controlled rainfall.[4] He admits that, in his own time, it would often have attracted Christian and Muslim hermits who were often 'weather-prophets and rain-makers',[5] probably not unlike the so-called νεφοδιώκαι or 'cloud-drivers'

---

[1] Hasluck (1929; 182).

[2] Delehaye (1892; 53f).

[3] Usener (1913; 198).

[4] On the personification of meteorological forces, see Lévi-Strauss (1966; 96).

[5] Hasluck (1929; 98f).

who in popular credence shifted clouds about the skies and are mentioned at least as late as the seventh century in the Sixty-first Canon of the Council in Trullo of 691-92.[1] The hagiographer lets us down in one respect, however, by failing to mention whether any other cultic buildings existed there, as for example a stone enclosure, a cairn, the tomb of a holy man or a even sacred tree.[2] All he mentions is the cross.

In comparison with the black stone's legendary flight from Palestine, Hasluck mentions a sacred stone at Alexandrovo near Uskub in the Balkans that was believed according to one report to have been levitated there from Mecca after the prayer of a Muslim holy man, citing an Islamic legend.[3] The structural similarity of this story to a pre-existing Greek or Bulgarian orthodox aetiology seems more plausible.

The *charismata* that the stone near the Latros monastery is said to have imparted to the Christian hermits are peculiar and sound rather like ecstatic or shamanic enthusiasms.[4] The name given to the Christian divinity or his messenger, the 'good spirit' (τὸ ἀγαθὸν πνεῦ'μα), is uncomfortably close to that of the so-called 'good daemon' (ὁ ἀγαθὸς δαίμων), a divinity named as the third in a triad with Men Askaenos and the Agdistean Mother of the Gods in a late second-century inscription from Eumeneia in Phrygia Paktiane.[5] At first sight it sounds quite similar to the Muslim dervishes, the successors of the Christian *paramonarioi*, whom Hasluck and his informants encountered while visiting shrines.[6] These men often presided over a Christian-Muslim synoikism at pilgrimage shrines whose sanctity had originally been associated with Greek saints and whose Turkish cult was seen as a species of 'unorthodox' Islam.[7]

*Religious Enthusiasm and Ecstasy*

Hasluck was much interested in the phenomena of religious enthusiasm in the early twentieth-century Anatolia, a subject that has been of particular interest to anthropologists. In his book on Cyzicus, he quotes a long section from a

---

[1] Rhalles and Potles (1992; 442f).

[2] Hasluck (1929; 99-104).

[3] Hasluck (1929; 198).

[4] Lewis (1989).

[5] *Inscriptiones Graecae ad Res Romanas pertinentes* (1927 no. 739).

[6] Hasluck (1929; 43f., 47f., 55, 69f.).

[7] Hasluck (1929; 49-59). On synoikism, see Ovsyannikov and Terebikhin (1994; 44-81).

physician named George of Cyzicus who was writing *circa* 1825. The latter mentions a thaumaturgic icon kept in a church near Cyzicus that was periodically the object of religious frenzy at the *panegyris* of the Dormition of the Mother of God held on 15 August. The writer was undoubtedly educated in classical Greek and saw this behaviour as a form of crypto-pagan possession descended in a line of direct continuity from the pre-Christian period. The text seems not to have been edited elsewhere and is worth quoting at length because it illustrates the easy lines of structural correspondence that are too often drawn in continuity arguments:[1]

> Here in August at the time of the *panegyris* a large body of people assembles from every direction, and a great festival is convoked becasue of the piety toward the *Theotokos*, and because of the miraculous activity of the icon (τὸ δὲ διὰ τὸ γενόμενον τερατούργημα τῆς εἰκόνος). I do not know when this custom was introduced among Christians, that a person should take the icon upon his shoulders and run as though possessed (ὡς ἐνεργούμενος), carrying it at times to steep and difficult places, at other times to rocks crags and rivers, while the rest of the people follow with wonderment and piety. As a result there occurs an altercation and emulation that the next one might shoulder the icon in order to accomplish the same disorderly behaviour. There are some who carry the icon without avail, since they do not run in a mad state but remain in their right minds, since they are not susceptible to its activity, nor do they minds remain queer from intoxication, nor do their have an irritable and agile hallucination. When I consider that such disorderly somersaults and leaps of the Corybants proceeded from the two roots, intoxication and hallucination, we also have disorders of the nerves that proceed from these two causes. As regards intoxication we have before our eyes what is in operation, but as regards hallucination and devotional enthusiasm, we have the Bacchic divine madness from the pagan revels, and from Turkish sources of information the dance of St Vitus and the frenzied movements and rotations of the dervishes. Wherefore it is proper that those who preside over our race spiritually should put a stop to these pagan ecstasies lest we become the laughing-stock of foreigners.

The text speaks for itself as an example of cultural criticism. The key terms are 'miracle working' (τερατούργημα) and 'as though being possessed' (ὡς ἐνεργούμενος). More literally, the participants behaved 'as though activated' by the numinous power of the icon. Hasluck mentions a structurally analogous behavioural phenomenon. The village has a hybridised Bulgar-Turkish place name:[2]

---

[1] Greek quoted from Hasluck's *Cyzicus* (1910; 25, note 1). Translation adapted from Trombley (1981; 169f., note 10).

[2] Quoted from Sir Arthur Evans, in Hasluck (1929; 210f).

Sir Arthur Evans found at Ibrahimovce, near Uskub (Macedonia), a Roman altar dedicated to Jupiter Optimus Maximus, which was used by the villagers as a rain-charm. It is generally kept face downward, but in times of drought Christians and Mohammedans, headed by a local *bey*, go together to the stone and, having restored it to its upright position, pour libations on the top, praying for rain. Evans remarks that the procedure has no parallels in ordinary Slavonic folk-usage, and suggests the use of the altar has been continuous since Roman times.

Hasluck disagrees with Evans' interpretation, but it can be seen from the tenth-century example at Latros that the genealogy of the ritual may well have passed through a Byzantine phase. We must therefore reject Hasluck's supposition that the 'rain-charm' was 'prescribed by a local dervish or sorcerer' and that it finds its origin in Turkish mythology. A story from Monastir might suggest a Greek origin for the ritual:[1]

[A] 'written stone' buried in a vineyard near Monastir ... was once dug up, but torrents of rain followed. It is now kept buried, because, if any one dug it up again, *it would never stop raining.*

A second example from late medieval Cyprus decisively confirms the Greek origin of the custom, thanks to its structural similarity to the Latros narrative:[2]

A rough boulder on the summit of Cyprian Olympus, which seems vaguely to have been connected with the ark of Noah, was formerly used as a rain-charm by the local Greeks. In times of drought it was lifted on poles, to the accompaniment of singing, by the peasants of the surrounding villages ... Here the position of the stone seems to have had more to do with its selection than the stone itself. Any mountain-top is an appropriate place for watching the weather, and particularly for rain-making, since mountain-tops attract rain-clouds.

Particular groups of Yuruks, the Bektashis at Kruya and Kizilbash all kept the 15 August festival in Hasluck's day; the latter seems to agree that its provenance, *sans* ecstatic behaviour, was Christian.[3]

---

[1] Hasluck (1929; 211).

[2] Hasluck (1929; 211f., note 3).

[3] Hasluck (1929; 100f).

*Possession, Exorcism and Numinous Stones.*

The phenomena of possession and exorcism are a constant feature of Late Antique and medieval Greek Christianity, particularly in Late Roman and Byzantine Anatolia. A considerable debate surrounds their behavioural causes and symbolic meaning.[1] The scholar has to exercise particular care in making cross-cultural and diachronic generalisations.[2] The main parameters are what possession and exorcism meant in pre-modern Greek religious belief and practice, not to mention broader questions about supposed activity of daemons.[3] The Sixtieth Canon of the Council in Trullo (691-692) forbids it:[4]

> It is decreed that those who pretend to be possessed and feign by foulness of manner this behaviour shall be punished in every way. Let them fall under the disciplines and penalties under which those fall who are truly possessed.

The Canon does not stipulate the causes of possession. It could well apply to the practice of 'prophesying in the spirit of Python' as recorded in a ninth-century account of Joseph Genesios,[5] feigning possession as a form of social or economic protest,[6] as seems to be partly the case in rural Galatia during the last decades of the life of St Theodore of Sykeon, or the performance of pre-Christian religious ritual in a state of ἐνθουσιασμός or 'divine possession'. If the latter, one thinks of an important remark of Cosmas of Jerusalem in his eighth-century commentary of the works of Gregory of Nazianzus, mentioning the persistent custom of self-castration in a state of 'divine possession':[7]

> [Following a description of the cult of Kybele:] Certain irrational pagans in the mountains of Caria practice self-castration even until the present day, as the story is, gripped by this ancient custom.

The key phrase is 'irrational pagans' (Ἕλληνες ἀλόγιστοι) which allows some interpretive scope for 'divine possession'. Hasluck has very little to say about this problem, but deals somewhat more extensively with the other side of the question, Christian and Muslim exorcism. It is worth pointing out  that

---

[1] Dodds (1973; 174, 196f., 201f., 204).

[2] Lienhardt (1961; 57-64, etc).

[3] Trombley (1993-4; i, 51f., 64f., 99-108, 314; ii, 88f., 97, 108f., 200-202, etc). Joannou (1971; 10-51).

[4] Rhalles and Potles (1992; ii, 440f).

[5] Genesios (1994; 42-45).

[6] Lewis (1998; 27-30).

[7] Cosmas of Jerusalem, *Scholia in Gregorii Nazianzeni Carmina, Patrologia Graeca* 38, col. 502.

'possessed' or 'enthused' behaviour exists in many primitive cultures, having structural similarities in individual behaviour and societal reaction wherever it occurs.[1] It therefore seems risky to posit that the ritual described by George of Cyzicus had its roots in the pre-Christian substrate; there is no evidence I am aware of suggesting it was possible to Christianise rites in this particular mode. Writing in the twelfth century, the Byzantine canonist Balsamon narrows the focus considerably, observing that 'possession' of the kind mentioned in the Sixtieth Canon of the Council in Trullo was used in popular divination by those who 'pretend to be possessed and as a means of livelihood proclaim the daemonic with the evil, satanic gaze of the prophetesses of the pagans'.[2] It is better to suppose that feigned 'possession' continued to exist outside this category, along the lines of the narratives found in the life of St Theodore of Sykeon, as will be seen later.

These themes are important because they contain *prima facie* evidence of another phenomenon that Hasluck discusses, so-called 'magic stones' with inscriptions on them, whose numinous power was used for divination, and in particular for the discovery of buried treasure.[3] A rationale for the interrelationship amongst these phenomena has never been worked out in detail. The custom of tomb-breaking ($\tau\upsilon\mu\beta\omega\rho\upsilon\chi\iota\alpha$) in Anatolia has a long history. An inscription from Thyatira in Lydia records the elaborate provisions made to prevent its occurrence:[4]

> F(l)avius Zosimos laid a coffin in a clear place that is just outside the city along the public road beside the precinct of Sambatha (the Chaldaean sibyl) within the enclosure wall of the Chaldaean (god) ($\dot{\epsilon}\pi\dot{\iota}$ $\tau\acute{o}\pi o\upsilon$ $\kappa\alpha\theta\alpha\rho o\upsilon^{\prime\prime}$ $\ddot{o}\nu\tau o\varsigma$ $\pi\rho\dot{o}$ $\tau\eta^{\prime\prime}\varsigma$ $\pi\acute{o}\lambda\epsilon\omega\varsigma$ $\pi\rho\dot{o}\varsigma$ $\tau\omega^{\prime\prime}$ $\Sigma\alpha\mu\beta\alpha\theta\epsilon\acute{\iota}\omega$ $\dot{\epsilon}\nu$ $\tau\omega^{\prime\prime}$ $X\alpha\lambda\delta\alpha\acute{\iota}o\upsilon$ $\pi\epsilon\rho\iota\beta\acute{o}\lambda\omega$ $\pi\alpha\rho\dot{\alpha}$ $\tau\dot{\eta}\nu$ $\delta\eta\mu o\sigma\acute{\iota}\alpha\nu$ $\dot{o}\delta\acute{o}\nu$) for himself by whom its was laid and for his sweetest wife Aurelia Pontiane, with no other person having the authority to put anyone into this coffin. Whoever dares or acts in contravention to this shall give 1,500 *denarii* in silver to the city of Thyatira (and) 2,500 *denarii* to the most sacred treasury, in order to become free in respect to the law of tomb-breaking ($\ddot{\epsilon}\xi\omega\theta\epsilon\nu$ $\tau\omega^{\prime\prime}$ $\tau\eta^{\prime\prime}\varsigma$ $\tau\upsilon\mu\beta\omega\rho\upsilon\chi\acute{\iota}\alpha\varsigma$ $\nu\acute{o}\mu\omega$). Two copies of this inscription have been written, of which the second has been put in the archive. It was done in the most distinguished city of Thyatira in the consulship of Catilius Severus, on the thirteenth of the month of Audnaios under Menophilos the public archivist.

---

[1] Lewis (1989).

[2] Lienhardt (1961; 57-64, etc.).

[3] Hasluck (1929; 207 and note 3).

[4] *Inscriptiones Graecae* (1927; 4. 1281).

Tomb-breaking often had motives besides the reuse of a sarcophagus, among them the theft of grave goods from pre-Christian funerary monuments that had gradually become concealed beneath the earth. At times these memorials eluded grave-robbers who resorted to occult practices directed to the subterranean divinities thought to control ground water and the fertility of the soil. This practice is reported at least as late as the mid-ninth century in the previously mentioned letter of Photius patriarch of Constantinople who mentions some rustics who sacrificed a dog to the katachthonian goddess Ge to compel the earth to yield up its hidden wealth.[1] A law dealing with treasure trove given at Constantinople by the Christian emperor Theodosius I recognises that the excavators were often prompted by such a divinity or by the guidance of fortune (*suadente numine vel ducente fortuna*).[2]

The life of Theodore of Sykeon (*ob.* 613) hegumen of the monastery of St George in the *territorium* of Anastasiopolis in Galatia, makes frequent reference to villagers breaking the ground looking for building materials.[3] The stones they found seem often to have come from semi-subterranean tombs of pre-Christian date. If the reports are accurate, whole villages gave way to possession hysteria after these excavations took place. This behaviour can be explained as a species of tabu sickness connected with an ongoing belief in the pre-Christian cult of the dead. Phrygia and Galatia are littered with funerary altars and inscriptions calling on the subterranean divinities (οἱ θεοὶ καταχθόνιοι) to torment (ὀχλέω) the grave breaker.[4] A good example of this is found in an undated inscription at Smyrna in which the sky gods and daemons under the earth are called upon to torment the tomb-breaker (οἵ τε θεοὶ οὐράνιοι καὶ οἱ κατὰ γη"ς δαἵμονες κεχολωμένοι αὐτω"ι καὶ γένει αὐτου" εἴασαν).[5] The life of Theodore of Sykeon uses language similar to that of the inscriptions, but substitutes the words daemons (δαίμονες) or spirits (πνεύματα) for 'gods'. Theodore was often summoned by the village clergy to perform mass exorcisms. In one instance, his life indicates that a villager who pulled blocks out of the ground was suspected of tomb-robbery (τυμβωρυχία). An incident like this occurred at the hamlet of Sandos in vicinity of Protomeria in Galatia I circa 600:[6]

---

[1] Photius, *Epistula* 1.20, *Patrologia Graeca* 102, col. 788.

[2] *Codex Theodosianus* 10.18.3 (2 March 390), in *Theodosiani Libri XVI* (1905).

[3] On the social background of this text, see Trombley (1985a, 2001). There is also a discussion of these materials in Mitchell (1993; 122-50).

[4] Trombley (1993-4; i, 331f.; ii, 106-9).

[5] *Inscriptiones Graecae* (1927; 4. 1479).

[6] *V. Theodori Syk.* §114 (Festugière 1970; 1, 89).

> The householder Eutolmios wished to enlarge his threshing floor. There was a small hill lying adjacent. While he was digging and leveling the circuit of the threshing floor, it happened that he dug into the adjacent hill and removed a stone from it.

The usual phenomena of hysteria followed, in which attacks by daemons on persons and animals were imagined. The villagers made a formal complaint to the civil governor of the province, alleging that Eutolmios had discovered buried treasure. The suspicion may have arisen because of an inscription incised on the stone that he removed. When the governor refused to hear the case, the villagers became violent and threatened to burn down Eutolmios' buildings. At this point the headmen of Sandos summoned Theodore of Sykeon who raised the symbol of the cross at the site and performed an exorcism ritual:[1]

> After putting in place the stone which had been extracted and filling up the excavation, he set up the image of the holy cross and remained there the entire night without sleeping, reciting the psalmody and praying to God (ἔστησεν ἐπάνω τὸν τύπον τοῦ τιμίου σταυροῦ, καὶ ἔμενεν ἐκεῖ ἄϋπνος ὅλον τὴν νύκτα ψάλλων καὶ εὐχόμενος τῷ Θεῷ).

Theodore's ritual is identical with that used to Christianize pagan temples, sacred groves and springs. This rather convincingly demonstrates the connection between the pre-Christian tabu and the obsessional behaviour exhibited by the Christian villagers, once word got out about the excavations. Structurally similar stories survive in medieval Greek and Ottoman period Egyptian folklore. In the latter instance, Christian clergy 'conjure the spirits back into the stone, after which it was again buried.'[2]

> There was often a *prima facie* suspicion that *tumuli* excavated toacquire building materials were tombs. For example, a report about a farmer named Timotheos at the village of Eukrai who dug up a small hill (βουνίον) seems to go back to an indictment or some other document:[3]
>
>> The civil governor of the metropolis of Ankyra at that time, Euphrantas, upon learning of this, sent to arrest the said farmer Timotheos and to impose fines because he had practised grave robbery (τυμβωρυχία).

The governor's police officials went to Eukrai and administered floggings because of the tabu sickness affecting the villagers:[4]

---

[1] *V. Theodori Syk.*§114 (Festugière 1970; 1, 90f.)

[2] Hasluck (1929; 208, note 2).

[3] *V. Theodori Syk.* §116 (Festugière 1970; 1, 92).

[4] *V. Theodori Syk.* §117 (Festugière 1970; 1, 92f.).

> But they were seized by uncontrollable laughter and begged that more blows be laid on ... Most of the men, with their wives and children, were cruelly possessed (χαληπω''ς ἐνεργου''μενοι) and caused great disorders and breakages.

Amongst other things, they killed domesticated animals, burned the communal and Timotheos' grain stocks, tried to kill him, ate all the food they could find, smashed household vessels, and beat anyone who tried to restrain them. The few who were not enthused (ὀλίγοι δὲ ἀνέργηντοι) then summoned Theodore of Sykeon, who came and performed an exorcism with the village clergy.

These modes of behaviour seem at first sight to have a structural relationship to the Christian ritual described by George of Cyzicus and to pre-Christian cults like that of Kybele where ecstatic behaviour and divine possession was an aspect of ritual. The incident at Eukrai suggests a sudden reawakening of a pre- or sub-Christian ritual consciousness, long suppressed by catechisation. The opening of a tomb protected by the subterranean daemons legitimised the lapse into ritually inspired, feigned possession; self-mutilation, a trait of worshipping Kybele, is not recorded, but the collective resort to mayhem may be structurally analogous.

Another incident of this type is reported at Eukrai *circa* 600. In this instance it concerns a sarcophagus whose removal evoked possessed behaviour in the same group of villagers. There is a strong likelihood that a the tomb had an inscription with a funerary imprecation, to judge from the first sentence of our witnesses George the monk's statement:[1]

> There was a marble sarcophagus standing in a certain place in their district that held the corpses of ancient pagans protected by daemons (πυάλου ... μαρμαρίνης ... ἐχούσης σκηνώματα ἀρχαίων ἀνθρώπων Ἑλλήνων ὑπὸ δαιμόνων φυλαττομένων). By their suggestion, a notion came to the householders of the village. They opened the sarcophagus, took its lid (σκέπασμα), brought it to the village and set it up for use as a trough. For this reason many persons, as well as their animals and fields, were troubled by daemons.

Theodore of Sykeon then performed the usual exorcisms, but ordered that the sacrophagus lid continue to serve as a trough and the tomb to be left open, lest they become a cause of numinous awe once more. George the monk saw the trough and learned the story behind it, including the local myth that it was

---

[1] *V. Theodori Syk.* §118 (Festugière 1970; 1, 94f.).

the spirits who had prompted the villagers to remove the lid and then to emplace it again:[1]

> [Theodore] did not permit the cover which had been taken to be restored to the spirits, *as they wished, when they asked it to be restored to its proper place*, but he left it for use as a trough. It is there today as a sign of his miracles.

*Jinn* were believed to dwell in ancient sarcophagi in Ottoman period Egypt.[2] This narrative framework seems plausibly to be of Christian provenance, to judge from the examples that have been seen.

At the risk of some repetition, it will be necessary to describe one last mass exorcism that Theodore of Sykeon carried out *circa* 610-613. In this instance, however, it concerns the population of an urban centre, the town of Germia. The behavioural structures are given a predictable cause:[3]

> In the aforesaid city John the bishop wished to build a cistern in the western part of the city and made a deep excavation. Because many ancient tombs were unearthed there, many of the unclean spirits fell on the people of the city, *both rich and poor*.

The author of the life of Theodore was perhaps a little surprised that the *wealthy* were affected by the tabu of tomb-breaking. The outbreak of hysteria lasted several days and attracted the attention of the patriarch of Constantinople, who sent the principal lawyer and protopresbyter of the Great Church to observe the exorcism. Theodore climbed into the excavation and is said to have forced the daemons back into the ground by invoking the powers of the Christian religion: the Pantokrator, the Theotokos, the archangel Michael who was thought to be the commander of the heavenly army and St George, the tutelary martyr of Theodore's monastery at Sykeon:[4]

> It happened that through his prayer [the daemons] were driven out by angelic power, so that the spirits in the afflicted persons cried out to themselves: 'Look! ... Komentiolos has come, and now Erebinthios is present; now Maxentios comes.' [Other names are called out.] [Theodore] roused each person as though from some condition of death, and fortified him with the sign of the cross, and asked if they saw anything. Each of them related what he saw as the sign of his healing, one a snake coming out of his mouth, another a dormouse, another a lizard, another a rat ...

---

[1] *V. Theodori Syk.* §118 (Festugière 1970; 1, 95).
[2] Hasluck (1929; 208, note 2).
[3] *V. Theodori Syk.* §161 (Festugière 1970; 1, 138).
[4] *V. Theodori Syk.*§161 (Festugière 1970; 1, 143).

One is tempted to suggest that the excavation displaced the ecology of the site, and that 'daemons' were folkloric projections into the vermin that scattered throughout the town as the digging continued. The life of Theodore gives a clear hint at this explanation:[1]

> He stood and prayed to the Lord to drive out all the daemons hidden in houses and hostels and to collect them in the place where they came out (... πρὸς τὸ ἐξελάσαι πάντα τὰ κρυπτόμενα πνεύματα κατ! οἴκους τε καὶ ξενεω'νας καὶ συναθροι'σαι εἰς τὸν τόπον ὅθεν ἐξη'λθον).

Hasluck provides a particularly apposite example of tabu sickness resulting from the movement of a stone bearing an inscription by a householder who was apparently a Muslim:[2]

> A Bulgarian peasant, living between Viza and Kirk Kilisse, found an inscribed stone, which he took to his house. His wife used it as a washing-block, but was at once visited by terrifying dreams and the farm animals began to die. Next the mother-in-law of the peasant trod on the stone and broke it; she died shortly after. The peasant was getting frightened, took the stone back to the place where he found it, and offered sacrifice (*kurban*) upon it.

The tutelary beings who produced these 'affects' would have been regarded as *stoicheia* or *jinn*, depending on whether the householder was Christian or Muslim.

*Conclusions*

It can be seen from the examples given that Anatolian Christianity effectively incorporated pre-Christian ritual where it did not directly undermine the new monotheism: 'possessed' behaviour is a good example of the limits of *Ritenchristianisierung*, being regarded as caused by a *numen alius generis*. The evidence has structural similarities to much of the material discussed by Hasluck, but difficulties still persist. By the time of the twelfth-century canonists Balsamon and Zonaras, categories of description that these commentators had learnt from the Greek *paideia* had begun to affect their description of phenomena, especially since it is not always clear that they had direct experience of behaviour they describe. The substrates concealed in their writings can perhaps be discovered in other late Byzantine texts. It remains to

---

[1] *V. Theodori Syk.*§161 (Festugière 1970; 1, 143).
[2] Hasluck (1929; 208).

identify the social and cultural factors that contributed to the survival of early medieval Greek religious behaviour into the Islamic period, but factors of discontinuity were also in play, including the population displacements that went on all through medieval period, entailing a mixing of folkloric traditions and religious beliefs. Whatever the outcome of this line of research, it is unlikely that Hasluck's groundbreaking work will be marginalised, thanks to the clarity of phenomenal detail he imparts to the evidence and the sureness with which he classifies geographically dispersed data.

*REFERENCES*

Anrich, G. (ed.) 1913 *Hagios Nikolaos; Der heilige Nikolaos in der griechischen Kirche*, Leipzig; Teubner.

Chadwick, H. 1966 *Early Christian Thought and the Classical Tradition*, Oxford, Clarendon.

*Corpus Iuris Civilis II. Codex Iustinianus*, 1954, ed. P. Krueger, Berlin; Apud Weidmannos.

Delehaye, H. (ed.) 1892 *Vita S. Pauli Iunioris in Monte Latro* (BHG 1474), trans. I. Sirmondi, Brussels; *Analecta Bollandiana* Vol 11.

Dodds, E. 1973 'Supernormal phenomena in classical antiquity', in *The Ancient Concept of Progress and Other Essays on Greek Literature and Belief* Oxford; Clarendon.

[Festugière] Georgios, of Sykeon 1970 *Vie de Théodore de Sykéôn. I. Texte grec,établi par André-Jean Festugière. (II. Traduction, commentaire et appendice par André-Jean Festugière.)* Subsidia hagiographica. no. 48., Brussels; Société des Bollandistes.

Frend, W. 1996 *The Archaeology of Early Christianity. A History*, London; Chapman.

Genesios. 1994 *Peri vasileion* ed. D. Tsougarakis, trans. P. Niavis, Athens; Ekdoseis Kanake

Hasluck, F. 1910 *Cyzicus*, Cambridge: Cambridge; University Press.

Hasluck, F. 1929 *Christianity and Islam under the Sultans*, Oxford: Oxford University Press.

Hefner, R. 1993 'Introduction: world building and the rationality of conversion', in *Conversion to Christianity*, ed. R. W. Hefner, Berkeley; University of California Press, 3-44.

*Inscriptiones Graecae ad Res Romanas pertinentes*, 1927 ed. R. Cagnat, Paris; Leroux.

Jaeger, W. 1961 *Early Christianity & Greek Paideia*, Cambridge; Mass; Belknap Press of Harvard University Press.

Joannou, P. 1971 *Démonologie populaire--démonologie critique au XIe siècle. La vie inédite de S. Auxence par M. Psellos*, Wiesbaden; Harrassowitz.

Kirsten, E. 1978 'Artemis von Ephesos und Eleuthera von Myra mit Seitblick auf St Nicolaus und auf Kommagene', in *Studien zur Religion und Kultur Kleinasiens ii*, eds. S. Şahin et al, Leiden; Brill, 151-176.

Lawson, J. 1964 (1910) *Modern Greek Folklore and Ancient Greek Religion* Cambridge; Cambridge University Press.

Lévi-Strauss, C. 1966 *The Savage Mind*, London; Weidenfeld & Nicholson.

Lewis, I. 1989 *Ecstatic Religion. A Study of Shamanism and Spirit Possession*, London; Routledge.

Lienhardt, G. 1961 *Divinity and Experience. The Religion of the Dinka*, Oxford; Oxford University Press.

Mitchell, S. 1993 *Anatolia. Land, Men, and Gods in Asia Minor II. The Rise of the Church*, Oxford; Oxford University Press.

Ovsyannikov O. and Terebikhin, N. 1994 'Sacred space in the culture of the Arctic regions' in *Sacred Sites, Sacred Places*, ed. D. Carmichael et al, London; Routledge, 44-81.

Ramsay, W. 1906 'The permanence of religion at the holy places in western Asia', in *Pauline and Other Studies in Early Christian History*, London: Hodder & Stoughton, 163-188.

Ramsay, W. 1908 'The orthodox church in the Byzantine empire', in *Luke the Physician and Other Studies*, London; Hodder & Stoughton, 141-168.

Rhalles G. and Potles, M. 1992 Σύνταγμα τῶν θειῶν καὶ ἱερῶν κανόνων, iii, Athens; Gregoriades.

Sevcenko I. and Sevcenko N. (eds and trans.) 1984 *The Life of St Nicholas of Sion*, Brookline; Hellenic College Press.

*Theodosiani Libri XVI cum Constitutionibus Sirmondianis* 1905 ed. Th. Mommsen, P. Krueger and P. M. Mayer, i-ii, Berlin; apud Weidmannos.

Trombley, F. 1981 *The survival of paganism in the Byzantine empire during the pre-iconoclastic period (540-727)*, Ann Arbor: University Microfilms.

Trombley, F. 1985a 'Monastic foundations in sixth-century Anatolia and their role in the social and economic life of the countryside', in *Byzantine Saints and Monasteries*, ed. Vaporis, N., Brookline, Mass; Hellenic College Press, pages 45-59.

Trombley, F. 1985b 'Paganism in the Greek world at the end of antiquity: the case of rural Anatolia and Greece', *Harvard Theological Review* Vol. 78, 327-52.

Trombley, F. 1993-94 *Hellenic Religion and Christianization c. 370-529* Leiden; Brill.

Trombley, F. 2000 'Religious experience in late antiquity: theological ambivalence and Christianization', *Byzantine and Modern Greek Studies* Vol. 24, 2-60

Trombley, F. 2001 'Town and *territorium* in Late Roman Anatolia (late fifth-early 7th c.) in *Recent Research in Late-Antique Urbanism* L. Lavan (ed.) *Journal of Roman Archaeology Supplementary Series*, Vol 42, Portsmouth, Rhode Island, 217-232.

Usener, H. 1913 'Übersehenes', in *Kleine Schriften* 4, Leipzig and Berlin; Teubner.

*Vitae Isidori Reliquiae* 1967 ed. C. Zintzen, Hildesheim; Olms.

Vryonis, S. 1971 *The Decline of Medieval Hellenism in Asia Minor and the Process of Islamization from the Eleventh through the Fifteenth Century* Berkeley and Los Angeles: University of California Press.

Vryonis, S. 1972 'Religious changes and patterns in the Balkans, 14-16th centuries', in *Aspects of the Balkans*, ed. Birnbaum, H. and Vryonis S., The Hague and Paris; Mouton, 151-176.

von Harnack, A. 1924 *Die Mission und Ausbreitung des Christentums in den ersten drei Jahrhunderten i-ii*, Leipzig; J.C. Hinrichs'sche Buchhandlung.

# 20. 'URBAN' AND 'RURAL' RELIGION IN LATE ANTIQUE CILICIA: FROM PAGAN DIVERSITY TO CHRISTIAN HERESY

## Afrodite KAMARA

The relationship between a 'high' culture (the imposition of a dominant political power) and a 'traditional' or 'low' culture (the survival of older forms of social or religious organisation) was an important underlying theme in Hasluck's historical research. In this respect he was the precursor of many a modern scholar of antiquity who has attempted to define the boundaries and meaning of *Hellenisation*, *Romanisation* or any other *-isation* in the ancient world. The present paper aims at examining the issue of such cross-cultural relations in two different dimensions: the relation between 'urban' and 'rural' and that between paganism and Christianity. Such a study may illustrate too just how difficult it is to eradicate deep cultural roots, even in times of major political change.

### The model

For over a century, scholars in the field of Greco-Roman religion neglected — deliberately or subconsciously — the study of the countryside which surrounded those admirable cities, abundant in monuments and institutions upon which they focused their attention. According to this general model, peasants did not experience existential anxieties; their religious behaviour was moulded rather by daily prayers and seasonal festivals than by their desire to reach higher spheres of contemplation. The same model of religious life for Asia Minor peasants was maintained whether considering Persian, Greek or Roman domination. Whilst the shift of political power was manifest in the cities by a change in the prevalent deities, these changes did not take deep root in the countryside where people worshipped primarily their ancestral gods and goddesses in an almost shamanistic way. With the advent of Christianity, things changed a little. The new religion maintained itself more or less within the boundaries of cities for the first three centuries. The fourth century AD, however, was marked by a turn towards the countryside, which manifested itself not only in religion, but also in the economic and social life of the

Roman Empire. Countryside settlements, which before were nothing but small villages, were enlarged to the point of becoming small towns. Although these settlements remained by and large dependent on the neighbouring cities in terms of administration, artistic creation and religious organisation, their land became now interspersed with rural churches and abodes of solitaries and ascetics. Church activity and funds were in part directed to the establishment of the Christian faith among the rural population and the presence and actions of holy men became a strong weapon in this aim, although their views conflicted sometimes with those standing high on the ecclesiastical hierarchy.

Although my exploration of these issues was originally intended to comprise a much larger area of Asia Minor, I have finally restricted my scope to Cilicia and Isauria.[1] The reasons lay in the geographical and ethnic diversity which this southeastern boundary of Anatolia presents. The Cilician Plain represents the typical Asia Minor landscape with a fertile soil, and a prevalence of cities. Rough Cilicia (Isauria), on the other hand, was, throughout antiquity, an area where civilized settlements often had to struggle against the invading force of the wilderness and its hostile inhabitants.

Demographically, the population of Cilicia and Isauria consisted of three main groups: Greeks and Romans, who formed the city élites, Cilicians, who had been integrated in the city system and accumulated wealth, and finally the inhabitants of the highlands above the Calycadnus valley, usually known under the name of Isaurians, often treated as barbarians prone to rebellion and banditry by their contemporaries. In some parts Rough Cilicia and Isauria

---

[1] The use of the term Isauria is confused both in the sources and in modern scholarship and thus needs some closer definition. Isauria was initially the surrounding territory of the city of Isaura on the Taurus mountain. The capture of the city and its destruction by Perdiccas led to the creation of another city close to the former one. The older city was repopulated at a given time and thus two cities emerged, Isaura Vetus and Isaura Nova, which eventually formed a δίπολις i.e. a common political and administrative entity. Isaura Vetus was made into the capital of Lycaonia after the creation of the *Tres Eparchiae* by Hadrian in 138 AD. Diocletian went a step further, as he created the province of which included most parts of Cilicia Tracheia. It is since the end of the third century, therefore, that the name Isauria came to denote Cilicia Tracheia. However, as described in the note below, this enlargement was not always followed by contemporaries, who continued to call the mountainous and most inaccessible range of Cilicia, close to Isaura and the decapolis, Isauria.

were a no-man's land.[1] In Hellenistic and early Roman times, Cilician piracy was the major threat in all naval activities and the coastland of Cilicia and Pamphylia was both a trap for the ships and a major marketplace for goods and slaves captured in sea raids. After the extinction of piracy by Pompey and the sedentarization of major part of those Cilician pirates, who were then transformed into merchants, a nuclei of banditry remained up on the highlands, where rural populations, normally living off animal husbandry, often found themselves excluded from all political participation and at the edge of famine.[2]

Another important factor for the choice of this particular geographical entity for this sort of comparative study lies in the nature of surviving evidence. According to Stephen Mitchell,[3] rural sanctuaries have not yet

---

[1] Whether Cilicians and Isaurians constituted different ethnic groups is a matter still in debate, and I am grateful to Mr Keith Hopwood for pointing out this to me during the presentation of this paper at the conference. Ramsay believed that the inhabitants of Isaura and the surrounding area constituted a separate tribe. The first mention of the Isaurians (*Isauroi* and *Isaureis*) is found in Diodorus (18.2), where it is mentioned that the inhabitants of Isaura enjoyed a period of political autonomy and great prosperity prior to the siege and capture of their capital by Perdiccas. Zgusta (1964) distinguishes Cilician from Isaurian names, although his distinction is based on the area where the linguistic testimonies were found, and not on a specific ethnic affiliation. The most recent and conclusive publication regarding the issue of the ethnic origins of the Isaurians is Burgess (1990). Burgess concludes that the paucity of linguistic or other evidence concerning the Isaurians offers evidence that the Isaurians were named so mainly because of their association with a specific municipality rather than constituting a distinct ethnic group. However, this attribution was so firmly established that, despite the administrative changes of the second and third century AD, the name Isaurian continued to be attributed only to the inhabitants of the inner parts of this territory, namely those who were still close to the initial area called Isauria. Late Antique sources, however, such as Zosimus and Eunapius, seem to realise the confusion regarding the term Isaurian and attempt to clarify it by explaining that the name was often used in order to denote more than one ethnic group at a given time. Burgess, referring to Jones, states that Isaurian has, by late antiquity, become an inaccurate and catch-all term, of designation for inland groups of that general vicinity which engage in periodic forays of banditry. The probable solution to the puzzle of the ethnic origin of the Isaurians is the following: the Isaurians, i.e. the inhabitants of the mountainous regions of Cilicia Tracheia, were descendants of the Luwian people known under the name Kedi/Kode?Kue/Cetae. They were pushed to the mountains by the Cilicians (Kelekesh?) when the latter raided the coastal regions and settled part of them.

[2] For Cilician pirates in Hellenistic and Roman times see De Souza (1999). Hill (1996; 4) thinks that the coastal cities of Rough Cilicia maintained a strong attachment to piracy as a means for complementing a poor economy. Equini Schneider (1999) interprets the presence in Rough Cilicia of three legions of the Roman army after the Diocletianic reform as a sign that the political situation was constantly unstable and the threat of revolt or banditry a permanent problem in the area. The military reinforcement of Cilicia by Diocletian was due to the chaotic situation following the Sassanian attacks and partial conquest of the area in the 260s. However, in the fourth century there were repeated uprises of the population, particularly the Isaurians. Ammian (XIV 2.17-19) attests to a serious Isaurian revolt in 354, appeased only through the efforts of Caesar Gallus, who had his see in Antioch at the time, as well as to a general period of bandits' attacks under Valens in 367-8 (XXVII.9.6 ss).

[3] Mitchell (1993; 16) 'Archaeology has virtually nothing to say about rural shrines in Anatolia, for none has been excavated. Only in mountainous districts, such as Pisidia and Isauria, where shrines were often cut from the rock, can we form some impression of their physical appearance. Here the rock face of a cliff or around a cave entrance, would be shaped as a shrine, with a place for an altar, votive niches or perhaps a statue. It is surely mistaken to argue that such architecture was characteristic of native or indigenous rural cults, and contrasted with the shrines of Greek or other imported gods, who warranted free-standing buildings. The distinction is due to geology and topography, not culture ... On occasion the architecture of the shrines was Hellenized since fragments of temple architecture are not unusual, but to build a naos was a sign that a community was wealthier and culturally more sophisticated than its neighbours.'

become the focus of serious archaeological excavation and study. On the contrary, they have often become prey to looters, which makes the attempt at a study even more difficult. In fact, it is only in Pisidia and Rough Cilicia that some conclusions regarding the appearance and function of such temples can be drawn, due to the fact that many rural sanctuaries in those two areas tend to be rock-cut and thus their façades (at least) remain unaltered. It is therefore possible to draw comparisons between religious worship in cities and countryside in both Christian and pagan times, as traces of rural sanctuaries have not been obliterated, as is often the case in other areas of the former Roman empire.

*Paganism in the cities and in the countryside*

Urban religion in Asia Minor throughout Roman Imperial times was dominated by gods of the Greek and Roman Pantheon, usually under attributes which reinforced civic institutions and loyalty to Rome and the emperor.[1] A few 'oriental' cults had permeated the Greco-Roman religious world and some of them acquired indeed the status of 'official' cults of the Empire, but their meaning and ceremonial expression was altered to match the tastes of their new adherents. The adoption of the ruler cult by almost all Asia Minor cities imposed a new layer of religious uniformity. On the other hand, worship of personified abstract notions, usually related to the prosperity of the city and to its particular cultural or economic features encouraged new religious conceptions.[2] The temples within the enclosures of the cities offered ample

---

[1] Numerous relevant inscriptions survive, of which I relate just a few. **Aegai:** Dedication to Augustus, Poseidon and Aphrodite (*CIG* 4443; Robert 1973; 163), dedications to Asclepius, whose worship was famous in this city (*CIG* 4442-4443 and 5616), dedicatory inscription in honour of a priest of Zeus, Hera, Athena and Ares (Heberdey-Wilhelm 1896: no. 39), altar dedicated to Zeus Heliopolitan (Heberdey-Wilhelm 1896: no. 43), altar dedicated to Dionysus, Demeter and the Emperors (Heberdey-Wilhelm: 1896: no. 44). **Mopsuestia:** Dedication to Marion, priest of Dionysus Kallicarpus (Heberdey-Wilhelm: 1896: no. 28), dedication of an altar to the god (without specification) and to the *demos* (people) (Dagron-Feissel : 1985:133, no. 86, pl. XXXV). **Iotape:** inscription commemorating the construction of temple for *divus* Traianus (Hagel-Tomaschitz:1998: 122, Iot 1a; CIG 4411a, IGR 833a), **Elaiussa-Sebaste:** Hermes on the reverse of a bronze coin of the city; Hermes was the tutelary deity of Corycus, and, apparently, of the whole area (*BMC* p. 235, no. 9). **Corycus:** Hermes (Oppian, *Hal.* III. 11. 8-9 characterises Corycus as city of Hermes and the *kerykeion,* symbol of the god, is to be found on several reliefs from that city); altar, in the museum of Silifke, dedicated to Hermes Corykeius for the good procreation and peace between the *Sebastoi* (Dagron-Marcillet-Jaubert: 1978: n. 42). **Cestrus:** Testimony to the ruler cult of Trajan and Hadrian in the small city (Bean-Mitford: 1962: 212-213, nos. 35 and 37); testimony to the cult of Zeus Megistos or Keraunios (Bean-Mitford:1962: 214, nos. 39-41). **Anazarbus:** dedication of an altar to an unnamed goddess by the chiliarch Lucius Aurelius Taruteinus Demetrius, priest of the *Sebastoi* (Dagron - Marcillet-Jaubert: 1978: n.3).

[2] A fortuitous example is the altar dedicated by a priest of Zeus, protector of the City and the Province, in the territory of Anazarbus in 99 AD (Dagron–Feissel: 1985:188, no. 109, pl. XLVI). See also the amazing metrical inscription related to an oracle from Antioch on the Kragus (Hagel-Tomaschitz: 1998: 38, AntK19).

space (literally and figuratively) for the dedication of altars and other votive offerings. People could thus express and publicise their piety, an act which gained them not only godly but also human favours. Religious evergetism, particularly when expressed in relation to the worship of the Emperor, of Rome or of the city's Tyche, had become intrinsically linked to civic benefactions. An interesting parameter, revealed by the epigraphic evidence, is that whereas Greeks and Romans sought religious offices in the major sanctuaries of cities and countryside alike, such as the cave temple of Athena in Tagai near Seleuceia, it was mainly Cilicians who reinforced the ruler cult, either by dedicating temples to the emperors or by assuming priesthoods in existing *Sebasteia*. Although this is a generalisation, one might say that in religious terms the Greeks and Romans were eager to gain the favour of the local gods and natural powers, whereas native Cilicians, adapted to the city-life, were eager to gain the favour of the political powers.

However, the gap between city and countryside was not definitive. Quiet sites in proximity to the cities were often considered more appropriate for religious worship than city temples. City dwellers commuted to those temples in times of need or of major religious festivals and the reverse itinerary must have been followed by peasants who visited the city temples.

The distinction between urban and rural therefore, in terms of religion, is not always very clear. It should be approached methodologically, in my opinion, by answering the question of who actually controlled each sanctuary; whether priesthoods were decided by and divided among members of a city élite, a group of professionals in religion, or the inhabitants of its neighbouring rural settlement. To some extent, though, the distinction between urban and rural has also an evaluating aspect, as temples of an urban character bore the features of grand architecture and urban art of high quality, whereas most rural temples followed the humble lines of daily life and low-quality artwork. Finally, in some cases at least, scholars notice a difference among the deities worshipped: rural sanctuaries are more often dedicated to local, pre-Hellenistic gods, who were amalgamated to their Greco-Roman equivalents, whereas urban sanctuaries are more clearly, as mentioned above, city- and state-oriented.

It seems that in Cilicia, and particularly in Isauria, the religious beliefs and acts of the inhabitants were directed towards the countryside to a large extent: summits, fountains and caves had a particularly intense religious and symbolic value in that area, which attributed to the most renowned sanctuaries an almost shamanistic character. According to the local religious imagery, subterranean cavities were the dwelling-places of gods or demons, vested with supernatural powers. Thus even in the immediate area around Seleuceia of the Kalykadnos lay four such caves: Sarpedonia akra (Sanctuary of the local hero Sarpedon), Holmoi, Tagai (Sanctuary of Athena Kanetis), and the more remote Yapılıkaya.[1] Although extensive reference to Christian sanctuaries and beliefs will be made below, we should mention here that the church of St Thekla close to the same city was actually erected around a small cave, in which the Saint spent her ascetic life. Although no archaeological evidence is available presently, archaeologists and historians presume that the cave was of some sort of religious use in pagan times as well.[2] About 25 kilometres to the east of the city, close to the neighbouring city of Corycus lay the famous *Corykeion antron*, today *Cennet Cehennem* (Paradise and Hell), where, according to the local mythological tradition, Zeus had imprisoned Typhon.[3] An impressive temple of Zeus sealed the opening of the cave.[4]

There is ample evidence from Rough Cilicia that caves, either natural or artificial, were related to the underworld as well. The territories of Seleuceia on the Calycadnus, Corycus and Elaiussa Sebaste are dispersed with rock-cut complexes combining the functions of tombs and temples. Inscriptions and symbols carved on the rock show that the God prevalent in those complexes was Hermes (under the attribute of *propompos?*).[5] Most of those rock-cut complexes are situated at a distance from the neighbouring cities or villages. In the case of Adakayalar and Yapılıkaya in fact they are quite isolated. Yet, other gods are epigraphically related with smaller caves and rock-cut sanctuaries, as attests an inscription from Anazarbus dedicated to Zeus, Hera and Ares by the priestess of 153 AD.[6]

---

[1] On Yapılıkaya see Durugönül (1989).

[2] See Hild-Hellenkemper (1990: 442): Da der Thekla-Kult bei Seleukeia in die römische Kaiserzeit zurückreicht, ist wohl auch hier die Bindung an eine bereits länger bekannte Hohle gegeben. Nicht auszuschliessen ist, dass hier an einen Athena (Parthenos) Kult, wie bei der Athena-Höhle in Tagai (mit unbekanntem frühbyzantinisches Kloster-Patrozinium) angeknüpft ist.

[3] On the myth of Typhon and the subsequent attempts to appease the titan's anger, see Robert, L., *BCH* 101, 1977, p. 116, n. 151.

[4] On Corykeion antron (not to be confused with the homonymous cave on the slopes of Mt. Parnassus on mainland Greece) see Hild-Hellenkemper (1990; 314-315); Keil-Wilhelm (1931; 214-219); Feld-Weber (1967: 254-278).

[5] See Durugönül (1989).

[6] Sayar (2000; no. 47, no. 52).

Apart from caves, cults focusing on high places were also evident in Rough Cilicia as they were in rural Northern Syria, with which our area of interest was in close cultural contact and administrative link,[1] particularly in late antiquity.[2] Examples of such sanctuaries are that of Zeus Astrenos, situated in the core of Isauria, near modern Hadim,[3] and Zeus Olybris, worshipped on the mountain above Anazarbus, but epigraphically attested also in Komana and Ankara. [4] An interesting cult related to natural phenomena was that of Poseidon Asphaleios and Ge Hedraia; the gods were worshipped as a preventive action against earthquakes, although the epigraphic testimonies usually followed an earthquake.[5]

Such sanctuaries were by no means frequented only by the rural population. They were places of high reverence and general worship. In fact, interms of their administration they were linked much more to the cities than to the villages and hamlets which surrounded them. An extremely interesting inscription from the area of Seleuceia, dated between 142 and 161 AD, mentions that the priesthood of the famous sanctuary of Athena Kanetis in Tagai was sold to Dionysidoros Theagenous following an auction.[6] The name, clearly Greek, belongs rather to a wealthy citizen of Seleuceia than to a peasant. We do not have sufficient evidence for the way priesthoods were filled previously, but by the mid-second century it is obvious that the decisive factor for their occupation was money. This proves that the sanctuary was actually controlled by the city élite, since we are still far from the fourth century, when economic élites of the rural areas made their appearance. On the other hand, as another inscription, this time from Iotape, proves,[7] Toues, son of Irdaouexes, clearly of Cilician origin,[8] had enough funds to build a temple in honour of Trajan, and had been vested with several civic offices in the past, namely three times a priest of the emperors, twice a *demiourgos*[9] and a gymnasiarch for

---

[1] About the historical and geographical links between Syria and Cilicia see Mellink (1964).

[2] On Syrian high-places see Callot and Marcillet-Jaubert (1984).

[3] Hagel and Tomaschitz (1998). Bean and Mitford (1970; nos. 123,124,126).

[4] Sayar (2000: nos. 44-47).

[5] **Anazarbos:** Sayar (2000: no. 49), **Alexandreia kat'Isson:** Jalabert, L.-Mouterde, P., *Inscriptions grecques et Latines de la Syrie*, III, 715 but also elsewhere in Asia Minor. For the cult of Poseidon Asphaleios see Mylonopoulos (1996; 92-99).

[6] Hagel and Tomaschitz (1998; 371, Sel.124).

[7] See Hagel and Tomaschitz (1998; 127, Iot. 9. Cf. IGR III, 831).

[8] For ethnic names, see Zgusta (1964).

[9] *Demiourgoi* in Roman Imperial times were called those inhabitants of the empire who had full citizenship and were able to undertake civic offices. See *Npauly*, 3, p. 446, Demiourgoi 2 (3).

lifetime.[1] Several inscriptions survive showing a particular link of native Cilicians with the emperor's cult.[2] As the acquisition of priesthoods became closely linked to the financial situation and political power of the priests-to-be, those honorary offices became dominated by members of the traditional city élites or of the local families which had access to wealth due to the development of commerce.[3]

Apart from shamanistic elements in Cilician religion, one has also to pay attention to pre-Hellenic cults of a special magical or ecstatic character. The best-documented such cult was found in Hierapolis Castabala. The name of the female goddess worshipped in that Cilician city – dominated over a brief period by the local royal family of Tarcondimotus[4] – has survived under different forms: Castabala or Artemis Perasia (or Persike, i.e. Persian) or simply Perasia or, as attested on an Aramaic late antique inscription, Kubaba. The goddess was certainly not Greek in her features. Her priestess, probably following a hereditary office, a privilege of the city's best families, would fall into ecstasy and walk over streams and rivers as well as over burning embers. This practice, attested by Strabo, has been used elsewhere in place and time as well: the Sicilian closed circle or family of Hirpi practiced the same thing in honour of Apollo, and the *anastenarides* in modern Thrace (northern Greece) still do the same on the namesday of St Constantine and St Helena, on the 21st of May. These instances, however, have something in common: although they inspire awe among spectators, they are considered as traces of 'alien wisdom', as something incomprehensible and intangible, as proof of some folkloric mysticism. The female goddess of Castabala had had her share of worship and dedications even by high-class Greeks and Romans, as the few inscriptions on the base of honorific statues prove; however, it had never become a highly appraised cult, fully accepted and exploited by Greek or Roman politics.

---

[1] The office of a *gymnasiarch*, i.e. superintendent of the gymnasium and the athletic contests held there remained one of the most prestigious honorary offices throughout the Roman period.

[2] See for example, Bean-Mitford (1970: no. 172) from **Cestrus** (mod. Macar Kalesi), Hagel and Tomaschitz (1998: 48), Aya7; 50, Aya 12 from **Ayasofya**, Hagel-Tomaschitz (1998): Iot 1, a, b; 3d; 9; 11b from **Iotape**, Hagel and Tomaschitz (1998): Kes3; 26a from **Kestros**. The number of such inscriptions is, of course, much more extensive and proves that the local élites of Cilicia consisted mainly of native Cilicians, as stressed also by Hopwood (1986: 345).

[3] In some cases those rich Cilicians were descendants of the renowned Cilician pirates, who were defeated by Pompeius in the 60s BC and were then permanently settled in the cities, undertaking commercial activity which thrived. See De Souza (1999). For the development of local, hellenized or non-hellenized élites, see Hopwood (1983:180-181).

[4] Tarcondimotus was a Cilician King who fought by the side of Octavian in Actium. His son, under the same name, was accorded privileges and bore the attribute *Philopator*.

Regarding religious activities and beliefs in urban and rural areas we can thus remark the following: whereas religion in the cities seemed to be dominated by the standard deities of the Greek and Roman pantheon, with the addition of ruler cult, which seems to have been prevalent in the second century AD, in the countryside prevailed Hellenized forms of local cults, which had their natural surrounding particularly in caves. These caves were sometimes transformed into proper temples, such as in the case of 'Korykeion antron' and the temple of Athena in Tagai near Seleuceia. In some cases they developed into the main cults not only of a rural area, but also of the neighbouring city. Thus, some of the major religious celebrations for Cilician and Isaurian cities took place *extra muros* (that is, outside of the city-walls). In these cases, however, one notices that city customs were dominant, especially since priesthood of such temples and cult centres passed, by means of donations, benefaction or simple auction, to the hands of the ruling city elite. City culture thus extended beyond the boundaries of the city walls and spread into the countryside, though without controlling it completely. These religious tendencies affected also the inhabitants of the more remote uplands of Isauria, and their inhabitans, the Isaurians.[1] From the little we know of them, we may suspect that the Isaurians did take part in the same religious festivals in the rural sanctuaries as did citizens and peasants, but not in an institutionalized and organised way.[2]

## Christianity in the cities and the countryside

Monotheism in Cilicia and Isauria as well as in the rest of the empire did not find its only expression in Christianity. At the time when Paul and his followers crossed the country and preached, addressing mainly the Jewish communities of the cities through which they passed, another monotheistic cult took root in some of the cities: the cult of Theos Hypsistos, sometimes appearing under a syncretistic garment as Zeus or Helios Hypsistos. In Cilicia and Isauria it is mainly attested in the city of Seleuceia.[3] Whether this cult developed under Jewish influence or whether it remained a purely pagan cult, is an issue which still remains open. The probability is, though, that any relation to the official Jewish cult should be excluded.[4] Also undecided is

---

[1] The most concrete study and presentation of the Isaurians has been done recently by Elton in Mathisen and Sivan (1996; 126-135); Elton (1996, 2000).
[2] The only inscription clearly mentioning an Isauros in a religious context is Bean-Mitford (1970; 131, no. 124) from Tamaşalık, presumably Astra in antiquity.
[3] Hagel-Tomaschitz (1998: Sel 98; 115; 116; 117).
[4] See Mitchell (2000).

whether Christian indoctrination appealed particularly to the adherents of this monotheistic cult or whether the perception of the Christian God was beyond the intellectual scope of those 'hypsistarians'. However, the percentage of hypsistarians in Cilicia is very small and too geographically restricted to allow us any generalisation. It is clear that this monotheistic cult was imported in Cilicia, probably from Pisidia or Phrygia, where it seems to have been much more widespread, and that it probably did not constitute a concrete Christian or Jewish heresy, but rather a version of pagan monotheism.

Contarary to the case of the cult of Theos Hypsistos, the spread of Christianity was rapid and gave rise to a complex religious scenario. In the first place, it has to be stressed that from the beginning Cilicia, both before and after its divisions, belonged to the sphere of administrative and cultural influence of Antioch-on-the Orontes. The Antiochene Church built on this pre-existing administrative and political structure in order to extend its influence northwards. Due to the fervent efforts of pioneers such as Ignatius of Antioch as well as to the attraction of the theological school of Antioch, all churches and bishoprics of Cilicia were soon subordinated to the Church of Antioch.

At least from the archaeological point of view, in the case of Cilicia we have much less information on urban Christianity than rural. The cities of the Cilician Plain, wealthier and thus probably rich in Christian sanctuaries and churches, as they were in pagan monuments and public buildings, have been largely built over and most of their early ecclesiastical buildings ruined. It is only through the discovery of epigraphic material that we can now reconstitute in part the early Christian history of this area. On the other hand, we are much better informed about the coastal cities of Rough Cilicia, where systematic archaeological studies of church buildings have yielded interesting results regarding the features and time-span of the expansion of Christianity.[1]

No house-churches have been discovered so far in Cilician Plain cities, and only a few buildings of early Christian churches have been excavated, the most important of which are situated in Missis-Mopsuestia. No miraculous interventions are recorded in this area. It seems that local Christianity was boosted by the persecutions: the main figures worshipped in the Mopsuestia-Anazarbus area were the martyrs Tarachos, Probos and Andronikos, for whom churches were built in the second half of the fourth century AD, as well as St Marinos and St Zosimus, the latter constituting an emulation of pagan

---

[1] See Hill (1996; 3-5).

Orpheus.[1] Christianisation must have been very well established by the fourth century AD, as no pagan inscriptions are to be found in the area of Anazarbus after that date.[2] Apart from St Tarachos, all other names are Greek or Roman, which makes us think that Christianity spread initially among the upper classes of the cities, maybe also among educated sections of the population.

As we move towards the coast, however, it seems that Christianity had to fight harder and with different means in order to defeat pagan cults. In the coastal regions the exponents of Christianity became healers or miracle-workers, sealing with their presence the pagan sanctuaries, especially those related to natural sites with a magical character. In Aegai, for example, the famous cult-centre of healing Asclepius,[3] the temple of the god remained in use until the emperor Constantine had it shut down.[4] Yet the reputation of the city as a healing centre — which apparently earned it a high income from visitors — was maintained by the substitution of the cult of Asclepius with that of the Saints Cosmas and Damianos, the doctor saints of the Christian world, as well as by that of St Thalelaeus, who also performed healing miracles. In the fifth century, an *extra-muros* church was built in honour of St Thecla, the local saint of Seleucia on the Kalykadnos, just to reinforce the function of Aegai as a pilgrimage centre for those who sought salvation from illness.[5]

The most amazing tales on the Christianisation of Rough Cilicia, however, survive in the *Life and Miracles of St Thecla* herself. The text, written in the fifth century, reflects various layers of the expansion of Christianity and the proselytising action of the saint, both before and after her heavenly ascension. The narration starts at the end of the first century AD, when St Thecla, persecuted in her hometown, Iconium, and in Syrian Antioch, where she went following Paul's footsteps, established herself in a small cave in the old necropolis of Seleuceia on the Kalykadnos, dedicated to a life of chastity and prayer. Thecla's abode was situated just above the sanctuary of Apollo Sarpedonios and on the pilgrimage road to the sanctuary

---

[1] See Maraval (1985; 355-6) on the local saints of Anazarbus and Mopsuestia. For the archaeological remains of the martyrion of Anazarbus see Gough (1952; 85-150) and for the association of St Zosimus with the Orpheus-myth see Halkin (1952; 252).

[2] Dagron and Feissel (1985; 157-200).

[3] Dagron and Feissel (1985; fn.4).

[4] The cult of Asclepius must have been judged particularly dangerous for Constantine to shut it down, as the usual practice of the emperor, at least according to the official imperial legislation, was to let sanctuaries function but to forbid sacrifices.

[5] See Maraval (1985: 354 and Soz.), *Hist. eccl.* (II 4-5 – GCS 50, p.57, 5-7 )on the cult of SS. Cosmas and Damianos, as well as Brocker (1976) on the cult of Saint Thalelaeus.

of Athena Kanetis at Tagai, the city's tutelary deity.[1] Her miracle-working powers caused the decline of those two sanctuaries,[2] as well as of two more, those of Aphrodite[3] and Zeus,[4] which she desecrated with the aid of her disciples. When the saint passed away, a monastery was built over the cave, which, through her grace, continued to perform miracles and to function as a pilgrimage centre. At the end of the fifth century, when the emperor Zeno came victorious out of his civil war with the usurper Basiliscus, he enlarged the monastery and adorned it with such buildings, that it surpassed the dimensions of a local, provincial sanctuary and became a major centre of pilgrimage. The case of Ayatekla or Meriamlık, as it is presently called in Turkish, can serve very well as an example demonstrating how a rural site, on the fringe of the city, becomes finally intrinsically linked to the city itself, while maintaining a certain autonomy.

Let us dwell a little longer on an incident during the pre-Zenonian phase of the monastery. At the time of the Monophysite strife, in the first half of the fifth century, when the Church of Antioch was imposing its theological views on its subordinate bishoprics, the leader of the monastery of St Thecla, Palladius, was following the monophysite doctrines of the rural clergy and the monasteries of the Antiochene.

We may suspect that the gap, made clear in the case of the Church of Antioch, estranged as she gradually became from the religious endowments of the city's *chora*,[5] was visible also in the case of the cities subordinate to Antioch, which gradually saw the monastic institutions trespassing the official theological lines towards Monophysitism. We may suspect also that

---

[1]  Dagron (1975; 53-59): 'She surrounded herself with a wall against the daemon Sarpedon, who had made his abode on that hoof on the sea [i.e. the small peninsula], and who made several people err in their faith by treachery and false oracles. She surrounded herself with a wall also against the warrior goddess Athena, who had made her abode like a vulture on a summit'.

[2]  Dagron (1975: miracles no. I and no. 2). A vivid description of the conversion of the temple of Athena Kanetis is the following (from miracle no.2): 'After Sarpedonius she [St Thecla] turned to the summit close to her abode, which was formerly called Mt. Cokysion, but as time went by the myth vested it with the name of the temple of Athena Kanetis, as if the mountain belonged to Athena. So she took the mountain away from the daemon and offered it to the dominion of Christ, to whom it belonged anyway by divine will. Until today the site is full of martyrs, like a high fortress is full of military officers, it is dwelled by holy men, as the fully armed Pallas, protecting the city, cannot bear with the insult made to her by the unarmed and naked virgin girl.'

[3]  Dagron (1975: miracle no. 3).

[4]  Dagron (1975: miracle no. 4).

[5]  The monasteries and clergy of the Syrian countryside became gradually strongly Monophysitic, following the doctrinal guidelines of the Church of Alexandreia, whereas the Church of Antioch, vacillating between one doctrine and the other, opted finally for 'Orthodoxy'. See Frend (1976). 'Chora' is a transliteration of the Greek word for territory, usually relating to the rural areas surrounding a city in antiquity.

the position taken by the monastery of St Thecla must have also been a way of winning over people in the countryside. Monophysism was a simpler doctrine, easier to grasp even for the uneducated peasants. At the same time the monks of St Thecla were exercising pressure on the city Church authorities, who apparently considered the monastery as a great asset.[1] The adornment of the site by Zeno, the emperor who sought to breach the gap between Monophysism and the Antiochene theology, can also be interpreted as a means of bending the resistance of the monks and reconciling the monastery with the official clergy of Seleuceia.

By the end of the fifth century, most important pagan temples in the Cilician countryside had been desecrated and transformed into churches, following the fate of the sanctuaries of Athena Kanetis and Sarpedon. Such was the end of the temple of Zeus at Cennet Cehennem replaced by a church,[2] and of the large temple of Hermes near Elaiussa-Sebaste (modern Ayas), in which a church was built. A smaller Hermes-temple, clearly a rural sanctuary, farther north and higher from Elaiussa at a site called today Çatıören, was also transformed to a church, proving that Christians, according the edicts of Theodosius I, who gave full support to the destruction of temples, conducted an organised eradication of all pagan cults in cities and countryside alike.

Despite the natural environment, Rough Cilicia and Isauria have many fewer stories about ascetics and monks to tell than, say, Northern Syria, although it is clear that by the fifth century, even the smallest villages were adorned with disproportionately large basilicas. It seems that the fear of bandits' raids caused Cilician monks to gather together in larger clusters; monasticism rather than asceticism was the norm there. The most impressive of those monastic endowments, set in a completely natural site, is that of Alahan monastery. No trace of a pre-existing pagan temple has been discovered yet, but the fact that the earlier of the three churches of the site was built over a cave, indicates that there, as well, some sort of struggle between pagan spirits and Christian monks had taken place. The monastery at Alahan was by far the largest monastic institution in the whole Cilicia, due to the generous donations of the emperor Zeno, a native of the area and probably the son of the abbot of the monastery, Tarasis. The site of Alahan is situated within the limits of Isauria. The imperial donation, apart from a family affair, had also the character of a gift to the belligerent Isaurians, Zeno's select military body, who apparently had been only recently Christianised, in order both to secure their loyalty, and, possibly, to refrain them from erring towards monophysitism or any other sort of heresy.

---

[1] On the appeal that Monophysism had on the population of the countryside, see Frend (1976).
[2] Hild and Hellenkemper (1990; 314-315).

In conclusion, in the Roman era, when paganism was still at its peak, Cilicia's religious life was associated with the countryside to a large extent; shamanistic elements had been infiltrated in the Greek and Roman religion following the general syncretistic pattern. Yet, the spread of the emperor's cult as well as the accumulation of wealth in the hands of native Cilicians, eager to display their loyalty and conformity to Roman patterns created a sort of religious uniformity, even temporarily. When Christianity spread, it tried to wipe out all traces of pagan religions, but it still conformed, apparently, to the innate shamanistic relation to natural elements and sites. Some of those sites became pilgrimage and monastic centres. The wealth they naturally accumulated, as well as imperial donations, offered these centres a great deal of autonomy. Their reputation as healing centres, as in the case of St Thecla as well as the control they exercised on the local population, as in the case of Alahan monastery, brought them often into opposition with the official clergy of the cities.

*REFERENCES*

Alföldy-Rosenbaum, E., Huber, G, Onurkan, S. 1967 *A Survey of Coastal Cities in Western Cilicia,* Ankara; TTK.

Alföldy-Rosenbaum, E., *The Nekropolis of Adrassus (Balabolu) in Rough Cilicia (Isauria),* Vienna; TAM 10 Ergänzungsband.

Bayliss, R. 1966 *The Ala Camii in Kadirli, transformations of a sacred monument,* MA dissertation, Newcastle upon Tyne.

Bean, G., and Mitford, T. 1962 Sites old and new in Rough Cilicia, *Anatolian Studies* Vol. 12, 185-217.

Bean, G. and Mitford, T. 1970 *Journeys in Rough Cilicia 1964-68,* Vienna; Österreichische Akademie der Wissenschaftern, Philosophisch-Historische Klasse 102, Ergänzungsband zu den Tituli Asiae Minoris 3.

Brocker, H. 1976 *Der heilige Thalelaius, Texte und Untersuchungen,* Münster; Forschungen zur Volkskunde; Heft 48, Verlag Regensburg.

Burgess, Jr. W. 1990 'Isaurian names and the ethnic identity of the Isaurians in late antiquity', *Ancient World,* Vol. 21, 109-121.

Callot, O. and Marcillet-Jaubert, J. 1984 'Haut-Lieux de Syrie du Nord', in *Temples et Sanctuaires,* Lyon; TMO 7.

Dagron, G. 1975 *Vie et miracles de St Thècle,* Subsidia hagiographica 62. Brussels; Société des Bollandistes.

Dagron,G. and Feissel, D. *Inscriptions de Cilicie,* Travaux et Mémoires 14, Paris; De Boccard.

Dagron G and Vérilhac, A. 1974 Une nouvelle inscription du temple de Zeus à Diocésarée-Uzuncaburc, *REA,* Vol. 76, 237-242.

Dagron, G. and Marcillet-Jauber, J. 1978 Inscriptions de Cilicie et d' Isaurie, *Belleten* 42, 373-420.

De Souza, P. 1999 *Piracy in the Greco-Roman World,* Cambridge; CUP.

Dupont-Sommer, A. and Robert, L. 1964 *La déesse de Hierapolis-Castabala,* Istanbul; l'Institut Français d'Archéologie de Stamboul.

Durugönül, J. 1989 *Die Felsreliefs im Rauhen Kilikien,* Oxford; BAR 511.

Elton, H. 1996 *Frontiers of the Roman Empire,* London; Batsford.

Elton, H. 1996 'Defining Romans, Barbarians and the Roman frontier', in Mathisen, R.W and Sivan, H.S. (eds.), *Shifting Frontiers in Late Antiquity,* Aldershot; Variorum, 126-135.

Elton, H. 2000 'The nature of sixth-century Isaurians', in Mitchell, S. and Greatrex, G. (eds.), *Ethnicity and Culture in Late Antiquity,* Cardiff; University of Wales Press, 293-307.

Equini Schneider, E. 1999 *Elaiussa Sebaste, campagne di scavo 1995-1997,* Roma; L'Erma di Bretschneider.

Feld, O. 1963-64 'Bericht über eine Reise durch Kilikien', *Istanbuler Mitteilungen* Vol. 13-14; 89-93.

Feld, O. and Weber, H. 1967 'Tempel und Kirche über der Korykischen Grotte (Cennet Cehennem) in Kilikien', *Istanbuler Mitteilungen,* Vol. 17; 254-278.

Frend W. 1976 'Popular religion and christological controversy in the fifth century', in Frend, W. *Religion Popular and Unpopular,* Aldershot; Variorum.

Gough, M. 1952 'Anazarbus', *Anatolian Studies* Vol. 2, 85-150.

Gough, M. (ed.) 1985 *Alahan: an early Christian monastery in Southern Turkey based on the work of Michael Gough,* Toronto; Pontifical Institute of Medieval Studies.

Hagel, S. and Tomaschitz, K. 1998 *Repertorium der Westkilikischen Inschriften,* Vienna; Verl. der Österr. Akad. der Wiss.

Halkin, F. 1952 'Une émule d'Orphée: la légende inédite de saint Zosime, martyr d'Anazarbe au Cilicie', *Analecta Bollendiana,* Vol. 70.

Hellenkemper, H. 1980 Zur Entwicklung des Stadtbildes im Rauhen Kilikien, *ANRW* 7.2 Berlin, 1262-1283.

Hild, F. and Hellenkemper H. 1990 *Kilikien und Isaurien,* Wien; TIB 5, Denkschr. 215.

Hill, S. 1996 *The early Byzantine churches of Cilicia and Isauria,* Aldershot; Variorum.

Hopwood, K. 1983 'Policing the hinterland: Rough Cilicia and Isauria', in Mitchell, S., *Armies and Frontiers in Roman and Byzantine Anatolia,* Proceedings of a colloquium held at University College, Swansea, in April 1981, Oxford; BAR int. series 156.

Hopwood, K. 1986 'Towers, Territory and Terror: How the East was Held', in Freeman, P. and Kennedy. D., *The Defence of the Roman and Byzantine East,* Oxford; BAR 297.i.

Hopwood, K. 1989 'Consent and Control: how peace was kept in Rough Cilicia', in French, D. and Lightfoot, C.(eds.), *The Eastern Frontier of the Roman Empire*, Oxford; BAR int. Ser. 553 (I), 191-201.

Keil, J. and Wilhelm, A. 1931 *Denkmäler aus dem Rauhen Kilikien*, MAMA III, Manchester; Manchester University Press.

Kirsten, E. 1974 'Elaiussa-Sebaste in Kilikien', in *Mansel'e Armağan, Melanges Mansel*, Ankara, 777-802.

Lewin A. 1991 Banditismo e civilitas nella Cilicia Tracheia antica e tardoantica, *Quaderni Storici* Vol. 26; Nr.1, 167-184.

Machatschek, A. 1967 *Die Nekropolen und Grabmäler im Gebiet von Elaiussa Sebaste und Korykos im Rauhen Kilikien*, Vienna; H. Böhlau, Kommissionsverlag der Österreichischen Akademie der Wissenschaften.

Maraval, P. 1985 *Lieux saints et pélerinages d'Orient: histoire et géographie des origines à la conquête arabe*, Paris; Cerf.

Mellink, M. 1964 'The Concept of Syro-Cilicia and New Developments in Anatolian Archaeology', *Compte rendu de l'Onzième rencontre assyriologique internationale organisé en Leiden du 23 au 29 juin 1962*, Leiden; Nederlands Instituut voor het Nabije Oosten, 34-38.

Minor, C. 1979 'The robber tribes of Isauria', *Ancient World* Vol. 10, 117-122

Mitchell, S. 1993 *Anatolia: land, men and gods in Asia Minor*, Two Vols, Oxford; Clarendon Press.

Mitchell, S. 2000 'The cult of Theos Hypsistos', in Athanassiadi, P. and Frede, M., *Late Pagan Monotheism*, Oxford; Clarendon Press, 81-148.

Mylonopoulos, J. 1998 'Poseidon der Erdeschütter. Religiöse interpretationen Erd-und Seebeben', in *Naturkatastrophen in der Antiken Welt*, Stuttgarter Kolloquium zu der historischen Geographie des Altertums, 6, 1996, Stuttgart, 92-99.

Rougé , J. 1966 'L'Histoire Auguste et l'Isaurie en IVe s.', *REG* Vol. 68, 282-315.

Sayar, M., Siewert, P. and Tauber, H. 1989 *Inschriften aus Hierapolis-Kastabala*, Vienna; Verl. d. Österr. Akad. d. Wiss.

Sayar, M. 2000 *Die Inschriften von Anazarbos und Umgebung*, Teil I., IK 56, Bonn; R. Habelt.

Strzygowski, J. 1903 *Kleinasien, ein Neuland der Kunstgeschichte*, Leipzig; J. C. Hinrichs.

Williams, M. 1992 'The Jewish community of Corycus', *ZPE* 92, 248-252.

Zgusta, L. 1964 *Kleinasiatische Personennennamen*, Prague; Orientalischen Institut in dem Verlagshaus der Tschechoslowakischen Akademie der Wissenschaften.

# 21. HAMSHEN BEFORE HEMSHIN: THE PRELUDE TO ISLAMISATION

Hovann SIMONIAN

In his writings, F. W. Hasluck has dwelt on the related topics of conversion to Islam and crypto-Christianity in Anatolia and the Pontos. His article on the crypto-Christians of Trebizond, however, focussed exclusively on Greek-speaking crypto-Christians.[1] Hasluck was possibly unaware of the existence of yet another Islamised community of crypto-Christians, this one of Armenian origin, inhabiting the district of Hemshin, in the highlands of the *sancak* of Lazistan. The *Hemshin*, or *Hemshinli*,[2] though, had been mentioned in a few western-language studies, including works by protestant missionaries E. Smith and H. G. O. Dwight in the 1830s, and by Vital Cuinet in his survey of the Ottoman empire, a source which R. M. Dawkins used when he listed the 'Hamchounlis' among the crypto-Christians of Turkey.[3]

Not too much blame should be laid on Hasluck, however, as the history of the Hemshinli is at many junctures mired in obscurity. It is to be regretted that Hamshen did not have its native historian, as both the paucity of existing sources and their laconic nature render the study of Hamshen Armenians and their Islamised descendants, the Hemshinli, an arduous challenge.[4] As examples, medieval Armenian chroniclers, such as Ghewond, and Stepanos Asoghik Taronetsi (Stephen Asoghik of Taron), provide us with only a few lines on the migration of Armenians to the Pontos and the foundation of Hamshen, which they believe to have occurred in the second half of the eighth century, while a third chronicler, Pseudo-Yovhannes

---

[1] Hasluck (1921; 199-202).

[2] In this article, 'Hemshin' and 'Hemshinli' rather than 'Hemşin' and 'Hemşinli' has been adopted to describe the Islamicized Armenians. 'Hamshen Armenians' will refer to their Christian ancestors and the descendants of those who refused conversion. 'Hamshen' will generally be used to designate the district prior to the Ottoman conquest, and 'Hemshin' for the period after it. Contemporary Turkish spelling will be reserved for Turkish words and modern toponyms, such as the districts (*ilçe*) of Hemşin and Çamlıhemşin. Armenian personal names and toponyms have been transliterated after a simplified version of the Classical and Standard Eastern Armenian system of the Library of Congress.

[3] Smith (1833; 324-25); Cuinet (1890; 121); Dawkins (1933; 268-69).

[4] Tashean (1980; 41-42); Edwards (1988; 408).

Mamikonean (John Mamikonean), in his history of Taron, places these events in the early decades of the seventh century.[1] A brief description of the geography and climate of Hamshen is given by the historian Hetum of Korykos (Frère Hayton) at the beginning of the fourteenth century.[2] A little more information is available on the principality of Hamshen during the fifteenth century thanks to the colophons (scribal memorials)[3] of Armenian manuscripts and the diary of Castilian ambassador Ruy González de Clavijo.[4]

The conversion of part of Hamshen's Armenian population to Islam and the exodus of those who remained Christians greatly reduced the access of Armenians to an already isolated region, and thus the ability of their scholars to gather material for a history of the district. Moreover, Armenian historians and ethnographers who studied the case of the Hemshinli placed most of the emphasis of their studies on the coercive nature of the conversion process and of the linguistic Turkification that followed a few centuries later, to the neglect of other aspects of the history of Hamshen/Hemshin. Turkish scholars, including local historians of Hemshinli descent, have been mainly concerned with the objective of establishing, or more correctly forging, the credentials of the Hemshinli as an authentic Turkic tribe having no links whatsoever with Armenians. Consequently, the history of Hamshen before Hemshin is often considered an enigma, particularly by those who lack the knowledge of the Armenian language. It is no surprise then that the title of a book recently published in Istanbul was *Hemşin Gizemi*, the mystery of Hemshin.[5]

The lack of knowledge about the history of Hamshen prior to Islamisation also has the unfortunate consequence of distorting any discussion of the latter phenomenon in Hemshin. Figures from an Ottoman *defter* of the early 1520s showing a high percentage of Muslims in the Hemshin *kaza* have

---

[1] Ghewond (1887; chapters 41-42); Ghewond (1982; 147-49); Stepanos Taronetsi (1883; 161-62); Stepanos Taronetsi (2000; 185-86); Yovhannes Mamikonean (1941; 283-85); Avdoyan (1993; 159-60 and 248-49).

[2] Dulaurier (1906; 129-30 and 268-69); Hetum of Korykos (1951; 15).

[3] Colophons are scribal memorials, usually written by the person whose task it was to copy the manuscripts. Alongside the arduous task of copying a long text, the scribe often inserted something about himself and about the conditions of copying, almost always including, in the Armenian case, the date, place and patron of the manuscript. In most cases the colophon was written at the end of copying, but not infrequently during the work. With the invention and progress of printing, the colophon became what we call now the front material or the information on publication. This information continued to be placed in textual paragraph form at the end of printed books into the Sixteenth century. I am indebted to Dr. Dickran Kouymjian for this definition of colophon.

[4] Clavijo (1999; 352-53); the most exhaustive survey of medieval sources on Hamshen is provided in the excellent article by Edwards (1988; 403-422).

[5] Haçikyan (1996).

led to the assumption that Hamshen Armenians were among the early converts to Islam in the Pontos. It has even been suspected that Islam had already made inroads in the region by the early fifteenth century. Mass conversion to Islam in Hemshin, however, is a later development, having mostly taken place in the seventeenth and eighteenth centuries. It is therefore important to properly establish the historical background of the district in the fifteenth and sixteenth centuries, including Christian-Muslim interaction, before moving to an analysis of subsequent periods of Hemshin history.

*Between myth and reality: The origins of Hamshen*

The genesis of Hemshin history can be traced to the period of Arab dominion over Armenia at the end of the eighth century. According to the historian Ghewond, twelve thousand men and their families, led by prince Shapuh Amatuni and his son Hamam, left their ancestral home of Oshakan in the Aragatsotn canton in the years 789-90 in order to escape the heavy taxes imposed by the Arabs. After an encounter in the canton of Kogh (now Göle, near the source of the Kur River) with Arab troops pursuing them, the fugitives reached the Byzantine-ruled Pontos, located to the north-west of Armenia.[1] Byzantine Emperor Constantine VI welcomed the two Amatuni *nakharar*s and the other princes accompanying them, bestowing honours upon them, their nobles and their cavalry, and granting the common people fertile lands in the region.[2] Another historian, Stephen Asoghik of Taron, placed these events a few decades earlier, in the 750s, but the political context of the late 780s, marked by a heavy climate of repression following the defeat of the anti-Arab Armenian revolt of 774-5 in which the Amatunis were prominent participants, makes the latter time period more plausible.[3] One should be careful here not to take the figure of 12,000 men literally, for it probably has more a symbolic significance than a statistical one. Armenian medieval historians, like their contemporaries throughout Christendom, dotted

---

[1] The Amatunis had acquired Oshakan in the fourth century. Their original domain was the Artaz canton, the modern-day Iranian district of Maku. The Artaz branch does not seem to have participated in the migration, for family members appear in possession of their domains in the ninth century, as vassals of the Artsruni Princes and later kings of Vaspurakan. The Armenian princes which held Maku and Artaz until the mid-fifteenth century could possibly be their descendants. A branch of the family may have remained in Aragatsotn itself, as the Vachutean princes which ruled in later centuries (twelfth to fifteenth centuries) over Aragatsotn and neighbouring districts claimed Amatuni descent. However, the validity of their claim is a subject of discussion among historians.

[2] Ghewond (1887, chapters 41-42); Ghewond (1982; 149); Grousset (1947; 320 and 338); Khachikyan (1969; 115-17); Edwards (1988; 404-05).

[3] Stepanos Taronetsi (1883; 161-62); Stepanos Taronetsi (2000; 185-86); Ghewond (1982; 134); Grousset (1947; 320 and 338).

their texts with Biblical references. The number twelve is a clear allusion to the twelve tribes of Israel, and Ghewond was probably making a parallel between Moses and Joshua taking their people out of servitude in Egypt, and Shapuh and his son Hamam leading Armenians to a new promised land away from Arab oppression.[1] Interestingly, the author of an 1898 article on Black Sea Armenians was told by an elderly informant of Hamshenite background that prince Hamam had come to the Pontos with a total of four thousand migrants.[2]

An account by a third chronicler, although it should be received with much caution, sheds some light on the situation in the territory settled by the Armenian migrants and the motivations of the warm welcome given to them by Constantine VI of Byzantium. In his history of Taron (now the region of Muş), Pseudo-John Mamikonean describes a war that takes place between Hamam, who is ruling over the Armenian settlers in the city of Tambur, and his maternal uncle, the prince of Georgia Vashdean. According to Edwards, this narrative could refer to events having taken place in the early ninth century, although Pseudo-John Mamikonean dates them to the early seventh century.[3] Shapuh's marriage to a Georgian princess raises the possibility that the Amatunis moved to Chaneti (Lazia) because they were already familiar with the region, over which their Georgian in-laws might have had a nominal or actual claim. Furthermore, the war between Hamam and Vashdean could represent a dramatised account of conflict having taken place between the Armenian settlers and their new neighbours.[4] The Byzantines generally encouraged Armenian immigration to win over soldiers for a future campaign against the Arabs. Edwards pertinently wonders whether they were not also recruiting in this case colonists who would help them bring order to border districts inhabited by unruly Tzan and other Kartvelian tribes over which the Byzantine administration had little control.[5] After rebuilding Tambur, which had been destroyed by the Persian (i.e. Arab) troops brought by Vashdean, Hamam called the city by his own name, Hamamashen (built by Hamam).[6] With time, Hamamashen became *Hamshen*, which came to designate the entire district inhabited by the Armenian immigrants and their descendants.

---

[1] Redgate (forthcoming).

[2] Muradeants (1898; 471).

[3] Edwards (1988; 405-06); Yovhannes Mamikonean (1941; 283-85); Avdoyan (1993; 159-60 and 248-49).

[4] Khachikyan (1969; 117).

[5] Edwards (1988; 406).

[6] Avdoyan (1993; 160).

Two other hypotheses concerning the origins of Hamshen deserve to be examined. The first and least plausible one links the foundation of Hamshen with the destruction of the Armenian capital Ani by the Seljukid Turks in 1064. A group of fugitives from Ani is believed to have found refuge in the forests of Hamshen, 'which until then had never seen any human face'.[1] This account, which was transmitted to nineteenth-century travellers by Hamshen Armenians and Muslim Hemshinli, remains widespread to this day in the oral tradition of both groups.[2] A Hemshin Mullah residing in Kyrgyzstan — where the Hemshin of Ajaria were deported by Stalin in 1944 — still took pride in the 1980s in being a descendant of Ani's inhabitants.[3] The popularity of this thesis, however, might have more to do with the prestige of Ani and the desire of many Armenians to trace their origins to the famed 'city of a thousand and one churches' than with historical fact. Migrants from Ani chose as their new homes cities that were important trading centres rather than a rural mountainous district such as Hamshen. Many did indeed move to the Pontos, but their destination was the city of Trebizond and not Hamshen.[4] Father Minas Bzhshkean was careful to note in his history of Pontos the differences in dialect and pronunciation between the Trebizond Armenians, who hailed from Ani, and the Hamshen Armenians.[5]

The final hypothesis concerning the origins of Hamshen connects it with the immediate districts to its south, Ispir and Pertakrag.[6] Following the initial settlement under Shapuh and Hamam Amatuni, the Armenianisation of Hamshen could have been advanced by a gradual infiltration of migrants from the south.[7] Similarities have indeed been noted between the dialect of the Khotorjur (Western Armenian Khodorchur) sub-district of Pertakrag and the one of Hamshen.[8] These parallels, however, could reflect contacts between the two districts throughout the centuries rather than a common origin. It is possible that the process of Armenianisation was completed when the newcomers assimilated the district's sparse Tzan population, if such a population existed at all. Anthony Bryer advances the attractive, yet

---

[1] Haykuni (1895; 296); Bzhshkean (1830; 84).

[2] Gatenean (1888; 2); Piro (1893; 3); Torlakyan (1968; 4).

[3] Vardanyan (1998; 7).

[4] Khachikyan (1969; 118-20 n. 12).

[5] Bzhshkean (1819; 82). This is also confirmed by Acharean (1947; 11).

[6] Ispir corresponds to the Syspiritis of classical times, to the Sper canton of Bardzr Hayk (Upper Armenia) province, and to the modern-day İspir *ilçe*. Pertakrag, also known as Peterek, was the Arseatspor canton of Armenian Tayk/Georgian Tao province, the Ottoman Keskim or Kiskim *kaza*, and the modern-day Yusufeli *ilçe* of the Artvin province.

[7] Khachikyan (1969; 119-20).

[8] See the forthcoming article by Bert Vaux. The present-day name of Khotorjur is Krakonaklar. The small valley is now part of the *ilçe* of İspir.

unfortunately unsubstantiated, supposition that the Hemshin, 'a singular people with certain traditional Tzan characteristics', were Armenianised by the Bagratunis of Sper/Ispir between the seventh and eleventh centuries.[1] Nevertheless, the hypothesis linking Hamshen with Ispir and Pertakrag is highly interesting, and very useful if only to remind us that despite the formidable Paryadres (Barhal) mountains, Hamshen Armenians were not isolated from their compatriots to the south. Hamshen may have thus been less an Armenian enclave in the Pontos than a northern extension of the Armenian settlements of Ispir and Pertakrag.[2] In later centuries, it is the large city to the south, Erzurum, which would attract the Islamised Hemshinli. In this context, one may agree with Bryer that 'any controller of Varoş (Varoş Kale, the upper castle of Hemshin) in the land of Arhakel would look to İspir, rather than to the remote and inaccessible Trebizond, for the nearest power'.[3]

*Geographical setting*

It is probably in the vicinity of Varoş Kale (at the altitude of 1,800 m.), also known as Yukarı Kale or Kala-i Bâlâ/Hemşin-i Bâlâ (from the Persian *bâlâ*, upper), that the semi-mythical town of Tambur, later Hamamashen and Hamshen, was located.[4] Ruins near the fortress seem to indicate the presence of a town of larger importance than the current villages around Varoş Kale.[5] In any case, the initial Armenian settlement on the north side of the Pontic mountains was in the highland district encompassing the valleys formed by two branches of the Fırtına river (the Prytanis, Portanis, or Pordanis of earlier times) — the smaller Hala (Khala) branch and the main Büyük Dere branch — and corresponding to the present-day Çamlıhemşin district of the Rize province. This heartland was protected from a northern intrusion by Aşağı Kale, or Zil Kale/Kala-i Zîr/Hemşin-i Zîr (from the Persian *zîr*, lower, alt. 750 m.), the former Kolonea/Kolona, located around 40 kilometres inland.[6]

---

[1] Bryer (1966; 192-94).

[2] Tashean (1980; 31).

[3] Bryer and Winfield (1985; 342).

[4] While Varoş and Kale-i Bâlâ refer to the same fortress, they also correspond to two separate villages near it. These villages are now mostly depopulated and used mostly in Summer as yaylas. Varoş is now Yazlık, and Kale-i Bâlâ is Hisarcık.

[5] Bryer and Winfield (1985; 337); Edwards (1988; 415).

[6] On Zil Kale, see Bryer and Winfield (1985; 341), Astill and Wright (1977-78; 28-48), and Bryer (1977-78; 49-56). I am indebted to Hagop Hachikian for his explanation of the meaning of *bâlâ* and *zîr*.

The easternmost section of the Pontic Alps was once known as the Paryadres (Barhal or Parhal) Chain, while the current appellation, the Kaçkar Range, refers to a more limited section of the mountains that forms the southern border of Hamshen. It is in this section that the Pontic Mountains, which run parallel to the Black Sea, reach their highest altitude, with an average of over 3,000 metres, and are closest to the coast, in some areas at less than fifty kilometres. On sunny days, one can see from the place where the Fırtına flows into the sea the Kaçkar (3,932 m.), the Tatos (3,560 m.), and the Verçenik (Varshamak or Varshambek in Armenian sources, at 3,711 m.) peaks. According to the authors of a travel guide to the region, 'those are some of the highest spots that can be seen at sea level anywhere on earth, rivaled only by a few points on the Andes and in New Guinea'.[1] Clear days, however, are rare, for the mountains hold the clouds coming from the sea, provoking abundant rainfall. Travellers to the region, such as the German botanist Karl Koch, have depicted the contrast between the valleys covered with mist and the sun-bathed mountain summits and pastures (*yayla*) above the line of clouds.[2] With a yearly average of 250 days of rain, Hemshin is the most humid area in Turkey and throughout the Black Sea region, its neighbour Rize receiving only 170 days of rain annually. The consequence of the rain is 'a natural flora of astonishing wealth and diversity: a quasi-tropical luxuriance that surpasses any other part of the Black Sea coast'.[3]

The other notable physical characteristic of Hamshen is its difficulty of access, if not outright inaccessibility. In addition to the Paryadres/Kaçkar Mountains to the south, entrance to the region from the coast is restricted by steep, rugged relief and dense forests, which also hinder travel and transport within Hemshin itself. Some of the paths are too narrow to be taken by horses and mules, leaving to humans the charge of sumpter beasts.[4] The quasi-permanent fog that covers Hamshen, as well as the impediment to access caused by its forests, mountains and ravines, have left a strong impression on the rare visitors or on writers who had heard of the district. In *La Fleur des histoires de la terre d'Orient*, Hetum of Korykos, of the royal Armenian house of Cilicia, the Frère Hayton of French sources, writes that

> In the realme of Georgi appered a gret meruayle, which I darred nat tell nor reherse yf I hadde nat sene it. But for bycause I was there and se, I dare say

---

[1] Nişanyan and others (1990; 117).

[2] Koch (1846; 32-33).

[3] Nişanyan and Nişanyan (2000; 140).

[4] Nişanyan and Nişanyan (2000; 140); Clavijo (1999; 352-53); Tumayean (1899; 164); for a physical description of the Pontos, see Bryer (1975; 118-20), Bryer and Winfield (1985; 1-7 and 54-57), and Planhol (1997; 53-54 and 132-33).

that in Georgi is a prouynce which is called Haynsen, the which is well of iii
dayes iourney of length or there about; and as long as this sayd prouynce
lasteth, in euery place is so great obscurite that no man is so hardi to come
into the sayd lande, for they can nat cum out agayn. And the dwellers within
the same lande sayde that often tymes there cometh noyse of men, cockes
crowyng, and horses neynge; and by a fludde that cometh out of that place
come tokens appering that there is resorting of people. Verily they fynde in
thistores of Armeny redyng, and Georgi, that there was a cruell emperour in
Persy name Sauorelx. This emperour worshypped the ydols, and cruelly
persecuted the Cristen men.... And than the sayd Cristen men made a gret cry
to Our Lorde God, and sone after came this great darknes that blinded
themperour and all his men; and so the Cristen men scaped, and the sayd
Emperour with his men taryd in the sayd darknes. And there thei shall abyde,
as they beleue, to the worldes ende.[1]

Hetum's work, including the passage on Hamshen, would be reproduced three
centuries later by English traveller Samuel Purchas, who believed that
'Hamsem' was the location of the original Cimmerian gloom of the Odyssey
(XI, 14).[2] Difficulty of access, however, did not imply complete isolation.
Medieval merchants and caravans travelling between the coastal regions to the
Armenian plateau sometimes went across Hamshen, borrowing a once paved
road along the Fırtına. Various mountain paths connected the district to Ispir
and Pertakrag (Peterek), on the other side of the Paryadres chain.[3] Father
Ghukas Inchichean (Injijian) of the Venice Mekhitarists informs us in his
early nineteenth-century *Geography* that every spring, 'Laz' people crossed
Khotorjur (now Sırakonak or Sırakonaklar), and by necessity Hemshin, to go
to Erzurum.[4] Later in the nineteenth century, it was the Armenian Catholics
of Khotorjur who hired Hemshinli guides to reach Rize via Hemshin.
Unfortunately, it was often 'Laz' — a generic appellation used to describe all
Muslims from the Pontos, including the Hemshinli — bandits who came
through these mountain paths from Hemshin to plunder Khotorjur. Other
tracks allowed communication between the Fırtına and parallel valleys.[5]

Throughout centuries, Hamshen Armenians spread from their heartland
in the Fırtına to the highland sections of neighbouring valleys, such as the
Adienos (Senes or Senoz Dere, the Kaptanpaşa *bucak* of the Çayeli *ilçe*) and
the Kalos or Kalopotamos (İkizdere) Rivers. The valley of the Zagatis River
(Susa or Zuğa Dere, the modern Pazar or Hemşin Dere) must certainly have

---

[1] Hetum of Korykos (1988; 14-15).

[2] Hetum of Korykos (1988; xi); Bryer and Winfield (1985; 337); Purchas (1614; 342).

[3] Khachikyan (1969; 126-27); Edwards (1988; 410); Bryer and Winfield (1985; 54-57 and 341-42); also see Rickmers (1934; 465-80), and Stratil-Sauer (1935; 402-10).

[4] Inchichean (1806; 133).

[5] Tashean (1980; 201 n. 200).

been one of the earliest they occupied. Hamshenite settlement follows the river almost along its whole length, coming to a halt at a short distance from the coast. The Susa Dere is thus likely to have constituted an integral part of the principality of Hamshen. Cihar (Kise) Kale, located eight kilometres inland from Pazar (Athenai/Atina), together with the two fortresses on the Fırtına, Varoş/Yukarı Kale and Aşağı/Zil Kale, appears to have been part of the defensive system of the barons of Hamshen. According to Anthony Bryer and David Winfield, these three fortresses, and even the castle of Athenai, on the coast, 'may be considered as a group on grounds of construction'.[1]

This raises the question of the northern borders of Hamshen. Did the principality of Hamshen have an outlet to the sea? Despite similarities in style with the inland fortresses, Bryer and Winfield doubt that the castle of Athenai (Pazar) ever belonged to Hamshen, as the emperors of Trebizond controlled the coast.[2] The locality closest to the mouth of the Fırtına, however, has an Armenian-sounding name, Ardeşen. Richard Kiepert's 1913 map of Asia Minor (*Karte von Kleinasien*) shows a promontory named *Armene* just to the east of Ardeşen.[3] Alexandre Toumarkine reports the story, told to him by Laz informants, that the villages of Seslikaya (Ağvan), Köprüköy (Temisvat), Çayırdüzü (Guvant), Akkaya (Pilercivat), and Duygulu (Telikçet), all located on the lower stretches of the Fırtına valley not very far from Ardeşen and the coast, were formerly inhabited by the Hemshin, prior to their expulsion by the Laz.[4] While the political boundaries of Hamshen might never have reached the coast, they were not very far from it. In subsequent centuries, large sections of the northern borders of the *sancak* of Hemshin, as described by Koch, were close to the sea.[5]

*The principality of Hamshen*

Aside from the commentary by Hetum of Korykos, the only other mention of Hamshen in historical sources in the six hundred years between the late eighth century and the early fifteenth is a reference to a monk from Hamshen who received a manuscript copied in Rome in 1240 while he was a resident there (Erevan, Matenadaran, manuscript no. 218).[6] A legend which could be linked

---

[1] Bryer and Winfield (1985; 337 and 339-40).
[2] Bryer and Winfield (1985; 337 and 339-40).
[3] Kiepert (1913); Tashean (1922; 25).
[4] Toumarkine (1995; 94 and n. 125).
[5] Toumarkine (1995; 94 and n. 125).
[6] Edwards (1988; 408).

to events that actually took place during that period is brought to us by ethnographer Sargis Haykuni. Two notables of 'royal race', Grigor and Martiros, come to blows after Grigor refuses to give his daughter in marriage to Artashen, the son of Martiros. The latter invades the territory of Grigor, vanquishes him, and marries his son to Grigor's daughter. Artashen then builds in the domain of his father-in-law, on the upper reaches of the 'large Hamshen river', a castle named after himself.[1] A curious fact here is the existence of the other Ardeşen on the coast, about the origins of which we know nothing, but a link between the two should not be excluded. One can reasonably wonder whether Ardeşen on the coast was founded by people from Artashen (in Western Armenian Ardashen).

If the 'large Hamshen river' meant the Büyük Dere, the main branch of the Fırtına, the tale transcribed by Haykuni could be a reference to the building of Varoş Kale. Koch, however, tells us of a yayla called Artä or Arta, near the sources of the Hala Dere, the smaller branch or affluent of the Fırtına.[2] A fortress on the Hala Dere filling the same role played by Varoş on the Büyük Dere, i.e. control of access to Hamshen from the south, makes indeed sense from a defence perspective. Bzhshkean mentions the existence of other castles along the Fırtına, in addition to Zil Kale.[3] One could easily imagine that these fortresses were built by either the main princes of Hamshen, or by lesser barons who held some of the affluents of the Fırtına or its adjacent valleys.[4] As an example, a booklet prepared in Hemşin Ortaköy (Zuğaortaköy, or Pazar Hemşin) for the occasion of the seventy fifth anniversary of the Turkish Republic mentions that in proximity to Kantarlı, the highest and southernmost village of the *ilçe*, stand the ruins of Mağlut Kale.[5] This fortress, however, is not included in any of the major works on the historical monuments of the region, and it could be no more than a minor building the importance of which has been blown out of proportion by local villagers.[6]

Not only Armenian, but also Georgian, Byzantine, Trapezuntine, and Turkish sources are silent about Hamshen. The answer to the question asked earlier about the absence of an indigenous historian in Hamshen might simply be, as judiciously discussed by Elizabeth Redgate, that there was no need for

---

[1] Edwards (1988; 408).

[2] Koch (1846; 105-06); Tashean (1980; 5, 13, 26, 74-78, and 113-14).

[3] Bzhshkean (1819; 97).

[4] Edwards (1988; p. 408).

[5] Sakaoğlu and others (1998; 29).

[6] Mağlut Kale is mentioned neither in Bryer and Winfield (1985), nor in the section on Hemshin of Sinclair (1989; 158-162), nor in Karpuz (1992; 59-61).

such a history, because there were no wars in Hamshen.[1] We can only deduce that the principality of Hamshen must have lived through these centuries as a vassal of the larger powers surrounding it, such as the Bagratuni Armenian kingdom, the Byzantine Empire, its successor, the Empire of Trebizond, the Jalayirids, and the Qara Qoyunlu and Aq Qoyunlu Türkmen Confederations. The Georgian option should also be considered, especially during the period of apogee of the Georgian kingdom, in the twelfth and thirteenth centuries. Links between Hamshen and Georgia might provide the rationale for Hetum's placement of his narrative on the darkness of Hamshen in the chapter on Georgia.[2]

Writing one century after Hetum, however, the Castilian ambassador Ruy González de Clavijo notes that he left Georgia — of which he considered Ispir (*aspri*) a part — to enter 'la tierra de Arraquiel' on the 13th of September, 1405.[3] The passage on Arraquiel in the diary he left has become what Bryer and Winfield call the *locus classicus* of Hemshin history.[4] Clavijo relates that the Muslims (*los moros*) of this land were discontented with their lord, named Arraquil (in Armenian Arakel or Arakeal, a first name meaning 'the apostle'), and asked the Muslim Lord of Ispir — the *spiratabec* or Atabeg of Ispir — to extend his authority over them. Accepting their proposal, the Lord of Ispir replaced Arraquil with a Muslim, to whom he gave a Christian deputy. Following a description of the rough mountains, narrow paths and lack of bread in the country, Clavijo says that the Castilians felt threatened by the men of Turkey (*con los de turquía*). The text here becomes confusing, for in the next sentence, these same men of Turkey, described as bad people of bad character (*mala gente de mala condición*) who would not let the envoys leave the region without giving them part of their goods, are also said to be Armenian Christians (*cristianos armenios*).[5] In the version edited by Argote de Molina and published in 1582, *turquía* is replaced by *esta tierra*, which would make the text more logical, but the two earliest manuscripts of Clavijo's diary, held in the Biblioteca Nacional de Madrid and the British Library, have unequivocally *turquía*.[6] Arraquiel thus appears to have been a land populated by both Muslims and Armenians, or alternatively, a territory raided by Türkmens who worried the Castilian diplomats, and inhabited by Armenians who extorted goods from them.

---

[1] Redgate (forthcoming).
[2] Hetum of Korykos (1988 ; 14-15).
[3] Clavijo (1999; 352).
[4] Bryer and Winfield (1985; 336).
[5] Clavijo (1999; 353); Edwards (1988; 417-18).
[6] Clavijo (1999; 54-55 and 353).

Based on this excerpt and on Ilia Zdanévitch's studies which indicate that Clavijo's itinerary led through the Kalopotamos Valley and not the Fırtına, Edwards comes to the conclusion that Arraquiel was not Hamshen, but a territory further to the west, on the Kalopotamos river.[1] The land of Arraquiel, along the Kalopotamos, populated by a mix of Turks, Armenians and Greeks, could not be, according to Edwards, the homogeneously Armenian Hamshen. It was rather a personal conquest of Arakel, and was hence named after him.[2] One could imagine a scenario under which a power vacuum in the Kalopotamos Valley, provoked by Türkmen infiltrations or other causes, gave Arakel the opportunity to intervene in this district and establish control over it. To do this, he had only to advance downstream from the Cimil Dere, a tributary river of the Kalopotamos, the valley of which had constituted an integral part of the Hamshen principality from much earlier on.[3] Dissatisfied with Arakel's domination, the Turks of the region, who by then probably constituted a sizable percentage of the population, called to their rescue the ruler of Ispir, who evicted Arakel from the Kalopotamos Valley and replaced him with a Muslim. This Muslim was given a Christian deputy to quell any discontent among the Greeks and Armenians of the district, who still made up the majority of the population. Centuries later, the Kalopotamos Valley, a 'corridor by which new settlers have entered the coastal lowlands from the Pontic mountains and from Anatolia', [4] was as mixed as it had been when Clavijo went through it. Its headwaters were populated by Hemshinli, while its lower sections were inhabited by other Muslims. Koch was the guest of Kumpusarowa Soliman Agha (Süleyman *Ağa* Kumbasaroğlu), the Hemshin Derebey of Cimil. The German botanist believed that the physiognomy of Süleyman *Ağa*, especially his profile, betrayed an Armenian origin and wondered if he was not a descendant of Hamam.[5] While Süleyman *Ağa*'s descent from Hamam is to be doubted, his adventures, including rebellion, imprisonment, escape, and even piracy — a remarkable feat for a mountaineer — could have deserved him a mention, if not a place of honour in the *mala gente de mala condición* category of Clavijo.[6]

---

[1] Zdanévitch (1964; 249-255); Zdanévitch (1976; 143-149); Edwards (1988; 416-20).

[2] Edwards (1988; 419).

[3] Cimil may even have contained a monastery of relative importance where manuscripts were copied. A Bible, restored in 1621 and known as *Cimili Awetaran* (the Gospel of Cimil), was originally copied there some three centuries earlier, in the early fourteenth century. This Bible was taken for safekeeping to a village in Ispir when Cimil was Islamized in later times (Sanosean 1904; 1).

[4] Meeker (1971; 343).

[5] Koch (1846; 23).

[6] Koch (1846; 31-32); also see Koch (1855; 112).

The main element arguing in favour of differentiation between Arraquiel and Hamshen, however, is the survival of the Hamshen Armenian princes for another eight decades. Arakel himself, or a namesake of his, is likely to have continued to rule over Hamshen, for a manuscript from the Koshtents monastery of the canton mentions that it was copied in 1422 'at the request of the baron of barons, Baron Arakeal and his son Ter (Lord) Sargis' (Jerusalem, St James Monastery/Armenian Patriarchate, ms. no. 1617).[1] The title of 'baron of barons' and of 'first baron' used in manuscripts leads us to believe that there were, below the paramount prince, secondary barons or chieftains in Hamshen. Sargis was probably a younger son who became the Bishop of Hamshen, for an addendum to the same manuscript was composed in 1425 'at the behest of Baron Dawit (David), baron of barons, ... during the patriarchy of the Lord Poghos, the kingship of Skandar pak, the barony of Baron Dawit, the episcopate of Ter Sargis'.[2] The Lord Poghos is the Catholicos Poghos (Paul) II (1418-1430), thus showing the continuing loyalty of Hamshen Armenians to the Armenian Apostolic — and non-Chalcedonian — Church. Skandar pak is Iskandar Bey of the Qara Qoyunlu (1420-1438), and his mention is a clear indication of where the allegiance of the Hamshen princes lay in the aftermath of Timur's invasions, namely with the Qara Qoyunlu to the south, rather than with Trebizond or one of the Georgian kingdoms. The connection between the barons of Hamshen and their Qara Qoyunlu suzerains is confirmed in yet another section of the same manuscript, which reproduces a letter sent to Baron Dawit by Khoja Shamshadin, an Armenian merchant from Trebizond, also known for his endowments of Armenian churches in Trebizond and Caffa in the Crimea. In his missive, Khoja Shamshadin requests Dawit to protect both Christian and Muslim travellers and not to levy excessive taxes on their merchandise. Dawit is also asked to obtain from the Lord of Sper (Ispir) a list of customs fees and other charges on goods being transported through his territory.[3]

To receive such a request from Shamshadin, Dawit must have clearly been on good terms with his neighbour, the Muslim Lord of Ispir and their common overlord, Iskandar Bey of the Qara Qoyunlu, and this fact must have been well known throughout the region. As discussed earlier, Hamshenite allegiance to a power holding Ispir to the south made sense from a geographical perspective, taking into account that the centre of gravity of the

---

[1] Edwards (1988; 409); Khachikyan (1969; 126). The West European title of baron had been adopted by Armenians at the time of the Crusades.

[2] Edwards (1988; 409); Khachikyan (1969; 126).

[3] Kachikyan (1969; 126-27); Edwards (1988; 410).

small principality lay so far up in the Kaçkar Range. It also made sense in the context of the period, when the Qara Qoyunlu, and then their Aq Qoyunlu rivals and successors were the dominant regional power. One cannot help question, however, whether religious issues did not play a role in the political orientation of the district. Hamshen was located in a predominantly Orthodox milieu, with Greek and Laz populations to the north, and to the southeast, the Georgians and Chalcedonian Armenians of Tao/Tayk, who followed the Georgian-Orthodox rite, but had kept the usage of the Armenian language.[1] In spite of this environment, Hamshen Armenians had clung to the Armenian Apostolic Church and its Monophysite, non-Chalcedonian faith. A small canton like Hamshen maintained three, and possibly four, monasteries, in the scriptoria of which a fairly large number of manuscripts were copied. Moreover, Hamshen also produced religious scholars, scribes and artists, known outside of their native region with the *Hamshentsi* epithet, and who served in places from the relatively close Baberd (Bayburt), Erznka (Erzincan), and Koloneia (Şebinkarahisar), to the distant Rome.[2] Ispir, which was exclusively Armenian well into the seventeenth century, and remained predominantly so until the exodus following the Russian-Turkish war in 1828, was Hamshen's only neighbour with a population belonging to the same Apostolic, non-Chalcedonian creed.[3] The importance of Ispir cannot be underestimated, for it constituted a link between Hamshen and other regions of Armenia, preventing Hamshen from becoming an isolated Armenian enclave in an Orthodox, Chalcedonian, sea. Good relations with rulers of Ispir were thus an absolute necessity for the princes of Hamshen. Religious affiliation also possibly answers the vexing question of the absence of any mention of Hamshen in Trapezuntine and Georgian sources, despite the prominent role played until the last decades of the sixteenth century by the Gurieli princes of Guria and the Jaqeli Atabegs of Samtzkhe in Chaneti (Lazia) and Tao, to the immediate north and south of Hamshen.

Dawit is remembered along with his young son Vard in the colophon of a manuscript copied in 1440 in the Khuzhka monastery of Hamshen (Matenadaran, ms. no. 7263). Another manuscript, copied in 1460 and now

---

[1] Tao/Tayk corresponds to the modern Turkish Yusufeli *ilçe* of Artvin, and the Tortum, Oltu, Narman, Olur, Şenkaya *ilçes* of Erzurum. On the Armenian-speaking Chalcedonians of Tao, see Yakovb Karnetsi (1919; 175-78), Tashean (1922; 66-67), and Grigorean (1969; 505-10). On relations between Armenians and Greeks in the theme of Chaldia and later the Empire of Trebizond, see Martin-Hisard (1980; 307-43), and Edwards (1992; 81-90).

[2] The monasteries are Koshtents, St. Khachik Hor or Khachekar, Varshamak, and Khuzhka. See Oskean (1951; 183-89 and 199), Khachikyan (1969; 132-34), and Edwards (1988; 408, 410 and 413-14).

[3] See Yakob Karnetsi (1919; 173-75), Miroğlu (1975; 114 and 117), Sahakyan (1996-97; 21-30), and Sahakyan (2000; 86-99).

held in Jerusalem (ms. no. 3701), informs us that the youthful Veke, son of Baron Vard, the Lord of Hamshen, was captured in that year by a certain Shahali and delivered by him to Sofun, 'whom they called Shekh'.[1] The unfortunate and misnamed child (Veke is an abbreviated form of Vigen, an Armenian first-name derived from the Latin *Vincentius*, meaning 'victorious') probably did not survive his captivity, for he is not mentioned further. We have no definitive answers about the identity of Shahali and Shaykh Sofun, but the latter was in all likelihood the Safavid Junayd of Ardabil, who had attacked Trebizond a few years earlier, around 1456.[2]

The Qızılbash attack was the forerunner of the fall of the principality of Hamshen. In 1474, it was still in Armenian hands, for Venetian ambassador Ambrogio Contarini, who wanted to meet Uzun Hasan, the Aq Qoyunlu leader, was advised by an Armenian of Caffa to sail to Tina (Athenai?), from where he could reach in a four-hour ride on horseback the castle of one Ariam, a subject of Uzun Hasan.[3] Ariam or Aram may have been the name of the new prince of Hamshen or of a secondary baron holding the valley of the Zagatis (Pazar Dere) river. His castle could have been Cihar, or the more enigmatic Mağlut, further upstream. The other information regarding Hamshen in the period following the Turkish conquest of Trebizond in 1461 comes from Ottoman sources. According to Mehmet Bilgin, who unfortunately does not provide any citation, the newly-acquired Ottoman areas of Rize and Atina (Athenai, the modern Pazar) were the targets of three large raids during the 1461-1483 period. The first of these attacks, the objective of which was plunder, was led by Georgians, the second by Georgians and Armenians, and the third by the 'Mamyan kafiri', i.e., the Gurieli Mamia or his successor Kakhaberi. The Armenians of Hamshen obviously come to mind, for they were the only ones who could have made an incursion into Rize and Athenai, given the vicinity of these towns to Hamshen.[4]

This type of activity — if it happened at all — must not have lasted long, for by 1489, Hamshen had fallen to the Ottomans. Its last prince, Dawit (II), was residing in that year in Ispir, where he sponsored a manuscript copied 'during our exile', now deposited in Erevan (Matenadaran, ms. no. 7638). The colophon remembered him as 'Baron Dawit, who was Lord of Hamshen, who has been exiled and has settled in the land of Sper by the nation of Chitakh

---

[1] Kachikyan (1969; 127-28).

[2] Kur_anskis (1977-78 ; 78).

[3] Bryer and Winfield (1985; 337); Zdanévitch (1964; 252); Barbaro and Contarini (1873; 116).

[4] Bilgin (1997; 32). The Prince of Guria Kakhaberi distinguished himself by his resistance to Turks. See Mourier (1886; 127).

(Ottomans)'. Two other figures were mentioned in addition to 'the holy Dawit', namely 'the prince of the Muslims Datay', probably the ruler of Ispir and the host of Dawit, and 'Sultan Eaghup, Lord of the Orient', i.e. Yakub, son of Uzun Hasan, overlord of Ispir and Hamshen prior to the Ottoman conquest.[1] Edwards believes that prominent Armenians of Ispir facilitated the migration of Dawit to Ispir.[2] That Dawit took refuge in Ispir and not Georgia is a further confirmation of his political loyalty to the Aq Qoyunlu. The hopes, if any, of regaining Hamshen, even with Aq Qoyunlu support, must have been quite dim. The Aq Qoyunlu were not a threat anymore to the Ottomans, and unlike his father, Yakub appeared to have maintained the most cordial of relations with the Ottomans, as shown by his correspondence with the future Sultan Selim, then governor of Trabzon.[3]

The most famous member of the princely family of Hamshen, however, was not Arakel or one of his successors, but the *vardapet* (doctor in theology) Yovannes Hamshentsi. This eminent scholar, called *rabunapet* (derived from Hebrew, and meaning 'head teacher') and a 'brave orator', around whom gathered students from all corners of Armenia, was first established in the Avag Monastery and then in the Surb Yakob (St James) of Kaypos or Kapos Monastery, both located at the foot of Mt. Sepuh (now Köhnem Dağı), in the region of the modern Erzincan. Yovannes, who died in 1497, is described in one manuscript as 'lord and captain of the Hamshen canton, son of a baron', and in another as being of 'royal race'.[4] This royal claim raises the question of the identity of the family ruling over Hamshen in the fifteenth century. Already in the tale transcribed by Haykuni, Grigor and Martiros, the two feuding notables, were said to be of royal lineage. This led Khachikyan to ponder a possible connection between the Hamshen princes and the Armenian royal Bagratuni dynasty, the origins of which were in Ispir. Khachikyan also suggested that the Hamshen princes may have descended from the Komnenoi of Trebizond through a female line, following a matrimonial link between the two houses.[5] A priest visiting the region of Erzurum in the 1870s mentions a small village populated by seven families of migrants from Hamamashen, 'which was called after Hamam Prince Bagratuni'.[6] The priest or the villagers who informed him could have simply confused Bagratuni with Amatuni. This

---

[1] Khachikyan (1969; 129); Edwards (1988; 411-12).

[2] Edwards (1988; 411).

[3] Bacqué-Grammont and Adle (1978; 215).

[4] Oskean (1951; 12-20 and 75-81); Grigor Vardapet Kamakhetsi (1915; 405); Khachikyan (1969; 131-32); Edwards (1988; 410-11).

[5] Khachikyan (1969; 131).

[6] Tashean (1980; 83 n. 80b).

confusion or mistake could possibly have been caused by a dynastic change, with the replacement at some point of the Amatunis by the Bagratunis of Ispir. In such case, the confusion of the villagers would reveal what the French call *un lapsus révélateur*. Regional history may have been rewritten by the new rulers, and the belief spread that Hamam was a Bagratuni, very much like the belief among Hemshinli in the modern Turkish Republic that they are an authentic Turkic tribe from Central Asia.

The later princes of Hamshen, however, could simply have belonged to a newly-emerged family, or had been descendants of Shapuh and Hamam Amatuni. In an age where the various Turkish and Mongol invasions had almost eradicated the Armenian nobility, descent from a princely house like the Amatunis, which by the fifteenth century was over a thousand years old — the first recorded Amatuni flourished in the fourth century — would potentially give immense prestige and allow a claim to 'royal' lineage. A possible confirmation of the Amatuni origins of the fifteenth century 'barons of barons' of Hamshen is provided in the list of Georgian princely families found in an annex to the 1783 treaty of Georgievsk between Georgia and Russia. In the section on houses of foreign origin is an Amatuni family, possible descendants of Dawit, the last prince of Hamshen.[1] This hypothesis would answer the question of what happened to Dawit and his family members after 1489, but in the absence of proof, this thought remains only a hypothesis.

### The Ottoman Period

The Ottoman conquest must have taken place a few years before 1489, because a *defter* dated from circa 1486 shows Hamshen as an Ottoman possession. It gives the names of two of its officials: Nişli Karaca is the *zaim* of Hemshin, and İsmail Bosna its *serasker*.[2] Already from this, the very first Ottoman document that mentions the district, Hamshen has taken the form Hemshin.[3] A *defter* from 1515 mentions Hemşin-i Bâlâ, the upper castle of Hemshin, with a garrison of 13 soldiers, two of whom are newly-settled Muslims, and

---

[1] Toumanoff (1983; 60). The claim of these neo-Amatunis, however, could have been fictitious. They may perhaps have been descendants of the Vach'utean family or of the Princes of Maku.

[2] Bilgin (1997; 30). According to Ömer Lütfi Barkan, who first studied it, this *defter*, which is not dated, was probably written between 1481 and 1486. See Lowry (1981; 18), and the discussion in Bostan (2002; 9).

[3] Hemshin is probably derived from *Hamshin*, the form taken by Hamshen when a suffix is added to it, as in *i yerkirs Hamshinu* (i.e., in our land of Hamshen).

gives the name of the district's *serasker*, one Ali. The brevity of information on Hemshin in the 1486 and 1515 *defters*, when compared with other *kaza*s of the Trabzon *liva*, demonstrates the very recent nature of the conquest. Hemshin had been annexed, its fortresses garrisoned, and Ottoman officials appointed there, but the district had yet to be fully absorbed into the administrative system of the empire. Hemshin is sometimes presented as a *vilâyet*, as is the case in a 1518 *defter*, or as a *nâhiye*, but it most often appears as a separate *kaza* of the Trabzon *liva* or *sancak*.[1]

In 1520, the Hemshin *kaza* contained thirty four villages and was divided into three *nahiyes*, Hemşin, Kara-Hemşin, and Eksanos.[2] The Hemşin *nahiye*, with fourteen villages consisted of the non-coastal section of the Susa or Zuğa Dere Valley (the modern Pazar or Hemşin Dere, i.e., the Hemşin *ilçe* of Rize), the valley of the Hala branch of the Fırtına, and the lower section of the Fırtına valley. Kara-Hemşin — a probable reference to the fog covering the region — consisted of the upper part of the Fırtına Valley and the Cimil Valley, and was composed of eleven villages. Eksanos, with nine villages, included the upper Senes or Senoz Valley, i.e., the present-day Kaptanpaşa *bucak* of Rize's Çayeli *ilçe*.[3] In addition to the upper castle Hemşin-i Bâlâ (Yukarı Kale/Varoş), the garrison of which had grown to forty men, the lower castle (Aşağı Kale), Hemşin-i Zîr, was noted for the first time and indicated as being manned by a garrison of thirty. The *defters* also mention the allowance received by these soldiers and their officers and their annual wheat and millet consumption. Mahmud Çelebi was the *zaim* of the *Kaza*, and Ali Koruk the *serasker*.[4]

That Hemshin was under Ottoman control in the 1520s is confirmed by the colophon of a manuscript anthology on the poetical works of Nerses Shnorhali and other authors, now deposited in the Free Library of Philadelphia (John Frederick Lewis Collection, ms. no. 123). The manuscript was written at the churches of Surb Astuatsatsin (mother of God) and Surb Siovn (Sion) 'in the monastery where the relics of the father St Khachik and St Vardan

---

[1] Bostan (2002; 23, 25, 39-40, 47, 101 and 221).

[2] Gökbilgin (1962; 322-23).

[3] *Defter* no. 387 provides the list of the villages of the Hemshin *Kaza*. The Eksanos *nahiye* includes the villages of Balahor, Çivitniz, Hahonç, Holvalı, Kağından, Mesahor, Meydân, Müsellemân-Komanos and Nolanih (?). The villages of the Hemşin *nahiye* are Abişlovih, Arovih, Aşodovih, Çinçiva, Hala, Müsellemân-Andervad, Müsellemân-Monvih(?), Müsellemânlar, Nahiye-i Kuş-ova, Nikorid, Pendavih, Sodsu, Viçna and Zuğa. The last *nahiye*, Kara-Hemşin, is composed of Askarakih, Baş, Bolvaç, Cimil, Çat, Makri-Toma, Molahiş, Ogovid, Tap/Tat, Varoş and Vartor (*387 Numaralı Muhâsebe-i Vilâyet-i Karaman ve Rûm Defteri*; 155-59).

[4] Gökbilgin (1962; 323); Bostan (2002; 101, 221, 277-83 and 453).

along with his companions have been placed for the glory and protection of our *gawar* (canton) of Hamshen'. It was completed on 9 June 1528, 'during the sultanate of Sulayman (I, 1520-1566), the reign of Skandar Pasha in Trabzon (Iskandar Pasha, 1513-1534), when our fortresses were controlled by the aghas Darveshali and Siminaws, during the episcopate of Ter (lord) Mart'.[1] Darveshali is probably Derviş Ali, while Siminaws corresponds to the Greek-sounding Siminos or Simonos, thus indicating that the latter was probably still Christian. In spite of Siminaws' possible Christian identity, it can be agreed with Edwards that 'one detects a certain air of resentment' at the mention of *our* fortresses being controlled by the *aghas*.[2]

Hemshin is absent from the *defter*s for the 1536 to 1553 period, during which, according to local Hemshinli historians, it was administratively attached to the Ispir *sancak*.[3] By 1554, a new *nahiye*, Kuşova, had appeared, thus increasing to four the number of *nahiye*s of the Hemshin *kaza*, while the number of villages was reduced by three to thirty one.[4] Given the location of Kuşova (Kuşiva, now Yolkıyı) in the Fırtına Valley, it can be deduced that this new *nahiye* was probably created by separating the lower Fırtına and Hala Valleys (now part of the Çamlıhemşin *ilçe*) from the Hemşin *nahiye*, leaving to the latter the valley of the Zuğa (Pazar) Dere.

Hemshin is not mentioned again in Ottoman sources until 1562, when its *ze'âmet* (fief) is attributed to Hasan Bey, the *sancakbey* (governor of a *sancak*) of Batum. In 1566, the Hemshin *kaza* was a dependent of the Gönye (Batum) *sancak*, to which it still belonged in 1583. No information can be gleaned from any of the *defter*s on which town or village was the administrative centre of the Hemshin *kaza*.[5] Armenian medieval cantons often lacked an administrative centre, and the Hemshin *kaza* was probably continuing this pattern.

In addition to administrative divisions and state officials, Ottoman documents provide us with figures on the population of Hemshin during the sixteenth century. According to the numbers provided in the famous 1962 article by M. Tayyib Gökbilgin, in the early 1520s there were, 682 *nefer*s or

---

[1] Mart is an abbreviated form of the Armenian first-name Martiros (Sanjian 1976; 677-84). Also see Mathews and Wieck (1994; 198-99), Bryer and Winfield (1985; 336 n. 9) and Edwards (1988; 412-13).

[2] Edwards (1988; 413).

[3] Sakaoğlu and others (1998; 14).

[4] Bostan (2002; 25, 40, 47 and 222).

[5] Bostan (2002; 40, 48-49 and 221).

soldiers, the religious affiliation of whom is not provided. This figure of 682 *nefer*s, taken either as privates or as bachelors, is obviously a mistake, since all of the fortresses of the Trabzon *sancak* had a total of 510 men in 1520. Gökbilgin also lists 671 households inhabiting the district's 34 villages, divided into 214 Muslim families and 457 Christians ones.[1] The recently published work by M. Hanefi Bostan provides slightly different figures for the same year, with a total of 670 households, divided into 214 Muslim and 456 Christian ones, 11 *mücerred* or bachelors, 3 Muslims and 8 Christians, and a more reasonable count of 70 *nefer*s. The total population of the Hemshin *kaza* was 3,619 individuals, with 1,331 Muslims and 2,288 Christians. According to a 1554 *defter*, however, first made available to us by Bostan, the Muslim population of the Hemshin *kaza* had dwindled to 16 families and one bachelor, i.e., a total of 81 individuals, while Christians were shown as numbering 706 families and 113 *mücerred*s, or 3,643 individuals.[2]

If we are to believe these Ottoman *defter*s, Hemshin had in thirty years been transformed from the *kaza* of Trabzon with the highest percentage of Muslims to the one with the lowest. Bostan believes that a mistake could have been made in 1520 by Ottoman notaries who registered all *müsellem* as Muslims, or that a great out-migration of Muslims had taken place in the intervening years, that is, between 1520 and 1554. Given the absence of any data on a Muslim exodus, it appears extremely likely that one of the two figures provided is simply wrong.[3]

The surprisingly high ratio of Muslims (32 per cent of households, 37 per cent of total population) in the 1520 *defter* has led to speculation as to whether Hemshin Armenians were early converts to Islam.[4] Conversion to orthodox or heterodox forms of Islam among Armenians happened frequently throughout the Middle Ages.[5] Early leanings of Hamshen Armenians towards Islam would help explain Clavijo's episode on the Muslims of Arraquiel petitioning the ruler of Ispir for the removal of their Christian prince. As we have seen, however, Arraquiel was probably not Hamshen, which continued to be ruled by its native Christian Armenian princes for almost another century after Clavijo's journey.

---

[1] Gökbilgin (1962; 323); Bostan (2002; 283).

[2] Bostan (2002; 221-23 and 260).

[3] Bostan (2002; 221-23 and 260).

[4] See Bryer (1966; 194) and Bryer and Winfield (1985; 336).

[5] Moosa (1987; 434). Also see Dadoyan.

The 1520 statistic is also thought-provoking because it makes Hemshin appear to be an enclave with an exceptionally high percentage of Muslims, while Islam had not yet made any inroads into any of its surrounding districts. Christians still predominated numerically in the rest of the Pontos, with a ratio of ten to one, in Ispir, with 96.5 percent of the population, and in Pertakrak (Kiskim), which still belonged to the atabegs of Samtzkhe.[1] Another aspect of this statistic is the less than 20 households per village figure, a low count even for a mountainous district, a possible indication of people hiding from the *kâtib* (notary) to avoid registration, and therefore escape taxation. Further, Hemshin still had a bishop in 1528, named Mart, and monastic activity, including the copying of manuscripts, appears to have continued unabated throughout the sixteenth century. It is difficult to imagine how 456 or 457 Christian families would have been able to sustain the three large monasteries of the region.[2]

The question which can then be raised is whether Ottoman control over Hamshen or Hemshin in the first half of the sixteenth century was consolidated enough to allow for a valid survey to be carried out. Hemshin was certainly in Ottoman hands during that period. A manuscript copied in 1531 informs us that Armenian boys were taken for the *devşirme* (child-levy) from 'Trebizond, Hamshen, Sper, and Baberd ... to the shores of the lake of Van, and who can describe the misery and tragedy of the parents' (Matenadaran, ms. no. 6272, p. 6).[3] However, Hemshin was very much a border district until at least the middle of the sixteenth century, which could explain the general brevity of *defter*s on the topic of the *Kaza*.[4] The province of Tao, to its south-east, was in the possession of the Jaqeli atabegs of Samtzkhe until it was taken by the Ottomans in 1549-50.[5] The colophon of a medical manuscript copied in Sebastia (Sebasteia, Sivas) in 1550 informs us that 'there was great mourning (among the Christians) in the city (of Erzurum) because they (the Ottomans) took control of the valleys of Tortum'.[6] The second district neighbouring Hemshin, Ispir, was occupied in the early years of the sixteenth century by the atabeg of Samtzkhe, Mzechabuk (1502-1515), who had thus taken advantage of the dissolution of the Aq

---

[1] Gökbilgin (1962); Bryer (1966); Bryer and Winfield (1985; 336); Miroğlu (1975; 114 and 117); and Sahakyan (2000).

[2] Sanjian (1976; 684); Oskean (1951; 183-88); Khachikyan (1969; 132-34); Edwards (1988; 412-13).

[3] Zulalyan (1959; 251).

[4] See Bostan (476, 479, 482, 514, 515, 518, 521 and 524).

[5] Brosset (1856; 217).

[6] Aghaneants (1912; 102).

Qoyunlu state following the death of Yakub.[1] We even know the name of the lieutenant and probable relative of Mzechabuk who was in charge of Ispir during all or part of that period, for a colophon added in 1512 to a manuscript originally copied in 1283 informs of the 'principality of Baron Kitevan over Sper (Ispir), from the Georgian nation'.[2] Mzechabuk, who pursued a policy of appeasement with the Ottomans, surrendered the keys of Ispir to Sultan Selim in October 1514 and the fortress of Hunut (now Çamlıkaya), in the Ispir district, a little later, in 1515.[3] In 1548, both Ispir and Bayburt were taken and destroyed by Shah Tahmasp.[4]

To the north of Hemshin lies Chaneti (Lazistan), the western part of which, including Athenai, was taken by the Ottomans in the immediate years following the conquest of Trebizond.[5] The rest of Chaneti, however, was alternately ruled by the Jaqelis of Samtskhe and the Gurielis of Guria until 1547, when the Ottomans took the area and built a citadel in Batumi (Bathys) and then one in Gonia (Göniye or Gönye).[6] Thus, until 1514, Ottoman access to Hemshin was rather restricted and only possible from the mouths of the Pazar or Fırtına rivers, in a region, Chaneti, which was more or less a constant theatre of war until at least 1547, and even later. The confiscation of Chaneti by King Bagrat of Imeretia in 1535 from the atabeg Qwarqware and its transfer to the Gurieli Rostom — an enemy of the Ottomans — might have further restrained access to Hemshin from the coast. This could explain the Ottoman administrative rearrangement of 1536 which, according to local Hemshinli historians, made Hemshin a dependency of the Ispir *sancak*.[7]

The political situation of the region during the first half of the sixteenth century could explain why the *defter*s of that period did not carry creditable figures. In contrast, the political conditions of the 1554 survey were certainly more propitious, as it was carried out when all of the region was under the firm control of the Ottomans, who had consolidated their conquests of the preceding years through a peace treaty signed with the Safavids in 1553.

---

[1] Bacqué-Grammont and Adle (1978; 216).

[2] Tashean (1980; 223-24).

[3] Bacqué-Grammont and Adle (1978; 221-23). The authors are mistaken in confusing Hunut, near Ispir, with Cinis, a place east of Aşkale and west of Erzurum.

[4] Tashean (1980; 231).

[5] Bryer and Winfield (1985; 337).

[6] Brosset (1856; 208-09, 213-15 and 256-57).

[7] Brosset (1856); Sakaoğlu and others (1998; 14).

*Epilogue*

The last manuscript to be copied in Hemshin which has reached us is dated 1630. The monk who copied the manuscript remembered in a colophon his tutor, the Bishop Ter Awetis from Pontos.[1] Ter Awetis not only hailed from the Pontos, but he was probably the same person as the Metropolitan Awetik, who was the Armenian Bishop of Trebizond until his death in 1648.[2] The first-ever mention of a bishop of Trebizond in a manuscript copied in Hamshen and the concomitant absence of reference to a local bishop could be interpreted as a sign of the decline or disappearance altogether of the Hamshen diocese, and of the annexation of its remains to the Trabzon diocese. The beginning of the process which would lead to the conversion to Islam of part of the Hemshin Armenians and the exodus of those remaining Christians appear as the obvious causes of this decline. However, the possibility should not be excluded that the very decline of the diocese itself, provoked by one event or another, facilitated the passage to Islam of a large section of its flock. In 1676, the Surb Pilipos (St Philip) chapel was consecrated in the small village of Kyan (now Kayabaşı, in the Yomra *ilçe* of Trabzon).[3] The builders of the chapel were in all likelihood refugees from Hamshen fleeing the Islamisation of their native district.

In the subsequent centuries, the population of Hemshin would experience several formative developments — the appearance of crypto-Christians known as the *kes-kes* (half-half in Armenian), the disuse of the Armenian language in Hemshin proper and its retention further east in Hopa, and the large number of Hemshinli who rose in the Ottoman political and religious apparatus. These and other developments would ultimately lead to the emergence of a distinct Hemshin or Hemshinli identity, the discussion of which, however, is beyond the scope of this paper.

*REFERENCES*

Acharean, Hracheay (H. Adjarian). 1947 *Knnutyun Hamsheni Barbari* (*Study of the Hamshen dialect*). Erevan; Erevan State University Press.
Aghaneants, Giwt A. Kah. (ed.) 1912 *Diwan Hayots Patmutean* (*Archives of Armenian History*), Vol. 10. *Manr Matenagirk, 15-19 Dar* (*Minor Documents, 15-19th Centuries*), Tiflis.

[1] Tashean (1980; 72-73 and 121); Edwards (1988; 413).
[2] Mkhitareants (1856; 37-39).
[3] Torlakyan (1981; 40-41 and 41n.); Safrastyan (1966; 42).

Astill, G. and Wright, S. 1977-78 'Zil Kale', *Archeion Pontou* (Athens), Vol. 34, 28-48.

Avdoyan, L. 1993 *Pseudo-Yovhannes Mamikonean, The History of Taron (Patmutiwn Taronoy): Historical Investigation, Critical Translation, and Historical and Textual Commentaries*. Columbia University Program in Armenian Studies, no. 6. Atlanta, Georgia: Scholars Press.

Bacqué-Grammont, J. and Adle, C. 1978 'Notes et Documents sur Mzé-_âbûk, *Atabeg* de Géorgie Méridionale (1500-1515), et les Safavides. Etudes Turco-Safavides V', *Studia Iranica* (Paris), Vol. 7, No. 2: 213-49.

Barbaro, J. and Contarini, A. 1873 *Travels to Tana and Persia*. Translated by William Thomas and Eugene A. Roy, and edited by Lord Stanley, London; Hakluyt Society.

Başbakanlık Devlet Arşivleri Genel Müdürlüğü 1997 *387 Numaralı Muhâsebe-i Vilâyet-i Karaman ve Rûm Defteri (937/1530)*, Vol. 2, Ankara; Osmanlı Arşivi Daire Bakanlığı.

Bilgin, M. 1997 'Rize'nin Tarihine Bir Bakış', in *Rize*, edited by H. Barışta and S. Başkan, Ankara: T. C. Kültür Bakanlığı.

Bostan, M. 2002 *XV — XVI. Asırlarda Trabzon Sancağında Sosyal ve İktisadî Hayat*, Ankara; Türk Tarih Kurumu.

Brosset, M. (ed.) 1856 *Histoire de la Géorgie: Depuis l'Antiquité Jusqu'au XIX$^e$ Siècle*. Part 2, *Histoire Moderne*, vol. 1. Translated by Marie-Félicité Brosset. St Petersburg: Imprimerie de l'Académie Impériale des Sciences.

Bryer, A. 1966 'Some Notes on the Laz and Tzan (I)'. *Bedi Kartlisa: Revue de Kartvélologie* (Paris) 21-22 (50-51): 174-195; reprinted 1988 in *Peoples and Settlement in Anatolia and the Caucasus, 800-1900*, London; Variorum Reprints.

Bryer, A. 1975 'Greeks and Türkmens: The Pontic Exception'. *Dumbarton Oaks Paper* (Washington, D.C.) 29, 1975: 113-149; reprinted 1980 in *The Empire of Trebizond and the Pontos*. London: Variorum Reprints.

Bryer, A. 1977-78 'Historical Note on Zil Kale', *Archeion Pontou* (Athens), Vol. 34; 49-56.

Bryer, A. and Winfield. D 1985 *The Byzantine Monuments and Topography of the Pontos*. Washington, D.C.: Dumbarton Oaks Research Library and Collection.

Bzhshkean, H. Minas Vardapet 1819 *Batmutiwn Pontosi vor e Seaw Tsov* (*History of the Pontos which is the Black Sea*). Venice; St Lazarus Monastery.

Bzhshkean, H. 1830 *Chanaparhordutiwn i Lehastan ew Yayl Koghmans Bnakeals i Haykazants Serelots i Nakhneats Ani Kaghakin: Sharagreal Handerdz Zanazan Banasirakan Teghekuteambk* (*Travels to Poland and Other Places Populated by Armenians Descending from Forefathers from the City of Ani: Annotated with a Variety of Philological Information*). Venice; St Lazarus Monastery.

Clavijo, R de. 1999 *Embajada a Tamorlán*, edited, introduced and annotated by Francisco López Estrada, Madrid; Editorial Castalia.

Cuinet, V. 1890 *La Turquie d'Asie: Géographie Administrative, Statistique, Descriptive et Raisonnée de Chaque Province de l'Asie-Mineure*, Vol. 1, Paris ; E. Leroux.

Dadoyan, S. 1997 *The Fatimid Armenians: Cultural and Political Interaction in the Near East*, Leiden; Brill.

Dawkins, R. 1933 'The Crypto-Christians of Turkey', *Byzantion* (Brussels) Vol. 8, No. 1; 247-75.

Dulaurier, E. (ed.) 1906 *Recueil des Documents des Croisades: Documents Arméniens*, Vol. 2, Paris; Imprimerie Nationale.

Edwards, R. 1988 'Ham__n: An Armenian Enclave in the Byzanto-Georgian Pontos. A Survey of Literary and Nonliterary Sources', *Le Muséon* (Louvain) Vol. 101 ; nos. 3-4; 403-22.

Edwards, R. 1992 'Armenian and Byzantine Religious Practices in Early Fifteenth-Century Trabzon: A Spanish Viewpoint', *Revue des Études Arméniennes* (Paris) n.s. 23; 81-90.

Gatenean, Yarutiwn. 1888 'Chors Tari Shavshet-Imerkhevum Shrjagayutean Ardiwnkits' (From the Result of a Four-Years Tour of Shavshet-Imerkhevi), *Mshak* (Tiflis) Vol. 16, No. 83, 23 July; 1-2.

Ghewond. 1887 *Patmutiwn Ghewondeay Metsi Vardapeti Hayots* (*History of Ghewond, the Eminent Vardapet of the Armenians*). Edited by Karapet Ezeants, St Petersburg; I. N. Skorokhodov.

Ghewond. 1982 *History of Lewond, the Eminent Vardapet of the Armenians*. Translation, Introduction and Commentary by Zaven Arzoumanian. Wynnewood, Pennsylvania; St Sahag and St Mesrob Armenian Church.

Gökbilgin, T. 1962 'XVI. Yüzyıl Başlarında Trabzon Livası ve Doğu Karadeniz Bölgesi'. *Belleten* (Ankara) Vol. 26, No. 102, April 1962; 293-337.

Grigor Vardapet Kamakhtsi. 1915 *Zhamanakagrut'iwn Grigor Vardapeti Kamakhetswoy kam Daranaghtswoy* (*Chronicle of Grigor Vardapet of Kamakh or Daranaghi*). Edited with an introduction and appendices by Mesrop Vardapet Nshanean. Jerusalem; St James Monastery.

Grigorean, Mesrop Ts.-V. G. 1969 'Hay-Kaghkedonakanneru Hetker Dzeragrats mech' (Traces of Chalcedonian Armenians in Manuscripts). *Handes Amsorya* (Vienna) Vol. 83, nos. 10-12; 505-10.

Grousset, R. 1947 *Histoire de l'Arménie des Origines à 1071*, Paris; Payot.

Haçikyan, L. 1997 *Hemşin Gizemi: Hamşen Ermenileri Tarihinden Sayfalar* (*The Mystery of Hemşin: Pages from the History of Hamshen Armenians*), revised, second edition, translated and edited by Bağdik Avedisyan, Istanbul; Belge Yayınları.

Hasluck, F. 1921 'The Crypto-Christians of Trebizond', *Journal of Hellenic Studies*, Vol. 41; 199-202.

Haykuni, Sargis 1895 'Nshkharner: Korats u Moratsuats Hayer' (Fragments: Lost and Forgotten Armenians) *Ararat* (Vagharshapat), No. 7 (July); 239-43 and No. 8 (August); 293-97.

Hetum of Korykos 1951 *Hetum Patmich Tatarats, Yegheal i Latin Orinake i Hay Barbar* (*Hetum the Historian of the Tatars, Translated from Latin into Armenian*). Translated by H. Mkrtich Awgerean, second ed. Venice; St Lazarus Monastery.

Hetum of Korykos (Hetoum) 1988 *A Lytell Cronycle: Richard Pynson's Translation (c 1520) of La Fleur des histoires de la terre d'Orient (c 1307)*. Edited by Glenn Burger. Toronto Medieval Texts and Translations, No. 6. Toronto/Buffalo/London; University of Toronto Press.

Inchichean, H. Ghukas Vardapet 1806 *Ashkharhagrutiwn Chorits Masants Ashkharhi: Asioy, Ewropioy, Aprikoy, ew Amerikoy* (*Geography of the Four Parts of the World: Asia, Europe, Africa, and America*) Part 1. Vol. 1. *Asia*, Venice; St Lazarus Monastery.

Karpuz, H. 1992 *Rize*, Ankara; Türk Tarih Kurumu.

Khachikyan, Lewon. 1969 'Ejer Hamshinahay Patmutyunits' (Pages from the History of Hamshen Armenians), *Banber Erevani Hamalsarani* (Bulletin of Erevan University), Vol. 2 (8); 115-44. Turkish translation, see Haçikyan.

Kiepert, R. 1913 *Karte von Kleinasien*. Folio A VI, *Tirabzon*. Berlin; Dietrich Reimer (Ernst Vohsen).

Kırzıoğlu, F. 1966 'Selim Çağında Hopa ile Arhavi Köyleri', *Türk Folklor Araştırmaları* (Istanbul) Vol. 10, No. 201 (April); 4038-40.

Kırzıoğlu, F. 1966 'Eski-Oğuz (Arsaklı-Part) Kalıntısı Hemşenliler', *Türk Folklor Araştırmaları* (Istanbul) Vol. 10, No. 203 (April); 4099-104.

Koch, K. 1846 *Wanderungen im Oriente Während der Jahre 1843 und 1844*. Vol. 2. *Reise im Pontische Gebirge und Türkische Armenien*, Weimar; Landes Industrie Comptoirs.

Koch, K. 1855 'Reise von Redut-Kaleh nach Trebisond (Kolchis und das Land der Lazen)', in *Die Kaukasischen Länder und Armenien in Reiseschilderungen von Curzon, K. Koch, Macintosh, Spencer und Wilbraham*, ed. Karl Koch, Leipzig; Carl B. Lorck.

Kurčanskis, M. 1977-8 'Autour de la Dernière Princesse de Trébizonde: Théodora, Fille de Jean IV et Épouse d'Uzun Hasan', *Archeion Pontou* (Athens) Vol. 34; 77-87.

Lowry, H. 1981 *Trabzon Şehrinin İslâmlaşma ve Türkleşmesi: Trabzon Örneğinde Osmanlı Tahrir Defterinin Şehirleşme Demoğrafik Tarihi İçin Kaynak Olarak Kullanılması*. Translated by Demet and Heath Lowry. Istanbul; Boğaziçi Üniversitesi Yayınları.

Martin-Hisard, B. 1980 'Trébizonde et le Culte de Saint Eugène (6$^e$-11$^e$ s)', *Revue des Études Arméniennes* (Paris) n.s. 14; 307-43.

Mathews, T., and Wieck, R. (eds.) 1994 *Treasures in Heaven: Armenian Illuminated Manuscripts*. New York/Princeton; Pierpont Morgan Library and Princeton University Press.

Meeker, M. 1971 'The Black Sea Turks: Some Aspects of their Ethnic and Cultural Background', *International Journal of Middle East Studies* (London) Vol. 2, no. 4; 318-45.

Miroğlu, İ. 1975 *XVI. Yüzyılda Bayburt Sancağı*. Anadolu Yakası Bayburt Kültür ve Yardımlaşma Derneği Yayınları, no. 1. Istanbul; Üçler Matbaası.

Mkhitareants, Abel Vardapet. 1857 *Vep Gaghtakanutean Hayots Trapizonu* (History of the Armenian Community of Trabzon). Constantinople; Masis.

Moosa, M. 1988 *Extremist Shiites: The Ghulat Sects*, Syracuse, New York; Syracuse University Press.

Mourier, J. 1886 'Batoum et le Bassin du Tchorok', *Revue de Géographie* (Paris) Vol. 19, July (51-62) and August (122-34).

Muradeants, Yakob. 1898 'Sew Tsovi Aperin' (On the Shores of the Black Sea). *Murch* (Tiflis) Vol. 10, No. 4 (April); 467-76, No. 6, (June); 831-38, and Nos. 7-8 (July-August); 1004-18.

Nişanyan, S., Landon T., and Gabriele O. 1990 *Zoom in Black Sea: A Traveler's Guide to Turkey's Black Sea Region*, Istanbul; Boyut Yayın Grubu.

Nişanyan, S. and Nişanyan, M. 2000 *Karadeniz: Meraklısı İçin Gezi Rehberi — Black Sea: A Traveller's Handbook for Northern Turkey*, Istanbul; Boyut Yayın Grubu.

Oskean, H. Hamazasp. 1951 *Bardzr Hayki Vankere* (The Monasteries of Upper Armenia), Vienna; Mekhitarist Press.

Piro. 1893 'Tachkats'ats Hayer' (Turkified Armenians). *Nor-Dar* (Tiflis) Vol. 10, No. 227 (21 December); 3.

de Planhol, X. 1997 *Minorités en Islam: Géographie Politique et Sociale*. Paris; Flammarion.

Purchas, S. 1614 *Pvrchas his Pilgrimage. Or Relations of the World and the Religions Observed in all Ages and Places Discouered, from the Creation vnto the Present*, second edition. London; H. Fetherstone.

Redgate, A. Forthcoming. 'The Foundation of Hamshen and Armenian Descent Myths: Parallels and Interconnections', in *The Armenian Communities of the Black Sea — Pontus Region*, ed. R. Hovannisian. Proceedings of the Tenth UCLA Historic Armenian Cities and Provinces conference May 2002. Costa Mesa, California; Mazda Publishers.

Redgate, A. Forthcoming 'Morale, Cohesion and Power in the First Centuries of Amatuni Hamshen', in *The Hemshin*, ed. H. Simonian. Peoples of the Caucasus Series. London; Curzon Press.

Rickmers, R. 1934 'Lazistan and Ajaristan', *Geographical Journal* (London) Vol. 84, No. 6 (December); 465-80.

Safrastyan, A. 1966 Kh. 'Kostandnupolsi Hayots Patriarkarani Koghmits Turkiayi Ardaradatutyan ew Davanankneri Ministrutyan Nerkayatsvats Haykakan Ekeghetsineri ew Vankeri Tsutsaknern u Takrirnere' (Lists and Reports of Armenian Churches and Monasteries Presented by the Armenian Patriarchate of Istanbul to the Turkish Ministry of Justice and Cults) *Ejmiatsin* Vol. 23, No. 6 (June); 41-47.

Sahakyan, L. 1996-7 'Baberd Gavari Teghanunnern u Etnik Kazme 16 d. Osmanyan Tahrir Davtarnerum' (The Toponyms and Ethnic Composition of the (Baberd) Bayburt Canton in Sixteenth Century Ottoman Tahrir Defters). *Iran-Nameh: Armenian Journal of Oriental Studies* (Erevan), Nos. 22-23 (6-7); 21-30.

Sahakyan, L 2000 'Sper Gavari Bnakavayrern Zhoghovrtagrutyune 16-rd Dari Osmanyan Tahrir Daftarnerum' (The Settlements and Demography of the Sper (Ispir) Canton in Sixteenth Century Ottoman Tahrir Defters). *Iran-Nameh: Armenian Journal of Oriental Studies* (Erevan) Vol. 35; 86-99.

Sakaoğlu, A., and others, eds. *Cumhuriyetimizin 75. Yılı Kutlamaları Çerçevesinde 1. Hemşin Bal, Kültür ve Turizm Şenlikleri, 22-23 Ağustos 1998*, Ankara; Hemşin Hizmet Vakfı.

Sanjian, A. 1976 *A Catalogue of Medieval Armenian Manuscripts in the United States.* Berkeley, CA; University of California Press.

Sanosean, M. 1904 'Speri Hnutiwnnere' (Antiquities of Sper / Ispir). *Arewelk* (Constantinople) Vol 21, No. 5579 (29 May); 1.

Sinclair, T. 1989 *Eastern Turkey: An Architectural and Archaeological Survey*, London; The Pindar Press.

Smith, E. 1833 *Researches of the Rev. E. Smith and Rev. H.G.O. Dwight in Armenia: Including a Journey Through Asia Minor, and into Georgia and Persia, with a Visit to the Nestorian and Chaldean Christians of Oormiah and Salmas.* Boston; Crocker and Brewster.

Stepanos Taronetsi (Asoghik) 1883 *Histoire Universelle par Etienne Açogh'ig de Daron.* Vol. 1. Translated and annotated by Edouard Dulaurier. Publications de l'Ecole des Langues Orientales Vivantes, no. 18. Paris ; Ernest Leroux.

Stepanos Taronetsi (Asoghik) 2000 *Patmutyun Tiezerakan (Universal History)*, translated, introduced, and annotated by Vardan H. Vardanyan. Erevan; Erevan University Publications.

Stratil-Sauer, G. 1935 'From Baiburt via İspir to Lâzistan', *Geographical Journal* (London) Vol. 86, No. 5 (November); 402-10.

Tashean, H. Yakovbos V. (Father Jacobus Vard Dashian). 1922 *La Population Arménienne de la Région Comprise entre la Mer Noire et Karin (Erzeroum): Rapide Coup d'Oeil Historique et Ethnographique*, translated by Frédéric Macler, Vienna; Imprimerie des Méchitaristes.

Tashean, H. Yakovbos V. 1980 *Tayk, Dratsik ew Khotorjur: Patmakan-Teghagrakan Usumnasirutiwn (Tayk, Neighbours and Khotorjur: Historical and Geographical Study).* Vol. 2. Vienna; Mekhitarist Press.

Torlakyan, B. 1968 'Hamshenahayer' (Hamshen Armenians). *Grakan T'ert'* (Literary Paper) Vol. 36, No. 21 (1432), 24 May; 4.

Torlakyan, B. 1981 *Hamshenahayeri Azgagrut'yune* (Ethnography of Hamshen Armenians). Haykakan SSH Gitut'yunneri Akademia, Hnagidut'yan ev Azgagrut'yan Institut. Hay Azgagrut'yun ev Banahyusut'yun, Nyut'er ev Usumnasirut'yunner (Academy of Sciences of the Armenian SSR, Institute of Archaeology and Ethnography: Armenian Ethnography and Folklore, Materials and Research), No. 13. Erevan; Publications of the Academy of Sciences of the Armenian SSR.

Toumanoff, C. 1983 *Les Maisons Princières Géorgiennes de l'Empire de Russie.* Rome; privately printed.

Toumarkine, A. 1995 *Les Lazes en Turquie (XIX$^e$-XX$^e$ Siècles).* Istanbul; Isis.

Tumayean, P. 1899 'Pontosi Hayere: Ashkharhagragan yev Kaghakakan Vichak Trapizoni' (The Armenians of the Pontos: Geographic and Political Situation of Trabzon). *Lumay: Grakan Handes (Luma: Literary Journal)* (Tiflis) Vol. 4, No. 2; 144-92.

Vardanyan, S. 1998 'Hamshentsi Musulman Hayeri Usumnasirutyan Patmutiunits' (Historiography of the Muslim Armenians of Hamshen). *Iran-Nameh: Armenian Journal of Oriental Studies* (Erevan) Nos. 29-31; 2-11.

Vaux, B. Forthcoming 'Homshetsma: The Language of the Armenians of Hamshen'. In *The Hemshin*, ed. H. Simonian, Peoples of the Caucasus Series, London; Curzon Press.

Yakovb Karnetsi (Jacobus of Karin). 1919 'Erzeroum ou Topographie de la Haute Arménie'. Translated by Frédéric Macler. *Journal Asiatique* (Paris) Vol. 13 (11$^{th}$ series), No. 2 (March-April); 153-237.

Yovhannes Mamikonean, Bishop of Mamikoneank. 1941 *Patmutiwn Taronoy (History of Taron).* Edited by Ashot Abrahamyan. Erevan ; Matenadaran.

Zdanévitch, Elie (Ilia). 1964 'Ruy Gonzales de Clavijo en Géorgie: Observations sur son Chemin d'Avnik à Trébizonde du 5 au 17 Septembre 1405', in *Actes du XII$^e$ Congrès International d'Études Byzantines, Ochride, 10-16 Septembre 1961*, Vol. 2. Belgrade; Nauc) no Delo.

Zdanévitch, Elie (Ilia). 1976 'L'itinéraire Géorgien de Ruy Gonzales de Clavijo et les Églises aux Confins de l'Atabégat', *Bedi Kartlisa: Revue de Kartvélologie* Vol. 34: 143-49.

Zulalyan, M. 1959 '"Devshirme"-n (Mankahavanke) Osmanyan Kaysrutyan mej est Turkakan ev Haykakan Aghbyurneri' (The 'Devshirme' in the Ottoman Empire according to Turkish and Armenian Sources), *Patma-Banasirakan Handes (Historico-Philological Review)* (Erevan), Nos. 2-3 (5-6); 247-56.

# 22. 'A LA MANIERE DE' F.W. HASLUCK. A FEW REFLECTIONS ON THE BYZANTINE-TURKISH SYMBIOSIS IN THE MIDDLE AGES

## Michel BALIVET

A hundred years ago, F.W. Hasluck tried to enumerate the many cases of Muslim-Christian symbiosis in the vanishing Ottoman Empire. Might be it possible to use the same fruitful methods for earlier periods, when the process of mingling among Christians and Turks in Anatolia and the Balkans was only starting? Is it even legitimate to compare different societies in the Middle Ages, such as those born of the Turco-Mongol nomad world in slowly Islamized Central Asia with those of Byzantium; urban, Mediterranean and Christian? And yet! For someone who deals with history, the Turkish past appears narrowly entangled with that of Byzantium between the eleventh and the fifteenth century. Peculiar analogies seem to emerge between the two societies in their educated or popular culture, in their toponymy and anthroponymy, their myths and *topoi*, customs and different behaviours. It really may be that in attempting to begin an explanation of these real or supposed similarities, Hasluck's method, a catalogue and systematic comparative inventory, remains the best.

Pure coincidence, real likeness, inter-influence, deliberate or casual syncretist process? Most of the time, the researcher finds it difficult to choose. He or she can only compare items of apparently common Byzantine-Turkish material and institute a survey of the different constituent elements of the melting-pot and the fusion that may have ensued, as Hasluck did and those afterwards who followed his method. In contrast, separatist analysis, be it either focussed on the Byzantine or Turkish side, has often taken the place of study on how the merging process has worked. If I may be forgiven for using a comparison with a cooking recipe (one that has its origin in the Turco-Byzantine geo-political area we're talking about) it is as if one wished, when preparing a vegetable *Macédoine* to deal only with the taste of turnip, carrot or green peas or beans, while neglecting the tasty interaction of the narrowly mingled vegetables, which alone explains the real alchemy of the said *Macédoine*.

We may speak of the Turco-Byzantine crucible as coming into existence after the Seljuk invasion and continuing until to the fall of Constantinople, Mistra and Trebizond in the middle of the fifteenth century. One notices clearly in that Balkan-Anatolian crucible the richness of the numerous elements of which it is composed. These elements are certainly of Turco-Byzantine origin. It is important though to maintain a sense of restraint, for they can also be of ancient Micro-Asia, Roman-Greek, Slavic, Uralo-Altaic, Persian-Arabic or Caucasian origin. This means that one can usually do no better than list a few types of 'resemblances' between the Turkish and the Byzantine elements which contribute toward that particular society, 'fused but not confused', which was the Anatolian and Balkanic Middle Ages.

Let us point out briefly, however, a few matters equally shared by the two societies: the fields are many, and sometimes unexpected, such as that of religion and mysticism. There are concepts which seem alike even in the vocabulary that is employed to describe them; for example 'the reverse of the mind' which represents repentance and conversion of the faithful, *metanoia*/μετάνοια,[1] *muqallib*,[2] or simplicity of the mystic's inner life — *nêpsis*/νῆψις, [3] and *sahw*.[4] The strict or laxist interpretations of the dogmas, according to 'akrivia' or '*economy*', as they are practised in Byzantium,[5] have their equivalent in the Muslim terms of *azîma*,[6] and *ruhsa*.[7]

One can easily compare different notions, that, for example, of the spiritual 'seal' — *sphragis*/ σφραγίς[8] and *khatm*;[9] patience — *hypomonê*/ὑπομονή[10] and *sabr*;[11] heart — *kardia*/καρδία and *qalb*;[12] where prayer and memory of God remain — *mnêmê tou Theou*/μνήμη τοῦ Θεοῦ and *dhikr*;[13] chain — *alysis*/ἄλυσις[14] and *silsile*[15] — that unites master and

---

[1] Syméon (1957; 97, 101).

[2] Massignon (1963; II, 105).

[3] *Philocalie* (1995; II, 858).

[4] Kalâbâdhî (1981; 215).

[5] Kaplan (1997; 60,77, 167).

[6] Massignon (1975; III, 190).

[7] Addas (1989; 67, 68, 199).

[8] Eusèbe (1952; I, 127).

[9] Chodkiewicz (1986; 227).

[10] Marc (1985; 275).

[11] Addas (1989; 248).

[12] Palamas (1973; I, 80); Abd al-Karîm al-Jîlî (1986; 25).

[13] Gardet (1952; 642-679).

[14] Syméon (1957; 81).

[15] Addas (1989; 175-177).

disciple; or the innermost war — *djihâd al-akbar*[1] and *hieros polemos/ ἱερο πόλεμο*[2] that the mystic undertakes. Also, but this may lead us too far, the mystic anti-conformism, so common in Islam and Byzantium, those they called on one side 'lunatics of Christ' — *saloi dia Christon /σάλοι διά Χριστόν*[3] — and 'people of guilt' — *malâmatîya* on the other.[4]

As it is well known, we shall leave aside that wide subject that consists of the use and remodelling at all levels (scientific, literary, epic, popular) of great figures of antiquity: Plato and *Aflâtûn*, Alexander and *Iskandar*, Galien and *Djâlînûs*, Apollonios of Tyane and *Balînûs*,[5] Hippocrate and *Lokmân Hekim*,[6] and even Buddha.[7] As Nixon discusses in this volume, Hasluck identifies a popular cult of Plato in Konya.[8] On Aristotle, a traveller in the Middle Ages says that '*at Stagyra, there is an altar on his tomb where they celebrate on his name day as if he were a saint*'.[9] Iskandar — Alexander and his vizier *Aristûtâlîs* are very famous among the learned people at the Ottoman court as early as the fourteenth century through the Turkish version of Alexander's epic, *Iskendernâme* by the poet Ahmedî.[10]

Folklore and mythology show a Turkish Cyclops, a fusion discussed for our age by Demetriou in this volume. The epic called 'Dede Korkut'[11] talks of a Tepegöz, 'He who has his eye on the top', that looks like Homer's Polypheme. Also present are the giants 'Forty cubits high' (*sarandapêkoi/σαρανδάπηκοι*) of the Greek popular tales.[12] One even notices the similarity in the very words of the tales: Polypheme, wounded, '… shouted like a wild animal and the rocks resounded';[13] Tepegöz 'had such a cry that the mountains and the rocks echoed'.[14] As for the Amazons in the ancient myth, against whom Hercules fights in Cappadocia,[15] we find a

---

[1] Rûmî (1990; 1423).

[2] Palamas (1987; 51).

[3] Baconsky (1996; 267-321).

[4] Gölpınarlı (1931; passim).

[5] Aflâtûn, Iskandar, Djâlînûs, Balînûs, cf. *Encyclopédie de l'Islam*, Leiden, 1991.

[6] Rollet (1992; 134-143).

[7] Clément (1951; I, 102).

[8] Hasluck (1926; II, 363-369).

[9] Mandeville(1993; 14).

[10] Ahmedî (1983).

[11] *Dede Korkut* (1998; 181-192).

[12] Mundy (1956; 287).

[13] *Odyssey*, book IX v. 395-396 : '(Πολύφημος) σμερδαλέ ᾤμωξεν· περὶ δὲ μέγα ἴαχε πέτρη.

[14] *Dede Korkut* (1985; Vol. II, 375): '(Tepegöz ) Şöyle na'ra urdı, haykırdı kim dağ ve taş yankulandı'.

[15] Grimal (1963; 31).

Turkish version which describes a group of female warriors in those same areas. The oldest Turkish chronicles which relate the conquest of Anatolia name these warriors *Bacıyân-ı Rûm,* 'Sisters of *Rum*').[1]

The rich lore surrounding number symbolism indicates that the Turks and the Byzantines used much the same key numbers. The cult of the Forty *Abdâl*[2] is just as important among the Muslim Turkish populations as the Orthodox veneration of the 'Forty martyrs of Sebasteia'.[3] The surveys of Andrew of Crete[4] and Theodore Studite[5] of the 'admirable dozen' of patriarchs and apostles with 'as many degrees of ascension in wisdom' remind one of the ideas of the Muslim mystic Ibn Arabî, who lived a long time in Anatolia, and who evokes in his treaty *The Wisdom of the Prophets (Fusûs al-hikam),* the twelve prophetic verbs, symbols of the Twelve Degrees of Wisdom.[6]

We may draw attention also to different, recurrent themes among the Byzantines and the Turks: the vivifying furnace (kaminos/$\kappa \acute{\alpha} \mu \iota \nu o \varsigma$) of the Byzantine liturgy based on the story of the three youngsters of Babylone who came unharmed out of the fire,[7] and the cauldron *(kazan)* of initiation of the dervishes and shamans, place of trance and union with God, where a child, instead of burning, finds divine reality and an adult becomes a child again.[8]

One could think too of interesting parallels between the Sleepers of Ephesus[9] and the Sleep of the hero the Oghuz Turkish epic;[10] parallels also, between the form of a dove (*eidos peristeras*/$\epsilon \tilde{\iota} \delta o \varsigma \ \pi \epsilon \rho \iota \sigma \tau \epsilon \rho \acute{\alpha} \varsigma$) which appears as the Holy Spirit during the very popular Byzantine Theophania celebration,[11] and the dove (*güvercin*) discussed in a very shamanic way in his hagiography (*Vilâyetnâme-ı Hacı Bektâş*) by the medieval Turkish saint, Hacı Bektaş on his arrival in Anatolia.[12]

---

[1] Aşıkpaşazâde (1949; 237-238).
[2] Mélikoff (2001; 141-142).
[3] *Synaxaire* (1990; III, 323-327).
[4] André (1986; 35).
[5] *Pentecostaire* (1994; 141).
[6] Ibn Arabî (1955, passim).
[7] *Synaxaire* (1988; II, 140-142).
[8] Mélikoff (1998; 62-63).
[9] Jourdan (1983, passim).
[10] *Dede Korkut* (1985; 166, 211, 243).
[11] *Synekêmos* (1976; 818).
[12] *Vilâyetnâme* (1958; 18).

According to Clement of Alexandria, the flute was invented in Phrygia.[1] They know too of the poetry of the Byzantine synaxaries which celebrate such or such saint as the 'flute of the mind'. On 25 January, in the prayer to the great Cappadocian theologian on his name day, Gregory the Theologian's teaching is compared to the melody of 'the shepherd flute' (*poimenikos aulos*/ποιμενικὸς αὐλὸς)'.[2] Nearby, in Konya, in the thirteenth century, Djelâleddîn Rûmî wrote his famous poems on the flute, the very instrument which leads to mystic union: 'the sound of the flute is fire, not wind; may he who lacks this fire be annihilated, it is the fire of Love which is in the flute *(âtaš ast in bange nây o nist bâd, har ke in âtaš nadârad nist bâd, âtaše ešq kandar ney fetâd )*'.[3] This flute is narrowly mingled with the dance (*semâ)*[4] of the whirling dervishes of Konya, just as it was in the Acts of John, a very well known text among the Byzantine theologians, where we see Christ dance in a circle with his apostles, saying: 'Grace dances; I want to play the flute; dance, all of you; he who doesn't dance ignores what is happening'.[5]

The similarities, homophonies, different processes of toponymic assimilation are often wavering and diverse, and not always easy to sort out. Alongside Greek names which the Turks didn't change, or very little, like Amasya, Ankara, Smyrna, Kayseri, are old Byzantine names often 'Turkified' by the means of puns, an efficient way of cultural appropriation. By pronouncing in his own way the Greek term *Anatolê*/'Ανατολή, *Ana-dolu*, a Turk would easily find the terms *ana*, 'mother', and *dolu*, 'full', and impute to it the idea of motherly fertility, which would not have been denied by Theodore II Lascaris talking of his 'mother' Anatolia.[6] This reminds us of the pun Mehmed II the Conqueror invented, starting from the name of Istanbul, of Greek origin, and turning it into *Islambol*, 'Abundance of Islam'.[7]

But what can be said of the Turcomans of *Karası*, an appellation which sounds Turkish but could come from the name of a town *Karesos-Akarasos*, which they controlled?[8] What of the tribe of *Germiyans* who became dominant in the thirteenth century, not far from the Byzantine region

---

[1] Clément (I; 104-105).

[2] *Synekdêmos* (1976; 847).

[3] in the *Mathnawî* (1990; 53).

[4] Balivet (2001; 75-80).

[5] *Actes de Jean* in Bovon, F. and Geoltrain, P. (1997; 975-976, 1002-1004).

[6] *Théodore II* (Delobette 1997; I, 277).

[7] 'Istanbul' (İnalcık 1991).

[8] Zachariadou (1993; III, 192).

*tôn Germiôn*/τω<sup>ων</sup>ν Γερμίων, mentioned by Ann Comnena a century before?[1] Or the dervish *Toklu Dede*, established in an old sanctuary of saint *Thekla?*[2] Or the Turcoman leader in the thirteenth century called *Salpakis*,[3] who reigned over the ancient region of *Salpakê*[4] or, finally, those *Bâbâï* dervishes[5] who rebelled in an area Strabon called *Babanomon?*[6] Some of the so-called etymological puns are rather simplified, for example a medieval Muslim author, roughly educated in Greek, explaining the purely Latin word *Optimates* by the 'province of eyes and ears', based according to him on two Greek words *aftia* (*ἀφτία*, ears) and *matia* ( *μάτια*, eyes).[7]

As for Turco-Byzantine anthroponymy, certain similarities make the analysis rather delicate. How can one identify with certainty the Byzantine in the Turkish names *Karyağdı, Karaca*,[8] *Akboğa*,[9] the Turks with Byzantine first names — *Durmuş son of Theodoros*,[10] *Therianos Bedreddîn*,[11] *Tatar son of Basil*.[12] Are we dealing with Greek-speaking Christians with Turkish family names or nicknames, with Byzantinized Turks with Christian first names and Turkish names, or with Turkified Christians with excusively Turkish names? *Gümüştekin* governor of *Harim*, a Latin converted to Islam, is known only by his Turkish name,[13] as well as the merchant, of Latin origin too, called *al-Sonkor al-Rûmî*.[14] You can find as well Turkish-speaking Muslims with two names, one Turkish and one Muslim — *Dâvûd* / *Kılıç Arslân*, etc...,[15] or with a Turkish name Islamised by homophony, which could well be the case of the founder of the Ottoman dynasty, *Osmân*, known by the Byzantine sources of the time under his Turkish title of *Ataman*.[16] Indeed, when one meets Turkish or Mongol names without precise reference to their religion, it may imply not Christians or Muslims, shamanists or even manicheists or Buddhists, but certain people coming from Central Asia to

---

[1] Comnène (1989; III, 192).
[2] Hasluck (1926 : I; 18, 57).
[3] Balivet (1999; 109-112).
[4] Robert (1937; 106-107, 321, 332, 338, 382).
[5] Ocak (1989; 60).
[6] book XII, 3, 39.
[7] Idrîsî (1999; 412).
[8] Beldicéanu (1983; II, 496, 481).
[9] Shukurov (1999; 33).
[10] Beldiceanu (1983 ; II, 479).
[11] Shukurov (1999 ; 20).
[12] Beldicéanu (1983; II, 479).
[13] Grousset (1935 ; II, 647).
[14] Chapoutot (1993; I, 302).
[15] Qalânisî (1952; 38).
[16] Pachymérès (2000; IV, 116).

Anatolia that the medieval Muslim sources name *kâfir Atrâk* (the 'Turkish unbelievers').[1]

Peoples of the steppe and Byzantines sometimes look alike and have done for a long time. Take, for instance, costumes and hair-style. Both wear *tzitzakion, skaramangion, skaranikon, kalyptra*.[2] Nicephoros Gregoras in the fourteenth century says his fellow countrymen 'drape in the robe of the Persian and the Mede'.[3] At both courts they played chess and polo.[4] Important words concerning the Turkish urban setting come from Byzantium: mansions along the sea coast named *yalı*, holy springs, *ayazma*, market *panayır* and so on.[5] Palaces in the Abbasid[6] and Seldjukid[7] style, Arabic inscriptions[8] or Persian frescoes,[9] are to be found in the imperial Byzantine town, just as Byzantine mosaïcs are in the Muslim capitals.[10] The Roman–Byzantine *forum* and the *meydân* of the Muslims, the Greek *acropolis*, and the Turkish *kule* are commonly used as synonyms by both parties (as in Ann Comnene 's writings, or in Trebizond).[11]

The court titles are mixed. Muslim titles such as *Amîr, Sayyîd* or *Çavuş* become part of the imperial court's hierarchy (*Myrsaïtês/Μυρσαΐτης, Tzaousês/Τζαούσης*),[12] just as Turkified Greek titles (*Efendi, Çelebî*) become the way to deign the Turks among other peoples.[13] An Arab chronicler in the fourteenth century, speaking of the State of Trebizond with regard to similarities between the Turks and Byzantines, finds that in fact the Empire of the Grand-Comnenes 'looks very much like their neighbouring Turkish principalities'.[14]

As a conclusion to this rough catalogue '*à la manière de*' F. W. Hasluck of real or supposed similarities between the Turks and Byzantines, we shall say that it is not always possible to give a satisfactory answer to the

---

[1] Qalânisî (1952; 246).
[2] Bréhier (1970; III, 45-46).
[3] Gregoras (1851; 29).
[4] Bréhier (1970; III, 62).
[5] Redhouse (1981 s.v.).
[6] Lemerle (1971; 27).
[7] Janin (1964; 122).
[8] Clavijo (1928; 87) and Buondelmonti (1897; 245).
[9] Kinnamos (1972; 171-172).
[10] Baynes-Moss (1948; 318).
[11] *meydân* , Bryer (1980; V, 134); *koula/κουλᾶ*, Anna Comnena (III, 22, 48).
[12] Balivet (1994; 115-123).
[13] *efendi, çelebî, EI* , s.v.
[14] al-Umarî (1838; 380).

question of the real or only apparent nature of these similarities, just as we can not, except in obvious cases, assert that the parallelism comes from a decisive influence of one society on the other. Indeed, in certain cases, one has to be careful when considering customs followed by either side in a given territory for the customs may have quite independent origins. The christic *Analypsis/ 'Aνάληψις* has nothing to do originally with the shamanic ascension of the Altaic 'Flying Man' *(Perende)*,[1] just as the founder of the order of the whirling dervishes, Mevlânâ, cannot be confused with Christ.

Nevertheless, in the narrow Turco-Byzantine cohabitation during the low Middle Ages, the smallest formal resemblance allowed popular assimilation and daring superimposition of different proptotypes of which we have many examples: the doctrine of Love and the miracles of Mevlânâ persuaded the Christians of Konya that, according to them, the Muslim mystic was the manifestation of Jesus for their time.[2] The resemblance of Saint George to the Koranic figure of Khidr allows the veneration of the Christian saint by Muslim populations, as F.W. Hasluck points out in several studies, [3] an idea that is followed up by Hopwood in this volume.

A spot of wishful thinking to finish with. The work of classification and interpretation of the many similarities between the Turks and the Byzantines, *à la manière de F.W. Hasluck*, has largely progressed through the surveys of people such as Beldiceanu, Bryer, Mélikoff, Ocak, Shukurov and so on. It must continue, not only by encouraging knowledge of Greek, but also in the future by as much as much as possible encouraging contact between those intending to work on the Islamo-Byzantine world and those who study similarly Turkish, Arabic and Persian. Through such close and creative scholarly collaboration, this process of research and learning may be maintained and even flourish.

*References*

Abd al-Karîm al-Jîlî 1953 *De l'Homme Universel*, translated by T.Burckhardt, Alger; Messerschmitt (Reprinted Paris, 1986).

Addas, C. 1989 *Ibn Arabî, ou la quête du Soufre Rouge*, Paris; Gallimard.

Ahmedî 1983 *Iskender-Nâme*, edited by I. Ünver, Ankara; Türk Tarih Kurumu.

---

[1] *Perende*, Mélikoff (1992), 156-157.
[2] Balivet (2001; 70-71).
[3] Hasluck (1926; 1, 48, 320, 326, 334 etc).

Al-Umarî 1838 *Mesâlik al-Absâr fî Memâlik al-Amsâr*, translated by E. Quatremère, in *Notices et Extraits des Manuscrits de la Bibliothèque du Roi*, XIII, Paris; Imprimerie royale.

André 1986 *Le Grand Canon de saint André de Crète*, Paris; Fraternité Orthodoxe en Europe occidentale.

Aşıkpaşazâde 1949 in *Osmanlı Tarihleri*, edited by C. Atsız, Istanbul; Türkiye Yayınevi.

Balivet, M. 1999 *Byzantins et Ottomans: relations, interaction, succession*, Istanbul; ISIS.

Balivet, M. 2001 *Konya, la ville des derviches tourneurs*, Paris; CNRS.

Baconski, T. 1996 *Le rire des Pères — Essai sur le rire dans la patristique grecque.*, Paris; Brouwer.

Baynes, N. and Moss, H. 1948 *Byzantium, an Introduction to East Roman Civilization*, Oxford; OUP.

Beldicéanu, I. 1983 *Le monde préottoman et ottoman à la lumière des archives de Turquie (fin XIIIe- milieu XVIe s.)*, thèse de Doctorat, Paris III, 1983.

Bovon, F. and Geoltrain, P. (eds) 1997 *Actes de Jean*, in *Ecrits apocryphes chrétiens*, Paris; La Pléiade.

Buondelmonti,C. 1897 *Description des îles de l'Archipel*, edited by E. Legrand, Paris; E. Leroux.

Bréhier, L. 1970 *Le monde byzantin*, vol. III: *La civilisation byzantine*, Paris; Albin Michel.

Bryer, A 1980 *The Empire of Trebizond and the Pontos*, London; Variorum Reprints.

Chapoutot-Remadi, R. 1993 *Liens et Relations au sein de l'élite Mamlûke sous les premiers sultans Bahrides (1250-1340)*, thèse de Doctorat, Aix-Marseille I.

Chodkiewicz, M. 1986 *Le Sceau des saints*, Paris; Gallimard.

Clavijo, R. Gonzalez de. 1928 *Embassy to Tamerlane,1403-1406*, translated by Le Strange; London; Routledge.

Clément d'Alexandrie 1951 *Les Stromates*, vol.I , col. *Sources Chrétiennes*, Paris; Éditions du Cerf.

Comnène, A. 1989 *Alexiade, règne de l'empereur Alexis I Comnène, 1081-1118*; *livres (XI-XV)*, Vol. III, Paris; Les Belles Lettres.

Dede Korkut 1985 *Dede Korkut kitabı*, in *Büyük Türk Klâsikleri*, vol.II, Istanbul; Ötüken.

Dede Korkut 1998 *Le Livre de Dede Korkut*, translated by L. Bazin and A. Gökalp, Paris; Gallimard.

Delobette, L. 1997 *Théodore II Lascaris: Eloge de Nicée, Eloge de Jean Vatatzès*, thèse de Doctorat, Paris IV.

Eusèbe de Cesarée 1952 *Histoire ecclésiastique*, Vol. I, col. '*Sources Chrétiennes*', Paris; Éditions du Cerf.

Gardet L. 1951 'Un problème de mystique comparée', in *Revue thomiste* N°3,

Gölpınarlı, A. 1931 *Melâmîlik ve Melâmîler*, Istanbul; Devlet Matbaası.

Grégoras, N. 1851 'Nicéphore Grégoras' in *Notices et extraits des manuscrits de la Bibliothèque Nationale*, vol. XVII, Paris; Imprimerie royale.

Grimal, P. 1963 *Dictionnaire de la mythologie grecque et romaine*, Paris; Presses universitaires de France.

Grousset, R. 1935 *Histoire des Croisades*, Vol.II, Paris; Plon.

Hasluck, F.W. 1926 *Christianity and Islam under the Sultans*, edited by M. Hasluck, Oxford; Clarendon Press.

Ibn Arabî 1955 *La Sagesse des Prophètes*, translated by T.Burckhard, Paris; Albin-Michel.

Idrîsî 1999 *La première géographie de l'Occident*, translated by Jaubert-Nef, Paris; Flammarion.

İnalcık, H. 1991 'Istanbul' in *Encyclopédie de l'Islam*, Leiden; Brill, Vol. IV, 234.

Janin, R. 1964 *Constantinople byzantine*, Paris; Institut Francais d'Etudes Byzantines.

Jourdan, F. 1983 *La tradition des sept dormants*, Paris; Maisonneuve & Larose.

Kalâbâdhî 1981 *Traité du soufisme*, Paris; Sindbad.

Kaplan, M. 1997 *La chrétienté byzantine du début du VIIe siècle au milieu du XIe*, Paris; SEDES.

Kinnamos, J. 1972 *Chronique*, translated by J. Rosenblum, Paris; Les Belles Lettres.

Lemerle, P. 1971 *Le premier Humanisme byzantin*, Paris; Presses Universitaires de France.

Mandeville, J. de 1993 *Voyage autour de la terre*, Paris; les Belles lettres.

Marc le Moine 1985 *Traités spirituels et théologiques*, transl. C-A. Zirnheld, col. 'Spiritualité orientale', No 41, Abbaye de Bellefontaine.

Massignon, L. 1963 *Opera Minora*, Vol. II, Beyrut; Dar al-Maaref.

Massignon, L. 1975 *La Passion de Hallâj*, Vol. III, Paris; Gallimard.

Mélikoff, I. 1992 *Sur les traces du soufisme turc*, Istanbul; Isis.

Mélikoff, I. 1998 *Hadji Bektach: un mythe et ses avatars*, Leiden; Brill.

Mélikoff, I. 2001 *Au banquet des Quarante*, Istanbul; Isis.

Mundy, C. 1956 'Polyphemus and Tepegöz', in *Bulletin of Oriental and African Studies*, Vol. XVIII, No. 2.

Ocak, A. 1989 *La révolte de Baba Resul*, Ankara; TTK.

Pachymérès G. 2000 *Relations historiques*,Vol V, Paris; Institut français d'études byzantines.

Palamas, G. 1973 *Défense des saints hésychastes*, edited by J. Meyendorff, Louvain; Spicilegium sacrum Lovaniense Administration.

Palamas G. 1987 *Douze homélies pour les fêtes*, translated by J.Cler, Paris; YMCA Press.

*Pentecostaire* 1994 *Pentecostaire*, translated by D. Guillaume, Parma; Dia. Apostolique.

*Philocalie* 1995 *Philocalie des Pères Neptiques* translated by J. Touraille, Paris; Brouwer/ J. C. Latté.

Qalânisî 1952 *Damas de 1075 à 1154*, translation of an extract from Ibn al-Qalânisî by R. Le Tourneau, Damascus; Institut français de Damas.

Redhouse 1981 *New Redhouse Turkish-English Dictionary*, Istanbul; Redhouse Press.

Robert, L. 1937 *Etudes anatoliennes*, Paris; E. de Boccard.

Rollet, J. 1992 *D'Esculape à Lokman Hekim*, Istanbul; Isis.

*Rûmî 1990 Mathnawî, La Quête de l'Absolu*, translated by E. de Vitray-Meyerovitch and D. Mortazavi, Paris; du Rocher.

Shukurov, R. 1999 'The Byzantine Turks of the Pontos', in *Mésogeios* No. 6, Paris; Herodotos ed.

Syméon 1957 'Syméon le Nouveau Théologien' in *Chapitres théologiques, gnostiques et pratiques*, col. '*Sources Chrétiennes*', Paris.

*Synaxaire* 1988 *Le Synaxaire*, vol. II, translated by Macaire de Simonos-Petras, Salonica;

*Synaxaire* 1990 *Le Synaxaire*, vol. III, translated by Macaire de Simonos-Petras, Salonica.

*Synekdêmos* 1976 *Megas kai Hieros Synekdêmos/Megav" kai; Jiero;" Sunevkdhmo"*, Athens.

Zachariadou, E. 1993 'The Emirate of Karasi and that of the Ottomans: two rival States', in *The Ottoman Emirate*, Rethymnon; Crete University Press; 225-236.

# 23. THE CRYPTO-MUSLIMS OF ANATOLIA

## Rustam SHUKUROV

My paper discusses the relationship between Christianity and Islam in Anatolia in the early stages of the Turkic conquest, a problem that was always within the scope of F.W. Hasluck's scholarly interests. In the exposition I would like to re-examine one of his favourite subjects, to the elaboration of which he dedicated perhaps the most pioneering and exciting pages in his writings: I mean the question of Anatolian heterodoxy, Christian elements in popular religion of the local Muslims, and Muslim influences within the beliefs of local Christians.

### Hafiz-i Abru's Evidence

The starting point of my analyses is a thought-provoking passage from the still unpublished Persian *Geography* of Shihab al-Din-i 'Abd-Allah-i Hafiz-i Abru (d. 1430). Hafiz-i Abru, native of Hirat in Khorasan, was a close friend and historian of Tamerlane (1370-1404), the famous Central Asian conqueror. Hafiz-i Abru was said to be an expert chess-player and one of the most educated and enlightened persons of his time. After the death of Timur Hafiz-i Abru became the official historiographer of Tamerlane's son Shahrukh, ruler of Iran in 1415-1447.[1]

Hafiz-i Abru is well known to modern scholars as the author of the extensive historical compilations *Dhayl-i 'Jame$^c$ al-tawarikh* and *Majma al-tawarikh*. The autograph manuscript of the latter, which belonged to the library of the Sultan Shahrukh and later passed to Istanbul (and is now in the Topkapı Saray Library), is illuminated with 142 famous fifteenth century miniatures; one or more other manuscripts of the same work have been also

---

[1] On Hafiz-i Abru's biography and historical works see Storey-Bregel (1972, 1; 341-9), Barthold (1897), F. Tauer (1963), and 'Introduction' by Bayani in his edition Hafiz-i Abru (1317/1939).

lavishly illustrated.[1] Hafiz-i Abru's numerous historical writings in Persian have been commonly considered a basic and reliable source for the history of Tamerlane and his successors. This is not surprising because, apart from his undoubted scholarly abilities, Hafiz-i Abru spent most of his life as a member of the king's entourage. He was therefore an eyewitness to many drastic events of his time and had access to the archives of the Timurid chancellery.

Hafiz-i Abru composed his *Geography* on the orders of the Sultan Shahrukh between 1414 – 1420 AD. It is an extensive work containing geographical descriptions of the climates of the world including the Muslim and Christian Mediterranean and Byzantine lands, often supplemented with historical sketches. The *Geography* is believed to have been based on the earlier Muslim geographical tradition, in particular, the works in Arabic of Hasan b. Ahmad al-Muhallabi and al-Idrisi, and the Persian compilation of Hamd-Allah Qazwini. However, it is obvious that Hafiz-i Abru considerably supplemented and enlarged his sources with an abundance of fresh information concerning the time of the Emir Timur and his successors.[2] For instance, the *Geography*'s historical account of Khorasan is widely acknowledged as an exceptionally important source of information for the history of Iran in the fourteenth and fifteenth centuries and has recently been published in Iran.[3]

It is worth noting also that Hafiz-i Abru was unable to finish his *Geography*, because Sultan Shahrukh ordered him to devote his activities to other extensive historical work. So, the *Geography* remained incomplete, and his narration, being obscure in many cases, apparently required further editing and emendation for which the author probably had had no spare time. Nonetheless, the surviving copies of *Geography*, most of which are illuminated with geographical maps, are not few, hence, one may think that the book was valued highly in the Persian-speaking world.[4]

---

[1] Ettinghausen (1955). For other illustrations see Grube (1962, nos. 37-40); Lentz & Lowry (1989, nos. 27-8); Robinson (1967, no.15); *Treasures of Islam* (no. 27); Curatola (1993, no. 227, p. 373-5).

[2] Krachkovski (1955; **4**, 234-6); Barthold (1963-77; **1**, 104, note 7).

[3] Hafiz Abru (Tehran, 1970).

[4] On the maps of Hafiz-i Abru's *Geography* see Harley and Woodward (1992; 127-8, 149-51 and fig. 6.12, 170, 390).

Here I make use of an unpublished chapter of Geography entitled 'Description of the Armenian land and Farangistan' (*dhikr-i diyar-i arman wa farangistan*) based on three manuscripts preserved in the British archives: two in London (British Library), one in Oxford (Bodleian Library).[1] This section contains curious and not entirely transparent information. In his account Hafiz-i Abru divided Armenia into two parts, namely Greater Armenia and Lesser Armenia. Within Greater Armenia Hafiz-i Abru distinguishes, as many other Muslim sources did, '[the land] relating to Azarbayjan' (that is Eastern Greater Armenia) and '[the land] relating to the country of Rum' (namely Western Greater Armenia). However, his further description of Western Greater Armenia introduces the following rather odd information. The passage in question reads as follows:[2]

و همچنین آنچه متصل مملکت روم است حاکم ایشان مسلمانست[a] و رعایا بعضی مسلمان و بعضی ارمنی باشند. فاما در دار الملک فرنج حاکم ایشان ترساست[b] و در میان ایشان مسلمانان باشند، اما ایشان آشکارا بر دین ترسائی باشند. و در زمانی که حضرت [A 90 // ] امیر صاحبقران انارالله برهانه فتح بلاد روم و شام فرمود ایلچی ایشان آمد و پیشکش و خدمات و آنچه وظیفه اذعان و انقیاد باشد بتقدیم رسانیدند. اما لشکر بار الملک ایشان نرسید و السلام علی من اتبع الهدی.[c]

---

[a] مسلمان نیست (C)
[b] نیز ترساست (C, B)
[c] علی من اتبع الهدی: B ندارد

---

[1] Hafiz Abru, Or. 9316 (British Library) – hereafter **A**; Hafiz Abru, Or. 1577 (British Library) – hereafter **B**; Hafiz Abru, MS Elliott 357 (Bodleian Library) – hereafter **C**. On the Oxford manuscript, see also *Catalogue* (1889, no. 33). On other manuscripts see Bayani 'Introduction' in Hafiz-i Abru (1317/1939); Storey-Bregel (1972; **1**, 342 note 54). At least two copies are probably preserved in Tashkent, see: *Sobranie* (1952; Vol. 6).

[2] Hafiz Abru, Or. 9316, fol. 89v-90; Hafiz Abru, Or. 1577, fol. 68; Hafiz Abru, MS Elliott 357, fol. 107v.

This is a translation of that remarkable passage:

> As to that [part of Greater Armenia] adjoining the country of Rum, their
> governor [i.e. 'the governor of the inhabitants of Greater Armenia'] is a
> Muslim and his subjects are partly Muslims and partly Armenians. In the
> Frankish capital city their ruler is a Christian. There are Muslims among
> them but openly they are of the Christian faith. When His Majesty Amir
> Sahib-Qiran [i.e. 'Emir Timur'] (May God elucidate his proofs [at the
> Judgment Day]!) deigned to conquer Rum and Syria their embassy came and
> presented numerous gifts, and reverences, and everything which was among
> the obligations of allegiance and subjection. However, the army did not
> reach their capital city itself. Blessing upon those who follows [God's]
> instructions!.[1]

In other words, Hafiz-i Abru asserts that there is a 'Frankish' country near
Western Greater Armenia, the ruler of which is a Christian; however, some of
his subjects, outwardly being in Christian faith, secretly confess Islam or, in
other words, may be designated, by analogy with the well-known phenomenon
of Crypto-Christians, *Crypto-Muslims*.


*Place and Time*


The passage starts with Hafiz-i Abru's statement that the westernmost part of
Greater Armenia bordering upon the region of Rum is under the Muslim
control and is populated by Muslims and Armenian Christians. This first
point of the passage presents no problem in its interpretation. The western
part of Greater Armenia was governed in Tamerlane's time by the Muslim
Emir Mutahhartan (1379-1403) and later by the Turkmens of the Aq-Quyunlu
and Qara-Quyunlu tribes,[2] and inhabited by both Muslims and Armenian
Christians. According to the Armenian sources, the local Armenians lived
inpeace with Mutahhartan and the Aq-Quyunlu leaders.[3]

---

[1] The fourth manuscript which I have had an opportunity to check, is preserved in National
Library of Russia in St. Petersburg (Hafiz Abru, Dorn 290). Judging by the catchwords, the
Petersburg MS lacks at least six quires, each of eight leaves, between fols. 235v and 236, 243v
and 244, 251v and 252. One or more of these missed quires probably contained the sections
(present in the two British Library's and Bodleian manuscripts) 'Armenian lands [belonging] to
Syria' (*bilad-i arman min al-sham*) and 'Description of the Armenian land and Farangistan'; the
latter section would have included the passage under discussion here. Moreover, the St.
Petersburg manuscript seems to have been bound (or rebound) wrongly, and the existing section
on Syria (fols. 238-243v), which in other manuscripts belongs to the first half of *Geography* and
precedes the mentioned descriptions of Armenia, is out of place, being found in the second half
of the manuscript in the middle of the description of Khorasan.

[2] Shukurov (1994; 36-41; Shukurov 2001; 216, 283-91).

[3] Sanjian (1969; 1425:9, 1435:2, 3); Metzopskii (1957; 69).

More questions arise when one tries to explain the subsequent narration. Which Franks are meant in Hafiz-i Abru's reference to the ruler of 'the Frankish capital city' and, hence, who was the sovereign of the Crypto-Muslims?

Muslim authors from the thirteenth century onward often designated both Constantinople and Trebizond Greeks as Franks and their lands as Farangistan.[1] Elsewhere in his work Hafiz-i Abru confirms this usage saying: ولایت ارمن در پیش مملکت فرنکستانست ('the region of Armenia is located by the side of the country of Farangistan').[2] Undoubtedly, 'Farangistan' and 'Frankish' here imply 'Byzantine lands' and 'Byzantine' respectively. Consequently, the discussed information about the ruler of 'the Frankish capital city' and his Crypto-Muslim subjects appears to be a sort of digression from the main subject and deals with the lands located *outside* Western Greater Armenia. But which particular part of the Byzantine world which, by the beginning of the fifteenth century, was divided between the European possessions of the Palaiologoi and those of the Grand Komnenoi in the Pontos is meant here?

It is reasonable to suggest that Hafiz-i Abru is discussing here an Anatolian Christian state adjacent to the farthest northwest edge of Greater Armenia. The only Christian state located on the northwest border of Greater Armenia which survived up until the time of Hafiz-i Abru was the Empire of Trebizond. This suggestion is also confirmed by earlier Muslim geographical usage well known to Hafiz-i Abru, such as in the Arabic geographical compilation of Ibn Khurdadbeh (d. 912) or the Persian Hudud al-alam (tenth century AD), that Armenia was contiguous to the Byzantine (Rum) province of Chaldia (*khaldiya* in Oriental sources).[3] As we know, after 1204 the major part of Chaldia had passed into the hands of the Grand Komnenoi of Trebizond constituting the main body of their possessions in the Pontos.

---

[1] For instance, the Pontic Greeks, the subjects of the Grand Komnenoi, are called 'Franks' in the following: in *Histoire des seldjoukides* (1952; 44), in the account on the events of 1214 in *Tarix-e al-e Saljuq* (1999; 87), in the fourteenth century in Aboulféda (1840; 393); referring to the events of 1243 in Ibn Bibi (1902; 238) and on the Saljuq conquest of Sinop in 1265-66 in Aksarayi (1944; 83). For similar usages see also Cahen (1951; 102) and Vryonis (1971; p. 234, note 550).

[2] Hafiz Abru, Or. 9316, fol. 89v; Hafiz Abru, Or. 1577, fol. 67v; Hafiz Abru, MS Elliott 357, fol. 107.

[3] Ibn Khordadhbeh (1889; 108). See also a Russian translation with additional bibliography and commentaries (Ibn Khordadhbeh 1986; 100) and *Hudud-al'Alam* (1937; fol. 37).

Further on Hafiz-i Abru relates that this Frankish ruler sent an embassy to Tamerlane with ample gifts, and Tamerlane's army did not reach the Frankish capital. Both statements of Hafiz-i Abru can be interpreted and confirmed by what we know about the interrelations between the Grand Komnenoi and Tamerlane. According to the well-known letter of Tamerlane to the Byzantine emperor John VII Palaiologos and some Oriental sources, in April and May of 1402 Tamerlane, at the beginning of his famous campaign against the Ottoman Sultan Bayazid I (1389-1402), stayed with his army near Erzincan, some fifty kilometres to the south of the Trapezuntine border. It is not impossible that just before this date, in 1400-02, the Trebizond emperor Manuel III Grand Komnenos (1390-1417), like his intimate allies John VII and the Erzincan Emir Mutahhartan, avoiding taking sides, outwardly recognised the sovereignty of Timur but simultaneously secretly negotiated with the Sultan Bayazid. I have suggested elsewhere that in about 1400 Bayazid restored Kerasous (lost by the Greeks in 1396-7) to Manuel III in exchange for Manuel's support against Timur. It seems that the intrigues of Manuel III outraged the Emir. Timur sent his army towards Trebizond and demanded that the Emperor Manuel III confirm his allegiance. Although Trebizond itself had not been attacked by Chaghatay troops, Manuel III, who probably visited Timur's camp in person, proved somehow his loyalty and, as a sign of his recognition of the supreme power of the Chaghatay Emir, promised to supply Timur with twenty battleships.[1] Very likely that it is this Trapezuntine embassy that Hafiz-i Abru implies.[2]

Therefore, one may suggest that Hafiz-i Abru in this passage is referring to the Grand Komnenoi, the rulers of the Empire of Trebizond. If so, Hafiz-i Abru's remark 'There are Muslims among them but openly they are of the Christian faith' also concerns the subjects of the Grand Komnenoi, the population of the Byzantine Pontos. Thus, this is a unique, albeit laconic, reference to the existence of Crypto-Muslims in Byzantine lands or more precisely, I suggest, in the Pontic region.

---

[1] The letter of Timur to John VII (more precisely, its Latin translation) has been much published and commented upon. For a discussion of the letter and, in general, on relations between the Grand Komnenoi and Tamerlane see Sanuto (1733; 797–798); Bryer (1966; 5); Bryer-Winfield (1985); Fallmerayer, S. (1827; 227-228); Alexandrescu-Dersca (1942; 123-124); Janssens (1969; 124-125); Brion (1963; 44); Miller (1962; 72). This information with additional interpretations and bibliographical references is summarised in Russian in my book Shukurov (2001; 260-292).

[2] It would be tempting to understand the passage on the 'Frankish embassy' as a reference to the well-known Palaiologan embassy to Timur accepted by the Emir in Altuntash near Ephesus in autumn 1402 (Alexandrescu-Dersca (1942; 86, 132), Matschke (1981; 66-7), Dölger (1965; 5, 74, no. 3199); Shukurov (2001; 283-4 and notes 77-78); cf. Schreiner (1975; 2, 371-3). That embassy attracted the attention of Persian contemporaries and its details undoubtedly were well known to Hafiz-i Abru, Shukurov (2001, *passim*). However, the whole context of Hafiz-i Abru's narration and, especially, the probable Pontic localisation of Hafiz-i Abru's 'Frankish capital' prompt me to prefer the Trapezuntine parallel.

I have already mentioned that Hafiz-i Abru has been recognised as a knowledgeable and trustworthy informant, possessing access to the state archives of his sovereigns and the best secondary sources of his time. It may be possible to rephrase this statement even more boldly; the information provided by Hafiz-i Abru, so far as I know, is unique for the entire body of Muslim (Arabic, Persian, Turkic) and Christian (including Greek, West European, Armenian and Georgian) primary sources of Anatolian history of the fourteenth and fifteenth centuries. To my knowledge, no other author or document has mentioned anything which can be interpreted as a hint to the existence of intact social groups of Crypto-Muslims in the Eastern Mediterranean. In the light of this, how should we appraise Hafiz-i Abru's comment? Is it an authorial misunderstanding, a mere editorial fault, or a unique reference to a real feature, formerly unknown and unrecorded by others, of the socio-religious life of this region? Is there any ground to believe Hafiz-i Abru's testimony, or, in other words, can Hafiz-i Abru's statement be confirmed or proved by known sources concerning the relationship between Christian and Muslim in Asia Minor?

I believe that it is plausible. Below I will present some points which might be helpful, beginning with the possible social conditions which could have begotten such a phenomenon as Crypto-Muslims.

*Demographic Data*

Some hints as to the phenomenon of Crypto-Islamicity may be found in the contemporary sources from various periods of Byzantine history. Maybe one of the earliest cases of that sort is represented by the *koubikoularios* Samonas, a confidential agent of the Emperor Leo VI (886-912) who is believed to have remained a secret Muslim while keeping high posts in the court hierarchy.[1] A less well-known case has been described by Constantine VII Porphyrogenitus (913-59) who accused the *protospatharios* Chase, originally a Muslim newcomer (Saracen) and later a confidant of the Byzantine emperor Alexander (912-913), of continuing to be 'a true Saracen in thought and manners and religion'.[2] There cannot be any doubt that openly both the *koubikoularios* Samonas and *protospatharios* Chase had to confess Christianity; otherwise, they would not have been allowed to occupy court offices. In other words, Samonas and Chase are the names of the earliest known Crypto-Muslims in

---

[1] See for instance: Jenkins (1948), Canard (1950).

[2] Constantine Porphyrogenitus (1967; 50, lines 202-203).

Byzantine history.[1] This means at least Crypto-Islamicity as such was not something entirely incredible in the Byzantine socio-religious experience; one may notice its traces, albeit infrequent and faded, in the primary sources. Nevertheless, the focus of my interest is not so much Muslim individuals, who occasionally by this or another way came to and settled in Byzantium, but a relatively large, ethnically and religiously compact group of Muslim newcomers.

Mutual and sometimes intensive interchange of population between Byzantium and the Muslim World took place from the very beginning of the Caliphate in the seventh century and up to the fall of Byzantium in the middle of the fifteenth century. However, one may notice an essential difference between the Arab and Turkic periods in the inter-relationship of Byzantium with the Orient. During the Arab period it is possible to distinguish three main categories of Asians who, aside from odd individuals, lived in compact fashion in the Empire: prisoners of war, merchants, and refugees from Muslim lands.

The most remarkable group of Muslim foreigners consisted of prisoners of war. Ibn Hawqal (late tenth century) mentioned prisons for the Arab captives in the themes of Thrakesion, Opsikion, and Voukellarion. Most prisoners though were probably kept in Constantinople. Some of these prisoners seem eventually to have returned to their homeland by way of ransom, exchange and so on. However, some of them were settled on free land or reduced to slavery. In the latter cases, the settlers and enslaved prisoners, being dispersed in different locations, ceased to maintain any intact unity, dissolving rather into a number of individuals. Being lost in the thick of the local people, they were quickly Christianised and mixed with them through intermarriage.

According to the Arab geographical tradition, Muslim merchants knew the Byzantine system of international trade well, including the most important markets and trade routes throughout the Empire, and, from the end of the ninth century onwards, frequented major Byzantine commercial centres. However, as in the case of prisoners, it seems that it was Constantinople only where there lived a relatively large permanent group of Muslim merchants. We return to this issue below.

---

[1] A similar example has been noted also by N. Oikonomidès for the twelfth century with reference to 'Danishmand-nama' in which the scholar detects the signs of the presence of crypto-musulmans (Oikonomidès 1983; 195-196).

From time to time groups of migrants, forced out of the Muslim countries, found asylum in Byzantium. Many of them belonged to different Christian rites. However, a few non-Christian Muslim groups were permitted to settle in Byzantine lands on the condition of their adopting Christianity. Among such migrants one may mention the Persian *khurramites* who escaped to Byzantium in the reign of Theophilus (829-42); the Moors who probably came from North Africa and lived in Southwest Anatolia (tenth century); twelve thousand Arab horsemen who migrated in 941 to Byzantine Anatolia with their families from Nisibis and so on. The Byzantine authorities usually divided such migrant communities into small groups and sent them to different parts of the Empire in order to facilitate their assimilation into the local population. As a rule the genuine ethnic and religious identity of such communities melted away in some decades or even more rapidly.

The distinct phenomenon of the Byzantine eastern periphery, the *acritic* zone, in which the population movement in both directions across the frontier was always quite intensive, must be kept in mind as well. Repeated changes of side for *acritic* and *thughur* warriors were not unnatural and, consequently, in the Byzantine frontier areas, there would have existed relatively numerous groups of renegades, who were formerly Muslim soldiers. This achieved a remarkable scale during the period of the Byzantine *Reconquista* of Syria in the tenth and early eleventh centuries. The assimilative tool of Christianisation, judging by the Byzantine epic 'Digenes Akrites', was operative in the case of the Arab *acritai* no less than in the mentioned instances of other migrants.[1] Nevertheless, immigrant Muslims on Byzantine soil either very soon lost their religious identity (as Muslim refugees and deserters) or constituted completely marginal communities of foreign subjects (as in the case of prisoners and merchants), unincorporated into Byzantine social structure and standing outside the Byzantine social organisation.

This general picture altered considerably during the period of the Turkish conquest from the mid-eleventh century onwards. The traditional categories of Muslim captives, merchants, travellers and vagabonds very soon were outnumbered by different sorts of migrants and settlers who spread all

---

[1] The most extensive informational resource for the Arab-Byzantine relations remains the classic work of Vasiliev and Canard (1935, **1–2**). So far there is no systematic and generalising review of the Arab presence in Byzantium, although particular aspects of it have been described relatively well in numerous studies; see, for instance: Canard (1964), (1973 studies 1, 15); Charanis (1972); Reinert (1998); Ditten (1993); Oikonomidès (1974); Balivet (1994, Chap. 1, esp. 12-14 and notes 10-12); Dagron (1994). On *khurramites* see Cheynet (1998). Further references to the relevant sources and literature may be found in these studies.

over the Empire. The harbingers of this future demographic change were the Turkmen mercenaries who appeared in Byzantium in large number as early as in the mid-eleventh century and in the course of the next few decades constituted a remarkable part of the Byzantine army. Indeed, the Byzantine authorities used Anatolian and Balkan Turks as the main manpower source for their armies. Numerous mercenary soldiers of Turkic race, enrolled for imperial service, probably usually served under the command of the Turkish military leaders who themselves had proved their loyalty to the ruling dynasty and were entirely integrated into Byzantine society such as Tzachas, Tatikios, Axouchos, Elchanes and many others. It is not impossible that originally some of them were chieftains amongst the Balkan and Anatolian Turkic nomads.

Among these military commanders were those belonged to the Byzantine nobility, as well as officers of the medium and low levels, scrupulously listed by Brand.[1] There are no exact figures for the number of Turks in Byzantine service, however, as Brand suggests, it must have been rather high to sustain the beliefs of the Crusaders that the Byzantines were in the alliance with the Turks. 'Hostility to Byzantium and suspicion of the emperors rose in the twelfth century, and the use of Turks contributed thereto'.[2] From the thirteenth-fifteenth centuries and, especially, under the Palaiologoi (1261-1453), the integration of Turkish mercenaries into Byzantine society continued and went so far that this process eventually amended remarkably the structural fabric of the Byzantine army. There appeared specific detachments of *mourtatoi* (from Ar. *murtadd* 'renegade'), *tourkopouloi* and *mixovarvaroi*, the soldiers and officers of which probably were Turks and half-Turks. The palace titles of Oriental (Turkic, Arabic and Persian) origin, such as *tzaousios* (possibly, a Sogdian word borrowed by the Turks: Tk. *çavus* initially 'messenger', later a medium rank officer), *ameralios* for admiral, *dragoumanos* (from Ar.-Persian *tarjuman*), which have been attested by the sources of the fourteenth-fifteenth centuries, entered the Byzantine *liste de préséance* and were obviously introduced to the Byzantine official hierarchy by these Turkish migrants.[3]

---

[1] Brand (1989; 1–25); see also more recent study with the additional fresh information: Necipoğlu (1999-2000).

[2] Brand (1989; 24). Brand estimates the number of Turks in the Byzantine ruling class as approximately one per cent (page 18-19). However, it should be kept in mind that Brand derives his figures from the anthroponimical data which records only those members of Byzantine high class who bore Turkish nicknames. Obviously, those individuals unknown to us of Turkic race who adopted purely Christian Byzantine names do not therefore appear. This has been noted also by Bádenas (1998; 182).

[3] Moravcsik (1983; **2**, 68, 197, 308-9, 327-8); Balivet (1999; 115-123), Bartusis (1989; 196ff); Savvides (1993); Zachariadou (1983).

The influx of migrants, in fact, was a part of a more extensive and crucial demographical transformation: that is the large-scale increase of the number of Turks in the Byzantine urban and rural population. From the eleventh through to the thirteenth centuries various Anatolian and Balkan rural areas controlled by the Byzantines were thereby colonised by Turks and Turkish-speaking population. We have eloquent indications of this from the contemporary Byzantine authors who complained of the partial or even complete Turkification of the particular regions of the Empire owing to this mass immigration by the Turks. John Kinnamos and Nicetas Choniates as early as 1142 complained of the Turkification of the frontier region of Phrygia.[1] According to Eustathios of Thessalonike, in 1178, under Manuel I Komnenos (1143-80), the capture of numerous Turkish women and children caused an influx of Turkish men to the Byzantine lands; the Turks became so many around Thessalonike that the region might well be called 'New Turkey, or the European land of the Turks.'[2] Eustathios of Thessalonike referred to the Cumans and Anatolian Turks among other nations found in Constantinople.[3] As a result, the Turks could be found in large numbers inside Byzantium both in cities and rural areas, becoming thereby an integral component of Byzantine social and political life.[4]

*The Byzantine Pontus*

This general picture is particularly true for the case of the Byzantine Pontos. Although the contemporary sources are not so lavishly detailed with regard to the Empire of Trebizond, undoubtedly, from the early thirteenth century onwards, Turks infiltrated into all social strata including peasantry, urban population and the imperial retinue. The most detailed demographic picture can be reconstructed only for the central region of Matzuka, located to the south of Trebizond. According to the anthroponymical data at least three percent of the Matzoukan population either were Turks or had Turkic or other

---

[1] On the turkicised Christian population of the islands in the lake Pousgouse (now Beyşehir Gölü) near Ikonium see: Kinnamos (1836; **I**, 10); Choniates (1975; 37). The passages have been commented upon many times, see, for instance: Chalandon, (1912; 181 note 3); Vryonis (1971; 459 note 54), for other references see Necipoğlu (1999-2000; 58 and index); Balivet (1994; 44); Shukurov (1999b; 228). On the Turkification of the frontier area of Chaldia see Choniates (1975; 226).

[2] Eustathios of Thessalonike in Regel (1892; 79), quoted and discussed in Brand (1989; 13). It is worth noting that men of Turkic race were mostly attracted by the fact that they did not have to pay a bride-price to the family of their future bride.

[3] Regel (1892; 94-95).

[4] The most comprehensive compilation of evidence as to the Turkic presence in Byzantium one may found in: Balivet (1994; 30-39, 1999; 2002), Necipoğlu (1999-2000).

Oriental routes.[1] The Turkic presence in Matzuka is also attested by toponymics. Beginning with the second half of the thirteenth century the toponymics of Matzouka included a number of place-names such as *Kalkana* (< Tk. *qalqañ*, 'shield'),[2] *Kapanin* (Tk. *qapan* 'mountain, hill',    cf. Pont. Gr. *kapanin* with the same meaning),[3] *Kara* (Tk. *qara* 'black'),[4] *Tzapresin* (probably from Pont. Gr. *tzapros* < Tk. *çarpık* 'crooked'),[5] and a few others which are hard evidence of the presence there of a Turkic population numerous and culturally consolidated enough to change native Greek and Georgian geographic nomenclature.

It is worth mentioning that Matzouka was the most fortified and defended region of the Empire, situated in the mountainous and in arduous terrain. One may suggest that in the limitrophe valleys to the west and east of Matzouka the presence of Turks might well have been even more substantial. Thus, by the first half of the fourteenth century, the south-western continental lowlands between Kerasous and Trebizond (i.e. west of Matzouka) were inhabited by the nomadic tribes of the Çepni, Aq-Quyunlu, Dukharlu and Boz-Doghan Turkmens.[6] A contemporary source asserts that in the mid-fourteenth century some Turkmens near Kerasous, probably the Aq-Quyunlu tribesmen, were the subjects of the Trebizond emperor.[7]

The same picture can be hypothetically reconstructed for the city of Trebizond which seems to have been flooded with the foreign soldiers of *amyrtzantarantai* (from Ar.-Per. *amır-jandar* 'emir of bodyguards'), *chourtziriotai* (from Tk.-Mon. *qurçi* 'bodyguard, archer') and *mourtatoi* regiments which apparently consisted of soldiers and officers of Turkic race. It is not out of the question also that in Trebizond, as in Constantinople, there existed a quarter of Muslim merchants which, as I suggested elsewhere, might well have been identical to the Maydan area in the eastern part of the city.[8]

---

[1] On Turks in the Pontic Byzantine society see Vryonis (1971; 460–461 n58–59), Shukurov (1999) with further bibliographical references.

[2] Uspenskii & Beneshevich (1927), no. 106.341 (late thirteenth century): *stasis tou Kalkana*.

[3] Uspenskii & Beneshevich (1927), no. 129.3 (second half of the fourteenth century): *merous tou Kapaniou*; Uspenskii & Beneshevich (1927), no. 134.5 (1415): *eis to Kapanin*; Uspenskii & Beneshevich (1927), no. 145.6 (fifteenth-sixteenth centuries): *sto Kapaniston*. For the etymology see Zerzelides (1961; 262).

[4] Uspenskii & Beneshevich (1927), no. 106.36 (late thirteenth century): *ek tou Kara*.

[5] Uspenskii & Beneshevich (1927), no. 175. 5 (1449): *to Tzapresin*; etymology see in Symeonidis, 168: *tzapros* < tk. *çarpık* 'verhext, krumm, schief.'

[6] Bryer (1975; 125, 132ff); Bryer-Winfield (1985; 102, 140-1, 173); Zachariadou (1983); Shukurov (2001; 227-50).

[7] Shukurov (1994; 59).

[8] Pseudo-Kodinos (1966; 345-7; Bryer (1975; 140-1); Shukurov (1999; 37).

One may also suggest that by the beginning of the fifteenth century, by the time of Hafiz-i Abru, the Byzantine Pontos might well have been much more Turkicised than the Balkan possessions of the Palaiologoi. The last statement, never having been strictly proved by numerical calculations, is based on the general impression, derived from the recent demographical studies on the Balkan population in which Greek and Slavic elements were predominant.[1] Such evidence, abundant in the primary sources, has been summarised and anthropologically and sociologically conceptualised in the important study of Speros Vryonis 'Manpower in Byzantine and Turkish Societies' in which may be found a detailed description of the typology of the Byzantine patterns of the acculturation of foreigners (Arabs, Turks, Latins, Slavs and so on). According to Vryonis, 'Turkish expansion into formerly Byzantine areas meant not only territorial expansion, but also demographic enrichment. To the degree that the Byzantines became less numerous, the more did they search for manpower outside their domains. Indeed, there were efforts by both principals to attract and utilize manpower which had its origin in the lands of the enemy.'[2]

Vryonis distinguishes two main tools of the incorporation of foreigners into Byzantine society: 1) bestowing to them imperial titles (or one may expand Vryonis's statement – bestowing that or another social status); 2) Christianisation of newcomers.[3] It only seems more reasonable to place Christianisation before the acquisition of social status because, according to Byzantine standards, as Vryonis's study shows, social standing was strictly prefigured by baptism.[4] The final stage of social incorporation of a newly baptized foreigner was marriage to a local woman; the next generation usually was bilingual or Greek-speaking.[5]

The territorial losses, which the Byzantines suffered during the Fourth Crusade and then, after the restoration of the Empire in 1261, inevitably led to the progressing augmentation of the density of Turkic population in Byzantium. Apart from casual Turkic immigration, the Byzantine authorities kept enlisting foreign mercenaries while the land and, respectively, indigenous

---

[1] See for instance Laiou (1975), Laiou-Thomadakis (1977) and especially, Chapter IV 'Names'.

[2] Vryonis (1975; 125). See also three other studies on the integration of foreigners: Laiou (1998) which deals with the cases of Slavs, Jews and Italians, Ivanova (1999) mostly on Slavs, and Bádenas (1998) on Turks.

[3] Vryonis (1975; 129-131); cf.: Bádenas (1998; 185).

[4] Vryonis (1975; 131).

[5] Vryonis (1975; 133-4). Laiou recently brilliantly demonstrated additional juridical and fiscal mechanisms of the accommodation of foreigners (1998).

manpower resources were constantly diminishing. From the thirteenth century onwards, in the words of Vryonis, the Byzantine military forces represented 'agglomerates of foreign mercenaries seeking temporary employment and ethnic enclaves settled in Byzantium. These included Latins, Cumans, Patzinaks, Uzes, Turks, Serbs, Bulgars, Vlachs, Georgians, Alans, and Albanians.'[1]

It is obvious that general insufficiency of local manpower, land and economic resources had to affect negatively the Byzantine assimilatory abilities (both confessional and ethnic), and many newcomers very likely had more opportunities to secure their own faiths and customs. The infiltration of Muslims into Constantinople became critical by the second decade of the fifteenth century just before the fall of the City when, according to the indignant report of the metropolitan of Medeia, the Agarenoi, i.e. Muslims, entered the City every day in flocks and nobody stopped them.[2] In the anthroponomical nomenclature of the Empire of Trebizond the pure Muslim names probably belonging to the unbaptised individuals appeared for the first time as late as by the first decades of the fifteenth century.[3]

To sum up, one may safely suggest that from the thirteenth to the fifteenth century Byzantine lands in general and the Byzantine Pontos in particular were inhabited by a considerable number of outsiders coming from the Muslim regions of Anatolia. It is of primary importance for my purposes to emphasise the fact that those migrants seem to have represented more and more often not so much temporary and incidental assemblies of individuals but a rather homogeneous and compact communities which hardly completely were assimilated with the local socio-religious patterns.

*The Status of Islam and Muslims*

There undoubtedly exists a confessional and ideological aspect of the problem which is connected with the autarkical core of the Byzantine self-identity in general. Canon law treated Muslims (Saracens, Ishmaelites etc.) like all other non-Christians and non-Orthodox heretics. The marriages of the Orthodox

---

[1] Vryonis (1975; 128). The purely mercenary character of the Late Byzantine army has been recently persuasively demonstrated by M. Bartusis (1992).

[2] Syropoulos (1971; 102). The passage has been discussed in more detail in Necipoğlu (1992; 160) and Balivet (1994; 35).

[3] In the year 1432: Amırzada or Amırça, a noble lady, a proprietor Shukurov (1999a; 11 no. 2), in the year 1432 Mahmud, a *paroikos* in the bandon of Rhizaion (Shukurov 1999a; 18 no. 23), in the year 1432: Shah Malik, a big proprietor (Shukurov 1999c; 21 no. 34).

persons with all infidels, including Muslims, were illegal. Orthodox women married to Saracens were to be not allowed to partake of the Christian mysteries. On the other hand, imperial legislation encouraged the local householders to accept newly baptised foreigners as grooms by substantial tax exemption, freeing them from paying *synone* and *kapnikon* for three years.[1]

Thus, generally, one may think that legally Byzantines did not distinguish Muslims (Saracens, Agarenoi, Ishmaelites) from other non-Christians and heretics. However, the matter might well have been more complex. Reinert has recently noted in his study on the Muslim presence in Constantinople[2] a paradoxical aspect of the Byzantine attitude towards Islam. Byzantines traditionally divided the non-Orthodox into three main groups: pagans, heretics, and Jews. However, there is no evidence that any ecclesiastical or imperial authority explicitly formulate the legal status of Islam and Muslims in the lands under the Byzantine jurisdiction. It is true that in canon law, as well as in Byzantine theological literature beginning with the polemical works of John of Damascus, Islam was usually construed as a sort of either heresy or paganism, while, according to imperial legislation, heretics and pagans were subjects to the punitive laws.[3] However, we know nothing of any official religious persecutions against Muslims. So, I incline to agree with Reinert who suggests that Byzantines left the legal status of Muslims 'vague and ambiguous, lest a groundwork for discriminatory or persecutory action be laid'[4]. *De jure* Muslims as a specific social and confessional category of population did not exist at all.

What could have been the consequences of such a puzzling legal status of the Muslims? First of all, we may safely suggest that in Byzantium there never existed Muslim social institutions based on confessional autonomy needed for the reproduction of Islamicity. The minimal social foundation of Islamicity consisted of the three basic types of institutions: *mosques* or the places for collective prayers and sermons; *qadi*s or Islamic judges because Muslims could not be judged by infidels, and *schools* for preservation and reproduction of religious knowledge. In other words, Byzantium lacked the minimal requirements for functioning there of an intact Muslim community and also, for free observation of Sharia Laws by Muslim individuals.

---

[1] Vryonis (1975; 131).

[2] Reinert (1998).

[3] See, for instance, the Ecloga's definition of a heretic, quoted by Reinert: 'a person who deviates, however little, from the Orthodox Faith and [who] is subject to the laws against heretics' (Reinert (1998; 149). Thoughtful remarks on the Byzantine religious tolerance and legal grounds of religious persecutions see: Alexander (1977; 253-9, 262)

[4] Reinert (1998; 149).

In this sense Byzantine attitude towards Muslims strongly contrasted with that towards Jews whose social life was regulated by an ample imperial legislation. The most important result of this legislation was that the Byzantines acknowledged licitness of Judaism: however discriminative this legislation, it allowed the Jewish community to survive and reproduce itself throughout the history of Byzantium.[1]

The existence of mosques and *qadi* court in Constantinople was a notable but, I believe, a unique exception of this general rule.[2] It seems that there existed two mosques in Constantinople. The oldest one was in the Praetorian prison which was constructed as a favour to the Arab general Maslama at the time of his siege of Constantinople (715-717). It was referred to throughout the tenth century by both Byzantine and Muslim authors, and was razed to the ground by the Constantinopolitan mob during a riot in 1200. That mosque was likely intended exclusively for Muslim prisoners of war. A different one presumably appeared sometime in the eleventh or twelfth century and served to the religious needs of the foreign Muslim merchants staying in Constantinople. It functioned apparently with several more or less durable intervals at least up to 1403. Generally, its localisation is uncertain, though for the period between 1189 and 1203 it is safely ascribed to the Muslim quarter of the city in the neighbourhood of the church of St Irene of Perama.[3] Likewise, due to the pressure of the Ottomans, in the late 1390s and then in 1430s, a *qadi* court was introduced in Constantinople just to meet the requirements of Muslim merchants, subjects of the Ottoman state.[4]

The Constantinople mosques of the eighth-twelfth centuries seem to have been the only ones on Byzantine soil. In general, Byzantines permitted the construction and re-construction of mosque or mosques in Constantinople only in the result of political or economical pressure of the Muslim rulers. Moreover, the congregation of Constantinopolitan mosques was consisted exclusively of prisoners, foreign merchants, and, one may suggest, of rare Muslim travellers and vagabonds. The same is true of the Constantinople *qadis*, whose clients were Muslim merchants. So, there can be little doubt that Constantinople mosques and *qadis* were intended not for 'local Byzantine'

---

[1] On Jews in the Byzantine Empire and Byzantine legislation on Jews see: Starr (1939), Parkes (1934), Sharf (1971), Sharf (1995) and more recent and comprehensive study of Laiou (1998; 162, 168-71; 179) on the legal foundations of Byzantine Jewry.

[2] For recent studies on the mosque in Constantinople, with further bibliographical references, see Janin (1964; 257-59); Balivet (1994; 35-6) and Reinert (1998).

[3] Reinert (1998; 128-9, 138-9, 141-2, 144-7).

[4] Necipoğlu (1992; 159-161). A *qadi* court possibly functioned in Constantinople for the first time in 1399-1403 (see Reinert 1998; 145-7).

Muslims but occasional and temporary visitors, subjects of the Islamic states. It is not impossible also that, sometime after 1204, the independent dynasty of the Grand Komnenoi, who deligently followed the traditional Byzantine political patterns, also permitted a mosque or mosques in their possessions which served to the needs of Muslim foreigners.

*Who were Hafiz-i Abru's Crypto-Muslims?*

So, it seems that, as a rule, Muslims, settled in Byzantium, willingly or not had to adopt Christianity. The founders of the renown Byzantine families of Tatikios, Axouchos and many others were converted Turks. *Mixobarbaroi* and *tourkopouloi* of Byzantine army also were Christians by faith. The problem of religious identity of large Turkish groups settled in Byzantine countryside is more complicated. However, due to anthroponymical data from both the Balkan and Pontic regions we know that the overwhelming majority of Turks bore Christian first names and therefore were baptised. Such Turkish Christians were an inevitable by-product of both Turkish conquests and defensive activity by the Byzantines. Voluntary Christianisation might well have been the only way for a Turkish migrant to socialise himself in the Byzantine society. The Qaramanli or Turkish-speaking Christians in Bythinia, Sivas, Kastamon, Niksar, Cappadocia, Alashehir-Philadelphia and other regions of Asia Minor, which, according to Vryonis, have been attested by the sources from 1437, initially partly or entirely might well have been these Christianised Turks.[1]

So, I conclude  that usually the only way for a Muslim migrant to enter Byzantine society and become a rightful subject of *basileus* was through conversion to Christianity. The absence of an alternative, the obvious inflexibility of the legal system with respect to Islam led either to the quick Christianisation of Muslim migrants, or to the formation of religious Christian and Islamic syncretism (which has been brilliantly described by Hasluck), or to an inevitable appearance of newly baptised Christians who continued to confess Islam secretly. Very likely, it was a latter group of neophytic Christian Turks that was implied by Hafiz-i Abru. These are my arguments to support the presence of Crypto-Muslims on Byzantine soil, especially, during the last decades of the history of the Byzantine world, when its general decline undermined its formerly strong assimilatory abilities. If Hafiz-i Abru's testimony, with which I opened my discussion, did not exist it would be necessary to invent it.

---

[1] Dawkins (1933), Vryonis (1971 ; 458–459).

REFERENCES

*Unpublished*
Hafiz Abru, *Geography*, St Petersburg National Library of Russia, Dorn 290.
Hafiz Abru, *Geography*, MS Elliott 357, Bodleian Library.
Hafiz Abru, *Geography*, British Library, Or. 1577.
Hafiz Abru, *Geography*, British Library, Or. 9316.

*Published*
Aboulféda 1840 *Géographie d'Aboulféda*, Paris; Reinaud.
Aksarayi, K. 1944 *Müsameret ül-ahbar. Moğollar zamanında Türkiye Selçukluları tarihi, mukaddime ve hasiyelerle tashih ve nesreden*, Ankara; Turan.
Alexander, P.J. 1977 'Religious Persecution and Resistance in the Byzantine Empire of Eighth and Ninth Centuries: Methods and Justifications,' in *Speculum*, **52/2**; 238-64.
Alexandrescu-Dersca, M. 1942 *La campagne de Timur en Anatolie (1402)*, Buchurest; Monitorul Oficial si Imprimeriile Statului, Imperimeria Nationala.
Bádenas P. 1998 'L'integration des Turcs dans la société byzantine (XIe–XIIe siècles). Échecs d'un processus de coexistence,' in *He Byzantine Mikra Asia (6os-12os ai.)*, ed. Lampakis, S., Athens, The National Hellenic Research Foundation, 179-188.
Balivet, M. 1994 *Romanie byzantine et pays de Rûm turc: Histoire d'un espace d'imbrication gréco-turque*, Istanbul; Isis.
Balivet, M. 1999 *Byzantins et Ottomans: Relations, interaction, succession*, Istanbul; Isis.
Balivet, M. 2002 *Les turcs au Moyen-Âge: des Croisades aux Ottomans (XI-XV siècles)*, Istanbul; Isis.
Barthold, V. 1963 *Sochineniia*, Vols. 1-9, Moscow; Nauka.
Barthold, V 1897 'Khafizi-Abru i ego sochineniia' in *Al-Muzaffariya. Sbornik statei uchenikov professora barona Viktora Romanovicha Rozena ko dniu dvadtsatipiatiletiia ego pervoi lektsii*, [=Barthold, 1963-1977 , vol. 8], St Petersburg; Akademia nauk, 1-28.
Bartusis, M. 1989 'The Megala Allagia and the Tzaousios: Aspects of Provincial Military Organization in Late Byzantium,' *Revue des Études byzantines*, **47**; 183-207.
Bartusis, M. 1992 *The Late Byzantine Army: Arms and Society, 1204–1453*, Philadelphia; University of Pennsylvania Press.
Brand, C. 1989 'The Turkish Element in Byzantium, 11th–12th centuries,' in: *Dumbarton Oaks Papers*, **43**; 1-25.

Brion, M. 1963 *Tamerlan*, Paris; A Michel.

Bryer A. 1966 'Shipping in the Empire of Trebizond', in *Mariner's Mirror*, **52**; reprinted in *The Empire of Trebizond and the Pontos*, London; Variorum collected studies series, 3-12.

Bryer A. and Winfield D. 1985 *The Byzantine Monuments and Topography of the Pontos*, two vols, Washington; Dumbarton Oaks.

Cahen, C. 1951 'Seldjoukides de Rûm, byzantins et francs d'après le 'Seljuknameh' anonyme', in *Mélanges Henri Grégoire*, Bruxelles; Institut de philologie et d'histoire orientales et slaves; secrétariat des éditions de l'Institut, **3**; 97– 106.

Canard M. 1964 'Les relations politiques et socials entre Byzance et les Arabes', in *Dumbarton Oaks Papers*, **18**; 35-56.

Canard M. 1973 *Byzance et les Musulmans du Proche Orient*, London; Variorum.

Canard, M. 1949-1950 'Deux épisodes des relations diplomatiques arabo-byzantines au X siècle,' *Bull. d'Et. Or. de l'Inst. fr. de Damas*, **XIII**; 51-69, reprinted in Canard (1973). *Catalogue of the Persian, Turkish, Hundûstânî and Pushtû Manuscripts in the Bodleian Library begun by ... Ed. Sachau... completed... by H. Ethé* 1889 Oxford; Clarendon.

Chalandon, F. 1912 *Les Comnènes. Études sur l'empire byzantin au XI et au XII siècles, vol. 2: Jean II Comnène (1118–1143) et Manuel I Comnène (1143–1180)*, Paris; A. Picard.

Charanis, P. 1972 *Studies on the Demography of the Byzantine Empire*, London;Variorum.

Cheynet, J. 1988 'Théophile, Théophobe et les Perses', in: *He Byzantine Mikra Asia (6os-12os ai.)*, ed. Lampakis, S. Athens; The National Hellenic Research Foundation, 39-50.

Choniates, N. 1975 *Historia*, ed. J. van Dieten, Vols. 1-2, Berlin–New York; Novi Eboraci: de Gruyter.

Constantine Porphyrogenitus 1967 *De administrando imperio*, Greek text edited by G. Moravcsik, English translation by R. Jenkins, rev. ed.,Washington; Dumbarton Oaks.

Curatola, G. 1993 *Eredità dell' Islam: Arte islamica in Italia*, Venice; Cinisello Balsamo, Amilcare Pizzi.

Dagron, G. 1994 'Formes et fonctions du pluralisme linguistique à Byzance (IX-XII siècle)', in *Travaux et Mémoires* **12**; 219-240.

Dawkins, R. 1933 'The Crypto-Christians of Turkey,' *Byzantion*, **8**; 247-75.

Ditten, H. 1993 *Ethnische Ferschiebungen zwischen der Balkanhalbinsel  und Kleinasien von Ende des 6. bis zur zweiten Hälfte des 9. Jahrhunderts*, Berlin; Akademie Verlag.

Dölger, F. 1965 *Regesten der Kaiserurkunden des Oströmischen Reiches von 565-1453*, Bd. 5. München; Beck.

Ettinghausen, R. 1955'An Illuminated Manuscript of Hafiz-i Abru in Istanbul, Part I', in *Kunst des Orients*, **II**, 30-44.

Fallmerayer, J. 1827 *Geschichte des Kaisertums von Trapezunt*, München; A. Weber.

Grube, E. 1962 *Muslim Miniature Paintings*, Venice; N. Pozza.

Hafizi Abru 1970 *Jughrafiya-yi Hafiz Abru: qismat-i rub'-i Khurasan, Harat*, edited by Mayil Harawi, Tehran; Bunyad-i Farhangi Iran.

Hafiz-i Abru 1317/1939 *Dhayl-i jami al-tawarikh-i Rashidi*, edited by Khanbaba Bayani, Tehran; Shirkat-i Tazamuni-i Ilmi.

Harley, J. and Woodward, D. (eds) 1992 *The History of Cartography*, Chicago; University of Chicago Press.

*Histoire des Seldjoukides d'Asie Mineure par un anonyme* 1952 Persian text published by F. Uzluk Ankara,

Hudud-al'Alam 1970 (1937) *The regions of the World, a Persian geography, 372 A.H.-982 A.D.*, translated and explained by the late V. Minorsky, with the preface by V. V. Barthold († 1930) translated from the Russian, second edition, London; Luzac.

Krachkovski, I. 1955-1960 *Izbrannye sochineniia*, 6 Vols. Moscow; Nauka.

Ibn Bibi (Mukhtasar) 1902 *Histoire des Seldjoucides d'Asie Mineure d'après l'abrégé du Seldjoucnameh d'Ibn-Bibi*, texte persan publié ... par M.H. Houtsma, Leiden; Brill.

Ibn Khordadhbeh 1889 *Kitab al-masalik wa'l-mamalik (Liber viarum et regnorum), et excerpta e Kitab al-kharadj, auctore Kodama ibn Dja'far.* quae cum versione Gallica edidit, indicibus et glossario instruxit M. J. de Goeje Lugduni-Batavorum; Brill.

Ibn Khordadhbeh 1986 *Kniga putei i stran*, translated and commentary N. Velikanova, Baku; Elm.

Ivanova, O. 1999 'O putiakh integratsii inoplemennikov v Vizantiiskoi imperii v VII–X vv. (preimuschestvenno na primere slavian),' in *Vizantiia mezhdu Zapadom i Vostokom*, ed. G. Litavrin, St Petersburg; Aleteia, 48-80.

Janssens, E. 1969 *Trébizonde en Colchide* Bruxelles; Presses universitaires de Bruxelles.

Jenkins, R. 1948 'The Flight of Samonas' in *Speculum*, **XXIII** 2; 217-235, (reprinted in *Studies on Byzantine History of the ninth and tenth centuries*, London; Varorium 1970).

Kinnamos, J. 1836 *Ioannis Cinnami epitome rerum ab Ioanne et Alexio Comnenis gestarum*, ed. A. Meineke, Bonnae; Corpus scriptorum historiae Byzantinae: Impensis Ed. Weberi.

Laiou A. 1975 'Peasant Names in Fourteenth-century Macedonia,' *Byzantine and Modern Greek Studies*, **1**; 71–95.

Laiou A. 1998 'Institutional Mechanisms of Integration,' in *Studies on the Internal Diaspora of the Byzantine Empire*, ed. H. Ahrweiler and A. Laiou, Washington, 1998; Dumbarton Oaks Research Library and Collection; 161-181.

Laiou-Thomadakis A. 1977 *Peasant Society in the Late Byzantine Empire. A Social and Demographic Study*, Princeton; Princeton University Press.

Lentz T. and Lowry G. 1989 *Timur and the Princely Vision*, Los Angeles; Los Angeles County Museum of Art

Matschke, K. 1981 *Die Schlacht bei Ankara und das Schiksal von Byzanz*, Weimar, Böhlau.

Metzopskii, F. 1957 *Istoria Timurlanka i ego preemnikov*, Baku, Elm.

Miller W. 1926 *Trebizond. The Last Greek Empire*, London; SPCK.

Moravcsik G. 1983 *Byzantinoturcica*, Bd. 1–2, Leiden; E.J. Brill.

Necipoğlu, N. 1992 'Ottoman Merchants in Constantinople during the First Half of the Fifteenth Century' in *Byzantine and Modern Greek Studies*, **16**; 158-169.

Necipoğlu, N. 1999-2000 'The Coexistence of Turks and Greeks in Medieval Anatolia Eleventh-Twelfth Centuries),' *Harvard Middle Eastern and Islamic Review*, **5**; 58-76.

Oikonomidès N. 1983 'Les Danishmendides, entre Byzance, Bagdad et le sultanat d'Iconium', in *Revue Numismatique*, 6 série, **25**; 189-207.

Parkes J. 1934 *The Conflict of the Church and the Synagogue: A Study in the Origins of Antisemitism*, New York; Atheneum.

Pseudo-Kodinos 1966 *Traité des offices*, introduc., texte et traduc. par J. Verpeaux, Paris; Éditions du Centre national de la recherche scientifique.

Regel, W. 1982 (1892) *Fontes rerum byzantinarum*, Vol. 1 Petrograd, 1892-1917; repr. Leipzig; Zentralantiquariat der DDR.

Reinert S. 1998 'The Muslim Presence in Constantinople, ninth-fifteenth century: Some Preliminary Observations', in *Studies on the Internal Diaspora of the Byzantine Empire*, ed. Ahrweiler, H. and Laiou, A. Washington, 1998; 125-150.

Robinson, B. 1967 *Persian Miniature Paintings from Collections in the British Isles*, London; HMSO.

Sanjian, A. 1969 *Colophons of Armenian Manuscripts (1301–1480). A Source for Middle Eastern History*, Cambridge; Harvard University Press.

Sanuto, M. 1733 *Vitae Ducum Venetorum*, in *Rerum Italicarum scriptores*, ed. Muratori, L. Vol. XXII, Milano; Rist. anastatica.

Savvides, A. 1993 'Late Byzantine and Western Historiographers on Turkish Mercenaries in Greek and Latin Armies: the Turcoples/Tourkopouloi,' in *The Making of Byzantine History. Studies dedicated to D.M. Nicol*, edited by Aldershot; Beaton, R. and Rouché, C., Variorum, 122-136.

Schreiner, P. 1975-1979 *Die byzantinischen Kleinchroniken*, Vols. I-III. Wien; Verl. d. Österr. Akad. d. Wiss.

Sharf, A. 1971 *Byzantine Jewry from Justinian to the Fourth Crusade*, London; Routledge.

Sharf, A. 1995 *Jews and other minorities in Byzantium*, Ramat-Gan; Bar-Ilan University Press.

Shukurov R. 1994 'Between Peace and Hostility: Trebizond and the Pontic Turkish Periphery in the Fourteenth Century', in *Mediterranean Historical Review*, **9/1**; 20-72.

Shukurov R. 1999a 'The Byzantine Turks of the Pontos,' *Mésogeios*, **6**; 7-47.

Shukurov R. 1999b 'Imia i vlast' na vizantiiskom Ponte (Chuzhoe, priniatoe za svoe)', in *Chuzhoe: opyty preodoleniia. Ocherki iz istorii kul'tury Sredizemnomoria*, ed. R. Shukurov, Moscow, Aleteia; 194-234.

Shukurov, R. 2001 *Velikie Komniny i Vostok (1204-1461)* (The Grand Komnenoi and the Orient, (1204-1461), St Petersburg; Aleteia.

*Sobranie vostochnykh rukopisei Akademii nauk Uzbekskoi SSR* 1952-67 ed. A. Semenov et al., Vols. 1-8, Tashkent; Izd-vo Akademii nauk UzSSR.

Starr, J. 1939 *The Jews in the Byzantine Empire. 641-1204*, Athens; Verlag der Byzantinisch-neugriechischen Jahrbücher.

Storey-Bregel, C. 1972 *Persian Literature, A Bio-bibliographical survey*, transl. into Russian and revised, with additions and corrections by Yu. E. Bregel, Vols. 1–3, Moscow; Nauka.

Symeonidis, Ch. 1971-1972 'Lautlehre der türkischen Lehnwörter im neugriechischen Dialekt des Pontos', *Archeion Pontou*, **31**; 17–231.

Syropoulos 1971 *Les 'Mémoires' du Grand Ecclésiarque de l'Église de Constantinople Sylvestre Syropoulos sur le concile de Florence (1438-1439)*, éd. et traduc. par V. Laurent, Paris; Institut Français d'Études Byzantines.

*Tarix-e al-e Saljuq dar Anatoli compiled by Unknown Author*, 1999 ed. N. Jalali, Tehran; Ayene-ye Miras.

Tauer, F. 1963 'Hafizi Abru sur l'historiographie', in: *Mélanges d'orientalisme offerts à Henri Massé*, Téhéran, Impr. de l'université; 10-25.

*Treasures of Islam*, 1985 ed. Falk, T., London; Sotheby's/Philip Wilson Publishers.

Uspenski A. and Beneshevich V. 1927 *Vazelonskie akty. Materialy dlia istorii krestianskogo I monastyrskogo zemlevladenia v Vizantii XIII–XV vv.*, Leningrad; Gosudarstvennaia publichnaia biblioteka.

Vasiliev, A. and Canard, M. 1935-1968 *Byzance et les Arabes*, Vols. 1-3. Corpus bruxellense historiae byzantinae, Bruxelles; Institut de philologie et d'histoire orientales.

Vryonis, S. 1975 'Byzantine and Turkish Societies and Their Sources of Manpower', in *War, Technology and Society in the Middle East*, ed. V. Parry and M. Yapp, London; OUP, appears also in Vryonis, S. *Studies on Byzantium, Seljuks, and Ottomans: Reprinted tudies*, [*Byzantina kai Metabyzantina*, Vol. 2] Malibu, California; 1981, Undena Publications; 125-40.

Vryonis, S. 1971 *The Decline of Medieval Hellenism in Asia Minor and the Process of Islamization from the Eleventh through the Fifteenth Century*, Berkley California; University of California Press.

Zachariadou, E. 1983 'Les janissaires de l'empereur byzantin', *Studia turcologica memoriae Alexii Bombaci dicata. Istituto Universitario Orientale, Seminario di Studi Asiatici*, series minor, XIX, Napoli, reprinted in E. Zachariadou 1985 *Romania and the Turks (c.1300-c.1500)*. London; Variorium.

Zachariadou, E. 1987 'Notes sur la population de l'Asie Mineure turque au XIV siècle', *Byzantinische Forschungen*, **12**; 223-231.

Zerzelides, G. 1961 'Hermeneutika tou toponymikou tes ano Matzoukas', *Archeion Pontou*, **24**; 245-290.

# 24. CHRISTIAN-MUSLIM RELIGIOUS SYMBIOSIS ACCORDING TO F.W. HASLUCK: COMPARING TWO LOCAL CULTS OF SAINT THERAPON

## Galia VALTCHINOVA

Among the numerous correspondences between Christian and Muslim religious life to be found in Hasluck's *Christianity and Islam under the Sultans*, Saint Therapon of Cyprus is an unusual example. His existence has been the object of two opposed interpretations: what other scholars see as a case of incorporation of a Christian saint cult into Islam is, for Hasluck, an ambiguous cult emerging from Islam itself. Yet, the same saint, or a martyr named 'Terapon' and presenting most of the features of the homonymous Cypriote saint, was celebrated in orthodox Christianity in Central Western Bulgaria during most of the Ottoman period (that is, the sixteenth to the late nineteenth century). Initially limited to Sofia (ancient Serdica or Sardica), devotion to this saint has gradually spread over a larger area, and he has come to be considered a local saint in the Znepole region, that is, the contact area of Bulgarian and Serbian populations, and celebrated as neo-martyr and victim of Ottoman persecutions.

The aim of this paper is to compare these local cults of a Christian saint named Therapon, and to discuss the social and cultural phenomena that appear to underlie them. Borrowing from Hasluck's observations on the creation of 'Greek' (Orthodox) neomartyrs, I shall treat the invention of saints, or the local re-invention of saints' cults as part of the politics of resistance in the Balkans under Ottoman rule. In such a way, I explore the relationship between the local/regional setting of Christian-Muslim symbiosis on the one hand, and the process of modernization and the creation of nation-states on the other. The theoretical aim of the paper is therefore to suggest a pattern, a correlation even, between religious symbiosis and tolerance, the changing use of saints' cults, and the nationalising process.

*Religious symbiosis*

'Religious symbiosis' is a popular term in humanities and cultural studies, used by F. W. Hasluck, among others. It is Hasluck's preferred expression to designate the complex and often contradictory reality of religious life in areas marked by centuries-long mixing of religious doctrines, traditions, and spiritualities. It does indeed appear a highly appropriate term to designate the religious co-existence of Christian and Muslim populations under Ottoman rule. A mixing, intertwining, *bricolage* between at least two Great Traditions of religious monotheism,[1] superimposed on a rich background of various polytheisms is the main characteristic of religious symbiosis in this setting. These characteristics make the term 'religious symbiosis' appear closely related to 'religious syncretism' and to a peculiar way of thinking religious life diachronically, or in evolutionary perspective. 'Symbiosis' is however a more neutral term, one that in the literature often appears to suppose or imply ethnographical work and first-hand experience. Accordingly, it appears a more relevant term for the immediately observable contexts of religious mixing that I shall describe here.

Religious symbiosis is partly characterised by the 'transference of sacred places', to which is dedicated most of the first volume of Hasluck's *Christianity and Islam under the Sultans*. Another characteristic of symbiosis is the 'transference' of sacred figures. This is a feature Hasluck has explored with much circumspection and prudence, urging against hasty judgements. Instead of speaking of 'borrowing' or 'assimilation' of saints from one faith into the other, he stressed the (at least relative) autonomy in the development of saints' cults in Christianity and in Islam. In this sense, he appears to give as much attention to the context in which such conflations could be produced as to the appropriation by Islam, or by Christianity of sacred figures of the opposite religion. It is the exchange of saints between these two Great Traditions, and especially the issue of how various logics could bring forth the development of a saint's cult over the centuries, that is the core of my investigation.

---

[1] The term is used in the sense of Redfield (1960).

*Prolegomena: Turabi-Arab-Therapon*

Among the examples of symbiosis of Christian and Muslim saints to be found in *Christianity and Islam*, the example of Saint Therapon near Larnaka in Cyprus is a peculiar one. Hasluck's description runs as follows:

> This is another ambiguous cult, first mentioned by Mariti. At the present day the sanctuary is still frequented by Turks and Greeks. By the former it is known as Turabi *tekke*, by the latter as S. Therapon. Turabi is the name of a wandering dervish from Kastamoni in N. Anatolia, who lived in the times of Mehmed II and was noted for his liberal views as to religions outside Islam. St Therapon is a well-known healer saint and healer in Cyprus where he has several churches; he is not, however, specially connected with Larnaka. As to the origins of a cult of this sort, it is impossible to be dogmatic. From the evidence we have it seems that it began as a secular cult of an 'Arab' *jinn* identified with Turabi ... If I am correct, we have here a cult shared by both religions whose origins were neither Christian nor Moslem, but secular. [I, 87].

'a saintly figure promoted from *jinn* or demon to *dede* or saint' [II, 734].

Let me now see the different approaches used in Hasluck's argument. First, he is careful to distinguish between what he has observed himself (the Muslim saint Turabi and the Christian Therapon venerated on the same spot, respectively in a *tekke* and in the nearby grotto), and a mid-eighteenth century description according to which a single saint 'Arab' has been venerated there by both the Greek and Turkish population. The two realities observed are related as two stages of evolution of the same phenomenon which is a good basis for tracing back the history of the cult. Mariti's evidence is given the same weight as his own observation and Hasluck does not question the production of evidence by an eighteenth century traveller. What matters is the confirmation that a 'saintly figure' has been venerated for centuries, albeit under various names, by both Christians and Muslims. Relying obviously on the sole traveller's testimony, Hasluck posits that 'saint Arab' is, so to say, an earlier stage of a century-long evolution culminating in the two saints venerated in the beginning of the twentieth century. The history of St Arab is considered against a properly Ottoman background, and Hasluck evokes the various meanings of the word 'Arab' that exist in Ottoman ('Turkish') culture, as well as the vast array of representations related to the 'Arab' in Christian cultures.[1] Following this logic, he seeks to explain the name of St Turabi both by reference to earlier Ottoman religious realities (the liberal-minded dervish from the mid-fifteenth century) and through etymology, perhaps based

---

[1] Hasluck (1929: II, 729-734; LVII. § 4 'The 'Arab' in Folklore and Hagiography'). I am not dealing here with his hint on St. Varvaros (II: 734), an issue which requires special treatment.

on Greek which, as he reminds elsewhere, is spoken by local Muslim (Turkish) population.[1] Seemingly Hasluck does not consider a possible interpretation of 'Turabi' as a corruption of the Greek name Therapon.[2] He mentions the existence of St Therapon in quite a general way and excludes a possible 'entry' to the Arab-Turabi issue through a Christian saintly figure.[3]

Hasluck's elegant construction of 'St Arab' and his original view concerning the Turabi/Therapon relationship is a fresh approach in a scholarship still largely dominated by the 'saints-successors of [ancient Greek] gods' theory. Many scholars of modern Greece and of Greek and Byzantine antiquities in the Ottoman empire contemporary to Hasluck stick to this theory as soon as they are faced with examples of Eastern-Orthodox popular devotion, with its resemblances to what was considered to be 'paganism'.[4] In the period when Hasluck reached his *akmè*, the dominating theoretical pattern of research on culture and religion throughout the Mediterranean is well exemplified by Lawson's (1910) *Modern Greek Folklore and Ancient Greek religion*[5] and the evolutionist perspective implicit within it. One does not consider the issue of 'popular', 'low' or unofficial levels: culture and 'religion' in the true sense of the term should only be 'high',[6] the mixture and the creolisation being either blamed as 'bastardised' (language, culture), or presented as a fruit of 'syncretism'.

Thanks to his master trope of *religious symbiosis*, Hasluck is successful in creating a richer and more balanced vision of cultural processes. The two volumes of *Christianity and Islam under the Sultans* make us feel

---

[1] He recalls this 'linguistic symbiosis' [expression mine] in his extensive correspondence with Richard Dawkins published post-humously as *Letters on Religion and Folklore*. Eg. Hasluck (1926: 66), 'As you know, Cypriote Turks talk it [the Greek language] in the villages'.

[2] This interpretation is forwarded in Delehaye's article on the Cypriot saints (Delehaye 1907: 248), concerning an *abba* Tarabô in Egypt. Hasluck knew about the study and even wrote a letter to the distinguished Bollandist in order to make a suggestion concerning the famous Three Hundred Alaman saints of Cyprus discussed there (cf. Hasluck 1926: 66). He does not take side with Delehaye's discussion about relationship of St. Therapon to these saints, nor does he mention the problem in his *opus major*.

[3] Modern Cypriot scholars prefer to approach this issue in precisely this manner: cf. Papagheorghiou A. (1993: 39), with a note on the fate of the *tekke* in question.

[4] Scholars like Hasluck and Dawkins were sensitive toward the suggestion that 'peeling' the ethnographic and folklore data gathered in 'Greece' and 'Turkey' could uncover an almost untouched antiquity layer. Cf. Dawkins (1906), an article which influenced many studies on carnival in both Greek *laografia* and in Bulgarian *etnografia* still in the 1960s and the 1970s.

[5] See especially Lawson (1910, Introduction and pp. 52-57). Lawson's book remained very influential in this respect even after his time. This state of mind points even in more recent studies, like the authoritative Blum & Blum (1965), who turn to *survivals* and the *religious syncretism* paradigm once they attempt to compare between modern Greek popular culture and ancient Greek practices and beliefs.

[6] Cf. Galatariotou (1993: 403-404) on Dawkins's theoretical background, see also Olsen in this work.

his special care in delineating local and historical contexts, his attempts to catch the profile of cultural interactions in their particular spot; in a sense, he foreshadows Geertz's much later concept of thick description. Nevertheless, in the case discussed here, it looks like Hasluck proceeds rather through chronological layers and in a selective way, paying attention to Christian realities within the Turkish-Ottoman layer only as far as they bear witness to religious symbiosis in its various forms. In our case, things could change when this ambiguous saint's cult is viewed from another side. Then, St Therapon 'of Cyprus' appears to be one the most adaptive figures of Greek-Orthodox culture in the island.

In the following pages, I shall try to give a more vivid and detailed picture of Saint Therapon's cult in Cyprus. This picture is compared to other cases of the same saint's cult within the Balkan-Anatolian Ottoman continuum Hasluck has studied, mainly from Central-Western Bulgaria. Finally, I shall try to separate 'symbiosis' — supposed or really attested — which is a core dimension of Hasluck's ambiguous cult, from the fabrication of saints and the manipulation of their cults as symbolic markers in ongoing social and political life.

### St Therapon of/in Cyprus: the legends, the cult

Hasluck's laconic remark that Therapon is 'well known in Cyprus' obliterates significant details which help to catch the very peculiarity of the cult of Saint Therapon in post-Byzantine Cyprus. Indeed, it is well established that the name of Therapon hides several saintly figures, all of which are lauded by dubious hagiographies but fervent devotions. Let me recall them.

Byzantine Menologia and Synaxars distinguish between two saints known under this name: the 'Cypriot' one and the 'Lydian' or 'Sardian' one. Both are commemorated in May, various manuscripts giving the dates of 14, 25, 26 or 27 of that month. The first saint known under this name is Therapon of Cyprus, *hieromartus*. He is said to have been a bishop on his native island who suffered martyrdom at an unknown date, perhaps under

Diocletian et Maximinus (284-305).[1] Putting aside the few extremely vague biographical details (such as the assertion: 'judging from his icons he must have been a monk'), the major part of the texts reproduce his *post mortem* miracles, exclusively related to healing. The true miracle-working power of the saint became manifest after his relics had been removed from the island, when it was besieged by the 'Saracens' or 'Agarenes', upon the saint's own request.[2] Brought to Constantinople, the corpse was put down in the church of Panaghia $\tau$ 'ελαῖα προσονομάζεται where it began to 'emit healing' (ιαματα).[3] The long lists of healing miracles appended to the various manuscripts of the *Vita* depict an universal doctor-saint, an image of *therapeutès* tailored to fit his proper name.

The other Therapon, the Lydian or Sardian [*Sardicensis*] one, is a *hieromartys* supposed to have lived in the third century.[4] According to his *Life and Passion* he was a priest in the cathedral church of Sardes, in the theme[5] τῶν Θρακεσίῶν in Asia Minor, and found his death in the persecutions of Emperor Valerian [250-253]. His martyrdom, depicted in naturalistic details, took place at Satala or Satalia, in 'a day's-walk distance' from Sardes, on the riverside of the Hermos river.[6] A giant oak is said to have miraculously sprung out where the saint's blood spilled over the earth. This tree exists right up to 'our days and time', asserts the anonymous hagiographer, and pieces stripped from its bark continue to provide healing to

---

[1] In *AA SS Maii* VI: 681-692 (under 27 May) he follows the other Therapon but the editors' commentary (col. 681) is revealing about the difficulties in distinguishing between the two. Migne, *PG*, 117, col. 473-475 (under May 25) reproduces the oldest known version, from *Menologion Basilii Porphyrogeniti Imp*, dating back from the end 9th-10th century (cf. Latysev's edition, St-Petersburg, 1910). Cf. le *Synaxarium Ecclesiae Constantinopolitanae* [further *SynEccl.CP*] in *Propylæum ad AA SS* Nov. cols. 709-710 (under May 26), with the editor's selection of other dates for commemorating the saint (May 14, 25 and 27). The Bollandist Fr. Halkin (*BHG* II, 295-296) retains only this Therapon under three dates (May 14, 26 and 27) and lists two kinds of hagiographical writings, *Miracula*, and *Laudatio et Miracula*. For the date of his martyrdom cf. *AA SS, op. cit.*, p. 681F : this conjecture of the early Bollandists is not accepted in *BHG*.

[2] Cf. Migne, *op. cit.*, col. 473 (twn Sarakinwn) and *SynEccl.CP*, col. 710: twn Agarinwn. The mention of an Arab attack or siege of Cyprus makes possible dating the transfer of relics to either 690-691 or to 806 according to Dawkins (1932 II: 56-57); for other possible datings and the period of Arab raids more generally, see Kyrris (1996: 176-202).

[3] *AA SS* op. cit., p. 680 D, p. 681, 682-683 note 5. On the church cf. H. Delehaye in *SynEccl.CP*, col. 710.

[4] Cf. *AA SS Maii* VI, cols. 680-681 (May 25, 26 and 27): 'in regione Thracesiorum' should not be confused with Thracia 'Europa regionem'. Cf. also Migne, *PG* 117, col. 473 (May 25); *SynEccl.CP*, cols. 710-712 (May 26 and 27).

[5] The mention of a theme (θέμα) dates the *Passion* to at earliest the mid-seventh century, when the theme arose as a new organizational unit in Byzantine administrative structure. Cf. Ostrogorsky, G (1973: 72-79) and Kyrris (1996: 177).

[6] The multitude of place names should be noted. On the place of martyrdom, the hagiographer mentions Synaon in Phrygia and Ancyra in Galatia. For the identifications of the places (putting aside Ancyra/ Ankara) see Jirecek (1897: 58), (links the place of martyrdom with mount Simav south of Brussa); Delehaye (1907: 248) and Kyrris (1993: 207) identify Satala/ Satalia with Antalia.

sick and ill people coming from all around (πᾶσαν νόσον καὶ πᾶσαν μαλακίαν ἰώμενον).[1]

Finally, a 'third' Therapon is reported, also from Cyprus. According to this legend, Therapon had distinguished himself as supporter of icons in 'his native northern country' and was miraculously delivered from a martyr's death inflicted upon him by 'infidel' iconoclasts. According to the same tradition he came to Cyprus after many years spent in Palestine, where he had become notorious for operating healing miracles. Once in Cyprus, his pious life and miracle-working made him famous to the point that the local archbishop granted him a bishopric 'near the sea'. Surprised by the 'Saracens' in his church when leading the Mass office, he was killed on the spot.[2] First published in Venice, this version concerning St Therapon of Cyprus was regularly reproduced in the Greek liturgical books, especially in the second half of the 18th and the early 19th century.[3] This print literature had great impact on the Slavonic books all over the Eastern-Orthodox world.[4]

The latter tradition relates St Therapon to the 'Three Hundred Alaman Saints', a puzzling product of local hagiography and/or of history-writing. Indeed, the *Three Hundred* are first mentioned in the Chronicle of Leontios Makhairas.[5] This Greek historian living in Lusignan Cyprus in the first half of the fifteenth century and writing for the Frankish court is famous for mixing Byzantine history-writing traditions with inspiration from Frankish chronicles.[6] The reality of the Three Hundred Alaman Saints of Cyprus has been challenged mainly by Western scholars,[7] and Hasluck is one of them. He shares his opinion with H. Delehaye, arguing that 'the entirely inexplicable 'German saints' [ἐξ ᾿Αλεμανις] of Cyprus were derived from a faulty rendering of᾿Ατταλέος τῆς Καραμανίας'.[8] Hasluck used to invoke the

---

[1] Cf. Migne, *op. cit.* col. 473 and Delehaye's conjecture in *SynEccl.CP*, col. 712, n. 8.

[2] For the legend's details see Sathas (1884: 407-8, 412-417), who accepts as authentic this Alaman saint Therapon.

[3] Kyrris (1993: 206-207). I am greatly indebted to Professor Anthony Bryer who pointed out and made available this article to me.

[4] Sergij Archimandrite 1997 [1901] III: 196.

[5] As far as I know, the most authoritative edition of this Chronicle remains the one by Dawkins (1932, I-II), under the title *Recital of the Sweet land of Cyprus*. Dawkins dedicates an long critical note to the issue of the Three hundred Alaman saints (II: 56-58), without taking side *pro* or *contra* their authenticity.

[6] I have no position on the much discussed issue of the nature of Machairas's *Chronicle* (historical writing in the 'true' Byzantine tradition or chronicle closer to the Frankish tradition and Latin standards), of his 'sources' and 'literary models'. Cf. Dawkins 1932 (II, Commentary), Galatariotou, C. 1993 (with recent literature quoted).

[7] That is, the Bollandists like Delehaye (1907: 248 sqq), Dawkins, R. (1932 II: 57-58). I shall discuss below the most recent analysis of the issue, Kyrris (1993).

[8] Hasluck (1926: 66).

linguistic/etymological argument (here, faulty rendering of Greek words; elsewhere, misinterpretation) when explaining transference of cultural *realia*.[1] This concept could point to a more general idea of 'invention of saints' which, unfortunately, remains implicit.

It should be stressed that the fantastic *Life* of the Alaman St Therapon of Cyprus is far from being the only dubious point of hagiographies relative to 'St Therapon'. All the three traditions quoted above present the signs of 'bastardised' hagiography, almost entirely weaved out of *topoi*, with little or no relevance to history. In fact, doubts about the real existence of any St Therapon already haunted the Bollandists working on the Greek *Vitae*. This critique is brought to its highest level by Father H. Delehaye in a series of works, amongst which his study of Greek-Cypriot hagiography.[2] Returning to the Three Hundred Alaman Saints, C. Kyrris also rejects as pure invention both the Therapon Cypriote and the Alaman St Therapon of Cyprus, retaining the Lydian /Sardian one as the only authentic saint bearing this name. Insisting upon trade contacts and economy, Kyrris's argument follows partly the suggestions of previous critics, including Hasluck's. He is perhaps the only author dealing with the Cypriot saints to underline the importance of socio-political mechanisms in the transference of a saint (for instance, of St Therapon from Asia Minor to Cyprus) and more generally, in the invention of saints (i.e. of the Alaman saints, corresponding to the demand for 'Western' oriented saintly figures by the Lusignan dynasty and to transformations occurring in 'Latin Cyprus'). Kyrris shows that the cult of St Therapon in Cyprus has mixed hagiographical writings from different centuries around which popular beliefs and folklore had flourished, with infinite adaptations to social and political contexts.

Be he Cypriot or Lydian, Saint Therapon remains fundamentally related to healing. Rooted in his very name,[3] the expectation of a healing effect is connected either to his miracle-working relics set in the Panaghia church of Constantinople, or to the miraculous oak tree allegedly sprouting on the spot of the martyr's death. The idea that both hagiographies only seek to

---

[1] The same approach is exemplified in the explanation of St. Arab (*Ch I*, I: 87). On a more general level, the discrepancy between spoken and written language is at stake.
[2] Cf. *AA SS*, op. cit., col. 681, and Delehaye in *SynEccl.CP*, col. 712. Cf. Delehaye (1907: 248: 'à croire que le culte de st. Thérapon aurait passé avec les reliques de Satalia en Chypre et y serait devenu populaire; que sa légende, déjà fort embarrassée dans le principe, se serait transformée en nouvelle version créée sous l'influence de traditions locales? Pareil fait s'est produit fort souvent dans des circonstances analogues. [...] St. Thérapon de Chypre ne serait autre que st. Thérapon de Sardes ou de Satalia, adopté par les Chypriotes'.
[3] The fact is already noted by Lawson (1910: 56).

justify the healing (*thérapeutès*) function of Saint Therapon has numerous adepts; the *Vitae* have already been interpreted in this sense by survivalist theories.[1] Without resorting to such an interpretation it is clear that devotion to St Therapon in the Greek-Orthodox area does refract the very meaning of healing/ healer, accessible to any speaker of Greek. This explains why, despite scholars' critique of the saint's hagiography and real existence, Therapon still enjoys high popularity in Cyprus and elsewhere on the Greek islands.[2] In Cyprus, a multitude of local devotions are attested from late Middle ages up to our days and time. Two local cults of Saint Therapon are signalled already by Machairas, in the villages of Sinda and of Kilani. Dawkins identifies them, respectively, as a 'now Turkish village lying at about 15 miles of Famagusta', and with a Greek (?) village 'about 8 miles [...] south of Troodos'.[3] The place where St Arab/ St Therapon has been worshiped, near Larnaka, is different from both of them, but it is always in the southern portion of the island where his cult is attested through mural paintings in several late medieval village churches.[4] Yet other, more recent examples of local devotions (*panegyria*) to St Therapon are reported in various *Himerologia* of the Cypriot Church.[5] According to evidence from elsewhere in insular Greece, the modern (mainly rural) celebration of the saint is explicitly associated with water and springs.[6] What is of real interest here is how this self-evident healing function changes (or has changed) over time, and to what extent a shift from 'healing' in general to more specific social functions of the cult could be expected. This is a topic which remains almost unresearched.[7]

---

[1] Cf. Lawson (1910: 54, 56). Russian philologist Shestakov D. (1910: 2, 198) based his himself on this text in postulating the 'folkloric origins' of many motives in Greek hagiography. It has also been supposed that in the case of the Lydian St. Therapon, we have a strategy to 'convert' a pagan cult of the tree into a Christian one. The procedure is fundamentally the same as Lawson's or even Dawkins's questioning of the Greek-Orthodox saints as successors of Olympic gods – a formula that has been launched in roughly the same time by French folklorist P. Saintyves (*Saints-successeurs des dieux: essai de mythologie chrétienne*. Paris, 1907).

[2] St. Therapon 'the Cypriot' is venerated on many Greek islands, especially on the Dodekannese: for this information I rely upon personal communications by Dr. E. Karpodini-Dimitriadi, Panteion University-Athens.

[3] Dawkins (1932, I, §32, p. 30; commentary II, p. 58, 61).

[4] P. ex. in the church of *St. Mamas* (end fifteenth century) at Louvaras, southward of Troodos mountains, in the *Panagia Katholiki* at Kouklia, near the ruins of Old Paphos, and in the cave hermitage of St. Sozomenus, in the area of Nikosia. Cf. Stylianou & Stylianou (1997: 254, 395, 511-12).

[5] See for instance Hmerologion Kuprou 1990, p. 124 (May 14), p. 129 (May 27), 174-175 (October 14), p. 181 (October 30). Cf. Delehaye (1907: 247) on St. Therapon still celebrated on October 14 at Angastina.

[6] On Keos island, he is venerated for curing eyes (data from Dr. E. Karpodini-Dimitriadi). Perhaps best attested is the devotion to St. Therapon on Lesvos island: see Schmidt (1871:81); Margari (1993).

[7] With the exception of Margari's (1993: 31, 32) brief study which hints at the relationship of the saint's celebration in Mitilini and the Greek national liberation struggle.

The many places in which St Therapon has been, or is, venerated as a local saint suggests a dynamic of devotional life which facilitates the implantation of a particular cult. Saints can move from place to place and are appropriated in local settings without the spread of their cults being necessarily bound to some *sacra* (their relics, a grave). On the contrary, the cult seems to have survived and to have been transmitted mainly through oral tradition. On this point, the hagiography of both the Cypriot and the Lydian Therapon are in accordance: the memory of the saint has survived for some centuries without written record till the time they have been captured in a *Life*, by word of mouth (ἐξ ἀγραφους παραδοσέως παρὰ τῶν προγενεστέρων) or even via images (...δηλοῦσιν αἱ εἰκόνες αὐτοῦ, ἐπὶ τοιχότης ἰδέας καὶ σχήματος αὐτον ἀναγράφουσαι).[1] The passages quoted are highly suggestive with regard to the intertwining of oral tradition, visual techniques and literary records which remains so characteristic of the Eastern-Orthodox religious cultures.[2] All this confirms the general impression of a cult extremely adaptive to local settings and to popular needs, and urges me to raise the question of how a saint's cult works not only through time, but within society.

### Tracking down the 'Bulgarian' Saint Therapon

Many of the questions raised in the case of St Therapon/St Arab observed by Hasluck in Cyprus surface, this time as background *data*, in the cult of St Therapon in Bulgaria. A martyr named 'Terapon' and presenting most features of the homonymous Cypriote saint was celebrated in Central Western Bulgaria throughout most of the Ottoman period. Initially bound to Sofia, ancient Serdica or Sardica — the Bulgarian capital today — the saintly figure gradually evolved to be considered a local saint and a neo-martyr from recent times, perhaps as a victim of Ottoman persecutions. This example of the saint's cult found on the opposite border of the Balkan-Anatolian Ottoman continuum that Hasluck has studied provides an interesting parallel to our case and a starting point for analysing the social and cultural processes, broadly speaking, involved in devotion to a Christian saint.

---

[1] For St. Therapon *hieromartus* of Cyprus see the *Menologium of the Emperor Basil* (Migne, *PG* 117, col. 473); *SynEccl.CP*, col. 710; cf. the commentary *ad loc.* in *AA SS*, Maii VI, p. 682. Note the special role of the image as 'carrier' of popular representations about a saint.

[2] For a modern interpretation of convergence between the oral and the written in the production of an Orthodox saint, see Dagron (1984: 160-163).

Worship of St Therapon in Sofia is attested still at the turn of the nineteenth century, when ethnographer (and former *komitadji* in the Macedonian struggle) E. Sprostranov conducted inquiries in the old churches of Sofia. He reported that in the church *St Paraskevi-[Petka]-the-Older*, in the centre of Sofia, people still used to venerate 'Saint Taraponti's oak'. According to information provided to him by some elderly churchgoers, the saint had been still more venerated several decades ago, in Ottoman times, by both Christians and Muslims, for 'curing mad people'.[1] Urged on by this intriguing remark, the father of Bulgarian ethnography and Orthodox priest D. Marinov visited the church in the first decade of the twentienth century, only to confirm the decline of the devotion. Nevertheless worship was still popular among 'peasants of the villages surrounding Sofia' who used to spend the night before his commemoration day, laying down in the church and trying to find a place to sleep near the truncated 'Taraponti's oak'.[2] Partly built into the northern wall which was supposed to date back from the sixteenth century, the latter trunk deserved the special attention of the ethnographer as a proof for pre-existing 'pagan' devotion to a 'sacred tree'. Nevertheless, the saint's reputation as healer of madness had already faded — a process perhaps prompted by the exodus of Muslim population during and after the Liberation war (1877-78).

Once the saint has been separated from its devotional centre, the *St Paraskevi-the-Older* church, and from the tree, its healing characteristic declined or disappeared. Already in the interwar period the oddly sounding saint's name had been chosen for a comic character in a series of short stories published in the most renowned Bulgarian humoristic journal. For most of the old Sofia population the saint became a synonym for corrupted priest and joyous drunkard as early as the 1930s.[3] Some devotional practice seem to have been preserved longer among people from the countryside. By the mid twentieth century, peasants of the village of Kâtina (now a suburb of Sofia) still venerated a votive stele dedicated to 'Saint Taraponti' who was considered as patron saint of one of the largest local families.[4] Taken as a whole

---

[1] Cf. Sprostranov 1907/1907: 3, 7-8, 12; the study of the church and the interviews date back from 1896-1899.

[2] Cf. Marinov (1982 [1914] : 351, 514).

[3] Cf. the inventory of data relative to the negative and pejorative image of the saint in the interwar period in Valtchinova (1999: 121 sq).

[4] Data from field work conducted by the author in 1999 and 2000. The veneration of family or lineage patron saints is a ritual practice related to the large family or *zadruga* (cf. Rhewbottom. 1974). On the cultural and geographical limits of the *zadruga* family in the Balkans cf. Todorova (1993).

however, active devotion to St Therapon in Sofia seems to have been limited to the church in question, and to have vanished shortly after the Liberation.

Another local devotion to 'Saint Therapon ' is recorded in the western most part of the old *sandjak* of Sofia, in the little town of Iznebol (now Trun). The most succulent and detailed description is provided by Czech historian Constantin Jirecek who visited the area a few months after its inclusion in the Principality of Bulgaria.[1] He was surprised to find people who told him in 1879, pointing at the rocky bank side of the local river, that 'Saint *Taraponti* lived there' and had suffered martyrdom on this spot, his blood causing a hole to form where it touched the earth. On the opposite bank side he could see the grotto where, according to the locals, 'Saint Petka (Paraskevi) dwelt'.[2] Was this a 'living memory' of ancestral beliefs rooted in the immemorial past, or the recent product of Orthodox activists? In a vast analytical excursus inserted in his travelogue, the Czech historian has opted for the second possibility, drawing on all the written data he was able to gather.[3] Oral data pointed in the same direction: if the name of the local river was Erma — a transparent allusion to Hermos from the *Life* of Therapon the Lydian, it was still unknown beneath the outskirts of the town where the 'Saint Taraponti' legend could be heard. However, by the time Jirecek has visited Trun, the cult of St *Taraponti* is attested for about two centuries in the town and throughout the Iznebol/Znepole area. Around the mid eighteenth century, the saint's name and commemoration day is popular enough to date a private event in the life of a local monk.[4] A manuscript collection of prayers and liturgical pieces produced in one of the local monasteries little before the middle of the eighteenth century gives the curious phrasing: 'to Saint Therapon [*Tarapontie*], *laudae znepolensia*'. His name has been inserted in the *invocatio* of a prayer which is normally addressed to a family or lineage patron saint.[5] This formula can be therefore be interpreted as derived from the saint's local identification, the logical end of the process of his appropriation.

---

[1] Inspired by his scientific interest in the Balkans, C. Jirecek became implicated in politics and became one of the 'builders of modern Bulgaria' as Minister of Public Instruction (1881-1882). Between 1879 and 1882, he realised several 'tours' throughout the Principality of Bulgaria and Eastern Rumelia. The observations gathered during these travels, published in his *Travels in Bulgaria* (1899) and still later in his *Memoirs* [*Dnevnici*], provide both abundant first-hand information for political, cultural and everyday life in Bulgaria, and analyses on historical issues.

[2] Jirecek 1899: 507 [1974: 560].

[3] Jirecek (1974: 559-60), also Jirecek (1897: 54-60), though the author does not use the word 'invention' or similar terms to characterise the nature of this fabulous hagiography.

[4] In a *marginalium* of an Evangel, Ms. n. 52, Sofia National Library, fol. 215, from 1759.

[5] Ms. n. 642 (132), Sofia National Library, fol. 18. Such prayers are attested mainly in celebrations like the aforementioned *slava*; in Znepole region, the holiday and the ritual itself is called 'saint' [*svetec*].

Given the necessity of some 'technical' time for the rooting of a cult, it is not unwise to date it back to early eighteenth or perhaps the late seventeenth century. Documents from the first half of the nineteenth century corroborate the importance of the saint's cult for the affirmation of a new-born regional identity.

Starting from this quite heterogeneous evidence, one could be tempted to adopt the stance of the 'pagan' background of the cult or the one of 'religious symbiosis' cherished by Hasluck, as indeed did the Bulgarian ethnographers quoted above. If one of them interprets the veneration of 'St Taraponti's log' at the Saint-Petka-the-Old church as evidence for pre-Christian religious practices, the other insists on the fact that 'Taraponti's oak' and the nearby *aghiasma* [source of holy water] have been frequented by both Christians and Muslims.[1] Notwithstanding the impression of versimilitude however, these devotions to St Therapon are examples of an invented tradition. To my mind, we have to deal with local 'Bulgarian' appropriation of the 'Greek' (or 'Cypriote') St Therapon, based on a concrete literary background. With time, the written support of popular legends has faded but legendary narratives have nurtured beliefs and ritual practices which have concatenated to form a seemingly coherent body of data to give the saintly figure consistency, and to project it onto the landscape and in the social life of local people. This process falls entirely within the limits, and the realm, of Eastern-Orthodox religiosity in the specific Ottoman context.

In the rest of this section and that following, I shall bring evidence as to my contention that this invention proceeds from adaptations of literary *Lives* to the then current social and religious life 'under the Sultans'. It is astonishing to follow the rising of a distinct Slavonic (and subsequently Bulgarian) hagiography of St Therapon. The evidence points to a late inclusion of this saint in South-Slavic hagiography, largely attributable to the Greek [Byzantine] one. There are very few Slavonic hagiographical pieces related to 'Saint Therapon ' prior to the Ottoman period.[2] It is not before the mid-sixteenth century that St Therapon appears in Bulgarian hagiography, and then in quite an impressive way. His name opens the list of 'local' martyrs inserted in the *Life of St Nicholas the New of Sofia* (henceforth LNNS).

---

[1] Cf., respectively, Marinov ([1914]: 43), and Sprostranov (1907: 3).

[2] Cf. Jirecek (1897: 55-56), (Ms. N. 54 from the Royal Library of Belgrade, a Synaxar from 1330 lost today): St Therapon 'presbyter of Sardi's church'. Cf. *Catalogue of Cyrillic Manuscripts of the Belgrade Library [Opis Chirilskih rukopisa]*, Belgrade, 1986, t. II, 1, p. 195 (ms. 94): *Life* of St Therapon 'bishop of Sardi', first quarter of the fourteenth century, and another 'hieromartys Therapon'.

Known through only one contemporary manuscript copy,[1] this *Life* is one of the two sixteenth century masterpieces of an original martyrology which flourished in Central-Western Bulgaria. A glimpse at the place and the circumstances surrounding the birth of this néomartyr helps to understand a little better the social context of this new hagiography.

The *Life* is produced to honour the memory of an Orthodox néomartyr of mixed ethnic origins who had suffered death in Sofia. In the sixteenth century Sofia is a large city, the centre of a *sandjak* which had to a play key role in the Ottoman grasp on the central parts of the Balkan peninsula. A transport and commercial crossroads, the city was also impressive in terms the variety of *millets* represented there: besides its Orthodox inhabitants and a considerable Muslim population, there were Catholics (organised around the community of Dubrovnik merchants), Armenians, and some Jews.[2] To judge from the multitude of church buildings, the importance of the metropolis and from its literary activity, Orthodoxy flourished in sixteenth century Sofia.[3] The same holds true for Islam: between the 1540s-1560s, Sofia is the home place of Balı Efendi, one of the most intransigent Suffi religious leaders of his time, who distinguished himself in battles against Muslim 'heretics'.[4] Fervent activists on both sides brought about increasing tensions between communities, and this holds true not only for Christians and Muslims. Besides Nicolas' martyrdom known only through Christian sources, the *sicils* report the case of a forced conversion of a Jew to Islam.[5]

Viewed in this context, the *Life* could be expected to go beyond simply recycling the old and well-known hagiographical clichés, and to take on more militant overtones. Effectively, the hagiographer Matthew the Grammarian — a Sofiote learned man and high-ranked member of the local clergy, adopts such a militant stance. He exhibits a strong sense of local identity, producing a special 'Praise to the illustrious city of Sofia' appended to the *Life* properly

---

[1] The copy is written in 1564 by Lazar of Kratovo. Located in the Sofiote church from where the cult radiated, this manuscript was found in 1899 by a Russian philologist, Polikhronij Syrku, who also edited it (cf. Syrku 1901; the *Vita* is reproduced in the second part, pp. I-CCLXXII).

[2] On Sofia in the 16th century v. Dinekov (1940) and Gradeva. [ms] with recent literature.

[3] By this time Sofia is encircled with Bulgarian-Christian villages whose population had various special statuses granted by the Ottoman administration. Most of these villages had monasteries or constructed impressive parish churches (cf. Kiel 1985: 57-85, 346-348), so that the Sofia area came to be considered as 'the little Mount Athos'. Bulgarian literary and art historians speak of 'Sofia literary and iconographical 'schools': cf. Dinekov (1940); Gradeva [ms].

[4] On Sofialı Bali Efendi see Clayer (1994: 65-80).

[5] Cf. Gradeva (1996).

speaking.[1] The city is proclaimed 'illustrious for its Christian antiquities' as well as for its saints, and this is precisely in order to support the latter claim that the hagiographer reproduces a list of 'glorious martyrs' who had purportedly suffered martyrdom in Sofia. St Nicolas is represented as 'crowning' the glorious deeds of a chain of martyrs which begins with Saint Therapon . Presented as a 'priest of the Holy *Sardakian* church', [2] the latter is said to have been a 'dweller of this place' and 'persecuted by criminals', to have been beheaded on a spot located at 'a day's-walk distance' outside Sofia. Not surprisingly, an enormous oak sprang up on the place his blood had spilled over: 'one can still see the giant tree' which 'provides cure and healing to all those who come led by their faith'.

The second major step in the Bulgarian appropriation of St Therapon is made two centuries later, in a still more programmatic piece of writing: the *Slav-Bulgarian history* [*SBH*] of the monk Paisij of Hilandar (1762). Once again, the saint is given place in the row of the illustrious neo-martyrs of Sofia: St George the New and St Nicholas the New. Although, he is now presented as 'a native from Trun' and as a priest in his native town. Significantly, this time he is said to have suffered martyrdom from 'Turks': seized while officiating in his church he has been brought to Sofia, within 'a day's-walk distance of his home'. By the time of Paisij, Trun long a centre of an Ottoman *kaza* is dependant upon the new sandjak centre of Nis, and upon the Nis bishopric. This affiliation is a recent one: several decades before, Trun was still listed in the Sofia Orthodox diocese.[3] My suggestion is that *SBH* echoed the religious-hierarchical dependency on Sofia It should be noted that this is not a mere 'echo': Paisij seems to give a 'native', local version of things, thus inverting the places of centre and periphery in the picture of an area which has long been culturally dominated by Sofia.

---

[1] The data on Matthew the Grammarian are summarised in Gradeva [ms]. We know from other sources that this erudite churchman had acquaintances within the so-called Kratovo circle (in the north-eastern part of today's Fyrom) and entertained personal ties with the copyist Lazar.

[2] Manifestly the rendering *Sardica* allows to associated *Sardae* with the ancient name of Sofia. For the two forms of the latter, Serdica/Sardica, and the marked events from early Christian history related to Sofia, see Barnard (1983).

[3] See Kiel (1985: 292-293) for the data and for a more general presentation of the discussion about possible affiliation of the *metropolis* (*mitropolija*) of Sofia to the Pec archbishopric by the end of 16th century. The issue is extensively discussed in Valtchinova (1999).

## The fabrication of a saint

This material from the central Balkan region allowed me to realise better the impact of the socio-political context on a seemingly 'purely religious' feature. In the following pages I shall explore different theoretical frameworks which may work to explain the cases of St Therapon's cult on both sides of the Eastern-Orthodox continuum in the Ottoman empire. First, the concept of 'invention of tradition', in the well known phrase by Hobsbawm and Ranger. It is now, I hope, beyond doubt that St Therapont has been reinvented to 'fit' either Sofia or the Trun/Znepole local setting. The invention of saints is largely attested throughout Christianity, for both medieval and modern times. It is best studied for the Catholic area of the Christian world: let me recall just R. Hertz's pioneer study[1] of the cult of St Besse in an Alpine valley, or Jean-Claude Schmitt's impressive book on the 'holy hound' Guignefort.[2] These works and the whole anthropological and sociological literature relative to the Christian saints' issue, has already piled up focus on another cardinal point: cults of saints raise and decline as a result of complex social interactions, appearing as a 'sociological test' for a human group.[3] There is no 'invention' or 'manipulation' of a saint's devotion (or even 'symbiosis') without some social need, broadly speaking. Third, many saints' cults do reflect the need for strengthen a collective or group identity, the sacred figure being invoked or venerated to obtain protection and power both in everyday life and on a symbolic level. Viewed in this perspective, any particular saint's cult appears as a product of complex interaction between legacy of the past and today's demand, between oral tradition and literacy.[4]

A return to the 'Bulgarian' St Therapon helps to illustrate this general assumption. The first 'invention of tradition' took place in Sofia around the middle of the sixteenth century, in the context of intensified confessional tensions in the otherwise tolerant Ottoman empire. The Christian-Orthodox response is high profile, resulting in the glorification of martyrdoms of local young men. Both of them are of mixed ethnic background. St George the New is a native of Kratovo while St Nicolas the New is from Ioannina, a sign of Christian solidarity.[5] Saint Nicholas the New's death as a martyr marks the

---

[1] Hertz (1983 [1912]).

[2] Schmitt (1979).

[3] Cf. de Certeau, M. (1974: 208). The guiding opus in this perspective is Brown (1981). For the Byzantine realm, these principles are outlined in Galatariotou (1991).

[4] This point is especially stressed by Hertz (1983 [1912]) and Schmitt (1979); also Brown (1981). For the term 'fabrication' [of a saint] see Schmitt J.-Cl. (1984) and Charuty (1995).

[5] St. George the New of Kratovo, or 'the Sofiote', suffered martyrdom in 1515. For the spread of both cults in 'Bulgaria' and 'Serbia' see Syrku (1901: 7-252).

true peak in the efforts deployed by local Orthodox elite towards production of neomartyrs.[1] The adaptation of the already approximate figure of 'Saint Therapon ' which mixes characters of the 'Lydian' and the 'Cypriote' is well in line with the production of martyrs. It reinforces the message carried out by the respective *Lives*. Once 'put into place', St Therapon comes to life, so to say, for a second time, and the material features of his 'presence' appear to support his devotion. With time, these 'natural' features have been integrated in a religious landscape associated with healing practices, thus becoming meaningful for both Orthodox and Muslims. Finally, it came to be seen as traces of pre-Christian times and vanished, once the modernising process started in the new Bulgarian capital city.

The case of St *Taraponti* of Trun is still more exciting. The cult should be brought in the periphery of the *sandjak* of Sofia in company of other saints, like St Nicolas the New or St Petka/Paraskevi, and at least in the beginning its implantation was dependant on these major saints.[2] Subsequently it developed to become quite an autonomous cult, taking on at least two specific social functions: supporting local identity and allowing the recognition of common identification within larger kin groups. This is precisely on this level of its evolution that the cult has been recaptured by the monk Paisij, to undergo further transformations. The monk-historian carries out further the task of the sixteenth century hagiographer: instead of putting Therapon as predecessor of the two most known Orthodox neo-martyrs in the 'Bulgarian lands', he transforms him as neo-martyr who had suffered himself death from local 'Infidels' [i. e. 'Turks']. The temporal chain is thus inverted and the invented 'martyr from Sofia' is taken out of the legend, only to be inserted in both local and 'national' history. This manipulation is quite understandable if we remember Paisij's heathen patriotic discourse and his struggle for 'raising the national consciousness.'[3] The case offered by St Therapon, already manipulated to fit the local realities elsewhere in 'Bulgaria' for anti-Ottoman struggle can thus hardly be overlooked. This is one of the most interesting achievements of rising nationalism promoted by Orthodox

---

[1] Delehaye (1922) and Hasluck himself (II, 452-59) show that the production of 'neo-Greek martyrs' results from the careful strategy of the Orthodox church under the Sultans.

[2] This assumption is based on the vision defended, among others, by Geary (1988), according to which the cults of saints could be seen as a peculiar form of accumulation and exchange of cultural capital (in the sense of Bourdieu 1980: 191-207). I have discussed extensively this issue elsewhere (Valtchinova 1999: 63-80).

[3] From late 19th century onward (and till today), this is the standard expression to designate Paisij's impact on further history-writing and on the concept of national history. The insistence on 'conscience' and 'memory' reflects the monk's famous phrase 'Don't forget your conscience and your faith' uttered in the Introduction to his *Slav-Bulgarian History*, as well as his complaint about Bulgarians' 'lack of memory' of the heroic deeds of their glorious ancestors.

itinerant monks in order to strengthen, or even to fuel process of maturing of 'the national' collective memory.[1] The case confirms that Orthodox clergy acted exactly in the same way as later lay elites in constructing 'national conscience' through invented traditions.

Once publicised as local devotion typical for Znepole, St Therapon /*Taraponti* underwent other transformations. Around the mid-nineteenth century, the cult was used as a kind of symbolic weapon by local activists struggling for the 'nationalization' of the Bulgarian church.[2] The curious trajectory of St Terapon's cult in Trun ended up with the inscription of the saint's life (*Life*) and 'deeds' in the local landscape which, on its turn, triggered popular beliefs and the folk legends. This local appropriation and, in a sense, the saint's 'naturalisation' is the last step in the evolution of his local devotion. It is fixed by C. Jirecek. Perhaps Jirecek's writings fuelled an ultimate wave of devotional fervour: this is precisely drawing on his narrative that local patriots did revitalize the cult, in the first decades of the 20th century. This revitalisation has much to do with concerns with local identity in a border area and with progressive political and cultural marginalisation of the region following its division after the First World War. But this is another story.[3]

Before concluding, let me ask a practical question: what, besides coincidence of name, do all these developments of a Greek saint's cult on the Slavonic periphery of the Orthodox world posses that might be relevant to the 'Turabi/Arab' issue that F. Hasluck has dealt with? The confrontation of the different patterns of evolution of the same Christian saint's cult creates a kind of primary field of study, an internal space of reference which could help understanding the general logic of this evolution better than conjectures about 'pagan origins' or Islamic influences. Just two points to make clear what I have in mind. In explaining the transformations undergone by St Therapon on 'Bulgarian' soil, the general stance adopted by native scholars is to seek 'errors' and 'mixing up' of names and places in the course of manuscript reproduction of saints' *lives*. Indeed homophony, onomastics or even low level of literacy can explain *some* developments in hagiographical tradition

---

[1] As in Serbia, in Ottoman Bulgaria monks and parish priests acted as myth-makers, adapting saints' *Lives* and Passions to both the local setting and the political context. In this respect cf. the general point made by Rogel (1977).
[2] For the Bulgarian church issue see the concise presentation in Crampton (1997: 66-76). It is precisely in the 1860s that the region of Trun became involved in the struggle. For data and the various interpretations see Valtchinova (1999: 83-90, 104 sq).
[3] A somewhat similar effect is outlined for the cult of St. Besse/Bessu by MacClancy & Parkin (1997).

during the Ottoman period. They can account for segments of the symbolic transformation — but they cannot explain the entire process of change-adaptation undergone by number of saint's cults in this period. As J.-C. Schmitt put it, the 'origin' matters little in terms of place or chronology: the essential is to understand in what historical conditions the cult has been constituted and sprang up. In the case of St Guignefort, the cult 'starts ... with a deep transformation of countryside all over Western Europe, a [social] change projected onto the landscape and the settlements [...], and reflects a new spatial correlation between the *seigneurs* and the village communities'.[1] In our case, it seems that social-economic transformations similar in length have been accompanied with change in kinship structures[2] and group solidarities which came to be expressed on a symbolic level. The *millet* system has also prompted the sense of a new kind of 'unity in the diversity', namely of religious unity countering the ethnic diversity of the Christian-orthodox population, at least in the first centuries of Ottoman domination. This unity could be fostered by new flows of economic exchange, and it resulted in the emergence of new 'regions' cutting across the former political borders. If so, we face a 'regional cult' of the kind outlined by R. Werbner.[3] Another mechanism of circulation-transformation of a saint's cult is outlined again by Schmitt, who speaks of 'distinct and largely autonomous cultural networks along which the information has been circulated. These networks are regional and may depend on [...] bishoprics. [...] Even minor change operated in the centre could have strong resonance once getting into wider circuit, especially on the periphery, as far as [the cult] absorbs oral traditions and folklore themes'.[4] The pattern delineated in the case of saint Guignefort fits perfectly the case of St Therapon re-invented in sixteenth century Sofia and his cult which, absorbing local traditions, had to undergo further adaptation in an peripheral area of the metropolis. All these observations might be also relevant for St Therapon's cult in Cyprus; this is a study which remains to be done.

Is it possible to reconcile Hasluck's 'ambiguous cult' with the 'invented tradition' and the 'fabrication of saints' approach? In general, the question is about complexity of devotional life — and the intricacies of

---

[1] Cf. Schmitt (1979 227-229).

[2] Cf. Todorova (1993: 133-158, chapter VI) for an extensive argumentation of the 'birth' of *zadruga* in the Ottoman period.

[3] 'In regional cults such flows [of goods, services, information and people through a network of centres] run across major political or ethnic boundaries. Hence the characteristic direction of the flows, along with the cult's distinctive topography, is of specific interest' – Werbner (1977: XI).

[4] Schmitt (1979: 171).

devotional logic, in a place where peoples and cultures had by the time Hasluck has observed the fruits of this long interaction mixed for more than ten centuries. Our comparison is suggestive about the ways it can be done, and namely emphasises the need not to underestimate the capacity of Christian cults of saints to adapt themselves to the infinite variety of local contexts and yet more, to adapt to social demand and to political circumstances, as indeed Hasluck later himself came to stress in his (posthumously published) first section to *Christianity and Islam*. Cults of saints can be powerful tools in fostering symbiosis in some circumstances; in others, on the contrary, they might foster distance and division. The same cult can bear one message in the context of Ottoman rule, quite another one in period of national awakening and still other in modern times when Christian saints are instrumentalised for the purposes of collective identity, of political or ethnic struggle. No matter whether the saint is 'real' or an 'invented': this is his cult that matters, and religious cult is always invented tradition in the sense of Hobsbawm and Ranger. Once the saint's cult enters public circulation, it follows the logic of religious life in its intricacies with social demand, politics, and culture, rather than conforming to claims about 'purity of faith' and authenticity of scriptural tradition. The same holds true for religious symbiosis: depending on historical circumstances and on sociocultural context, such symbiosis might be either a powerful cultural orientation triggered from 'below', or indeed a rhetorical device promoted from 'above'.

*REFERENCES*

Barnard, L. 1983 *The Council of Serdica 343 A.D.* Leeds; Leeds University Department of Theology and Religious Studies, Sofia; Synodal Publishing House.

Blum, R. and E. 1965 *Health and healing in rural Greece*, Stanford; Stanford University Press.

Bourdieu, P. 1980 *Le sens pratique*, Paris; Minuit.

Brown, P. 1981 *The Cult of the Saints: Its Rise and Function in Latin Christianity* Chicago, The University of Chicago Press.

Clayer, N. 1994 *Mystiques, etat et société: Les Halvetis dans l'aire balkanique de la fin du 15ᵉ s. à nos jours*, Leiden; Brill.

Certeau, M. de. 1974 'Hagiographie', in *Encyclopædia Universalis*, vol. 8 (7è publ.), 207-209.

Charuty, G. 1995 'Logiques sociales, savoirs techniques, logiques rituelles', *Terrain* 24 (n° spécial 'La fabrication des saints'), 5-14.

Christian, W. Jr. 1981 *Local Religion in Sixteenth-Century Spain*, Princeton; Princeton University Press.

Crampton, R. 1997 *A Concise History of Bulgaria*. Cambridge; Cambridge University Press.

Dagron, G. 1984 'Frontières et marges: le jeu du sacré à Byzance', in *Corps écrits 2*. Paris; P.U.F. (1982), 159-166 [reprinted in 1984. *La romanité chrétienne en Orient. héritages et mutations*. London; Variorum Reprints, XII].

Dawkins, R. 1906 'The Modern Carnival in Thrace and the cult of Dionysos' in *Journal of Hellenic Studies* 26; 191-206.

Dawkins, R. [Edited with a translation and notes by] 1932. *Recital concerning the Sweet land of Cyprus, entitled 'Chronicle'*. Vols 1-2, Oxford; Clarendon Press.

Delehaye, H. 1907 'Saints de Chypre', *Analecta Bollandiana* Vol. 26; 161-301.

Delehaye, H. 1966 [1921] 'Greek Neo-Martyrs' in *Mélanges d'hagiographie grecque et latine*, Bruxelles, Sté des Bollandistes; 247- 255.

Dinekov, P. 1940 'Relations between Turks and Bulgarians in Sofia in the 16th century' in *In memoriam P. Nikov, Bulletin of the Bulgarian Historical Society*, Vols. 16-18, 196-211.

Galatariotou, C. 1991 *The making of a saint. The life, times and sanctification of Neophytos the Recluse*, Cambridge; Cambridge University Press.

Galatariotou, C. 1993 'Leontios Machairas' *Exegesis of the Sweet Land of Cyprus*: Towards a Re-appraisal of the text and its Critics' in A. Bryer and G. Georghallidis (eds.), *The Sweet Land of Cyprus, Papers given at the 25th Jubilee Spring Symposium of Byzantine Studies*', Birmingham; Research Centre for Byzantine Studies; Nicosia, Cyprus Research Centre, 393-413.

Geary, P. 1988 'Sacred commodities: the circulation of medieval relics' in A. Appaduri (ed.) *The Social Life of Things. Commodities in Cultural Perspective*, Cambridge; Cambridge University Press, 169-191.

Gradeva, R. 1996 'On the issue of the religious atmosphere in the Ottoman Empire: Sofia in the mid-16th century' [in Bulgarian] in *The Bulgarian 16th Century Collection of papers on Bulgarian history and culture in the XVIth century* Sofia; National Library, 149-185.

Gradeva R. [in press] *Apostasy from Islam in the Balkan Provinces of the Ottoman Empire* [in Bulgarian], Sofia: University of Sofia Publishing House.

Hasluck, F. 1929 *Christianity and Islam under the Sultans*. Edited by M. Hasluck, two vols, Oxford; Clarendon Press.

Hasluck, F. 1926 *Letters on Religion and Folklore*. Annotated and edited by M. Hasluck, London; Luzac & Co.

Hertz, R. 1983 [1912] 'Saint Besse. A Study of an Alpine Cult', in Wilson, S. (ed.) *Saints and their Cults: Studies in Religious Sociology, Folklore, and History*, Cambridge; Cambridge University Press, 55-100.

Hobsbawm, E. and Ranger, T. (eds.) 1982 *The Invention of Tradition*. Cambridge; Cambridge University Press.

Jirecek, C. 1897 'Das Christliche Element in des Topographischen Nomenklatur des Balkanländer', *Sitzungsberichte der Kaiserl. Akademie der Wiss. in Wien, Phil.-Hist Classe*, Bd. CXXXVI, Wien.

Jirecek, C. 1899 *The Principality of Bulgaria*. Vol. II. *Travels throughout Bulgaria*, Plovdiv; HGDanov [re-published 1974, Sofia; Nauka & Izkustvo Publ.]

Kiel, M. 1985 *Art and Society of Bulgaria in the Turkish Period. A sketch of the Economic, Juridical and Artistic Precondition of Bulgarian Post-Byzantine Anr and its Place in the Development of the Art of the Christian Balkans, 1360/70-1700. A New Interpretation*. Van Gorcum; Assen/ Maastricht.

Kyrris, C. 1993 The 'Three Hundred Alaman Saints' of Cyprus: problems of origin and identity. A Summary. — In: A. A. A. Bryer & G. S. Georghallidis (eds.), *'The Sweet Land of Cyprus'. Papers given at the 25th Jubilee Spring Symposium of Byzantine Studies*, Birmingham, March 1991, Nicosia; 203-235.

Kyrris, C. 1996 *History of Cyprus*, (second enlarged ed.), Lampousa Publications; Nicosia.

Lawson, D. 1910 *Modern Greek Folklore and Ancient Greek religion*. Cambridge ; Cambridge University Press.

MacClancy, J. & Parkin, R. 1997 'Revitalization or continuity in European ritual? The case of San Bessu' in *Journal of the Royal Anthropological Institute* (N.S.), Vol. 3; 1, 61-78.

Margari, Z. 1993. 'L'arbre sacré d'Aghios Thérapon, à Lesbos', *Etudes et Documents balkaniques et méditerranéens* 17, [Paris, LAS], 31-34.

Marinov, D. *Narodna vjara i religiozni narodni obicai [Popular faith and popular religious customs]*, Sofia, 1914 (= *Sbornik za narodni umotvorenija*, vol. 28; new ed. 1981 Sofia; Izkustuo).

Ostrogorski G. 1973 'Die Entstehung der Themenverfassung', in *Zur byzantinischen Geschichte (Ausgewählte Kleine Schriften)*, Darmstadt; Wissenschaftliche Buchgesellschaft.

Papagheorghiou, A. 1993 'Cities and countryside at the end of Antiquity and the beginning of the Middle Ages in Cyprus' in *The Sweet Land of Cyprus*; 27-51.

Redfield, R. 1960 *The Little Community, and Peasant Society and Culture*, Chicago; University of Chicago Press.

Rhewbottom D. 1974 'The saint's feast and Skopska Crna Goran social structure', *Man* (N.S.), Vol. 11, 18-34.

Rogel, C. 1977 'The Wandering Monk and the Balkan National Awakening' in W. Haddad & W. Ochsenwald. (eds.), *Nationalism in a Non-national State: The Dissolution of the Ottoman Empire*, Ohio University Press; 77-101.

Sathas, C. 1884 'Vie des Saints Allemands de l'Eglise de Chypre', *Archives de l'Orient latin* II, 2, 405-426 [separately paginated, 1-26].

Schmidt B. 1871 *Volksleben der Neugriechen*, Leipzig; Teubner.

Schmitt, J.-C. 1979 *Le saint lévrier: Guinefort, guérisseur d'enfants depuis le 13$^e$ siècle*. Paris; Flammarion.

Schmitt, J.-C. 1984 'La fabrique des saints', *Annales ESC*, mars-avril, 286-300.

Sergij, A. 1901 *Polnyj mesjacoslov Vostoka [Complete Menaion of the Eastern Church]*, vol. I-III, Vladimir [Photo-reprint Moscow, Synodal Editing House, 1997].

Shestakov, D. 1910. *Issledovanija v oblasti slavjanskih skazanij o svjatyh [Studies in the realm of popular narratives on saints]*, Warsaw; for the author.

Sprostranov, E. 1906/1907 'Belezhki i pripiski po sofijskite carkvi' [Notes and *marginalia* found in the churches of Sofia]. — *Sbornik NU*, vol. 22-23, 1-18.

Stylianou, A. and J. 1997 *The painted churches of Cyprus. Treasures of Byzantine art.* second ed., Leventis Foundation; Nikosia.

Todorova M. 1993 *Balkan Family Structure and the European Pattern. Demographic Developments in Ottoman Bulgaria*, New York; American University Press.

Werbner, R. 1977 'Introduction', in; R. P. Werbner (ed.), *Regional Cults [=ASA Monographs* 16] London, Academic Press; ix-xxxvi.

Valtchinova G. 1999 *Laudae Znepolensia: Local religion and identity in Western Bulgaria.* Sofia, M. Drinov Academic Publishers.

# 25. THE CONVERSION OF CHRISTIAN AND JEWISH SOULS AND SPACE DURING THE 'ANTI-DERVISH MOVEMENT OF 1656-76'

Marc BAER

*Conversion to Islam in the Ottoman Empire*

From the beginning of Ottoman rule at the beginning of the fourteenth century to the dissolution of the Ottoman Empire in the early twentieth century, much of the Christian population in Anatolia and Rumelia became Muslim. Generations of historians have sought to determine why they changed religion, who facilitated their conversion, and the characteristics of the Islam they joined. It is generally agreed that two means of conversion were most significant: the devshirme, or levy of Christian boys who were converted and trained to be the administrative and military elite, and the proselytization of sufis. In the first instance, the state played a direct role in compelling conversion from the fourteenth to seventeenth centuries.[1] According to Ottoman historian Sa´deddin, by the end of the sixteenth century 200,000 Christians had become Muslim by this process.[2] The relation between sufis and the state is more complex.[3] The Bektashis, for example, were linked to the Janissaries, the infantry corps made of devshirme recruits. But it is not clear to what extent sufis acted in concert with the sovereign. Did sultans send sufis as an avant-garde to colonize and proselytize, or did state institutions and incorporation follow the trailblazing path of errant dervishes more or less uncontrolled by the political power? Either way, sufis were probably as significant a force in conversion as the devshirme during the same period. As Michel Balivet has written, 'the most original phenomenon in the diffusion of Islam in the Balkans is the essential role played by dervishes--more or less heterodox--that accompanied the Ottoman political progression in Europe.'[4] According to V.L. Ménage, Muslim 'holy men' were the dominant religious

---

[1] See Wittek (1955), Ménage (1965, 1966), İnalcIk (1965), Itzkowitz (1972:49-53), and Demetriades (1993).

[2] Ménage (1979:65-6).

[3] See Hasluck (1929:1v, 1:56, 1:85-6, 1:89, 1:158, 1:336; 2:372, 2:402, 2:429-30, 2:436, 2:439, 2:500-1, 2:526, 2:570, 2:573, 2:576, 2:581-2, 2:586-7, and 2:591), Tschudi (1960:1161-3), Birge (1937), Barkan (1942), Vryonis (1971, 1972, 1990), Ocak (1981, 1998: 136-202), Balivet (1994, 1995, 1999), Kafadar (1995:62-90), and Gölpınalı (1966:89-119).

[4] Balivet (1999:53).

figures among Turkish nomads and peasants 'and the strongest influence in the conversion of rural Anatolia.'[1]

While scholars have paid considerable attention to these two major conversion processes, the responsibility of Ottoman sultans and valide sultans (mothers of the sultan) has received little attention. The aim of this study is therefore to shed light on an era in Ottoman history when conversion policies and practices, influenced by a turn to piety, moved in directions demonstrably not encompassed by devshirme or by sufi influence. In the late seventeenth century the Ottoman Empire witnessed mass conversion of Christians in Rumelia and the Mediterranean. Many of these men and women likely converted for socio-economic reasons. The unraveling of the devshirme system had significant effects upon the ability of men to convert and enter the military class, an avenue that had not been as open in earlier centuries when the government relied upon restricted numbers of professional troops.[2] Christian and Jewish women converted to divorce and remarry, and children became Muslim to run away from home.[3] Slaves owned by non-Muslims converted in order to be re-purchased by Muslim men of high social status.[4] Other non-Muslims, however, were either directly compelled to convert by Mehmed IV, who reigned between 1648 and 1687, or his mother Hatice Turhan Sultan, or had their conversion facilitated by the dynasty and administration.

Unlike earlier centuries when sufis aided the conversion of non-Muslims and had a close relation with the Ottoman dynasty and administrators, in the second half of the seventeenth century the state attempted to crush many sufi orders and end what they considered their 'heterodox' practices. The leading men and women of state were pious individuals whose religiosity was manifest not only in the suppression of 'innovations' practiced by Muslims, but in an unprecedented emphasis on converting Christian and Jewish souls and space in the inner circle of the dynasty and administration, Istanbul, and the areas of Rumelia through which

---

[1] Ménage (1979:59).

[2] İnalcık (1980) and Greene (2000).

[3] Numerous cases can be found in the Islamic law court records of Istanbul, particularly from the districts of Hasköy, a predominantly Jewish area on the Golden Horn; Beşiktaş, which included several Bosphorus villages and had a mixed population of Armenians, Jews, Orthodox Christians, and Muslims; and Istanbul proper, which was as diverse as Beşiktaş.

[4] These conversions were based on the principle that non-Muslim men could not marry Muslim women, non-Muslim parents could not raise Muslim children, and non-Muslims could not own Muslim slaves. Conversion did not free a slave. But when a slave's owner fathered her children and acknowledged paternity, the children would be born free, and the mothers would be freed and become inheritors upon the master's death.

the sultan and his retinue passed or visited. While it is difficult for a modern scholar to determine precisely why these figures turned to piety, there can be no doubt that their religious policies were quite different than those of their predecessors.

## The 'anti-dervish movement'

Unlike earlier periods, in the late seventeenth century the leading men and women of the Ottoman dynasty and administration sought to sever links to most sufis, and reform their own behaviour and that of other Muslims. They supported the Kadızadeli movement, which aimed to replace the Islam practiced in Istanbul with a religion purified of especially Sufi 'innovations.' It championed restrictions on practices they felt the Prophet Muhammad had not sanctioned. Mehmed IV, Hatice Turhan (d. 1683), and Grand Vizier Köprülü Fazıl Ahmed Pasha (d. 1676) supported the movement's last leader, Vani Mehmed Efendi (d. 1685), who became their spiritual guide. They targeted many sufis and their popular devotional acts, including the Mevlevi playing of reed pipes and whirling. The grand vizier ordered the razing of sufi lodges and places of pilgrimage, and exiled sufi leaders such as the Halveti shaykh Niyazi Mısri (d. 1694), a vocal critic of Vani Mehmed Efendi and Fazıl Ahmed Pasha.[1] The efforts of the reformers led to violence between Muslims, and even bloody clashes within the mosques of Istanbul as Kadızadeli preachers fought with preachers affiliated with sufi orders that had lost royal favour. Vani Mehmed Efendi encouraged the grand vizier and sultan to defend the empire from the attacks of Christian powers and even go on the offensive, launching sieges of Crete (relaunched in 1665) and Vienna (1683), while at the same time strengthening Sunni Hanafi Islam in the imperial domains.

*Christianity and Islam Under the Sultans* contains a short section entitled 'The Anti-Dervish Movement of 1656-76.'[2] Hasluck narrates the key events that began with the appointment of Köprülü Mehmed Pasha as grand vizier in 1656, and ended with the death of his son and successor in office, Fazıl Ahmed Pasha two decades later. The author argues that the Bektashi-Janissary combination was dangerous for sultans from the time in the sixteenth century when the link between the two was officially recognized, to when the Janissaries were disbanded and murdered in 1826. As evidence for the

---

[1] Gölpınarlı (1953:167).
[2] Hasluck (1929:2:419-23).

danger they posed, Hasluck notes Janissaries deposed two sultans in the seventeenth century. But the third quarter of the seventeenth century was a period of hope in an otherwise gloomy era, for that was when the two Köprülüs hindered Janissary political power and cracked down upon the 'heterodoxy' of the Bektashi. Hasluck also mentions the rise of Vani Mehmed Efendi, who he terms 'the religious counterpart' of the grand viziers, a preacher that 'opposed lawlessness in religion as they in politics.'[1]

Hasluck was correct to point out the anti-sufi aspects of the era. The work of more recent scholars has provided much insight into the reformist activities of Fazıl Ahmed Pasha and Vani Mehmed Efendi and the rise to importance of the Kadızadeli movement.[2] In troubled times, a moral rejuvenation was viewed as a means of restoring the empire to greatness. However, Hasluck overlooked the fact that the coin of piety has another side: the 'anti-dervish' movement affected Christians and Jews, whether in Istanbul, the inner circle of the palace, or the areas through which the sultan and his retinue passed. Hasluck emphasized the significance of Fazıl Ahmed Pasha and Vani Mehmed Efendi. Research based on Ottoman archival and literary sources reveals the importance of two other figures, valide sultan Hatice Turhan and Mehmed IV. They both were pious people who had a close relationship with Vani Mehmed Efendi. According to Ottoman writers, Hatice Turhan's piety was manifested in the important decisions to compel Jewish palace physicians to convert to Islam, and following fire in 1660, build the Mosque of the Valide Sultan (or *Yeni Cami*, New Mosque) on the waterfront in Istanbul, expelling Jews and turning over their property to Muslim foundations in the process. Christian space in Galata and Istanbul was likewise Islamised. At the same time, Mehmed IV, discounted by historians as a 'do-nothing' sultan and overshadowed in the historiography by the Köprülüs, in fact, played a significant role in the conversion of commoners in the regions in Rumelia in which he travelled on the hunt and military campaign. In all these episodes the

---

[1] Hasluck (1929: 2; 423). Hasluck's brief discussion of the political and religious trends of the period serves as background to that which most interested him, the origin, history, and remaining fragments of the tomb and cult of Saint Polycarp or Saint John in İzmir, which was revered by two faiths. The tomb was transferred from Muslims to Orthodox Christians by 1657. One could quibble with the factual information, language, interpretation, and overlooked issues in these few pages. There is no evidence that the 'anti-dervish movement' caused the tomb of Saint Polycarp to change hands. After all, if it had been the site of 'heterodox' rites, why wouldn't the grand vizier have it destroyed as he did other dervish lodges and tombs? Vani Mehmed Efendi rose to power along with Fazıl Ahmed Pasha in 1661, not 1664. One would be wary today of using the phrase 'national revival,' to refer to the seventeenth century. The terms 'disease,' and 'superstition,' are not the most polite words for describing popular religious practices.

[2] Ocak (1979-83), Thomas (1972:106-10), and Zilfi (1986, 1988:146-59). See also Çavuşoğlu (1990).

valide sultan and her son played a direct role in the conversion of people and places. Finally, the conversion of the rabbi and messianic claimant Sabbatai Tzevi serves as another example of the palace cracking down on a 'lawless heterodox' movement, here Jewish, during the period. Thus the piety of the leading figures of the era, including the sultan and his mother, was manifested not only in the opposition to certain Sufi groups and practices, but also in the Islamisation of people and space.

*Hatice Turhan: the sultana as convert-maker*

When Mehmed IV ascended the throne in 1648, he was but seven years old. His mother, Hatice Turhan, and grandmother, Kösem Sultan, fought for power in the palace.[1] The former won the contest in 1651 when she had Kösem Sultan murdered. Throughout her son's reign, Hatice Turhan was one of the most powerful figures of the state. Accordingly, the decisions she made were implemented and had great ramifications, especially for Christians and Jews in the imperial capital and in the sultan's inner circle. One of her important decisions was to compel Jews serving in the palace to convert to Islam.

The head of the privy physicians was the most important medical figure in the empire because he appointed all physicians, oculists, and dentists, and since he treated the sultan with whom he was on intimate terms. In the sixteenth century members of the Jewish elite usually held that position.[2] One cannot dispute the impressive record of Jewish physicians in the sixteenth-century Ottoman court. But over the course of the seventeenth century the number and proportion of Jewish physicians decreased greatly as many of those who wished to remain in office converted to Islam. In previous centuries some individual Jews had faced hostility in the palace because of their positions concerning foreign affairs, but it was not until the late seventeenth century that the group as a whole lost its once significant place.[3]

---

[1] Kösem Sultan was the mother of Murad IV, who reigned from 1623 to 1640, and Ibrahim I, who was in power from 1640 to 1648.

[2] Galanté (1938), Lewis, (1952, 1984:130), Birnbaum (1961), and Heyd (1963).

[3] A Jewish poem concerning physician Moshe Benvenest's exile to Rhodes in 1584 is discussed in Benayahu (1971-8). The physician was apparently a member of the court faction punished for supporting peace with Spain, and not France.

The conversion of the Spanish Jewish physician Moses son of Raphael
Abravanel illustrates the phenomenon. He became Hayatizade Mustafa Fevzi
Efendi, and was head physician from 1669 to 1691.[1] We learn of the
physician's conversion from the treatise of the Kadızadeli palace preacher
named Kurd Mustafa, which has not been utilized by modern scholars.[2] The
treatise was dedicated to the mother of the sultan and completed around 1676.
Its author lauds her for her piety, and gives two examples. The first is the
construction of an imperial mosque complex in Eminönü, Istanbul. The
second is the conversion of the head palace physician, Hayatizade. While
narrating the history of the mosque, Kurd Mustafa juxtaposes two stories of
Jews in palace service. The first concerns sixteenth-century valide sultan
Safiye Sultan's companion Esperanza Malkhi, referred to by the Greek term
'lady' (kyra).[3] The kyra served as purveyor of goods and services to the harem
and was intermediary with foreign embassies.[4] The author calls her 'the
accursed Jewish woman' who 'unjustly caused many people to be oppressed
and transgressed.'[5]

In order to explain the piety of Hatice Turhan, the author contrasts the
close relationship Safiye Sultan had with the kyra with Hatice Turhan's
compelling Hayatizade, another Jew in palace service, to convert to Islam.[6]
Although Hayatizade was an exceptional physician, because he had not
become a Muslim, 'she was not pleased that he should take the noble pulse
and diagnose the maladies of his excellency.'[7] Therefore, she ordered that as
long as Hayatizade 'did not wear the crown of Islam on his head, or don the
cloak of the faith on his shoulders,' he was not granted permission to give
medical treatment to the sultan. As long as he did not 'ennoble himself with
the teaching of Islam and distinguish himself from among the Jews with the
banner of Islam' he could not be chief palace physician. Although  we  do  not

---

[1] For more information about the life of this physician see Galanté (1938:13-4). Hayatizade's
name combines the Hebrew word, 'hayat,' for tailor, since his father was a Jewish tailor, and
the Persian suffix 'zâde,' which means 'son of.' Hayatizade's grandson not only became
shaykh al-Islam, but until the twentieth century his descendants resided in Vaniköy, Vani
Mehmed Efendi's village on the Bosphorus in Istanbul.

[2] Kürd Hatîb Mustafa.

[3] For a discussion of the term see Galanté (1926:3-5).

[4] Lewis (1984:144), Peirce (1993:225-6), and Benbassa and Rodrigue (2000:38).

[5] Kürd Hatîb Mustafa, fol. 18b. Rebellious cavalry (sipahi) who blamed her for their pay of
debased coins murdered her in 1600. Peirce (1993:242-3).

[6] Silâhdar Fındıklılı Mehmed Ağa (1928:2:578) corroborates this fact.

[7] All quotes in this paragraph are from Kürd Hatîb Mustafa, fols. 19a-b.

know the actual mechanics of his conversion, we do know that he indeed became a Muslim.[1]

### Islamizing space

Along with compelling Jewish palace physicians to become Muslim, Hatice Turhan also made the decision to Islamise space in Istanbul. Following two fires which devastated the city in the spring and summer of 1660, the first in Galata and the second in Istanbul, the valide sultan decided to recommence construction of an imperial mosque in Eminönü, which along with being the city's main harbor and commercial sector, was the site of the main concentration of Jews.[2] Safiye Sultan had laid its foundations at the end of the sixteenth century, yet its construction had been abandoned shortly after.[3] After the fire Hatice Turhan ordered its completion, along with the Egyptian (Spice) Market, imperial tomb complex for Hatice Turhan and other members of the dynasty, and other structures. For this reason she is compared to Safiye Sultan, who was not able to complete the mosque. Kurd Mustafa described the act as an expression of her piety:

> There is no end to the pious works of her excellency, the valide sultan. Just as her laudable moral qualities are many, so, too, are her works. Among them is the noble mosque whose match has not been seen and whose peer has not been heard, which she constructed in the place known as Eminönü in the well-protected city of Istanbul.[4]

The construction of the mosque greatly affected Jews in the city. Qur'anic verses in the completed mosque concern the Prophet Muhammad's expulsion of the Jewish Banu Nadir tribe from Medina.[5] That banishment was mirrored a millennium later by the expulsion of Jews living in the district from Hoca Pasha, bordering the walls of Topkapı Palace in the east, to Zeyrek in the west. According to Ottoman historians, they were expelled across the Golden

---

[1] Hayatizade joined a long line of Jewish palace physicians who had converted to Islam. For example, Mehmed II's physician, Hekim Yakub, became a minister in the government (*vizier*), most likely after converting to Islam. See Birnbaum (1961) and İnalcık (1989:526). Hayatizade eventually died a Muslim imprisoned in the infamous Yedikule. Defterdar Sarı Mehmed claimed he was dismissed because he did not take proper care of Süleyman II. Defterdâr Sarı Mehmed (1995:398). Silahdar, however, wrote that Muslim physicians engineered his downfall when Mehmed IV died. Silâhdar Fındıklılı Mehmed Ağa (1928:2:578-9).

[2] For the Istanbul fire see 'Abdi Pasha, fols. 128b-29b and Silâhdar Fındıklılı Mehmed Ağa (1928:1:183-4).

[3] Thys-Şenocak (1998:62-3).

[4] Kürd Hatîb Mustafa, fol. 18a.

[5] Thys-Şenocak (1998:67).

Horn to Hasköy, upon threat of death, despite a hefty bribe, and prohibited from resettling.[1] An imperial decree ordered Jews to sell the properties they owned to Muslims, and entrust their endowments to Muslim foundations.[2] In accordance with a legal opinion (*fetva*) issued in these circumstances, Jews were not allowed to reclaim synagogues that had completely burned in the fire, even though they were considered buildings that had existed at the time of the Ottoman conquest of the city.[3]

Armenians, Catholics, and Orthodox Christians in Galata and Istanbul were also affected by Islamisation policies. Churches that burned in the fires of 1633 and 1660 accrued to the state treasury where they were sold at auction.[4] Many were actually purchased by Christians in the summer and fall of 1661. Yet imperial decree and Islamic law court records of Istanbul narrate how most were reclaimed by the state the following spring and summer, and new structures built on the property were razed.[5] Christians had apparently broken their pledge only to build houses and not churches on the properties.[6] Catholics, who were especially concerned since they were allowed to maintain churches only in Galata, managed to hold on to several properties, some of which still exist, such as St George and San Pietro.[7] Yet the Catholics of Galata, like the Jews of Eminönü, saw former domiciles and places of worship taken over by Muslims as part of an imperial policy of Islamisation.

Scores of churches in re-conquered Bozcaada (1658) and newly conquered Crete (1669) were likewise converted into mosques. Kurd Mustafa writes the following about Bozcaada:

> In short, we seized the aforementioned island from the hands of the enemies of religion. The call to prayer was read in the mosques and Friday mosques, drowning out the churchbells, and the candle of Islam illuminated every corner of the churches.[8]

---

[1] Silâhdar Fındıklılı Mehmed Ağa (1928:1:218) and Kürd Hatîb Mustafa, fols. 22a-b. See for example the Islamic law court records of Istanbul (hereafter IŞS) 9, fol. 143b, 4 29 September 1661.

[2] See for example IŞS 10, fol. 82a, 5 June 1662.

[3] Zeytoun/Izdin: IŞS 9, fol. 52a, 8 July 1661 and IŞS 10, fol. 82a, 5 June 1662; Alaman/German: IŞS 9, fol. 85a, 31 July 1661 and IŞS 9, 216a, 18 December 1661; Little Istanbul: IŞS 9, fol. 86a, 13 August 1661; Dimetoka: IŞS 9, fol. 177b, 27 October 1661; Aragon: IŞS 9, fol. 216a, 18 December 1661; Antalya and Borlu: IŞS 10, fols. 113b-14a, 16 September 1661; and Borlu: IŞS 9, fol. 143b, 29 September 1661. See Heyd (1953:300-5).

[4] IŞS 9, fols. 83b-96b, fols. 142a-157a, and fols. 247a-253a; IŞS 10, fols. 82a-95a and fol. 156b.

[5] IŞS 10, fol. 156b, 9 May 1662.

[6] IŞS 10, fol. 156b, 9 May 1662.

[7] St. George: IŞS 9, fol. 96b; San Pietro: IŞS 9, fol. 96a, 17 August 1661.

[8] Kürd Hatîb Mustafa, fol. 10a.

According to Silahdar, the fourteen churches found within the citadel of Candia were converted into mosques for Mehmed IV, Hatice Turhan, Grand Vizier Fazıl Ahmed Pasha, and other officials, and seventy-four other churches were transformed into mosques as well.[1] Echoing what had occurred in Istanbul, the former Jewish neighborhood in Candia 'was endowed in its entirety to the mosque of the queen mother' in the city.[2] For Silahdar, these spaces formerly 'filled with polytheism and error' became 'illuminated by the light of Islam.'[3] Defterdar Sarı Mehmed relates how the citadel of Candia contained many monasteries and chapels. In order to replace them with mosques, the Ottomans first destroyed the 'idols' and 'images' they found so that those ancient abodes of idols became, like the luminous heart of the believer, free of the filth of polytheism; and those abodes of graven images narrow and dark with the darkness of infidelity became, like the heart of the people of firm belief, purified and stripped of the marks of error. [4]

The names of villages in Rumelia and Istanbul were also Islamised. In Istanbul a forest preserve on the Bosphorus north of Üsküdar called Priest's Preserve (*Papaz korusu*) was given to Vani Mehmed Efendi in the 1660s. He restored a small mosque, and built a medrese and over a dozen seaside mansions, including his own, in the adjoining village. A wealthy Jewish Hasköy vintner family was evicted from the village, which became known as Vaniköy.[5] According to Abdülbaki Gölpınarlı, Vaniköy was one of only two areas in Istanbul where sufis, especially Hamzavi Mevlevis, never set foot.[6]

*Mehmed IV: The sultan as convert-maker*

While leaving Filibe in 1667, Mehmed IV's party alighted in 'Priest Village' (*Papaz köyü*) whose name they changed to 'Islamic' (*İslâmiyye*).[7] What was Mehmed IV doing in Priest Village? Mehmed IV was a particularly mobile ruler. This sultan spent most of his long reign not in Istanbul, but in Edirne, or more correctly, in the environs of Edirne and eastern Thrace. In fact, he

---

[1] Silâhdar Fındıklılı Mehmed Ağa (1928:1:525-6). For more detail on the conversion of churches into mosques in Crete see Greene (2000:78-87).
[2] Greene (2000:84).
[3] Silâhdar Fındıklılı Mehmed Ağa (1928:1:525-6).
[4] Defterdâr Sarı Mehmed (1995:15-6).
[5] Kayra and Üyepazarcı (1993:94-5).
[6] Gölpınarlı (1953:168). They blamed Vani Mehmed Efendi for the murder of ninety-year-old Beşir Ağa and the drowning of forty of his disciples at Kadıköy Feneri in 1662. For this reason they cursed him and his village, and called him 'Vani the Murderer' (*Vani-i cani*).
[7] ʹAbdi Pasha, fol. 248b. The entry is dated 14 December 1667.

spent most of his time hunting, which earned him the nickname, 'Avcı Mehmed,' 'Mehmed the Hunter.' While this sultan has been criticized for his apparent love of leisure and inattention to the affairs of state, in fact, the sultan's frivolous activities had serious consequences for non-Muslims.[1] The registers of the Ottoman court's distribution of cloaks and turbans reveals how several hundred Christian and Jewish children, men, and women converted to Islam in his presence. They changed religion at ceremonies at his travelling court whether he was on the hunt, or less frequently, on military campaigns to Ukraine, when he travelled to Rumelia to observe naval campaigns between Ottoman and Venetian forces, and when he journeyed to Istanbul on occasion.[2]

Most converts appeared before the sultan to convert when he was hunting. Mehmed IV utilized the *battue* (*sürgün avı*), a hunting technique that required dozens, hundreds, even thousands of commoners who formed a huge arc around the sultan's hunting party and moved through the forest beating the brush and flushing the prey toward the hunters. Massive numbers of peasants could be assembled. For example, ´Abdi Pasha relates how on one Sunday the sultan used as many as 35,000 peasants to drive animals through a forest preserve where he killed over sixty deer.[3] Many of these drovers became Muslim, especially in the district of Silistre in the towns and forests nearest Edirne. The sultan also converted peasants he happened upon while hunting such as a drover and his son who were attending the birth of a calf.

The sultan privileged his boon companion and historian ´Abdi Pasha by narrating to him his conversion of a peasant while on the chase in the winter of 1665 in Pasha Köy, a favorite hunting ground less than two days journey from Edirne.[4] They brought the drover before the sultan. The sultan spoke to him without intermediary asking, 'Are you a Muslim?' When the cattle drover stated that he was a non-Muslim (*dhimmi*), the sultan called him to the true religion. 'Come,' he said, 'become a Muslim. Let me give you a means of livelihood and God will forgive all your sins. In the afterlife you will go straight to heaven.' Although the sultan offered Islam to him more than once, the non-Muslim refused. The sultan's attendants quickly alerted  the

---

[1] For an assessment of his reign, see Baysun (1957).

[2] One finds nearly two hundred converts in documents maintained today in Istanbul. See BBA, Ali Emiri Tasnifi, IV. Mehmed. Several hundred more converts are documented by sources located today in Sofia. See A. Velkov (1990).

[3] ´Abdi Pasha, fol. 247b. The entry is dated 11 December 1667.

[4] ´Abdi Pasha, fols. 161a-62b. The incident occurred 12 March 1665. The story is also related in Mehmed Râşid (1865-6:1:94-5) who omits the sultan's speech contained in ´Abdi Pasha's narrative, but provides the additional information that the sultan's servants that pressured the cattle drover to convert were African eunuchs of the harem (*enderûn ağaları*).

peasant that 'the one speaking with you and saying to you, 'be a Muslim,' is none other than his eminence the majestic emperor, the Refuge of the Universe in person.' That was enough to convince the drover: 'with alacrity he accepted Islam and his son followed him.' The sultan rewarded the man for his decision with a fifteen-akçe per day gatekeeper position, and a purse of coins, and the cattle drover and his son were assigned to the Old Palace in Edirne. The sultan came from the ride in state and related the event to 'Abdi Pasha in person. 'Today,' he said, 'I did not, in truth, simply go on the chase. Rather, by divine wisdom, while pursuing a rabbit I chanced upon a cow giving birth, and while watching the spectacle, in my presence Islam became divinely facilitated to that fellow. Therefore, that is a cow of divine guidance.' He ordered that they purchase the cow with its suckling calf, and place it in the palace's privy garden.[1]

*Sabbatai Tzevi: converting the messiah*

The converted drover was not the only new Muslim to take up a gatekeeper post in the palace in Edirne, for Sabbatai Tzevi joined him a year later. The messianic movement led by this rabbi is well known.[2] In 1665, Jews in Izmir declared him the messiah, and he made his way to Istanbul in the winter of 1666, apparently intending to depose the sultan. Three Ottoman historians narrate how he was instead arrested, imprisoned, and eventually called to a meeting of the imperial council in Edirne where he became a Muslim rather than a martyr.[3] Vani Mehmed Efendi was in attendance; Mehmed IV observed proceedings from a window. Jewish sources claim Hayatizade served as the rabbi's translator although there is no evidence of this relationship in the Ottoman accounts.

The Sabbatean movement could not have come at a worse time for Ottoman Jews. This was the period of the 'anti-dervish movement,' as Hasluck reminds us, when the state was cracking down on all forms of ecstatic or 'heterodox' religious expression. It is no coincidence that Fazıl Ahmed Pasha and Vani Mehmed Efendi were concerned about putting an end to an

---

[1] The author also relates how the drover had dreamed of converting before the encounter described in this narrative. But if this was the case, the reader wonders why he was so slow to accept the change of religion.

[2] The classic account of the messianic claimant's life and beliefs is Scholem (1973). But see more recent reassessments, including Idel (1993, 1998:154-211) and Liebes (1993:93-113). For accounts of Sabbateanism in its Ottoman context, see Zilfi (1988:146-57) and Hathaway (1997).

[3] 'Abdi Pasha, fols. 224 a-b, Silâhdar Fındıklılı Mehmed Ağa (1928:1:431-2), and Mehmed Râşid (1865-6:1:133).

affair which caused the empire's Jews and those of surrounding regions to flock to be near their messiah while engaging in antinomian behavior. Their acts caused social strife among Jews, and tension between Jews and non-Jews.

Renamed Aziz Mehmed Efendi, the rabbi was bathed, robed in sumptuous garments, given a purse of coins, and a ceremonial palace gatekeeper position. Many of his followers, including his wife, also became Muslim. Aziz Mehmed Efendi was given a salaried position in the palace and taught the fundamentals of Islam by Vani Mehmed Efendi. The former messiah reportedly converted many Jews between 1666 and 1672. Jewish and European sources claim many came to the court of the grand vizier to become Muslim.[1] According to Jewish sources, Aziz Mehmed Efendi, accompanied by Vani Mehmed Efendi's men, urged Jews to convert to Islam and many were given turbans at the royal preacher's residence.[2] Jews also wrote that he invited rabbis to dispute with him in the imperial audience hall in the palace in Edirne as the sultan and his preacher observed the proceedings. European observers noted that after his conversion Aziz Mehmed Efendi strolled through the streets of Istanbul with a large retinue of turban-wearing Jewish converts to Islam and preached in synagogues to win more converts.[3]

Despite being a Muslim, the former rabbi continued to engage in Kabbalah. He encouraged his followers to retain a belief in his messianic calling and practice the Kabbalistic rituals and prayers that he taught them. The former rabbi and his converted followers prayed in Hebrew; Aziz Mehmed Efendi was reportedly even seen wearing a Jewish skullcap and phylacteries (*tefilin*).[4] Because he continued to practice Judaism, the convert was exiled to Ülgün/Dulcigno on the Adriatic in Albania in 1673. Before he died there three years later, the same year Fazıl Ahmed Pasha passed away, he married a Jewish woman from Salonica whose brother led the first community of Sabbateans (Dönme).[5]

---

[1] Scholem (1973:729).

[2] Scholem (1973; 847).

[3] Scholem (1973; 859, 874).

[4] Scholem (1973; 874-5).

[5] Their descendants maintained hybrid religious beliefs and practices until the early twentieth century. Despite assimilating into secular Turkish society, their identity remains highly controversial. See Baer (1999).

*Conclusion*

This study focuses on one factor in the conversion of Christians and Jews to Islam during the late seventeenth century, namely the role of the sultan and sultana. A devotion to purifying Islamic practices of Sufi 'innovations' led to a harsh new approach to Muslims, especially in the imperial capital. Anti-Sufi reforms in turn went hand-in-hand with the Islamisation of space and people in the period from 1656 to 1676. The conversion of space and the transference of urban sanctuaries, or the conversion of churches into mosques, was an important aspect of Islamisation. In the third quarter of the seventeenth century, Christian and Jewish space in Istanbul, and Christian churches in Bozcaada and Crete were Islamised. Several hundred Christians and Jews converted in the presence of the pious sultan and sultana, in the heart of the palace, and in remote forests in Rumelia. The desire to convert a proclaimed Jewish messiah also reflects the anti-Sufi aims of Fazıl Ahmed Pasha and Vani Mehmed Efendi since they did not tolerate any manifestations of 'unorthodox' behavior, especially when desiring a quiet home front while launching a massive siege of Crete.

Hasluck praised the Köprülü era since the Ottoman dynasty reasserted its control over Bektashis and Janissaries. That period did not last long enough for the sultan, however. Janissaries defeated on the Habsburg front dethroned Mehmed IV in 1687. Yet, unlike his predecessors Osman II (reigned 1618-22) and Ibrahim I (reigned 1640-8), he was not executed. In fact, the dethronement of these three rulers may have had more to do with debased coins and military defeat, and thus economic and political reasons, than with differing views of Islam.[1] While in power, Mehmed IV and his mother Hatice Turhan were successful in expressing their religiosity. In addition to displaying the usual 'symbols of power and legitimation' including public festivals for the circumcision and weddings of royalty as had other sultans and valide sultans before them, Mehmed IV and Hatice Turhan, by converting individual non-Muslims and Islamizing spaces, added their version of piety and beneficence to the vocabulary of rule.

Much of previous scholarship has been devoted to the conversion of non-Muslims who served in the administration and military, and the sufi role in conversion in earlier centuries, such as when sufis demonstrated the links between Christianity and Islam. This study is thus significant for describing the direct role that the palace and dynasty could play in bringing non-Muslims into the fold. The reader should not have the impression that the Ottomans were always driven to convert non-Muslims, or that the raison d'être of the state was to create Muslim populations. Rather, it should be noted that a turn to piety among the leading men and women of the dynasty and administration could affect Christians and Jews. Conversion to Islam was not only the path of those who entered state service, realized the truth of Islam as demonstrated by sufis, wished to change their social and familial circumstances, or benefit from those aspects of Islamic law that were superior to their own religious law. The decision to convert to Islam could be instigated by the sovereign and his mother, who normally did not interfere in the religion of imperial subjects.

*REFERENCES*

*Archives*

Başbakanlık Osmanlı Arşivi (BBA, Prime Ministry's Ottoman Archive), Istanbul:

> Ali Emiri Tasnifi, IV. Mehmed: 504, 608-9, 626, 1169-72, 1642, 1676, 1710, 1729, 1732, 1986, 2175, 2187-9, 4454, 4523, 4766, 4820, 4823-4, 5145, 7016, 9845, 9853, 9911, 9915, 9928, 9946, 9957, 10273-95, 10297-8.

> Küçük Ruznamçe (KR): 3413-31.

> Istanbul Müftülüğü, Şer'iye Sicilleri Arşivi (Office of the Istanbul Müfti, Islamic Law Court Records Archive), Istanbul:

> Beşiktaş Şer'iye Sicilleri 23/73 (1659-61)- 23/85 (1687-90)
> Hasköy Şer'iye Sicilleri 19/8 (1661-2)- 19/11 (1679-87)
> Istanbul Şer'iye Sicilleri 8 (1660-1)-18 (1675-6).

*Sources ottomanes sur les processus d'Islamisation aux Balkans.* 1990. *Traduction des Documents,* A. Velkov et al, Sofia: Éditions de l'Academie bulgare des sciences, Serie sources-2.

*Literary sources*

ʿAbdurrahman ʿAbdi Pasha. *Vekāyi'nāme.* Köprülü Library, Istanbul. MS. 216.

Defterdâr Sarı Mehmed. 1995. *Zübde-i Vekayiât.* Ankara; Türk Tarih Kurumu Basımevi.

Kürd Hatîb Mustafa. *Risāle-i Kürd Hatīb.* Topkapı Sarayı Müzesi, Istanbul. MS. Eski Hazine 1400.

Mehmed Râşid. 1865-6. *Târîh-i Râşid.* 2 vols. Istanbul; n.p.

Silâhdar Fındıklılı Mehmed Ağa. 1928. *Silâhdar Tarîhî.* 2 vols. Istanbul; Devlet Matbaası.


*Published*

Baer, M. 1999 'Revealing a Hidden Community: Ilgaz Zorlu and the Debate in Turkey Over the Dönme/Sabbateans,' in *Turkish Studies Association Bulletin* 23.1; 68-75.

Balivet, M. 1994 *Romanie byzantine et pays de Rûm turc: Histoire d'un espace d'imbrication gréco-turque,* Istanbul; Les Éditions Isis.

Balivet, M. 1995 *Islam mystique et révolution armée dans les Balkans ottomans: Vie du Cheikh Bedreddin, 'le Hallâj des Turcs' (1358/59-1416),* Istanbul; Les Éditions Isis.

Balivet, M. 1999 *Byzantins et Ottomans: Relations, interaction, succession,* Analecta Isisiana XXXV, Istanbul; Les Éditions Isis.

Barkan, Ö. 1942 'Osmanlı İmparatorluğunda Bir İskan ve Kolonizasyon Metodu Olarak Vakıflar ve Temlikler I: İstila Devirlerinin Kolonizatör Türk Dervişleri ve Zaviyeler,' in *Vakıflar Dergisi* 2: 279-386.

Baysun, C. 1957 'Mehmed IV,' in *İslâm Ansiklopedisi,* 7;547-57.

Benayahu, M. 1971-8 'Rofeh he-hatzer rav Moshe Benvenest ve-shir al-higliyito le-Rodos me-rav Yehudah Zarko,' in *Sefunot* 12, Sefer Yavan II; 123-44.

Benbassa, E., and Rodrigue, A. 2000 *Sephardi Jewry: A History of the Judeo-Spanish Community, 14-20ᵗʰ Centuries,* Jewish Communities in the Modern World no. 2. Berkeley and Los Angeles; University of California Press.

Birge, J. 1937 *The Bektashi Order of Dervishes,* London; Luzac & Co.

Birnbaum, E. 1961 'Hekim Yakub, Physician to Sultan Mehemmed the Conquerer,' *Harofe Haivri: The Hebrew Medical Journal* 1; 222-50.

Çavuşoğlu, S. 1990 'The Kadızadeli Movement; An Attempt of Şerʾiat-Minded Reform in the Ottoman Empire.' Ph.D. diss., Princeton University.

Demetriades, V. 1993 'Some Thoughts on the Origins of the Devşirme,' in *The Ottoman Emirate (1300-1389),* ed. E. Zachariadou, Crete; Crete University Press, 23-31.

Faroqhi, S. 1994 'Crisis and Change, 1590-1699,' in *An Economic and Social History of the Ottoman Empire*, Volume Two, 1600-1914, ed. S. Faroqhi et al, Cambridge; Cambridge University Press, 413-636.

Galanté, A. 1926 *Esther Kyra d'après de nouveaux documents*. Constantinople; Fr. Haim.

Galanté, A. 1938 *Médecins juifs au service de la Turquie*. Istanbul; Imprimerie Babok.

Gölpınarlı, A. 1953 *Mevlânâ'dan Sonra Mevlevîlik*, Istanbul; İnkilâp Kitabevi.

Gölpınarlı, A. 1966 *Simavna Kadısıoğlu Şeyh Bedreddin*, Istanbul; Eti Yayınevi.

Greene, M. 2000 *A Shared World: Christians and Muslims in the Early Modern Mediterranean*, Princeton; Princeton University Press.

Hasluck, F. 1929 (1973) *Christianity and Islam Under the Sultans*, ed. Margaret Hasluck, two vols. Oxford; reprint, New York; Octagon Books.

Hathaway, J. 1997 'The Grand Vizier and the False Messiah: The Sabbatai Sevi Controversy and the Ottoman Reform in Egypt,' in *Journal of the American Oriental Society* 117.4: 665-71.

Heyd, U. 1953 'The Jewish Communities of Istanbul in the Seventeenth Century,' in *Oriens* 6: 299-314.

Heyd, U. 1963 'Moses Hamon, Chief Jewish Physician to Sultan Süleyman the Magnificent,' in *Oriens* 16: 152-70.

Idel, M. 1993 ' 'One from a Town, Two from a Clan' _ The Diffusion of Lurianic Kabbala and Sabbateanism: A Re-Examination,' in *Jewish History* 7.2: 79-104.

Idel, M. 1998 *Messianic Mystics*, New Haven; Yale University Press.

İnalcık, H. 1960 'Arnawutluk,' in *Encyclopaedia of Islam, New Edition* (*EI²*), 1:650-8.

İnalcık, H. 1965 'Ghulam-Ottoman Empire,' in *EI²*, 2:1085-91.

İnalcık, H. 1980 'Military and Fiscal Transformation in the Ottoman Empire, 1600-1700,' in *Archivum Ottomanicum* 6: 283-337.

İnalcık, H. 1989 'Jews in the Ottoman Economy and Finances, 1450-1500,' in *Essays in Honor of Bernard Lewis: The Islamic World from Classical to Modern Times*, ed. C.E. Bosworth et al, Princeton; The Darwin Press, 513-50.

Itzkowitz, N. 1972 *Ottoman Empire and Islamic Tradition*, Chicago; The University of Chicago Press.

Kafadar, C. 1995 *Between Two Worlds: The Construction of the Ottoman State*, Berkeley and Los Angeles; University of California Press.

Kayra, C. and Üyepazarcı, E. 1993 *Mekânlar ve Zamanlar: Kandilli, Vaniköy, Çengelköy*, Istanbul; İstanbul Büyükşehir Belediyesi Kültür İşleri Dairesi Başkanlığı Yayınları.

Kiel, M. 1985 *Art and Society of Bulgaria in the Turkish Period*, Maastricht; Van Gorcum.

Lewis, B. 1952 'The Privilege Granted by Mehmed II to His Physician,' in *Bulletin of the School of Oriental and African Studies* 14: 550-63.

Lewis, B. 1984 *The Jews of Islam*, Princeton; Princeton University Press.

Liebes, Y. 1993 *Studies in Jewish Myth and Jewish Messianism*, trans. Batya Stein. New York; State University of New York Press.

Ménage, V. 1965 'Devshirme,' in *EI²*, 2:210-3.

Ménage, V. 1966 'Some Notes on the Devshirme,' in *Bulletin of the School of Oriental and African Studies* 29: 64-78.

Ménage, V. 1979 'The Islamisation of Anatolia,' in *Conversion to Islam*, ed. N. Levtzion, New York; Holmes & Meier, 52-67.

Ocak, A. 1979-83 'XVII Yüzyılda Osmanlı İmparatorluğunda Dinde Tasfiye (Püritanizm) Teşebbüslerine Bir Bakış: Kadızâdeliler Hareketi,' in *Türk Kültürü Araştırmaları* XVII-XXI/1-2: 208-25.

Ocak, A. 1981 'Bazı Menâkıbnamelere Göre XIII-XV Yüzyıllardaki İhtidalarda Heterodoks Şeyh ve Dervişlerin Rolü,' in *Osmanlı Araştırmaları* 2: 31-42.

Ocak, A. 1998 *Osmanlı Toplumunda Zındıklar ve Mülhidler (15.-17. Yüzyıllar)*, Istanbul; Tarih Vakfı.

Peirce, L. 1993 *The Imperial Harem: Women and Sovereignty in the Ottoman Empire*, New York; Oxford University Press.

Scholem, G. 1973 *Sabbatai Sevi: The Mystical Messiah, 1626-1676*, trans. R.J. Zwi Werblowsky. Bollingen Series XCIII. Princeton; Princeton University Press.

Thomas, V. 1972 *A Study of Naima*, ed. N. Itzkowitz, New York; New York University Press.

Thys-Şenocak, L. 1998 'The Yeni Valide Mosque Complex at Eminönü,' in *Muqarnas* 15: 58-70.

Tschudi, R. 1960 'Bektashiyya,' in *EI²*, 1:1161-3.

Vyronis, S., Jr. 1971 *The Decline of Medieval Hellenism in Asia Minor and the Process of Islamisation from the Eleventh through the Fifteenth Century*, Berkeley and Los Angeles; University of California Press.

Vyronis, S., Jr. 1972 'Religious Changes and Patterns in the Balkans, 14-16th Centuries.' In *Aspects of the Balkans*, ed. H. Birnbaum and S. Vryonis, Jr., The Hague; Mouton, 151-76.

Vyronis, S., Jr. 1990 'The Experience of Christians under Seljuk and Ottoman Domination, Eleventh to Sixteenth Century,' in *Conversion and Continuity: Indigenous Christian Communities in Islamic Lands, Eighth to Eighteenth Centuries*, ed. M. Gervers and R. Bikhazi, Papers in Mediaeval Studies, no. 9. Toronto, Pontifical Institute of Mediaeval Studies, 185-216.

Wittek, P. 1955 'Devshirme and Shari´a,' in *Bulletin of the School of Oriental and African Studies* 17: 271-8.

Zilfi, M. 1986 'The Kadızadelis: Discordant Revivalism in Seventeenth-Century Istanbul,' in *Journal of Near Eastern Studies* 45.4: 251-69.

Zilfi, M 1988 *The Politics of Piety: The Ottoman Ulema in the Post-Classical Age* (1600-1800), Minneapolis; Bibliotheca Islamica.

# 26. A SHARED HERITAGE: BYZANTINE AND OTTOMAN VIEWS OF THE CLASSICAL MONUMENTS OF ISTANBUL

## Keith HOPWOOD

> Once upon a time, a King had a very beautiful daughter. She was called Belkis (the name of the Queen of Sheba in the Arabic tradition). He promised her hand to the man who could provide the most useful and beautiful amenity for his city. Two men stepped forward to compete. One built a wonderful palace; the other, an equally fine aqueduct. The King could not decide who had won. He prayed to Allah, and, in the morning he found he had two very beautiful daughters, whom he could bestow on both the talented builders.[1]

This story comes from a place called Belkis, in Southern Turkey, which had two very prominent ancient remains: a theatre (the palace), and an aqueduct. The story is therefore a fairly obvious aetiological myth linking the name of the village to its most visible monuments. We cannot, of course, speculate on the nature of the myth-making here: did the village-name Belkis come from the myth, or the myth from the name? We know that there never was a King of Belkis, or of its predecessor, classical Aspendos, and we also know that the theatre was the gift of a local aristocrat of the late second century AD, since the dedicatory inscription (and, very rarely in classical antiquity), the architect's name have been preserved.[2] By the time the process of myth-making started, not only had the original function and chronological context of the building been lost, but also the ability to read dedications in Greek.

For many scholars, this is unproblematic. The Turkish conquest of Asia Minor killed, evicted, or assimilated the Byzantine-Greek population and represented a complete break with the Byzantine-Classical tradition.[3] A glance at the better-documented process of turning the history of (in this case) the late antique period into myth, can be traced in the Metropolis of Constantinople itself, where demotic (or pseudo-demotic) texts from both the middle-Byzantine and Ottoman periods have survived.

---

[1] Told in the guide to the Antalya region by N. Keskin (n.d). The story is alluded to in Hogarth (1925; 208). It does not appear in the latest guide to Aspendos (Özgür, 1988).

[2] *IGRR* III 803 for the donor inscription.

[3] İnalcık (1969-70).

What I hope to show is that both traditions evolved along similar lines and that there is a closer relationship between these texts than has been previously noted. Stefane Yérasimos in his *La fondation de Constantinople et de Sainte Sophie dans les traditions Turques*[1] does suggest the possibility of a link in his footnotes but dismisses it as historically impossible. This is because he subscribes to the notion that the population of Constantinople/Istanbul like that of Asia Minor was almost completely replaced in the years after its capture by the Turks in 1453. This is based on an important article by Halil İnalcik, the leading Turkish Ottoman historian. He was heavily influenced by M. Fuad Köprülüzade, whose *Foundation of the Ottoman Empire* of 1935, and still considered definitive in the Turcophone tradition, ends with eleven hypotheses (unproven),[2] of which one is that the Byzantines were either killed or driven out of the areas of Turkish conquest in the heartlands (as opposed to the later Balkan and other conquests). This seems to me to be untenable for several reasons.

*First*, the survival until 1926 of substantial Greek minorities within mainland Turkey. Nineteenth century travellers report these as indigenous 'Ionian' Greeks.[3]

*Secondly*, the continuity and blending of religious traditions, attested by Hasluck in his two-volume *Christianity under the Sultans*, researched before the exchange of populations.[4]

*Thirdly*, my own research into the conquest of Asia Minor between 1071 and 1350 shows that Byzantines and Turks on the high plateaux of Asia Minor had to work together to form viable state structures to ensure their self-protection.[5] Patronage and protection rather than ethnic cleansing were the basis of the Seljuk state as attested by Hasluck and its successor emirates of which the Ottoman emirate was one, if we subscribe to this Hasluckian notion. We should therefore look for a shared tradition in which change should occur as a series of innovations by different (usually anonymous) authors to create new, overlapping images of the past.

---

[1] Yerasimos (1990).

[2] İnalcık (1992; 111-7).

[3] See, for example, Ramsay (1897; Ch. X; Hogarth (1925; 54-6).

[4] Hasluck (1929) passim.

[5] Hopwood (1992), (1993), (1997).

## Constantinople/Istanbul

Constantinople has always been a fertile place for mythmaking: the French scholar Ebersolt in 1918 could write of the city:

> Cette superposition de quatre civilisations a créé cette ville étrange, moins pure qu'Athènes, moins riche que Rome, mais tormentée, passionnante, énigmatique.[1]

Indeed, a city derived from the four traditions of Greece, Rome, Byzantium and Turkey should offer much material for the making of a myth. Its original decoration, by Constantine, of monuments brought from pagan temples all over the Eastern Empire, emphasised its status as an art gallery and museum of these formally venerated objects of a cult that was soon to be suppressed. Religious objects were redefined as works of art. Pagan culture was always suspect to the medieval Christians. St Basil the Great had hesitated much concerning what parts of the pagan literary canon might be assimilated within the Christian curriculum.[2] The city of God was enigmatic from its very foundation.

The Byzantine sources we are to consider date from the eighth and ninth centuries and are known as the *Patria*[3] — accounts of the marvels of the city very much like the better studied *Mirabilia Urbis Romae*.[4] They are anonymous, and very rarely refer to the classical textual based tradition. The authors intersperse personal observation, incident and received tradition. Although the tradition has literary antecedents, Dagron sees in them a 'littérature de la rue'[5] — an attempt by men of moderate education to make sense of what they see around them.

When I gave an earlier draft of this paper in London, I was censured for proclaiming the existence of this 'middle brow' literature, which had an existence independent of the 'higher' genres of historiography and theology. I should, my critics averred, have taken note of Gramsci's dictum that culture is a hegemonic, 'top-down' construct which involves all genres within the sphere of upper class ideology. I cannot agree with this criticism. Carlo

---

[1] Ebersolt (1918; 10).

[2] The *locus classicus* is the essay by St Basil discussed by Wilson (1975). On this problem in general, see Wilson (1983; 8-12).

[3] Edited by Preger (1901). See now the new edition of the *Parastaseis Syntomoi Chronikai* by Cameron and Herrin (1984).

[4] Greenhalgh (1989).

[5] Dagron (1984; 5).

Ginzburg in his magnificent *The Cheese and the Worms*[1] shows the intellectual formation of a sixteenth century Italian miller whose views were an idiosyncratic fusion of both 'high' and 'low' cultures: such, I believe are the *patria*.[2]

By the eighth century, even these monuments had been de-contextualised. The Arab invasions of the seventh century had seriously affected the city, not only by the harrowing events of two sieges, but also by the capture of Egypt and its crucial grain supply. By the eighth century, many areas of the city within its walls were deserted, and the monumental centres of the old city stood isolated, or as today occupied by an invasive flood of domestic space.[3]

One way of dealing with this was to emphasise the alien nature of the monuments and the danger they posed to the god-fearing inhabitants.

> One day we went off to the Kynegion with Himerios the honourable *chartularios* to investigate the statues there, and found among them one that was small in height and squat and very heavy. While I was wondering at it and not getting on with my enquiry, Himerios said 'You are right to wonder, for he is the builder of the Kynegion'. When I said 'Maximian was the builder and Aristeides the architect', immediately the statue fell from its height, which was great, and dealt Himerios a great blow and killed him on the spot. I was afraid, for there was no-one else there, except for the men who were holding our mules, and they were outside the steps. Terrified of being hurt myself, I dragged him by the right foot to where they throw the convicts, and tried to throw him in, but in my terror I let go of my load at the edge of the bank and ran away and sought asylum in the Great Church. When I told the truth about what had happened, I was not believed until I resorted to confirmation by oath, since I was the only one who had seen the event at the time. So the dead man's relations and the friends of the emperor went with me to that place, and before approaching where the man lay fallen, stared in amazement at where the statue lay fallen. A certain John, a philosopher, said 'By divine providence, I find it so in the writings of Demosthenes, that a man of rank would be killed by the statue. And he told this at once to the Emperor Philippicus (711-3) and was commanded to bury the statue in that place; which indeed was done, for it was impossible to destroy it. Consider these things truly, Philokalos, and pray that you do not fall into temptation, and take care when you look at old statues, especially pagan ones (*Parastaseis* 28).

---

[1] Ginzburg (1992). Original Italian edition 1976.

[2] It is worth comparing the poem of Constantine of Rhodes on the buildings from the early tenth century. Here, Constantine is 'hijacking' the tradition of *patria* for the 'higher' literary genres. The text is discussed in Baldwin (1985; 169-76).

[3] On the desertion of Constantinople, see Mango (1996; 128-9).

I have cited this passage at length, because it encapsulates all the themes of the *Patria*. Here we have a Byzantine 'Indiana Jones' investigating the material traces of a 'mythical' past and caught alone in a very nasty enclosure. We hear of intra mural burials elsewhere in the *Parastaseis*:

> In the time of Leo the Isaurian (717-41) many *thematia* were destroyed because the man was irrational. At that time the Trizodon, as it is called, was removed. It was in the hollow place before St Mokios. Up to that time many people used to perform astronomical calculations by it and tombs of pagans (hellenes) and Arians are buried there, and many other corpses (5d).

Both places, therefore, harbour some potentially restless dead.[1] The anonymous author and Himerios are going statue-hunting in the Kynegion.[2] Our author is puzzled. Then Himerios makes a suggestion which the author caps 'Maximian was the builder and Aristeides the architect' — it looks as though they are piecing out, with their imperfect grasp of epigraphic Greek, the inscription on the statue base, like the mythmakers in Belkis, who have no context for their monuments. Unlike them, the protagonists here share the language and culture of the third or fourth century dedicatees, but like them, also lack the context.[3]

A similar imperfect grasp of the context of an inscription may be seen in *Parastaseis* 38 where we hear that:

> Constantine the Great was acclaimed after defeating Azotios and Byzas and Antes, the Blue Faction shouting 'you have taken up the whip again and as though young again you race madly in the stadium'.

The text has been preserved both in stone and the literary tradition.[4] It was an acclamation not to an emperor, but to the famous sixth-century charioteer Porphyrius.[5] It is clear that the author can read the inscription, but is capable of reattributing it from its dedicatee, Porphyrius, to the earlier emperor Constantine. This decontextualisation of material in the Middle Ages has been

---

[1] For this term, see Johnston (1999).

[2] Cameron and Herrin (note ad loc.) describe the Kynegion as a place of execution: a suitable place, therefore, for stories of supernatural events. Mango (1981; 343) identifies the Kynegion with the ancient amphitheatre of Constantinople, a rich source of statuary and inscriptions. This emphasises the cultural break between the Byzantines of the eighth century and those of the fourth and fifth centuries. See Mango (loc. cit.), and Mango (1980; 77-81).

[3] This goes further than the 'lack of continuity' mentioned by Dagron (1984; 29). New interpretations of place-names, and new creative misreadings of texts have fragmented the experience of the late antique world for the medieval observer.

[4] *Palatine Anthology* xv. 44.5-6. For commentary, see Cameron and Herrin ad loc. Cameron (1973; 109-111).

[5] On whom, see Cameron (1973) passim.

noticed by Vickers in the case of the Classical tradition of rhetoric in the West.[1] It seems to apply to the East also. Constantine's defeat of Byzas and Antes should alert us to the chronological dislocation and decontextualisation within these texts. For the moment we should return to the former text where the death of Himerios is mysteriously foretold by Demosthenes. It is difficult for us to associate the fourth century B.C. Athenian orator with a fourth century A.D. construction, yet that anachronism neither worried the author, nor the élite company before whom the revelation of the oracle takes place.[2] We might also hesitate at the oracular powers granted to the classical orator. Equally, the anachronism of opposing Constantine and Byzas in the second extract shows how far removed the author of the *Parastaseis* was from the ancient chronographic tradition: the events associated were 1,000 years apart. Constantine did indeed fight Licinius for control of Byzantium: the tradition conflates that struggle with the replacement of the name Byzantium with Constantinople. It also assimilates Constantinople to the Roman tradition, by giving Constantinople two founders, Byzas and Antes, like Roman Romulus and Remus.[3] The reconstruction of a Constantinopolian past is evident.

Chronological inexactitude is evident in other areas of the tradition. Earlier philosophers are associated with major works in the capital: Galen (early second century A.D) is associated with Constantine (early fourth century AD and Zeno (late fifth century AD) *(Parastaseis* 40). A major figure is the legendary first century sage and wonder-worker Apollonius of Tyana. He appears in the *On Statues* (79) as a founder of statues, and elsewhere (103) as being summoned by Constantine to bless the monuments.

Inevitably, in a Christian context, there was much speculation as to how these wonder-workers achieved these miracles, given that such miracles could only be performed by God. In the third century, the answer had been that these acts were the work of demons.[4] By our period, given the rarity of appeals to demons, the agency was left to nature, which had been prevailed upon by the sages, but worked at the command of the Deity.

---

[1] See Vickers (1988; 214-53).

[2] Notice that our protagonists have to be redeemed by a member of the élite and that such a prestigious expert pronounces the definitive closure of the adventure. He does so, of course, in terms that are desperately 'middlebrow'.

[3] Constantinople was the New Rome: she should therefore have two founders like the first Rome. Byzas was well attested, having given his name to Byzantium.

[4] Most succinctly expressed at Lane Fox (1986; 444).

For the statues and columns associated with these figures worked wonders. The death of Himerius was an instance of their power, and a warning to those drawn to investigation of the pagan past and draws attention to the potentially sacrilegious danger of researching for *Patria* materials! We see statues as a recompense for the false murder set up by the assassins (*Parastaseis* 7), building on an ancient tradition of statues as recompense for misdeeds.[1] We find statues whose (presumably indecipherable) inscriptions foretell the future (*On Stelae* 61 & 62) as well as the last days of the city (*On Stelae* 50). These are *tetelesmenoi* which, via Arabic, gives both English and Turkish Talisman or Tilismen.[2] The cross reference of the cultures provides the crucial word.

Equally, some columns have specific functions. We hear of a column in the Zeugma, which supported a statue of Aphrodite: this statue was the sign to test women and girls, whether rich or poor, whose chastity was suspect. If anyone thought that a girl had lost her virginity and this did not reveal itself naturally, her parents and friends would say "Right, let's go to the statue of Aphrodite and, if you have remained chaste, the proof will be made there". If the girl who approached the statue was blameless she passed unharmed, but if she had lost her virginity, as soon as she was near the column, would she or no, a sudden power overwhelmed her spirit and she raised her skirts and showed her genitals to everyone ... But the sister-in-law of Emperor Justin (II 565 — 75) had the statue destroyed because one day when the rain stopped her from travelling by boat on her way to Blacharnae she passed the column on horseback and this princess, guilty of adultery, exposed herself. (*On Stelae* 65).

We shall see that a statue of Aphrodite was famed by the Ottomans, but for different purposes. In modern times, the column of Marcian is now known as the *Kız Taşı* (Maiden's Column) which is now thought to have similar powers.[3]

A major break with the past was the forgetting of former institutions. As a 'New Rome', Constantinople also had to have a Senate House, which by the eighth century had lost any political importance. *Parastaseis* consequently derives Senate, from its founder Sinatos,[4] and sees it as an ordinary palace. There are hints also, that there was an eliding of Justinian and his family and

---

[1] *Parastaseis* 7. On this issue generally, see Faraone (1992).

[2] Faraone (1992; 4)

[3] Sumner-Boyd and Freely (1973; 256-7).

[4] *Parastaseis* 43.

his great church, for the *Parastaseis*[1] gives the name of his wife as Sophia, not Theodora, and the *On Stelae* (62) gives the wife of Justinian's prefect, who built the church, her (historical?) name of Sophia.

Much of this material resurfaces in the anonymous Turkish manuscript of 1491[2] and Evliya Çelebi's *Seyahatname*. It may be no accident, as there were Byzantine survivors in Istanbul and Mehmed II himself patronised the historian Kritovoulos and employed the patriarchate to strengthen the Greek community of Istanbul.[3] The historian Oruç records that Mehmed II collected books and experts to inform him of the nature of the antiquities of Constantinople.[4] What is pertinent is that both texts recontextualise the material in a new framework of world history. Whereas the Byzantine texts had been dealing with details of their urban environment, the Ottoman texts situate these within a vastly different grand scheme. Stefane Yérasimos, who published the 1491 manuscript, sees it as an attempt to rein in Mehmet II's attempts at world power.[5] I cannot agree. If Constantinople has been founded by Solomon, Yanko ibn Madyan, Alexander the Great, Puzantin of Hungary, Heraclius of Rome and Constantine the Great, it cannot be anything other than a seat of world power.

Let us begin with Solomon. There is no extant monument attributed to him, but the 1491 manuscript attributes to him a palace at Cyzicus[6] to which all the antiquities of the world were brought. This is then pillaged by Yanko to begin the great city of Islambol (full of Islam). Both Greek and Turkish texts state that the columns of Haghia Sophia came from Cyzicus and we know from early Ottoman chronicles that Cyzicus was the capital of Orhan's son Süleyman. The Ottoman dynasty is hijacking the myth of the ancient importance of Cyzicus (or is the myth hijacking the Ottoman dynasty? Solomon is later seduced by his wife into idol-worship and loses the support of heaven.

He is succeeded as a major founder by Yanko ibn Madyan, allegedly in the early eighth century BC. To Yanko are attributed most of the talismans in Istanbul, including the obelisk of Theodosius I. Consequently, modern

---

[1] *Parastaseis* 81.

[2] Yerasimos (1990).

[3] *ODB* 1159, Runciman (1968; 165-85).

[4] Cited in Yerasimos (1990; 99).

[5] Yerasimos (1990; 2).

[6] Almost certainly the temple of Hadrian, still extant in the fifteenth century. See Hasluck (1910; 10-12, 187-9). This temple was listed by Kedrenos in the eleventh century as one of the seven wonders of the world. See Baldwin (1983; 258).

scholars have identified him with that conqueror. The chronology and the sense of the narrative forbid this identification. Yanko is a purely mythical figure. Indeed, if Yérasimos is to be believed, it is a 'ghost name', deriving from a false reading of an Arabic text.[1]

Yanko, however, is accredited with the hippodrome obelisk. Here Evliya describes it:

> This is also an obelisk of red-coloured stone covered with various sculptures and situated in the At-Meydan. The figures on its sides tell the different features of the city. It was erected in the time of Yanko ibn Madyan, who is represented on it sitting on his throne, and holding a ring in his hand, implying symbolically, "I have conquered the whole world, and hold it in my hands, like this ring". His face is turned towards the East and kings stand before him, holding dishes, in the guise of beggars. On another are the figures of 300 men erecting the obelisk, with the various machines used for that purpose.

This is a direct description of the monument, transported to the new Ottoman chronological scheme. Yanko's stance in the relief hints at the universal monarchy ascribed to him in the Ottoman tradition. The kneeling kings emphasise his dominion. Here, the Ottomans read correctly the iconography of the monument since Theodosius is holding the laurel of victory in the chariot races, and the 'kings' are captive barbarians. Here, a comprehensible relief is recontextualised into a new scheme of universal history where Evliya's personal observation, tales from Greek and Turkish inhabitants of İstanbul combine with the Ottoman/Islamic world story.

Another monument to Yanko further emphasises his status as world conqueror.

> There is a lofty column of white marble, inside of which there is a winding staircase. On the outside of it, figures of the soldiers of various nations, Hindustanis, Kurdistanis and Multanis, whom Yanko ibn Madyan vanquished... Subsequently at the birth of the Prophet, there was a great earthquake by which all were thrown down topsy-turvy, and the column, itself broken in pieces: but having been formed by talismanic art, it could not be entirely destroyed.

Evliya here is referring to the column of Arcadius (400) set up to commemorate the expulsion of the Goths. Its base alone survives, though much of it survived into the seventeenth century to beseen by Evilya and

---

[1] Yérasimos (1990; 65).

drawn by Freshfield. It is frequently represented in the views of the trade processions by Ottoman miniaturists. It was therefore integrated into the imperial ceremonial of the sixteenth and seventeenth century Ottoman state.

Removing talismans could be dangerous:

On the site of the baths of Sultan Bayezid Veli (II: 1481 - 1512) there was a quadrangular column (tetrapylon) eighty cubits high, erected by an ancient sage named Kirbariya, as a talisman against the plague, which could never prevail in Islam ... as long as this column was standing. It was afterwards demolished by that sultan, who erected a heart-rejoicing *hamam* in its place; and in that very day one of his sons died of the plague, in the garden of Daud Pasha outside the Adrianople gate on an elevated platform; since which time plague has prevailed in that city.

The talismanic nature of these monuments is evoked by Evliya's description of the serpent column, originally installed in İstanbul by Constantine the Great and a monument which also appears prominently in the *Surname-I Hümayun* (*Imperial Book of Festival*) of 1582. The Ottoman tradition dated this monument to a later stage in the chronology (though well before its actual date):

A sage named Surandeh, who flourished in the days of error under King Puzantin, set up a brazen image of a triple-headed dragon in the At-Meydan in order to destroy all serpents, lizards, scorpions and suchlike poisonous reptiles: and not a poisonous beast was there in the whole of Makedoniyyah. It has the form of a twisted serpent, measuring ten cubits above and as many below ground. It remained thus buried in the mud and earth from the making of Sultan Ahmed's mosque, but uninjured, until Selim II, surnamed the drunken, passing by on horseback, knocked off with his mace the lower jaw of that dragon which looks to the West. Serpents then made their appearance in the Western side of the city, and since that time have been common in every part of it. If, moreover, the remaining heads should be destroyed, Istanbul will be completely eaten up by vermin.

The damaged talisman is backed up by six further in the Altı-Mermer (Hexakionon) district which repel flies, gnats, storks, wolves and ensure the cocks to crow. All these fell in the earthquake that accompanied the birth of the Prophet, but, like the statue that crushed Himerios, are indestructible. They were also the work of Philip of Macedon, Plato, Hippocrates, Socrates and Pythagoras. The Greek tradition was clearly alive and well, although the talismans in the Ottoman tradition are more apotropaic than predictive.

The column of Constantine also acquires magical powers:

> In the Tavuk-bazaar, there is another needle-like column formed of many
> pieces of red emery stone and a hundred royal cubits in height. This was
> also damaged by the earthquake which occurred in the two nights during
> which the Pride of the World was called into existence; but the builders girt
> it round with iron hoops, as thick as a man's thigh, in forty places, so that
> it is still firm and standing. It was erected a hundred and forty years before
> the era of Iskender; and Konstantin placed a talisman on top of it in the orm
> of a starling, which once a year clapped its wings and brought all the birds
> of the air into the place.

The Great Church of Aghia Sophia had attracted Byzantine myth-making: the
Ottomans had to fit it also into their system. The links with Solomon are
deeply Byzantine, for Justinian is alleged to have compared his church with
Solomon's Temple with the words "Solomon, I have surpassed thee".[1] It is
almost certain that this embodiment of the superiority of the New over the
Old Testament was not lost in the imagination of Christianity's Islamic
successor. The manuscript of 1491 believes the structure was built in memory
of the founder's wife Sofia (not the Church of Holy Wisdom), an idea hinted
at in the Greek *Patria*. Evliya sees it as the mausoleum for the founder Ai Sof
(strangely, for he has some understanding of Greek). However, he is interested
in the traditions of Hızır, the Green man of Islamic tradition, who guarded the
waters of life. Hızır seems to have helped the builders, (in place of the
nameless eunuch of the *Patria*). Hızır was the Islamic syncretism of St
George[2], the patron saint of Cappodocia and the frontiersmen of Byzantium,
who assimilated most to Turkish ways.

If Hızır/St George is a major conceptual link between Byzantines and
Turks, I would also argue that the same is true of Ottoman shrine of Eyüb
Ansari. Eyüb was the standard-bearer of the Prophet who was killed in one of
the early sieges of Constantinople. Mehmet the Conqueror discovered his
tomb after a revelation by the Shey-ül Islam Akşemsettin. However, it seems
fairly certain that one of the terms of peace between Arabs and Byzantines had
been the honouring and preservation of the tomb of Eyüb. The Arab
community in the city would have kept the site known. Here was a common
tradition presented as a re-foundation.

---

[1] By the author of one of our *Patria*, Preger (1901, Vol. 1; 105).
[2] Greenhalgh (1989).

This material casts considerable light on both societies living among earlier ruins and the ways they came to terms with them. Both texts show the awakening of interest in antiquity by societies that were just experiencing considerable population growth attested by Greenhalgh (though at different dates) for Western Europe. The Byzantine tradition reflects the fragmentation and myth-making of the Middle Ages; the Ottoman sets this arcane knowledge into narrative of 'utter antiquity' like its contemporary Elizabethan England. But the *Patria* and Evliya's travel-journal reflect alongside the intellectual tradition the experiences of the ordinary *İstanbullu* over a thousand years which created a shared heritage in this 'tormented, passionate and enigmatic city'.

*REFERENCES*

Baldwin, B. 1983 'The Development of a Byzantine Theme' in *L' Antquité Classique* 52, 253-9.

Baldwin, B. 1985 *An Anthology of Byzantine Poetry*, Amsterdam; J.C. Gieben.

Cameron, A. 1973 *Porphyrius the Charioteer*, Oxford; Clarendon Press.

Cameron, A. and Herrin, J. 1984 *Constantinople in the Early Eighth Century: The Parastaseis Syntomoi Chronikai*, Leiden; Brill.

Dagron, G. 1987 *Constantinople Imaginaire: Études sur recueil des Patria*, Paris; Presses universitaires de France.

Deacy, S. and Pierce, K. (eds) 1997 *Rape in Antiquity: Sexual Violence in the Greek and Roman Worlds*, London; Duckworth.

Ebersolt, J. 1918 *Constantinople Byzantine et les Voyagers du Levant*, Paris ; E. Leroux.

Farah, C. (ed.) 1993 *Decision Making and Change in the Ottoman Empire*, Kirksville; Thomas Jefferson University Press at Northeast Missouri State University.

Faraone, C. 1992 *Talismans and Trojan Horses: Guardian Statues in Ancient Greek Myth and Ritual*, Oxford, New York; Oxford University Press.

Freely, J. 1974 *Stamboul Sketches*, Istanbul; Redhouse Press.

Ginzburg, C. 1992 *The Cheese and the Worms: The Cosmos of a Sixteenth-Century Miller*, London; Penguin.

Greenhalgh, M. 1989 *The Survival of Roman Antiquities into the Middle Ages*, London; Duckworth.

Hasluck, F. 1910 *Cyzicus*, Cambridge; CUP.

Hasluck, F. 1929 *Christianity and Islam under the Sultans*, Oxford; Clarendon.

Hogarth, D. 1925 *The Wandering Scholar*, Oxford; Oxford University Press.

Hopwood, K 1992 'Low-Level Diplomacy between Byzantines and Ottoman Turks', in Shepard and Franklin (eds), 151-8.

Hopwood, K. 1993 'Peoples, Territories and States: The Formation of the Beğliks of Pre-Ottoman Turkey', in Farah (ed.), 129-38.

Hopwood, K. 1997 'Byzantine Princesses and Lustful Turks', in Deacy and Pierce (eds), 231-42.

Hopwood, K 2000 'Living on the Margin: Byzantine Farmers and Turkish Herders', *Journal of Mediterranean Studies* 10, 1-2, 93-106.

İnalcık, H. 1969-70 'The Policy of Mehmet II in Istanbul', *Dumbarton Oaks Papers* 23-4; 231-49.

Johnston, S. 1999 *Restless Dead: Encounters between the Living and the Dead in Ancient Greece*, Berkeley; University of California Press.

Keskin, N. (n.d.) *Antalya: A Dazzling Paradise of Nature, History and Sun*, Istanbul; Güzel Sanatlar.

Köprülü, M. 1992 *The Origins of the Ottoman Empire*, NewYork; Albany State University of New York Press.

Lane Fox, R. 1986 *Pagans and Christians*, Harmondsworth; Viking.

Mango, C. 1981 'Daily Life in Byzantium', *Jahrbuch der Österreichischen Byzantinistik* XXXI/1, 337-53.

Mango, C. 1993 'The Development of Constantinople as an Urban Centre', in C. Mango, *Studies on Constantinople*, Ashgate; Variorum.

Özgür, M. 1988 *Aspendos*, Istanbul; NET Türistik Yayınlar.

Preger, T. 1901 *Scriptores Originum Constantinopolitanarum*, Leipzig; Lipsiae.

Ramsay, W. 1897 *Impressions of Turkey During Twelve Years' Wanderings*, London; Hodder & Stoughton.

Runciman, S. 1968 *The Great Church in Captivity: A Study of the Patriarchate of Constantinople from the Eve of the Turkish Conquest to the Greek War of Independence*, Cambridge; CUP.

Shepard, J. and Franklin, S. (eds) 1992 *Byzantine Diplomacy*, Ashgate; Variorum.

Sumner-Boyd, H. and Freely, J. 1972 *Strolling through Istanbul*, Istanbul; Redhouse Press.

Vickers, M. 1988 *In Defence of Rhetoric*, Oxford; Clarendon Press.

Wilson, N. 1975 *St Basil on the Value of Greek Literature*, London; Duckworth.

Wilson, N. 1983 *Scholars of Byzantium*, London; Duckworth.

Yérasimos, S. 1990 *La Fondation de Constantinople et de Sainte-Sophie dans les Traditions Turques*, Istanbul; Institut français d'études anatoliennes.

# PART FIVE

# TRAVELLERS,
# EMPIRE AND NATION

# 27. TRAVELLERS IN THE OTTOMAN EMPIRE AND TOPKAPI PALACE

Ömür BAKIRER

Travellers to Ottoman lands in general and to the capital Istanbul in particular have always been an interesting research topic for scholars. Though many have written on this subject, the criticism may be made that it has not been treated systematically. First of all a complete catalogue, including number and gender of travellers and how many of them have contributed written or visual information in the form of books or albums is missing. Secondly, a complete list of the libraries, both in Turkey and outside, that house these travelogues or albums in their collections, is also lacking.[1] Indeed, according to Eyice, though there have been many attempts to compile such a list or lists, not one has yet been thoroughly realized.[2]

This paper therefore makes no attempt to mention all the names, nationalities and works of travellers who have visited Istanbul with such growing interest through the centuries. It is only a brief account of those travellers, artists, writers and others who had a glimpse of the royal residence, Topkapı Palace, from a distance or had the privilege to enter it for one reason or another. Most of these visitors were not hesitant or indifferent to what they saw and therefore shared their experiences generously by writing or drawing what aroused their interest, what they learned by communicating with the native people or other travellers, and what they experienced during their stay. These verbal or visual documents are of primary importance in recording the architecture of the palace and the changes that took place from its establishment until the end of the nineteenth century.

However, there is one essential drawback with these documents. This is their subjective nature. In their visual representations, some artists at least have not drawn exactly what they saw but they have added their personal interpretations or their previous experiences to the subject. One example that illustrates this is the panorama drawn by Wilhelm Dilich, during the early

---

[1] Tayanç (1972; 39-42, 42-47).
[2] Eyice (1996; 9-10).

seventeenth century, where he has distorted the domes and minarets of all the buildings by reinterpreting them according to his recollections of a European town. Likewise, in their written descriptions, writers have paraphrased what they learned or what they were told, in the light of their own cultural background. We shall return to this issue throughout my discussion below.

*Background: The Palace and the first visitors to Istanbul*

After the conquest in 1453, Mehmed II the Conqueror (1444-1446; 1451-1481) had two royal residences constructed, one after the other. The first, the so called *Saray-ı Atik-i Amire* (Old Palace) was built in the central part of the city, on the third hill in place of the Byzantine Theodosius Forum and completed in 1454. A few years later, in 1459, as this palace became too crowded, the Sultan decided to construct a new one, larger than the first, and better located.[1] He selected a magnificent site for the *Saray-ı Cedid-i Amire* (New Palace) on the northern end of the first hill, on the area once occupied by the ancient acropolis of Byzantium. It was surrounded by a defensive wall and guarded by towers which extended from the Byzantine sea walls along the Golden Horn and met the walls along the sea of Marmara, altogether measuring around five kilometres. The palace was renamed Topkapı (Cannongate) during the nineteenth century, after the main sea gate added to the defensive walls during the reign of Mahmud I (1730-1754). When Abdülmecit I (1839-1861) moved his residence to the newly constructed Dolmabahçe palace, Topkapı became the residence for the widows of dead Sultans.

Almost the entire plan of the Topkapı Palace, with the exception of the harem (the ladies quarters) and the so-called Fourth Court was laid out and built by the Conqueror himself between 1459-1465. Monumental and elaborate gateways, large courts coming one after the other, small scaled buildings and halls lined on both sides of the courts, were arranged to reside in majesty on the elevated site of the acropolis and planned with utmost care to increase privacy. The accumulation of administrative and service units in the first two courts gave them a rather public aspect, thus they were easy to enter. In the third and later constructed courts privacy came first. Entry was therefore restricted. Until the late seventeenth century, only doctors and those who came

---

[1] The following brief description pertains only to the architecture of the Palace. It is summarised from several sources some of which are listed below: And (1994; 99-100); Arslan (1992a; 71-73); Eldem and Akozan(1982); Kuban (1996; 323,334), Seçkin (1998), Goodwin (1971) Necipoğlu (1991; 2-10), Uzunçarşılı (1945; 16-20).

for specific services could enter, which made this section more and more desired by those who could not see what was going on behind the gates.

The harem was largely constructed during the time of Murad III (1574-1495), with extensive additions and reconstructions chiefly under Mehmed IV (1648-1687) and Osman III (1754-1757); while the isolated pavilions of the Fourth Court date from various periods. On three occasions, in 1574, 1665, and 1856, serious fires devastated large sections of the palace, so that while the three main courts have preserved essentially the arrangement given to them by Mehmed II, many of the buildings have either disappeared or have been reconstructed and redecorated in later periods.

From the first days of its construction, the palace has been a centre of interest for travellers, especially because it was completely concealed with the encircling, high defensive walls. Foreigners could enter the Third and Fourth Courts only with special permission. However, those who were not accepted usually found a way of viewing it even if from a distance. The best way was to look at the palace from the sea while passing in a boat or to view it across from Pera, where all the embassies were located after the seventeenth century. This is why most of the panoramic views are drawn from one or the other of these two spots. However, during the first quarter of the nineteenth century and the reign of Mahmut II (1808-1839), a special permission 'firman' had to be issued for noteworthy foreigners who wished to enter the palace.

Before the eighteenth century, foreigners who arrived as individuals or in groups of two or three were interested mainly in cartography. It is perhaps possible to see a relation between these and the pilgrimage maps destined to enlighten travellers during stopovers on their way to the Holy Land. Therefore, the earliest visual documents that present information for the urban environment of the city and the location of the two palaces are the maps made by westerners, before and after the conquest of the city, and by Ottoman miniature painters during the early and later part of the sixteenth century.

Of course, with its unique geographic and topographic position, Istanbul has always been an interesting stop for visitors and travellers. According to Tekeli, the earliest known map of the city is by the Florentine priest Christophoro Buodelmonti, from 1422.[1] This map does not include scientific and accurate information, but depicts the overall character and topography, the walls and main buildings without too much interest in the

---

[1] Tekeli (1994; 556-557); Kuban (1998; 44-45, 1994; 156); Kayra (1990; 21, fig.2).

specific features of the single buildings and important districts. This lack of detail and accuracy leads it to be regarded a 'picture-plan' or 'engraved-plan' similar to many other examples of the period.[1] A second map by the German mapmaker and scientist Hertman Schede, was published in 1493, fifty years after the conquest, yet it still depicts the urban environment of Byzantine İstanbul. Kuban sees it as 'a complete fantasy', perhaps drawn even without seeing the city.[2] Although general and rather abstract, these two maps give the opportunity to view the location of the two palaces before their construction.

Another map, a bird's eye view of the city, is by Giovanni Andrea Vavassore, from the first half of the sixteenth century.[3] This one depicts the area around the Golden Horn and Pera, and shows only some of the transformations that took place during the reign of Mehmed II. For instance, the Old Palace is shown, but in place of the New Palace it still depicts a Byzantine building. It is believed that this served as a base map for several others prepared during the sixteenth century and later.

Perhaps a contemporary of Vavassore, from the Ottoman side one may mention the famous artist Matrakçı Nasuh who also included a 'picture-plan' of Istanbul in his Mecmua-i Menazil from 1535-37.[4] Here both palaces are depicted in their correct locations and in detail.[5] Still another late sixteenth century map by Veli Can is included in the Hünername I[6] from 1582 where the plan of the palace shows the gates and courts in correct order.[7]

As well as warfare, conquests, and encouraging projects for urban renewal in his new capital, Sultan Mehmed II is also responsible for promoting, if not initiating, diplomatic and cultural relations between the Ottoman Empire and the West.[8] The Sultan had a personal interest in culture, arts, science and made a rich collection of objects d'art, manuscripts, maps, albums, paintings and even Christian relics.[9] In accordance with these interests, and aided by his friendly relations with the city of Florence, artists

---

[1] Kayra (1990; 21-22), Ebersolt (1996; 44-47). Buedelmonte's plan accompanies a written description of the Hippodrom area, Kuban (1998; 44-45).

[2] Kuban (1998; 44-45).

[3] Tekeli (1994; 3/556-557), thinks that it might be after 1530), Kuban (1998; 44-45, 1994; 556), Kayra (1990; 45, fig. 29 detail).

[4] İÜK, T5964.

[5] Yurdaydın (1976; TSM H1523, fol.15 verso, 16 recto and verso, 17 recto and verso), Kayra (1990; 46, fig. 30).

[6] TSM, H1523.

[7] Anafarta (1969), And (2002; 330).

[8] Arslan (1992a; 15), Mansel (1996; 189-191).

[9] Necipoğlu (1991; 135).

like Constanzo da Ferrera and Gentile Bellini and from Verona the painter Matteo de Pasti, were invited to the palace. According to Necipoğlu, Bellini was to devise wall paintings for the private apartments of the Sultan.[1] However, it appears that he ended up painting the well-known portrait of the Sultan, and making his medallion, but the more essential project in consideration was never realized.

The beginnings of more permanent diplomatic and commercial relations with the West may be attributed to the sixteenth century, when the Ottomans were particularly prominent in politics and in warfare.[2] During the reign of Sultan Süleyman the Magnificent (1520-1566), the boundaries of the Empire were extended. Western European countries, who feared both the Ottoman army and the Ottoman triumphs, began sending diplomatic envoys and embassies to Istanbul in order to learn more about the Ottoman economic, diplomatic and military structure. The capital was interested in receiving not only these ambassadors, merchants and traders but they also welcomed craftsmen, artists and others, even though they themselves were not yet interested in establishing permanent embassies abroad.[3] The only occasion when they did send a diplomatic envoy or a temporary ambassador to the West was when they wished to extend an invitation to a festivity or to support the military ambitions of another country.

The first permanent French ambassador arrived in Istanbul in 1535, during the reign of Sultan Süleyman I, the Magnificient. The Sultan was a supporter of diplomatic relations with France, as they shared a similar interest in monarchy and power. French ambassadors were therefore privileged, an advantage which lasted until the French revolution in 1789.[4] Furthermore, the French embassy provided the leading framework for scholarly and artistic exploration of the Empire. For that reason ambassadors began to bring with them artists and initiated a tradition that continued for the next two centuries.[5]

The first Austrian ambassador, Baron Ogier Ghiselin de Busbecq, arrived in 1554 at a time when the Ottoman-Austrian relations were not that friendly, yet he stayed until 1562, extending his interest in Ottoman culture and arts. He contributed descriptions in the so called "letter form" that initiated

---

[1] Necipoğlu (1991; 135-136).
[2] Arslan (1992a;15-17), Mansel (1996; 189-191).
[3] Arslan (1992a; 15-17, Mansel (1996; 189-191).
[4] Arslan (1992a; 15-17, Mansel (1996; 189-191), Eyice (1996; 11).
[5] Mansel (1996; 191), Eyice (1996; 9-46).

a new literary genre and was popular even during the following centuries.[1] Busbecq was accompanied by the Dutch artist Melchior Lorichs, who stayed in İstanbul until 1559 and made the well known and perhaps the largest panoramic view of the city, now in the University Library at Leiden.[2] This detailed visual account depicts most of the monumental edifices in the city in elevation, including the Palace and the Elçi Hanı (ambassadors' inn), the early residence of the ambassadors and artists who arrived in the city.

Among other sixteenth century artists, the names of Pieter Cocke van Aelst, and Nicola de Nicolay are at the forefront. Nicola de Nicolay accompanied a French embassy to Istanbul in 1551. In his book, *Discours et historie véritable des navigations, prégrinations et voyages faits en Turquie*, published in Lyon in 1567, he collected a number of previous travellers accounts. The woodcuts that accompanied the text are considered the first accurate images of the Ottomans that reached the West.[3] Flemish Pieter Coeck van Aelst was in İstanbul in 1525, during the early years of Sultan Süleyman's reign. His panoramic view of the city, represented with people in the foreground and buildings in the background, was initially intended to be woven as a carpet upon his return. But the project was never realized, and the drawings were published after his death by his wife. The album, dated 1553, was named *Ces Moeurs et facons de fairs de turcs avecq les Regions y appertenantsz ont este au vif contre faitez par Pierre Coeckd'alost lui estant en Turquie*.[4]

This century is also the period when interest in all aspects of antique culture began strongly to be felt in Europe. At the beginning, this interest stayed within the boundaries of Italy and the Italian archaeological sites, yet toward the end of the century it covered all the countries in the Mediterranean basin, including the Ottoman lands and the capital. Intellects like Tavernier, Thévenot, Chardin, Bernier, and Dreux who were lovers of antique culture and arts, visited antique sites on the Aegean coast, wrote their impressions and made sketches which were later produced as engravings to illustrate the texts. Such works were highly admired when they were published and distributed in

---

[1] The letters of Busbecq remain a classic account of the Empire and are published in several languages, see *Turkish Letters of Ogier de Busbecq, Translated from the Elzivir edition of 1633*, by Edward Seymour Foster, Oxford 1927 or Busbecq 1555, *Türkiye'yi Böyle Gördüm*, translated by A.Kurutluoğlu İstanbul: Kervan Kitapçılık. Ebersolt (1996; 83-85), Kuban (1998; 44-45, Mansel (1996; 214).

[2] Ebersolt (1996; 84-85), Necipoğlu (1991; 42, pl.251-f).

[3] The book was translated by T. Washington as *The Navigations, pregrinations and voyages, made into Turkie in 1585*, Mansel (1996; 214), Eyice (1997; 9-10).

[4] Eyice (1997; 91-92).

the western countries.[1] Another important manifestation of the era is the picture albums that record certain historic incidents with drawings comparable to the Ottoman miniature style. One such example is a pictorial narrative compiled, around 1586, for the Habsburg ambassador Johannes Lewenklau. It comprises a series of illustrations recording a procession where the Austrian ambassador is carrying presents to the Sultan as a tribute.[2]

*The seventeenth century and after*

During the seventeenth century there is a noticeable increase in the number and type of the travellers, as well as in the type of documents they begin to produce. The growing fascination of the westerners in Ottoman life and customs is one reason for this increase in the number of visitors. There was also an advance in the establishment of permanent foreign embassies. Mansel writes, 'Soon after the middle of the sixteenth century no other capital welcomed so many embassies. Ambassadors came to Constantinople from London and Paris, Stockholm and Samarkand, Goa and Fez. In 1628, by no means an exceptional year, ambassadors from Vienna, Warsaw, Moscow, Isfahan and Delhi arrived to pay their respects to the Sultan. Power was the draw.'[3]

After 1600, the ambassadors who had lived at the centre of the city in the so called *Elçi Hanı* during the previous century, began to establish themselves in Pera on the hill above Galata, with a direct view across the Golden Horn and the Sultan's palace.[4] Each embassy began to construct a spacious and luxurious 'palace', where they lived with their attendants, visitors and artists who accompanied them. Altogether the inhabitants of an embassy could reach to a number between fifty and a hundred.

Ambassadors were known as the 'Sultan's guests'. They rode to the palace on the Sultan's horses, were admitted into the second court with stately ceremonies, dined with the Grand Vizier in the Porte or in a private kiosk and rarely they were given the privilege of admission to the Sultan's throne room. In these occasions the parties spoke different languages, they wore different costumes, altogether they had different customs, beliefs, and religions but as

---

[1] Arslan (1992a; 15) Mansel ( 1996; 214).
[2] Necipoğlu (1991; 42, Pl.33 a_q), And (1994; 102-106).
[3] Mansel (1996; 189-192), Arslan (1992a; 15-17), Kuban (1998; 44-45).
[4] Mansel (1996; 189-194).

always they shared the same interests in monarchy, power and financial matters.[1] The ambassadors were either invited to attend and take part in the festivities or were given the opportunity to watch and even to record them. The Ottoman festivals were organized to celebrate occasions such as wedding ceremonies, births in the royal family, circumcision of the imperial princes, enthronement, and religious days.[2] The attendance of foreign visitors in these ceremonies is recorded in the Turkish sources starting from the late sixteenth century onwards. Surname-i Humayun from 1582 and Surname-i Vehbi from 1720 are good examples. On pages where the Sultan, his viziers and attendants are shown watching the festivities there may be seen also the representations of some members of the diplomatic emissaries residing in the capital, watching the parades in the locations reserved for them.[3]

The ambassadors or the artists who accompanied them documented the architectural and urban environment where the parades took place, the Sultan and his family, the officials, organizers and finally the ordinary people who attended, individually or in groups, were depicted in their special garments. The medium of these representations was water colours, oil paintings, engravings and even drawings in the Ottoman miniature style. Most of these drawings were collected in albums that were distributed in western countries and which introduced them to the Ottoman world, culture and arts. Therefore, among the several privileges given to foreign visitors, entrance to the palace grounds, attending ceremonial festivals and permission to record these occasions may have been most effective in collecting data for the imperial capital and its populace.[4]

The second reason for the increase in the number of written and visual documents, during the seventeenth century, is perhaps the advance in the Ottoman interest in the West. In 1607, the first Ottoman diplomatic envoy was sent to France. This was an official occasion when the Westerners met the Ottomans in person whom they had come to know from books and from their military legends. During 1669-70, the second Ottoman envoy, headed by Suleyman Paşa as ambassador, arrived in France and created diplomatic alliances that were promising for both parties. After these occasions the Ottoman impact on French culture and literature began to be felt stronger than before as specific types of literary works began to be devoted to the

---

[1] And (2000; 28-29), Mansel (1996; 192-94).

[2] Mansel (1996; 189-194).

[3] For the Surname-i Humayun (TSM H1344) from 1582, And (2002; 257-262). For the Surname-i Vehbi (TSM A3595) from 1720, Atıl (1999; 95-45), Renda (1977; 35-36).

[4] Renda (1977; 18-19), Kuban (1998; 44-45), Mansel (1996; 189-194).

introduction of this little known culture. Among them the 'letter form', initiated during the sixteenth century, gained in impetus and continued to be popular throughout the following centuries.[1]

The earliest account from the first half of the seventeenth century is by Ottavio Bon (1551-1622), the Venetian Balio, who was in Istanbul between 1606-1609, during the reign of Ahmed I (1603-1617). It is stated that, Bon's account of Istanbul is based on accurate first hand information that was provided from Domenico Gerosolomitano, the physician of Murad II. It is also possible that he made friends with a member of the palace and collected information even on the more private residences, he himself was not able to enter.[2] According to Goodwin, Bon is the most reliable among all the western diplomats and travellers who were active between 1453 and the end of the seveneenth century.[3]

Bon's description of the physical condition of the palace starts with the main gate: 'at the first entrance into the Seraglio, there is a very large and stately gate', and continues slowly proceeding through the First, Second and Third Courts.[4] These descriptions were sent to Venice as a large report or manuscript entitled, *Il Seraglio del grand signore descritto a Constantinopoli nel 1608*, which is now kept in the libraries of St Mark and Marciana.[5] The early version of this manuscript was published after his death in 1625. A new version, with additions made by John Graves, was published in 1650. The story of Bon's manuscript is interesting. Robert Withers, who was in Istanbul between 1610-1620, was given a copy of this manuscript by the Venetian ambassador. He translated it and made some additions himself. Still later another Englishman, John Greaves, who was in Istanbul in 1638, was given this English translation, which he edited and published in 1650 in London. Furthermore other scholars, like Samuel Purches in 1624 in England and Michel Baudier in 1625, in France made references to his work in their own publications.[6]

Another account from the early years of the seventeenth century is by Thomas Dallam who was not an ordinary traveller but had a specific mission. On the occasion of the accession of Mehmed III (1595-1603) Queen Elizabeth

---

[1] Renda (1977; 18-20).

[2] Bon (1996; 11-16), Kuban (1996; 323-327).

[3] Bon (1996; 11-20).

[4] Kuban (1996; 325-327).

[5] Whithers (1996; 2-4).

[6] Whithers (1996; 2-4).

I of England, wished to renew the capitulations and sent the Sultan some presents among which there was also an elaborate organ. Thomas Dallam, the builder of the organ travelled to Istanbul, visited the Palace every day for a month while he supervised the installation. He is one of the few outsiders who was let into the privacy of the harem and the Fourth Court, therefore his observations are extremely interesting. *The Diary of Master Thomas Dallam 1599-1600*,[1] contains descriptions of the Fourth Court and the *İncili Köşk* (Pearl Kisok) where the organ was installed. These are considered as observations of an eye witness.[2]

The Englishman George Sandys, (1578-1644), reputed as a poet and traveller, set out for the Levant in 1610, stayed with the English ambassador in Istanbul for some time and later pursued his journey to Egypt. His observations and comments published as *Relation of a Journey to the Turkish Empire* (London 1632) are considered to be careful and accurate, in contrast to his contemporaries. For instance, his descriptions of the sea shore kiosks and especially the *Yalı Köşkü* (Shore Kiosk) have provided guidelines for restoration studies.[3] M. de Montconys arrived in 1648. His travel notes were published as *Journal des Voyages de M. de Montconys publi par le sieur de Liergue, son fils*.[4] From the second half of the seventeenth century there is John Covel who was in Istanbul between 1670-1679, and his travel notes accompanied with engravings were published in 1693.[5]

Among the famous travellers of this century are Guillaume Joseph Grelot and Cornelius de Bruyn, who have presented their views of the capital both in written and visual format. G. J. Grelot in 1672 executed two panoramic views of Topkapı Palace which were published in *Relation Nouvelle d'un Voyage de Constantinople*, (Paris 1680-1681). One is looking from the Golden Horn in side elevation, the other is a birds-eye view of Topkapı together with Üsküdar Palace opposite.[6] This panorama is considered the most important work of the century. Kuban, mentions that 'the elevation of the Palace, facing the Golden Horn is a true document, certain sections are out of scale but the palace, palace grounds and some of the kiosks, like the *Sepetçiler Kasrı* (Basketmakers' Kiosk ) and *Yalı Köşkü* (Shore Kiosk) are

---

[1] Published in *Early Voyages and Travels in the Levant*, ed. Bent (1903).

[2] And (1994; 102-108).

[3] Fedden, (1958; 10), Eldem-Akozan (1969; 176).

[4] Ebersolt (1996; 107), Kuban (1996; 44-45).

[5] Ebersolt (1996; 146-148), Kuban (1996; 44-45).

[6] Ebersolt (1996; 138-141), Kuban (1996; 44-45).

better proportioned and given with all their details'. The accuracy in the representation of these specific buildings has made them accepted as trustworthy documents and together with several others they have been utilized as visual sources during the preparation of restoration drawings by S. H. Eldem.[1]

Cornelius de Bruyn arrived in Istanbul in 1678. He was more of a painter than a writer and he was mostly engaged in engravings. In *Voyage au Levant* (Delf 1698, Paris 1714), de Bruyn's panorama of İstanbul shows the sea front elevation of the palace, like Grelot's, as he too has viewed it from the Golden Horn. It is claimed that there are vital defficiencies in his work. His drawing is schematic and abstracted with certain details that do not exactly correspond to that of the city and seem to be copied from Grelot's panorama.[2] Nine years later, in 1686, Francesca Scarella made two other panoramas from the same spot, both showing a bird-eye view of the palace together with the small sea-shore kiosks.[3] It would not be appropriate to leave the seventeenth century without mentioning the most famous Ottoman traveller of the time, Evliya bin Derviş Mehmet Zilli, better known as Evliya Çelebi, who has given a long description of the palace in the written account of his travels which might be a useful complimentary source to some of the visual documents.[4]

According to Arslan, the eighteenth century gave rise to a new trend or a different impetus in relations between the Ottomans and the Europeans.[5] As before, there are several reasons that encouraged the positive and negative aspects of these relations and contributed to the development of new art forms both in visual and written format. From the diplomatic point of view, with the Treaty of Karlowitz, signed in 1699, the Ottomans lost political power in Europe. In addition, they fell behind technological and scientific developments in the West. This decline, at least in certain institutions, initiated a growing Ottoman dependence on the West. This is reflected in the rise in the power of the Europeans, who began to obtain more privileges than before.[6]

---

[1] Eldem-Akozan (1969; 171-185), Kuban (1996; 45-46).
[2] Ebersolt (1996; 148-151), Yerasimos (1994; 325).
[3] Necipoğlu (1991; pl. 31 a,b).
[4] Çelebi (1846).
[5] Ebersolt ( 1996; 166-167).

[6] Arslan (1992a; 16), Mansel (1996; 204).

As a consequence of this shift in power, during 1721-1722 Ahmed III (1703-1730) sent a diplomatic envoy to France to research scientific, military and cultural matters. The leader of the group, the so-called 'Twenty-Eight Mehmet Çelebi' presented a report to the Sultan upon his return. An assessment of the army based on this report made it clear that radical reforms were needed, and this initiated a new interest in western technology.[1] Mahmud I (1730-1754) followed by providing scientific and technical assistance, inviting professionals in these fields. His successor, Mustafa III (1757-1774) was yet more enthusiastic in seeking similar support. During his reign, Baron de Tott, a Turkish-speaking officer of Hungarian origin arrived under the guidance of the French ambassador, M. de Vergenes. Tott was 'trusted and housed by the Sultan', helping to organize the defense of the city, supervising modernization in several fields, besides encouraging the establishment of military institutions for education.[2] Furthermore, he contributed a detailed written description of the city concentrating on the Byzantine monuments and their state of preservation as well as on the social life in and around the city. Yet his descriptions collected in his, *Mémoires du Baron Tott sur les Turcs et les Tartars*, in two volumes (Amsterdam 1785), are considered a rather sharp and antagonistic account of the Ottomans.[3]

Mustafa III, who concentrated and supervised developments mainly to do with technical and scientific matters, did not have a particular liking for the arts. Yet he also was not actively against them and during his reign western artists continued to live and work in the embassies, and the privileges that were given earlier continued without restrictions. His followers Sultan Abdulhamid I (1774-1788) and Sultan Selim III (1788-1807) were rather more liberal and gave the artists and travellers permission to stroll in and around the city freely and make drawings as they wished.[4] Perhaps it was this liberty that increased the number of ambassadors and diplomats visiting İstanbul towards the end of the eighteenth century.

Now more than before, almost all the ambassadors were accompanied by artists who prepared drawings to accompany the written descriptions. These were later etched to be printed as engravings, thus an engraver was also included in the team for the final product. It appears that, during the process of engraving, the drawing may gain or loose some details, which may explain

[1] Arslan (1992a; 16-17), Mansel (1996; 203-204), Kuban (1996; 44-45), Renda (1977; 18-19).
[2] Renda (1977; 18-19) Mansel (1996; 203-204) Arslan (1992a; 17-18).
[3] Gölen (1998; 69).
[4] Arslan (1992a; 18-20), Renda (1977; 19-27), Kuban (1996; 44-45).

the rather careless handling in some of the illustrations. With improvements in the techniques of printing these travelogues were quickly published, as books or albums and in large numbers. They became popular as they informed the westerners on the Ottoman lands, customs and ways of life. This interest showed its impact on European literature, music, theatre, ballet and opera, as new themes inspired from the Ottoman culture began to be created. Literary works with a romantic approach to eastern countries and writing on new ideas as if they were taking place in an exotic eastern land created new literary forms. Furthermore, while in the previous centuries only the rich could travel in the east, during the late eighteenth and early nineteenth century, members of other classes could travel easily. Conditions were better as railways and boat-lines opened. Diplomats, tradesman, ordinary travellers, and even those seeking for adventure were on the road.[1]

During the eighteenth and nineteenth centuries, travellers and artists visiting Istanbul were of two types. Those of the first group were affiliated to the embassies, where they stayed, worked, and accompanied the ambassadors in their excursions to make drawings for them. As before, the French embassy welcomed and supported more artists than the others. Within the framework of these activities, Kont Choiseul-Gouffier (1752-1817), arrived as the French ambassador in İstanbul in September, 1784.[2] He had already published the first volume of his *Le Voyage pittoresque de la Grèce* in 1782 and the book was one reason for his appointment as ambassador to İstanbul. Besides bringing in military and naval staff for technical assistance, he was accompanied by two known artists, Jean Baptiste Hillair and Louis-Françoise Casses.[3] As the result of the permissions given by Abdülhamit I and Selim III, these two artists and others found suitable working conditions, both in the capital and the suburbs where they could travel freely.[4] In 1776, Gouffier, accompanied by Jean Baptiste Hillair, who had already worked for him for the drawings in the *Voyage pittoresque*, made his first journey to the Levant. During this excursion, Hillair prepared most of the drawings for the second volume of Gouffier's *Voyages pittoresque de la Gréce*.

Louis-Francois Cassas (1756-1827) arrived in Istanbul together with Gouffier, in September 1784. Cassas, stayed in the city for a short time, then went to Egypt and Syria, to make drawings for the ambassador. Landscape

[1] Boppe (1998; 109-110) Masel (1996; 205, 214) Renda (1977; 18-19) Kuban (1996; 45).

[2] Boppe (1998; 109-110) Mansel (1996; 205, 214) Renda (1977; 18-19) Kuban (1996; 45), Renda (1994; 2/386).

[3] Mansel (1996; 205-214) Renda (1977; 18-19) Kuban (1996; 45).

[4] Boppe (1998; 114), Renda (1994; 2/386).

drawings from İstanbul, general plans and views from Bursa, as well as panoramic views of the city and its single monuments were among his repertoire of drawings.[1] Other travellers who were welcomed in the French embassy were, the French artist and writer Antoine-Laurent Castellan (1772-1838),[2] and the artist Armand Charles Caraffe (1762-1822).[3] Castellan arrived in İstanbul in 1795 and was employed as a technical draughtsman in the Arsenal at the Golden Horn. The first section of his memoirs was published in 1808, under the title *Lettres sur la Morée* . This was followed by a second volume in 1811. Castellan contributed several panoramic views of the palace as seen from the sea, together with the sea shore kiosks. Caraffe on the other hand was more interested in the social life of the city and made drawings of people rather than buildings and views.

The Swedish embassy, followed the French in supporting travellers. Muradgea D'Ohsson, historian and diplomat was born in İzmir in 1740. He worked for the embassy between 1763-1782 and in 1795, D'Ohsson became the Swedish ambassador. He had spent twenty years with research on Ottoman chronicles and had planned to write a history for the reign of Selim III, yet he was persuaded to write a description of the diplomatic state of the Empire rather than its history.[4] It ended up with his monumental work, *Tableau générale de l'Empire Ottoman* in three volumes, (Paris, 1787-1820). The engravings included panoramic views, exterior and interior elevations and they were made mostly by l'Espinasse and Le Barbier who were related to the embassy during his office, as well as Jean Baptiste Hillair, who as mentioned above was affiliated to the French embassy during the same period. [5]

In summary, Gouffier and D'Ohsson were very effective in receiving travellers. During the period of ambassador D'Ohsson; L'Espinasse, Le Barbier, and during the period of ambassador Gouffier; Caraffe, Hillair and others were affiliated to the embassies in one way or another. In relation to the new approaches of the period, perhaps more important was the work of François Kauffer, an engineer who accompanied Gouffier in the embassy. During 1785-1786, Kauffer, together with an assistant, visited every street and district, making notes and taking measurements. These analytical studies were then used to prepare an accurate and scaled plan of İstanbul.[6] Here we have  the

---

[1] Yerasimos (1994; 2/386).
[2] Özel (1994; 2/385).
[3] Tekeli (1994; 3/556-557).
[4] Arslan (1992a; 73-70), Renda (1994; 2/386).
[5] Arslan (1992b; 113-118).
[6] Boppe (1998; 109-115), Mansel (1996; 215).

first example for the second group of maps which were drawn usually after the second half of the eighteenth century and all through the nineteenth and twentieth centuries. These were seriously realized depending on the current technological opportunities of survey and representation, thus reflecting the process of advance in map making, in contrast to the first group, from the fifteenth and sixteenth centuries, which were 'picture-maps' without accuracy and combined plan and elevation features together. The first maps of their kind by Kauffer were followed by the maps of Hellert, Kammar, Constantna, Daves, Stolpe and finally Moltke.[1]

The second group of travellers, active during the late eighteenth and early nineteenth century, were those not affiliated to any patron but who traveled for themselves and recoded whatever suited their fancy. Among them William Henry Bartlett (1809-1854) was mainly interested in topographic views. The results of his various trips in distant lands were exhibited at the Royal Academy in London, during 1831-1833. His trip to Istanbul in 1835, followed this exhibition. The engravings made after his drawings were illustrated in *The Beauties of the Bosphorus* (London 1839) prepared by Miss Julia Pardoe.[2]

Thomas Allom (1804-1872), is another traveller who was not directly related to any embassy. Allom was trained as an architect, and designed several official buildings in London before setting out for the Orient in order to experience a new culture. As part of this trip, which took place between 1836-1838, he visited Istanbul, where he made drawings, including views from the palace and from single buildings which later illustrated the well known book *Constantinople and the Scenery of the Seven Churches of Asia Minor* (London, 1845) by Robert Walsh a priest at the English embassy in İstanbul.[3]

Other visitors to İstanbul also trained as architects are Antoine-Ignace Melling (1763-1831), Gaspare Trajano Fossati (1809-1883), and his brother Guiseppe Fossati (1822-1891). Melling and the Fossati brothers arrived without any official duty, yet shortly after their arrival they became affiliated to the palace, Melling as a designer and architect and Fossati as a restorer-architect. Antoine-Ignace Melling arrived in 1795, worked for Selim III and his sister Hatice Sultan as the architect, landscape architect, designer and painter . He worked in the construction of a new palace, the so-called Neshebat

---

[1] Boppe (1998; 109-110), Mansel (1996; 205, 214), Renda (1977; 18-19).
[2] Arslan (1992b; 113-118).
[3] Boppe (1998; 114-120).

Palace for the Sultan and the arrangement of its garden. During his free time
he went around the city making drawings. He was given special permission to
enter the private courts of the palace. He made panoramic drawings of the
Topkapı Palace from various spots and angles creating unique visual
documents. He recorded too the architectural characteristics of other famous
palaces of the time publishing them in his *Voyages Pittoresque de
Constantinople et des Rivers du Bosphore, d'apres les dessns de M.Melling,
architecte de l'Empereur Selim III, et dessinateur de la Sultan Hadidge sa
soeur*, ed. .M.M.Treuttel et Würtz,( Paris 1819).[1]

The elder of the Fossati brothers, Gaspare Fossati studied architecture
at the Academy of Brera between 1822-27. In 1833 he was in Russia with a
post as palace architect and in 1836 he was appointed to build the new
Russian embassy in İstanbul. He was joined by his brother Guiseppe and the
two were engaged in the construction of new buildings as well as in
restoration projects, among which the restoration of the Hagia Sophia is the
most important. This work was thoroughly documented in *Ayasofya of
Constantnople as Recently Restored by Order of His Majesty the Sultan
Abdul Medjid*, London, 1852.[2] Fossati included engravings in this work
showing the church together with the main entrance and the first court of the
palace.[3] The drawings of Melling and Gaspare Fossati have a special place in
the nineteenth history of Ottoman architecture and of Istanbul, as they have
both contributed to the documentation of the architectural heritage of the city
as well as adding new buildings to its repertoire. Furthermore, Fossati's
restoration projects initiated new considerations for the preservation of the
architectural heritage of the city.


*Conclusion*

Travellers, merchants, diplomats, historians, artists, writers and others, with
their numbers increasing after the second half of the sixteenth century, visited
the Ottoman Empire with different aims and interests. One common
contribution of these visitors was recording their observations and
investigations in travellers' books or travelogues. Today we can evaluate these
books as valuable written and visual documents carrying information on the
physical environment and monuments as well as the daily life, habits,
customs, culture, and the social institutions of the Ottoman Empire both in
the capital and in the provinces.

[1] Arslan (1992b; 113-118).
[2] Cengiz, (1994; 326-327).
[3] Arslan (1992b; 113-118).

This paper gives a brief account of the foreign travellers who have visited the Ottoman capital Istanbul and the Topkapı Palace and have contributed travellers books that contain written and visual information on the palace. The written accounts are descriptions and the visual documents are cityscapes, city panoramas, interior and exterior elevations delineated as drawings and engravings. If this study had intended to examine the works of all the travellers who were in the capital during the seventeenth and nineteenth centuries, it would have been necessary to mention a number of others who have helped to shape the process of recording the monuments within their surroundings. However, this would highly extend the limits of the paper.

One may wonder why the written and visual records of foreign visitors are so important to study the architecture, social life, customs and the people of the Empire. This phenomenon is interpreted by Kuban who states that: 'in medieval Turkish culture miniature painting was the only means of visual expression, therefore the cityscapes or representations of single buildings, which became quite customary in historic manuscripts especially during the sixteenth and seventeenth centuries, are delineated as miniatures. In most cases these miniatures give us idealized views rather than direct views, although they can sometimes add the third dimension vaguely. Therefore the engravings of the western travellers are considered the only sources for us until the mid-nineteenth century when Turkish painters begin to make drawings and paintings.'[1] As for the written documents, Ottoman historians of the period have given only very general descriptions of the palace, as they were rather hesitant or timid to write anything in detail on the Sultan's private dwelling, considering it impolite.

Therefore, foreign travellers have left us invaluable information with which to study the architecture of the Topkapı Palace. The palace, constructed by Mehmed II, during the late fifteenth century, underwent simple repairs, restorations or remodeling after serious fire hazards or it was altered and additions made according to the wishes of the Sultans. The documents from different centuries help for the study of these changes and can give certain guidelines for restitution projects, though the essential hindrance, the 'subjective' nature of these documents, resulting from the individual interpretations of the artists and the craftsmen remains. Both with regard to the palace and other monuments this is largely overcome with the entry of photography during the nineteenth century,[2] yet then of course the precise documentation and exact reproduction that they give rise to may seem to cease to be a work of art.

---

[1] Kuban (1998; 44-45).
[2] Özendeş (1996; 75-79).

REFERENCES

Anafarta, N. 1969 *Hünername Minyatürleri ve Sanatçıları*, İstanbul; Yapı Kredi.

And, M. 1994 *İstanbul in the Sixteenth Century*, İstanbul; Akbank.

And, M. 2000 *40 Gün, 40 Gece, Osmanlı Düğünleri, Şenlikleri, Gecit Alayları*, İstanbul; Toprakbank.

And, M. 2002 *Osmanlı Tasvir Sanatları, 1. Minyatür*, İstanbul; İş Bankası.

Arslan, N. 1992a *Gravür ve Seyahatnamelerde İstanbul*, İstanbul; Büyükşehir Belediyesi Kültür İşleri Daire Başkanlığı, No.9.

Arslan, N. 1992b 'Osmanlı Sarayı ve Mimar Antoine-Ignace Melling', *Osman Hamdi Bey ve Dönemi*, İstanbul; Tarih Vakfı, 113-118.

Arslan, N. 1996 'Gravürlerin 19.Yüzyılda İstanbul'un Kültür Sanat Ortamındaki Yeri', *19.Yüzyıl İstanbul'unda Sanat Ortamı*, 14-15 Mart 1996, İstanbul; Lebib Yayıncılık, 63-74.

Atıl, E. 1999 *Levni and the Surname, The Story of an Eighteenth-Century Ottoman Festival*, İstanbul; Koçbank.

Bent, J. (ed.) 1893 *Early Voyages and Travels in the Levant* London; Hakluyt.

Bon, O. 1996 *The Sultan's Seraglio, an Intimate Portrait of Life at the Ottoman Court*, London; Saqi Books.

Boppe, A. 1998 *XVIII.Yüzyıl Boğaziçi Ressamları* (trans.N.Y. Celviş) İstanbul; Pera Yayıncılık.

Boppe, A. 1911 *Les Peintres du Bosphore au dix-huitième siècle*, Paris; Hachette.

Boppe, A. 1989 *Les Peintres du Bosphore au XVIII $^e$ siècle*, Paris; ACR Edition.

Dallam, T. 1903 *The Diary of Master Thomas Dallam 1599-1600*, in Bent (ed.).

Busbecq, O. 1881 *The Life and Letters of Ogier Ghiselin de Busbecq*, 2 vols. ed. C. Foster and J. Daniel, London; Kegan Paul.

Çelebi (Evliya Efendi) 1846 *Narrative of Travels in Europe, Asia and Africa in the seventeenth century*, trans. Hammer-Purgstall, London; Oriental Translation Fund of Great Britain and Ireland.

Cengiz, C. 1994 'Fossati, Gaspare', *Dünden Bugüne İstanbul Ansiklopedisi*, Vol. 3, 326-327.

Davis, F. 1970 *The Palace of Topkapı in Istanbul*, New York; Scribner.

Ebersolt, J. 1918 *Constantinople Byzantine et les Voyageurs du Levant*, Paris; Èditions Ernest Leroux.

Ebersolt, J. 1999 *Bizans İstanbulu ve Doğu Seyyahları*, trans. İ. Arda, İstanbul; Mataş.

Emler, S. 1963 'Topkapı Sarayı Restorasyom Çelışmaları', in *Türk Sanatı Tarihi Araştırma ve İncelemeleri*, I; 211-312.

Eldem, S. and Hakkı-Akozan, F. 1982 *Topkapı Sarayı:Bir Mimar Araştırma*, İstanbul; Kültür Bakanlığı.

Eldem, S. and Hakkı-Akozan, F. 1969 *Köşkler ve Kasırlar* İstanbul; DGS Matbaası.

Eyice, S. 1973 'İstanbul'un Ortadan Kalkan Bazı Tarihi Eserleri', *Tarih Dergisi*, no. 27, 133-179.

Eyice, S. 1996 '19.Yüzyılda İstanbul'da Batılı Mimarlar, Ressamlar, Edebiyatçılar', *19.Yüzyıl İstanbul'unda Sanat Ortamı*,14-15 Mart 1996, İstanbul; Lebib Yayıncılık, 9-46.

Eyice, S. 1998 'xvııı.Yüzyılda İstanbul'da İsveçli Cornelius Loos ve İstanbul Resimleri (1710'da İstanbul)', in *18.Yüzyılda Osmanlı Kültür Ortamı*, İstanbul; Lebib Yayıncılık; 91-130.

Fedden, R. 1958 *English Travellers in the Near East*, Bibliographical series, London, New York;

Goodwin, G. 1971 *History of Ottoman Architecture*, London; Thames & Hudson.

Goodwin, G., 1990 'Gaspare Fossati di Morcote and his Brother Guiseppe' in *Journal of Islamic Environmental Design*, vol.1, 122-127.

Gölen, Z. 1998, 'Baron de Tott'un Seyahatnamesine Dair', *Bilge*, Yaz 17, 69-71.

Kayra, C. 1990, *Istanbul Mekanlar ve Zamanlar*, İstanbul: Ak Yayınları.

Konyalı, İbrahim Hakkı, 1942 *İstanbul Sarayları*, İstanbul.

Kuban, D. 1996 *İstanbul an Urban History, Byzantion, Constantinople, İstanbul*, İstanbul; Economic and Social History Foundation.

Kuban, D. 1998 *İstanbul Yazıları*, İstanbul; Yapı Endüstri Merkezi.

Kuban, D. 1994 'Gravürler', in *Dünden Bugüne İstanbul Ansiklopedisi*, Vol.3: 417, 423.

Mansel, P. 1996 *Constantinople, City of World's Desire, 1453-1924*, London; John Murray.

Necipoğlu, G. 1991 *Architecture, Ceremonial and Power, The Topkapı Palace in the Fifteenth and Sixteenth Centuries*, MIT Press.

Necipoğlu, G. 1997 'The Suburban Landscape of Sixteenth century Istanbul as a Mirror of Classical Ottoman Garden Culture', in *Gardens in the Time of the Great Muslim Empires*, ed. A. Petruccioli, Leiden, New York, 32-71.

Oberhummer, E. 1902 *Konstantinopel unter Sultan Suleiman dem Grossen aufgenommen im Jahre 1559 durch Mechior Lorichs*, Munich.

Özendeş, E. 1996 'İmparatorluk Başkentinde 19.Yüzyıl Fotoğrafçılığı' *19.Yüzyıl İstanbul'unda Sanat Ortamı*, İstanbul; Lebib Yayıncılık, 75-79.

Purchas, S. 1905 'Relation of a Journey begun an.Dom: 1610', in *Purchas His Pilgrims*, Vol.8, Glasgow, 110-171.

Renda, G. 1977 *Batılılaşma Sürecinde Türk Resim Sanatı, 1700-1850*, Ankara; TTK.

Renda, G. 1994 'Cassas, Louis-Françoise', *Dünden Bugüne İstanbul Ansiklopedisi*, Vol. 2: 386.

Renda, G. 1994 'Caraffe, Armand Charles', *Dünden Bugüne İstanbul Ansiklopedisi*, Vol.2: 385.

Seçkin, N. 1998 *Topkapı Sarayı'nın Biçimlenmesine Egemen olan Tasarım Gelenekleri Üzerine Bir Araştırma*, Ankara; Atatürk Kültür Merkezi.

Tayanç, M. 1972 'Türkiye ile İlgili Seyahatnameler' *Belgelerle Türk Tarih Dergisi*, No.57: 42-47; No.58: 39-42.

Tekeli, İ. 1994 'Haritalar', *Dünden Bugüne İstanbul Ansiklopedisi*, vol.3, Kültür Bakanlığı, Tarih Vakfı, İstanbul, 556-560.

Uzunçarşılı, İ. 1945 *Osmanlı Devletinin Saray Tekilatı*, Ankara; TTK.

Whithers, R. 1996, Büyük Efendi'nin sarayı, trans.C.Kayra, İstanbul; Mataş.

Yurdaydın, H. 1976, *Beyan-ı Menazil Seeferi Irakeyn*, Ankara; TTK.

Yerasimos, S. 1994, 'Castellan, Antoine, Laurent', *Dünden Bugüne İstanbul Ansiklopedisi*, Vol.2, 386.

Yerasimos, S. 1994, 'Bruyn, Cornelius', *Dünden Bugüne İstanbul Ansiklopedisi*, Vol. 2, 325.

Yerasimos, S., 1994, 'Grelot, Guillaume Joseph', *Dünden Bugüne İstanbul Ansiklopedisi*, Vol.3, 423-424.

# 28. COLONEL LEAKE'S VIEW OF THE TURKS

## Malcolm WAGSTAFF

The Revolutionary and Napoleonic Wars (1792-1815) brought educated and articulate west Europeans to the Ottoman Empire in unprecedented numbers. Some British travellers ventured there because the usual haunts of the Grand Tour in France and Italy were closed to them, except for a brief period during the Peace of Amiens (1802-03). Other British subjects travelled in the Near East as soldiers, sailors, diplomats and advisors. Frenchmen and Russians travelled in the Ottoman domains for similar reasons. Some of these western visitors published accounts of their experiences, unlike many of the merchants and consuls who resided longer in the Empire and had more detailed knowledge of its peoples but were generally silent. Although most travellers probably had some schoolboy knowledge of ancient Greek, few spoke the contemporary languages of the Ottoman Empire. They were not only dependent on their dragomans for guidance and information, but also quietly separated from the populations of the territories traversed and the towns visited. In any case, many travellers were more interested in ancient sites and ancient history than in contemporary conditions. Accordingly, many western travellers seem to have relied more on what they had read in preparation for their tours than upon first-hand observation and face-to-face discussion when they came to write their own accounts of what they allegedly experienced. They often readily retold the prejudices of their times, not least about Turks and the Ottoman Empire. Their audiences expected no less. Unfavourable stereotypes were perpetuated.

A notable exception to the majority of western travellers to the Ottoman Empire appears to be Colonel Leake. He travelled in several provinces at the beginning of the nineteenth century and left monumental accounts of some of his travels, notably those in what is now Greece. These impress the reader with their austere and laconic style, their meticulous descriptions of topography and their precise information about contemporary social, economic and political conditions. Thus, Leake's view of the Turks is likely to be treated as more authoritative than that of many of his contemporaries. In fact, there are grounds for questioning this supposition.

Below I provide a brief introduction to Colonel Leake, set out the basis on which his view of the Turks could have been formulated and then outline what those views were. A few conclusions are drawn. I suggest that Leake may have been more reliant upon stereotypes of Oriental and Islamic despotism than one might have supposed.

*Colonel Leake (1777-1860)*

In his address to the anniversary meeting of the Royal Geographical Society in 1860, the President described Lieutenant-Colonel William Martin Leake (generally known simply as 'Colonel Leake'), who had died at the beginning of the year, as 'a model geographer'.[1] The basis for that assessment was primarily Leake's work on the topography of ancient Greece and Athens. In his topographical work on Greece, published in the 1820s, 1830s and 1840s but based on field work carried out twenty to thirty years earlier,[2] Leake attempted, on the one hand, to locate the settlement and topographical names found in the ancient authors and, on the other hand, to provide the ancient names for the sites where ancient remains survived. His publications on ancient Athens were dedicated to locating the districts and individual buildings mentioned by the ancient writers, chiefly Pausanias who wrote in the second century AD, and to identifying the surviving ancient remains. Leake's topographical work remains significant to this day. He saw sites and structures which have since disappeared; he combed through the ancient authors with great thoroughness; and his deductions were based on careful comparison of the literary, epigraphical and numismatic evidence with the topography, frequently as he had seen it himself.[3]

Leake was not only a considerable scholar; he was also a recognised Philhellene. His biographer noted that when Leake was buried in Kensal Green Cemetery, London, 'he was followed to the grave by M. Tricoupi, the Minister of the King of Greece, who had expressed a desire to make this public acknowledgement of the respect and gratitude of his countrymen'.[4] The Greeks were grateful not only for Leake's researches on the ancient topography of Greece but also for the support which he gave to the liberation of Greece from Ottoman rule. His sympathies for the Greek cause are clear in his

---

[1] De Grey and Ripon (1860).

[2] See bibliography.

[3] Wagstaff (2001).

[4] Marsden (1864; 41).

*Historical Outline of the Greek Revolution*,[1] the first account in English of the background and early stages of the uprising. He published a defence of the Greek right to the small islands of Cervi (Elafonisos) and Sapienza which lie off the south coast of the Peloponnese (Morea) and were claimed by Britain as part of the Ionian Islands, under British protection since the Vienna Treaty of 1815.[2] In letters to the press, he supported the efforts to liberate Crete in the 1840s, and in the 1850s he went on to publish pamphlets condemning the British policy of supporting the Ottoman Empire which led to the Crimean War.[3] Yet Leake's support for Greek independence was qualified. For example, and perhaps significantly, he was not a member of the London Greek Committee which raised money for the provisional governments set up by the revolutionaries. In a published letter to his friend, William Richard Hamilton, he went so far as to say that he did not 'believe it desirable or possible to erect a Greek empire at Constantinople' and 'even considered the independence of a portion of Greece premature' while the nation was divided by 'a line of separation'.[4] The expectation, then, might be that Leake, the Philhellene, would have a negative view of the Turks. Comments about Turks — their behaviour, monuments and institutions — form a minor strand in the social and economic thread woven into his topographical and political publications. Almost a hundred years later, Hasluck himself drew freely upon this material for his book, *Christianity and Islam under the Sultans*.[5]

*Leake's Sources*

In the introduction to his *Historical Outline of the Greek Revolution,* Leake claimed to be 'acquainted with ... the customs of the two contending parties'.[6] This might suggest that his view of the Turks was founded essentially upon personal experience. There is a good deal of evidence to support the idea.

As a young officer in the Royal Artillery with experience in the West Indies, Leake was seconded to the British Military Mission sent to assist the Ottoman Empire following the French invasion of Egypt (1798-1802). He spent seven months (217 days) in and around Istanbul, based at Levend Çiftlik

---

[1] Originally published anonymously in 1825 and then reprinted under Leake's name in 1826.

[2] Leake (1850).

[3] Leake (1851, 1853, 1854, 1855a, 1855b and 1857).

[4] Leake (1855a).

[5] For example, Hasluck drew upon Leake's *Travels in Northern Greece* (1835) in locating *tekkes* of Bektashi dervishes (Eg. pp. 532 n.3; 533 n.5; 534 n.1; 541 n. 2; 542 n.1) and for his discussion of the encouragement given by Ali Pasha of Ioannina to the Bektashis (Eg. 590-91).

[6] Leake (1826, 6-7).

and Büyükdere. After crossing Anatolia in January, 1800 and visiting Cyprus, he spent three or four months at Alanya (on the south coast of Anatolia) recovering from jaundice. Subsequently, Leake was attached to the Ottoman army gathering at Jaffa and went with it across Sinai when Egypt was invaded in 1801. A journey up the Nile to just beyond the cataracts (October 1801-February, 1802) was followed by brief visits to Syria (April-June, 1802) and Greece (June-September, 1802).

In 1804 Leake was sent to Greece as a military advisor to the Ottoman authorities, then expecting a French invasion. Greece was part of the Ottoman Empire. Arriving at Aghii Saranta on the coast of Epirus on 20 December, 1804, he had his first meeting with Ali Pasha of Ioannina in his family stronghold of Tebelene. The Vizir was the most powerful Ottoman governor in Greece at the time, with a reputation for intrigue and ferocity. Leake travelled extensively in Greece over the next two years and spent a total of about 45 days in Ali Pasha's lake-side capital, Ioannina, during which he had several interviews with the Vizir.[1] His mission ended when he was arrested at Salonika in February, 1807, during the brief war between Britain and Turkey. Diplomatic efforts secured his release after some eight months confined to the house of the Janissary Sergeant-Major (*Bash Tchaoush*), Hadji Bakym Oglu, alias Hadji Mustapha Aga.[2] Before Leake returned home, Sir Arthur Paget, the British plenipotentiary newly sent to the region to re-establish peace with the Ottoman Empire, took the opportunity to use Leake's acquaintance with Ali Pasha to sound the governor on his intentions should the Ottoman dominions in Europe be partitioned between France, Russia and possibly Austria, as seemed likely following the Treaty agreed at Tilsit between Napoleon and the Czar. Leake and Ali had a brief clandestine meeting on a beach north of Prevesa on the night of 12 November, 1807.

After a few months at home, Leake was sent as British resident to Ali Pasha of Ioannina in 1808. When not in the capital city, or at the mountain resort of Kalarytes and the port-town of Prevesa, he spent much of his 13 months' residency travelling.[3] This allowed him to complete his topographical studies in Epirus and central Greece, though these were interrupted briefly in the autumn of 1809 when Byron and Hobhouse came through and had their celebrated interview with Ali Pasha. Leake left Prevesa rather hastily and in fear of his life, probably in April,1810.[4] He did not return to the Ottoman Empire.

---

[1] 10 June – 3 July, 23 October – 11 November, 1805.
[2] The spellings are Leake's own.
[3] Leake (1835; Vol. 4).
[4] Leake's journals and diplomatic correspondence come to an abrupt end around 1 May, 1810.

Although he served as British military observer with the army of the Swiss Cantons during Napoleon's 'Hundred Days' and remained in the army until 1823 (apparently on full pay), Leake devoted much of his time from 1810 until his death in 1860 to scholarly activity and to the work of societies such as the Royal Geographical Society and the Royal Society of Literature.[1]

During his travels Leake met many administrators, military commanders and landowners who were Turks. He was particularly well acquainted with Ali Pasha of Ioannina, but also met one of his rivals, Ibrahim Pasha of Berat, as well as — reputedly — the most powerful man in eastern Macedonia, Ismail Bey of Serres.[2] He talked to Mehmet Vanli, the governor of the Morea, at Tripolitsa (Tripolis) in March, 1805 and possibly again in May the same year and in March, 1806.[3] He encountered Möse Musa Pasha for the first time in February, 1806, when he was governor of Epakto, but they met again in November when he had returned as governor of Salonika.[4] Möse Musa Pasha was a significant person. Although the Sultan's preferred candidate for the governorship of Egypt in 1806, he was out-manoeuvred by the Albanian from northern Greece, Muhammed Ali. He subsequently became one of the conspirators who removed Sultan Selim III from the throne in 1807 and for several months was one of the most powerful figures in Istanbul.[5] In addition to these powerful figures, Leake met less important provincial and town governors, as well as the commanders of various fortresses and various landholders, such as Nuri Bey of Corinth.[6] He heard comments on the behaviour of these Turks from various Greeks, chiefly locally powerful individuals, but almost certainly also from his Greek and Albanian guides. These were supplemented by anecdotes collected in 1807 while under house arrest at Salonika.[7] As already mentioned, impressions of the Turks, comments and stories about them, appear in Leake's topographical works as part of the daily record of his travels. The journal format provides the basic structure of these books and the material is derived from a diary written at the time. Occasional comments on Turks appear in Leake's other publications, while the characters and motivations of important officials such as Ali Pasha of Ioannina and Ismail Bey of Serres are given extensive treatment in his despatches to the Foreign Office. Leake, then, seemed well placed to have an informed and considered view of the Turks.

---

[1] Leake was a founder member and a vice-president of both societies.

[2] Leake (1835; Vol. 2, 356-57; Vol. 3, 202-203).

[3] Leake (1830; Vol. 1, 85-114; Vol. 2, 47-48; Vol. 3, 383-85); Manuscript Journal 2, 12 March, 1805.

[4] Leake (1835; Vol. 2, 610; Vol. 3, 236-37).

[5] Shaw (1971; 276-86, 290-91).

[6] Leake (1830; Vol. 3, 257); Manuscript Journal 14, 21 April, 1806.

[7] Manuscript Journal 18.

*Leake's View of the 'Turks'*

What were Leake's views? Some preliminary remarks are necessary before answering the question. First, like the *Book of Common Prayer*[1] and many of his British contemporaries, Leake frequently used the word 'Turk' to mean any Muslim, specifically in his case any non-Albanian Muslim.[2] Occasionally, though, he specifically described those families claiming descent from the leaders of the original Ottoman conquests as *Osmanlı*.[3] Secondly, when generalising about the character and behaviour of 'Turks', Leake rarely differentiated explicitly either between the provincial governors, military commanders and local landholders, on the one hand, and the ordinary Muslim population, on the other hand, or between the rural and urban components of the latter group. In many cases, though, it is clear that his comments are specifically about the more powerful Muslims; the exceptions will be mentioned later. Third, despite some degree of ambiguity, Leake specifically differentiated two distinct groups of 'Turks', the *Koniáridhes* (note the use of the Greek plural) and the *Yurúks*. The *Yurúks* lived in Macedonia and Thrace where they 'have villages and have become cultivators', unlike their namesakes in Anatolia who followed a wandering life like Kurds and Turkomans.[4] The *Koniáridhes* were the reputed descendents of settlers brought in from the Konya area at the time of the Ottoman conquests, like the original *Yurúks*, and lived in groups of small villages near Serres in Macedonia and Turnavo in Thessaly. Leake described the *Koniáridhes* as a poor and inoffensive people. Although armed, they were 'peaceably disposed' so that their 'name was a bye-word of contempt among the Albanians, who esteem nothing but the power derived from the sword and the tufék'.[5] Fourth, Leake did not produce any systematic discussion of the 'Turks' in his publications. Even his *Historical Outline of the Greek Revolution*, where he described the Albanian and Greek populations of emergent Greece, lacks a section specifically devoted to 'Turks'. Leake's views, therefore, must be compiled from remarks and comments scattered across his publications and official despatches.

---

[1] The third collect for Good Friday: 'O merciful God, who hast made all men, and hatest nothing that thou hast made, nor wouldest the death of a sinner, but rather that he should be converted and live; Have mercy upon all Jews, Turks, Infidels, and Hereticks (sic), ...'
[2] For this reason, 'Turk/s' will now appear in parenthesis.
[3] Leake (1835; Vol. 3, 249).
[4] Leake (1835; Vol. 3, 175).
[5] Leake (1835; Vol. 1, 174; Vol. 3, 357).

When we attempt to reconstruct Leake's views of the 'Turks' from these materials, I think we can recognise three groups of comments: views about 'Turks' as rulers, views about the personal character of 'Turks' and views on their living conditions. My quotations are taken principally from Hasluck's source, Leake's *Travels in Northern Greece*, published in 1835.

Like many of his contemporaries, Leake thought that Turkish rule in Greece depended entirely on 'horse and sabre'.[1] The 'Turks' were 'a nation of soldiers', of great endurance and fanatical courage.[2] Despite the privileges allegedly given to the Christian subjects of the Empire by 'Mahomet II' (Mehmet the Conqueror), Leake maintained that their disabilities had increased over time. Turkish rule had become oppressive. Early in his literary career, Leake attributed this to the degeneracy of the present generation of 'Turks' as soldiers and to the corruption of government at every level.[3] He gave several examples of extortion in his *Travels*, commenting in *Travels in Northern Greece*, for example, that under the current governmental system everyone felt danger in displaying wealth, while property and life were insecure, even for the 'most favoured subjects'.[4] Although Leake believed that conditions were better on *vakıf* (mortmain) and royal property, what he once called 'Turkish desolation' could be observed everywhere.[5] For instance, the ruined and collapsing houses noticed in Anapli (Nauplion), as well as the silted-up harbour and the undrained marshes at the head of the bay, were attributed to 'the effects of Turkish domination'.[6] Alternative explanations such as the decline of trade in the port and erosion in the hinterland, were not even considered.

Towards the end of his life Leake went far beyond 'degeneracy' in explaining what he saw as the character of Turkish rule in his own time. It had more fundamental structural origins.

> The Musulman of the present day, conscious of his inferiority to civilised Europe in arts and arms, is submissive until the moment arrives when by fraud and treachery, or by open violation of the most solemn engagements, he can find an opportunity for the indulgence of his vindictive and cruel disposition. These qualities, *inherent in the religion and the race*, are habitually exercised even amongst themselves, with relentless cruelty.[7]

---

[1] Leake (1825; 8).
[2] Leake (1854).
[3] Leake (1825; 32).
[4] Leake (1835; 249).
[5] Leake (1835; 108, 249).
[6] Leake (1830; Vol. 2, 357-60).
[7] Leake (1858; 18-19). Emphasis added.

On the other hand, Leake acknowledged that Ali Pasha of Ioannina had brought peace and stability to the territories which he administered. A trivial example will illustrate the point. On 18 November, 1805, Leake's party stopped to dine at the little village of Kurbáli, on the road from Trikkala to Larissa in Thessaly. The men were absent with their flocks, but the strangers were received by 'the women without fear — one of the favourable traits of Ali's government'.[1] Ali Pasha's authority rested on his reputation for ruthlessness but was backed by his Albanian soldiers — hardy, active and skilled with the musket, as Leake described them.[2]

Leake characterised individual 'Turks' as idle and rapacious, bigoted, insolent, profligate and greedy for gain.[3] He believed that except for the *Koniáridhes*, they considered 'agricultural labour a degradation'.[4] On the other hand, they delighted to display their weapons.[5] Some young *Osmanlıs* were spendthrift to an extreme. Leake heard, for example, of a certain Hassan Efendi who went through an inheritance of 10,000 piastres and seven *çiftliks* (estate farms), ending up as a clerk in the *Mekherné* at Salonika.[6] To maintain their extravagances, as well as to recoup themselves for the purchase price of their offices, Leake maintained that 'Turkish' landholders and governors squeezed the peasants (mostly, but not exclusively Christians in Greece) and extorted as much revenue as they could. 'The corn, after deducting the Vezir's portion, suffices only for a small part of the consumption of the inhabitants ...' Leake noted of Ali Pasha's *çiftlik* of Kraniá.[7] He believed, in fact, that extortion was the root cause of the widespread poverty and desolation which he saw throughout Greece. On the other hand, Leake was told by foreign merchants in Salonika that the 'Turkish' landed proprietors in the neighbouring plains were 'persons of the greatest stability in Turkey; and the Frank merchants who bargain with them for their corn, cotton and tobacco, can, without much risk, make advances upon their crops.[8] In general, Leake concluded, 'Turks' showed 'more honour and honesty than their Christian subjects', though it was 'a poor commendation'.[9]

---

[1] Leake (1835; Vol. 1, 430).

[2] Leake (1835; Vol. 1, 346).

[3] Leake (1835; Vol. 2, 108).

[4] Leake (1835; Vol. 3, 174).

[5] Leake (1835; Vol. 1, 203).

[6] Leake (1835; Vol. 3, 249). More detail is given in *Manuscript Journal* 17, 17.

[7] Leake (1835; Vol. 1, 300).

[8] Leake (1835; Vol. 3, 249).

[9] Leake (1835; Vol. 3, 256).

Leake generalised his experience of encounters with Ottoman officials into a comment about there being a 'certain manly politeness' about the 'Turks'.[1] However, he thought that strangers could be deceived by this. Superficial politeness towards visitors from western Europe covered

> a rooted aversion to all European nations, as well as to the individuals who have the misfortune to have any dealings with these plausible barbarians. Though in the most splendid aera (sic) of their history their feelings may have been those of contempt, founded upon ignorance, fanaticism and the pride of conquest, it has been changed by their weakness and their dread of the Christians of Europe, into a mixture of fear and hatred. Thus there are two things which the European who has any political dealings with the Turk, should never lose sight of: 1, that he hates us: 2, that he fears us.[2]

Although Leake describes the serais (palaces) of some of the governors and the state in which they lived, he has little to say about the living conditions of ordinary 'Turks'. What comment he provides largely refers to urban communities and probably to the lower orders of their 'Turkish', ie. Muslim, populations. Towns 'entirely Turkish'[3] and the quarters where they lived generally appeared neglected and run-down. At Grevena, for example, the Turkish quarter had 'a ruinous and wretched appearance, like all the Turkish villages of Greece', [4] while at Epakto (Naupaktos) the 'Turks' lived 'in ruinous houses in misery and poverty, too proud to work, and by their insolence and oppression preventing the Greeks from settling here'.[5] Even Salonika, one of the most important towns in the Ottoman Empire at the beginning of the nineteenth century and a place which Leake knew fairly well, bore 'the usual characteristics of a Turkish town; no attention is paid to cleanliness or convenience in the streets'.[6] Unfortunately, Leake says nothing about this aspect of Larissa (Turkish Yenişehir) which he called 'the most Ottoman town in Greece to the southward of Saloníki'.[7]

---

[1] Leake (1835; Vol. 3, 256).

[2] Leake (1835; Vol. 3, 255-56).

[3] Phrase is from Leake (1830; Vol. 2, 360).

[4] Leake (1835; Vol. 1, 304).

[5] Leake (1835; Vol. 2, 609).

[6] Leake (1835; Vol. 3, 239).

[7] Leake (1835; Vol. 1, 440).

*Conclusion*

Leake's views of the 'Turks' are largely negative, as expected. Surprisingly, though, they are not very different from those of many of his contemporaries,[1] despite his first hand experience of seeing, meeting and dealing with them. Accusations of misrule, inefficiency and tyranny, intolerable pride and scorn for the rest of the world, neglect of agriculture and property, all elements in Leake's view of the 'Turks', were part of the image of the 'Turks' standard in western Europe by the end of the eighteenth and the beginning of the nineteenth century.[2] The novelist, John Galt, for example, expressed similar sentiments. Writing from Athens on 10 March, 1810, about the time when Leake was leaving Greece, he noted:

> The Turks here may be considered as domiciliated military: they are idle and insolent. The young, from their earliest years, imitate the practices of the old. A Turkish lad, just entering his teens, carries his pipe, tobacco-pouch, and pistols, with all the gravity of his father; he frequents the coffeehouses and the baths with the same arrogance, and passes the time in reveries equally mystical and useless. The Greeks, on the contrary are all activity and industry.[3]

It is a mixture of observation (Turks lounging in coffeehouses) and reading ('domiciliated military'). There is no serious analysis. Are Leake's views any more soundly based?

His direct acquaintance with the ordinary Muslim populations of Greece, let alone of elsewhere in the Near East, was largely limited to Albanian escorts and hired janissary guards; his guides were probably Christians. His hosts were generally the wealthier and more educated members of local Christian populations — doctors, merchants, land owners, bishops. He often had letters of introduction to them and they alone had the space to accommodate the traveller and his party. Doubtless, they had their own agendas when they talked with their guest. Unlike many of his contemporaries, Leake could communicate directly with them. He spoke Greek and possibly Albanian, though not necessarily Turkish. His Christian hosts, who were not only literate but also, in some cases, had travelled and resided in central and western Europe, probably told him about the oppression and extortion which they endured from the 'Turks'. Their views seemed to be confirmed in the under-use of land and the neglect of the physical fabric of

---

[1] Angelomatis-Tsougarakis (1990; 100-04).

[2] Daniel (1966; 11-17, 77-84); Çırakman (2002; 132-72).

[3] Galt (1813; 140-41).

towns and villages which Leake observed. He appears uncritical of the implied link to despotism and offers no alternative explanations for the perceived desolation. No doubt his Christian contacts suggested that they could run things much more effectively. Although they were looking to their own advantage (and, in practice, Greek landowners were no better than 'Turkish' ones in their treatment of the peasants), the Greek national movement was beginning to have an effect, influenced by the spread of education and the infiltration of ideas from revolutionary France. The views of his Greek hosts and travelling companions fitted those of the English Philhellene.

Leake's knowledge of Muslim rulers and landlords was better than his acquaintance with ordinary 'Turks', but with the partial exception of Ali Pasha of Ioannina, it was not very close. One of Leake's responsibilities on his first mission to Greece was to sound out the Ottoman governors on their likely support for the Sultan if the French arrived and related Christian uprisings took place. He was also required to advise on their military preparations, including the improvement of fortifications.[1] In any case, he needed the governors' permissions to travel, to secure horses and accommodation, and, where necessary, to provide an escort. He carried imperial *firmans* (orders) requiring their cooperation. Thus, Leake encountered the 'Turkish' *aǧas, beys, voyvodas* and *pashas* in formal meetings arranged for business reasons. Like other western travellers, he was usually received politely and provided with the coffee, *glika* and pipe which good manners required. On the other hand, the Ottoman officials were more suspicious of a foreign soldier than an English *mi'lord*. Encouraged by the French agents also active in Greece at the time, they must often have regarded Leake as a spy.[2] In the circumstances, Leake was perhaps justified in interpreting their politeness as superficial.

In general Leake's experiences of the 'Turks' confirmed his expectations. The sources of these prejudices are more difficult to locate, but there are some possibilities. First, Leake's paternal uncle, James Lee, was a Levant merchant who had spent much of his life in the Ottoman Empire.[3] He may have influenced his nephew's views even before young William went out to the Near East. Secondly, references in his published works show that Leake was well read in the available travel and scholarly literature in both English and French covering the region. He may have imbibed more than ancient

---

[1] FO78/57; Acc. 599/85492.

[2] For example, Leake had difficulty in visiting the fortress of the Palamidi at Nafplion, while Nuri Bey refused permission to visit the fortress of Acrocorinth, Leake (1830; Vol. 2, 360-61; Vol. 3, 257).

[3] Acc. 599/84616.

history and topographical detail. Thirdly, a catalogue of Leake's books made towards the end of his life shows that he possessed several of the standard works of his time on the Ottoman Empire.[1] It is difficult to prove that he acquired or even read them before he visited the Near East, but they were certainly instrumental in constructing the view of the Turks shared by Leake's contemporaries.[2]

The uniform view of the 'Turks' found in travellers, essayists and political thinkers of the eighteenth century has been attributed to a shared classification of the Ottoman Empire as a despotism. Aslı Çırakman has argued that, following Montesquieu's influential *Spirit of the Laws* (1749), the eighteenth century view was that despotism should be seen as more than a political system. Despotism, in fact, defined the nature of society. The existence of despotism and its characteristics were deduced in turn from such defining principles as the natural climate of the region concerned, human nature and the type of religion followed.[3] Thus, both a warm climate and Islam automatically produced the despotism of the Ottoman Empire and its ruling 'Turkish' elite. The travellers knew, then, what they would expect, when they visited Ottoman provinces: oppression, corruption and the neglect of land and buildings would be evident; arrogance, ignorance and laziness were to be expected. Leake's views reflect these deductions so closely that it is tempting to conclude that, like his contemporary William Eton (a copy of whose work he possessed),[4] he was operating with a framework of expectations derived ultimately from Montesquieu.[5] While *The Spirit of the Laws* does not appear in Leake's catalogue of his library, Rycaut's *Present State of the Ottoman Empire* is there.[6] It was Montesquieu's major source of information on the Ottoman Empire. Rycaut's identification of the 'maxims' on which the Ottoman system was alleged to be based provided Montesquieu with material both for the formulation of his 'laws' and their testing with apparently empirical data.[7]

---

[1] *A Catalogue of Books having reference to my Collection of Coins and Antiquities* ... dated 29 March, 1858 lists as in Leake's library: d'Ohson, I. de Mouradja, *Tableau Général de l'Empire Othoman* (Paris 1788), Eton, W. *Survey of the Ottoman Empire* (London 1801), Habesci, E. [Alexander Gika] *The Present State of the Ottoman Empire* (London 1784), Rycault, P. *The Present State of the Ottoman Empire* (London 1667), and Thornton, T. *The Present State of Turkey* (London 1807).

[2] Çırakman (2002; 132-72, 185-92, 201-08).

[3] Çırakman (2002; 105-32).

[4] Eton (1801).

[5] Suggested by Çırakman (2002; 145).

[6] See note 1 previous page. It may have been one of the rare first editions, Anderson (1989; 42).

[7] Çırakman (2002; 111-114).

Finally, Leake's acquaintance with Ali Pasha of Ioannina and his subordinates, as well as a pattern of travel largely confined to Ali's domains, may have helped to confirm preconceived ideas. Leake heard about, and to an extent experienced at first hand, the particularly oppressive, ruthless and rapacious regime of a very powerful provincial governor. Moreover, he encountered it at a time of uncertainty, tension and stress for the Ottoman Empire. The Empire was caught up in the world war generated by the French Revolution. France and Russia threatened invasion and partition. Both sought to ferment rebellion amongst the subject peoples and encouraged moves towards independence by the provincial governors. Serbia was already in revolt (1804). Wahhābi fanatics had captured Mecca (1803) and Medina (1804) and gone on to invade Syria and Iraq (1805). Forceful measures were necessary to contain and prevent other uprisings, on the one hand, and to raise extraordinary taxes to pay for additional troops to defend the Empire, on the other. At the same time, the division in Ottoman society over the westernisation programme introduced under Selim III (1789-1807) weakened central authority and eventually produced the *coup d'etat* of which Leake's acquaintance, Möse Musa Pasha, was a part. Ali Pasha skilfully exploited the situation to strengthen his quasi independence and to increase the extent of his domains. He played-off the French and the British in a convoluted diplomatic game, and Fleming has argued that he deliberately played the part of the Oriental despot with westerners to secure their support.[1] His officials and Albanian soldiers were certainly diligent in occupying unprotected towns and villages on his borders, controlling the population of his domains and exacting taxes, knowing that failure meant death. Seeking to make sense of such a complicated situation, Leake may have overlooked the extraordinary context of the time and space in which he made his observations. All too easily, he may have slipped into interpreting his first-hand information in terms of the accepted model of despotism, thus allowing his experience to confirm the west European stereotype of the 'Turks'.

*REFERENCES*

*Published works by William Leake*

1821.    *The Topography of Athens*, London; John Murray.
1825.    *Historical Outline of the Greek Revolution*, London; John Murray.
1830.    *Travels in the Morea*, 3 vols., London; John Murray.

---

[1] Fleming (1999; 156-80).

1835. *Travels in Northern Greece*, 4 vols., London; J. Rodwell.

1846. *Peloponnesiaca: A Supplement to 'Travels in the Morea'*, London; J. Rodwell.

1850. *The Claim to the Islands of Cervi and Sapienza*, London; L. Booth.

1851. *Greece at the End of Twenty-three Years' Protection*, London; J. Rodwell.

1851. [Pacificus] *One Word for Russia and Two for Ourselves*, London; John Murray.

1854. *A Letter to Colonel Chesney of the Royal Artillery by an Old Brother Officer who has Served Many Years in Turkey*, London; L. Booth.

1855. *A Postscript to the Letter to Colonel Chesney*, London; L. Booth. [Vetus] *The Object of the War*, London; L. Booth.

1857. *The Late War by a Christian*, London; L. Booth.

1858. *Some Reasons for Reform and the Ballot in a Letter to Richard Cobden, Esq., from a Retired Officer of Artillery*, London; L. Booth.


*Archival*


Acc. 599: *Martin Leake Papers*, Hertfordshire Record Office, Hertford; /84616 (Microfilm), *Memoir of his Father, Himself and His Family by John Martin Leake* (c.1829). /85492, 'Instructions to Captain W.M. Leake, Royal Artillery, from Lord Harroby', 28 August, 1804.

FO 78/57 *Foreign Office Papers, Turkey: Captain W.M. Leake, Turkey and Egypt*, Public Record Office, Kew: 'Instructions to Capt. Leake' [added in pencil, 'July, 1804'].

Martin Leake, W. *A Catalogue of Books having reference to my Collection of Coins and Antiquities which by my Will I have Bequethed and desired to go along with such coins and Antiquites upon the Trusts therein mentioned* 29 March, 1858, Classics Faculty Library, University of Cambridge.

*Notebook 18*: Classics Faculty Library, University of Cambridge: 'W.M. Leake Notebooks'


*Other published sources*


Anderson, S. 1989. *An English Consul in Turkey: Paul Rycaut at Smyrna, 1667-1678*, Oxford: Oxford University Press.

Angelomatis-Tsougarakis, H. 1990. *The Eve of the Greek Revival: British Travellers' Perceptions of Early Nineteenth-Century Greece*, London: Routledge.

Baggally, J. 1938. *Ali Pasha and Great Britain*, Oxford; Blackwell.

Çırakman, A. 2002. *From the 'Terror of the World' to the 'Sick Man of Europe'*, New York, Oxford: Peter Lang.

Daniel, N. 1966. *Islam, Europe and Empire*, Edinburgh: EUP.

De Grey and Ripon, Earl 1860. 'Address to the Royal Geographical Society of London; Delivered at the Anniversary Meeting on 28 may, 1860', *Journal of the Royal Geographical Society* Vol. 30; cxiii-cvvi

Fleming, K 1999. *The Muslim Bonaparte. Diplomacy and Orientalism in Ali Pasha's Greece*, Princeton, New Jersey; Princeton University Press.

Galt, J. 1813. *Letters from the Levant*, London; Cadell & Davies.

Hasluck, F. 1929. *Christianity and Islam under the Sultans*, edited by M.M. Hasluck, Oxford; Clarendon Press.

Marsden, J. 1864. *A Brief Memoir of the Life and Writings of the Late Lieutenant Colonel William Martin Leake*, London (privately printed)

Plomer, W. 1970. *The Diamond of Jannina: Ali Pasha, 1741-1822*, London; Cape.

Shaw, S. 1971. *Between Old and New. The Ottoman Empire under Sultan Selim III, 1789-1807*, Cambridge, Mass; Harvard University Press.

# 29. RELIGION AND PLURALITY IN OTTOMAN CULTURE: THE ORTHODOX COMMUNITY IN SALONICA IN THE 1840s

## Bülent ÖZDEMİR

Many aspects of Ottoman society have been analysed in the context of either nationalist movements or the *millet* system but little attention has been paid to the unique character of Ottoman society simply as 'Ottoman'. What were its basic characteristics? How did this divided society manage to find common elements? This is potentially a very wide topic, but in this paper we will look at the Orthodox community of Salonica in the first half of the nineteenth century in the light of archival documents and contemporary travellers' accounts. After a general survey, the paper tackles certain more specific issues such as the rise of the Greek merchant class, the authority of church, forced conversion and apostasy.

It may be argued that the nineteenth century Ottoman reforms were shaped above all by continuing social changes. These broad socio-economic changes (an increase in production and trade, urbanisation, immigration, demographic development) intensified at the beginning of the nineteenth century and altered in turn the basis of Ottoman society, including traditional social formations and the structure of communal organisation. Religious communities as distinct entities were as influenced as the rest of the society, and responded according to their ability to resist and change under contemporary conditions. When these developments threatened the basic structure of the Ottoman state, the state also responded by the promulgation of a series of measures whose purpose was to preserve the existence and integrity of the Empire. I would argue that all the nineteenth century reforms should be seen in the light of this reactive state policy, which incidentally marked a reiteration of existing policy rather than a totally innovative approach. Those aspects of the reforms concerning in particular the non-Muslim subjects of the Empire ranged from greater representation in local administration to permission to build new churches and schools. Along with these new privileges, there were also new obligations such as military service and changes in taxation.

*Salonica*

In the early nineteenth century, the Orthodox community of Salonica constituted one fifth of its total population. More precisely, according to the Ottoman census of 1831, 21.7 per cent of the total population of the city was Orthodox Christian. While the Greek-speaking population witnessed a relative decline in the early nineteenth century, other Orthodox sectors of the population such as Bulgarian and Vlach had been nurtured by continuous immigration to the city.

We do not have specific data with respect to the number of Bulgarians in Salonica, because the Ottoman officials treated the Orthodox population as one group regardless of ethnicity. However, that books were published in the 1850s in Bulgarian, albeit spelt in Greek characters, suggests that a number of Bulgarians were living in the city in the early nineteenth century.[1] In 1839, according to Blunt, the British consul in Salonica at that time, there were in Salonica two Greek schools, with four school masters in total and 35 scholars. At the beginning of the nineteenth century, there had been only one Greek school which had to suspend its activities during the Greek Revolution but was reopened in 1828.

Blunt does not supply exact information concerning the time of the establishment of the second school, but, in 1845, a school for girls was founded attached to a former boy's school.[2] The first Greek printing and publishing house was established by Garbolas Miltiadis in Salonica in 1850. The number of churches in 1839 is given as twelve, with one Archbishop, eight bishops, and twenty-seven priests. Also, there were two monasteries, with twenty-two monks. The church of Aghios Andonis served the Orthodox population of the city as its only hospital. The total number of major Greek commercial establishments is given as eleven in 1839,[3] the best-known being Kaftandzoglou, Paikos, Rogotis, Skambalis, Papatheos, Kakos, and Balanos.[4]

---

[1] See FO 195 / 100 Blunt to Ponsonby 25 January 1839 and Anastassiadou (1997; 67).
[2] Anastassiadou (1997; 65).
[3] FO 195 / 100 Blunt to Ponsonby 25 January 1839.
[4] Vacalopoulos (1988; 301-307).

## The Tanzimat and After

Arguably, already by the time of the Tanzimat reforms, the status of the Orthodox community was in some respects almost equal with that of the Muslims in the Ottoman Empire. Indeed, in terms of conspicuously poor or wealthy people these changes may have had little meaning. For the poor, both Christians and Muslims, there was not much change in their daily lives because they still shared the same fate, which was to work in the field and struggle. For wealthy people, for instance for a flourishing Christian, the reforms provided a better framework within which to achieve a more comfortable life, but in practical terms, such men had already achieved success and substantial freedom in their actions.[1] Nevertheless, the reforms certainly had some immediate impacts. Henceforth, the head of the Orthodox community could take part in the provincial council as an equal member and intervene with the local authorities with respect to the affairs of the town. Obstacles to the construction of new churches and cemeteries were removed. The principle of equal taxation was put into effect, though this was regarded in some social circles as a mixed blessing and most of the notables of the Orthodox community objected to paying the same as ordinary taxpayers.

It is true, though, that the non-Muslim subjects in general appear to have thought that their conditions would improve after the reforms had begun to be implemented. We are told in the reports that the non-Muslim people of Salonica were daily gaining courage and beginning to realize the benefits held out to them. It is interesting to note that some Greeks, formerly Ottoman subjects but at this time citizens of the newly established Greek state, may have been tempted to emigrate from independent Greece into the Ottoman Empire. I quote Consul Blunt:

> I believe that there exists but little sympathy among the Greek *reaya* in Turkey for those of Greece. The state of the *reaya* is now so different to which it was prior to the Hatt-ı Sheriff of Gülhane. They are generally speaking more free than supposed, and perhaps more so than they could expect to be in Greece. There are certainly exceptions, but in no case, to any extent approaching even the brutality of former times. It is a well-known fact that numerous Greek families would have crossed the frontiers and returned to their old rulers under the impression that they would have been happier and more free in Turkey than in Greece.[2]

---

[1] A contemporary traveller Adolphus Slade remarked in his observations that the Greeks were more prosperous in the cities and the countryside than the Muslim compatriots, but the Greeks still complained as if they were the poor and oppressed. Slade (1832, I; 128-129).

[2] FO 78 / 531 Blunt to Canning 10 November 1843.

*The Rise of Greek Commerce*

The rise of a Greek-speaking urbanised merchant class is a well-argued facet of the eighteenth century Ottoman Empire.[1] Nevertheless, along with factors such as the influence of Western ideas and the Enlightenment, the role of the Orthodox Church, the negative effects of Ottoman rule, and the ancient roots of pro-nationalist feelings noticed already in thirteenth century Byzantium, it occupies a place in the debate about the emergence of nationalism in the Balkans.[2] Equally, with regard to the nineteenth century, a frequently-debated idea concerning the idea of nationhood among the Orthodox is the question of whether there existed such a feeling among the people because of the influence of these merchants or whether this is to be seen as a construction of recent historiography and should be disregarded.[3]

As far as Salonica was concerned, the ambitions of the Greek Orthodox people to live under the newly established Greek state were hard to realise in the 1840s since their region remained part of the Ottoman Empire until 1912. If it was the case, as is argued in much of the literature, that the growing power of the Orthodox merchant class and their relatively new and free-thinking ideologies played an important role in the process of the creation of national feeling among the Greek people, one may ask why did it not emerge more forcefully in Salonica, which had a considerable number of wealthy Orthodox merchants and families, and why were there so few efforts to mobilise the Greek population to participate in the Greek State from 1830 onwards? Quite the contrary, the Greek merchant class chose to remain in Salonica, with growing mercantile power, and seemed pleased with the protection provided by the European powers and the new reform measures of the Ottoman government.[4]

At least part of the reason must be lie in their well-being. The Orthodox merchants had been engaged as muleteers in the import-export trade before they became the agents of the European merchants. In time, they became the main import-export merchants, and consequently moneylenders and bankers. The result of large business and the concentration of capital paved the way for the development of more cosmopolitan interests than nationalist ones.

---

[1] Clogg (1982; 185-207). See also Stoianovich (1960) and Clogg (1981).

[2] Clogg (1982; 188) also see Kitromilides (1990; 26-33), Xydis (1968), Sugar and Lederer (eds. 1971).

[3] See Clogg (1981).

[4] Kasaba, Keyder, and Tabak (1986) suggest that the political impact of the merchant class was not uniform because of 'the historical conjunctures in which the bourgeoisie moved to prominence, their physical and social surroundings, and the economic processes that supported their ascent were all important in determining their political choices and influences.' p. 124.

However one decides the exact reason, it seems that in this case at least one cannot give much credit to the role of the merchant class in the ideal of achieving national independence. It should be remembered that their being neutral or apolitical concerning most of the developments was a consistent position and most of those with commercial interests were inclined to take a pragmatic approach to politics. They were more concerned about their interests and consequently the preservation of the *status quo* in the Ottoman Empire than in venturing into a national struggle, which might end in a fiasco and cause them to lose everything.[1] Stoianovich classified the Orthodox merchants' attitudes towards national independence as follows: 'one — perhaps the largest — group of merchants did not originally think in terms of political independence. Another group favoured political independence only if it did not entail social revolution, or entail only the transfer of wealth from one small group to another, that is from the Turks and Muslims to themselves. A third group, numerically small but active, desired national independence even at the cost of social revolution.'[2] According to Richard Clogg, the third group was also for the most part not big merchants but small entrepreneurs and the members of the petty bourgeoisie.[3]

In turn, this implies that the tendency to regard every social movement as one provoked by the abusive system or the shortcomings of Ottoman local administration is mistaken. The improving conditions of the Christian notables as wealthy merchants, *çiftlik* (large farm holders)[4] and entrepreneurs led them to disregard the Christian *reaya*, and there is no reason to suppose that they were more tolerant than the Muslim notables. This can be seen more clearly in the post-Tanzimat era by which time the Christians eventually acquired the right to possess land. In economic matters, Christian merchants were not inclined to favour the Christian *reaya* on account of their religious affiliation. Contemporary travellers' accounts are full of information regarding the Greek notables' arbitrary exercise of power over and mistreatment of their co-religionists. These men were often depicted as insolent, degenerate, proud and also as public robbers, monopolists. 'The travellers' characterisation of the notables as 'Christian Turks' echoes the views of the Greeks themselves.'[5] It appears therefore that the elite of the Orthodox community in Salonica as in the other parts of the Empire, may be seen in the 1840s as being comfortably wedded to the improving of the Ottoman system of government, and they were not agents of rapid social change.

---

[1] Stoianovich (1960; 303).

[2] Stoianovich (1960; 306).

[3] See also Clogg (1982; 104).

[4] There were a considerable number of Christian and Jewish *çiftlik* holders in Salonica according to the Ottoman *sicils*. See for instance, Sicil 231:14, 3 *Muharrem* 1251.

[5] Angelomatis-Tsougarakis (1990; 79). See also Clogg (1982; 102).

*The Church*

After the conquest of Constantinople, the Ottomans continued the previous Islamic states' general policy of granting and recognising non-Muslim communities' extensive privileges with respect to their internal organisation and communal affairs.[1] Since Islam regards Christianity as a religion and respects the Christians as the 'people of the book', and Jesus Christ as a prophet, the Orthodox church was recognised as an official body to supervise both the religious and civil affairs of the community in the Empire. According to İnalcık, from the beginning, to protect the rights of non-Muslims in the Ottoman Empire was considered 'a command of God and a duty of the State' by the Ottomans.[2] Moreover, the Orthodox Church was particularly recognised as the most respected religious community in the hierarchical structure of the Empire.[3] Before the eighteenth century, traditionally the candidate for the Patriarchate was proposed to the Sultan by the holy synod of the Patriarchate, which was believed to be composed of Metropolitans who were mostly close to İstanbul, and thereafter an imperial *berat* (permit) was issued for the confirmation of appointment.[4]

The first change in this structure of the organisation of the Patriarchate came in the eighteenth century in opposition to the growing power of certain Greek families of Istanbul (Phanariots) over the civil and administrative affairs of the Orthodox community. In 1755, the popular masses and especially the guilds of Constantinople were admitted by Patriarch Cyril V to take part in the administration of church affairs. But two years later, in 1757, this practice was abolished by an imperial order obtained from the Ottoman government. Fearing that the control of church affairs would pass to lay representatives, the Orthodox clergy proposed another reform in the composition of Synod, which mainly protected the interests of the clergy by leaving the election of the Patriarch and the administration of the affairs of the community to the Metropolitans.[5] However, this protection of their interests did not last long

---

[1] Bowen and Gibb (1950; 215-16). Hitti (1951; 716). There are several explanations of this issue in the literature: that Mehmet the Conqueror granted the privileges because of his policy over Europe, which served to split Christianity into two camps, or his financial considerations, which served to collect more tax from the non-Muslims, or that Constantinople was not captured by force but surrendered by capitulation. For the elaboration of the above arguments see Papadopoulos (1992; 1-26). See also Arnakis (1952; 235-251) Runciman (1965), Frazee (1969; 1-8). According to İnalcık 'from the beginning Ottomans followed a policy of tolerance and protection of the Orthodox Church. This policy proved to be beneficial to both the Church and the new rulers.' İnalcık (1993; 20).

[2] İnalcık (1993; 18).

[3] Bozkurt (1989; 32). Ware (1964; 2).

[4] Bozkurt( 1989; 29), Papadopoulos (1992; 41).

[5] Papadopoulos (1992; 49-55).

and around the middle of the nineteenth century, mostly middle class people objected to this system and wanted to participate in the administration of communal affairs.

The nineteenth-century Ottoman reforms included religious communities in their scope. The Tanzimat decree of 1839 did not deal directly with reforms with respect to the Orthodox Church. However, in 1847, the Ottoman government intervened for the first time in the internal affairs of the Orthodox Church by ordering that three secular members be added to the members of the Synod.[1]

A considerable segment of the educated Christian population in Salonica seems to have opposed the new reform measures of the Tanzimat, as happened elsewhere throughout the Empire. Historically, not only the Greek speakers but also other non-Greek-speaking people of the Ottoman Empire including large numbers of Slav, Vlach and Bulgarian Orthodox peoples were regarded as beholden to the Ecumenical Patriarchate. Unlike in the West, the Orthodox Church created a unique identity in which faith and ethnicity was blended; and the Church became the sole representative of this identity.[2] Bishops of the cities and towns were the most influential figures among the Orthodox population regardless of their ethnic origin. One scholar writes of this as: 'The absence of social stability in agrarian societies due to the lack of a permanent ruling elite [which] maximised the clergymen's influence and the local chieftain's (klephtes) patronage.'[3]

The Orthodox clergy were highly educated persons, and intelligent enough to see and comprehend the ongoing changes in Ottoman society. These changes certainly would have suggested to them that, potentially at least, their own established interests were in danger. Their living conditions were relatively better than those of the ordinary people, and any reforms were likely to reduce the dependence of the flock on them. Therefore, from this point of view, any measure which could change the old and established order could be dangerous to them, including the introduction of taxation on Christian religious endowments and consequently the decrease in their sources of income.[4]

---

[1] Bozkurt (1989; 30).
[2] Karpat (1986; 139).
[3] Gounaris (1995; 409-418).
[4] İnalcık (Tanzimat 101).

The Ottoman government had long ago realised the importance and power of the church for the Empire.[1] For instance, when the negative effects of French revolutionary propaganda were felt to be dangerous among the people of the Empire after 1798, the Ottoman government, though its attitudes were more liberal towards the French revolution than those of most European states, tried to protect its interests by utilising the ecclesiastical anti-Westernism. The book, *Dhidhaskalia Patriki* (Paternal Teaching), was written by the Patriarch Anthimos of Jerusalem and published in Istanbul in 1798. The intention of publishing and distributing this book in the Ottoman Empire was to show how dangerous were French revolutionary ideas to believers and to prevent the Orthodox subjects of the Empire from falling into these atheist traps.[2]

During the Tanzimat, the Ottoman government tried to reduce resistance to the reforms by offering new positions to the Church connected with their implementation. According to the reforms, Bishops or the heads of the Christian communities in the towns would be the members of the newly established local Councils.[3] Just like the other powerful bodies (government officials, merchants, landowners) of the towns, bishops were still hesitant and confused as well as reluctant to accept the position assigned to them in the provincial administration of the Empire, because of the idea that the new measures would change their old-established power and influence upon society. But, in a very short time, the clergy of the Orthodox Church, like the others (tax-farmers, local government officials), had adapted to the new system.

Parallel to the irregularities committed by the local government officials and the *beys* in the interior, the members of the Greek Church such as bishops in the cities and towns in their capacity as a part of the administrative body were in some ways involved in exploitation.[4] In the Ottoman local administration, the church undertook certain duties regarding the Christian subjects of the Sultan. First of all, they were delegated to represent the Christian community in all matters in general. After the Tanzimat reforms were implemented, they became members of the local councils. They were also awarded the right to present Christian petitions to

---

[1] According to some scholars, this can be traced back to the reign of Sultan Mehmet the Conqueror who was fully aware of the importance of the Patriarchate as representing Eastern Christianity, and consequently its divisive effect on the Western Church. Arnakis (1952; 236).

[2] Clogg (1969; 87-116).

[3] For remarks on the Church in the Balkans, see Sugar and Lederer (1971).

[4] On the Orthodox Church as a negative factor in the eyes of travellers, see Angelomatis-Tsougarakis (1990).

the authorities, at both the local level and in Istanbul, and to send delegations to the capital. Most importantly, they were delegated to extract and to forward certain taxes such as *zabitlik* or tithes from the Christian community to the local authorities. As we see from contemporary reports, the bishops were thereby encouraged to participate in a most injurious plunder of the Christian reaya. According to Consul Blunt, a bishop's visit to a village put fear into the Christian reaya greater than that felt towards the Ottoman authorities, partly because the Bishop travelled with their retinue on horseback as in former times, a form of processional travel that incurred very considerable expense, an expense that was supported by the Christian *reaya*.[1]

The rate of *zabitlik* was fixed by measure, but the bishops took a certain proportion according to the quantity of produce. Each year they increased the measure while paying a fixed amount to the local authorities. The Christian *reaya* were not strong enough to raise any objection on this subject. Consul Blunt reported that in the time of the Greek Revolution, some of the Christian *reaya* of Salonica went to the bishop and remonstrated with him about the increases in local expenses, and some of them threatened to write to Istanbul, but the matter was not followed up. The Orthodox bishop threatened to denounce them to the authorities as persons who had engaged in revolution.[2]

In another case, some Ionian subjects under British protection in Salonica were forced to pay *cizye* by the Greek Bishop according to the general obligations of the Orthodox Community, in spite of the opposition of the governor of Salonica. Then, the bishop declared that if they did not want to pay the tax, they would cease to be considered as Christians by the Greek Church and would be deprived of the ceremonies of the church. As this case shows, the higher clergy did not hesitate to invoke religious authority against the Christian people if these people opposed the decision of the local government authorities.[3] Consul Blunt reports, with respect to the plundering of the Christian *reaya* by the Greek clergy, that the common expression amongst the Christians in the interior in those days was: 'We are free as far as regards the Turks, but when shall we be liberated from the bishops?'[4] On this

---

[1] FO 195 / 176 Blunt to Ponsonby 30 January 1840. In a recent study on Cyprus during the Tanzimat reforms, the same kind of maladministration of communal affairs by the Church is emphasised. According to the author, this triggered the reform process even before the Tanzimat in the 1830s. See Dionyssiou (1969; 12).

[2] FO 195 / 176 Blunt to Ponsonby January 1841.

[3] FO 195 / 100 Charnaud to Ponsonby 28 May 1834.

[4] FO 195 / 176 Blunt to Ponsonby 20 January 1841.

subject, the contemporary travellers' accounts echo the same kinds of complaints. Most of the reports depicted the clergy as ignorant, stupid and inactive. Their identification with the Ottoman authorities and notables gave travellers a bad impression and consequently they depicted the clergy as preoccupied principally by their own interests and merciless in exploiting their own flock.[1]

## After Greek Independence

After the establishment of a sovereign Greece in the Balkans in 1830, the region around Salonica was unavoidably embroiled in the problems and disorders which arose between the two countries arising from the exchange of peoples, especially Greeks who retained strong ties with the region. In 1842 the border controls between the Ottoman Empire and Greece were still not very strict for travellers coming from the two countries. People from both sides of the border commonly crossed the frontier for a number of reasons such as visits to relatives, trade, and so on. From the reports, it appears that these activities sometimes created problems for the authorities of that region. For instance, if a Greek citizen resided in a town for a prolonged period he was sometimes obliged to pay *cizye* as the Orthodox subjects of the Ottoman Empire did; or when they travelled with arms, they were not allowed to retain them without producing a certificate of permission. Similarly, the parties on the Greek side were equally alive to the least provocation, in order to blame any event on 'Turkish barbarity and oppression.'[2]

According to the reports, the Greek Consul in Salonica was persistently on bad terms with the local authorities. He refused to contact the local authorities in person and merely sent his vice-consul, who was the father-in-law of the Russian Consul, in order to present the cases. Further problems arose from the fact that affairs of a trifling nature were left entirely in the hands of the interpreters, who were well known for their cupidity and impertinence. The consuls themselves imagined that it was not becoming to their dignity ever to treat affairs personally with the local authorities. It was observed by Consul Blunt that even in simple affairs the Greek Consul, for example, forced matters to the point of a dispute, because of the influence of the Russian Consul, Mr. Valliano. As understood from Blunt's reports, the conduct of persons in the employ of the Greek Consulate after the

---

[1] Hobhouse (1813; 297), Leake (1835; IV; 281-82), Walpole (1818; 174, 201-202).
[2] FO 78 / 490 Blunt to Canning 11 October 1842.

appointment of the Greek vice-consul, Haci Dobrodosco, was sufficient to cause irritation to the authorities. Consul Blunt says: 'when a Greek commits a crime and is captured by the local authorities, he is always given up to the Greek Consul upon his promise that he is going to be punished, but it is never done.'[1]

There do appear have been attempts to incite Christian people to rise against the Ottoman authority through the official Greek representatives during the 1840s. After the Tanzimat reforms, these efforts usually failed. Consul Blunt reported the following reply of the Christian people to the Greek spies: '... we have nothing to complain against the Turks, but the tyranny and oppression of the Bishops, and we will have nothing to do either with Hellenes or Russians for what could we do, were we inclined to join you and throw off our allegiance when England and France are with the Sultan?'[2]

*Some reflections on society*

Conversion was a common phenomenon in a multi-faith society such as Salonica. When a person wanted to convert to any other religion, he had to do so in front of local authorities, including the *müfti*, heads of the Orthodox and Jewish communities and sometimes the foreign consuls. Conversion from Islam to the Christian or Jewish faith was prohibited; and if this happened, the punishment according to Islamic law was death. When a person who converted to Islam decided to return to his previous faith and declared so in front of the authorities, their first act was to persuade them to desist through disputation. If this effort failed and the person insisted on their apostasy from Islam, the death penalty was carried out by the authorities.[3] In 1844, through the continuous efforts of British Ambassador to Istanbul Lord Canning, new effectual measures were taken by the Ottoman government to remove the punishment of the death penalty for apostasy cases, replacing it with imprisonment.[4]

---

[1] FO 195 / 100 Blunt to Ponsonby 20 June 1839.

[2] BPP, Blunt to Canning 3 May 1849, No: 79, p. 46.

[3] According to Kemal Karpat, if one willingly converts to Islam that makes one subject to Muslim law, and can still be enforced against one when one decides to return to one's previous faith. Karpat (1983; 259-266).

[4] FO 78 / 555, Canning to Aberdeen, 23 March 1844. According to Islam, conversion from Islam to any other religion is considered as a total rejection of the truthfulness of the Islamic faith and consequently requires capital punishment. In contrast, conversion from Christianity to any other religion and even within Christianity from one sect to another is very common and to some extent acceptable.

From the conquest of the Balkans in the fifteenth century to the end of the Empire, there was no policy of forced conversion. 'Most of the great Balkan families and smaller *tımar* holders converted to Islam during the sixteenth century not as the result of Ottoman pressure, but in consequence of their realisation that this was a necessary first step on the road to becoming full Ottomans' says Stanford Shaw on this issue.[1] Richard Clogg has cited the following ten reasons from a contemporary account:

> 1) love of civil liberty, 2) in consequence of the fatigues of slavery and particular vexations, 3) to enjoy the luxurious privileges of polygamy, 4) to preserve their property from Muslim usurpation, 5) to enjoy freedom in their manner of dressing, 6) to get rid of a capital condemnation, 7) to free their children from slavery, 8) from want of religion, a sentiment of honour, 9) from a taste for arms, and often with a design to avenge himself on a Turk who has ill treated him, 10) from despair, or from a state of drunkenness.[2]

Consul Blunt reported the following incident relating to apostasy from Christianity in Salonica:

> A Greek *reaya* presented himself to the Pasha saying that he wished to embrace the Mohammedan faith. His Excellency told him to go and reflect, and gave him a week to consider. The man who is a native of Ionina returned still resolved to abandon his faith, but the Pasha having in the meanwhile made inquiries with respect to this individual, and finding that he wished to become a Muslim purposely to escape the payment of some trifling debts. His Excellency rejected him.[3]

In former years, the debts of a prospective convert had generally been paid by the Muslims; after that the individual was accepted as a true convert to Islam. The above case clearly defines the position of the Ottoman authorities towards the status of Christian people in Ottoman society. In other words, depiction of the Ottoman authorities' aggressive behaviour towards the Christian *reaya* in which the former perceive the latter as potential candidates for Islamisation, as found in a number of accounts, needs closer examination. For example, the following cases cited by Blunt:

> a)   A boy of nine years of age, taken by some Turks and persuaded to apostatise. When he was brought before the Council he declared that he was a Christian and was liberated.

---

[1] Shaw (1963; 65).
[2] Cited Clogg (1973; 30).
[3] FO 195 / 240 Blunt to Canning 21 August 1845.

b)  A monk of the Oriental Church named Pappa Isaiah, presented
himself before the Council at Serres, about two months since, and
apostatised to the Muslim faith, and took the name of Isa Efendi.
He repented shortly after and went to Mount Athos and from there
to Greece. He returned a few days since to Serres, and presented
himself to the Greek bishop of that place and told him of his
determination of recanting before the whole Council. The Bishop
advised him not to do this. The monk would not however follow
the Bishops advice but presented himself before the Council,
dressed as a monk, and declared himself a Christian. Ömer Pasha
and the Council were horror-struck and ordered that the monk
should be immediately beheaded. The bishop reminded the Pasha of
the Sultan's promise in favour of the Christians, and the monk
was imprisoned.[1]

A final example is a very good indication of changes in the thinking of the
people in Salonica that the *Tanzimat* brought about. Blunt reported:

In a recent case of a Greek woman's embracing Islam, prior to the
ceremony, Vasıf Mehmet Pasha called the Molla and told him to speak with
all due respect for the Greek bishop, who would be present, and that when
asking the woman if she with free will left her religion, he must say the
'Christian religion' and not ... *gâvur*.[2]

*Conclusion*

We conclude; the Orthodox community of Salonica in the early nineteenth
century was not an agent of modernisation as argued, for example, by
Davison.[3] It must be considered no more than a part of a general
transformation of the Ottoman social structure which had started in earlier
centuries and intensified in the nineteenth century, one that affected many
different aspects of the community, including attitudes to one another, as
illustrated in the above examples re. apostasy and conversion. If the Orthodox
community of Salonica is to be taken into consideration, it can be argued that
it was changing within the boundaries of this general Ottoman transformation
and played its own distinctive role. Nevertheless when confronting the
problems of the time (economic, social, educational and administrative), the
common people of Salonica from different communities underwent similar
experiences. There was no separation between Jewish, Muslim and Orthodox
people, who had shared an extended common past during their centuries-long

---

[1] FO 195 / 240 Blunt to Canning 21 August 1845.

[2] FO 195 / 240 Blunt to Canning 3 May 1844.

[3] Davison (1982; 319-337).

cohabitation. The new reform measures of the *Tanzimat* were concerned with the socio-economic problems of Ottoman society without making religious and ethnic distinctions between the peoples of the Empire, who were as we have illustrated in the case of the Orthodox community in Salonica were in any case themselves internally diverse. Thus, the Orthodox community of Salonica was both affected by and was also responsive to the Tanzimat reforms. It was not though the instigator of that change. It was not convinced enough of its merits to take a leading role. It was also not convinced, at least in any unified way, as to the merits of independence. In sum, it was, in many and diverse respects, an integrated part of the *status quo*.

## REFERENCES

*Archival*

FO 195 / 100 Charnaud to Ponsonby 28 May 1834.
FO 195 / 100 Blunt to Ponsonby 30 May 1837.
FO 195 / 100 Blunt to Ponsonby 25 January 1839
FO 195 / 100 Blunt to Ponsonby 21 March 1839.
FO 195 / 100 Blunt to Ponsonby 20 June 1839.
FO 195 / 176 Blunt to Ponsonby 20 February 1840.
FO 195 / 176 Blunt to Ponsonby 30 January 1840
FO 195 / 176 Blunt to Ponsonby January 1841
FO 195 / 176 Blunt to Ponsonby 20 January 1841.
FO 195 / 240 Blunt to Canning 3 May 1844.
FO 195 / 240 Blunt to Canning 21 August 1845.
FO 78 / 490 Blunt to Canning 11 October 1842.
FO 78 / 531 Blunt to Canning 10 November 1843.
FO 78 / 555, Canning to Aberdeen, 23 March 1844
BPP, Blunt to Canning 3 May 1849, No: 79, p. 46.
BPP, Blunt to Canning 3 April 1849, No: 79, p. 43.

*Published*

Anastassiadou, M. 1997 *Salonique, 1830-1912: une ville ottomane à l'âge des Réformes*, Leiden; Brill.
Angelomatis-Tsougarakis, H. 1990 *The Eve of the Greek Revival: British Travellers' Perception of Early Nineteenth Century Greece*, London; Routledge.

Arnakis, G. 1952 'The Greek Church of Constantinople and the Ottoman Empire', in *Journal of Modern History*, Vol. 24, No. 3; 235-251.

Bowen, H. and Gibb, H. 1950 *Islamic Society and the West : a study of the impact of western civilisation on Moslem culture in the Near East*, Vol. 1, Part 1. London; Oxford University Press.

Bozkurt, G. 1989 *Gayrimüslim Osmanlı Vatandaşlarının Hukuki Durumu 1839-1914*, Ankara; Türk Tarih Kurumu.

Clogg, R. 1969 'The 'Dhidhaskalia Patriki' 1798: An Orthodox Reaction to French Revolutionary Propaganda', in *Middle Eastern Studies*, Vol. 5, No. 2, (May); 87-116.

Clogg, R. 1973 'A Little-known Orthodox Neo-Martyr, Athanasios of Smyrna, 1819', in *Eastern Churches Review*, Vol. 5, No 1, Spring, pp 30-38.

Clogg, R. 1981 'The Greek Mercantile Bourgeoisie: 'progressive' or 'reactionary'?' in Richard Clogg, (ed.) *Balkan Society in the age of Greek Independence*, London; Macmillan Press, 85-111.

Clogg, R. 1982 'The Greek Millet in the Ottoman Empire' in B. Lewis and B. Braude (eds.) *The Functioning of Plural Society Vol I., Central Lands*, New York; Holmes and Meier, 185-207.

Davison, R. 1982 'The Millets as Agents of Change in the Nineteenth Century Ottoman Empire' in Lewis and Braude; 319-337.

Dionyssiou, G 1969 'The implementation of the Tanzimat reforms in Cyprus (1839-1878)', Unpublished MLitt. Thesis, University of Birmingham.

Frazee, C. 1969 *The Orthodox Church and Independent Greece, 1821-1852*, Cambridge; CUP.

*Gounaris*,B. 1995 'Social Cleavages and National 'Awakening' in Ottoman Macedonia', in *East European Quarterly*, Vol. 29; 409-418.

Gülsoy, U. 1989 '1828-29 Osmanlı-Rus Savaşı'nda Rumeli'den Rusya'ya Göçürülen Reaya', unpublished MA thesis, Istanbul; Marmara University

Hitti, P. 1951 *History of the Arabs*, fifth edition, London; Macmillan.

Hobhouse, J. *1855 Travels in Albania and Other Provinces of Turkey in 1809 and 1810*, 2 Vols, new ed., London; John Murray.

İnalcık, H. 1973 'The Application of the Tanzimat and its social effects', in *Archivum Ottomanicum* 5, 97-128.

İnalcık, H. 1993 'The Turks and the Balkans', in *Turkish Review of Balkan Studies*,

    Vol. 1, pp 9-41.

İnalcık H. 1982 'Ottoman Archival Materials on Millets', in Lewis and Braude (eds.), 437-441.

Issawi, C. 1982 'The Transformation of the Economic Position of the Millets in the Nineteenth Century', in Lewis and Braude (eds.), 261-285.

Karpat, K. 1983 'The Situation of the Christians in the Ottoman Empire: Bulgaria's view', in *International Journal of Turkish Studies*, Vol. 4, No. 2; 259-266.

Karpat, K. 1986 'Ottoman Views and Policies', in *Greek Orthodox Theological Review*, Vol 31, Nos 1-2, pp. 131-155.

Karpat, K. 1983 'The Situation of the Christians in the Ottoman Empire: Bulgaria's view', in *International Journal of Turkish Studies*, Vol. 4, No. 2; 259-266.

Kasaba, R., Keyder, Ç, Tabak, F. 1986 'Eastern Mediterranean Port Cities and Their Bourgeoisies,' in *Review* Vol. X, No. 1, (Summer); 121-135.

Kinglake, A. 1908 *Eothen*, London; J.M. Dent & Sons Ltd.

Kitromilides, P. 1990 'Imagined Communities and the Origins of the National Question in the Balkans', in M. Blinkhorn and T. Veremis (eds.), *Modern Greece: Nationalism and Nationality*, Athens; Sage-ELIAMEP; 26-33.

Leake, W. 1835 *Travels in Northern Greece*, 4 vols, London; J. Rodwell.

Lewis, B. and Braude, B. 1982 (eds.) *The Functioning of Plural Society Vol I., Central Lands*, New York; Holmes and Meier.

Senior, N. 1859 *A Journal Kept in Turkey and Greece*, London; Longman.

Papadopoulos, T. 1992 *Studies and Documents Relating to the History of the Greek Church and People under Turkish Domination*, second edition, Hampshire; Variorum.

Runciman, S. 1965 *The Fall of Constantinople, 1453*, Cambridge; CUP.

Shaw, S. 1963 'The Ottoman View of the Balkans', in Jelavich, C and B. (eds.), *The Balkans in Transition*, Berkeley; University of California Press.

Slade, A. 1832 *Records of Travels in Turkey, Greece, etc....in the years 1829, 1830 and 1831*, two vols, London; Saunders and Otley.

Stoianovich, T. 1960 'The Conquering Balkan Orthodox Merchant', in *Journal of Economic History*, Vol. 20; 234-313.

Sugar, P. and Lederer, I. (eds.) 1971 *Nationalism in Eastern Europe*, Seattle; University of Washington.

Todorov, N. 1983 *The Balkan City, 1400-1900*, Seattle; University of Washington Press.

Vacalopoulos, C. 1988 *Southeast European Maritime Commerce and Naval Policies*, Thessaloniki; Institute for Balkan Studies.

Vucinich, W. 1963 'Some Aspects of the Ottoman Legacy,' in *The Balkans in Transition*, edited by C and B. Jelavich, Berkeley; University of California Press.

Walpole, R. 1818 *Memoirs Relating to European and Asiatic Turkey...*, London,

Ware, T. 1964 *Eustratios Argenti, A Study of the Greek Church under Turkish Rule* Oxford; Clarendon Press.

Xydis, S. 1968 'Medieval Origins of Modern Greek Nationalism,' in *Balkan Studies*, Vol. 9; 1-20.

# 30. FIELD OF DREAMS: ETHNOGRAPHICAL MAPS AND THE ETHNE OF MACEDONIA, 1842-1906[1]

İpek YOSMAOĞLU

'La Macédoine est un champs d'illusions où rien n'est vrai'.
Maurice Gandolphe, 1904.

The current inventory of ethnicities inhabiting the geographical region called Macedonia no longer constitutes the conglomeration, whose variety and fluidity had inspired a French chef to throw together all the leftover vegetables in the kitchen and name the concoction 'salade macédonienne'. Unlike the niçoise, the macedonienne never became a culinary classic; but the international problem that gave the salad its name persevered through the establishment of nation states, two world wars, a civil war, and the fall of communism, to be recorded in the annals of the human sciences as a classic case of ethnic conflict. My interest here is in the past of the conflict rather than its contemporary aspects.[2] In the latter half of the nineteenth and the beginning of the twentieth centuries, a great number of maps were published, which depicted the several different ethnic groups inhabiting this region that was still part of the Ottoman Empire. My purpose is to discuss the nature of these maps as historical documents that can further our understanding of the formation of national identities and nation-states in the region. The preparation, publication and dissemination of these maps do not simply constitute the by-product of a disinterested involvement with the geography of less-known parts of the world. I contend, rather, that this process reveals a complex set of relations involving the ways in which the Balkans were perceived in Europe, the Balkan elite justified their territorial claims, and the inhabitants themselves were appropriated in a conflict that was in practice not confined to two-dimensional representations.

---

[1] The maps discussed here are all from the Gennadius Library of the American School of Classical Studies at Athens. I would like to take this opportunity to express my gratitude to the School and the library staff, especially Dr. Charis Kalliga for their support and assistance. I am also indebted to Professors Rif'at Abou-El-Haj, Xaris Exertzoglou and Malcolm Wagstaff, who read earlier versions of this paper, for their invaluable suggestions and criticisms.
[2] Arguably the most interesting insights into the recent past of the issue have come from the discipline of anthropology. Karakasidou (1999), Danforth (1995) and Brown (2003).

*Historical Background*

Given that the maps of 'Turkey-in-Europe' produced during this period were largely the product of the contemporary political and cultural climate, I will begin with a brief account of the major developments that shaped those years before moving on to a discussion of ethnographic cartography. The Macedonian Question, which would eventually culminate in one of the bloodiest episodes in the history of the Balkans, namely the Balkan Wars of 1912-1913, was formally recognized as an international problem for the first time after the Treaty of San Stefano that had concluded the Russo-Ottoman War of 1877-1878. The Ottoman Empire, having suffered a terrible defeat that nearly ended with the Russian army entering the imperial capital, was forced to consent to extremely harsh terms that stripped it of most of its holdings in the Balkans. A great part of the territory including almost all of Macedonia[1] was accorded to the newly established principality of Bulgaria.

The borders of this 'Great Bulgaria' extended from the Danube in the north to the Aegean Sea in the south, and the Black Sea in the east to Uskub (Skopje), Ohrid and Monastir (Bitola) in the west excluding Edirne, Eastern Thrace and Selânik (Thessaloniki) — dimensions that might satisfy even the most ambitious of Bulgarian nationalists. However, San Stefano's immediate affect was to alter the European balance of power — a concern much larger than the survival of a fledgling Balkan state. Britain was especially disturbed by increasing Russian influence in the Mediterranean and, being a Russian client-state, Great Bulgaria did not last very long; Britain asked that the peace treaty be revised. A Congress was convened in Berlin in June, where all major European powers were represented and delegates of the Ottoman Empire and other Balkan states were merely present. The treaty, signed on 13 July 1878, re-established the European status-quo; Ottoman rule was restored in Macedonia. Bulgaria no longer had access to the Aegean and it was split in two principalities, the Southern principality of Eastern Rumelia staying under nominal Ottoman suzerainty. It joined the Danubian principality in 1885.

---

[1] It is practically impossible to give a geographical definition of Macedonia, especially during the period specified here, since Greeks, Bulgarians and Serbs all attributed different borders to the region. It is commonly accepted that the Ottomans never used the term Macedonia, but documents from the Ottoman archives prove that the term was used occasionally, if not officially, in correspondence especially after it acquired international popularity. *Webster's Geographical Dictionary*'s 1949 edition describes Macedonia as 'a Region in Cen. Balkan peninsula., N.W of the Aegean Sea, with somewhat indefinite boundaries but including Macedonia division of Greece, most of the middle Vardar valley in SE Yugoslavia, and SW Bulgaria W of Mesta river' (p. 647). The three provinces of the Ottoman Empire, namely, Selânik, Kosova and Monastir roughly correspond to this region, which will be the definition adopted here for the sake of convenience.

Any historical account of the origins of the Macedonian Question also needs to mention the religious schism that deepened the divisions between the Christian inhabitants of Macedonia. Until 1870, the year that the independent Bulgarian Exarchate was founded, the Ecumenical Patriarchate of Constantinople was the single authority over all Orthodox subjects of the Ottoman Empire.[1] Although the Exarchate was not the first Orthodox Church to become independent of the Patriarchate, its emergence had an enormous impact on the Patriarchate's power. Unlike the previous cases where church autonomy had been preceded by political independence from the Ottoman Empire, now a rival Church was established in Istanbul that could potentially challenge the Patriarchate's authority *within* the Empire, which included the right to collect taxes, establish and regulate schools, and issue marriage licenses — in short, to oversee all civil and ecclesiastical aspects of the lives of the Ottoman Empire's Orthodox subjects. The other implication, more important for Macedonia was that Slavic speakers could now be distinguished officially from the Greek Orthodox (*Rum*), a default category that they been placed in due to their association with the Patriarchate. Consequently, the Exarchate could use that distinction to further its own sphere of influence, which dovetailed with that of Bulgarian nationalists.

In 1893, the Internal Macedonian Revolutionary Organization (IMRO), which would eventually play an important part in the turmoil that preceded the Balkan Wars, was founded in Salonika.[2] IMRO at least nominally, was seeking autonomy for Macedonia and freedom for all Macedonians. However, it was associated with Bulgarian interests in the area because its ranks were occupied by a large portion of Bulgarian-educated teachers and because it made extensive use of the Bulgarian Exarchate's influence. Its pro-Bulgarian leanings were also betrayed by its reluctant but pragmatic collaboration with a similar, but Sofia-based, organization called the Supreme Committee that supported the annexation of Macedonia by Bulgaria.[3] IMRO managed to set up a very complicated and well-organized movement especially in the provinces of Monastir and Selânik, and even started to act like a shadow government collecting (or extorting, depending on one's position) taxes, establishing tribunals, and recruiting soldiers for their cause.

---

[1] Stavrianos (2000; 373).

[2] Perry (1988).

[3] In contemporary Macedonian nationalist narratives however, IMRO (or VMRO) is enshrined as the symbol of Macedonian people's 'national awakening' at the end of the nineteenth century. For a general literature review see Danforth (1995; 42-55).

After a couple of failed attempts, IMRO finally succeeded in initiating a general revolt in August 1903, known as the Ilinden Uprising. The uprising was a concerted effort that started with the insurgents cutting telegram lines, attacking railroads, and massacring Moslem villages. Except for Krushevo, which the insurgents took over for a couple of weeks and even proclaimed a republic, the plan did not make significant progress, and it was completely suppressed by the end of the month.[1] In this respect the attempt had ended in failure.

Considering however, that the expectation had not been the total defeat of the Ottoman Army, but to incite reprisals which would direct European attention to the area, it can be said that, in a certain sense, the guerrillas did achieve their goals. As they were retreating to the mountains or beyond the border, non-combatant locals took the devastating blow inflicted by Ottoman troops and *başıbozuks* (irregulars); entire villages were burnt down, inhabitants killed, women raped. By the beginning of 1904, the Ottoman Empire had reluctantly accepted a new reform programmeme that was initiated by Russia and Austria, and that would remain in place until 1909. The Mürzteg Programme, as it came to be called, involved extensive European control over the vilayets of Kosovo, Selanik and Monastir through a supervisory 'agents' system. It was eventually extended to include the representatives of other European Powers, Britain, France and Italy.

Factors such as the Ottoman perception of the plan as an imposition, the conflicts between the powers themselves, lack of financial assistance and the increasing violence and polarization in the countryside all limited the reforms' capacity to improve the living conditions in the region. The vicious circle — guerrilla attacks followed by retaliations — became even more violent especially after the formation of Greek and Moslem bands employing similar tactics. Peasants were forced to declare their allegiances to competing sides, which made them further vulnerable to attacks. As soon as a village had announced itself as either Exarchist or Patriarchist, they were harassed by the other side. The period between 1902 and 1918 was characterized by civil war, war, and expulsion for the inhabitants of Macedonia, and they were to experience more of these scourges again.

---

[1] The short-lived Krushevo Republic has a special place in the construction of Macedonian nationalism; for a discussion see Brown (2003).

*Ethnography, the science of 'human races'*

As far as the present discussion is concerned, perhaps equal in importance to this politically charged atmosphere was the development of a tradition of explorers' writings on 'Turkey-in-Europe' in the nineteenth century. Their purposes were not limited to descriptions of ancient temples, but set out to inform the European public about the climate, geography and, most importantly, the contemporary inhabitants of these regions. According to Maria Todorova:

> The Balkans ... as a distinct geographic, social and cultural entity, were 'discovered' by European travelers only from the late eighteenth century on, with the beginning of an awareness that the European possessions of the Ottoman Empire had a distinct physiognomy of their own that merited separate attention apart from their treatment as mere provinces of the Ottomans or simply as archaeological sites. Until then, the Ottoman Empire was treated as a unity in Europe and Asia.[1]

The reasons for this new interest included on the one hand the perceived transformation of the Ottoman Empire from a considerable military power into a decrepit political entity, whose imminent dissolution raised questions about its potential colonization and/or partition and the fate of fellow Christians living under its sway; and on the other, a growing enthusiasm with the newly developing discipline of ethnography, the science of 'human races'. Needless to say, the latter motivation was not entirely independent of the first, and could even be characterized as an off-shoot of it. The 1910 edition of Encyclopedia Britannica described ethnology and ethnography as:

> sciences which in their narrowest sense deal respectively with man as a racial unit (*mankind*), i.e. his development through the family and tribal stages into national life, and with the distribution over the earth of the races and nations thus formed. Though the etymology of the word permits in theory this line of division between ethnology and ethnography, in practice they form an indivisible study of man's progress from the point at which anthropology leaves him.[2]

This definition hints that by the first decade of the twentieth century, the discipline of 'ethnography' could be distinguished, if slightly, from its sister 'anthropology'. Anthropology at this stage was strictly occupied with the study and analysis of societies who were still at the initial stages of their 'evolution', whereas ethnology could potentially deal with those somewhat

---

[1] Todorova (1997; 62).
[2] *Encyclopedia Britannica* 11th edition, vol. 9; 849.

closer to the final stage, but still 'primitive' in comparison with Western European societies. The same paragraph also reveals a notion that was prevalent especially in the second half of the nineteenth century that human communities, much like growing biological organisms, passed through progressive stages in a linear evolutionary continuum, the culmination of which were nations.

In this respect, Ottoman Macedonia made up an extremely rich source to be tapped for ethnographical purposes, not only because of the variety of 'races' inhabiting it with their different languages, customs and half-formed national consciousness, but also because of their unique quality as communities frozen in time, sheltered from the progress that had transformed the rest of Europe. 'The Volksmuseum of Europe'[1] could serve as a perfect laboratory for the European ethnographer, who, wittingly or unwittingly, would help invent the 'nation' even where it had not been before, thanks to the power of scientific labeling and classification.

We should also not lose sight of the fact that the two interrelated concepts, namely the unquestionable legitimacy of the nation state and the superiority of Western civilization, were among the premises that influenced the way a majority of — if not all — ethnographical studies and maps of the Ottoman Empire were done. The latter concept was often expressed in explicit fashion pointing out the elements that distinguished the local communities from Europeans either by what they lacked (comfortable housing, organized police, etc.) or what they had (ornate headgear, superstitious practices, etc.) In many cases, it was acceptable for the 'ethnographer' to ridicule those who would today be considered his or her 'informants'. For instance, G. F. Abbot, author of a book on the folklore of Macedonia,[2] sponsored and published by Cambridge University, recorded his impressions of the villagers' dance at the festival of Virgin Mary in Petritch (village in the province of Serres) with the following words:

> Notwithstanding this weight of wool and metal, they danced with great perseverance and an air of truly Christian resignation. Bagpipes –the favourite instrument of the Bulgarian—supplied the local equivalent for music. Round this squealing band a wide circle footed it slowly and exceedingly stupidly ... The dance consisted of a one step forward, one backward, and one to the side, without any variation whatsoever. A melancholy refrain Sospita Yanno, Sospita Yanno [sic], drawled out in sleepy and sleep-begetting tones, accompanied the sad measure.[3]

---

[1] Todorova (1997; 63).
[2] Abbott (1903a). He was also the author of *Songs of Modern Greece* (1900).
[3] Abbott (1903b; 174).

Two decades after the publication of Said's *Orientalism*, it is fairly easy to detect and predict the rhetoric of these texts and to diagnose a 'hegemonic discourse'. However, it is not my purpose to discuss these rather obvious and crude 'Orientalisms', or condemn ethnographic work done during the second half of the nineteenth century per se. In fact, as the example of Amie Boué testifies, there were exceptions to these mainstream representations of 'local races' in ethnographical studies.[1] Rather, I wish simply to emphasize that ethnography, like any other discipline, was not independent of the practitioner's political and cultural milieu, which, at this particular point in time, included an assumption about the 'incomplete' quality of the communities under study that made them inferior to the Western prototype.[2]

The other concept mentioned earlier, by which the nation state was privileged as the most evolved form of human organization was influential in a relatively more subtle yet pervasive manner. It was not only expressed in generic discourses on the deplorable conditions of life in the European territories of the Ottoman Empire, but it also penetrated the epistemological foundations of certain disciplines such as ethnography and geography that were occupied with phenomena that could presumably be analyzed objectively and systematically with the aid of statistical data. For instance, it was expressed, time and again, at meetings of geographical societies or in prestigious geographical journals that the Ottoman Empire's inability to produce detailed statistics of its population of the Ottoman Empire was both an indication and a cause of its backwardness. 'I certainly should never expect Turkey to survive unless she consented to become statistical like the rest of Europe',[3] declared Dr. Farr, during a meeting of the Statistical Society in 1877 in London, epitomizing more than one prevalent notion among Western European scholars concerning the present state and the future of the Ottoman State.

When one looks at the literature on the population and resources of the Ottoman Empire during the period in question however, it becomes clear that being 'statistical like the rest of Europe' did not simply include producing

---

[1] Amie Boué was not an ethnographer by training, he was a geographer, but he did produce one of the best ethnographical accounts of the Ottoman Balkans in the first half of the nineteenth century (Boué 1840).

[2] For a masterful analysis of travelers' literature on the Balkans with its nuances and development from the sixteenth into the twentieth century, see Todorova (1997).

[3] Quoted in E. G. Ravenstein (1877; 466). Ravenstein, in another article that he had dedicated to the 'Distribution of the Population in the Part of Europe Overrun by Turks' had also voiced this complaint himself: 'Some statistical information on the populations of that part of Eastern Europe which is now devastated by the Turkish hordes will prove acceptable at the present time. It is scarcely necessary to state that no regular census of the population has ever been taken.' Ravenstein (1876; 259-261).

numbers such as the value of exports and imports from major ports, the population of cities or population density of the empire by region, etc., because these numbers *were* available in consular reports, Ottoman state almanacs, and publications of some European scholars.[1]

What they did not include — at least until the Ottoman census of 1905-1906 — were figures showing the distribution of 'different races' or 'nations' within the whole.[2] From the point of view of the Ottoman imperial government there was no pressing need to register the subjects of the empire according to 'racial' categories, because the censuses were taken mainly for the purposes of estimating potential tax revenue and the number of soldiers to be recruited, for which wealth and religion were the only two relevant categories of information. It must also be remembered that, even after the uprisings of the early nineteenth century that succeeded in carving out independent nation states out of the Ottoman Empire, it could hardly be argued that a significant part of the Empire's population identified themselves with reference to a national category — as opposed to religious, social or local. When national/ethnic identity was added to the Ottoman census questionnaire in 1905, the census clerks had a difficult time registering individuals who could not decide what exactly they were, let alone which 'nationality', as it was the case in Zervi, where villagers expressed to Ottoman census authorities in September 1905 that they were neither *Rum* nor *Bulgarian*, but Christian Orthodox and wanted to be recorded as such, contravening the point of the

---

[1] There are records of an Ottoman census held in 1831, and another one in 1844, the results of which were published by Ubicini. A very detailed census of the Tuna Vilayeti (Danube Province) was taken in 1866, as part of the reforms under way there. In addition to these, the *salnâmes,* or yearbooks provided information on population, which were used by authors like Ritter zur Helle von Samo (*Die Völker des Osmanischen Reiches,* 1877) to compute general statistics. The first comprehensive census was taken during Abdülhamid II's reign, in 1881, the results of which were presented to the sultan in 1893. The final Ottoman census was carried out in 1905/6. (See Kemal H. Karpat's classic study on Ottoman population (1985). Karpat considers Urquhart (1833) and Ubicini (1851) among the Europeans who published relatively more reliable data on the Ottoman Empire because they had direct access to Ottoman provincial sources as well as general surveys. For the European literature concerning Ottoman population statistics Karpat refers his readers to Engin Akarli's unpublished M.A Thesis (1970) for a complete bibliography. Some of the titles from this period worth mentioning are, Ofeicoff [A. Shopov]. (1887) and J. Ivanoff (1920).

[2] The categories for the 1881/82-1893 census were: Muslims, Greeks, Armenians, Bulgarians, Catholics, Jews, Protestants, Latins, Monophysites (Syriacs), non-Muslim Gypsies, Foreigners. To these categories were added in 1906/1907: Cossacks, Wallachians, Greek Catholics, Armenian Catholics, Maronites, Chaldeans, Jaconites, Samaritans, Yezidis, Gypsies (without religious distinction). See tables I. 8. A (pp. 132-133) through I. 16. A (pp. 166-167) in Karpat (1985). To give the reader a general idea about the figures, according to the 1905 census the total population of the three provinces of Monastir, Selânik and Kosova was 2, 417, 840, of which 1,127,775 were recorded as Moslem; 628,253 Bulgarian; 564,067 Greek; 59,552 Jewish; 26, 042 Vlach. According to the same figures, in Monastir Moslems constituted 40% of the total population, Greeks 35%, and Bulgarians 24%. In Selânik, these percentages were 45.5, 28.6, and 17.2; and in Kosova, 56.5, 2, and 40 respectively (calculations based on the data published by Karpat).

census process to provide an ethnographic picture of the three provinces of the Ottoman Empire.[1] The striking fact remains that despite all the complaints about lack of reliable statistics, European scholars did continue publishing data that purportedly showed the 'distribution of races in European Turkey', which would — and could — never account for villages like Zervi.

Another point deemed 'unscientific' by European ethnographers (and politicians, travelers, journalists, etc.) was that these 'races' were allowed to cohabit and intermingle at all, obstructing the attempts to designate one certain area to each group. This was understood to be a deliberate policy decision on the part of the Ottoman Empire, after the well-known dictum 'divide and conquer'. For instance, H. N. Brailsford, the writer of *Macedonia: Its Races and Their Future,* and an active member of the British Relief Mission after the uprising of 1903 remarked:

> Macedonia lies confounded within three *vilayets* (i.e. provinces), which correspond to no natural division either racial or geographical ... The result is that no race attains a predominance, and no province acquires a national character. The natural arrangement would have been to place Greeks, Servians, and Albanians in compartments of their own, leaving the Bulgarians to occupy the centre and the East.[2]

It is hard not to notice that the *natural* arrangement suggested by Brailsford also happened to accord most of the three European provinces of the Ottoman Empire to the 'Bulgarian element'. Although it was not clearly spelled out, this arrangement would inevitably also involve the deportation of Greek, Serb, and Albanian populations — if one were to count only those cited by Brailsford — and probably the expulsion of the Muslim population, which did not figure in most European designs for the region anyway. More importantly, such an arrangement presumed a knowledge of who exactly were the Greeks, Albanians, Bulgarians and Turks, and, as self-evident as it may seem looking out from the homogenous confines of the nation-state, these tags were by no means easily assigned in Macedonia even as late as the turn of the twentieth century. Even though one might read Brailsford's remarks as the exaggerated claims of a propagandist, this was exactly how the 'national unity' of states arising from the remains of the Ottoman Empire (including its heir apparent) was achieved: expulsion, deportation, wholesale massacre, and failing all that, enforced assimilation, until everyone was placed 'in compartments of their own'.

---

[1] (Prime Ministry Archives, Istanbul. Papers of *Rumeli Umum Müfettişliği* [General Inspectorate of Rumeli]) TFR.I. SL 87/8623. Most of the problematic cases involved villages that had been recorded either as Exarchist or Patriarchist out of fear, but wanted to change their status. Another frequent problem concerned dissenting individuals or households in villages that had been registered *en masse* under a certain category.

[2] Brailsford (1903; 7).

It is significant that although he did complain about the lack of proper compartmentalization, the 'ethnographical map of Macedonia' that Brailsford published as an appendix to his work indicated a more or less homogenous Bulgarian population as the dominant element in Macedonia, with some corridors of Turkish settlements and the Chalkidiki peninsula inhabited mostly by Greeks forming the main exceptions. Pockets of Vlachs, Pomacks and Serbs, denoted by small symbols were the only sign of intermingling on this map.

The inconsistency in Brailsford's assertions that 'no race attains a predominance' and his map showing Bulgarians as the 'predominant race' is reminiscent of Bianconi's complaints in 1877 about the lack of reliable statistics on the population of the Ottoman Empire in the same book where he published his own statistics produced from dubious sources.[1] Both authors had a preconceived idea about what the numbers and/or the maps *should* look like, and both authors had a claim on the correct *scientific* method of determination, measurement, and visual representation of their subject matter. The crucial difference was that Bianconi had painted the entire area accorded by Brailsford to the 'Bulgarian race' with the colours of the Greek territory.

It is interesting to note that Bianconi also explicitly stated in the introduction to his work that a good ethnographic map of the region—such as his own—was indispensable for statesmen 'to fix the limits of various independent States that might be formed in the Balkan peninsula'.[2] The twenty-nine-year difference between the publication dates of Bianconi's (1877) and Brailsford's (1906) maps do not necessarily correspond to a specific shift in trends from pro-Greek to pro-Bulgarian maps, as one might extrapolate when presented with these two isolated cases. In fact, starting the chronology from an earlier point, it becomes clear that Bianconi's map was among the first ones supporting Greek claims in Macedonia.

---

[1] See F. Bianconi (1877, especially 13-21). This is a perfect example of how certain 'authoritative' sources on statistics of Ottoman population were fabricated simply by the practice of copying a previous work and declaring it as the most 'reliable' without providing any tangible proof why these figures were better than any other. Bianconi's figures (pp. 22-26) relied largely on those provided by 'Stanford', (1877) supplemented by a few British Consular reports and the author's own observations from the time when he worked in the region as an engineer for the French railroad company that built the 'Jonction Salonique-Constantinople'. The so-called Stanford tables, in turn, were again 'estimates' and the author himself cited another 'authority' as the most reliable source. This 'reliable and objective' source was Henri Mathieu's *La Turquie* (c. 1857), in which the author stated that he had made every effort to approach the 'truth' but he still did not pretend to be giving exact figures (p. 44).

[2] Bianconi (1877 ; 1). All translations in this paper are mine unless otherwise noted.

*Arranging the 'Races of Turkey-in-Europe'*

H. R. Wilkinson, in *Maps and Politics*, notes that the map published by the Pan-Slavist scholar Schafarik (an Austro-Hungarian subject of Czech origin) in 1842 'virtually revolutionized the prevailing ideas on the distribution and character of the peoples of south-eastern Europe', and ' ... set the fashion for nearly all ethnographic maps of this area'.[1] One might want to take this with a pinch of salt since the Serbian scholar Jovan Cvijić remarked in 1906 that having been published in Tchech, Schafarik's *Slovansky Národopis* 'remained unknown to other cultured nations'.[2] Nevertheless, even Cvijić recognized that the map was ground breaking in its classification and labeling of six major groups currently inhabiting the Balkan peninsula; namely, Albanians, Turks, Serbo-Croats, Greeks, Bulgarians and Romanians.

In 1847, Amie Boué, the French geographer published a map in Berghaus's Atlas, seven years after the publication of his seminal work on the Ottoman Empire's European territories, *La Turquie d'Europe*. In this map, he attributed an even larger territory to the Bulgarians than Schafarik, and denoted Turks only in a few major cities.[3] However, Boué was not so much interested in questioning the legitimacy of Ottoman rule in the Balkans than suggesting methods to bring it on par with other European states.[4] According to his writings, this did not necessarily involve exchanging the imperial source of authority with a national one, but a confidence in the potential for reform within the existing framework. Obviously, what he implied was not the potential of the Empire to reform itself, but the potential of modernity to change everything within the reach of railroads.

Yet, Boué's map made such a good case for the Bulgarians that it was reproduced during the first decades of the twentieth century a few times in other ethnographical works and Atlases favouring the Bulgarian side in the struggle for Macedonia; the scholar's reputation no doubt providing a veneer of scientific objectivity to works that might otherwise be considered propaganda.[5] In 1861 came the publication of another pro-Bulgarian map,

---

[1] Wilkinson (1951).

[2] Cvijić (1906; 19).

[3] Boué (1840 ; 37).

[4] Boué considered the Ottoman Empire another European state rather than an aberration in the continent as Bianconi did. It is worth noting that he compared it to mostly Spain, sometimes to England and France, and occasionally in a favourable manner. (See for instance Boué 1840; II, 158).

[5] For instance, V. Kntchev [or Kantchev], *Macedonia, with eleven maps*, Sofia, 1900, quoted by Cvijić (1906; 30-31).

prepared by Gustave Lejean, a consul of the French government published in
*Petermann's Mittheilungen* based on the data he had collected during two
trips made in 1857 and 1858. Lejean candidly expressed in the introduction to
his work that the 'ethnographic study of the Ottoman Empire' was no longer
an 'object of purely scientific curiosity'. He separated himself from earlier
ethno-geographers with a stated position that language could not be used as a
criterion to determine nationality in 'Turkey' since 'religious hatred and
political inequality' had caused people to adopt languages that did not
correspond to their races.[1] He proposed as a replacement the criterion of
'history'. The final outlook still favoured Bulgarians in Macedonia. His map's
most striking feature in contrast with earlier examples was a great block of
Turkish settlement in North East Bulgaria, covering regions that normally
were attributed to Romanians.

The period from 1842 to 1877 was characterized by a predominance of
maps that favoured the depiction of large Slav settlements, specifically
Bulgarians, in South Eastern Europe. After this point, the representations on
the maps, the criteria used to determine nationality, and also the nationality of
the maps' authors began to diversify. Even the 'Bulgarianness' of Macedonian
Slavs, which had been accepted as more or less self-evident, came to be
questioned. While maps favouring one particular group continued to be the
norm, there appeared a few exceptions that questioned the representation of
homogenous distributions, and factors such as school enrollment were
introduced as more reliable measures of national consciousness. Perhaps the
most important development was that the Balkan elite itself got increasingly
involved in the production of these maps ending the monopoly of European
scholars on the subject.

I would like to address this last development in some detail, but let me
first introduce some of these maps that were among the most significant in
chronological order.[2] In 1876, Heinrich Kiepert, arguably the most prominent
geographer in Europe at the time, published his *Ethnographische Übersicht
des Europäischen Orients,* which was another addition to the pro-Bulgarian
maps of the region. This was followed in 1877 by two pro-Greek maps, first
the one known as the 'Stanford Map', and second, Bianconi's. The same year,
another map by the pro-Greek scholar Synvet was published. This map was
quite modest in its claims in comparison with others prepared by
Greek authors; it attempted to challenge pro-Bulgarian representations  not by

---

[1] Lejean (1861; 1- 2).
[2] Wilkinson (1951)..

negating their versions, but by stressing the existence of dense 'Turkish' settlements all over the Balkan peninsula, and showing that the Greek population of the Ottoman Empire had been grossly underestimated.[1] Synvet, a French philhellene, was a teacher at *Galatasaray Lisesi* (a prestigious educational institution for the Ottoman bureaucratic elite at the time; it today still functions as a high school), which raises the possibility that his motivations could have been of a more imperial order, in contradistinction to the nationalistically driven authors of other 'Greek maps'.[2]

The following year witnessed the publication of two important maps by Carl Sax and a new map by Heinrich Kiepert. Carl Sax's map can be distinguished as the only map of the region during this period that attempted to represent complexity rather than 'preponderance'.[3] According to Cvijić, there was some merit in Sax's work, but 'the well-known, peculiarly Austrian, bureaucratic methods made him tear nations into atoms'.[4] The Serbian scholar did have a point, for Sax cited no less than twenty-one groups in his classification, and his concern with justifying Austrian intervention in the region did not go unnoticed. One might even go as far as to suggest that this was the first 'pro-Austrian' map of the Balkans.

On the other hand, Sax's peculiar method legitimately called into question the 'racio-linguistic' criteria that had hitherto been the norm; as he pointed out, the importance of religion had been neglected, and what he called

---

[1] He adjusted the numbers produced by community registers by referring to records of syllogues, or literary organizations. Kemal Karpat notes that the figures he calculated proved to be exaggerated 'when the Ottoman census of 1881/82-1893 gave the first truly comprehensive account of the Greek population' Karpat (1985; 49).

[2] Synvet's figures were largely based on the results of a two-year old survey done by order of the Patriarchate with the purpose of determining the number of Orthodox households that would contribute to a light tax for supporting Bishoprics (*La Carte Ethnographique de la Turquie d'Europe et denombrement de l'Empire Ottoman*). A year later he published *Les Grecs de L'Empire Ottoman: etude statistique* (Constantinople, 1878) where he supplemented these figures by those provided by membership registers of 'syllogues', or Greek cultural organizations, which he believed gave a more accurate picture. By this count, the numbers had increased significantly; the Greek population of Macedonia, which was estimated at 474,000 originally, was now reported as 587,860.

[3] According to Wilkinson, Sax had access to reputable sources; he was aware of all the previous literature, had served as the Austrian consul in Adrianople and could also tap into the information gathered by other Austrian officials, who 'by virtue of their geographical position and their immense experience in dealing with diverse nationalities, commanded sources of information not available to the French or British or even to the Russians.' (1951; 77). Wilkinson's remark about the unique Austrian 'experience in dealing with diverse nationalities' is rather curious in its neglect of the diverse populations that the French and the British had to 'deal with' in the colonies. One cannot help wondering whether this was because of an implicit assumption that those colonized populations required and cultivated more of an 'anthropological' interest rather than an 'ethnographic' one. It seems likely that Wilkinson made an interesting — and valid — distinction between multi-national and colonial empires.

[4] Cvijić (1906; 24).

a sense of 'group consciousness'; or the sum of elements that keep a community together, had not been taken into account.[1] It was a refreshing break from the mainstream; what remained unclear however, was how Sax himself had been able to measure 'group consciousness' among the peasants of the Balkans exhaustively enough to chart it on a map.

During the decade following the Berlin Conference, there was less enthusiasm for new maps of the Balkans. It took another eleven years until the first (well-known) map supporting Serbian claims in the region was published by Spiridon Gopčević in 1889[2] which was severely criticized as a pure propaganda piece. This map was also the first one among those mentioned so far to use the term 'Macedonia' in its title. Ten years later, the Greek Scholar Nicolaides published another 'ethnographic and linguistic map of Macedonia', and the term Macedonia started turning up more and more as political rivalry became concentrated in the region.

The controversy was also no longer limited to the pro-Greek and pro-Bulgarian sides, but included now the Serbian side, which did not give up after Gopčević's 'initial failure'.[3] An anonymously prepared pro-Serbian map known as the Serbian University Map was published in 1891. Other maps of the period worth mentioning were those of Gustave Weigand (1895), which may be classified among pro-Bulgarian maps; Richard von Mach's map (1899), in which ethnographical representation was based on the distribution of Serbian, Bulgarian and Greek schools; a map published anonymously in Sofia in 1901[4]; another anonymous map showing Christian schools in Macedonia (1905), and Brancoff's maps showing the Christian population and Christian Schools of Macedonia (1905).

---

[1] Wilkinson (1951; 77).

[2] Strictly speaking, Spiridon Gopčević was not the first to publish a pro-Serbian map of the region, his most important predecessors being M. S Miloyevitch in 1873, Colonel Dragashevitch in 1885, and M. Veselinovitch in 1886, see Cvijić (1906; 29). It seems that Gopčević earned the reputation because his work became widely available to European scholars after its publication in *Petermann's Mittheilungen*.

[3] Wilkinson notes that 'it is a firm axiom of the propagandist ... that an initial failure may be turned into an ultimate success by the simple process of reiteration', and Gopčević 'provided the Serbs with their initial failure.' (1951; 103).

[4] According to Cvijić, there was 'no doubt that this edition belongs to the Bulgarian Ministry of War', (1906; 31).

The most significant example of maps prepared with school data is the anonymous 'Carte des Ecoles Chrétiennes de la Macédoine' published in Paris in 1905.[1] Brancoff's (alias Mishev) map of Christian schools, in rebuttal, charged that Greek schools were protected by the Ottoman government whereas Bulgarians could not even get a permit to open up a school in areas where the population had joined the Exarchate, but given enough time, Bulgarian schools would prevail because they offered better education.[2]

The trend of ethnographical maps based on school data was largely the invention of Greek propagandists who were despairing at the notion, gaining firmer ground in Western Europe, that Macedonia was largely inhabited by a Slav population.[3] The first generation of ethnographical maps claiming Macedonia as Greek, however painstakingly prepared, failed to undo this perception. The school criterion was introduced as a new basis because it provided the map makers with numbers that could be easily accessed and hardly challenged.

These figures also happened to favour Greek schools, which, despite the relatively recent rivalry of Bulgarian and (to a lesser extent) Serbian schools, benefited from the authority of the Patriarchate as well as the material and human support of the Greek state and the Greek bourgeoisie. More importantly, this criterion combined consciousness and culture as the main determinants of national identity rather than racial or linguistic factors, thereby emphasizing the element of free will, and invoking the charisma for European public opinion of Greek culture and its classical heritage. It seems that these attempts were not entirely in vain after all; to cite an example, Eduard Driault wrote at the dawn of the Balkan Wars:

> The Greeks know that they have formidable enemies, that the Turk is still strong, that the Slavs are more numerous in Macedonia. But Hellenism is not a simple question of races; it is an idea, an intellectual and moral force, made by the rational support of free men to principles that established the grandeur of ancient Greece and that are the essential sources of European civilization.[4]

---

[1] According to Cvijić, 'there is nothing which represents better than this chart the gigantic efforts of the Greeks to Hellenise these two vilayets.' (1906; 32). School statistics in favour of Greeks were initially published in the form of statistical tables, but the visual impact of a map was certainly stronger. For statistics see, *The Population of Macedonia, Evidence of the Christian Schools* (1905), and Stephanopoli (1903).

[2] Brancoff (1905 ; 77-79).

[3] Even in a mainstream source of general information such as *Encyclopaedia Britannica,* the population of Macedonia was described as follows: 'The greater part of Macedonia is inhabited by a Slavonic population, mainly Bulgarian in its characteristics; the coast-line and the southern districts west of the Gulf of Salonica by Greeks, while Turkish, Vlach and Albanian settlements exist sporadically, or in groups, in many parts of the country.' 'Macedonia,' (1910 ; 17, 216).

[4] Driault (1912 ; 282).

*Questioning Maps, Questioning Authority*

Three maps published by two authors during this period deserve a closer analysis here in order to expose certain ideological elements that found a hospitable environment in the medium of ethnographical geography. The first is the map known as 'the Stanford Map' published in 1877. Apparently the Stanford map was not taken very seriously in Europe, with the exception of Britain, but the fact that it was translated into various languages and included in Wilkinson's selection in 1952 suggests that it did have a certain impact if only in terms of being the 'initial failure' of the Greek side.[1] The author managed to remain anonymous, although it was clear that he was a member of the Greek intellectual elite.[2] It turns out, that the author was Ioannis Gennadios, who held the post of Greek chargé d'affairs in London at the time, and would later serve as the Minister to London and to the Hague.[3]

In the pamphlet that accompanied the map, Gennadios argued that 'the different nations and races inhabiting European Turkey and the western portion of Asia Minor ...are all more or less marked by a confusing diversity of origin, language, national character, political condition, social status, intellectual development and religious persuasion'. Since these categories could not be matched to religious or linguistic principles either, it was, in his words 'an abortive, not to say an impossible, undertaking to establish in a graphic representation the distribution and intermixture of race, language, and creed in Turkey'.

Instead, Gennadios suggested that 'a practically useful ethnological map' would 'explain and represent the actual relations in which those nations stand toward one another'.[4] These relations were revealed in Gennadios's work through a method that employed a hybrid of historical and cultural claims, religious influence, and occasional references to statistical data. He insisted that the area north of the Balkans was characterized by long-time Bulgarian

---

[1] Wilkinson (1951; 75). Carl Sax's verdict on this map was that 'it cannot even be mentioned seriously', while Kiepert said that it 'extended Greek pretensions to the utmost limits possible to man' Cvijić (1906; 23). Many thanks to my colleague Margarita Poutouridou for the translation.

[2] It seems that even Kiepert was not able to figure out the identity of the author, his inquiries having been answered by only the information that he was Greek. See letter from Kiepert to Paparrigopoulos, published in Svolopoulos (1992; 366). Cvijić (1906; 22) did disclose Gennadios' name as the author, but the knowledge must have remained obscure since Wilkinson cited the author as anonymous (1951; 71).

[3] Gennadios is today remembered more as a bibliophile than a diplomat. He donated his impressive collection of books and manuscripts to the American School of Classical Studies at Athens that keeps the collection in a separate library building that carries his name.

[4] *Ethnological Map of European Turkey* (1877; 2).

settlement, whereas the South had remained purely Greek, and even the so-called Bulgarians of Northern Macedonia and Thrace were Greek. In his own words:

> During a period of darkness, internal convulsions and administrative prostration, the mixed Greek and Bulgarian populations of those regions were gradually merged into a new and common body, neither purely Bulgarian, nor purely Greek, but appertaining to both races. This mixed people may be appropriately designated as 'Bulgarophone Greeks', for it is easily proved that Greek is the prevalent element in its constitution. The outward features of this race differ considerably from those of the Bulgarians north of the Balkans; the latter are clearly of the Mongolian type, whereas South of the Balkans we find the Caucasian, and very frequently the purely Greek type. Their dress is identical with that of the Greeks whereas a Bulgarian is always distinguished by the unavoidable pootoor — breeches large and full to the knee and tight around the leg to the ankle — and the characteristic cylindrical-shaped cap, or calpak of black sheep skin. Their language is not only more smooth and much softer than that of the Northern Bulgarians, but it contains an immense admixture of Greek words, wholly incomprehensible to a pure Bulgarian ... In their churches, their schools, and their correspondence they always use the Greek language, which they understand and study.[1]

One of the most striking characteristics of this excerpt is the way Gennadios presents costume as a distinguishing feature of the Bulgarian 'race'. This is hardly surprising given that the term 'race' had not yet gained the strictly biological sense — especially one deriving from the colour of skin — as it would during the first decades of the twentieth century, and language, customs, habits and religious beliefs were counted among the 'mental' factors that distinguished one group from another.[2] Race was also used almost interchangeably with the term nation, and could even be determined by social class, the working classes constituting an inferior group. It is also worth noting that the 'race' Gennadios associated Bulgarians with was not Slavs, a group recently discovered by a sympathetic European audience, but Tartaric hordes descending upon Eastern Europe.[3]

---

[1] *Ethnological Map* (1877; 13).

[2] Ravenstein (1850; 2).

[3] More specifically he described them as 'a mixed people formed by the fusion of Mongolian and Hunnish tribes, with much Tartaric blood in their veins ... It is true that owing to a close contact with Slav races the Bulgarians, during their descent upon the Balkan peninsula, absorbed into a widely different dialect a large proportion of Slavonic words. But the Bulgarian language contains also a considerable Turkish element; and by a similar process the Slavs of Turkey have adopted many Bulgarian words, the roots of which are not to be found in Slavonic'. [Gennadios] 1877; 11. The Bulgarians had been classified among the Southern Slavs by A. Balbi in 1828 in his *Atlas Ethnographique de Globe ou classification des Peuples Anciens et Modernes d'après leurs langues* (cited by Wilkinson, 1951; 29) and this classification was more or less the norm especially among ethnographers who gave precedence to linguistic affiliation.

The 'non-aryan' roots of Bulgarians was a favourite topic especially of authors who wanted to give credence to Greek claims in the Balkan peninsula.[1] The implication was that Bulgarians were racially inferior. According to an evolutionary hierarchy that was highly credible in Europe at the time, the Causasian and Greco-Roman types — among which the Slavs were numbered — represented the apex, whereas Tartars and other 'Turco-Mongolian races' were placed towards the bottom of the pile.[2]

What Gennadios managed to accomplish with this pamphlet was nothing less than to devise a mechanism through which the European rhetoric about superior and inferior qualities of races could find their way back into the discourses of self-perception generated by the subject cultures. The map may have been considered a failure, but the vogue Gennadios started gave the Greek elite a powerful weapon to fight against the claims of romantic Slavophiles: the weapon of cultural and racial superiority. Ioanna Stephanopoli, in a pamphlet she published on the populations of Macedonia would echo Gennadios's words when she argued that 'Bulgarians are not Macedonians, and Macedonians are not Bulgarians', and, 'if they are proud of belonging to the Family of Aristotle, of Alexander, of the Diadochoi, they [the inhabitants of Macedonia] would find it demeaning in their own eyes to be confused with the 'peoples without glory' who have not added even the smallest stone to the edifice of civilization that humanity has been erecting for centuries.[3]

An even more impressive example by which a 'race's fitness to rule' was expressed through ethnographic cartography was a map published by Heinrich Kiepert, professor of geography at the University of Berlin, who was considered by many in Europe including Bismarck, to be the best cartographer

---

[1] For instance, according to Driault, they 'are not pure Slavs, they seem to be Slavicized Tartars', Driault (1912; 286). The 'non-aryan' quality of Bulgarians was such a respected notion that even advocates of the Bulgarian side in the struggle for Macedonia, such as Brailsford had to come up with apologetic explanations as to the racial purity of Macedonian Slavs: 'They [Macedonian Slavs] are not Serbs, for their blood can hardly be purely Slavonic. There must be in it some admixture of Bulgarian and other non-Aryan stock ... On the other hand, they can hardly be Bulgarians, for quite clearly the Servian immigrations and conquests must have left much Servian blood in their veins, and the admixture of non-Aryan blood can scarcely be so considerable as it is in Bulgaria. They are probably very much what they were before either a Bulgarian and or a Servian Empire existed—a Slav people derived from rather various stocks, who invaded the peninsula at different periods.' Brailsford, (1903; 101).

[2] This notion inevitably affected general perceptions about different ethnic groups of Ottoman Europe and consequently their entitlement to political sovereignty. Ravenstein, for instance, argued in a paper presented to the Statistical Society in London in June 1877 that the critical difference that legitimized the Russian empire and disqualified that of the 'Turks' was the fact that Russians were 'intellectually superior to the races they govern, while the opposite is true of the Turkish Empire' (Ravenstein 1877; 438). Needless to say, the British in India or Ireland or any other part of the world were sanctioned by the very same principle.

[3] Stephanopoli (1903; 7).

of the times.[1] This map, published only two years after the appearance of the cartographer's well-known *Ethnograpshiche Übersichtskarte* displayed an image that was almost the exact negative of its predecessor.[2] In the first map Kiepert had allocated most of the region of Macedonia to the Bulgarian 'race' Thrace was shown as half Turkish and half Greek, further north, a more or less similar proportion was observed between Turks and Bulgarians. This map had such a good reception in Europe that it was actually used as a reference at the Congress of Berlin — clear praise for its objectivity. [3] Kiepert's second map was also accompanied with a *Notice Explicative sur la Carte Ethnocratique des Pays Hellèniques, Slaves, Albanais, et Roumains*, which basically argued that it was a mistake to base political boundaries on ethnographic maps. To correct this mistake, a new style called *ethnocratique*, was introduced. The new method consisted of:

> the separation of South-Eastern Europe according to divisions or groups of race, and, to the possible extent, *natural* frontiers, historical requirements, traditional affinities, and to assign to each division or group a single colour. This colour would not claim rigidly that the constituent parts of each section are occupied exclusively by a single race, it would only indicate the race that would be preponderant.[4]

If we could ignore the conditions that preceded the composition of this text, the above quote might perhaps be read as positive indication that Kiepert was disturbed by the impact his earlier map had, and attempted to undo some of the propaganda generated by its publication. On the other hand, being the 'pop-geographer' that he was, there is no indication that Kiepert would ever shy away from a little publicity. In fact, his correspondence with Konstantinos Paparrigopoulos before the compilation of this map raises more than a few question marks about Kiepert's motivations to publish it.[5]

---

[1] Wilkinson (1951; 67).

[2] Reimer (1876) and Kiepert (1878).

[3] Wilkinson notes Bismarck's high regard for Kiepert and mentions that his map was used at the Congress of Berlin and 'was regarded as part of Bismarck's 'honest brokerage'. (1951; 67-68). It must be noted however, that Kiepert's maps used at the Congress of Berlin were prepared under Russian sponsorship (See Karpat 1985; 26), were first published in Russian, and according to Paparrigopoulos, were translated into French after Bismark's orders to be used at the Congress (see Paparrigopoulos's correspondence with P. Argiropoulo in Dimara (1986; 348.)

[4] Kiepert (1878; 5). Emphasis mine.

[5] France, Ministère des Affaires Etrangères, A.A.E; C.P, Grèce, 106: Tissot (Athènes) à Waddington, 6 Mars 1878; 25 Mars 1878, Annexe à la Dépêche Politique d'Athènes, No 35 du 25 Mars 1878, published in Svolopoulos (1992 ; 361-370).

Perhaps unknown to most of Anglophone academia, Konstantinos Paparrigopoulos (1815-1891) is regarded to this day as one of the greatest names of Greek national historiography.[1] At the time of his correspondence with Kiepert, he was among the members of *Εύλλογο " προ " Διάδοσιν των Ελλινηκών Γραμμάτων* [Society for the Dissemination of Greek Letters, henceforth S.G.L.], which took an active interest in ethnographical maps of 'European Turkey'.[2] Feeling the need to counter the alarming prestige Bulgarians seemed to have with ethnographic cartographers — confirmed by the recent recruitment of Europe's best; Paparrigopoulos took it upon himself to persuade Kiepert to draw a new map on S.G.L's orders (which were in fact Paparrigopoulos's own), the expenses of which would be met by the same organization.[3] The historian left for Berlin in July 1877 with this goal in mind.

During his stay in Berlin, Paparrigopoulos apparently convinced Kiepert to draw a new map of the regions comprising roughly of the Peloponnese, Thessaly, Epirus, Macedonia, Thrace and Eastern Rumeli. At this first encounter between Kiepert and Paparrigopoulos, the Greek historian apparently specified certain demands concerning the limits of the map, and how it would be 'coloured'. During the year that passed between this meeting and the publication of the final version of the map, Kiepert and Paparrigopoulos maintained a correspondence, over the course of which the German cartographer changed his earlier depiction of the region almost entirely, in line with Greek claims, despite his initial reservations concerning the colouring of certain regions and the name(s) to be printed on the map. The first disagreement regarded two 'transition zones', the first one around Karaca Dağ and Orta Dağ (Meson Oros or Strednagora), and the second the upper valleys of the Strymon and Vardar (Strimonas and Axios).

Kiepert was in favour of drawing the line demarcating Greek 'ethnocracy' from that of the Bulgarians a little more south than Paparrigopoulos argued should have been. The first region was, Kiepert asserted, 'exclusively inhabited by Bulgarians'. As for the second region:

---

[1] The only biography of Paparrigopoulos written in English, to my knowledge, is the unpublished Ph.D. dissertation of Kontos (1986). A well-researched and extensive biography in Greek is Dimara (1986). According to Antonis Liakos, Paparrigopoluos's magnum opus *History of the Greek Nation (1860-1874)*, was the definitive 'grand narrative and introduced a new style to national historiography ' by replacing the third person hitherto favoured by Greek historians with a pronounced use of 'we', and even more significantly, by introducing a continuity into the Greek nation's genealogy that incorporated the Byzantine past and 'turned the national identity into a native-produced one.' Liakos (2001; 33).

[2] Dimara (1986; 336), Svolopoulos (1992; 358).

[3] Dimara (1986; 343), based on Alexander Rizos Rangavis's memoirs.

> ... I made it extend in a way that may seem exaggerated to you, though it is justified by the fact that we don't find any Greeks there (except for merchants and teachers at schools established here and there in some towns) and finally because Bulgarians constitute the large majority also in the southern part of Macedonia, which is indicated as Greek territory.[1]

Kiepert asked to be informed of any alterations in the borders that he had suggested, in which case, he further demanded, Paparrigopoulos's or another committee member's name be cited as the 'colouring author'. Even though we do not have Paparrigopoulos's reply among the documents published by Svolopoulos, it is possible to infer from Kiepert's letter dated 9 October 1877 from Naples that the historian did not accept Kiepert's proposed modifications. Kiepert was surprisingly accommodating in his response, when he stated that 'he [Kiepert] perfectly appreciated the reasons and the facts' presented by Paparrigopoulos to prove that the southern part of Macedonia was more than half-Greek. Concerning a revised version of the map, he pointed out it was impossible to draw an exact line from memory and suggested to Paparrigopoulos to send a 'sample of the entire map' coloured in correspondence with his corrections.

However, even the flexibility that Paparrigopoulos seems to have magically cultivated in Kiepert had its limits, and the name proposed by Paparrigopoulos for the map, 'Chart of Greek Lands' obviously transgressed them, when the cartographer retorted: 'I have nothing to object to Πίναξ των Ελληνικών Χωρών [Chart of Greek lands], except for the fact that at least half of the area represented on the map includes lands that were never either Hellenic or Hellenized, like Serbia, Wallachia, Danubian Bulgaria, Montenegro, Northern Albania.'[2]

Paparrigopoulos's letter to Kiepert dated 16 February 1878 from Athens reveals that the letter and the latest colour proof of the map sent by the cartographer had not settled the differences concerning the limits of Greek dominance in the regions of Thrace, Macedonia and Epirus. Paparrigopoulos was also not very happy about Kiepert's objection to the title of the map and pointed out that it was enough to take a look at Kiepert's own proof to see that 'these lands [Hellenic or Hellenized] fill up more than three quarters of the whole map'.[3] In addition, the cartographer had repeated his demand concerning

---

[1] Svolopoulos (1992; 365).

[2] Svolopoulos (1992; 366).

[3] Svolopoulos (1992; 368). The title of the final and published version of the map suggests that this became the only compromise Kiepert could obtain from Paparrigopoulos.

placing the authorship for colouring under someone else's name, and despite
their previous conversations, the Kingdom of Greece had been given 'a colour
different than other Hellenic lands'. This last 'mistake' seemed to be the straw
that broke the camel's back: Paparrigopoulos was indignant:

> As you see, Professor, your last work is far from corresponding to the first
> arrangements, to which you had kindly given your complete consent. It
> goes without saying that it is impossible to accept these modifications. We
> cannot but attribute them to a simple misunderstanding; we also have the
> firm hope that after the considerations we hereby presented to you, you will
> kindly give M. Reimer the necessary instructions in order to place the
> different colours conforming to the basis established by you and that we
> hastened to accept.
>
> We have sent a telegram to M. Reimer in order to stop all further work on
> the map, until an agreement can be reached between us.[1]

The bluff seems to have worked, because Kiepert's final letter dated 25
February 1878 from Berlin was almost apologetic in its acceptance of the
terms suggested by Paparrigopoulos:

> I did not, in any manner want to anticipate by this temporary sketch
> (which, as M. Reimer told me should not represent anything other than a
> sample of the style of colouring) the definitive decision about the frontier
> lines to adopt. I had thought instead with M. Reimer that the printing of
> the map (the corrections of which are at the moment on lithography
> stones) should be deferred for a short term, from what it seems, when it will
> be possible to present in it the new frontiers of Bulgaria, Serbia, and
> Montenegro established by the peace [Treaty of San Stefano] ... However,
> if you absolutely want to be in possession of a certain number of samples
> of the map, intended for the needs of the moment, we can print and colour
> them, according to the instructions and corrections that you would like to
> send.[2]

In the same letter Kiepert implored, yet again, that another name along with
his be published as the colouring author, afraid that he would be found
accountable by critiques who would not know, in his words, to 'distinguish
between the very different trends of this map, and the ethnographic maps' that
he had published earlier. In the end, it was again Paparrigopoulos who
prevailed, even though it seems to have taken another three to four months of
convincing — the details of which are unfortunately not documented. We do
learn from a letter by Paparrigopoulos to his protégé Argiropoulos that it was
around June that the final agreement was made. In the same letter, it is hard to

---

[1] Svolopoulos (1992; 369).
[2] Svolopoulos (1992; 370).

miss a certain element of irony in Paparrigopoulos's style when he uses of the title 'the eminent geographer' [ο επιφανή " γεογράφο "] repeatedly when referring to Kiepert: 'The eminent geographer (who nowadays is busy with the translation of his Russian maps of Asian borders into French for the conference [of Berlin] on Bismarck's commission), the eminent, well, geographer was persuaded to colour our chart the way we wanted it to be from the beginning; and even better, under his name.'[1]

It is hard to say whether Kiepert's reluctant acceptance of the 'arrangements' with Paparrigopoulos, which were the complete opposite of his earlier map could be attributed to his sincere conversion to the Greek cause.[2] What can safely be argued is that Paparrigopoulos surpassed even Gennadios's genius in his subversion of European ethnography against itself manipulating not merely its apparatus, but its *authority*. The literal issue of authorship of the map that required Paparrigipoulos's most strenuous efforts, and Kiepert's last objection to overcome was also the most important symbolic element of the map, communicating the scientific authority to the public embodied in the geographer's authorship.

Gennadios had claimed that authority by remaining anonymous and giving the impression that the map was prepared by a British author.[3] By contrast, Paparrigopoulos usurped the already existing and unquestionable authority of Kiepert by making sure that his name was the only one to be printed on the map and the text that accompanied it (written however, by Paparrigopoulos himself), deliberately misleading the reader. The result was so convincing that even the otherwise meticulous and thorough Wilkinson was tricked into stating: 'In the explanation accompanying the map Kiepert outlined the difficulties inherent in the production of an ethnographic map and he maintained that the use of such maps for drawing up political boundaries was a malpractice which no geographer ought to countenance.'[4]

It is extremely significant, in my opinion, to note that the Kiepert-Paparrigopoulos map was essentially a protest against all other ethnographic maps in principle, questioning their legitimacy or even relevance, in terms of helping determine national borders. I must also note that the correspondence and the bargaining preceding the publication of the *Tableau Ethnocratique* is

---

[1] Paparrigopoulos's letter to Argiropoulo, Dimara (1986; 348).

[2] Which would be somewhat ironic given his earlier reaction to the 'Stanford Map'.

[3] The confusion created was enough that Dimara, as recently as 1986, page 343, cited 'the famous English Edward Stanford'.

[4] Wilkinson (1951; 75).

available to the historian today only because Paparrigopoulos himself had chosen to disclose it to the representatives of European Powers in Athens, months before he had guaranteed the publication of the map under his terms.[1] The letters were attached to a memo, in which Paparrigopoulos argued that while no one would dispute the merits of Kiepert's geographical work, the same certainty could not be sustained for its ethnographical component, because Kiepert himself was 'far from believing in the absolute value of the data we have on the population of the diverse races of the Orient.'[2]

It is difficult to gauge the exact magnitude of the impact that the Kiepert-Paparrigopoulos map had in Western Europe. It is likely that it remained somewhat obscure in comparison to Kiepert's previous work,[3] but its importance lay in its capacity to transform the faith the Greek public had in their stakes in Macedonia. Paparrigopoulos gave the Greek nation the much needed reassurance that ethnography was not an exact science that could determine borders. If maps were to be drawn in order to 'display the races of the Orient', the heritage of Greek civilization was a more justifiable principle than sheer numbers in determining their colours.

### Ethnographical Maps: A Discourse of Power?

In a much-quoted article the late geographer J. B. Harley made the following observation about cartography:

> The way in which maps have become part of a wider political sign-system has been largely directed by their associations with elite or powerful groups and individuals and this has promoted an uneven dialogue through maps. The ideological arrows have tended to fly largely in one direction, from the powerful to the weaker in society ... Maps are preeminently a language of power, not of protest.[4]

Harley's conclusion has a strong appeal. It would allow us to conceptualize all the ethnographical maps presented in this paper as essentially discourses of power that can be deconstructed with the same methods that we would use for a text. Rather than going with a such a prescribed framework however, I

---

[1] This is why we do not know how exactly he convinced Kiepert to publish the map under his name. See Svolopoulos (1992; 360).

[2] Svolopoulos (1992; 361).

[3] Cvijić does not mention the original, but he does refer to Nicolaides's rendering of it (1899) and notes that he was 'astonished to see Kiepert's name on this map,' (1906; 32).

[4] Harley (1988; 300-1).

would like to point out that the brief history of ethnographic cartography presented in this paper demonstrates the potential of those 'ideological arrows' to go in more than one direction.

The distinction between the powerful subject who drew the maps and the weak object who was represented proved to be at least as contingent as the distinction between 'Exarchists' and 'Patriarchists' of late nineteenth-century Macedonia. The maps we have reviewed show that a specific kind of scientific knowledge, a kind of 'knowledge as power', which was originally introduced as a tool in the disposal of colonialist Europe to analyze, classify and process foreign peoples and cultures was skillfully appropriated and deployed by the elite of the very same cultures in order to articulate their own agendas of regional domination. In this sense, maps could demonstrate a 'language of protest', and, as the case of Paparrigopoulos suggests, even a language of subversion. We also saw that terms like 'elites and powerful groups' that abound in the vocabulary of such a conceptualization fail to register the differentiation within these groups that directly influenced their contribution to the enterprise of ethnographical map-making.

Harley's conceptualization of maps as texts that can be deconstructed in a post-structural sense has raised criticisms especially with respect to its essentialized notion of ubiquitous hegemony, and its tendency to look for conspiracy within the whole discipline of cartography.[1] On the other hand, some of the conceptual tools that Harley has introduced do allow for an analysis of cartography that goes beyond uncritical citing and organizing of evidence. It is not an analytical requirement to adopt Harley's entire deconstructionist paradigm to use these tools, which can facilitate a more profound understanding of not only scientific, but also political and cultural processes that ultimately determined the variety in the shape of contemporaneously published maps of a given region. In a similar vein, Jeremy Black notes: 'Harvey's claim that 'whether a map is produced under the banner of cartographic science — as most official maps have been — or whether it is an overt propaganda exercise, it cannot escape involvement in the processes by which power is deployed' can be amended by substituting 'analysed' or 'described' for 'deployed.'[2] Black's remark makes a crucial distinction between the processes that are inherent, inevitable and often unconsciously influential to map-making, and a sinister and deliberate manipulation of knowledge that perpetuates a position of power.

---

[1] For a balanced critique, see Black (1997; 19-25). Black also provides a bibliography of critiques and positive reviews of Harley in the same book, see p. 169, footnote no. 2.

[2] Black, *Maps and Politics,* p. 24.

Returning briefly to the maps presented in this paper with these warnings in mind, I would like to raise the question 'in what way did these cartographic images help us visualize the three-dimensional outlook?' The preferred method of representation of different groups across a given territory was *chorochromatic*,[1] meaning that a colour was assigned to each group which in turn was used to indicate the areas on the map where that group was 'preponderant'. Looking at the monochrome reaches of a given group on such maps, the first illusion that is created is that even the uninhabitable places like mountain tops, marshlands, or riverbeds have a national attribution.

An obvious problem arising from the use of this technique combined with complications of small-scale representation is that the dots that seem scattered within a block of colour — representing cities — might actually indicate more people than the background itself, the countryside. In addition, Macedonia is made up of a collection of medium sized plains, divided by mountain ranges that never form linear and unyielding chains. In such a geographical setting, and given the special historical conditions that fostered the 'cohabitation' of communities of different religious or linguistics affiliations, sharp divisions within valleys is not a phenomenon to be expected. Another important element missing from these representations are indicators of *patterns* of settlement, which we know, were characterized by a large number of small and scattered hamlets. Therefore, on a basis of day-to-day life, differentiation *within* the smaller regions was more relevant than differentiation across the broader region of Macedonia.[2]

Could this complexity be mapped had the nineteenth century ethnographer been equipped with precise census data (which we do not have access to even today), today's state-of-the-art devices to chart exact locations of villages, and a miraculous ethno-meter that would measure and record a standardized national allegiance index for each person? Alternatively, would our energies be better spent if we were to direct them away from such speculations to a full-scale deconstruction of each and every one of these maps?

---

[1] Monkhouse and Wilkinson (1952; 28). I am grateful to Prof. Wagstaff for providing this information.

[2] Another method of representation, apparently available to the cartographers I have been discussing, but never utilized, is exemplified by the map of the *sancak* (administrative unit) of Serres produced by the French Gendarmerie in 1905. Each village was marked by a dot and underneath the dot was a line whose colour represented a nationality. If the village was thought to be mixed, the line was of multiple colours, each colour making up the length of the line roughly in proportion to the percentage of the population that was, say, Bulgarian or Greek. Ministère des Affaires Etrangères, Constantinople (E/ Macédoine) no. 147, Dossier 1, Mars 1905.

I would argue that the ethnographic maps presented in this paper have a certain quality of transparency that renders their deconstruction in a strictly post-structural or iconographic sense redundant. Likewise, the argument that they served a political agenda can be an exercise in stating the obvious. On the other hand, an exclusively positivist evaluation focusing on the 'accuracy' of various representations not only undermines the importance of a critical approach in their use as *historical* sources, but also makes the assumption that this 'accuracy' was attainable had the precise data been available. This is a faulty assumption because, as Black asserts, 'the limitations of the map-medium are more than 'technical' and non-controversial; the questions involved are more than merely a matter of which projection or scale to select, and with such choices seen as 'technical,' rather than as involving wider issues.[1] Therefore, I would argue that a deconstruction of ethnographical maps, in fact, *is* necessary — necessary to the extent that each deconstruction also implies, by definition, a contextualization.

The 'limitations of the map-medium' are even more complicated in the case of ethnographical maps since they give the impression that it is possible and intellectually justifiable to depict constantly evolving and contingent phenomena such as 'ethnic consciousness' in a static and reified fashion. The importance of the choices available to the map-maker and of the decisions she or he makes are underscored by the fact that the product of these decisions do not merely represent a topographical image, but a very potent suggestion as to how the territory that Harley called 'a socially empty space' is to be filled. It is naïve (if not essentially wrong) to pretend that the ethnographical map-makers could not foresee the political uses that their projections would be put into. The maps depicting ethnic homogeneity as an ideal were catalysts in a process that inevitably culminated with that homogeneity in practice; a process that was very painful for those who did not fit the 'scale'. Let us end with Harley's observation:

> The abstract quality of the map, embodied as much in the lines of a fifteenth-century Ptolemaic projection as in the contemporary images of computer cartography, lessens the burden of conscience about people in the landscape. Decisions about the exercise of power are removed from the realm of immediate face-to-face contacts ... Any cartographic history which ignores the political significance of representation relegates itself to a 'ahistorical' history.[2]

---

[1] Black (1997; 17).
[2] Harley (1988; 303).

*REFERENCES*

*Archival*

Prime Ministry Archives, Istanbul. Papers of Rumeli Umum Müfettişliği [General Inspectorate of Rumeli]) TFR.I. SL 87/8623

Ministère des affaires Etrangères, Nantes. Constantinople Serie E, Macédoine.

*Published*

Abbott, G. 1900 *Songs of Modern Greece*, Cambridge; Cambridge University Press.

Abbott, G. 1903a *Macedonian Folklore*, Cambridge; Cambridge University Press.

Abbott, G. 1903b *The Tale of a Tour in Macedonia*, London; Edward Arnold.

Akarlı, E. 1970 'Ottoman Population in Europe in the 19th Century', unpublished M.A Thesis University of Wisconsin-Madison.

Bianconi, F. 1877 *Ethnographie et statistique de la Turquie d'Europe et de la Grèce*, Paris: A. Lassailly.

Black, J. 1997 *Maps and Politics*, Chicago; University of Chicago Press.

Boué, A. 1840 *La Turquie d'Europe, ou observations sur la géographie, la géologie, l'histoire naturelle, la statistique, les moeurs, les coutumes, l'archéologie, l'agriculture, l'industrie, le commerce, les gouvernements divers, le clergé, l'histoire, et l'état politique de cet empire*, Four volumes, Paris; Chez Arthus Bertrand.

Brailsford, H. 1903 *Macedonia, Its Races and Their Future*, London; Methuen & Co.

Brancoff, D. 1905 *La Macédoine et sa population chrétienne*, Paris.

Brown, K. 1995 *Of Meanings and Memories: the National Imagination in Macedonia*, University of Chicago, Department of Anthropology, unpublished doctoral dissertation.

Brown, K. 2003 *The Past in Question: Modern Macedonia and the Uncertainties of a Nation*, Princeton; Princeton University Press.

Cvijić, J. 1906 *Remarks on the Ethnography of the Macedonian Slavs*, translated from the second edition, London; Horace Cox.

Danforth, L. 1995 *The Macedonian Conflict, Ethnic Nationalism in a Transnational World*, Princeton; Princeton University Press.

Dimara, K. 1986 *Κωνσταντίνο " Παπαρριγόπουλο ", η εποχή του, η Ζωή του, το έργο του*, Athens; Morfotiko Idryma Ethnikis Trapezis.

Driault, E. 1912 *La Question d'Orient depuis ses origines jusqu'a nos jours*, (5ème edition) Paris; Librairie Felix Alcan.

'Ethnology and Ethnography' 1910 *Encyclopedia Britannica*, 11th edition, New York, Vol. 9, 849.

[Gennadios] 1877 *Ethnological Map of European Turkey and Greece with Introductory Remarks on the Distribution of Races in the Illyrian Peninsula and Statistical Tables of Population*, London; Edward Stanford.

Harley, J. 1988 'Maps, Knowledge, and Power,' in Cosgrove, D. and Daniels, S. (eds.), *The Iconography of Landscape: Essays on the Symbolic Representation, Design and Use of Past Environments*, Cambridge; Cambridge University Press, pages 277-312.

Ivanoff, J. 1920 *La Question Macédonienne au point de vue historique, ethnographique et statistique*, Paris; Librairie J. Gamber.

Karakasidou, A. 1999 *Fields of Wheat, Hills of Blood, Passages into Nationhood in Greek Macedonia*, Chicago; University of Chicago Press.

Karpat, K. 1985 *Ottoman Population 1830-1914: Demographic and Social Characteristics*, Madison; University of Wisconsin Press.

Kiepert, H. 1878 *Tableau Ethnocratique des pays du sud-est de l'Europe par Heinrich Kiepert* with *Notice Explicative sur la Carte Ethnogratique des pays Helleniques, Slaves, Albanais et Roumains, dessiné par M. Henri Kiepert*, Berlin; Imprimerie de Kerskes & Hohmann.

Kontos, D. 1986 'Konstantinos Paparrigopoulos and the Emergence of the Idea of a Greek Nation', Unpublished PhD dissertation, University of Cincinnati.

Lejean, G. 1861 'Ethnographie de la Turquie d'Europe' in *Mittheilungen aus Justus Perthes' Geographischer Anstalt über Wichtige Neue Erforschungen auf Dem Gesammtgebeite der Geographie von Dr. A. Petermann*, Gotha; Justus Perthes.

Liakos, A. 2001 'The Construction of National Time: The Making of the Modern Greek Historical Imagination', in *Mediterranean Historical Review*, Vol. 16 (2001), 27-42.

'Macedonia' 1910 *Encyclopaedia Britannica*, 11th Edition, New York, Vol. 17, 216.

Mathieu, H. c. 1857 *La Turquie et ses différents peuples*, Paris.

Monkhouse, F. and Wilkinson, H. 1952 *Maps and Diagrams: Their Compilation and Construction*, London; Methuen, New York; Dutton.

Ofeicoff [A. Shopov] 1887 *La Macédoine au point de vue ethnographique, historique, et philologique*, Phillippopoli; Imprimerie Centrale.

Perry, D. 1988 *Politics of Terror*, Durham and London; Duke University Press.

*The Population of Macedonia, Evidence of the Christian Schools*, 1905 London; Ede, Allom and Townsend.

Ravenstein, E. c. 1850 *Illustrations of the Principal Varieties of the Human Race, arranged according to the system of Dr. Latham, Descriptive notes by Ernest Ravenstein*, London; James Reynolds.

Ravenstein, E. 1876 'Distribution of the Population in the Part of Europe Overrun by Turks', *The Geographical Magazine*, London; October, 1876, pp. 259-261.

Ravenstein, E. 1877 'The Population of Russia and Turkey, ' *Journal of the Statistical Society*, Vol. XL (September).

Reimer, D. 1876 *Ethnographische Übersichtskarte des Europäischen Orients*, Berlin; D. Reimer.

Svolopoulos, K. 1992 'Ο Κωνσταντίνο " Παπαρρηγόπουλο " και η Χαρτογράφηση τη " Χερσόνησου του Αίμου απο τον Χαϊνριχ Κιπερτ', in Αφιέρωμα ει " τον Κωνσταντίνον Βαβούσκον, Thessaloniki ; Ekdoseis Sakkoula.

Stavrianos, L. 2000 [1965] *The Balkans since 1453*, New York; New York University Press.

Stephanopoli, I. 1903 *Grecs et Bulgares en Macédoine*, Athens; Imprimerie Anestis Constantinidis.

Todorova, M. 1997 *Imagining the Balkans*, New York; Oxford University Press.

Wilkinson, H. 1951 *Maps and Politics: A review of the Ethnographic Cartography of Macedonia*, Liverpool; Liverpool University Press.

# 31. GREEKS WHO ARE MUSLIMS: COUNTER-NATIONALISM IN NINETEENTH CENTURY TRABZON

Michael E. MEEKER

*Introduction*

Until recently, the later Ottoman Empire was commonly perceived as a fossil of the early modern period, unable to cope with internal and external challenges, and so condemned to a relentless spiral of decline. Over the last two decades however, historians and sociologists have explored how Ottoman officials and subjects confronted and managed a changing military and commercial environment. As a result, we can now understand more clearly how features of the late Ottoman world arose as contemporary, even innovative, adaptations to circumstances of the seventeenth, eighteenth, and nineteenth centuries. The new understanding has been achieved in no small part by attending to the gap between official pretensions and practices. State officials often cloaked ruling strategies in a rhetoric of imperial centralism and absolutism; nonetheless, the archival record they left behind can be examined to expose systematic policies of compromise and negotiation with local elites.

This raises the possibility that an ethnographic approach, such as we find in the writings of F. W. Hasluck, might be another way of uncovering the working, as opposed to the idealized, relationship of Ottoman state and society. With this idea in mind, I want to question a prejudice that recent research has more or less left in place. A narrow circle of high officials is presumed to have been responsible for devising and applying each program of reform during the late Empire and early Republic. The top-down character of the modernization process has been deemed inevitable, given that the provincial rural population was politically fragmented, culturally backward, and economically impoverished.

The example of the old province of Trabzon is not in accord with this assessment. In its eastern and western coastal districts, local state-societies of post-classical origin consistently adapted themselves to the changing policies and institutions of the centralized government. As a consequence, combinations of state officials and local elites determined the course and outcome of each successive program of reforms. Both insiders and outsiders failed to understand the state-societies of the old province of Trabzon, however, since their existence was improper, even illegal, by the measure of formal state institutions, whether reformed or unreformed.

*Early Consular Perceptions: The Old Imperial System*

In February 1814, the tenth year of his residence in the town of Trabzon, consul Pierre Dupré reported that Süleyman Pasha, the provincial governor, was assembling a large military force for the purpose of invading the outlying districts and destroying the local elites who dominated them. Already, one of the local elites had been arrested and imprisoned while another had fled the province in order to seek sanctuary elsewhere. As the consul had explained in his earlier reports, the local elites in question lived in semi-fortified mansions, maintained large retinues, and mobilized hundreds of men in arms. They sometimes made war against one another, laying siege to their rivals' residences, even within the precincts of the provincial capital itself, but they also occasionally came together to oppose the government, sometimes forcing state officials to take refuge in the citadel or leave the town altogether.

The early French consuls, Dupré in Trabzon and Fourcade in Sinop, recognized this situation as something familiar rather than strange. They considered the local elites as representatives of a feudal system much like that of thirteenth century France. By this understanding, the consuls saw the local elites as a second government separate and distinct from the first government of state officials. Accordingly, they called the local elites 'chiefs' and 'lords', sometimes using a French terminology (*chef, seigneur*) and sometimes an Ottoman terminology (*agha, bey*) as though the latter were the equivalent of the former.

The thesis of two governments was consistent with consular interests, or should I say, consular desires. At any given moment along the southern Black Sea coast, some group of local elites was usually engaged in military actions, sometimes in competition with their peers, sometimes in defiance of state officials. As long as the local elites remained in place, the threat of endemic civil disorder limited the transit trade through the coastal towns, hence restricted the expansion of French commerce. Accordingly, the consuls were pleased to believe that the 'little despots' of all the coastal districts were an expendable feudal appendage to the official imperial regime. In accordance with this conception, they recommended that their government assist the Ottomans in suppressing them.[1]

The early consuls were not mistaken in thinking that civil disorders, arising from quarrels among various combinations of local elites and state officials, inhibited the transit trade, especially through the town of Trabzon. But otherwise, they had an imperfect understanding of the place of the local elites in the structure of imperial state and society. Those individuals whom the consuls considered to be the chiefs and lords of the coastal districts were in fact the more prominent of a larger number of local elites in each district. Furthermore, all these local elites, both the greater and the lesser, were associated with an even larger number of ordinary individuals in each district.

In this regard, the majority of the Muslims in the old province of Trabzon comprised a hierarchical network of interpersonal association that was part of, rather than separate and distinct from, the imperial regime. In fact, state officials and local elites did not really consist of two entirely different groups of individuals. A certain number of the local elites in the coastal districts were consistently appointed to state offices, and a certain number of state officials consistently established themselves as local elites in the coastal districts. The crisscrossing of state officials and local elites was the feature of a *society-oriented* state system that came in the company of a *state-oriented* social system.[2]

Such an arrangement had begun to take shape during the later seventeenth century with increasing local participation in imperial, military, and religious institutions. As such, it was an artifact of the imperial regime that brings to mind the late modern rather than the early medieval history of western Europe. That is to say, the relationship of society and state in Trabzon anticipated a nation-people represented by, and participating in, a nation-state. However, this relationship was not associated with a 'nationalist' concept of a people who spoke a native tongue, abided by native manners and customs, and belonged to a native land.

---

[1] Dupré on centralized government and commerce, MAE CCCT L. 1, 1801-1811, No. 59, June 6, 1807; Fourcade on aghas resembling the feudal system of France, MAE CCCS, No. 3, 16 Brumaire, An XI (Nov., 1802]; Fourcade on centralized government and commerce, No. 18, 30 Prairial An XIII [June, 1805]; Fontanier (1829: 17-18) on aghas resembling feudal system of France; Fontanier on centralized government and commerce, MAE CCCT L. 3 1825-1835, No. 11, Jan 27, 1831.

[2] Some observers commented on the close relationship of state and society in the province of Trabzon. See Decourdemanche (1874; 361) who visited the coastal region sometime in the 1850s.

Accordingly, Süleyman Pasha most certainly would not have agreed with the consuls on the necessity of destroying the local elites altogether.[1] During the period in question, the greater and lesser local elites were indispensable for carrying out the most elementary governmental functions, collecting taxes, organizing militias, arresting fugitives, enforcing court orders, and so on. Rather, Süleyman Pasha was assembling military forces in order to gain greater control over the local elites. He was ready to make examples of a number of them by imprisoning or executing them, but even in these instances, he would allow their brothers, sons, or nephews to succeed them. These were the standard procedures by which the provincial governors of Trabzon attempted to redress the distribution of power between state and society in the coastal region.

*The Prophecy of Zadek*

After completing his report, Dupré appended a curious document that he introduced as: 'Summary of a prophecy that has been communicated to me by Monsieur Theodosia, Archbishop of Erzurum.' My translation of the French follows:

> Zadek the hermit lived in the mountains of Germany where he died around a hundred years ago. Before his death, he had lapsed into a deep sleep for three days and then upon awakening he had called his friends to his side. He told them that he had received a revelation and asked them to write down what he had heard. // He first stated that there would be a revolution in France during which the French would invade Egypt. // He predicted that the Emperor of France would force the submission of all the powers of Europe and principally that of Austria. Afterwards he would go into Anatolia where he would establish Christianity. Then he would go into Jerusalem where he would find the Stone of Salomon containing an immense treasure. He would build a city the dimensions of which Zadek designated. From there, the Emperor of France would go into Persia and conquer it. Finally he predicted that he would bring about the union of the churches, and that the Christian religion, as well as the dynasty of the Emperor, would continue to exist until the end of the world. Zadek concluded by stating that he had only seven hours to live, after which he uttered his last sigh.[2]

---

[1] Higher state officials, including Süleyman Pasha, probably encouraged the early consuls to think of the local elites as usurpers of authority who lacked legitimacy. But these same state officials, including Süleyman Pasha, were oftentimes little different in their origins from the most prominent of the local elites.

[2] MAE BPMT L. 2 (1812-1824), No. 23, Feb. 10, 1814.

Hasluck tells us that prophecies of a conquest by a Christian emperor were common among both the Muslims and the Christians of the later Ottoman Empire.[1] By his account, such predictions came to life during unsettled moments, always in a new form to suit the occasion. The prophecy of Zadek was in all likelihood a learned edition of a more popular version, since its elements were more or less common knowledge in northeastern Anatolia in 1814. Both the Christians and Muslims were well aware of the French Revolution, the Napoleonic wars, and the French Empire, however imperfect their understanding of the actual character of each. The Christians and the Muslims also believed, or should I say knew, that the French had both the ability and the intention to affect the fortunes of the Ottoman Empire. They even anticipated that the French might invade and occupy the coastal region, the example of the Napoleonic invasion of Egypt serving as precedent.[2]

Otherwise, the popular version of the prophecy would appear to have been polished by an Orthodox churchman for the benefit of a French consul. Zadek predicts that the Emperor of France will bring about the restoration of the Byzantine Empire. Interestingly, this accomplishment anticipates a restoration of the form but not the content of the Ottoman Empire. The French Emperor is to realize the ambitions of Mehmet the Conqueror and Süleyman the Magnificent. All the lands of the classical imperial regime at its furthest extension, together with all the lands of its western and eastern antagonists, will be united in a world rule based on the true religion. The emperor from the west replaces the sultan from the east, Christianity replaces Islam, and Jerusalem replaces Mecca.

The archbishop and the consul were thinking along the same lines but in different registers. Both were considering how centralized governmental authority might suppress provincial social formations that did not serve their interests. Retrospectively, they were of a 'reactionary' rather than a 'progressive' disposition by the measure of the coming age of nations. In contemplating the province of Trabzon, both were inclined to place their bets on a revival of dynastic absolutism, whether neo-Byzantine or neo-Ottoman.

---

[1] Hasluck (1921; 200-01). See also Balivet (1999).

[2] Local knowledge of the French Empire can be inferred from the remarks of Rottiers (1829; 179-80), Beauchamp (1813: 2: 270, 276), and Fourcade on the Laz arrival in Sinop, MAE CCCS, folio p. 191. Other circumstances indicate that the local elites of Trabzon were also apprised of events in Moscow and Cairo.

In contrast, the state officials and local elites of the coastal region accepted that the centralized state system came in the company of local social systems. That is to say, the relationship of state and society in Trabzon was ahead rather than behind the times since it anticipated the age of nations.

*Bureaucratic Centralism and Nationalist Ideology*

As it happened, state officials did succeed in reigning in local elites in the eastern coastal region. By 1840, the governor of Trabzon was in a position to deploy large numbers of troops anywhere in the eastern coast region at short notice. Once convinced of this capacity, the local elites no longer dared to assemble military forces in order to challenge state officials. By 1850, the central Ottoman government had reorganized the provincial government in accordance with new methods and technologies of bureaucratic administration. Just as the early consuls had predicted, military pacification and bureaucratic centralization did result in a rise in the transit trade through the town of Trabzon. By 1860, thanks to the steamboat and telegraph, the town of Trabzon was part of mercantile networks that reached into western Europe, and many of the residents of the provincial capital, especially Christians, enjoyed a new level of prosperity and security.

With these developments, consular officials lost interest in the character of the social formations in the coastal districts since they were no longer an obstacle to the expansion of the transit trade.[1] Indeed, the later French and British consuls presume that the local elites had been entirely suppressed during the 1830s.[2] Yet, state and society were still coordinated in the coastal districts. The local elites still represented hierarchical networks of interpersonal association.[3] State officials still turned to local elites to assist them in carrying out elementary functions of government. Local elites still became state officials, and state officials still became local elites, almost certainly in larger numbers than before, given the expansion of bureaucratic government. By comparison with what had once been the case, the local elites and state officials were now more consistently partners than competitors.

---

[1] Although the later consuls did take an interest in treatment of the Christian minorities, they devoted most of their attention to trade and commerce.

[2] The British joined the French in the provincial capital in 1820 after the Treaty of Adrianople (Bryer 1970; 33).

[3] These networks also survived the Young Turk Revolution of 1908 as well as the declaration of the Republic of Turkey in 1923. See Meeker (2002; Chap. 8 and Chap. 9).

The later consuls did not understand that the relationship of state and society during the 1870s was in many ways similar to what it had been before the 1840s. They regarded the collusion of local elites and state officials as a problem of governmental corruption characteristic of sultanic centralism and autocracy. By this estimation, they regretted the fictive suppression of the fictive medieval world of old Trabzon.[1] While the early consuls had called for the reinforcement of the centralized government as the antidote for an endemic feudal anarchy, the later consuls indulged themselves in nostalgic recollections of lords living in castles, surrounded by knights and troubadours, who protected ordinary villagers from the rapacity of the Ottomans.[2] The inconsistency of consular opinion arose from an invariant prejudice. Both the earlier and later consuls viewed the relationship of state and society in Trabzon to be improper and illegal by the measure of centralized bureaucratic government. They differed only in condemning either local elites or state officials as principally responsible for a condition of misrule.[3]

As for the Orthodox Christians of the old province of Trabzon, they became more, rather than less, interested in the local state-societies, but not because they wanted to understand their place and function in the Ottoman Empire. The rise in the transit trade had benefited the Pontic Greeks in the coastal towns, and the higher level of prosperity and security had encouraged Aegean Greeks to migrate into the coastal region.[4] Growing in wealth and numbers, the Orthodox Christians became more confident, and hence, more imaginatively nationalist.[5] And so inevitably, they began to ponder the patterns of state and society in Trabzon precisely because these patterns were not what they should have been by the criteria of the emergent age of nations.[6] In other words, the local state-societies of Trabzon challenged the way in which the Orthodox Christians contemplated who they had once been and what they might now be.

---

[1] The local elites begin to be idealized from the very moment of their military pacification. See Slade (1833).

[2] Koch (1855; 110-11) is one of the first observers to romanticize the local elites as medieval lords and knights. For the later period, see Palgrave (1887; 17) and Biliotti, PRO FO 195 1329, May 12, 1880. Cf. Bryer (1969; 193).

[3] For an example of a later consul who became hopelessly confused about who was really responsible for misgovernment, local elites or state officials, see the discussion of Biliotti, PRO FO 195 1329, May 12, 1880, in Meeker (2002; 254).

[4] Bryer (1970; 49-51).

[5] Palgrave, 'the Greeks aim at mastery not equality' in PRO FO 195/812, No. 6, April 17, 1867, as quoted in Bryer (1970; 51).

[6] For more on the Ottoman Greeks in Asia Minor, see Gondicas and Issawi (1999) on society and economy, and Gerasimos (1999) on identities and perceptions.

In some parts of the old province of Trabzon, there were large numbers
of Muslims who spoke Kartvelian (Lazi), Armenian (Hemşin), and Hellenic
(Pontic) dialects, that is to say, languages that were once associated with
Christian peoples. By a nationalist accounting of history, these Muslims
stirred mixed feelings of despair and hope. Their ascendants seemed to have
betrayed their ethnic identity by converting from Christianity to Islam, and
yet, they also seemed to have held fast to their ethnic identity by continuing
to speak their original 'Christian' languages. In any event, the combination of
a Muslim faith and a 'Christian' language stood unquestionably as evidence of
a horrible outrage by its very inappropriateness.

In other words, as the Greeks of Trabzon became imaginatively
nationalist, the local state-societies became increasingly unacceptable, even
incomprehensible, to them. For this very reason, the local state-societies of
the coastal districts became subjects of analysis and worry. In this regard, the
district of Of became an intense focus of interest, not because it was the only
place where there were large numbers of Greek-speaking Muslims, but rather
because the Oflus presented especially difficult problems for a nationalist
accounting of history.

Before considering nineteenth century explanations of how Greeks
became Muslims in the district of Of, I shall first summarize what can be
established by ethnographic and archival evidence.

### The District of Of: Greeks who are Muslims

The large majority of the inhabitants of the district of Of were still Christian
a century after the conquest of Trabzon (1461 C.E.). [1] During the second
century of Ottoman incorporation, the Muslim population gradually increased
by immigration of Turkic-speaking Muslims and by conversion of Greek-
speaking Christians. [2] By the end of the seventeenth century, the large
majority of the inhabitants of the district were probably Muslim, but perhaps
only incipiently Ottomanist Muslims. By the middle of the eighteenth
century, most of the male inhabitants of the district had some kind
of affiliation, official or unofficial, legal or illegal, with imperial, military, or

---

[1] The contribution by Shukurov to this volume raises the possibility that some of the Christians
of Of may have been crypto-Muslims at the time of Ottoman incorporation. Since the number of
Muslims remains very low during the first century of Ottoman rule, there would have been only
a small number of crypto-Muslims in Of at best.

[2] For a more detailed account of the history of conversion and immigration in the district of Of,
together with a full citation of the evidence, see Meeker (2002; Chap 5).

religious institutions. The inhabitants of the district of Of had become an ottomanist provincial society, homogeneous at the level of imperial identification and participation, even if heterogeneous at the level of ethnic and linguistic background.

The lower, eastern quadrant of the district had been open to settlement by large numbers of Turkic-speaking peoples from Erzurum. Here a Turkish dialect became the language of assimilation, and many of the villagers were affiliated with imperial regiments and militias. The upper, western segment of the district had been a refuge for Christians during the sixteenth century but most had converted to Islam by the close of the seventeenth century. Here a Greek dialect became the language of assimilation, and many of the villagers were religious teachers or students. These patterns were relative rather than absolute. There were individuals in upper western Of who were officers or soldiers just as there were individuals in lower eastern Of who were teachers or students.

Since the Oflus had become an ottomanist provincial society by the middle of the eighteenth century, one must question whether the population of the district of Of should be described in ethnic terms at this time. Both the Greek-speakers and the Turkic-speakers were composite populations, the result of multiple arrivals from various locations of Turks, Greeks, Kurds, Albanians, and Bosnians, if not also some number of Lazis, Armenians, and Georgians. The Turkish dialects and Greek dialects that were spoken in the district were languages of assimilation suffused with an imperial vocabulary drawn from literary Turkish, Persian, and Arabic. The efficiency of this transformation was a consequence of the importance of itinerant occupations in the district. The very same Oflus who were occasional soldiers and students were also occasional tradesmen, craftsmen, and labourers in the towns and villages of the Balkans, Anatolia, the Caucasus, and the Crimea.

Toward the middle of the nineteenth century, most outsiders considered the district of Of as a *terra incognita*. The appointees of the provincial governor were sometimes unable to take up their posts in the district of Of, and those who did so were obliged to arrive in the company of a sizable military force. Even after the pacification of the local elites, French, British, and German travellers were often advised to avoid the district by both officials and consuls so that the Oflus were seldom visited and described in print. As a consequence, the Oflus were regarded as mysterious and dangerous. They were said to be brigands and pirates, preoccupied by endless vendettas among themselves, and otherwise given to raiding, extortion, or kidnapping. They were said to provide sanctuary for rebels and outlaws from all parts of Trabzon since their villagers were marginally under the control of the centralized government.

The reputation of the Oflus did contain grains of truth; nonetheless, it was grossly exaggerated. Like other Trabzonlus, the Oflus were clannish, having strong social bonds among themselves, but suspicious and distrustful of strangers. However, the Oflus were not isolated from the outside world, even if the outside world was isolated from them.[1] Indeed, the district was *terra incognita* because its inhabitants had been so successful in assimilating imperial institutions and insinuating themselves in the imperial regime. They had been so successful, precisely because of their ethnic mixtures, the Turkic elements being closer to the later military (*yeniçeri*) institution and the Hellenic elements being closer to the later religious (*medrese*) institution. By virtue of a hierarchical network of interpersonal association, derived from imperial identification and participation, the Oflus fended off government interference in local affairs even as they also penetrated official and non-official circles in the provincial, even in the imperial, capital. In other words, the district of Of was actually one of the best examples in the old province of Trabzon of the displacement of ethnicity by imperial identification and participation.

By the mid-nineteenth century, however, the local state-societies of the coastal region had become virtually indecipherable. Several decades of imperial reforms had erased the policies that had fostered imperial social formations in all the old province of Trabzon. At the same time, observers of a nationalist orientation, such as the Greeks, but also the British and French consuls, had begun to focus on those features of the population that indicated ethnicity. As a consequence, the Oflus became harder rather than easier to understand, and hence, more than ever, available for mythic invention and elaboration.

*A Greek Nationalist Outlook*

The Orthodox Christians had always had an explanation for Muslims who spoke 'Christian' languages. Such a circumstance was said to be the result of

---

[1] See Karl Koch's (1855; 110-11) account of the district of Of during his visit there in the 1840s. He specifically notes that the reputation of the Oflus as brigands and pirates was little more than an ignorant prejudice.

the perfidy of a high state or church official of the Byzantine period. The official had betrayed his own people by forcing them to convert *en masse* solely in order to win Ottoman favor. In the case of the Greek-speaking Muslims of Of, it was a Bishop Alexandros. In the case of the Lazi-speaking Muslims of Arhavi, it was a Prince Lazerew.[1] These older traditions acquired a new colouring with the advance of a nationalist outlook and expectation during the second half of the nineteenth century. Poutouridou summarizes the still current traditions of forced conversion as follows:[2]

> The most popular version of events that is found in nearly all the histories of the period attributes the mass conversions to a quarrel between Alexandros, bishop of Of and the Metropolitan of Trabzon, sometime in the middle of the seventeenth century. Alexandros took the drastic step of converting to Islam, and as Iskender Bey, 'satrap' of Trabzon, became 'enraged at the Greek population ... and converted many of the churches remaining in their hands into mosques and hamams, mercilessly exacted burdensome taxes ... and threatened them with conversion or death. It was in this time that the inhabitants of Of were converted.'[3]

As the summary indicates, Bishop Alexandros of Of, having become İskender Bey of Trabzon, replaced legitimate and supportive Byzantine institutions with illegitimate and oppressive Ottoman institutions. In this regard, the old tradition of Bishop Alexandros was a story of the overturning rather than the restoration of Byzantium, and so, a negative version of the prophecy of Zadek. That it is to say, it was imperial rather than nationalist in orientation.

Now, the old tradition of Bishop Alexandros had attributed him an Oflu origin. This meant that the Oflus, 'Greeks who were Muslims', became a symbol of the forced conversions that the apostate churchman had brought about in all the coastal region during the seventeenth century. During the nineteenth century, however, the Oflus acquired a new significance. According to Poutouridou, the new renditions of the old tradition claimed that the Oflus had 'sacrificed their orthodox faith in order to retain their language and customs'. So the Oflus became a symbol of a substratum of Greekness underlying what was merely the appearance of Muslimness. In other words, the Oflus were perceived as a Greek people resolutely attached to a Greek homeland. The tradition of Bishop Alexandros was becoming more imaginatively nationalist and so less imaginatively imperial.

---

[1] Fontanier (1834; 299) mentions that the Bishop of Of and the Prince of the Laz had led their peoples into Islam. The bishop and the prince are probably both apocryphal figures. For the former, see Janssens (1969; 173).

[2] Poutouridou (1997-1998) cites the following works as nineteenth century examples: T. Evangelidis, *A History of Trabzon from the Earliest Times to the Present* (Odessa 1898); S. Ioannidis, *History and Statistics of Trabzon and Surrounding Areas* (Constantinople 1870); P. Triandafyllidis, *The Greek Race in the Pontos, or Pontica* (Athens 1866) and *The Fugitives* (Athens 1870).

[3] Poutouridou (1997-1998; 50). I have omitted several significant footnotes from the citation.

Outside observers had always confused the Greek-speaking Muslims in the district of Of with groups of crypto-Christians in the province of Trabzon. So nationalist accounts of the district soon supported the idea that the Oflus were Greeks by citing reports that they preserved Christian holy books and relics and celebrated Christian rites and holidays. Curiously, these notions were not impeded by other evidence that the Oflus had identified with and participated in imperial institutions. From the first half of the eighteenth century, it was common knowledge that the numbers of religious teachers and students in the district of Of exceeded every other coastal district. But during the nineteenth century, outsiders began to see these religious teachers and students as an indication of Byzantine continuity, that is, a legacy of an older tradition of priests and monasteries, or alternatively, as an indication of Ottoman disaffection, that is, a means for evading imperial military service. The stubbornness of these perceptions is truly remarkable. When the Oflus eventually became notorious as advocates of hard-line responses to foreign intervention, outsiders viewed their 'fanaticism' as an attribute of their recent conversion, hence further evidence that they were unnaturally Muslim. The coherence of local identification with and participation in imperial institutions in the district of Of was consistently interpreted as a symptom of an Ottoman violation of national destiny.

*The First Oflu Tradition of Conversion: The Story of Osman Efendi*

The Oflus seem to have always accepted that large numbers of conversions occurred in their district sometime after the Ottoman incorporation of the coastal region in the fifteenth century. From the mid-nineteenth century, however, there were differing traditions about who was converted, who converted them, and why they converted. The earliest citation of such a tradition of which I am aware appears in the *History of Trabzon* by Şakir Şevket, published in the year 1877. By this account, a certain Osman Efendi from the learned class (*ulema*) of Maraş had occasion to come to Of about a century after the Ottoman conquest of Trabzon. Eventually, but only after a great deal of effort, Osman Efendi succeeded in convincing the priests and villagers of the district of Of to accept Islam.[1]

The tradition of Osman Efendi takes the form of a venerable religious genre, that is to say, the biography of a member of the learned class. Almost certainly, it would have originated among upstanding members of the learned

---

[1] See Karadenizli (1954; 46) for a Turkification of Şakir Şevket (1877/1294; 98).

class (*ulema*) in the province of Trabzon, and most probably, in the district of Of. In this regard, it is not so much a story about the Oflus as a story about Osman Efendi. Yet, the tradition is oriented to the question of how Christians became Muslims in the district of Of and so stands as a reply to the Orthodox account of Bishop Alexandros. Indeed, the tradition of Osman Efendi concedes the event of a mass conversion in the district and so concedes that all the inhabitants of the district were the descendants of Christians. The explanation for such concessions, I suggest, was an intent to compose an effective rebuttal.

By accepting the doubtful thesis of a mass conversion of priests and villagers, members of the learned class in Of transformed a myth of religious oppression during the seventeenth century into a myth of religious naturalization during the sixteenth century.[1] That is to say, members of the learned class had co-opted the perception of the Oflus as an integrally Christian people in order to represent them more perfectly as an integrally Muslim people. All this suggests that the tradition of Osman Efendi must have first been composed sometime in the nineteenth century. Any earlier than this, members of the learned class would have had fresh memories of the gradual and complex process of Islamization. More to the point, they would have been less pressured by Greek nationalism to respond to a claim that the inhabitants of Of had been Christians who were forced to become Muslims.

But there is another matter that points to the late nineteenth century origins of the tradition of Osman Efendi. By buying into the event of a mass conversion, those who invented and circulated the tradition of Osman Efendi were gaining an advantage over another opponent, one that was inside rather than outside the district. Not all, but probably most, of the religious teachers and students in Of were patrilineal descendants of converted Greek-speakers. Not all, but probably most, of the military officers and soldiers in Of were patrilineal descendants of immigrant Turkic-speakers. Any story of Islamization by conversion therefore tended to elevate the local status of the religious teachers and students just as any story of Islamization by immigration tended to elevate the local status of military officers and soldiers. This means that the tradition of Osman Efendi is an argument, not only of Muslims against Christians, but also an argument of the old imperial religious establishment against the old imperial military establishment, or to use local terminology, an argument of hodjas against aghas.

---

[1] By contemporary polemics, Muslims claimed that conversion occurred soon after Ottoman incorporation in order to exaggerate the antiquity of current belief and practice, while Christians claimed that conversion occurred soon after Ottoman incorporation because they were the result of intimidation and violence. Ottoman registers indicate that no significant number of conversions to place from Christianity to Islam during the first century of Ottoman rule.

Today, in the district of Of, one can hear stories of Islamization by conversion and stories of Islamization by immigration. Most probably such alternative versions have been in circulation ever since the seventeenth century. That Şakir Şevket had cited the tradition of Osman Efendi in his *History of Trabzon* is an indication that the hodjas were prevailing over the aghas at the moment of its publication. They were prevailing, I would suggest, because the hodjas had a better response to Greek nationalism than the aghas. I will return to this point later in the paper.

*The Second Oflu Tradition of Conversion: The Story of the Maraşlılar*

An alternative tradition of mass conversion was circulating in the district of Of during the final decades of the Ottoman Empire. This so-called 'story of the Maraşlılar' also appears to have been the work of members of the learned class but it had been composed with a popular rather than a scholarly audience in mind. The alternative tradition also refers to a mass conversion during the sixteenth century, attributing it to the efforts of two rather than one member of the learned class from Maraşlılar. As we shall see, this story of the Maraşlılar is more mythical than historical in its formulation by comparison with the story of Osman Efendi.

Hasan Umur, a local historian of the district of Of, cites the story of the Maraşlılar in the first of his three books, *Of and the Battles for Of*. While this book was not published until 1949, Umur (b. 1880, d. 1977) reports that he heard it from his village religious teacher, presumably sometime in the late nineteenth century when he was his student. Umur was interested in the alternative tradition as a source for understanding the history of the district of Of, but only if it could be supported by other kinds of evidence. My translation of his presentation of the alternative tradition follows:

> Everywhere in the world one always encounters some number of legendary stories regarding historical personages. I am recording the story of the Maraşlılar as it was related to me by our [village] hodja, Karakaşoğlu Ahmet Efendi.
>
> Supposedly, during the time of the Great Caliph Hazreti Ömer [634 to 644 C.E.], there was a dispute between the Islamic and Christian religions. After an exchange of notes and the conclusion of an agreement between Caliph Ömer and the Istanbul Emperor, the latter saw fit to send two Christian learned men of religion from Trabzon to the City of Light [Medina] and wrote to the King of Trabzon [to help him with this task]. The King of Trabzon saw fit to make his selection from among the Oflus since

the greatest of the Christian learned men of religion were to be found in that district. Sending the two men to Istanbul, he managed to bring them to the favorable attention of the Emperor by describing for him their excellent qualities. Eventually, these two learned men of religion from Of reached Medina and came into the presence of the Caliph. When they saw his simple way of life, his great and boundless justice, his compassion before Muslims, and his majesty before unbelievers, overcome by his excellent qualities and without even entering into the dispute, they immediately (*tereddütsüz*) accepted Islam. But now faced with the circumstance [of their conversion], they did not return to Of but settled instead in Maraş, the water and air of which closely resembles that of Of.

A thousand years later [assuming lunar years of the Hicri calendar, this would have been about 1010 A.H. or 1600 C.E.], two descendants of these two persons from among the Islamic men of religion [of Maraş] were informed in their dreams that the attainment of the right path of Divinity by the people of Of, the district from where their own forebears had come, was dependent on their going there. They came to Of, and in a short period of time, the people of Of were honoured (*şereflendi*) with the religion of Islam. One of the two learned men from Maraş died in Paçan [Maraşlı] village where he was buried. The other died in the higher reaches of the district of Of as he was returning to his own country. This is the story of the deceased hodja.[1]

Umur cast doubt on the tradition both as an account of the conversion of the Oflus and as an account of the Maraşlılar, even though he accepted that conversions has taken place as a result of efforts of members of the learned class. He reminded his readers that villagers did not speak either Turkish or Greek with the same accent and did not use the same vocabulary in different parts of the district. This indicated that groups of Turkish-speakers as well as groups of Greek-speakers had arrived at different times and had come from different places. In other words, any story of a mass conversion had to be doubted since the Oflus were a composite population. He also tells his readers that he had visited the reputed grave of one of the two Maraşlılar sometime around 1910 in Paçan [Maraşlı] village in the upper western valley of Of.[2] He found that the grave was little more than a pile of stones, lacking any inscription. When he asked the villagers how they knew that the stones marked the grave of one of the two Maraşlılar, they replied that this had been revealed to someone in a dream. Umur comments that the graves of a number of learned men from Of had been preserved and venerated for many years. How then was it possible that the graves of the two Maraşlılar had been neglected

---

[1] Umur (1949; 8-9).

[2] The grave was commemorated by a monument some years later, and this monument was refurbished on one or more occasions. It featured an inscription in Latin letters when I saw it in the 1970s.

and forgotten when they were otherwise celebrated by tradition? In all probability, the pile of rocks did not mark the grave of one of the Maraşlılar.

We can agree with Umur that the alternative tradition contains little reliable information about what happened in the district of Of after it became part of the Ottoman Empire; however, it may tell us something about the way in which the Oflus were thinking about their place in the imperial regime during the late nineteenth and early twentieth century. For even if the alternative tradition reaches us in the language of the Turkish Republic of the 1940s rather than the Ottoman Empire of the 1880s, its plot appears to be intact.[1]

Unlike the story of Osman Efendi, the story of the Maraşlılar does not take the form of a biography. Instead, there are two unnamed members of the Christian learned class (âlim) who depart from Of and two unnamed members of the Muslim learned class who return a thousand years later. This mythic device accomplishes three functions. It temporalizes the process of conversion so that it spans the period between the founding of the first Muslim community in Medina and the opening of the second century of Ottoman incorporation of Trabzon. It collectivizes the process of conversion by describing it as the movement of an entire community from Christianity to Islam. It territorializes the process of conversion by situating one grave further down and another grave further up the upper western valley.[2] The story therefore takes the form of a local history of a specific people living in a specific land but situated in the world history of all the Muslims (umma) living in all the land of Islam (dâr al-islâm). The accomplishment of a single individual named Osman Efendi has slipped into the background while a people of a land among other peoples in all the world has come into the foreground.

Like the story of Osman Efendi, the story of the Maraşlılar also concedes the occurrence of a mass conversion. So both versions would appear to be responding to Orthodox Christian traditions of Bishop Alexandros. But now the alternative tradition has directly and explicitly engaged the nationalist

---

[1] Since Umur writes that he heard the tradition from his childhood teacher and that he knew of the tradition by the time of his visit to Paçan [Maraşlı] village, I conclude that the version he cites was in place by no later than the 1910s, but probably dates from no later 1880s.

[2] The territorialization was extended sometime in the 1970s or 1980s when an old grave located near the coastline of the eastern border of the district was attributed to a third individual from Maraş; so there is now a tomb in Paçan [Maraşlı] village, one near Eskipazar, and one in Yente [Çayıroba] village. I did not meet anyone in Of who questioned the story of the Maraşlılar, but many Oflus do not accept that the tombs commemorating them were their true burial places.

oriented version, since it is a story of a people attached to a land. This idea is not a particularly salient aspect of Islamic belief and practice, but it is at the very foundation of nationalism.[1] In this respect, the story of the Maraşlılar has made further concessions in order better to insist on differences. The people of the land form a community, not by language or custom, but by their openness to the truth, supplemented by God's favor. So the Oflus are a nation by religion not a nation by ethnicity.

This substitution of religion for ethnicity would seem to emphasize the role of a clerical elite, hence learning and argument. This is not quite the case. The two priests are chosen first by a king and then by an emperor because of their excellence as scholars. They travel to Medina to engage in a debate with Caliph Ömer concerning the relative merits of Christianity and Islam. However, the story here tells us that religious truth is not best mediated by argument and evidence. Here is the sentence that describes the conversion of the two priests before Caliph Ömer: 'When they saw his simple way of life, his great and boundless justice, his compassion before Muslims, and his majesty before unbelievers, overcome by his excellent qualities and *without even entering into the dispute*, they immediately accepted Islam.' The two priests convert as a result of their direct personal witness of the qualities of an individual to whom the truth has been revealed. The story then places this direct personal witness in the lineage of the people of the land.

Now the story has to be admired for its grace and dignity in the local context. The people of Of were descended from immigrants and settlers who included groups of Turkic, Greek, and Kurdish peoples, not to mention more solitary representatives of other ethnic groups of Anatolia, the Caucasus, and the Balkans. At the time it was circulating, the very large majority of the inhabitants of the district was Ottoman Muslim. So the story of the Maraşlılar construed an otherwise ethnically heterogeneous population as a homogeneous community. This is an admirable accomplishment if one considers that it would have been easy to promote resentment and hostility among the inhabitants of Of by emphasizing differences in language, custom, memory, and history. In the larger imperial context, of course, the story pointed to the precedence of the Muslims in regard to the smaller but nonetheless considerable numbers of Christians.

---

[1] I have to concede that Umur might have had some interest in 'nationalizing' the tradition when he was writing his book in 1949. See Meeker (2002; Chap. 9). Still, I would argue that Umur was repeating the tradition more or less as he had received it, since he was interested in criticizing it rather than using it to support his own nationalist outlook.

This brings us to an aspect of the alternative tradition that both aligns it and opposes it to nationalism. In the story, Caliph Ömer is the Muslim counterpart of the Christian king and the Christian emperor. Here we should recall that the late nineteenth century, when this story had begun to circulate, was one in which kings and emperors were beginning to claim they represented specific nations.[1] Moreover, the kings and emperors in question were almost all Christian just as the nations they claimed to represent were also almost all Christian. This should alert us to signs that the story of the Maraşlılar might be suggesting that a Muslim nation was different from a Christian nation just as a caliph was different from a Christian king and emperor. Such a contention is embedded in the story. The Emperor of Byzantium communicates bureaucratically by writing, first with the Caliph Ömer and then with the King of Trabzon. In doing so, he makes an arrangement for a debate and then searches his realm for men of learning. As has already been noted, the two priests discover instead a truth in the personal presence of the Caliph so that no argument takes place and no evidence is presented.

Now this story of the Maraşlılar is circulating rather late in the period of imperial bureaucratic modernization, at a moment when state officials were engaged in the codification, that is to say, bureaucratization, of the imperial legal system, an effort that did not spare the sacred law of Islam. So the story harbours more than a criticism of nationalism based on ethnicity, it also harbours a criticism of a state system based on bureaucratic supervision. The story points to a Muslim nation where personal religious virtues are the basis of social relations that are in turn the basis of centralized governmental authority. This is the vision that appears before the priests as they gaze upon the Caliph and observe 'his simple way of life, his great and boundless justice, his compassion before Muslims, and his majesty before unbelievers.' This is the old form of imperial legitimacy that moved downward and outward among ordinary Muslims, where it became the basis of complaints lodged against the verticality, legalism, and luxury of the imperial state system during the post-classical period.

During the period of bureaucratic modernization, the old form of imperial legitimacy had acquired new significance and importance for the state-societies of the coastal region. The aghas in the coastal districts of the province of Trabzon had gradually lost their military positions and functions in the course of the nineteenth century. At the same time, they had become

---

[1] See Anderson (1991).

more systematically integrated within the centralized bureaucracy. So the hierarchy of interpersonal networks in the coastal districts not only remained in place but acquired new kinds of power and authority as the population came under more systematic bureaucratic surveillance and supervision. The image of Caliph Ömer in the story of the Maraşlılar is a critique of this new kind of agha composed by a new kind of hodja. This dates the story of the Maraşlılar to the 1870s or 1880s, the period during which religious brotherhoods, such as the Nakşibendi and Kaderi, first set down roots in the district of Of. From this period, a local academic tradition of teaching and learning, based on argument and evidence, was supplemented by a local tradition of religious leadership and association, based on charismatic religious virtues. [1]

Before leaving the alternative tradition, I must now mention its most remarkable feature that I have so far passed over in silence. The story of the Maraşlılar emphasizes the identity and destiny of a people attached to a land, at the expense of any reference to the founding and extension of the Ottoman Empire. In this respect, the story of the Maraşlılar contrasts with the story of Osman Efendi. It explains how the Oflus became a Muslim society by personal witness of the truth of Islam rather than how a member of the learned class of the Ottoman Empire missionized the Oflus. The story of the Maraşlılar is then every bit a myth of nation and not at all a myth of empire. If this is correct, we can also say that the Oflus were neither mired in backward feudal practices nor passive targets of state reforms during the late nineteenth century but actively coming to grips with nationalist ideology, religious revival, and bureaucratic centralism. Nonetheless, the Orthodox Christians of Trabzon were unable to recognize this trend of counter-nationalism in the district of Of, precisely because its inhabitants symbolized the impropriety and illegitimacy of state and society in the Ottoman Empire. To press home this last point, I shall conclude by citing the comments of one of the most knowledgeable of the later British consuls.

### Consul Biliotti Describes the Muslims of Trabzon

I have noted that the British and French consuls lost interest in the local elites of Trabzon once the latter were no longer in a position to challenge the

---

[1] In the district of Of, it is generally believed that religious leaders of religious brotherhoods did not arrive until the Hamidian period. Their emergence among the religious teachers and students of Of would have almost certainly been associated with criticism of the academic and bureaucratic character of the old imperial religious establishment. As a late indication of this shift, see Gologlu's (1975; 54) citation of Şakir Şevket, where he refers to 'Osman Efendi' by using expressions, 'Şeyh Osman' and 'Maraşlı Şeyh,' that do not appear in the original text.

centralized government. On occasion, however, the consuls did comment on the Muslims of the coastal region, usually insisting on their 'hybridity' and 'anarchy' in negative terms. I shall consider the reports of British Consul Alfred P. Biliotti because some of his remarks would seem to be an exception to this generalization.

Biliotti was the son of a family of Italian origin linked to the island of Rhodes, apparently his birthplace. He had first entered the consular service in 1856, at the age of 23, on the island of Rhodes, his residence at that time, and was assigned to Trabzon in 1873 where he remained as a consul until 1885.[1] By his Levantine background, he could himself be described as a member of a new imperial citizenry that arose during the later nineteenth century, one that was composed of civil servants, professionals, and businessmen. At the moment of his arrival in Trabzon, he was entirely familiar with the multi-ethnic and multi-religious character of the provincial population, and unlike other British and French consuls he had immediately grasped the peculiar character of its Muslim majority:

> Of the other [districts] of the Southern Black Sea coast, I shall not speak in detail, for, although heterogeneous in origin and character, the Mussulmans inhabiting them may be considered as having homogeneous affinities by religious conviction and political ties with the Ottoman Empire, to which they are not adverse ...[2] It may be said, on the contrary, that the different elements forming these populations have lost all distinction of races, and that [Tiberians], Byzantines, Armenians, Turcomans, &c., are all blended together, and form, with the descendants of the Janissaries and [Sipahis], a single body of faithful Mussulmans and patriotic Osmanlis.[3]

More an oriental than an orientalist, Biliotti understood that most of the Muslims of Trabzon formed a kind of imperial nation, even though they were of diverse ethnic and linguistic backgrounds. But he concedes this point only in order to assert the precedence of the Orthodox Christians. When Biliotti used the phrase, 'a single body of faithful Mussulmans and patriotic Osmanlis' in his consular report of 1873, he was thinking as a late imperial

---

[1] Biliotti presumably knew Italian, French, Greek, and Turkish, as well as English. He became British vice-consul of Rhodes at age 23, serving their from 1856 to 1873. He also served as a consular official in Crete from 1885 to 1899, and in Salonica until his retirement to Rhodes in 1903 (s. v. Biliotti, *Who was Who*). He was an amateur 'classical' archaeologist, like other members of his family, carrying out digs of Greco-Roman sites under the sponsorship of British patrons, such as the Earl of Derby (Biliotti 1974 [1874]). David Barchard tells me that Wyndham Graves, Biliotti's consular successor in Crete, considered him to a 'native' of Rhodes.

[2] In the complete passage, Biliotti seems to refer to all the Muslims of the southern Black Sea coast *except* those in the province of Trabzon; however, a reading of the entire report confirms that he has in mind the Muslims in Trabzon, except for other groups he had just mentioned.

[3] Biliotti, Sept. 25, 1873 as quoted in Şimşir (1982: 73). Also see a similar reference to the Muslims of Trabzon by Biliotti in PRO FO 195 1141 Jan. 1877.

citizen. That is to say, he was arguing the legitimacy of the Ottoman government as the legitimate representative of an Ottoman population. In asserting the case for the Ottoman Empire (which might well have been doubted by at least some of his superiors) he was also arguing that the Orthodox Christians of Trabzon were best suited to lead and direct the regional Ottoman population. The Orthodox Christians were the only large, stable community in the province (unlike some of the Muslims who fragmented and divided). The Orthodox Christians were steadfastly opposed to Russian rule (unlike some of the Muslims who were rebels and separatists).[1] So Biliotti was asserting the existence of an imperial nation in Trabzon in 1873 as he was asserting that the precedence of the Orthodox Christians was necessary for the viability of this imperial nation.

A decade later, Biliotti had turned decidedly sour on the Muslims of Trabzon. The cause of this change in sentiment was almost certainly due to a shift in official policies in the late Ottoman Empire. As Deringil has recently demonstrated, Sultan Abdülhamit II (1876-1909) pursued linguistic, religious, and educational policies whereby imperial rule would be buttressed by an imperial people. In other words, the Ottomans had turned to policies of imperial nationalism during the same period that the English, French, German, and Russians had turned to policies of imperial nationalism. The only difference was the reliance of the former on a religious as opposed to an ethnic nationalism. These new official policies would raise a question about the position of the Orthodox Christians in the province of Trabzon even as they would lend a fresh legitimacy to the state-societies of the coastal districts. Accordingly, Biliotti's argument that the Orthodox Christians might lead and direct the Muslim population had been overtaken by events. Iin response, he began to insist on the impropriety and illegitimacy of the state societies of the coastal region.

During 1885, his last year as consul in Trabzon, Biliotti found an occasion to comment on the large Muslim majority in the coastal districts between Batum and Trabzon. He would have had precisely the population of these very districts in mind when he had described the Trabzonlus as 'children of Janissaries and Sipahis harvested from the Tiberians, Byzantines, Armenians, and Turkomans.' But now, this insightful even if overly romanticized observation was replaced with scorn and ridicule. In the course of a lengthy report on secular schools among both the Muslims and Christians,

---

[1] To make this case, Biliotti exaggerates the numbers of Orthodox Christians near the provincial capital while emphasizing the dispersion and instability of the Muslims.

he paused to comment on the plethora of religious teachers, students, and
academies among the Muslims between Batum and Trabzon:

> The number of medressés [higher religious academies] is especially great
> eastward of Trebizond. // The majority of the inhabitants of these districts
> are the descendants of Byzantines who began to embrace Islamism about
> 150 years since [1885 - 150 = 1735]. // Numerous medressés may have been
> necessary at that period for the purpose of instructing proselytes, but their
> usefulness is no longer apparent. One of the present undeniable results of
> these institutions is to enable the youths attending them to evade
> conscription. Another probable result is to entertain a feeling of hostility
> toward Christians at large, for hardly any live in these districts. Furthermore
> no progress seems to be made in good moral[s], as the native population
> eastward of Trebizond is more addicted to brigandage and murder than in any
> other part of the Vilayet. // Not withstanding their so thoroughly learning
> the Turkish language, they continue to use in familiar intercourse, a corrupt
> Greek dialect called Lazico ... Another *remarkable fact* is that with all their
> fanaticism they still stick to Christian Customs and traditions, and that the
> families that furnished Christian priests in bygone time, are those in which
> the greater number of mollahs are to be found. // They preserve with
> reverence their sacred books, the sacerdotal vestments and emblems of their
> forefathers and put the greatest faith in their healing power. They impose
> the former on sick persons and to drink the communion cup is reserved as
> the last hope of recovery in desperate cases of disease. Pilgrimages with
> offerings in a renowned Byzantine monastery, that of Soumela, at eight
> hours distance from Trebizond, dedicated to the Virgin, are not unknown
> occurrences. But in spite, or perhaps, because of all this, the Mussulmans
> Eastward of Trebizond, especially those of Of, are the most fanatical in this
> vilayet. [My italics].[1]

Biliotti had indeed related a series of remarkable facts. By his account, the
populations in the eastern districts were almost all Muslim, in contrast to
other parts of the coastal region. On the other hand, this had not always been
the case since they still spoke older Byzantine languages among themselves
and still preserved Christian scriptures, vestments, and relics. Yet, at the same
time, they were now among the most 'fanatical' of the Muslims in all the
province, having come to know Turkish thoroughly and to specialize in
Islamic teaching and learning. On the other hand, these accomplishments
notwithstanding, the many mollahs and medreses that existed in the eastern
districts had no apparent effect on morals whatsoever, since the peoples of the
eastern districts specialized in robbery and homicide. All told, these signs of
having used their former accomplishments as Byzantines for the purpose of
new accomplishments as Ottomans were to no avail. For one could not say
what the function of mollas and medreses should have been, save to
enable them to avoid conscription (in that part of the province that had always

---

[1] PRO FO 195/1521, 'Report on the Schools in the Vilayet of Trebizond,' May 1885.

provided large numbers of soldiers for the Porte) and to encourage hostility toward Christians (who however were virtually non-existent among them). If Biliotti's superiors believed this section of his consular report, they would believe anything.

Each negative observation in the cited passage was one that outsiders commonly applied to the Greek-speaking Muslims of Of. So Biliotti was describing all the districts between Batum and Trabzon by the swarm of rumours that had been provoked by these Greeks who had become Muslims. For Biliotti, as for other ethnic and linguistic nationalists, the people of Of had become a symbol of the unacceptability and incomprehensibility of the state societies of Trabzon. As for the people of Of, their specialization in religious teaching and learning would put them in a position to benefit from the new top-down official policies; nonetheless, they had begun to travel the road of an imperial nationalism long before the idea had occurred to state officials.

## REFERENCES

### Archives

MAE CCCS: Republic of France. Ministère des Affaires Étrangères. Correspondance Consulaire et Commerciale. Turquie, Sinope. SANS: 1801-1811.

MAE CCCT L.: Republic of France. Ministère des Affaires Étrangères. Correspondance Consulaire et Commerciale. Turquie, Trébizonde. Livres 1-13: 1800-1901. BPMT: Bulletin Politique et Militaire de Trébizonde. An official characterization of some of these consular reports.

PRO FO: United Kingdom. Public Record Office. Foreign Office. Consultation of consular reports classed under 195/ 4, 101, 173, 225, 812, 1238, 1329, 1381, 1420, 1521, 2135; 524/ 1, 2; and 526/ 8.

### Published

Anderson, B. 1991 *Imagined Communities: Reflections on the Origins and Spread of Nationalism,* London; Verso Press.

Balivet, M. 1999. 'Textes de fin d'empire, récits de fin du monde; à propos de quelques thèmes communs aux groupes de la zone byzantino-turque' in *Les traditions apocalyptiques au tournant de la chute de Constantinople,* edited by Benjamin Lellouch and Stéphane Yerasimos, Paris: L'Harmattan; 5-18.

Beauchamp, M. 1813. 'Mémoire géographique et historique du voyage de Constantinople à Trébizonde,' in *Voyage en Perse, en Arménie, en Asie Mineure, et à Constantinople* by Jaques Morier, Vol. 2; 261-320.

Biliotti, A. 1974 [1874] 'Report on Saddak, the Supposed Site of Ancient Satala' *Anatolian Studies* Vol. 24; 225-44.

Bryer, A. 1969. 'The Last Laz Risings and the Downfall of the Pontic Derebeys, 1812-40.' *Bedi Kartlisa* Vol. 26; 191-210.

Bryer, A. 1970. 'The Tourkokratia in the Pontos: Some problems and preliminary conclusions.' *Neo-Hellenika* Vol. 1; 30-54.

Decourdemanche, J. (alias Osman Bey). 1874. 'Lazistan' *Izvestija Imperatorskogo Russkogo Geograficeskogo Obscestua* Vol. 10; 356-64.

Deringil, S. 1998. *The Well-Protected Domains: Ideology and the Legitimation of Power in the Ottoman Empire, 1876 — 1909* London; I. B. Tauris.

Fontanier, V. 1829. *Voyage en Orient, entrepris par ordre du gouvernement français de 1821 à 1829* Paris; Librairie Universelle.

Fontanier, V. 1834. *Voyage en Orient, entrepris par ordre du gouvernement français de 1830 à 1833* Paris; Librairie de Dumont.

Gerasimos, A. 1992. *The Greeks of Asia Minor: Confession, Community, and Ethnicity in the Nineteenth Century* Kent, Ohio; Kent State University Press.

Gologlu, M. 1975. *Trabzon Tarihi: Fetihten Kurtuluşa Kadar* Ankara; Kalite Matbaası.

Gondicas, D. and Issawi C. 1999. *Ottoman Greeks in the Age of Nationalism: Politics, Economy, and Society in the Nineteenth Century* Princeton, NJ; The Darwin Press.

Hasluck, F. 1921. 'The Crypto-Christians of Trebizond.' *Journal of Hellenic Studies* Vol. 41; 199-202.

Janssens, E. 1969. *Trébizonde en Colchide* Brussels; Presses Universitaires de Bruxelles.

Karadenizli, K. 1954. *Trabzon Tarihi* (Turkification of Şakir Şevket) Ankara: privately printed.

Koch, K. 1855. 'Reise von Redut-Kaleh nach Trebizond' in *Die Kaukasischen Länder und Armenien* edited by K. Koch, Leipzig; C. B. Lorck, 65-114.

Meeker, M. 2002. *A Nation of Empire: The Ottoman Legacy of Turkish Modernity.* Berkeley; University of California Press.

Palgrave, W. 1887. *Ulysses or Scenes and Studies in Many Lands* London; Macmillan and Co.

Poutouridou, M. 1997-1998. 'The Of Valley and the Coming of Islam: The Case of the Greek-Speaking Muslims', *Deltio Kentrou Mikrasiatikan Spoudon* Vol. 12; 47-90.

Rottiers, Le Colonel [B.] 1829. *Itinéraire de Tiflis à Constantinople* Bruxelles; Chez H. Tarlier.

s. v. Biliotti, Sir Alfred. 1929. In *Who was who, a companion to 'Who's who', containing the biographies of those who died during the period 1916-1928*. London: A. & C. Black limited.

Şakir Ş. *Trabzon Tarihi* 1877/1294. Istanbul.

Şimşir, B. 1982. *British Documents on Ottoman Armenians*, Vol. 1; 1856-1880. Ankara: Türk Tarih Kurumu Basımevi.

Slade, A. 1833. *Records of Travels in Turkey, Greece, etc. and of a Cruise in the Black Sea, with the Capitan Pasha, in the years of 1829, 1830, and 1831*, 2nd ed., 2 vols, London; Saunders and Otley.

Umur, H. 1949. *Of ve Of Muharebeleri*, Istanbul; Güven Basımevi.

Zürcher, E. 1999. 'The vocabulary of Muslim nationalism.' *International Journal of the Sociology of Language*, Vol. 137; 81-92.

# 32. 'WE GOT ON WELL WITH THE TURKS': CHRISTIAN-MUSLIM RELATIONS IN LATE OTTOMAN TIMES

Renée HIRSCHON

The puzzle addressed in this chapter arises from a period of intensive anthropological fieldwork in the 1970s in Kokkinia (officially known as Nikaia), a locality settled by Anatolian Christians in the 1920s who were expelled under the terms of the 1923 Lausanne Convention, the compulsory population exchange between Greece and Turkey. The epistemological issue relates to the ways in which history is constructed, given that different versions of past events and conditions may coexist. I am concerned specifically with the various and contradictory depictions of relations between Christians and Muslims in the last phase of the Ottoman Empire.

In short, the question is how are we to interpret a sharply contradictory picture, in this case presented within the Greek context.[1] On one hand, the official discourse of hostility engenders everyday stereotypical views, expressed in stock phrases such as 'The Turks are barbarians' (*oi Toúrkoi eínai várvaroi'*), and the cliché designation of the Ottoman period as '400 years of slavery' (*tetrakósia chrónia sklaviá*). On the other, there are many accounts of the uprooted refugees themselves whose first hand recollections are recorded in archival and oral history sources, and can be starkly juxtaposed and summarised in a frequently repeated phrase: 'We got on well with the Turks' *(kalá pernoúsame me tous Toúrkous)*. In this contradiction between the official historiography and that of oral narratives, independent contemporary accounts play a critical role. The contribution of Hasluck's writings to our understanding of life in the final decades of the Ottoman period, as well as the accounts of other foreign commentators and travellers, is here most valuable. For those concerned with the verifiable nature of historical records, they constitute independent corroborative evidence for the evaluation of the historical (as opposed to mythical) basis of oral accounts since they provide an independent source of information. As will be shown, the overall picture is

---

[1] A parallel examination might be conducted from the Turkish side, with undoubtedly interesting comparative results.

more differentiated than that of the prevalent nationalistic discourse and corroborates the generally benign view of the refugees themselves.

I have, therefore, been provoked into a critical examination of our understanding of the past, essentially to re-assess the significance of the memories of the displaced Christians of the Ottoman Empire within the prevailing context of commonly accepted ideas of history. The direct source of this information was the *Mikrasiates* and their descendants, who had to pay the price of the failed irredentist attempt to accomplish the *'Megali Idea'* for a Greater Greece, which culminated in the defeat of the Greek army in Anatolia in 1922. Living on a daily basis in Kokkinia, a poor refugee settlement in Piraeus, I was fortunate enough to become familiar with the perceptions of life in the Greek state of these people — the last of the Ottomans — and their memories of their homeland.

The voices of the Asia Minor refugees (*Mikrasistes prosfyges*) who were settled in Piraeus, in other urban quarters, in ordered settlements on the outskirts of villages in northern Greece, and on the islands, were ignored for decades. The national trauma of a defeated ideal had left wounds which went too deep. While I was doing my fieldwork, very little was heard about this mass of uprooted people and their subsequent fate in the Greek state (the influx had represented one in four of the Greek population). It was only after the fiftieth anniversary of their expulsion that increasing attention began to be directed to this painful chapter in modern Greek history. In sharing daily life with these people, I heard many articulate testimonies about life before their expulsion; these were not elicited through direct questioning but were expressed unsolicited in everyday contexts. These were woven into everyday activities in Kokkinia, a place far removed from their roots, at first utterly alien, and even decades later, never quite a homeland.

This made me reflect on the way in which memory and narratives about the past (which are at risk of being lost) operate in creating cultural continuity, and are connected with the present. These thoughts returned to me when, from the late 1980s I became Professor at the University of the Aegean on the Greek island of Lesbos only seven miles off the Turkish coast. My office in Mytilini had an uninterrupted view across a tranquil expanse of water to coastal settlements opposite (*apénanti)*: on clear days you could even see the houses. At that time, one of considerable tension in the relations between the two countries, the words of people in Kokkinia kept coming to mind: 'We got on well with the Turks — it was the politicians who brought the hatred' (*kalá pernoúsame me tous toúrkous, i politikí mas férane to mísos*).[1] The challenge presented by this message, so contradictory to the received wisdom that an ancient hatred divides Greeks and Turks, is the focus of this paper. Grim parallels with the fate of the peoples of the former Federal Republic of Yugoslavia as they engage in belated nation-state formation add a dimension of political relevance to this work.

The aftermath of the 1999 earthquakes and the current rapprochement between Greece and Turkey at the diplomatic political level has verified dramatically a long-ignored but little-known insight — the deep repository of good will and sense of commonality at the popular level which was so much part of the narratives of the people of refugee origin who settled in Kokkinia and other parts of Greece.

*History as myth*

In embarking on some kind of historical anthropology,[2] we have to engage with the challenging question of 'what constitutes history?' Opposing approaches can be discerned and, odd as it may seem to those involved in postmodernist discourse, textual analysis and other critical pursuits, the objective nature of history as a factual and definitive record of past events is promulgated even now by some historians with a more positivist approach. The objective veracity of history is a viewpoint usually held in opposition to what is seen as the subjective and mythical quality of personal narrative about the past, and is by no means an outmoded view in some academic institutions where oral history and tradition may be treated with scepticism, caution and even summarily dismissed for its 'unreliability'.

Nevertheless, the effect of post-modernism on both history and anthropology is striking and has clearly led to a convergence of approaches. A fruitful blend is to be found in the work of Elizabeth Tonkin, a social anthropologist long-concerned with oral history. She argues forcefully for dissolving the dichotomy between objectivist and subjectivist history as well as between history and myth. All of these oppositional types she regroups into a generic and inclusive category in which they are redefined as various 'representations of pastness'. According to this approach, a more useful distinction is that of 'history-as-lived' and 'history-as-recorded', implying a

---

[1] Hirschon (1998; 30).
[2] Cf. Cohn (1987; 42ff).

complementary set of relations between oral and written history, and between personal narratives and documents.[1]

As a social anthropologist and not a historian, I have concentrated on personal narratives, oral accounts and allusions, those which are the people's own stories — the 'his-stories' or (more so in my experience) the 'her-stories'. The narratives of the older generation, particularly those of the women, rich in detail and in emotional evocations, provided colourful pictures of the diversity of Anatolian towns in the early part of the twentieth century, of a cosmopolitan and heterogeneous mix of peoples, and of a way of life whose passing was imminent. The people I knew in 1972 were young adults before the expulsion and most of them have now passed away. Their vivid memories constitute a source of oral social history which it is incumbent upon us to record and to evaluate.

My motives for this contribution are, therefore, to re-call and thus re-vive — 'to give life to' — what might otherwise be the lost voices of Anatolia. In this I am following Tonkin's reminder that 'people without access to authoritative voices … are hampered in their representations of the past both to themselves and to others'.[2] When the institutional structures to retain these informal accounts are lacking, where there is no active concern with oral and local history, she notes that the danger of losing the narratives is acute. My endeavour here is a kind of salvage operation, to circumvent the possible loss of one kind of 'representation of pastness'.

In re-calling the personal accounts, however, one is also confronted by another and countervailing 'representation of pastness', that of the official and publicly propounded history. A marked disjunction exists between state history-as-recorded, that taught in schools, in textbooks, and expressed in the everyday views of most citizens. The Anatolian voices I heard did not represent the past in the same way. How different are the his- and her -stories of those who actually lived in those places from those that are re-written, re-vised, and re-formed in a nationalistic framework which leads to a purposeful distortion of the Ottoman past.

The intention then in this paper is to construct a view of the past, which might reconcile the contradictions between the 'history we are taught' and the 'history they have lived'. It should remind people in these now

---

[1] Tonkin (1991).
[2] Tonkin (1991; 26).

separate societies that they once shared an amicable past, one which they have allowed to be forgotten, or to be purposefully distorted. In this endeavour, the work of Hasluck plays an important part. Inherent in this task is the suggestion floated in Sider and Smith that the anthropologist's task of 're-presenting local voices' also extends furthermore to 'make these voices matter'.[1] Their call to relate our work on the past as it is remembered to the contemporary world, that in which it is taught, has direct political import and even policy implications.

*Difference as identity*

In 1972, conducting doctoral research in Kokkinia, a poor locality in the metropolis of Athens-Piraeus (population 86,000 in 1970 in the unbroken urban expanse of over 4 million), I rented the front room of a refugee shack on one of the main roads of the district. My first surprise was learning that a slummy district where I was living, not far from the port, ostensibly no different from other parts of the city, was not just a part of the urban metropolis inhabited by Greeks -'*Ellines*' — but by people whose self-designation clearly differentiated themselves from the society around them.

This was a refugee settlement, established in the 1920s for the mass of destitute and traumatised people who had fled or been expelled from the Anatolian and Black Sea areas, from Thrace and Kappadocia, following the Greek army's rout in 1922.[2] I was surprised to discover that the people with whom I was living, Greeks by all objective criteria without any distinguishing features of difference, consistently referred to themselves as 'refugees', '*prósfyges*', or 'Asia Minorites', '*Mikrasiátes*'. My landlord was Prokopi, born in Ankara in the 1890s, then in his seventies, who had a small kiosk selling bread and cigarettes, and his wife Marika was a devout woman from the small town of Sungurlu near Ankara. Within days of unpacking my things in a rented room in the home of this elderly couple, I became aware of a set of categories which I had not expected. 'We Mikrasiates don't do things like that', Marika would say, referring to whole range of activities, from food preparation to housekeeping, to speech and comportment, recreation, religious observances. 'Those Greeks...', other women friends would tell me, 'they don't know how to ... ', describing in derogatory terms the incompetence of

---

[1] Sider and Smith (1997;13).
[2] Pentzopoulos (1962).

the locals in every possible range of activity.[1] Further, in complaining about government or administrative matters, they would deplore their treatment by 'those Ellines — what they've done to us..' (*aftí i Ellines, ti mas kánane..*) The fact that some fifty years after their arrival they expressed a strong sense of identity which marked them off from the rest of the Greek population, from the 'locals' whom they characterised with a number of derogatory labels, is of considerable interest in itself, especially as it applied as much to the original refugees as it did to their children and grandchildren, the second and third generations.[2]

What became abundantly clear as I got to know them, living on a daily basis and sharing in the everyday round of activities for over a year, was that this sense of identity was promoted by the frequent and vivid references to life in their homeland, (*stin patrída*), by the many tales and accounts of the experiences of the older people in their villages and towns. Indeed, it was a world of many layers, the physical environment imbued with images of past and distant places, co-existent and co-incident, such was the force of the continual narrative process. The older people, among them my close friends — Avraam from Nigdi/ Niğde, Prokopi from Ankara, Marika from Sungurlu, Margaro from Vourla/Urla, Olympia from Magnisia/Manisa, Koula from Pergamo/Bergama, Athina from Antalya, and Eliso from Brusa/Bursa — painted such graphic pictures of the world they had inhabited in their youth that I, though a complete stranger to the eastern Aegean, became so familiar that I felt I had shared with them that way of life in the last phase of the Ottoman period.

One remarkable common theme in the verbal accounts of these refugees is that relations with their Turkish neighbours had been good, and that for long periods there were harmonious relations with other groups. 'We got on well with the Turks', men and women alike were wont to say, '*Kalá pernoúsame me tous Toúrkous*'. This theme recurred with great regularity accompanying, too, the accounts of the exodus from their homes. Even within hair-raising narratives recalling all the terror and pain of uprooting, of loss of family members, the dislocation of arriving in turmoil in the unprepared, ill-endowed Greek state, it is notable that they could nonetheless distinguish their experience of daily life with their neighbours from the traumatic events of their displacement. The fact that these people had been violently uprooted, had lost their families, homes, property, employment, makes the quality of these

---

[1] Hirschon (1998; 30-35).
[2] Tsimouris (1997).

statements even more remarkable. The first point to note then is the lack of bitterness and rancour, and the absence of generalised hatred for Turkish people, even though they had reason to express such sentiments.

The second noteworthy point is the common conclusion: 'It was not the ordinary Turk who provoked the troubles' they would say. 'Our relations with Turks were good, it was the politicians who stirred up the trouble'. They attributed the hostilities between their communities to interference by the 'Great Powers'. Again and again, the conclusion would be 'The politicians made us hate one another'.[1] In more specific discussions on the changing position of the Christian populations of the Empire, the increasingly negative climate at that time was attributed to the influence of the Young Turks, a nationalistic movement of the first decades of the twentieth century, a time when new political aspirations were being fostered.[2]

The conviction that troubles were largely stirred up by politicians and 'the Great Powers' is a politically informed explanation. It might be attributed to the fact that Kokkinia was an area of marked left-wing orientation, a politicised locality, with a long-time record of supporting the Communist and other left wing parties.[3] But it is worth noting that the same views are also expressed orally and are recorded in the archival accounts of refugees settled in various rural locations, and from villages in northern Greece where both left and right wing allegiances developed.[4]

Arguments against the veracity of oral accounts of the past are sometimes categorically dismissive, attributing to them the romanticism and nostalgia to which uprooted exiles are held to be inescapably subject. The viewpoint taken here is, however, that these perceptions should be taken into account and evaluated seriously. As Tonkin reminds us, every oral narrative is contextual and should be heard as an interaction specific to the context. These oral accounts (archival sources from the late 1950s and 1960s, my fieldwork from the 70s) undoubtedly relate to the time and place of their happening. Nonetheless, given the nature of the forced expulsion from their homeland and their deep personal losses, the overall absence of acrimony and of generalised hatred or bitterness towards Turkish people presents a challenge to

---

[1] Hirschon (1998; 30).
[2] Zürcher (1998).
[3] Hirschon (1998; 46-8).
[4] Veremis (2003).

interpretation.[1] This is particularly striking since it contrasts with the stance of antipathy and belligerent hostility found among many younger Greeks in the 1970s, exacerbated after the Cyprus events in 1974.

*Text-ures of the past: history as lived*

In the accounts about life in Anatolia the awareness of social diversity was a striking feature. I was impressed by the familiarity which people of the older generation had with the existence, ways and customs of other groups, more evident among those from towns, but also among people from villages depending on the exact place of origin. Frequent references were made to the customs and ways of others: besides the most common references to Muslims, there were many to Jews, Armenians, Gipsies, Europeans of various nationalities, and to Levantines.[2] The majority of Ottoman Christians had lived in a multi-ethnic and diverse society, they had everyday knowledge which incorporated 'otherness' as a common human experience. A quality of cosmopolitanism permeates the accounts of the past given by these refugees. This contrasts with the world view of their contemporaries, local Greeks whose social experience derives from a strong emphasis on ethnic homogeneity, an experience similar in this respect to those who have grown up in the Turkish Republic. The importance of contact with the different ways of others is that it produces familiarity, removes the threat of the unknown, and may create the preconditions for greater respect as well as understanding.

In the oral accounts which refer to intercommunal relations, one feature is clearly revealed: the close interaction of Christians and Muslims and the extensive knowledge of the ways of others that existed in their multiethnic society, a sense of familiarity and of mutual accommodation.[3] A typical statement is that of Anna K. (b.1881) from Brusa: 'The Turks loved us, we lived well together. Greek and Turkish children sometimes threw stones at one

---

[1] In validating the oral tradition, a Greek folklorist has noted that 'The historical value of these texts is due to the fact that no one later can undertake with the same competence or authenticity the role of the first-hand witness' (Meraklis, 1992; 794). Indeed, the field of oral history and that of the study of narrative have achieved the status of disciplines in their own right. The use of outsiders' accounts, those of western observers as sources must also be carefully evaluated, for they are equally selective, often revealing more about the writer and his or her worldview than providing independent descriptions about a situation. The use of such sources poses some epistemological problems which are relevant to the content of this presentation but will not be dwelt on here.

[2] Abundant corroborative evidence of the diversity of populations and their relationships is provided by outsiders; contemporary writings on the region abound with descriptions of the various groups, see e.g. Lane Poole (1889), Ramsay (1917).

[3] Hirschon, forthcoming.

another, but we mothers stopped them. As long as Russia was there, we were the kings'.[1]

Revealed here is another theme, that of having a superior position despite being a subject people. This is conveyed in commonly heard phrases, such as 'We were well-off there — we had the Turks as our servants', or in the kindly but somewhat patronising way in which they recalled the Turks as slow, well-intentioned, lazy, or as lacking initiative. Paschalis S. (b.1882) was from an all-Greek village (previously mixed) called Dağsarsı/ Dansari/, 22km west of Brusa, having 140-60 houses. He was a Turkish speaker, and expressed some characteristic attitudes, saying:

> Turks didn't bother us at all there, they were afraid of us, not we of them. But we loved them and they loved us, we had a great friendship. If they did bother us, they were in for big trouble. We were well-off there. It was the Macedonian Turks who came from over here — they were fanatical and they spoiled them. Anyway we didn't pay any attention to the Turk ( .. *then díname pentára*..). We had no cause for worry (*then mas anisichoúse típota*).[2]

Alexandros K. (b.1881) from Demirtaş/Demirdesi, a large village of six to seven houses ten kilometres north of Brusa, asserted that they felt secure because of the size of their village. Sometimes they would beat up the Turks a bit, but usually they had few contacts besides commercial dealings (*aliverísi*). But he also added, 'They used to come to us if they wanted ouzo, we had good ouzo. Sometimes at *Bairami*, they would bring sweets to their acquaintances'.[3] This social dimension is a common theme, revealed in many other accounts.

*Language*

An interesting by-product of the cultural mix in this area was the extent of bilingualism. In the region of Brusa some of the so-called 'Greek' villages were predominantly Turkish-speaking. At school in Baylacık/Yialatzik, for example, they were taught Karamalidika (i.e. Turkish written in Greek script). In church, even though the Liturgy was in Greek, the Gospel was read in Turkish so that they could understand it. In Dağsarısı/Dansari where most people were Turkish-speaking, teaching at school was in Turkish and Greek,

[1] KMS: B.136.
[2] KMS: B137.
[3] KMS: B 138.

for a Greek teacher had been brought in from outside. In Demirtaş/Demirdesi, a large Greek-speaking village, bilingualism was widespread for the men knew Turkish, and through contact with co-workers, those women who worked in the silk industry in Brusa also spoke Turkish.[1]

It was striking that, in Kokkinia in the 1970s, many of the older people, the first generation of refugees, were barely literate but nonetheless were bilingual in Turkish (pre-Republican) and Greek, and those who had lived in larger cities were familiar with other languages and customs to some degree. This was quite unlike their contemporaries, monolingual and literate Greeks who had grown up in the nation-state. In Kokkinia during the early 1970s, cinemas regularly showed Turkish films. These were especially popular among the older women who praised them for their high moral tone (*semnótita*). In the households, I heard Turkish proverbs quoted, and naughty children were threatened with 'the stick of Sultan Mehmet'.

The importance of multilingualism is not to be taken lightly. It is little acknowledged that many thousands of Orthodox Christian newcomers to the Greek nation state in the 1920s were entirely Turkish-speaking or bilingual. This diversity was largely lost in the decades that followed. The loss was pointed out by the director of the archaeological museum in a Greek provincial town who recalled that, as a child, she had spoken Turkish to both her grandmothers who were from Asia Minor. When she went to school, however, she began to see the Turks as the enemy, and became ashamed of her heritage. She now feels angry that she was deprived of her bilingualism and the richness that this would have offered her. The suppression of minority languages is by no means confined to Greece; indeed, it is a common feature in the process of creating the nation-state as a homogeneous entity. An encouraging sign of change is the interest Greek students are now showing in learning Turkish, and the number of courses offered in universities.

*Ritual*

In everyday conversation in Kokkinia, references to other groups in Ottoman society occurred most often with regard to ritual life — to celebrations of the life cycle such as marriages, and to major religious festivals. These occurred spontaneously, usually at times of festivity. In Kokkinia, I heard many reminiscences about life in their homeland neighbourhoods as women recalled

---

[1] KMS: B136,137,138.

their relationships with those of other communities. Muslim customs of marriage and circumcision were described and I was told how food was exchanged between Greeks and Turks at the major festivals of Ramazan and Easter. References to the customs of Armenians were less common, depending on the place of origin, while the customs and practices of Jews were familiar to Anatolian Greeks from the towns.

In references to the contacts between Christians and Muslims, the striking feature is the impression of amicable and mutually tolerant relations. A characteristic anecdote is that of Constantina L. (b.1912) from Esmes, near Ismit/Nicomidia.

> With the Turks we were like brothers. At our weddings, our baptisms and all the Greek festivals they joined in, wearing their embroidered costumes, their cartridge belts, and firing deafening pistols. Not only did they celebrate with us, they treated us (*mas kernoúsane*) and threw their money about (*skorpoúsan pantoú leftá*). At Turkish festivals we all enjoyed ourselves, and danced '*antíkrista*[1]

Similarly, quoted in his biography, Athenagoras, Ecumenical Patriarch of the Orthodox Church in the 1960s, makes this clear statement about the kind of relationships he recalled:

> In my village there were both Turks and Christians, but we lived peacefully together; the Muslims were invited to christenings and in turn Christians were the guests at circumcision feasts. It was a sort of biblical coexistence and we all felt that we were the children of Abraham. The Muslims ate mutton and lamb during the festival of Baihram and we Christians ate the Easter lamb.[2]

A degree of religious and cultural borrowing exists as a feature in all mixed communities, and one obvious example is the practice of pilgrimage to the Holy Land by Anatolian Orthodox Christians. Although, pilgrimage is not prescribed as an act of grace in Christian dogma — indeed the injunction is to worship God in any place — nonetheless, Christians have indeed practised pilgrimage from at least the fourth century AD. Among Anatolian Christians, the aspiration was to visit Jerusalem, to worship at the Holy Places, and to be 'baptised' in the river Jordan. On their return they would prefix Hatzi/-enna to their name. Many Greek surnames starting Xatzi- show how widespread this custom was. This example of cultural borrowing indicates the significance of communication in a shared discourse with their Muslim neighbours.

---

[1] Quoted in Meraklis (1992; 799).

[2] Vaporis (1986; 7).

The fact that religious elements are borrowed does not shake the central commitments of the believer, and the process of syncretism is integral to the development of all religious systems in contact with others. The salient point is that the co-existence of different faiths may lead to the growth of mutual respect, and to the recognition that grace may be attained in different ways and through a variety of practices. Appropriation of holy sites by the conquering religion is described in various examples provided by Hasluck.[1] He remarks on the frequenting of Christian shrines by Turks as a commonplace.[2] Another example is provided by baptism, the most important rite in conferring Christian identity. Hasluck notes how it was accorded respect by Muslims, and many accounts exist of Muslim mothers who took their children to a priest for immersion in holy water, since they believed in its beneficial effects.[3] This is not to suggest that conversion followed immersion in holy water, nor does the use of the Christian cross as a charm or phylactery. Rather it demonstrates a mutual respect for and recognition of the power and verity of different faiths.

The accounts of foreign writers provide independent evidence and corroborate accounts of the quality of intercommunal contacts. Here, Hasluck plays a key role with abundant references to ritual observances and to practices at particular holy places, thus validating the accounts of the Asia Minor refugees about their life before the expulsion. In addition, there are mentions of saints or priests, of emirs and dervishes who are called on for healing by followers of the other faith.[4] For example, St John the Russian, widely known among Asia Minor Christians for his miraculous powers, was revered also by Muslims.[5] My landlady Marika and others from the locality told me how his shrine in Urgup/Prokopi was regarded as holy by local Muslims and visited for blessings from far and wide.

Among the other Christian saints who were respected by Muslims, particularly mentioned is St George. Describing life in Brusa when she was a young girl, Anna K. recalled how on St George's day Turks went up to his shrine on Mt Uludağ/Olympus and prayed. St George was particularly revered by Muslims; he was called Xidirilles and his day on 23rd April has a seasonal significance, for it is always near Easter/Pascha. In Brusa, Anna K. recalled how the Turks waited eagerly to get the dyed red eggs which, when broken,

---

[1] Hasluck (1929;11-13, 21ff).
[2] Hasluck (1929;66).
[3] Hasluck (1929; 34).
[4] Hasluck (1929; 8, note 1).
[5] Hasluck (1929; 65).

'would bring on the summer heat'. Greek women would dye large numbers of eggs, even sending them to the dye-shop (*vapheíon*) so that they could share them out, together with Easter bread (*tsouréki*) to friends and neighbours. 'In return' she said, 'they would give us sweetmeats, that is, the *sarailides*, the wives of *pasádes* did this — the poor couldn't always reciprocate'.[1]

This was by no means unique: even today the widespread popularity of St George is attested by the huge crowds numbering tens of thousands who visit the island of Büyükada/Prinkipo on his name-day where his church is venerated. A recent volume dedicated to the settlement of Erenköyü/Renkioyi (ancient Ofrinion in the Troad) similarly describes how the main church dedicated to St George with its miracle-working icon was much revered by Muslims who would come for the forty days before the Saint's day bringing votive offerings (*támata*).[2]

The belief in the healing powers at the holy shrines of others is well documented. For example, the Church of St Dimitrios in Salonika 'was ... to some extent adopted as a place of healing by the Moslems'.[3] Similarly, the Mosque of Eyyub in the City was reverenced by Christians and this 'attracted to it a Greek clientele' for healing at its sacred well.[4] The Church of St Amphilochius in Konya was 'a pilgrimage for both religions'[5] and many other examples are described for both sides. Healing at the 'holy springs' (*ayiásmata*) was another practice frequently mentioned. The vivid descriptions of the town of Brusa always mention the abundance of water sources. Thus Anna K. recalled how :

> Turkish women used to go to our holy springs, they'd bathe and become well because of their faith. Many of us who didn't have the same faith wouldn't benefit. They would even come to our priest and would be healed. They'd say to us 'You go to the *hotza* to be read over'. But we would say 'It's not allowed' (*then kánei*).[6]

These quotations are by no means confined to Brusa, a multi-ethnic town, and its region. There were many hundreds of other mixed settlements, each having its own tradition, history, and dynamics. The expulsion of the Christian population in 1922-3 marked a radical break in the long-term, though not

---

[1] KMS; B 136.

[2] Giannakopoulos (1995; 29, 70-1).

[3] Hasluck (1929; 16).

[4] Hasluck (1929; 79, 82).

[5] Hasluck (1929; 17).

[6] KMS; B 136.

necessarily constant, mixture of different population groups in Asia Minor settlements. The consequence of the events of 1922-1923 for Turkey, emerging as a nation-state with a radically new set of institutions, as indeed for the whole of the region, was that its Ottoman diversity was suppressed. For the modern Greek state, too, greater homogeneity was achieved with the expulsion of most of its Muslim populations.[1] Its inter-religious and diversified past has been relegated to silence, as have the landscapes of Asia Minor. But nonetheless something has been preserved in the vibrant memories of those who lived in that period.

The message of these narratives, carrying a benign picture of relations between different communities, is poignantly summarised in the words of Anna K. In 1922, at the age of 41 she abandoned everything with the news of the Greek army's defeat and fled in panic from Brusa her home town to the port of Mudania. Some forty years later in Athens, this is what she said:

> When we left in 1922, the Turks were crying and didn't want to let us go. "We will hide you," they said, "We'll protect you. It's only a storm and it'll blow over..." (*Bóra eínai kai tha perási*)... We weren't treated badly at all.[2]

*The nation-state view*

A study of national history teaching on both sides of the Aegean sheds light on the situation of long-term tension between these nation-states. This factor is a primary consideration in explaining the contrasting dispositions expressed by sections of the Greek population. The indigenous Greeks had been educated in the nation-state and had no contact with Turks, while this has been paralleled for the younger generations of Turks. Official recognition of the importance of history teaching is shown in the rapprochement between the two countries in the present phase of 'post-seismic' diplomacy. One of the first commitments in the meetings of the Foreign Ministers of Greece and Turkey was to revise existing text books. It is worth noting that the same concerns were expressed in the period of the Davos meetings (February 1988) with several initiatives taken on both sides of the Aegean, but then political tensions over Cyprus and the Aegean brought that to a stop.

---

[1] See Hirschon 2003.
[2] KMS; B136.

Millas, a Greek of Istanbul, has provided a valuable analysis of school text books. He points out how the treatment of the past by both countries displays common themes, and that it has changed little over the past 50 years. The main difference is that in Turkish texts Greece is less important and features in a limited way, while in Greek ones the Turks occupy a prominent place — they are the primary enemy.[1]

He notes that the similarities in treatment are extensive: on each side, texts are founded in notions of their own superiority, on their prior claims to civilisation, and each explicitly discredits the other's achievements, and glorifies their own expansionist territorial conquests while those of the other are vilified. An interesting pattern emerges in which history is biased on both sides and in rather similar ways. Each side depicts the other as uncivilised. A graphic example in the Greek case is found in a sixth form textbook (unrevised in 1990). Here the Turks are described as 'savages ... without civilisation ... who did not grant a single right to the enslaved nation'.[2] Yet in direct contradiction the following chapter refers 'without comment to the privileges granted under the Ottoman Empire to its Greek-speaking population'. Turkish school texts provide a mirror image and are just as judgmental: Greeks are shown as 'aggressors (who) acted with cruelty, killed the Turks without pity'. Turkish boys and girls are warned to 'be very wary and cautious with this neighbour'. 'Slaughters' and 'massacres' are always committed by the other side while the same activities are shown as benevolent by those who perpetrate them.[3]

Millas concludes with an assessment of the damage done by these school texts which distort historic events, ignore 'the complexity of life and the way ethnic groups change and evolve', and essentialise the differences between the two nations. 'Children are left to conclude that the other side was always in the wrong and their own side is almost perfect'. In periods of rapprochement 'even the governments which authorise the use of these text books admit their harmfulness'.[4]

The pervasive and insidious effects of this nationalistic teaching of the past is also detectable in general histories and in the advanced texts used in universities. In an unpublished paper 'Greeks, Turks and Historiography',

[1] Millas (1991; 24).
[2] Millas (1991; 26).
[3] Millas (1991; 27-29).
[4] Millas (1991; 29-32).

Millas analyses the bias and implications of nationalistic attitudes, however nuanced and sophisticated the treatment.[1] He examines the work of four well-known historians on both sides and finds, disturbingly, that their descriptions of the same period of Ottoman rule depict it in quite a different way — entirely positive from the Turkish side and wholly negative from the Greek side. He characterises some historians as those who write for the state and play an 'important role in "building a nation"' but, even while others distance themselves from this project claiming neutrality, their work also reflects what he calls an 'ethnic' bias.

I have referred to Millas' analysis to pinpoint this central issue, increasingly recognised and researched,[2] that the teaching of history within the ideological confines of the nation-state leads to a distorted view of the past, one that rests upon sharp distinctions between 'us' and 'them', often in a confrontational stance. The practical and policy implications of this realisation relate to the exercise of writing history, particularly in forming the attitudes of the young. Though it might be impossible to achieve a balanced view, it remains to be recognised that the 'representation of pastness' must be fuller than that of history-as-recorded alone. In addition, it needs to incorporate the experience of those who have lived it. Oral narratives have an important role, and the dichotomy between myth and history must be dissolved in order to enrich our understanding of past events and situations.

*Conclusion*

My intentions in this chapter have been to present a fuller picture of the quality of relations between Muslims and Christians in the last phase of the Ottoman Empire based on the memories of those who had first hand experience of the times. It serves to remind us of a more positive and benign climate, not represented in textbooks or in the official versions of the past. Stories of persecution and barbarity in Greco-Turkish relations are all too well-known. The voices of people who have lived through the events tell these and many other stories which are in danger of being lost if ignored, so that this endeavour also constitutes a salvage exercise. I have purposefully concentrated on accounts of amicable contacts and, given that this constitutes a selective and partial view, it could be seen as a romanticised view of the

---

[1] Millas (1997).

[2] Scholars on both sides of the Aegean are investigating this problem. For example, see Avdela 2000, Koulouri 2002, and the proceedings of an international conference held in Istanbul in 1995, published in Turkish (Berktay and Tuncer, 1998).

Ottoman past. The veracity of these accounts, however, is corroborated by the records of independent writers, important among them being the writings of Hasluck.

This approach to historiography is forcefully advocated by Samuel and Thomson and by Tonkin who uphold the significance of oral accounts.[1] As these narratives challenge the received view of history in this region they should act as a corrective to the common and widely-held attitude that enmity between Greeks and Turks is a permanent, historical and longstanding fact. Phrases such as 'implacable enmity', 'ancient' and 'atavistic hatred' informed all political discourse in the 'pre-seismic period' before 1999 and are still used in news reports. However, research into various periods of the past shared by peoples from this region reveals a far more complex picture, with varied and differentiated relationships between them. Even taking into account the element of nostalgia and romanticism which might colour the sentiments of the uprooted, and the contextual influences which affect their expression, these testimonies must be incorporated in the writing of history in its fullest sense. In answer to those who would devalue their importance, it is well to remember that even 'The mythical elements in memory ... need to be seen both as evidence of the past and as a continuing historical force in the present'.[2] Only in this way can a fuller 'representation of pastness' be created through a common history, expressed in one Greek word 'synistoria', which will provide a more balanced understanding of the situation at different periods.[3]

The silent voices given public expression here demonstrate a kind of tolerance which provides a model to be emulated. In the present period of political instability and in the contemporary context of fluctuating tension in this region, politicians would do well to consider the voices of the Asia Minor past which convey an important and timely message for all of us.

---

[1] Samuel and Thompson (1990), Tonkin (1991).

[2] Samuel & Thompson (1990; 20).

[3] An example of such an approach from both Muslim and Christian viewpoints is the volume *Orthodox Christians and Muslims* edited by N.M. Vaporis (1986).

*REFERENCES*

*Archives*

KMS. Kentro Mikrasiatikon Spoudon /Centre for Asia Minor Studies, Athens,
    unpublished archives.

*Published*

Avdela, E. 2000 'The Teaching of History in Greece', *Journal of Modern Greek
    Studies*, vol.18 (2); 239-53.
Berktay, A. and Tuncer, H. 1998 *Tarih Egitimi ve Tarihte 'Öteki' Sorunu* (*History
    Education and the 'Other' in History*), Istanbul; Tarih Vakfı.
Cohn, B. 1987 *An Anthropologist among the Historians and Other Essays* Oxford;
    Oxford University Press.
Collingwood, R. 1947 *The Idea of History*, Oxford; Clarendon Press.
Giannakopoulos, G. 1995 *O Teleftaíos Ellinismós tou Renkioyi* Athens;
    Asprovalta.
Hasluck, F. 1929, Christianity and Islam under the Sultans, edited by M. Hasluk,
    Two Vols. Oxford; Clarendon Press.
Hirschon, R. 1998 Heirs of the Greek Catastrophe, second edition, Oxford, New
    York; Berghahn Books.
Hirschon, R. 2003 (ed) *Crossing the Aegean: The Consequences of the 1923
    Population Exchange between Greece and Turkey*, Oxford, New York;
    Berghahn Books.
Koulouri, C. 2002 *Clio in the Balkans: The Politics of History Education*,
    Thessaloniki; Centre for South-East European Studies.
Lane Poole, S. (ed) 1878 *The People of Turkey*, by a Consul's Daughter, 2 vols,
    London; John Murray.
Meraklis, E. 1992 'Ellinotourkika tis Mikras Asias', *I Lexi*, vol. 112, Nov-Dec;
    793-801.
Millas, H. 1991 'History Textbooks in Greece and Turkey', *History Workshop
    Journal*, vol. 31; 21-33.
Millas, H. 1997 'Greeks, Turks and Historiography' unpublished paper, presented
    at the conference *Exploration of a Cultural Heritage: History of the Turkish
    and Greek Communities in the Ottoman World* (Bosporus University, April
    1997).
Ramsay, W. 1917 *The Intermixture of Races in Asia Minor* London; British
    Academy.

Samuel, R. and Thompson, P. (eds) *The Myths We Live By*, Routledge; London.

Sider, G. and Smith, G. (eds) 1997 *Between History and Histories: the Making of Silences and Commemorations*, Anthropological Horizons 11, Toronto, Buffalo; University of Toronto Press.

Tonkin, E. 1991 *Narrating Our Pasts: The Social Construction of Oral History* Cambridge; Cambridge University Press.

Tsimouris, G. 1997 'Anatolian Embodiments in a Hellenic Context: The Case of Reisderiani Mikrasiates Refugees', unpublished Ph.D. thesis, University of Sussex.

Vaporis, N. (ed) 1986 *Orthodox Christians and Muslims*, Brookline, Mass; Holy Cross.

Veremis, T. '1922: Political Continuities and Realignments in the Greek State' in Hirschon (ed) 2003.

Zürcher, E. 1998 *Turkey: A Modern History* London; I. B. Tauris.

# 33. MUSLIM EXPERIENCE OF 'FEAR AND SHAME': THE CASE OF THE POMAKS IN GREECE

## Fotini TSIBIRIDOU

The marginality of Islam in the Balkan nation-states after the dissolution of the Ottoman Empire may be seen as analogous in many ways to Said's idea of 'Orientalism'. This thought becomes even more worthwhile when we realize that the dominant vernacular value code of some marginal Muslims, amongst them, both men and women, instead of being 'honour and shame' is 'fear and shame'. This represents a significant departure from the dominant stereotype for Mediterranean people as reflected in Western anthropology up until, and even after, the 1970s.[1]

By studying a group of Muslim Slav speakers, known as 'Pomaks', in Greek Thrace I try here to examine these issues in analysing one version of the 'Muslim myth' in the Balkan area. Such myth-making is closely connected to certain aspects of the social construction of ethnic, cultural/religious and gender identities in the region. Using the metaphor of 'myth' instead of 'religion' helps, first of all, to avoid the *de facto* use of the concept of religion; the latter, according to Talal Asad's reflection, an analytical category with a historically specific meaning which serves the needs of western liberal thought.[2] Moreover in this way we can clearly define, right from the beginning, the course of Islam in the region, and note indeed that it changes: starting as a mystic experience[3] and emerging as an orientalistic mythology, the 'retrogressive', which is one of the connotations of the 'Muslim' in the framework of Balkan prejudices and ignorance today. Like any other myth, this one too implies and contradicts notions regarding human relationships and the representation of human experience.[4] Man's relationship to nature, the relationship of the natural to the supernatural, the healthy to the unhealthy, as well as gender relationships and the relationship to social

---

[1] Peristiany (1965), (Herzfeld 1980).
[2] Asad, (1993: 54).
[3] Hasluck (1973); Norris (1993).
[4] Campbell (1998: 253).

'others' are all supported by contradicting discourses as a result of asymmetrical and unequal social relationships in the specific social network of which the Pomaks are a part.

## Ethnographic writing

The 'myth' metaphor also corresponds to the process of problematizing ethnographic writing.[1] This problematization includes the narrative process of the ethnography as well as the participant-observation politics of the ethnographic experience. In my case, being a native of my research area, I began this project in order to discover the other half of myself. I was born and brought up in Thrace, in a middle-class Greek-Orthodox Christian family. I took part in the practices of my Greek-Christian education always conscious of the fact that some other practices were occurring as 'big secrets' within the community around me, although nobody would talk about them. My curiosity as a child grew into a struggle in my teens, a struggle to include my Muslim peers in our social group as the restrictions on our interaction were mounting. Leaving the area in order to seek an understanding which my familiarity would not allow me was the obvious consequence. Anthropology has helped bridge the gap of that familiarity and the flight from it, since this area became the field of 'native anthropology', this hybrid form of the observer/observed, professional/personal situation with an overtly-reflexive analysis on both levels. Since 1984, this long-term fieldwork in the villages and cities of Thrace (Christian and Muslim, rural and urban population, old and new inhabitants) has given me access to data which allows me to undertake a comparative project — still in progress — 'looking for the Muslim myths in the Balkans'.[2]

To understand 'Islam' in the everyday life of these people is one major aim of this work, first of all, because minority groups in the Balkans have been described during the last ten centuries mostly on the basis of 'religious' criteria, and also because religion is a central political issue today. Yet 'Otherness' seems to be one of the most important functions not only of Muslim but also of Christian myths in the Balkans. Defining the relation with the 'other' social/human being is a priority for the agro-pastoral societies in the Balkans, just as defining the relation of human beings to the

---

[1] Clifford and Marcus (1986).

[2] A first analysis of this project has been presented at the American Anthropological Association annual meeting, in December 2001, to be published the *Journal of Modern Greek Studies* under the title: 'Looking for the Muslim myths in the Balkans'.

surrounding animal world in the tropical forests or the Indian native spaces, is a priority in their respective mythology.[1] People think not in rational and critical terms concerning their relation to the Other; but rather define the Other through stereotypes. This is also the case in the modern ethnic and national myths in the Balkan area.[2] In sum, on the basis of my fieldwork into these 'Muslim myths', I would suggest grouping the topics that the researcher has to deal with, as follows:

1.  The history of Islam in the Balkans and heritage of the Ottoman past.
2.  Inner hermeneutics/orientalisms based on religious or other criteria.
3.  Embodied mystical experiences both in Sunni and Bektashi versions of Islam (such as a kind of spirit possession of a part of the human body, the evil eye, as well as sorcery and 'paganistic' practices, known by Orthodox Christians as well, or Bektashi mystical 'Sufi' practices).
4.  Power relationships in the politics between different groups (for instance magico-religious and secular leaders, conceived as 'liminal' persons in the case of the Pomaks and discussed below).
5.  Traditional gender segregation with particular reference to stereotypes of women in the modernization/re-Islamization process.
6.  Material conditions typical of agro-pastoral societies, along with moral principles of the 'limited good' kind.

Here, we are going to investigate parameters which contribute to the dominance of the moral value code of 'fear and shame' within a marginal Muslim group of Pomaks; the latter seeming to be one of the vernacular versions of the 'Muslim myth' in the Balkans.

*The fieldwork area*

The fieldwork area in question is situated in a mountainous region of Thrace in Northeastern Greece. Since the incorporation of this part of Thrace into the Greek nation-state in 1920, the population comprises a Christian majority and a Muslim minority, the latter mainly Turkish-speaking. This cohabitation

---

[1] Campbell (1998).
[2] Smith (2000).

dates from the early Ottoman period, and goes back as far as the fourteenth century. A large part of this Muslim minority is now claiming a 'Turkish ethnic identity'. Slav-speaking Muslims, known as 'Pomaks', also inhabit the highlands of Rhodopi, and as a marginal part of the Muslim minority, have been moving from being silent on their identity to becoming more overtly assimilated into the Turkish-speaking majority, who declare themselves 'Turks'. However, the last five years have also seen greater self-assertion and the appearance of a nascent ethnic identity amongst the Pomaks, one more self-consciously 'Pomak' than before.[1] I am a part of this game, with multiple roles, in that my presence as ethnographer helped to create new dynamics equally in the understanding of my informants and my self.

I will try to describe the local version of the Islamic 'religion' among Sunni Pomaks. Their version contains beliefs and practices at the interface of religion and sorcery (beliefs in the *dzins*, evil eye, sorcery, and so on). These practices are embodied within power struggles of a religious, secular and metaphysical nature. These so called 'isolated' people are part of a strong unequal social game based on deep hierarchical principles. Poverty and marginality, economy, politics about 'Otherness'; these are the dominant influences against which the social actors must construct their profile. In all these 'religious' practices two figures become dominant: the *hodza* (Sunni priest) and certain old women. By describing specific practices and cases, I will attempt to reveal the apparent connection between these figures, which represent 'exogenous/liminal power'. This kind of power is very important, if not dominant, in the way local, socio-cultural and ethnic identities, are constructed.

### History and heritage in the Balkans

It is also important to examine these data within the socio-historical context, one that may be considered as emerging through a *longue durée* process within a Balkan region that is inhabited by Christians, Muslims, ethnic minorities and majorities, marginal and dominant groups in a mutual social hierarchy. Because of this there is a prevailing logic of dichotomy, an 'us and them', in every particular group of the area.[2] The game is regulated by hegemony practices, which are exercised by real persons or invisible things possessing some mystical power. The strong discrimination between different

---

[1] See Tsibiridou (2000, Chapter One).
[2] Cohen (1985).

groups and the determination of the 'other' in this society takes place not between equals but through hostile definitions which reinforce the dominance of perpetual binary but unequal oppositions.

## 'Internal orientalisms'

Dichotomies dominate the symbolic construction of the communities in Thrace: dichotomy between Christians and Muslims, as well as between 'in-group' and 'out-group'. This dichotomy is, among other constructions, the product of long-lasting policies exercised by the various authorities. In addition, Thrace is the only Greek province where Christians and Muslims (*Sunni* and *Kızılbaş*) of various categories, i.e. refugees, old inhabitants, Turkophones, Slavophones, Gypsies, and Armenians, coexist. This heritage, with in-group/out-group 'differences' and paradoxes has generated, for centuries now, inner hermeneutics based mostly on religious criteria which has resulted in what Maria Todorova calls 'internal orientalisms'.[1] It is not by accident that in all these orientalistic discourses constructing 'Otherness', women's appearance and behaviour is objectified and used as proof of men's religiousness: 'they are not like us, their women are 'open' (bodily and linguistically speaking)'.[2] 'They are not like us, they are *sofou* (very religious persons)'. The latter are saying: 'We are the real Muslims; our neighbours are savages, fake Muslims'.

More specifically, in the area of fieldwork, the triptych language-religion-nomination seems to work as a criterion for internal differentiation among them.[3] Therefore, a group of villages to which the village of our main fieldwork belongs appears to be inhabited by similar people neither extremely religious nor its opposite — rather, in their own words, fun-loving people who stick together due to the fact that they consume alcohol in public. The others, who are called *sofou*, are by self-ascription teetotalers ('up here we are all the same, you are not going to find any alcohol up here'). At the same time they attack verbally their neighbours, the Kizilbash/Bektashis, accusing them of secret orgy practices and of monopolizing the organization of festivities in the area. Let me stress that these symbolic practices such as organizing annual festivals result in social prestige of great importance to the social identity of men. There is too another paradigm of controversial

---

[1] Todorova (2000).

[2] For similar instances, see Nagata (2001).

[3] See Tsibiridou (2000; 29-80) for a more detailed discussion.

collective identity. It concerns a central village in the area, about whose people the surrounding villages say: 'They are no longer Pomak!', or still 'that they used to be Pomak ... they will be Pomak again ... but now they are not'.

The need to understand the origin and the establishment of such controversial discourses has led me in my case study to search for comparative data, both historically and geographically. In the nationalistic Greek literature regarding the Pomaks, they are presented as 'the descendants of the ancient Thracian tribe of the Achrian'. In travel reports from the eighteenth and nineteenth centuries such terms as *agrian, dagli* (mountain people) are said to be used as definitions by outsiders to refer to populations of the mountain area of Rhodopi: 'Which the Turks call *ahrian*' or even 'Turks who do not know their language'. However, the term *ahrian* has been used since the seventeenth century for Christians who converted to Islam. The term *Pomak* appeared very late, after the mid-nineteenth century. If we exclude the favorite 'historical myths' of scholars in all three countries Greece, Bulgaria, and Turkey interested in the origin of the Pomak and their ethnic substance, the most important information on the Pomak community comes from fieldwork conducted by fellow researchers in Bulgaria. They mention that the term *Pomak* is used even today to refer to Gypsies who, formerly Muslims, have converted to Christianity. In general, in Bulgaria the term is synonymous with 'non-real Muslim'.

The terms *Pomak* and *ahrian*, which define one who has converted to another religion, are also used metaphorically to describe a 'non-trustworthy person'. Religious conversion makes somebody capable of changing his mind in other social matters too. A typical example of this is the fact that Greek-speaking refugees from Bulgaria, when referring to someone in Thrace who is not trustworthy may say even today: 'Don't trust him, he is an *agrianis*'. It seems that these populations during a long period of four to five centuries have been marginal due to their religious peculiarity, their linguistic particularity, and their spatial isolation and poverty. At the same time, because of these peculiarities, historical conjunctures and power policies, they have had to 'alter' or 'differentiate' their attitude towards the 'outsiders'. In many cases their attitude was not in concurrence with but was adjusted to the conjunctures and demands of the particular political and/or religious authority.

With a legacy of 'internal orientalism' based on religious-cultural criteria these people have progressed from the twentieth into the twenty-first century — from the problem of division into nation-states to the present dilemma of ethnic claims. In the modern era, identities are constructed by all those representatives of authority who mediate, moving in a liminal space, between the socially stratified groups of Thrace. In the global context which supports ethnic movements, these ethnic (re)constructions rest upon re-interpretations of Islam, either in order to adopt a 'Turkish identity' or the 'ordinary Muslim Greek' or the 'faithful Pomak', in contrast to the stereotype of the 'unfaithful, untrustworthy defector' of the past.

*Power and network principals*

The representatives of minority groups and marginal people are always people with power. The lower the status of a group is, the greater their fear and their dependence on those people with 'power' and 'authority'. People in 'power' inside the agro-pastoral community always have connections with the authorities and people in power who live outside. The main accomplishment of these liminal *personae* is that they can speak outside languages (Turkish in the past, Greek now). In the way of life in the mountains, such figures may also be represented as female (old woman in black who like ghosts terrify men, old women with sorcery skills, old women who 'cast lead' in order to exorcize the evil eye, old women who threaten couples).

Social relations and networks such as these function on different levels:

1. At the level of community: we inside the community are without power/others outside the community have the power.

2. At the level of house/body: inside the house/body we are protected and self-controlled/outside the house/body we are exposed and in danger of losing control, and being punished because of transgressions.

3. At the level of gender: the men's world concerns the strict socio-political game/women's world is outside of this socio-political game, a fact that creates an association between some women with power and other male *personae* in power, from outside. All are conceived as 'others'. This is one side of the vernacular version of the gender-segregated world in the Balkans and the Mediterranean area.

In the discussion below, we will talk about women, secular and religious power, conceptions and representations of socio-corporal integrity, transgressions and self-control. We will also discuss hypotheses concerning the efficiency of this dichotomizing world and the totalizing character of power: religious, secular and metaphysical, as well as its polluted nature. On the other hand, in this context of strong interdependence of the social actors, religious practices usually are closer to the practical and mystical myth-making dimension of religion than to the theological and fundamental form of the monotheistic Protestantism in the West.[1] In the Balkans and Anatolia area Christian orthodox and Muslims share common practices and a pagan heritage incorporated into the monotheistic versions of religion that they now pursue.

*The balance of 'poverty' practices*

In addition to the time-honoured practice of gossip, which may aim at social control and or practically at the obtaining of a particular good or want, the sorcery practices of the past continue to be used, usually by certain old women. Examples of this are:

> Jealousy drives some women with extra-ordinary capacities to use *dzadilik* practices which are aimed at men and their material property (fields, sheep etc.). They translate that person's name as '*somebody who is related with this action*'. Women are not influenced by this negative practice. *Dzadilik* is more effective during the Holy Week of the Orthodox Christians, and especially on Good Friday and Good Saturday.

> Control over mating; every choice of mate is at risk because old women may intervene and exercise *karatchalik*, which aims at the dissolution of the relationship between men and women. There is a typical narrative about *karatchalik*, provoking feelings of anguish in the audience, revealing the risk the society incurs from the women (see below). They translate it as '*the action by means of which somebody puts himself between two others*'.

> Control over a man's social behaviour; an intervention either by such women and some special *hodza* may render a man a-social, a-sexual or over-sexual, or provoke abnormal behaviour and psychological problems (*pravina*). In the few cases that this happens to women, they become ab-normal. These women, victims of *pravina* become aggressive to themselves and they escape into another reality (grave psychological problems, like deep depression or syndrome of persecution). They translate *pravina* as '*the action by means of which somebody is doing something*'.

---

[1] Asad (1993).

*Evil spirits and socio-corporal integrity*

Such sorcery practices must be studied in combination with 'religious' beliefs and practices. I strongly believe that every religion must be seen in its local version, because theological beliefs and 'religious' practices are transformed by social relationships at the same time that they are transforming them. The realization of the mystery of life and the integration of the individual are acquired through specific beliefs and practices, beyond theology and the scriptures. In our case, cosmological views and social behaviour alike are both interpreted within the framework of Islamic religion albeit here religion is used not in a theological sense, but in a practical version, which combines pagan beliefs and practices that they hold in common with Orthodox Christians as well. More specifically, Islamic and Christian versions in this area, between the Balkans and Anatolia, sometimes share pagan traditions that concern social control, power and conceptions about the human body and illness.[1]

'Here people do not care about God and his Prophet, Mohamed whom you can't touch or see. Here people care only about *dzinia* and *peri*, these things which are materially analogous to the human body', said one of my Pomak informants, an educated person. Islam as a theological and cosmological practice in this local version, concerns principally the relation and the personal dealings of people with these spirits, called 'he-them' or 'it' (masculine, plural or neutral in Greek) who test men and women perpetually. These invisible powers (*dzins, peri*) are also called by the Pomaks *edzinlie*. They live in outside places called *kirda, vonka, pot*, spaces outside the house, the neighborhood, the road. These invisible powers can harm the human body when men reciprocate aggressively to provocation or when men transgress particular rules. These invisible spirits may take the form of small animals such as a cat, frog, turtle and so on.

Let us consider these beliefs, and also their associated healing and avoidance practices. *Dzins* may enter and take possession of a body organ, thus causing illness such as blindness, paralysis or a stroke. It is therefore important to avoid antagonising them, something that may be done through certain transgressions, or through aggressive behaviour:

---

[1] Hasluck (1929).

Don't throw hot water outside your house at night because you may burn them. Don't shake the tablecloth outside the house at night and most importantly don't urinate outside the house because you may urinate on them. This makes them furious. Before any action, you ask for permission by saying, a prayer, the *bismila*. Even before touching something you say this. At times a *dzin* appears in a different guise and asks for bread in order to test you. In that case you must give it something and let it go. The worst thing you can do is to kick it; in that case harm will come to you at once. These happenings may take place during the day, but mostly at night, until about 4 o'clock in the morning...

From the structural point of view, what seems to pose a threat is contact by the inside with the outside; the inside of the body and the house with everything outside. This link occasionally becomes explicit, in that the inside of the house may be identified with the inside of the body, for example; the heart with the main wooden pillar of the house, the head with the roof and so on. The emphasis on avoiding aggression toward the *dzin* is reflected in that there is a general avoidance of overt aggression in village society. The avoidance of hostile acts in child-rearing, for instance, as well as general abstinence from verbal aggression is paralleled by an avoidance of loud voices and music. Anyone who violates this code of silence is either deviant or crazy, or in a state of 'crisis', such as victims of sorcery, puberty, or liminal situations like wedding celebrations.

Returning to the *dzins*, there is no way of protecting oneself from them other than through the use of charms made by *muskatzi* (healers). The *muskatzi* make charms called *muska* and *karatchale* by placing inside amulets writings from old Egyptian astrological books, blue stones and a piece of *karachalik*, literally 'black wood'. The healers derive their power from the fact that they are the owners of these books, and therefore can communicate with them: 'These people deal/have dealings with the *dzins*'. In the case of illness the one who suffers must look for someone even more powerful than the *muskadzi*, such as special *hodzas* (Sunni priests) 'who are strong enough and have the power' to cure. However, it is important to mention here that when I asked my informants about the ways they can be protected, their answers concerned mainly the method of curing, emphasizing their blind dependence on all those 'who know about these things', or 'have the power'. In general, everyone must be very cautious to avoid revealing whatever has to do with the internal world of the body and the house otherwise their bodily, social or mental well-being may be endangered. Therefore, they are extremely cautious regarding not only the way they behave, but also the way they express themselves. A good illustration of this is the prevalence and force of the 'evil eye'.

*Evil eye as social control*

Whatever people in this community lack in expressive voice, they make up in abundance through the use of their eyes. The eyes are the most visible body parts of women. It is through the eyes the game of love is carried out: 'She looked at me and I got the message that she is going to wait for me to finish my military service and come back'. 'You look at her and if she's got a sweet eye, you approach her'. The whole of social activity is subject to control exercised by the eyes. *Nazar*, literally meaning 'eye' or 'look' is associated with acts of envy, and in particular greediness (*taxmakia*), 'of the greedy man whose eyes are never satisfied'. *Nazar* is the effect of a 'look' on somebody, who, once affected, loses his/her ability to communicate. *Nazar* is connected with desire and is not of a deliberate nature. Even parents may exercise it unwittingly on their children. This is caused by the power of the eye. To protect themselves from this phenomenon they resort to 'whatever can distract the eye': a red piece of cloth in tobacco fields and gardens, animal skulls in stockyards. Strong desire results from deprivation: the ill, the odd, the very religious, widows or sullen people supposedly have the ability to cast the evil eye. Whoever is lacking happiness risks 'leaving for the other world with his eyes wide open' from desire. Men and women who have been breast-fed by two women, as well as blue-eyed people — which may apply to a large proportion of the population — and dissatisfied people are potentially suspect where the evil eye is concerned. Sensitive people may also 'qualify': 'the ones who are healthy and kind do not need to use red pieces of cloth'. Plants and animals as well as people are equally susceptible to the evil eye. Flowers in gardens and tobacco plants, whatever is alive may wither and die, just as man struck by the evil eye does. To protect themselves from it people wear a charm called *karatchale*, which consists of a black twig and a blue stone *sintsae*.

For a cure the victims first resort to the woman of the house, who will say the *bismila* (prayer) and also may spread the ashes of burnt sheep horn on children's cheeks. For animals they may carry out a *mevlut*, an exorcizing prayer read by the *hotza*. However, if symptoms (dizziness, weakness, temperature, insomnia in babies) do not stop, they go to one of the two women in the village who 'cast the lead': that is, cast molten lead into water and perform a ritual over the afflicted person. This covers the whole body, from head to toe and includes ritual cleansing with water at the end. The noise made by the hot lead seems to put a halt to the evil eye's power; the cleansing with water gives the life back to the body.

The evil eye is always associated with overt desire. Fear of its being triggered acts as a form of social control that emphasises the importance of being master of one's bodily and material needs, the danger of excess or attracting overt attention. By virtue of the evil eye, financial, social and natural differentiations between people become emphasised, and may influence the health of the human body. In turn, the body may be protected when a charm is placed between the body and external world. The charm is named *karachale*, after the kind of sorcery (*karatchalik*) which splits up couples. The charm seems to be of a female nature and is usually placed on the breast. In all the above cases, salvation and therapy come from 'outside', from the specialized *hodza*, in the same way salvation-protection comes from the 'outside' *mouskadzi*, the healer who makes charms to protect people against the evil eye and the spirits such as *dzins* and *peri*. In this respect, therefore, the *Hodza*, the old women and the *mouskadzi* hold the well-being in their hands of those who are at risk of affliction.

## The hodza

From the social point of view, men go to the mosque in part because they want to be seen by the others and particularly by the *hodza*. It is characteristic that this is particularly noticeable in the *mahala*, the Muslim/Pomak quarter of the town. There, the *hodza* who has dealings with various employers can also help them find work. The *hodza* is *diavasmenos*, literally 'able to recite' or learned. He can recite the holy language of Islam, Arabic, and speaks the other dominant languages like Turkish and Greek, an ability that gives him power within this marginal minority of Slavic, and today more prominently, Turkish speakers. An important role of the *hodza* is his capacity for removing the evil eye, *nazar*, unlike the situation in the villages where it appears to be largely women who act in this capacity. Another function of the *hodza*, 'he who has the power', is his involvement in the cure or the prevention of sorcery.

## Female power, the old women

In the socio-political game, women seem to be classified as 'outside' or liminal (in-between) *persona*. In people's representations, 'an old woman in black' threatens to harm men who circulate in and around the neighborhoods (*mahalades*), which become inhabited by strange powers, such as these ghostly old women, during the night. One should note that the dress code for all women includes a long black dress, which could make all women potentially frightening. Real old women, on the other hand, are thought to wish to undermine any mating between the young and only too willing to intervene using sorcery in order to separate them.

In order to grasp how the idea of women as such an alien, but potentially powerful figure is formed and manipulated, one should study the whole spectrum of social relationships both inside and outside the community. The first and most characteristic of these social relationships is the strict discrimination of the sexes in everyday practices as well as the paradox of the kinship organization, such as the unbroken bond between a mother and her daughter despite tradition for a bride to relocate to her husband's house after marriage. As marriage is patrilocal, a woman is considered to be a lifelong stranger in the groom's family. It is not uncommon when a woman dies for her to be buried next to her own blood kin. Husbands constantly complain that their relationships their wives are difficult because women's mothers come between couples.

The old woman, as a threat to the mating process, becomes a symbol of threat to reproduction *per se*. Here it is possible to draw an interesting comparison between the Pomaks and the Bedouins of Egypt.[1] There is a well-known story in the Balkan and Mediterranean regions of two young lovers who die when separated. They are buried side by side and on their graves grow male and female plants that become entangled (white-red roses or male-female palm trees). When the evil person who is responsible for separating the two lovers becomes aware of the entwined plants s/he viciously separates them. In the case of the Bedouins who live in unilinear descent groups and where a preferential marriage to the paternal cousin is observed, the evil person is this parallel cousin of the girl. In the case of the Pomaks, who practice bilateral consanguinity when looking for a mate, the evil person is an older woman. This comparison between these two cases helped me understand and perceive how characteristics of the culture became primordial: the first refers to the continual bond between mother and daughter, the second to fear of old women's knowledge.

---

[1] Abu-Lughod (1988).

## Power and knowledge

In this society knowledge and power are conceived as identical. Old women and the *hodza* may therefore appear homologous to those who are the community's representatives, the *muhtars*, to the outside world, 'who know how to speak the other two dominant languages' (Turkish and Greek). This ranking system, which operates on invisible structures (inside versus outside), and on binomial oppositions (knowledge=power versus fear=shame) is not only a product of western thought and of my structural and binary representations but constitutes, whether consciously or unconsciously, part of the vernacular categorization. It is important to try to understand the nature of this foreign and alienated power experienced by people. To do that, we have to see the metaphors of this power and the emotions that it provokes. For example, there is a marked fear of the deceased, despite the fact that some villages are surrounded by cemeteries. The *hodza* and some old women perform the ritual cleansing of dead bodies; this pollutes and empowers them at the same time. The association of pollution and power is apparent from some typical expressions. For instance, they refer to the old women who clean the dead bodies and perform *dzadilik* (sorcery practice concerning the material goods of the person) in the same way they call the clever and mafioso hodza, *lera* which literally means 'dirtiness'. It is indicative that there is a common expression in Thrace for the fact that someone has been spoiled: 'You have become a hodza': power is thus represented in itself as being polluted. People are afraid of those in authority, but there is little respect for them.

## Permanent 'crisis' and modernization

In the rural context, for an individual to ignore proper behaviour constitutes in itself a crisis, something that may also become associated with links with the 'outside' such as a man who mixes with outsiders, challenges authorities, wastes money, has an affair with 'foreign' women, looks for 'fake love' or leads a wild life. Such a man may be supposed to be bewitched by sorcery. Upon relocation to the cities, however, circumstances, which were considered a deviation due to sorcery become daily practice to the extent that one can conclude that life in the city, at least till now, means a condition of permanent 'crisis'. Men in the city live their everyday life between two worlds, the world of a Christian modern city, and the world of the marginal Muslim neighborhood (*mahala*). This fact, in combination with the main cultural practice of experiencing their socialization as a deviation-violation of authority rules, results in a condition of permanent, obligatory marginality. It is characteristic that this marginality is considered as a suspended condition even at the imaginary level. For example, many people repeatedly dream about 'being in the nasty position of falling into a void', or 'feeling the earth tremble under the feet'.

On the other hand, the modernization process forces people to encounter a more scholastic form of the faith, one within which 'fundamental values' of the 'orthodox beliefs' appear more strongly than previously. These Sunni Pomaks, for instance, have to prove that they are good Muslims, because they want to be accepted by the broader group of the Muslim minority, on which they are dependent. At the same time, in the context of internal orientalisms, they are rejected by them, as 'retarded' ones, Pomaks, 'people from the mountains'. For similar reasons, but different motives the mystical Muslims, the Kizilbash, Pomak or not, identify themselves with the minority group of Alevis in Turkey, whose picture is associated with modernist ideas and secularism. Women, in this case are 'open' (open in the double sense of not wearing headscarfs or veils, and possessed of outgoing personalities) instead of the others who are 'closed'.[1]

In a global situation today which appears to encourage the emergence of ethnic movements, the suspended condition of the Pomaks lends itself to such modern myths,[2] this time with the support of an 'external power', that of a Greek nationalist businessman. The new attempts to get an ethnic identity rest upon re-interpretations of Islam: either in order to adopt the 'Turkish identity' or the 'ordinary Muslim Greek' or the 'faithful Pomak', in contrast to the stereotype of the 'unfaithful, untrustworthy defector' of the past. The protagonists of the Pomak ethnic movement are trying to reverse all these negative stereotypes by encouraging people 'not to be ashamed and afraid to be a Pomak'. They say all 'Pomaks are religious persons'; although this is not true but, they have to dissociate Pomaks from the secular Kemalist Turks, as the elite of the Turkish speakers claim to be in Thrace. What remains true though is the vestigial sense of 'fear/shame'; the two words in their language are very similar (*stramo/srano*), and they are used indifferently, one in the place of the other. Every time I asked for clarifications they used to give me the stereotypical answer: 'To be afraid, or to be ashamed is the same'.

---

[1] For a similar comment, see Ahmed (1991).
[2] Banks (1996).

This case study is an example of the complications the researcher has to deal with in the case of a Muslim 'myth in the Balkan area'; complications which have to do with power relationships, modes of designation, discriminations and prejudices. A comparison with other case studies in the other main Balkan areas inhabited by Muslims (Albania, Kosovo, Bosnia and Bulgaria)[1] could help further to clarify the situation. Such a comparative approach works like a mirror aimed at enriching our analytical categories and expanding our theoretical discourse.

These marginal people seem to rely upon a presupposition of a form of 'exogenous' power in order to function. They depend on the socio-cultural conditions prevailing in the larger multi-cultural and multi-religious area with unequal social status for the protagonists. So, the exogenous power is viewed as belonging to liminal *personae*, such as certain women, the Sunni priests, the *muhtars* and the healers. If we attempt to compare this situation with others, we see that in respective multi-cultural and multi-religious situations found under the weight of hegemonic practices — see for example the case of colonial power in Nepal — there exists the development of magico-religious practices where women and inferior casts have a leading role.[2] A similar ambiguity is found in other related situations with regard to the place of these leading figures between the outside and the inside world where sorcery practices serve the role of promoting factional rivalry, splitting the community and thus redefining the social hierarchy.[3]

All in all, my main hypothesis for this version of Islam is this: in order to reproduce themselves as social beings the dichotomy logic becomes a *modus operandi* seeking to deal with their stigma. As Ervin Goffman described it:[4] to keep genders apart, dissociate in-group/out-group, in-house/out-house, in-body/out-body. In this way the control of the external power as well as the self-control of the social behaviour are both embodied in the management of the stigma. The stigma of the marginality and minority status derives from the interiorization of images about them projected by other people, wherein they are seen as 'different', 'marginal', 'perfidious' and the people 'without knowledge', vernacularly expressed by the Pomaks themselves through 'fear and shame' feelings and practices of 'silence'.

---

[1] Zhelyazkova, Nielsen, Kepell (1995); Bringa (1995); Duijzings (2000).
[2] Gellner (1992) .
[3] See the analysis of African cases by Mary Douglas (1970).
[4] Goffman (1963).

All research concerning religious belief and practices in the Balkan area — and beyond for that matter — must not begin with the theological, but with the practical side. The latter can be seen as a 'mythical text' in its local version, with a particular story, full of metaphors, tropes, metonymies, binarisms, symbolisms and mystical experiences. This 'text', in our case, is fragmentarily understood by people helping them to realize not so much the mystery of life and the connection with God, but the individual's integration in the (human/animal) world and the particular social condition. All the above, together with the long process of transformation into a marginal minority have led to the adoption of general practices of silence and severe self-control.

*REFERENCES*

Abu-Lughod, L. 1988 *Veiled Sentiments. Honor and Poetry in a Bedouin Society*, Berkeley, Los Angeles; University of California Press.

Ahmed L. 1991 'Early Islam and the Position of Women: The Problem of Interpretation', in N. Keddie, and B. Baron (eds), *Women in Middle Eastern History*, New Haven; Yale University Press.

Asad, T. 1993 *Genealogies of Religion. Discipline and Reason of Power in Christianity and Islam*, Baltimore and London; The Johns Hopkins University Press.

Banks, M. 1996 *Ethnicity: Anthropological constructions*, London; Routledge.

Bringa, T. 1985 *Being Muslim the Bosnian way. Identity and Community in a Central Bosnian Village*, Princeton New Jersey; Princeton University Press.

Campbell, J. 1988 *The Power of Myth* (in Greek), Athens; Iamvlichos.

Clifford J. and Marcus, G. (eds.) 1986 *Writing Culture: The Poetics and Politics of Ethnography*, Berkeley, Los Angeles; University of California Press.

Cohen, A. 1985 *The Symbolic Construction of Community*, London; Tavistock Publications.

Douglas, M. 1970 *Witchcraft Confessions and Accusations*, London; Tavistock Publications.

Duijzings, G. 2000 *Religion and the Politics of Identity in Kosovo*, New York; Columbia University Press.

Eliade, M. 1990 *Dictionnaire des Religions*, Paris; Plon.

Foster, G. 1965 'Peasant Society and the Image of Limited Good', *American Anthropologist* (676): 293-315.

Gellner, D. 1992 'Identity Systems of Highland Burma: 'Belief', Akha, zah, and a Critique of interiorized notions of ethno-religious Identity', *Man (N.S)* 27, 799-819.

Goffman, E. 1963 *Stigma. Notes on the Management of Spoiled Identity*, Englewood Cliffs, NJ; Prentice-hall Inc.

Hasluck, F. 1973 (1929) *Christianity and Islam under the Sultans*, New York; Octagon Books.

Herzfeld, M. 1980 'Honor and Shame: Problems in the Comparative Analysis of Moral Systems', *Man* 15: 339-351.

Lévi-Strauss, C. 1962 *Pensée sauvage*, Paris; Plon.

Nagata, J. 2001 'Beyond Theology: Toward an Anthropology of 'fondamentalism' ', *American Anthropologist 103 (2)*: 481-498.

Norris, H. 1993 *Islam in the Balkans*, London; Hurst.

Peristiany J. (ed.) 1965 *Honour and Shame. The values of Mediterranean Society*, London; Weidenfeld and Nicholson.

Smith, A. 2000 *National Identity* (in Greek), Athens; Odysseas.

Todorova, M. 2000 *Imagining the Balkans*, New York; Oxford University Press.

Tsibiridou, F. 2000 *Les* Pomak *dans la Thrace grecque. Discours ethnique et pratiques socioculturelles*, Paris; L'Harmattan.

Zhelyazkova, A., Nielsen J. & Kepell J. (eds) 1995 *Relations of Compatibility and Incompatibility between Christians and Muslims in Bulgaria*, Sofia; International Center for Minority Studies and International Relations.

# 34. HASLUCK, MOUNT ATHOS, AND THE RECONSTITUTION OF MONASTIC LIFE IN POST-SOCIALIST ROMANIA

## Alice FORBESS

While a great deal of insight has been gained regarding the affect of the 'socialist experiment' on political and economic structures in Eastern Europe, its impact on religion, particularly on the Orthodox Church, remains little studied. Partly, the reason for this is the fact that, in contrast to the spectacular transformation of other institutions, the Orthodox Church seems to have remained remarkably impervious to change. Considered the most conservative of the major branches of Christianity, Orthodoxy gives the impression that 'historical developments in other areas of life such as economy and politics have only altered certain outward aspects of the Church'.[1] Indeed, in Romania, the Church has constantly stressed its role as a guardian of tradition and national values and its opposition to modernity and industrialisation. Yet, it has also demonstrated, in practice, an uncommon ability to adapt to repeated radical changes in the political, social and economic environment, even maintaining its active involvement in social and political life under the socialist regime. My paper examines this flexible response to change from the viewpoint of monastic establishments, internal structures of the Church that were portrayed, in official discourse, as guardians of tradition.

Although not directly focused on Hasluck´s subject matter, the paper follows the line of intellectual inquiry opened by him, and develops parallels to his diachronic study of Mount Athos monasteries. More specifically, it examines how historical contingencies in the nineteenth and twentieth centuries have changed monastic praxis at a famous Wallachian convent. The central question is: have monastic traditions introduced in Wallachia by monks from Mount Athos between the fourteenth and nineteenth centuries, survived to the present-day as organisational realities 'on the ground', as writers within the Orthodox Church would have us believe? Or, should the recent fascination

---

[1] Stewart (1994; 139).

among religious and laypeople with Mount Athos and its traditions be interpreted as an attempt within the Romanian Orthodox Church to re-introduce to monastic life traditions now considered more ´authentic´ than the existing arrangements? In 'Christianity and Islam under the Sultans', Hasluck argued that 'a survival of religious tradition is so far from inevitable that it is only probable under favourable conditions. A violent social upheaval such as conquest may possibly, and a change of population in an area will probably obliterate such traditions altogether'.[1] This premiss implies that the survival of religious traditions in is a matter to be explained rather than assumed. Hence, I shall examine here how several changes of population in Romanian monasteries and convents have impacted upon the survival of traditions.

My argument is that, under the influence of major demographic, political and economic changes 'Athonite' traditions portrayed in church-endorsed literature as the most 'authentic' form of Orthodox monastic praxis have survived only in the sense of broad 'family resemblances' between Greek and Romanian monasticism. The re-emergence of Mount Athos monastic traditions as symbolic devices central to post-socialist Orthodox discourse should be seen, rather, as a symptom of change, in the sense that more radical innovation is being forestalled through an attempt to revert to an imagined, ´pure´ tradition, formerly brought to Wallachia by Athonite monks.

The end of socialism gave rise to a free religious market in which the Romanian Orthodox Church, an autocephalous institution aspiring to the status of national church (80 per cent of Romanians are Orthodox) found itself competing not just against former rivals, most notably the Catholic, Greco-Catholic and some Protestant denominations, but also against alternative spiritual systems, such as yoga, Daoism, various forms of new age healing, magical practices and so forth. Strictly forbidden during socialism, and glimpsed only through samizdat copies, these novel spiritual practices now received a great amount of popular interest.

The immediate reaction of the Romanian Orthodox Church was to stress its own rich mystical tradition as the 'correct' alternative to these systems which, in its philosophy and vocabulary, Orthodox mysticism broadly resembled. This counter-offensive brought the monastic tradition, formerly obscure, to the forefront of the Church's public discourse, conferring overnight notoriety upon hermitages and monasteries across the country, which began to draw large numbers of pilgrims and monastic recruits. An

---

[1] Hasluck (1929; 3).

important element of this revival was the Athonite mystical tradition of hesychasm, a system of ideas and practices introduced in Romanian monasteries by Greek monks from the fourteenth century onwards. The influence of monks from Mount Athos on the development of Romanian monasticism was stressed by Church writers who argued that these authentic traditions of 'true' monasticism had been kept alive in Romanian monasteries and convents, in spite of historical upheavals.[1] This focus on the purity of monastic traditions represented, I would argue, a reaction to the Church's loss of legitimacy as a result of its open co-operation with the socialist state — a well-known illustration of which was the Patriarch's acquiescence to the demolition of a number of ancient churches by the Ceausescu regime. Consequently, Church literature and public activities (conferences, workshops, pilgrimages, youth organisations) focused strongly on mysticism, hesychasm, and monastic life, portrayed as the mainstay of authentic Orthodoxy.

Yet, since the collapse of socialism, Romanian monasticism has been undergoing a period of re-configuration, because the continuity of the system has been disrupted by the socialist government's decision in the early 1960s to expel from monasteries and convents all monastics between the ages of eighteen and fifty-five. A consequence of this 'reform' was the breakdown the system of apprenticeship central to ensuring the continuity of monastic communities. This system, through which novices were adopted and instructed by elder members on a one-to-one basis, had produced cohesive communities, integrated across age barriers and held together by strong, family-like connections. Contrastingly, present-day communities tend to be divided between old members, unable, due to advanced age and physical ailments to train novices, and young ones, most of whom tend to be only summarily acquainted with traditional monastic practice and ideology. The necessity to redefine monasticism's place in relation to post-socialist society, and the concomitant breakdown of former structures of monastic life have created a field for innovation in monastic practices. In this context, the Church's claim of fidelity to the Athonite 'Rule' can be seen as an attempt to circumscribe innovative tendencies within clear, accepted boundaries, by reaffirming continuity with older traditions.

The following discussion is divided into three sections. The first explores the history of relations between Mount Athos and Wallachian monasteries, which were quite intense until the mid-nineteenth century, and outlines their historical, political and economic context. The second section

---

[1] For example, Pacurariu (1996), Balan (1982), Remete (1996), Savin (1996).

examines what specific elements define ´Athonite´ monasticism. Finally, the third section completes the picture with an ethnographic account of changes within monastic life in Wallachia, based on the memories and insights of living informants from Mora convent.[1]

*Historical links between Wallachia and Mount Athos*

Although the contemporary Romanian Orthodox Church emphasises the constitutive influence of monks from Mount Athos on the organisation of Romanian monasticism, it remains silent regarding the fact that most Wallachian monasteries were for 150 years actual colonies (*metochi*, monastic estates) of Mount Athos and other Greek monasteries. Anxious to stress the Church´s essentially Romanian character, and its historical defence of national values, church writers remain silent regarding this Greek domination within the Church, and it was only through my fieldwork at Mora that I discovered that the monastery was actually inhabited, for half of its existence, by Greek rather than Romanian monks.

Athonite influence in Wallachia began to make itself felt in the fourteenth century, when Romanian monasticism was being standardised and brought under ecclesiastical control. At this time, St Nicodimos, an Athonite monk of Serbian or Romanian origin, founded several of the oldest monasteries in Wallachia. From the Middle Ages onwards, the growing threat of Ottoman conquest brought Christian religion to the political foreground, as autochthonous princes in the Romanian provinces sought to forge alliances with other Christian nations in order to stem Ottoman expansion. Often as acts of thanksgiving for military victories, these rulers frequently founded monasteries, generously endowing them with estates and gold. As a rule, Athonite monks were brought in as abbots to the new monasteries, in order to organise life according to the highest standards.[2]

At the beginning of the sixteenth century, the Romanian Principalities were constrained to accept Ottoman suzerainty, although they were not annexed through military conquest. One of the conditions of this surrender was respect for the autochthonous religion, and thus there were no serious attempts to introduce Islam north of the Danube. The consolidation of Ottoman control over the Principalities was accompanied by the growth of Greek political and

---

[1] The name of the convent and those of informants have been changed.
[2] Pacurariu (1996).

religious influence in these provinces. As Stewart points out, Ottoman suzerainty actually enhanced the status and political influence of the Greek Orthodox Church.[1] This was due to the ascendance of wealthy Greeks from the Phanar district of Constantinople (henceforth called Phanariotes) to high political appointments within the Ottoman Empire and through their wealth, connections and political skills. From the beginning of the eighteenth century, Sultans began appointing Phanariote governors over the Romanian principalities, instead of the less reliable autochthonous princes. In order to consolidate their power, these governors appointed Greek monks to high ecclesiastical positions, and began the practice of 'dedicating' the wealthy Romanian monasteries to Greek ones. Consequently, Greek monks acquired control of the Romanian monasteries, which were formally declared *metochi* (monastic estates) of Mt. Athos and other Greek monasteries, to which they sent two thirds of their annual revenues. As Hasluck notes, the Romanian princes, and later the Phanariote governors were 'after the fall of Constantinople the greatest benefactors of the [Athos] monasteries', which they endowed with money, buildings, and especially land.[2] According to Seton Watson as a result of land donations by local princes and the practice of 'dedicating' local monasteries to Athonite ones, by the mid 1800s, Greek monasteries controlled the remarkable proportion of a fourth of the total surface of Wallachia and a third of Moldavia.[3]

The contemporary Orthodox discourse focuses on the positive aspects of Greek Orthodox involvement in Romania, stressing the harmony of mutual relations between the sister churches throughout the ages.[4] Yet this is what an official publication of a Wallachian diocese said about Greek monks in 1908: 'we saved them from cold and hunger, and they strangled us. They strangled us, the enemies, and we forgave them. We warmed the snake at our breast and it filled us with venom'.[5] As Seton Watson remarks, due to widespread corruption and abusive taxation, by 1862 'the Greek monk was the very opposite of an asset to the [Romanian] state', forming 'a parasitic class, at once alien and incompetent'.[6] Given the strong resentment of the Romanian populace, beggared by the excessive taxation practised by the Phanariote governors and their official appointees, including Greek monks, it is not perhaps altogether surprising that the first decree (1862) passed by the newly

---

[1] Stewart (1994; 140).
[2] Hasluck (1924: 64).
[3] Watson in Pacurariu (1996; 307).
[4] Balan (1982).
[5] Rautu (1909; 32, my translation).
[6] Watson in Pacurariu (1996; 307).

formed Romanian state (comprising Moldavia and Wallachia, united under a Romanian prince) proclaimed the seizure of all monastic estates by the state, as well as the expulsion of all Greek monks from the country, and a ban on speaking the Greek language within the Church.[1]

## The monastic traditions of Mt. Athos

Orthodox monasticism does not include a plurality of separate orders and Rules, as is the case in the Catholic Church, but rather, several variant forms of monastic community organisation. All monasteries follow the 'Rule' of St Basil of Caesareea, but, as Hasluck pointed out, 'this is not a Rule in the Western sense since it laid down only the ethical code of the monastic life: the actual rule observed [is] the *typikon* of the individual monastery which, being varied, was not applicable to the whole [Mount Athos] community'.[2] Thus, since Athonite monasteries vary in organisational structure and rules guiding day-to-day practice, we can not speak of a single form of monastic organisation specific to Mount Athos. Instead, as Hasluck describes in his monograph, patterns of organisation, co-existing even at Mt. Athos, can be placed along a continuum between two opposite conceptions of monastic life present in the canonised writings of the Church Fathers: the eremitic and the coenobitic traditions. Both consider mystical union with God through contemplation the central goal of the monastic's life, but they differ regarding the methods prescribed for achieving it. The older of these traditions, the

---

[1] In his book on Athos, Hasluck tells us the Athonite perspective on the matter: 'In Rumania the causes of the quarrel are ultimately economic. [The princes of the Transdanubian provinces had been the greatest benefactors of Athonite monasteries after the fall of Constantinopole], and the vast estates of the Community and various Athonite monasteries in Moldavia and Wallachia at the time of their alienation brought in a revenue of about £120, 000 yearly. Most of these lands, often attached originally to Rumanian monasteries which were made dependent on Athos, were dedicated by Rumanian princes in the sixteenth century. ... They were administered either by monks who spent but a short time in the country or by bailiffs whose luxury became proverbial. One third only of their revenues stayed in the country, the rest going direct into the coffers of Athos. Prince Couza's government in 1861-2 confiscated the whole of these monastic lands with their church furniture and documents. For this high-handed action, the government sought justification in (1) the alleged corrupt state of the clergy, especially the monks, (2) a quibble on the meaning of the words *inchinare* (dedicate) and *metochi* (monastic estate), and (3) exaggeration of the clauses in the foundation charters which dealt with the obligations of the monasteries to their tenants. The usual conditions of the bequests seem to have been that the sovereign monastery was entitled to the *surplus revenues* of the metochi and in former cases a definite (small) sum was to be set aside annually for a special local charitable purpose ... It is extremely probable in the nature of things that abuses existed. But the real reason of the confiscation was that which necessitated the similar but less drastic cutting short of the monasteries in Greece (1834), viz. that a medieval system is incompatible with the modern state: in the case of Rumania this was aggravated by the fact that money went out of the country. Athos never acquiesced in the seizure, and refused all offers of indemnity on this account' (1924: 64-6).

[2] Hasluck (1924: 24).

eremitic (from the Greek *eremos*, meaning desert) argued the mystical goal was best achieved through complete withdrawal from the world and a focus on strict ascesis.[1] Contrastingly, the coenobitic conception of monasticism, refined by St Basil, argued that the individualism of the eremites led to the sin of pride, and that only life within an integrated community allowed monastics to fulfil the Christian injunction to practice charity.[2] This conception later became prevalent, helping to bring the monastic movement under the control of the Byzantine Church.

Mount Athos was originally an independent territory inhabited by eremitic monks (hermits), who resisted the construction of large monasteries, arguing that it interfered with their solitary way of life. Although the coenobitic communities eventually prevailed and flourished, the tension between the eremitic and coenobitic ideals has persisted at Mt. Athos to the present day.[3] Hermitages coexist with monasteries, but are usually placed under their authority, rather than remaining independent. As a compromise between the strong individualism of the eremites and the equally extreme emphasis on obedience and sharing of the coenobites, a third form of organisation, called idiorythmic evolved. In such communities, monks were allowed a certain amount of autonomy, could own individual possessions and occupy paid positions within the monastery.[4]

In conclusion, we can not speak of a single 'Athonite model' of monastic organisation. Rather, the distinguishing characteristic of monasticism at Mount Athos is the strictness with which the general rules common throughout Orthodoxy are enforced and lived. For instance, these are the features of Athonite life, described by a contemporary monk living at the mountain: (i) continual prayer, day and night; (ii) genuflexion (*metanoia*); (iii) strict and frequent fasting; (iv) constant repetition of the Prayer of the Heart; (v) foregoing sleep (*priveghere*); (vi) following the complete programme of prayer and religious services (including the all-night service, from midnight to dawn); (vii) work, in the daytime, while saying the Prayer of the Heart; (viii) constant meditation of the hour of death and eternal life; (ix) eating only once a day, only vegetarian food,[5] and also the interdiction on all females from entering the Mountain.

---

[1] Lawrence (1994; 3-7).
[2] Lawrence (1994; 9).
[3] Makarios Simonpetridis (2002).
[4] Hasluck (1924: 74).
[5] Sova in Balan (1988: 615, my translation).

In comparison, these are the present-day monastic rules at Tismana, a Wallachian monastic establishment founded by an Athonite monk in the fourteenth century: '(i) frequent confession; (ii) personal example in monastic living; (iii) the study of holy books and theological education of the novices; (iv) humility and obedience'.[1] Indeed, in most Wallachian monasteries and convents, ascetic practices such as fasting, vegetarianism, intensive prayer and work regimes are less severely enforced, while at Athos they are usually compulsory.

Although at Mount Athos coenobitic monasteries are still prevalent, most present-day Romanian monasteries and convents are organised according to the more relaxed idiorythmic model. As a compromise to the eremitic ideals, monastics are allowed, if they so wish, to retreat to hermitages and practice stricter forms of ascesis in the latter part of their career. Such a step normally marks passage into a higher stage of monasticism called 'the great division' (*schima mare*), which implies also a vow of silence, fasting and vegetarianism, all night prayers and solitude, that is, stricter ascetic practices commonly associated with Athonite monasticism.

From this section, it is important to note, as Hasluck observed, that within Orthodox monasticism, variations occur in a different way than in the Catholic case. First, a certain degree of flexibility is built into the system, allowing each diocese and leadership of individual monasteries to spell out and alter the *typikon*, the rules governing daily practice in each establishment (i.e. the schedules of work and prayer, the possibility of paid employment, etc.). Second, when the reform of a monastic establishment is deemed necessary, this is accomplished through a stricter enforcement of existing rules, rather than the creation of a new Rule. Thus, Romanian monasteries can be said to be organised according to the Athonite model in the same sense in which all Orthodox monasteries are, that is, they share St Basil's 'Rule' and basic organisational structures. In the light of these observations, the Romanian Church's claim that its monasteries are organised according to the Athonite model can be upheld only in a weak sense, implying the persistence of general 'family' resemblances.

---

[1] Gligor in Balan (1988: 712-4, my translation).

*Hesychasm*

Although we can not speak of an 'Athonite Rule' as such, there exists an ascetic tradition, *hesychasm*, which was developed at Athos and later introduced, by Athonite monks, in Wallachia. In order to ascertain to what extent the Athonite influence survives in Wallachian monasteries, I shall look for traces of this tradition in present-day monastic practice. Official Church discourse in Romania, particularly after the collapse of socialism, has stressed the centrality of hesychast ideology and practice in Romanian monastic spirituality,[1] but I shall ask whether hesychasm has indeed persisted as a lived-in reality, in spite of historical upheavals, or whether it is, rather, in the process of being re-introduced from above, in an attempt to restore former (idealised) standards of spirituality.

Hesychasm is a set of conceptions and contemplative practices developed by the Athonite monk St Gregory Palamas, (1296-1359). He argued that the embodiment of Christ had, in effect, transformed the substance of the created world by bringing into it the charismatic energies of the Holy Spirit. Since this event, each individual has held divine essence within his own soul. Consequently, mystical enlightenment could be reached through inward concentration, achieved by practising, in solitude, a set of contemplative techniques.[2] This argument recalls the tensions between the eremitic and coenobitic monks at Mt. Athos, and upholds the eremites' point of view, defending their solitary, contemplative lifestyle.[3] Palamas' best known contribution to ascetic technique is the 'prayer of the heart', which consists of the incessant repetition of a formulaic prayer (such as, 'Lord Jesus, have mercy on me, the sinner') with each breath, in such a way that it eventually becomes a refrain repeated unconsciously by the mind.

How did hesychasm fit within the context of Orthodox dogma? It is important to point out that Palamas´ ideas did not represent a radical departure from the views of the Church, but rather, gave further emphasis to a mystical bias already strong in the Orthodox conception of Christianity. 'Orthodoxy is

---

[1] Pacurariu (1996), Balan (1982), Remete (1996), Savin (1996).

[2] Ware (1963: 77-78).

[3] The view that God resided within each person and that one could know God directly by looking within probably sounded too close to gnosticism, and attracted charges of heresy against the hesychasts. In 1341, a Synod was held in Constantinopole to consider the 'hesychast controversy'. Palamas defended himself by pointing out that he drew a distinction between God's essence — unknowable —and his uncreated charismatic energies, which were one with God, but also knowable. He was cleared of the charges owing, it seems, a great deal to the outspoken support of Athonite monks. Subsequently, he was made a bishop and beatified during his lifetime.

conceived to be a living tradition, a continuous hermeneutic interaction in which individuals are guided by the Holy Spirit toward consistent interpretations of both Scripture and the existing body of tradition'.[1] The centrality of mysticism (the premiss that true religious knowledge is mystical, revelatory and derives from direct experience of divine realities) to Orthodox dogma reflects neo-Platonist philosophy (i.e. Plotinus) and the exegetic tradition of the School of Alexandria (Origen, Clement of Alexandria). These writers stressed the allegorical, hidden meaning of scriptures, and the necessity of attaining mystical enlightenment as a pre-requisite to a more thorough understanding and interpretation of scripture. The key ingredient to achieving mystical knowledge is charisma,[2] defined as an uncreated energy emanating directly from God and extraneous to the created world, which elevates the individual to a level where direct knowledge of the divine is possible.

The Church, as the successor of the apostles, holds the monopoly of charisma, and thus, the monopoly over the production, legitimization and dissemination of religious knowledge,[3] but not all members of the clergy have equal access to the knowledge and power conferred by mystical enlightenment. In the eyes of the public, the consumers of religious goods and services, there exists a clear hierarchy, according to which the highest charismatic power, and therefore, efficacy in prayer, healing, foretelling the future and so on, belongs to the monks and hermits rather than parish priests, or even high clerics, who are seen as being too involved in worldly matters. Therefore, it is mainly to monks or nuns with special reputations of saintliness that pilgrims turn when in need of confession, advice, intercession through prayer, or healing. After the collapse of socialism, the newly published literature on Mount Athos and hesychasm helped bring these already present conceptions to the forefront of public discourse and thus, Mount Athos and its traditions became symbols of the power of Orthodoxy, expressed through its initiated monks and nuns.

In conclusion, Mount Athos and hesychasm became, in the post-socialist decade, symbols of a vitality of faith, super-imposed on the already existing monasteries, convents and hermitages, to whom they conferred an

---

[1] Stewart (1994; 140).

[2] This mystical conception of knowledge rests on the following assumptions (i) true knowledge is hidden and available only through the mediation of divine charisma, which lifts the ego above its cognitive limitations, to a state of 'mystical union', placing it on the same level as Divinity, where true knowing can occur; (ii) such mystical knowledge is essentially non-discursive, because divine reality surpasses all description — although discourse based on revelation does exist, for instance, the Patristic writings which are canonised; (iii) synthetic knowledge (such as the mystical), which is holistic (involves mind, emotions, soul, and body), is considered superior to rational discrimination, which is divisive (analytical).

[3] Bourdieu (1971).

aura of mystery and power. These symbols proved very compelling in the context of the uncertainty brought on by the transition from socialism. As a result, monasticism became the most popular and prominent structure within Romanian Orthodoxy during this period of re-configuration and monks and nuns with reputations of saintliness began to attract pilgrims in the thousands. Official Church discourse contributed to this popular trend by portraying monastic establishments as the guardians of authentic Orthodox faith and tradition during the communist times, when many clerics were seen to support the oppressive regime. According to this perspective, authentic spiritual traditions inherited from Athos had remained within monasteries and hermitages, untouched by upheavals in the secular world.[1] In the next section, I shall consider how change and tradition appear to those who lived within one such convent.

*Athonite traditions and the case of Mora Convent*

I began my research at Mora Convent under the impression, garnered from the wealth of literature published in the post-socialist period on hesychasm, mysticism and monastic traditions, that hesychasm constituted an important part of the ideology and practice of contemporary Romanian monasticism. There were good reasons to suppose that Mora might preserve such traditions, as it is considered one of the greatest monastic establishments of Wallachia. The community had been founded by Athonite monks, and it had been inhabited by Greek monks until the middle of the nineteenth century. However, one of the first things that struck me, as I began to gain an inside view of this community of 60 nuns, was the shortness of their memory regarding the history and monastic traditions of Mora. The medieval atmosphere of this fortress convent, with thick high walls and high iron-clad gates, contrasted with the fact that almost none of the nuns knew what had happened there before the 1950s. Even the nun acting as a historical guide to visitors knew only the 'official account' of the convent's early history, but very little about life there in the nineteenth and early twentieth centuries.[2]

There were, I discovered, possible reasons for this absence of memory regarding the intimate history of life at Mora. There had been four radical changes of population at the convent in the past two hundred years. The Greek

---

[1] Balan (1982), Pacurariu (1996).

[2] For example, she did not know about the fact (well remembered by older villagers from the area) that, in the 1920s, the Romanian royal family frequently used the convent as a summer retreat, and even added new buildings to the compound.

monks were expelled, replaced by Romanian monks who, in turn, abandoned the monastery, which was then converted into a convent. The nuns were expelled by the socialist regime in the early 1960s, and, in the 1980s, the community was reconstitution with nuns who did not originate from the area of the convent but from remoter regions. As a result, there remained at Mora only two elderly nuns of local origin, who had personal memories of life there before the socialist changes.

Inter-generational communication seemed very superficial, and most younger nuns showed little interest in what the older ones had to say: the system of monastic apprenticeship, whereby senior nuns 'adopt' and initiate novices into monastic life, was not functioning. Formerly, this system of family-like connections between elder and younger nuns had produced continuity in monastic communities and contributed to integrating them across generations. Its breakdown was a long-term consequence of the 1962 socialist reform of monastic establishments, which expelled all nuns and monks between the ages of 18 and 55, aiming to re-integrate them in society. The removal of young and middle aged monastics produced long term demographic changes and still affects the pattern of monastic life. The community I found at Mora was divided between elderly, ailing nuns no longer able to assume the training of novices, and young ones, many of whom were acquainted only superficially with monastic practice and ideology, from books rather than direct instruction. Thus, however strong Mora's former links with Greece, changes in the monastic population created radical discontinuities between the present and earlier patterns of life. What I found was not the continuity of tradition stressed in official Church discourse but rather, a picture of repeated and indeed forced dynamic transformation.

Eventually, I discovered an ideal informant in the person of Mother Veselia, a tiny elderly nun (born in 1919) raised at Mora from the age of three by two aunts who were nuns. Her parents, members of a large local family, had given her up because they had too many children (a common reason for monastic recruitment at that time). Intelligent and inquisitive, Veselia educated herself by studying books and documents in the convent's archives, and had a keen memory of events there during her lifetime. Younger nuns did not, however, benefit from her knowledge, because, due to a conflict with Mora's leadership, Veselia had never returned to live inside the convent after the 1962 expulsion, preferring to remain, living as a nun, in a small house outside the convent gates.

When I asked her about Mora's connections with Mount Athos, she replied: "No, you won't find anything like Athonite monastic life here, there aren't any more links with Mount Athos". For her, Athos represents an exotic and remote place, closely connected to the central figures of Christianity, an epicentre of the faith, where monks lead an exemplary life, in marked contrast to the misbehaving young nuns at Mora nowadays:

> Over there, it is not allowed for the 'female part' to go, ever since the Saviour ascended to Heaven. He gave gifts to the Virgin and the Apostles, and each went to [missionise]. They drew lots, and the Virgin fell to Mount Athos. Because there was the God Apolon, they say he was so high you could see him from Constantinople. He was an idol of gold, but they say he was their god. I read somewhere that they still preserve there the gifts that the magi brought to Jesus, some little grains of incense, you can imagine how they got there, where they might have come from, to get to Mount Athos. There were many hermits, and holy fathers [at Athos], so sanctified by the land itself that the novices that came there to do obedience used to see during liturgy: a monk and an angel, a monk and an angel, just like that!
>
> Now, go in our convent among the sisters to see what [the young nuns] are doing. They talk, giggle, I don't know what! At Athos, the rule was thus: no one talks during the obedience chores. Because only this way you can lead monastic life. But here, the novices have not shed 'the world' at all. They know everything that is going on in the world outside. Can you expect miracles, when our novices sneak out to go to the discotheque? Because I've seen them, but I don't care!

What did she know about the Greek monks who had lived at Mora? 'Oh, I always felt admiration for the Greek monks that lived here, because they improved and beautified the monastery'. In particular, she liked to remember the last Greek abbot, a monk from Meteora named Hrisantos, under whose leadership Mora achieved the height of its prominence and wealth — he controlled several surrounding monasteries and their estates, and ran a flourishing cattle trade as far as Budapest and Vienna. However, Hrisantos´ memory is highly controversial: in church publicity he has come to symbolise the corrupt and predatory side of Greek monks. A contemporary archbishop who is a well-known literary figure, wrote a strange fictional short story drawing on accounts of Hrisantos' life. In this strange story, the immensely wealthy and powerful abbot is plagued by an unusual virility and is sexually aggressive towards laywomen and nuns alike. After his death, Hrisantos' body, buried under the floor of the Mora church, continues to excite women pilgrims, who tempt the monks, leading to the gradual abandonment of the monastery by the confused monks. Later, the body is exhumed and found to be completely undecayed, and it is discovered that Hrisantos had had an incestuous relationship with his mother in Greece. Through a further chain of events, Hrisantos' dead body attempts to rape a nun, also dead but undecayed, who turns out to have been his daughter.[1] I cite this story because it shows that the stereotype of the corrupt and predatory Greek monk, a result of the Phanariote colonisation, also persists in the historical imagination, alongside its opposite, the image of the saintly Athonite hermit Nicodimos, who brought hesychasm to Romania. It is interesting, furthermore, that the 'positive coloniser' Nicodimos was ethnically 'adopted', as church writers argue he was a Romanian (born in the Vlach community of northern Greece) and Serbians claim he was ethnically Serbian, whilst Hrisantos remains decidedly alien and Greek. Furthermore, a distinction is drawn between Nicodimos, an authentic monk, and Hrisantos, a false one who, Anania suggests, was really a common criminal who had taken refuge within the Romanian church.

At Mora, two of the Greek abbots are still remembered, the first, an Athonite monk named Ioannis, who built a church for the neighbouring village, and Hrisantos, who built adequate living quarters for the monks and surrounded the monastery with a high wall to protect its gold from brigands. Generally, they are seen as opposites: one is good, the other bad, one a true monk, the other using religion for power and profit, but Mother Veselia had a more nuanced view:

> they say Hrisantos was found undecayed fifty years after his death, but I, who am alive, have washed his bones. They found his remains accidentally, under the church floor, when they changed the pavement. I said I wanted to be the one to wash his bones, because I care very much about the monks who were here before, because they did something for the place! It is true that Hrisantos sent gold out to his Greek monastery, but he also organised the economic activity of the monastery, making a great deal of money and improving living conditions for the monks. Unlike many abbots before him, who allowed the place to decay and crumble, and the monks to live in unhealthy conditions, he left something durable in his wake.

It seems Hrisantos became a symbol of the Greek monks' corruption partly through the unfortunate timing of his period of power — immediately before the expulsion of the Greek monks from Romania in 1862. This is what a 1908 monograph on the monasteries in the area, published by the diocese, has to say about this change of population at Mora:

> This holy monastery, built for Romanian monks, had become, by the middle of the last century, a cave of Greek brigands, a place for the spoliation for Romanians, for the enrichment of the riffraff of Greece and

---

[1] Anania (1990: 230-77).

the Phanar, a place of corruption and promiscuity of Greek snakes. And the prototype of the beast-man, corrupt, thief and corrupting is that sinister figure of the Gold Monk, the Abbot Hrisantos. Elders still preserve fresh the memory of the horrors perpetrated by this devil in monk's habit, from whose claw no family escaped without being dishonoured, no girl uncorrupted (*necinstita*). At the local fair, he used to set up his tent [and pick out, from the crowd, women he wanted]. ... Such a long time the Greeks have sucked out the fortunes of this country, and so outraged was the local population, that on the portrait of I. Merisescu [the Romanian abbot that followed Hrisantos] it is written: '*the first Romanian abbot*'.[1]

It is clear that, even by Hrisantos' time, the strict Athonite way of life was no longer being practised by the monks at Mora. After the Greek monks' departure, there was an attempt to reform monastic life, substituting Romanian monks for Greek. However, the loss of economic independence through the seizure of monastic estates—and the subsequent dependence of monasteries on state subsidies—led to rapid decay of all monastic establishments in the area. In just thirteen years, Mora was abandoned altogether and the remaining monks moved to another monastery, which was also later abandoned for lack of resources and recruits. Another neighbouring monastery was temporarily converted into a prison to keep it from falling into ruin.[2] Thus, Wallachian monasteries that had formerly flourished nearly ceased to exist in the wake of the Greek monks' expulsion. However, although this reform happened to be associated with the end of Greek colonisation, it was, as Hasluck observes, due essentially to the fundamental incompatibility of the medieval system of large monastic estates with the modern state which was just at that point coming into being.[3]

In 1872, these largely empty monasteries were converted into convents. For nearly fifty years, the new population of nuns at Mora was allowed to live in a very independent, loosely organised community. They had separate households and supported themselves by working their own land and keeping cattle. Such laxity is untypical of Orthodox monastic life, and was due to the Diocese's weakened and disorganised condition following the seizure of monastic estates.[4] When, in the 1920s, the Romanian Orthodox Church achieved the status of an autocephalous institution, the monasteries and convents were again reformed. The practice of private ownership was abolished (because it led to economic inequalities among nuns), and communities organised according to the idiorythmic model also present at Athos. The nuns

---

[1] Rautu (1908; 37, my translation).

[2] Rautu (1908).

[3] Hasluck (1924; 66).

[4] Rautu (1908).

at Mora resisted the introduction of this new, stricter regime and many (including Veselia's aunts) left the convent in protest, taking their possessions with them rather than surrendering them to the community. Such disobedience shows the nuns were accustomed to a high degree of independence. Eventually, the threat of excommunication brought most of the dissenters back to the convent.

According to Veselia, the new regime emphasised hard work, obedience to the leadership and attendance at all religious services, but discouraged education and theological training. The abbess stressed above all equality among nuns, rejecting educated novices because their superiority might produce inequalities in the community. At this time, after World War I, monastic recruits were mainly of local peasant stock — either surplus children of local families like Veselia or war orphans. Nearly all the elderly nuns I have met joined the convent as children, and expulsion from the convent by the socialist reform was particularly traumatic, because it obliged them to learn to survive in a world entirely alien to them.

This expulsion, in 1962, brought on the most recent change of population at Mora. At that time, the recently elected abbess M. highly educated herself, introduced a new emphasis on theological education for nuns. In 1940, she opened a theological seminary at the convent, suspended by the communists a few years later. Nevertheless, M. managed to maintain her position and keep the convent open with a minimum of staff. Later the state's attitude towards monasticism relaxed, and the convent was again allowed to recruit novices.

M. was born in Transylvania, and according to Veselia, she encouraged Transylvanian novices to join, promoting them to positions of power in the convent. This is quite likely because, during my stay at Mora, I noticed that nuns tended to form groups on the basis of their regional provenance. As a result, the newest population of Mora is dominated by Transylvanians, who hold the dominant positions, and includes nuns from diverse regions, but none from the local area.

After the collapse of socialism, Mora received more than thirty young novices, but not all remained to take their vows. The pattern of recruitment has changed as a result of social and economic contingencies. About half of the novices came from poor or broken families, and thought their disadvantaged background had significantly contributed to their decision to join. Others came from the urban middle class (several with university degrees) and were recruited through monk-confessors, churches and Christian student organisations. Having known them for two years, I think most of the novices joined with a genuine desire to practice spiritual discipline, but most felt monastic life was not what they had expected, because of an excessive emphasis on work rather than spiritual guidance and activities. Part of the problem is, again, economic: in order to sustain itself, the convent is exploiting its potential as a tourist attraction, and has even opened a hotel inside the grounds. As one nun put it, 'the world has come into the convent and as a result we have little privacy and time for our spiritual needs, whereas monastic life ought to be a retreat away from worldly matters'. The constant stream of tourists with expensive equipment and enjoyable lifestyles, so tantalisingly close, yet forbidden, is quite distracting for the novices, and several told me they would leave the convent if they had the skills (education, work experience) to support themselves.

### How enduring are Athonite traditions in Wallachia?

After socialism collapsed, Romanians began to explore areas of knowledge and activity previously forbidden, and as a result, there was an intense kindling of interest in religion and spirituality. Curiosity was stimulated by the media and by a profusion of publications on spiritual matters, which appeared almost overnight. In this context, several monasteries and convents acquired national fame, drawing large numbers of pilgrims on account of the rumoured spiritual efficacy of the prayers and rituals practised there. Hermits and monks acquired saintly reputations, published books of spiritual advice and insights, appeared on television shows, and were sought by pilgrims from both urban and rural backgrounds. The Orthodox Church, which was now facing increased competition in the religious field (from other forms of Christianity as well as alternative spiritual systems) stressed its own mystical tradition as 'correct', and in this context, hesychasm, considered an 'authentic' tradition preserved in Romanian monasteries became prominent. Yet, while lay spiritual practitioners began to exploit this niche by teaching classes of hesychasm to the urban middle classes, Archbishop Anania, confessed that: 'of all the great Romanian monastics I have interviewed, none claimed he actually practised the prayer of the heart' central to hesychasm. 'We may conclude that, [although there may be some monastics who do not say they practice this form of meditation out of modesty], *this form of prayer, formerly widespread [in Romania] is on the point of disappearing completely'* (my italics).[1] This is tantamount to saying that Athos-style monasticism is practically non-existent in Romania, particularly as Anania adds that Father Cleopa, a famous Romanian hermit, had to go to Mount Athos to learn the proper way of practising this prayer, which is no longer taught properly in Romania.[2] This suggests that, rather than being locally taught, passed on from master to novice, hesychasm was being re-discovered through post-socialist popular literature, and re-introduced into monastic life by monks and nuns interested in experimenting with such techniques. Mount Athos and its monastic traditions provide a point of reference for Romanian Orthodoxy, an idealised image of how ´real monasticism´ ought to be (and, monks and nuns often told me, is not). My research suggests that, in the past as now, whenever monastic communities were considered to have become too lax, they were reformed along the lines of the Athos ideal — that is, through a stricter enforcement of existing rules, and reversion to more severe work and prayer schedules — a pattern Hasluck also discovered at Athos.[3]

*Frasinei*

Rigour in enforcing rules varies from one monastery to another, and in present-day Wallachia, only the monastery Frasinei is commonly described as truly 'Athonite'. Unlike Mora, Frasinei was never inhabited by Greek monks, being founded in 1848 around the time their domination was ending. Interestingly, the founders intended it to be an 'experiment in true monasticism', unlike any other monastery in Wallachia, and to organise the community brought an Athonite monk as the first abbot.[4] This choice suggests that even at a time when Greek monks were generally considered corrupt Mount Athos remained a potent symbol of high monasticism.

However, Frasinei is atypical of Wallachian monasteries for several reasons. First, it is relatively new, and its connections to Greek monasteries much more superficial than those of Mora and other older, ´dedicated´

---

[1] Anania in Balan (1988; 598).

[2] This is how an Athonite monk explains the performance in a letter to his novice: 'Mystical prayer must flow like a river, be completely non-intentional. In order to achieve this, first you must repeat the prayer fast, to keep the mind from straying. You must send it into the heart, because the mind feeds the soul. First, you say the prayer a few times while breathing once, later, as the mind gets used to staying in the heart, you say it with each breath.' My translation. Iosif (1996; 3-4).

[3] Hasluck (1924; 74).

[4] Rautu (1908; 45).

monasteries. Secondly, special efforts were made to maintain Frasinei as close to Athos standards as possible: women are still excluded from entering its grounds, and the monastery was exempted from the 1864 seizure of estates through special dispensation from the prince, thus ensuring independence from state interference, and economic viability.[1]

After the collapse of socialism, Frasinei acquired the reputation of a centre of high spirituality, fuelled by the exceptional strictness of the regime of life, which impressed all pilgrims. This is how a man who had been to many monasteries throughout Romania described life there:

> It is a disaster, over there, worse than in jail. It is very rough there, you can't make a move, nothing! I think life is better even in labour camps than there. They [the monks] can't make any move. Their confessors won't allow them. And all their time is scheduled, all of it! I have been in the army, but never have seen anything like conditions there, they work them harder than in the army![2]

In recent years, monks from Frasinei have frequently travelled to Mt. Athos for training, and they have begun to 'colonise' other monasteries and hermitages in the area, introducing what are considered to be higher standards of practice, closer to the Athos ideal. For instance, Patrunsa, in 1995 a small mountain hermitage with five monks, has been reorganised by a monk from Frasinei into a monastery of thirty monks, and its spiritual fame has been steadily increasing, as has the number of pilgrims it draws.

If monasticism is undergoing a period of revival, reconfiguring its meaning and role in relation to contemporary society, the most daring innovation I came across was still based on hesychasm, and belonged to a monk from Frasinei. In the 1990s, Fr. Ghelasie has applied hesychast ideas to health, developing a system of holistic therapy meant to cure disease through diet and spiritual exercise. Conceived at a time when, due to the novelty of religious freedom, exotic ideas were flooding the religious market, this system is an attempt to set the record straight on bio-energetic and occult methods of healing. Ghelasie describes, 'hesychast sacro-therapy' as a synthesis, transcending, though not rejecting, science, and his stated goal is to

---

[1] Rautu (1908; 45).

[2] My impression was that this pilgrim was quite likely a member of the (post-socialist) secret police sent to keep an eye on pilgrimages — he did not 'look the part of the pilgrim', and his zeal for going to monasteries contrasted with his lack of basic understanding of Orthodox religion (a lack which he demonstrated later in the conversation). However, I am convinced he was quite sincere in these comments, and, being an army man, he must know what he is talking about.

reintroduce miraculous healing to medicine. Accordingly, he borrows from the vocabulary of science and bio-energetic healing terms such as: energy, yin, yang, alkaline, acid, or neutral. He starts from the assumption that the fall of mankind has severed 'created energies' (present in living things) from divine 'un-created energies' — charisma — the key element that sustains and restores life, producing 'mechanical-biological torn energies', which, being severed from the life-sustaining divine source, are dead and disease producing. Consequently, only divine charisma can restore the energetic balance and health. For this reason, Ghelasie argues, all other healing systems outside of Orthodoxy are ineffectual, as humans alone can not correct energy imbalances without divine charisma. Disease is defined as an imbalance between the three components of living things, identified by Ghelasie as alkaline, acid and neutral, terms he also identifies as yin, yang and neutral. Healing is effected through diet,[1] and eating represents a 'holy mystery' (a sacrament), an act whereby divine charisma can enter the human body and sustain life. Since cooking is considered a way of killing food, balance is to be restored by eating raw foods, and hesychast bread made of crushed wheat and water left in the sun to dry. This bread, symbolising the body of Christ, is, according to Ghelasie, the perfect food, encompassing a balance of the trinity of elements.

In 1995, when I came across Ghelasie's books, there was a great deal of interest in his system, and many informants believed hesychast sacro-therapy to be a highly advanced idea, fit for the twenty-first century. Yet, a few years later enthusiasm had subsided, and I did not meet anyone, either in the diocese town or in the villages around Mora, who actually applied this form of therapy. Perhaps this was partly due to the strictness of the diets recommended, which made them unpracticable to most meat-loving Romanians, but the tendency towards a decrease in interest regarding spiritual and occult matters seemed more generalised. If the early nineties brought a sudden revival of religion and spirituality, the latter part of the decade saw a reversal of this trend. For instance, when a bio-energetic healer began practising in my village, patients flooded in queuing up for hours, but two years later he stopped practising there altogether for lack of patients. People said it cost too much, and, although they claimed they 'felt something' when he worked on them, they did not see significant improvements to their health. Pilgrimages to monasteries and convents continue to be organised regularly, but many formerly enthusiastic  pilgrims became disenchanted. A young

---

[1] Diseases are classified in terms of the three basic elements, and treated with specific diets of raw vegetables and fruits, classified on the basis of aspect and colour into telluric and solar, passive and active.

professional man, who, as a student, made a hobby of pilgrimages, told me: 'I don't go to Frasinei any more, they are just a bunch of homosexuals, these monks. I once saw an old hermit touch a young man in an indecent manner'.

## Conclusions

Micro-level research is limited in its time scale, making it difficult to assess long term trends, yet I think localised data highlights the uncertainties and dilemmas of the post-socialist religious revival, the tension between the Church´s tradition-orientedness and the contingencies inherent in a rapidly-changing social, economic and political environment. Moreover, a diachronic view appears to suggest that, within the past 200 years, the Church, like Romanian society itself, has weathered not one, but several relatively intense transitions. Amidst all this change, the Orthodox Church continued to view itself as 'an unalterable totality, a whole pattern of faith transmitted through the ages.[1] To use Bloch's term, it has cultivated a 'platonic style of memory', which is past-oriented, denies temporal change, dismissing it as insignificant, and stresses its unchanged essence and continuity with origins. Bloch contrasts this style of remembering with 'Aristotelian memory', which is present-oriented, eagerly incorporating new elements, and stressing the importance of adaptation.[2] The disparity between the representation of Orthodox monastic life in public discourse and its (no less significant) practical, lived-in realities is due to this 'platonic' de-emphasis of imperfect reality in favour of ideal type.

How did Romanian monasticism reconstitute itself after the revolution of 1989? The revolution could not produce a discontinuity in time, a sudden break with the past, or a return to pre-communist values: the past remains in the present. For instance, Mora's leadership has maintained the priorities set during socialism, to preserve and restore the architectural compound, cultivate good relations with the political elite, foster tourism. Meanwhile, several of the nuns complained to me that 'true monasticism is no longer practised here'. Yet, considering Mora's history from Hrisantos onwards, it is hard to see when 'true monasticism', in the sense of active pursuit of the mystical goal through dedication to ascesis, was actually a focus of this convent's life. Most often, the community was too busy adapting to economic and political changes to concentrate much on anything else.

---

[1] Ware (1980: 318, qtd. in Stewart).
[2] Bloch (1998).

Does this mean that the true Orthodox mystical tradition is waning? In Orthodox monasticism, as in any other vocation, reconciling ideal types of religious experience with everyday life is a contingency rather than a choice. Monastic life has not survived unchanged, but it has managed to always maintain a degree of relevance in relation to the present, to keep up recruitment and work out strategies of adaptation. One strategy for managing change, I have tried to show, is the periodic re-appropriation of an idealised standard issuing from a renowned spiritual centre — Mt. Athos — and the justification of innovations in terms of established traditions, such as hesychasm. The idea of mystical knowledge as the only authentic religious knowledge allows room for innovation, and at the same time permits the Church to maintain its monopoly of knowledge. While, in discourse, Romanian Orthodoxy preserves 'the quality of an ever actual present, in the living light of Tradition',[1] in practice, it is perhaps closer to the doctrine of Patriarch Justinian, the first appointee to this position during socialism, who, in his manifesto 'Apostolatul Social' (the social discipleship) set out to prove the possibility of conciliation between communism and Christianity. He argued that Orthodoxy rested on a complementarity between 'tradition' and 'renewal', a dialectical model meant to demonstrate that Orthodoxy is capable of adapting to the new society.[2]

*REFERENCES*

Anania, V. 1990 *Amintirile Peregrinului Apter*, Bucharest; Cartea Romaneasca.
Balan, I. 1982 *Vetre de Sihastrie Romineasca*, Bucharest; Editura Institutului Biblic al Bisericii Ortodoxe Romane.
Balan, I. 1988 *Convorbiri Duhovnicesti* (1,2), Roman; Editura Episcopiei Romanului si Husilor.
Bloch, M. 1998 *How we think they think: anthropological approaches to cognition, memory, and literacy*, Boulder, Co; Westview Press.
Bourdieu, P. 1971 'Genese et Structure du Champ Religieux', *Revue Francaise de Sociologie* XII, 295-334.
Bria, I. 1981 *Dictionar de Teologie Ortodoxa*, Bucharest; Editura Institutului Biblic si de Misiune al Bisericii Ortodoxe.
Crainic, N. 1993 *Sfintenia si Implinirea Sufletului: curs de teologie mistica 1935-36*, Iasi; Editura Mitropoliei Moldovei si Bucovinei.

---

[1] Lossky (1974; 164).
[2] Gillet (1997; 41).

Ghelasie, G. 1994 *Hrana Harica: Retete Complementare la Medicina Isihasta*, Bucharest; Editura Neva.

Gillet, O. 1997 *Religion et nationalisme: l'idéologie de l'Église orthodox roumaine sous le régime communiste*, Bruxelles ; Éditions de l'Université de Bruxelles.

Hasluck, F. 1924 *Athos and its monasteries*, London; Kegan Paul, Trench, Trubner & Co. Ltd.

Hasluck, F. 1929 *Christianity and Islam under the Sultans*, two vols. Edited by M. Hasluck. Oxford; Clarendon Press.

Iosif, G. 1996 *Marturii din viata monahala*, Bucharest; Editura Bizantina.

Lawrence, C. 1984 *Medieval monasticism: forms of religious life in Western Europe in the Middle Ages*, London; Longman.

Lossky, V. 1974 *In the image and likeness of God*, London; S.P.C.K.

Pacurariu, M. 1996 *Istoria Bisericii Ortodoxe Romane*, Galati; Ediutra Episcopiei Dunarii de Jos.

Rautu, M. 1908 *Monografia eclesiastica a judetului Valcea*, Ramnicu Valcea; Imprimaria Judetului si a Comunei R. Valcea.

Remete, G. 1996 *Dogmatica Ortodoxa*, Alba Iulia; Editura Episcopiei Ortodoxe.

Savin, I. 1996 *Mistica si Ascetica Ortodoxa* Sibiu; Tipografia Eparhiala.

Simonpetridis, M. 2002 'Interview' in *Ortho Logia, Romanian Orthodox Spirituality Journal*, Online edition: www.ortho-logia.com.

Stewart, C. 1994 *Demons and the Devil: moral imagination in modern Greek culture*, Princeton; Princeton University Press.

Verdery, K. 1991 *National ideology under socialism: identity and cultural politics in Ceausescu's Romania*, Berkeley; University of California Press.

Verdery, K. 1996 *What was socialism, and what comes next?* Princeton, NJ; Princeton University Press.

Ware, T. 1963 *The Orthodox Church*, Harmondsworth; Penguin.

Weber, M. 1993 *The Sociology of Religion*, Boston; Beacon Press.

.

# PART SIX

# ARCHAEOLOGY, HERITAGE AND IDEOLOGY

# 35. HERITAGE AND NATIONALISM IN THE BALKANS AND ANTOLIA OR 'CHANGING PATTERNS, WHAT HAS HAPPENED SINCE HASLUCK'?

Mehmet ÖZDOĞAN

Crucially, Thrace is located between Europe and Asia. Considered a threshold, it has always been a resource when searching for enlightenment on events that may have taken place in either of these continents. However, it is now evident that Thrace did not always play that active role in cultural history that is so often envisaged. In fact, its place as a cultural bridge has varied considerably in time from an active 'transmitter' to becoming marginal. Almost mirroring its changing position, the interest of historians in the region has also varied; this latter interest, however, has changed not so much according to the available facts but with changes in political trends.

In earlier years, the ancient cultures of the Near East were taken to be the ancestors of European civilization, thus stimulating theories based on diffusionist models. Accordingly, Anatolia and Thrace's role in cultural history was reduced to being a bridge transmitting ideas or peoples from the Near East to Europe. However, later, when European nations began working for a 'European Identity' that excluded all foreign influences it became almost embarrassing to mention the presence of foreign elements that contributed to the formation of European cultures. Thus, Thrace, lying in between South-eastern Europe and Anatolia, became an 'archaeologically uninteresting' marginal zone. More recently, with the onset of global trends, new intellectual approaches such as pluralism or multi-culturalism have become fashionable and Anatolia is again being looked upon for the roots of European civilization. Besides these general trends, nationalism and communism, and their impact in the formation of local schools of archaeology, have also played a significant role in designing research strategies in this critical zone.

*Thrace: barrier or a land bridge?*[1]

South-eastern Europe, or the Balkans is located on the threshold of Europe and Asia. Eastern Thrace, the small peninsula protruding from the Balkans towards Anatolia, constitutes the main point of contact between these land masses. Besides its strategic position, it is also on the narrow neck of the main maritime route connecting the Aegean with the Black Sea. Thus, Eastern Thrace, or the region around the Sea of Marmora holds a central position between four distinct cultural entities: the Balkans, the Aegean, Anatolia and the Pontic littoral. It is mainly due to this position that the region has conventionally been regarded as a cultural bridge transmitting peoples, ideas or commodities between distinct cultural spheres. In this respect, Hasluck evidently sensed the significance of this region; his work both at Kırklareli, the heartland of Eastern Thrace, as well as on the Kapıdağ peninsula may be considered a reflection of this understanding. The pioneering work of Hasluck was not taken further, however, and Thrace became one of the archaeologically least-explored regions.

As the significance of Thrace has been acknowledged by almost all scholars, the reasons beyond the paucity of research in this region are worth questioning; the research strategies that govern archaeological field work are not sufficient to answer this question alone. Changing trends in politics — not only in the region, but more significantly in Western Europe — stand out as the main factor, as they had an impact in designing socio-historic theories, that directly or indirectly influenced research strategies. In reality, local and globular political trends are intermingled with each other in an inseparable way; nevertheless, here, for the sake of clarity, we shall consider them under different headings.

*Our variable: the changing role of the Balkans in cultural history*

In the course of the last decade or so, our knowledge of the sequence of cultures in Thrace has increased considerably. An overview of recent evidence has been extensively published elsewhere,[2] so here we shall restrain from going into any particular details. However, there are a number of points

---

[1] This phrase was formulated some years ago by David French, one of the only scholars to have mastered the archaeological assemblages of the near East as well as those of the Balkans (French 1986).

[2] See especially Özdoğan (1996a, 1998b, 1999).

relevant to the general position of Thrace in between Europe and Asia that are worth mentioning within the context of this paper in order to stress the changing role played by Thrace in cultural history.

Like any other region that is located at the meeting point of distinct geographical entities, Thrace occupies a central position at the same time being marginal to everything around it. This is vividly exemplified in recent history. During the period when the Ottoman Empire extended from the Balkans to the remote parts of the Near East, Thrace held a central position, but it became a marginal area when the Empire disintegrated. This pattern appears to repeat itself in much of prehistory. During the Neolithic period, at the time when Neolithic economies were expanding from Anatolia to Europe, Thrace was active as a cultural bridge transmitting this new way of life from one continent to the other. Even then, this was not an event that developed on a single track; as evidenced by our excavations at Hoca Çeşme, it involved endemic movement of Neolithic farmers, but simultaneously, as indicated by the sites of the Fikirtepe culture in Eastern Marmora, acculturation of local food gatherers was also taking place.

Following the establishment of farming economies in South-eastern Europe, during the time of the so-called 'Vinça' culture, there seems to be an active interaction going through the Sea of Marmora. However, by the beginning of the Late Chalcolithic, Thrace became an area marginal to all of its surroundings, an invisible border being established along the Sea of Marmora. This is an episode that is worth stressing as it demonstrates how the role of a region can change in time. The Neolithic way of life that led to the establishment of farming villages both on the Anatolian plateau, as well as in the Balkans, had been developing up the end of the Chalcolithic Period as a rural economy, primarily based on farming, without any apparent sign of development towards social complexity.

However, in the semi-arid and arid regions of the Near East, a social dynamic was proceeding on different lines. The developments in the Near East that led to complex social structures are too intricate even to be summarized within this paper.[1] Nevertheless from a synoptic viewpoint it is possible to say with some justification that in the arid regions of the Near East, establishing irrigation systems became indispensable due to the risk of drought. Surplus production, which in other areas would not attain surplus value, became an important asset in such dry areas. This eventually stimulated the development of more complex systems, known as the formation of urban and state economies.

---

[1] For details see Özdoğan (1996b).

This new form of society had developed in Syro-Mesopotamia, an area lying to the south of the Anatolian plateau; surplus production had no value in Anatolia or in the Balkans, where environmental possibilities are considerably more extensive than in the southern flat-lands of the Near East. However, as surplus value production became incorporated with an organised bureaucratic system, the state model of society began to extend its reach, eventually becoming a 'world system'.

The expansion of this model to Anatolia began by the early stages of the Late Chalcolithic Period and became fully established in the third millennium. Even though the eventual model of urbanisation that developed in Anatolia was considerably different from that of the Mesopotamian one, it still resulted in radical changes in social structure. Thus, in Anatolia the life-style that developed by the Late Chalcolithic is basically different from that of the earlier periods. The changes should not be regarded only as the establishment of urban centres but more significantly as transformations in social structure, in economy and in technology. Thus, gradually Anatolia became a part of the Syro-Mesopotamian system. Considering the limitations of transportation, it is self evident that the western parts of the Anatolian plateau may be considered as being on the fringes of this new system.

The development of urbanisation in Anatolia coincided with the onset of a new cultural formation in the northern parts of the Balkans, the Gumelnitsa-Cucuteni culture. This new formation, the Gumelnitsa-Cucuteni culture, compared to the previous cultures in the Balkans is highly sophisticated and evidently became a centre of attraction. However, the components of this culture are totally different from those of Mesopotamian and Anatolia, with no indications of a complex socio-economic structure that would eventually lead to urbanization or to state formation. Thus, during the fourth millennium BC, two alternative core systems were developing, one in the Near East and the other in the Northern Balkans, leaving Thrace in the middle.

The marginal position of Thrace during this period is well reflected in the archaeological record. Among the prehistoric cultures of Bulgaria, the Gumelnitsa-Kocadermen group is certainly the most prolific. It is during this period that there is a marked increase in population, exploitation of metal sources including copper and gold, and the manufacture of highly sophisticated ceramics that are fired in high temperatures. Moreover, this is the time of 'mound-building' in Bulgaria, meaning that there is a continuum in settlement sites leading to the accumulation of archaeological debris of considerable thickness. However, Eastern Thrace is almost void of any habitation during the Late Chalcolithic Period; all we could find datable to this period are rather small flat settlements, some revealing Pre-Cucuteni and/or early Gumelnitsa types of sherds.[1]

We are conscious of the limitations of surface surveys and that any survey, no matter how professionally conducted, may overlook numerous sites. However, if there had been numerous mound sites similar in size to those of Bulgaria, we would certainly have encountered at least a few, and one would expect prestige objects of this culture to turn up in local museums. There is then some justification to come to the conclusion that during the Late Chalcolithic Period Thrace isolated, 'external' or 'marginal' to the then developing World Systems.

The 'fault-line' that became established during the Chalcolithic Period was sustained throughout the entire span of the Bronze Age;[2] however, this time developing on different lines. On the Anatolian side, states developed by the end of the Bronze Age into Empires. In contrast, in the Balkans nomadic life based on herding was introduced. This drastic difference in socio-economic systems further deepened the break between the two regions. Several millennia passed by before Thrace gained a central position again. Even the Hellenistic, Roman and Byzantine Empires did not provide Thrace with a more central position, as their control over northern Balkans was never complete. It is only when the Ottomans established their domination over Anatolia and the Aegean as well as the Balkans that Thrace regained a central position.

What we have presented above is an over-simplistic overview of the evidence; it is clear that real life is much more complex then we have summarized. However the general trend is discernable, and the role assigned so often to Thrace by looking at its location on a map is not supported by the evidence found in the field. It is at this point that the impact of political thinking that defines archaeological research becomes so significant.

---

[1] For details see Özdoğan (in press).

[2] This, of course does not mean that there was no contact through two millennia; during the Early Bronze Age the territories demarcated by this fault-line considerably shifted their position, at times to include littoral areas of Eastern Thrace. Especially towards the end of the Early Bronze Age, there seem to be Anatolian attempts to override this boundary, as indicated by the Kanlıgeçit (Karul 2002) and the Galabovo assemblages (see also Leshtakov 2002 on the problems related to the Bronze Age fault-line).

*Lack of mutual understanding: the impact of political blocks*

As already noted above, Thrace as a whole was a part of the Ottoman Empire until the beginning of the twentieth century, when it was divided up between Turkey, Greece and Bulgaria. This partition had far-reaching consequences, and must be treated as much more than a simple change of political borders. The new state boundaries also became the external limits of larger, but hostile ideological blocks. The most apparent outcome was that military priorities overshadowed cultural concerns, which became evident after the Second World War when most of the region was closed to archaeologists. Only after the disintegration of the Soviet Block did the invisible wall that divided up Thrace along Turkish and Bulgarian lines disappear and it became possible for cultural scientists to have look at the other side.

However, the boundary that passed through the middle of Thrace was so strong that the archaeological schools on either side had in the course of the subsequent fifty years developed on completely distinct lines. Thus, even after the removal of political restrictions, it was still difficult for one side to develop an understanding of the other.

Archaeologists working on the Turkish side, both Turkish or foreign, had been educated under the strong impact of 'Mesopotamia-Centric' traditions. For almost all of them, the cradle of the civilization was in the east. Anatolia constituted the boundary of prehistoric civilizations; there was nothing of interest further away, on the Balkan peninsula for example. The archaeological data that became evident especially during the cold war years was so alien to them that even fabulous assemblages such as Lepenski Vir or Varna Cemetery were not only ignored but met with considerable scepticism.

During the last fifty years, the dating of Southeast European prehistoric cultures has gone through revolutionary changes. Cultures that were thought to be third millennium BC prior to the implementation of radiometric dating methods were now understood to be as early as sixth millennium. Needless to say, this change in the dates had radical consequences for the prehistory of the Balkans, thus bringing a new perspective in cross-cultural relations between the East and the West. Anatolian archaeologists who had been trained to consider more recent dates for European prehistory, found it rather difficult — and even in some cases impossible — to accept this radical change. There is still considerable suspicion, in spite all evidence, on the fourth millennium dating of Varna finds for example.

In fact the archaeological data that has accumulated during the last fifty years in South-eastern Europe is so bulky and varied that, for any Anatolian or Near Eastern archaeologist who has not already been following up the subject, it stands now as a scary task even to approach. Thus, the archaeological perspective of those working in Anatolia practically stops by the Sea of Marmora, the other side being conceptually vague and distinct. Very few envisage that the other side is as near as anywhere on the plateau.

The same, more or less, holds true for colleagues working in Southeast European archaeology. They have grown up almost totally removed from the developments that have taken place during the last fifty years in Anatolia. The extent of their knowledge is often simply the discoveries of James Mellaart;[1] the scale of the changes in Anatolian archaeology remains far from their comprehension. Limitations in acquiring data from the other side is not enough to explain the apparent divergences between Anatolian and Balkan archaeologies. The basic discrepancy in the development of the archaeological traditions stands out as a more important obstacle.

Immediately following the disintegration of the Soviet block, there were some attempts by specialists on either side to learn from the other, but these soon faded away due to the differences in archaeological language.[2] In Balkan archaeology there is an emphasis on pottery sherds, occasionally leading to what can properly be named as 'sherdology', which results in almost totally ignoring assets such as cultural assemblages. Accordingly when Balkan archaeologists have had the means to reach Anatolian data, their main concern has been to look for selected items, ignoring the overall cultural framework. This has inevitably led to the formulation of some absurd analogies, such a comparing a simple palisade system with massive fortifications. Accordingly the break between the Balkans and Anatolia can be considered as an intellectual border, one developed in time under the impact of different regimes.

---

[1] Needless to say, there have always been exceptional cases, such as Bouzek, Makkay or Chernyh who tried to keep up with Anatolia and the Near East, but these have remained exceptional cases and they were not significant in the formation of thinking in Eastern block schools of archaeology.

[2] Strangely enough, this trend is reflected in the works of West European colleagues taking an interest in the region. Most of the recent publications on the prehistory of Europe, still overlook the archaeological data from north-western Turkey.

*The impact of nationalism, national identities and national policies*

Archaeology has always been intermingled with nationalism. National states in their formation process have always looked upon archaeology to build up and to define their national identities. Certainly Thrace, divided up between three national states that emerged from the ruins of the Ottoman Empire is no exception. However, as the concept of nationalism in Greece, Bulgaria and Turkey has developed on different lines, Thrace presents an interesting and unique case. We consider that for a proper understanding of Thracian archaeology, it is worth considering each as a separate entity.

*National Archaeology in Greece and the Impact of Hellenism*

The beginning of the Renaissance marked a great rise in interest among European intellectuals in the ancient Hellenistic cultures of the Aegean. This in time stimulated a feeling of highly romanticised admiration. As the modern Greek speaking ethnic communities of the Ottoman Empire were seen as the direct descendants of ancient Hellenistic cultures, they were highly treasured by the Europeans, who in turn had a significant impact on the creation of a distinct Greek nationalist feeling.

As to be expected, soon after its separation from the Ottoman Empire, the Greek state looked upon the Hellenistic cultures for its identity[1] and established a national school of archaeology. From the beginning, archaeology became an asset of official ideology and in doing so developed a selective approach to the past. Prehistoric and historic cultures not related to Hellenism were looked down as 'others' and in some way of less value. Thus, most of archaeological research was focused on the core area of Hellenistic cultures, that is, in the Aegean, leaving out Thrace as an auxiliary region. This should not be taken to mean that there was no research conducted on the Greek side of Thrace; since early years there has always been some research done, which has considerably intensified during the last decade or so. But, nevertheless, the official stance,[2] did not stimulate research, on Thrace or on early prehistory in general. In this respect, the exceptional stand that Greek archaeologists took during the discussions concerning the origins of neolithization in Europe is of interest. It should be remembered that the debate peaked between 1970 and 1980, the time when relations between Turkey and Greece were at their worst.

---

[1] See especially Alexandri (2002).
[2] As noted by Fotiadis (2001).

Whereas most European theoreticians defended the independent origins of farming and rejected the idea of an intrusion from Anatolia, the leading Greek prehistorians continued to look toward the East, to Anatolia as the origin of Neolithic economies.[1]

## The Case of Bulgaria: Archaeology and Propaganda

Promoted by Russia, the emergence of Bulgaria as a national state was rather sudden, an event not even expected by the Bulgarians themselves. During the Ottoman period, the Greeks and the Bulgarians illustrate distinct cases of the retention of ethnic memories. Ethnic Bulgarians or the 'Bulgarian speakers' of the Ottoman Empire were always concerned to distinguish themselves from other Orthodox communities. The remote memory of the Bulgarian kingdom, the semi-national state that existed before the takeover of this region by the Ottomans perhaps helped to sustain this identity. In contrast, amongst the Greek communities of the Ottoman Empire, later to be the subjects of Greece, Orthodoxy was much more apparent then national or linguistic identity; they were known as *Rum* or simply as Orthodox communities. Thus, the Bulgarian state, consciously or unconsciously, did not need the help of archaeology to build up a national identity; Bulgarians, the new subjects of the national state, already had an ethnic-based identity while Greece had to develop a national identity derived from past history, and thus needed archaeology as a tool. Thus, while Greek state was actively involved in archaeology since the beginning, Bulgaria did not develop a national policy until the establishment of the Communist regime. This does not necessarily imply that there was no local archaeology in Bulgaria; on the contrary by the last years of nineteenth century, there were local Bulgarian archaeologists active in the field and museums were founded. It was one, however, with no indication of any selective approach to the past — except to the remains of the Ottoman period.

The lack of visually attractive ancient sites, either of the Bronze Age or of antiquity, stimulated prehistoric archaeology to develop in Bulgaria more than in Turkey or in Greece. That in the communist regimes of the Soviet Block archaeology as a discipline had been considered a historic science further stimulated this trend. Archaeologists of the communist regimes received their basic education in history and not in archaeology, and then became more or less self-made archaeologists. This inevitably resulted in a lacuna in the basics of archaeological science. Bulgarian archaeology became categorical, showing

---

[1] See for example Theocharis (1973).

more interest in artefacts (or in most cases in sherds) than issues such as cultural process or theoretical frameworks whereby we may understand the past.

The recovery of Varna cemetery in 1972 marks the beginning of a new approach in Bulgarian archaeology. The sensation stimulated by the unexpected discovery of rich and early finds, including numerous gold objects, gave the Communist regime a unique chance to use archaeology as a means to propagandise in the West. Here, it should be noted that in those years Bulgaria was almost in total isolation, not only from the Western Block, but also to a degree from other Socialist states of the Balkans, as it was the only genuinely pro-Russian body in the area. Thus the excitement aroused in the West by the Varna finds provided Bulgaria a unique opportunity.

Here, it should also be noted that the discovery of the Varna cemetery came at just the correct moment, at a time when the 'anti-diffusionist' movement was at its peak and European cultural historians were busy trying to devise a new culture-historic profile for Europe. As already noted above, during those years, the picture that was being envisaged was an independent European identity, a culture that began and developed on the European soil without any intrusions from outside. This ideology had to look at the distant past and select convincing evidence. Stimulated by the then Communist Party members and senior Bulgarian archaeologists, the Bulgarian regime came to consider archaeology as a tool to achieve just that aim.

With its lavishly decorated painted pottery and figurines, the Early Neolithic cultures of Bulgaria, or the so-called Karanovo I culture, soon became a prime target. In thirty years, over a hundred early Neolithic sites were investigated, numerous Bulgarian exhibitions sent to Europe and archaeologists who were also members of the Communist Party took the liberty of freely travelling and lecturing in Western countries. Likewise the Varna finds, with gold and copper finds, were immediately taken as the eventual proof of metallurgy having earlier beginnings in the Balkans than in Anatolia.[1] Moreover, after the discussions on the Tartaria tablets provoked by this activity, Bulgarian archaeologists began to draw a picture of Late Chalcolithic Period almost similar to that of the Near Eastern Uruk culture. Various scenarios were devised to verify parameters of complex societies,

---

[1] There have been a number of publications on the presence of metallurgy in early Vinça horizon. See for example Jovanoviç (1971). For a more recent assessment, see Pernicka (1993).

writing, metallurgy, organized trade, development of urban centres in the Balkans. This trend, on its most extreme was formulated as '*Ex Balcanae Lux*' to contravene '*Ex Oriente Lux*' (Todorova 1978).

The impetus triggered by the finds in Bulgaria was so high that some Western archaeologists fell into the trap of developing abstract theories by using negative or non-existent data.[1] The growing excitement in the West, stimulated Bulgarian archaeologists to such a degree that, work became focused on recovering showy objects or ceramics, omitting all other components of culture. This, regrettably led to hasty and not always properly documented excavation of numerous important sites. A drastic consequence of this wave was therefore the selective publication of excavated material

The biases were so strong that an artificial past was created on highly selective grounds; if any new evidence did not confirm what was already said, it was disregarded. This not only affected our understanding of the Bulgarian cultural sequence, but had its impact on the whole of the Balkan peninsula. In our survey of Eastern Thrace, initially we were bewildered by finding numerous artefactual assemblages that had no apparent parallels in the Bulgarian archaeological publications. The fact that we were able to trace these assemblages up to the Turkish-Bulgarian border was even more striking. The insistence of our Bulgarian colleagues, to whom I had shown the material, that such types do not occur in their territory further complicated the matter, as further away, on the other side of Bulgaria, in Yugoslavia, Hungary or in Romania similar material was present. It seemed that if the territory covered by Bulgaria would be omitted, it would be much easier to understand the prehistoric sequence of the Balkans. Nevertheless, recent work in Bulgaria is less biased when looking at prehistoric cultures and thus things are gradually coming back to normal.

Yet another outcome of looking at the past as objects — or as sherds — has been the fragmentation of cultural assemblages. Needless to say, this is directly related to the definition of culture; in the Balkans cultures are defined according to the stylistic differences in pottery. As each colleague had a certain sherd or pottery element in mind in defining cultural territory, artificial cultural areas have been created. This inevitably led to the 'Balkanisation' of the past. Numerous cultural areas have been defined, each given a distinct

---

[1] A brief survey of European literature of the 1970s and 1980s would reveal numerous papers on the beginning of domestication in the Balkans, even of species of which wild species are not present in that area.

name and each colleague claiming to be the specialist of that culture; this resulted in inconceivable endless discussions on the possible interaction and chronological position of those groups. By the 1990s the picture drawn of prehistoric Balkans became so complicated that even the specialists of these countries found themselves in the midst of chronological equations.[1] Happily this too has died out a little during the last decade.

While Bulgarian prehistorians were thus busily engaged, archaeologists with interests in historic periods took a totally different line. The Iron Age cultures of Bulgaria, with the exception of some finds from the tumuli, lack visually impressive finds. So an ethno-cultural approach was developed, not however taking Bulgarian identity, but Thracian as the basis for its enquiry. It is of interest to note that this approach was developed by the senior archaeologist members of the Communist Party. Thracology Institutes were founded, not only in Bulgaria but also in Romania. Some wealthy individuals living in the West who still maintained good relations with their homeland were convinced through these new institutes that the ancient Thracians were the most civilized of all past nations, and a new ethno-cultural theory was developed. Thracians and Thrace took the central position in this new 'post-racist Indo-European' approach. Even if this stimulated some scientific work in the field, it also led to the formulation of absurd theories.[2] These also faded away after the disintegration of the Soviet Block.

*Archaeology in Turkey: 'Anatolia-ism' and the impact of 'Mesopotamia-centric' approaches*

The modern Republic of Turkey is an offspring of the Ottoman Empire. Even though it is generally assumed that Turks, or Turkish speaking groups, constituted the core of the Empire, the Ottomans never identified themselves with their Turkish speaking subjects. Moreover, Turkic speaking persons were looked down as being untrustworthy. Turk in the ethnic sense was used by Westerners, and it seems evident that there was no-one in the Empire who called himself as a Turk, even though there were Turkish speakers. The

---

[1] This was especially apparent in discussions related to the Vinça culture. In a decade or so there have been about 10 international meetings to discuss the chronology of Vinça culture; the outcome utilised almost all possible combinations of the alphabet in their attempt to designate phases.
[2] Such as a paper delivered to the VIth International Meeting of Thracology in Florence entitled the 'Thracian impact on Pre-Colombian America' or in designing world maps where all civilizations originate from Thrace.

concept of nationalism was imported to the Ottoman Empire, as late as the 1890s, when the disintegration of the Empire gained pace.[1] Even then, to be identified as Turk, was considered to be humiliating. Thus when Atatürk formed to new Republic of Turkey, he also had to create a nation and assign a reputable identity.

As the Turkish-speaking groups had originated in Asia, and moved into Anatolia as late as the eleventh century, looking at Central Asian origins for cultural identity seemed to be the most plausible solution. At least this was the expectation of most of the early republican ideologists working with Atatürk. On the contrary, Atatürk took a different line and designated Anatolia as the homeland. A historic-linguistic theory was developed in 1930s as the official stand of the state which associated some of the proto-historic cultures of the Near East with Turkish identity. These included the Sumerians and the Hittites, two cultures whose linguistic origins were not clearly defined in those years. The word Sumer accorded well with the phonetic characterization of Turkish; for the Hittites a new name, 'Eti' was created. This artificial history fulfilled its objective; the desperate Turkish speakers of the Ottoman Empire gained a new spirit and full-heartedly accepted their identification as 'Turk'. In this respect it is of interest to look at some of the given names during those years that are derived from Sumerian literature, 'Akurgal' and 'Sargon', are two Turkish archaeologists among many with Sumerian names.

This move of Atatürk to create a history was necessary at that time. Alongside other issues, it also created a sense of 'Anatolia-ism', incorporating all of Anatolian past cultures into the official state policy. If Atatürk had preferred to take the other line, that of looking to Asian origins, it seems possible that the new Republic would have identified itself only with the Turkic heritage of the peninsula, that is the Seljuk and Ottoman. However, the Anatolia-centric approach actually adopted embraced all cultures that lived in Anatolia, regardless of their ethnic or linguistic origin. This is well demonstrated in the distribution of Turkish state financed archaeological expeditions: those of Hellenistic or Roman cultures have always dominated over others.[2]

---

[1] In the Ottoman Empire, Turk as the name of the nation was first suggested in 1874; such an identification was met with considerable opposition from the Ottoman intellectuals who considered being called 'Turk' a humiliation. For further discussion on this see Berkes (1975; 64) or Güvenç (1996; 21-33).

[2] The Pan-Turkist or Turanist groups have always looked at Central Asian origins; initially they were happy with Atatürk's identification of Sumerians and Hittites as being of Turkish origin, but since then have kept protesting against governmental support of Greek-Roman or Byzantine sites.

Atatürk's ideology turned to archaeology; especially to the protohistoric cultures of Anatolia. In this respect, archaeology has been involved in the ideology of the state. However it has not been selective of the past according to ethnic origin. It has been more interested in 'civilization', thus looked particularly to Mesopotamia. With regard to Thrace, the name 'Trak' was considered as being of Turkish origin; thus Atatürk took a personal initiative in late 1930s and assigned A.M. Mansel to start excavations in Thrace. This resulted in the recovery of numerous rich Thracian tumuli. Later, after the death of Atatürk, these theories were forgotten and interest in Thrace soon died out.

For a proper understanding of Turkish archaeology, it is also necessary to have a look at the Ottoman archaeology. Archaeology came into Ottoman Empire as an imported concept early in the eighteenth century within the process of Westernization. The Ottoman Empire was essentially an eastern state, though for over five hundred years the only eastern state that confronted the West. Developments taking place in the West, including new concepts and ideas, were followed in the Ottoman Empire relatively earlier than in other Eastern states, and there was too an intentional process of Westernization.

Simplifying a much more complicated reality, it does appear legitimate to agree that the traditional view of the past in the East is that it has no time dimension; it is an amalgamation of legends, myths and fiction. The past is to be believed and not to be questioned or proved. Thus, in a way it is chronologically flat. However, in the Western way of thinking that developed with the Renaissance, the past is to be questioned and to be proved against a time-scale. The Ottomans prior to the partition of Peloponnesus from the Empire were in the possession of all areas that were of interest to the first generation of archaeologists; from the late sixteenth century the Empire received visits from antiquarians and interested explorers who were in search of ruined cities. The Ottomans, for long, ignored them. Ruins were ruins. However, by the early decades of the eighteenth century, when Western explorers began concentrating more concretely on ruins, sculptures and, especially when they began excavating, the Ottoman bureaucracy began to feel uneasy and initiated preventative measures. But as the Empire at that time had weakened considerably, the control on the European explorers was only partial.

At the same time, the Ottoman Empire was undergoing a process of Westernization. Newly emerging intellectuals, as well as some bureaucrats, were trying to replace or rejuvenate traditional institutions with those designed in a more western style. Needless to say, this was not an easy process and met with considerable resistance from the traditional groups. Nevertheless, compared to the other societies that attempted to make similar transformations, the Ottomans were much more successful. In part this is due to the fact that the process of Westernization was mostly stimulated by the Sultan himself, with the support of the army. Thus, military officers throughout the nineteenth century constituted the main body of newly emerging intellectuals. It is not a coincidence that the first museum to be opened in the Ottoman Empire was the military museum, founded in 1846 in Istanbul.

Already from the beginning of the nineteenth century, a number of Ottoman aristocrats had been sending their children to Europe, mainly to France, to be educated in the 'Western' style. Even though they were expected to become scientists or engineers, some became interested in arts and literature, such as Osman Hamdi Bey, whose life is described so well by Eldem in Volume One of this work. The first generation of Ottoman archaeologists had met and worked with the western archaeologists of their time, who were mainly concerned with Greek or Roman cultures. Thus, in the introductory phase of archaeology in the Ottoman Empire, 'Classical Archaeology' was considered an essential component when regarding the past. Even the new Imperial Museum was constructed as an imitation of Classical architecture. In this respect, it is possible to say that if there is any selection of the past in the foundations of Turkish and or Ottoman archaeology certainly it has been anything but Turkish. It is mainly for that reason that the medieval remains of Turkey have been, and are still, overlooked and not considered as a part of archaeology. Finally, it may be noted that most of the Turkish archaeologists of the Republic were educated by the German school of archaeology, with a Mesopotamia-centric, diffusionist approach. This orientation remains with us today. The lack of interest in the archaeology of Thrace displayed by Turkish archaeologists is partly a consequence of this.

In this paper we have tried to cover a wide range of issues, from archaeological data to nationalism to international politics. With such a wide scope, we do not think that it is possible to formulate a simple or even acceptable conclusion. However, to return to the beginning, we can conclude that the archaeology of Thrace is as important and interesting as any other region, if one can avoid biases due to political interferences.

## REFERENCES

Alexandri, A. 2002 'Names and Emblems: Greek Archaeology, Regional Identities and National Narratives of the Turn of the 20th Century', *Antiquity* Vol. 76; 191-199.

Berkes, N. 1975 *Türk Düşüncesinde Batı Sorunu*, Istanbul: Bilgi Yayınevi.

Bouzek, J. 1985 *The Aegean, Anatolia and Europe: Cultural Interrelations in the Second Millennium B.C.*, Praha: Çekoslovenska Academia.

French, D. 1986 'Anatolia: Bridge or Barrier?', *IX. Türk Tarih Kongresi I*; 117-118.

Foiadis, M. 2002 'Imagining Macedonia in Prehistory, ca. 1900-1930' *Journal of Mediterranean Archaeology*, Vol. 14.2; 115-135.

Güvenç, B. 1996 *Türk Kimliği*, Istanbul: Remzi Kitabevi.

Javanoviç, B. 1971 'Early Copper Metallurgy of the Central Balkans', in *Actes du VIII Congres International des sciences Prehistorique et Protohistoriques*, 131-141.

Karul, N. 2002 'Einige Gedanken über das megaronzeitliche Tor in Kanlıgeçit' in Aslan, R. et al. (eds.) *Mauer Schau. Festschrift für manfred Korfmann* II, Stuttgart; Verlag Bernhard Alber Greiner, 665-671.

Leshtakov, K. 2002 'Alabovo Pottery and a New Synchronisation for the Bronze-Age in Upper Thrace with Anatolia', *Anatolica* Vol. 28; 171-211.

Özdoğan, M. 1996a 'Tarihöncesi Dönemde Trakya. Araştırma Projesinin 16. Yılında Genel Bir Değerlendirme', in *Anadolu Araştırmaları XIV*; 329-360.

Özdoğan, M. 1996b 'The Neolithization of Europe: A View from Anatolia. Part 1: The Problem and the Evidence from East Anatolia', *Procilo XX*; 25-61.

Özdoğan, M. 1998a 'Ideology and Archaeology in Turkey', in Meskell, L. (ed.) *Archaeology Under Fire. Nationalism, Politics and Heritage in the Eastern Mediterranean and Middle East*, London; Routledge; 111-123.

Özdoğan, M. 1998b 'Tarihöncesi Dönemlerde Anadolu ile Balkanlar Arasındaki Kültür İlişkileri ve Trakya'da Yapılan Yeni Kazı Çalışmaları', *TÜBA-AR* 1; 63-93.

Özdoğan, M. (1999) 'Northwestern Turkey: Neolithic Cultures in Between the Balkans and Anatolia' in In: M.Özdoğan (ed.) *The Neolithic in Turkey*, Istanbul; Arkeoloji ve Sanat yayınları, 203-224.

Özdoğan, M. (*in press*) 'The Fourth Millennium in Eastern Thrace: an Archaeological Enigma', in *Festschrift für Viera Pavukova*.

Pernicka, E. 1993 'Eneolithic and Early Bronze Age Copper Artefacts from the Balkans and Their Relation to Serbian Copper Ores', *Praehistorische Zeitschrift* Vol. 88; 1-54.

Renfrew, C. 1969 'The Autonomy of South-East European Copper Age', *Proceedings of the Prehistoric Society* 35; 12-47.

Renfrew, C. 1976 *Before Civilization, The Radiocarbon Revolution and Prehistoric Europe*, London: Penguin Books.

Theocharis, D. 1973 *Neolithic Greece*, Athens; National Bank of Greece.

Todorova, H., 1978 *The Eneolithic in Bulgaria*, Oxford; British Archaeological Reports International Series.

# 36. CYCLOPS' CAVE: APPROPRIATIONS OF ANCIENT THRACE

## Olga DEMETRIOU

*Introduction*

My concern in this paper is to discuss possible ways in which the past may be conceptualised and linked to the present. I will particularly concentrate on material provided by my Turkish informants in Komotini, northern Greece in 1998-99 and then I will try to explain how I think their being members of the Turkish minority community in Greece may be related to their way of conceptualising this issue.[1] In doing this, I will offer these views as alternatives to mainstream historiographic ones (mainly Greek but also Turkish), and will try to explain how the two may relate to each other. In other words, I will be examining how the local past is appropriated, how it is differently appropriated and what this difference may mean.

*History*

For Greek scholars, the historical starting-point is located in antiquity, when Thrace was inhabited by *Thrakiká Fíla* (Thracian races), and more specifically, when these races were invaded by the Achaeans.[2] Stilpon Kyriakides (1887-1963), a Greek Komotinian folklorist who gave his name to the street passing

---

[1] Komotini is the capital of Rhodoppe, the department of Western Thrace with the largest concentration of Muslims. The whole of the Muslim minority of Greece numbers roughly 110,000 people and is dispersed in the towns and villages of Western Thrace, which borders Bulgaria and Turkey. Komotini has a population of roughly 40,000, half of which are Muslims and the other half Greek Orthodox. The Treaty of Lausanne of 1923 guaranteed the presence of the Muslim minority in Greece, by exempting it from the compulsory exchange of Muslim and Orthodox populations between Greece and Turkey respectively at the end of the war between them. At that time, excluding the Muslim minority of Thrace from the exchange seems to have been a counteracting substitute for the exemption of the Greek Orthodox minority of Istanbul – through the presence of which Greek nationalists were able to keep alive the hope of restoring Byzantium to its former glory. This hope formed the backbone of the Great Idea, which envisioned Asia Minor in a Greater Greece whose capital would be Istanbul. The total defeat of the Greek army in 1922 by the forces of Kemal Atatürk shattered this idea irrevocably.

[2] This designation is apparently used in its Homeric context to mean antiquity's generic 'Greeks' (from the twelfth century BC tribe).

in front of the current Law School of the University of Thrace, wrote
extensively on local history. It is indicative that one of his main concerns was
to suggest a link between ancient and modern Thracians, and he went to great
lengths to link the nationalist discourse of descent from ancient Greeks (and
more specifically Athenians) to their contemporary peripheral Thracian
identities. He explained that these races were in fact civilised and that they
accepted the Achaic invasion as a civilising mission — the relative degrees of
this 'civilisation' are implicit but nevertheless easily deduced.[1] It is in fact
this implicit hierarchy that leads him to the conclusion that it was the failure
of Thracians 'wholly to assimilate Hellenic civilisation' that eventually caused
the Greeks to drive them to the north. Thus, he assures his audience in
Komotini in the 1950s, they can be certain that "we are not Hellenised
Thracians... [but rather] Hellenes of Hellenic descent" (then ímetha thilathí
exellinisméni Thrákes. Polí mállon pistévo óti ímetha Éllines ex Ellínon).[2]

I think that the image of this Athens-educated professor returning to his
native town to lecture local Greeks on its history captures well the dynamics
between contemporary peripheral and central identities in the search of a
unifying discourse of ethnic beginnings and ethnic continuity. This was of
course, in the aftermath of the Balkan Wars and the Asia Minor 'disaster' —
three decades on, in fact, which would have given the Greek state ample time
to shift its emphasis away from the idea of a Greater Greece and concentrate its
nation-building efforts on the territory under its control. The opening addresses
indicate that the audience attending Kyriakides' Thrace lectures in 1953, 1954
and 1959 largely consisted of Eastern Thracian refugees. His emphasis on
homogeneity and common descent, as much as his passing references to his
own ties to the town and the 'locals', fits this nation-building goal very well.
In this sense, Kyriakides could be said to belong to a school of public
intellectuals that propounded the state's positions on Greek historical
continuity and common descent. Indeed, whether explicit or not, there seemed
to be agreement in Kyriakides' intellectual milieu on the role of Greek
academia in this effort. For this reason, it is worthwhile to turn to the context
of his working environment in a little more detail.

One of Kyriakides' recurring appointments in the 1950s and 1960s was
to the board of the Thessaloniki-based Institute of Balkan Studies. This
Institute was founded in 1953 with a mission to extend the work of the
Society for Macedonian Studies and is still at the forefront of Greek research

---

[1] Kyriakides (1993; 9-10).
[2] Kyriakides (1993; 9-10).

in the fields of archaeology and history in the Balkans. In its own words, it focuses on 'the systematic investigation of the conditions prevailing in the sensitive area of the Southern Balkans both before and after the Macedonian Struggle'.[1] I would argue that the choice of this specific historical point testifies to the Greek orientation of the Institute's viewpoint. I should also mention here that in the Greek name of the Institute (shortened to IMXA for *Íthrima Meletón Hersonísou tou Émou*), the area is designated not through the rendering of 'Balkan' to Greek (which would make it *Valkanikón Meletón*) but through recourse to the ancient Greek name of the mountain *Émos*. This emphasises further the Greek-ness (or rather Hellene-ness) of Balkan heritage, setting the research focus of the Institute geographically and temporally within national (and nationalist) bounds.[2] It is exactly the diachronically unchanging character of this focus that exemplifies the relationship between Kyriakides' quest of national description (documenting the territorially 'compacted' national culture) and the subsequent employment of academic research for nationalist purposes. Several of the Institute's publication and research titles make this explicit: 'Thrace from antiquity to the present day' (a recent project), 'Greeks of Albania' in 1994, 'The Greek Nation, 1453 — 1669' in 1976, 'Northern Hellenism in the pre-amble of the Macedonian Struggle (1878-1894)' in 1983.

The latter two titles illustrate this point, because they belong to works by Apostolos and Konstantinos Vakalopoulos (both proponents of ideas similar to Kyriakides'), whose historical research, although a generation apart, is permeated by the same ideological conviction of the glory of the 'Greek Nation'. The Greek version of the book with the same title is an eight-volume history, published between 1961 and 1988 as the highpoint of Apostolos Vakalopoulos' career (begun in 1935). Born in 1909, he served on the Institute's committee at various points between 1968 and 1984, many of which coincided with Kyriakides' appointment — a situation that allows for a speculative reconstruction of an environment where ideas were shared and exchanged while research policy was being formed. Their friendship actually seems to predate these appointments, since in 1953 Apostolos Vakalopoulos published a volume in honour of Stilpon Kyriakides' 25-year-long career

---

[1] www2.hyper.gr/imxa/ research.html: 26/10/01, my emphasis.

[2] Herzfeld has discussed extensively the implications of the opposition between 'Greek' and 'Hellenic' identity during the formative years of the Greek state and the debate over the designation of demotic or purified Greek as the official language. The latter was linked to images of ancient Greece and contemporary high culture, while the former was related to ideas about Byzantinism/Ottoman subjugation, and thus impurity as well as Orthodoxy/popular religion and hence oriental, low-class tastes (1987).

(1926-1951).[1] The volume was interestingly, entitled *Historical traditions of Greek refugees from Suyut.*

Konstantinos Vakalopoulos seems in this respect to be not only genetically but also intellectually a direct descendent of this generation (unlike, for example, Kyriakides' daughter, Alki Nestoros, who would later question the politics of Greek ethnology). Born in 1951, he studied in Greece and London and was involved in historical research at the Institute between 1977 and 1986. He has written extensively on the history of Northern Greece including an impressive volume on Thrace entitled *History of Northern Hellenism: Thrace.*[2] In it, he is primarily concerned to prove that Thrace has always been Greek, and that such it should remain. Interestingly, this is a rather more direct approach to the same political issue of homogeneity that Kyriakides was addressing some four decades before.

In short, there seems to be a genealogy of Greek scholarly historical research concerned not only with similar areas and topics, but also with identifying similar ideologies and driven towards similar ends. Yet within this nationalist scholarship individual interests and aesthetics are discernible, showing that what is termed 'official' in fact covers a variety of viewpoints, whose convergence is interesting exactly because of divergences in discipline, time, topic and style. The language, although noticeably different in form because of its demotic version in the second generation, also employs to a large extent similar imagery. Interestingly, people are largely absent from these stories. They primarily deal with wars, colonisations, attacks, all of which take place in the landscape, rather than among people. The closest allusion to living human beings is the idea of 'civilisation' (*politismós*), or 'tribes' (*filés*), both of which belong to the past and appear as a single mentally perceptible unity. In the case of Thrace, it could be argued that this conceptual homogeneity serves well (in a political sense) the restoration of an imagined[3] contemporary nation-state in the face of an opposite reality. The contemporary Thrace of these works was in fact very much a heterogeneously populated area, in contrast to the many other parts of Greece. It was 'polluted' by the presence of a minority that was everything (modern) Greek identity was defined against – Muslim in religion and Turkish in descent, language and

---

[1] Kyriakides had in fact been publishing research on Greek folklore even before 1926 (Kyriakides, 1922), see Mundy (1956; 287, ft 2).

[2] Vakalopoulos (1990).

[3] I am here employing a somewhat corrupted view of Anderson's theory, with emphasis on the untenability of such a 'nation-state' rather than on its conceptual production Anderson (1991).

national sentiment.[1] Thus, if not wholly, it was at least partly the de-legitimisation of the presence of these people in a 'genuinely Greek' place that these works seem to be geared towards.

The first generation of these studies was produced at a time when memories of World War Two and the civil war were still fresh, when fears of a new attack by Turkey or Bulgaria were not entirely unjustified, and when the demographic results of the Greco-Turkish war of 1923 were, as mentioned before, clearly visible. The next generation, on the other hand, had the much more rhetorical 'Macedonian issue' to content with, at a time when academia in Greece acquired a very discursively militant character. Apostolos Vakalopoulos' work had in fact been quoted in the Court of Human Rights during the trial of Sidiropoulos against Greece for sanctioning his right to declare himself a Slav. Thus, much more vocal than his predecessors Konstantinos Vakalopoulos asks in 1990 in a Greek newspaper column, 'what we (implicitly referring to the state) are doing for our Thracian compatriots and where the Institutes of Thracian studies are' — an indication of what he considers to be the role of Greek area studies research centres.[2] And in another article, he underlines that 'knowledge of the historical past is the basis for the continuation of our ethnic/national identity'.[3]

*Archaeology*

It is in this spirit that a number of archaeological expeditions (some not surprisingly supported by the Institute of Balkan Studies) were and still are carried out in various parts of Thrace. Such excavations seek to establish continuities of civilisation not only on the Greek, but also on the Bulgarian and Turkish sides of the current border. The main difference between them hinges on the fact that the '[demonstration of] a reified view of ethnicity, particularly in [the] adherence to the model of 'Hellenisation'' is not a prerogative of nationalist archaeology, but an application of 'colonialist assumptions... [that] pervade even the more theoretically sophisticated literature [on archaeology]'.[4] This gives the Greek thesis more credence

---

[1] I here use 'descent' to indicate the conceptualisation of identities as defined by lineage and blood in a general sense, which ultimately makes them national –i.e. it refers to the Greek notion of nationality, which is highly 'ethnic' (centred on concepts of blood and lineage).

[2] Vakalopoulos (1990; 162).

[3] Vakalopoulos (1990; 149).

[4] Owen (2000; I).

internationally, posing the Turkish and Bulgarian archaeological search for continuities against this hegemonic Hellenisation thesis.

One of the few volumes that illuminate the issue of Eastern Thracian archaeology (i.e. Turkish appropriations) emphasizes the lack of archaeological work and particularly excavations on the Turco-Bulgarian border.[1] It quickly becomes obvious, however, that the findings already uncovered are important for what they reveal about the first and second centuries AD (when the area came under the Roman Empire), i.e. that locals seem to have had trade relations across the Black Sea and the Balkans. This period is not mentioned in the Greek works – an omission that points to a clear shift in the designation of periods of historic significance. Indeed, from the Turkish archaeological point of view, the Greek colonisation seems to have been no more important a turning point in local history than others that followed it. In fact, as Özdoğan argues in this volume, Thrace seems to have enjoyed, on a European scale, fluctuating amounts of archaeological interest in direct proportion to its contemporary value as a bridge for cultural exchange or as unadorned border of cultural continuity. Interestingly, a theme that seems important in archaeological works is the quality of relations between the 'indigenous' Thracian population and its conquerors. In the same way that Kyriakides described the amicable relations between 'civilized' Thracians and 'civilized' Achaeans (the subjugation of the former being based on precisely this common but qualitatively differential civility), Onurkan points out Thrace's good relations with Rome from 100 B.C. up until 15 AD [2]

Bulgarian Thrakology on the other hand, appears more directly concerned with combating Greek claims of descent. According to the Bulgarian view, Thracians appeared as 'something akin to freedom fighters' in contradistinction to their image on the Greek side of the twentieth century border as 'savages'.[3] (Greek archaeology was presumably unconvinced by Kyriakides' argument for 'civilised' Thracian tribes.)

Bulgarian nationalism has subsequently appropriated the Thracian past as a civilisational meeting point. In Owen's words, '[t]he introduction of ancient antiquity into Bulgarian identity demanded a view in which ethnicity was now based not upon physical descent (i.e. having Slav or Bulgarian blood in one's veins), but upon a distinctive mix of cultural influences in the

---

[1] Onurkan (1988).

[2] Onurkan (1988; 106).

[3] Owen (2000; 39).

territory which gave rise to the distinct and unique nature of Bulgaria as an entity'.[1] In the course of post-socialist nationalism, this mosaic model gave way to a view of ethnic hierarchies, with the Thracians being viewed as culturally superior to the Greeks.[2] Thus, despite the fact that 'civilisational merging' outlooks seem more reliable than 'point of origin' ones, evidently both of them have equal ability to push the boundaries 'between deliberate political use of archaeology... and the general submersion of archaeology in... nationalist discourses'[3].

Between these points of 'amicable relations' on the one hand and 'colonisation' on the other, processes of contact seem much more complex under a less reductive lens. Through an examination of the period of Philippic and Alexandrian Macedonia (c. 360 B.C.) Archibald argues that relations between the Macedonian and Odrysian kingdoms were very different in relation to most descriptions of cultural amicability. Instead, 'the province of Thrace was unlike any other territory associated with the invading force'.[4] It was an area where 'the barbarian divide hurt most keenly',[5] where '[t]he ordinary inhabitants... had... no direct access to the cultural life of their rulers'[6], and where ultimately, '[t]he potential common links of geography [between Greek colonists and Odrysian princes and their followers] needed specific personal initiatives and concrete acts of cooperation in order to actualise which of the possible directions they envisaged would emerge as the dominant ones' [page 316]. This excerpt emphasises particularly well the degree of complexity that accounts of the local past should consider, if they are to be more (social) scientifically than politically engaged (and indeed, the impossibility of achieving complete separation between the two). And it shows in this sense, the relevance of situated-ness in the present in accounts of the past.

Owen takes one such present, namely the national one, to task for its skewed views on Thracian antiquity. Although not explicitly attentive to the question of the possibility of attaining a privileged position of neutrality, she does provide a good case for why this present should be particularly prejudiced in its assessment.[7] She argues for the need to take into account the implication of local populations in the process of cultural contact and shows

---

[1] Owen (2000; 47).

[2] Owen (2000; 47-52).

[3] Owen (2000; 41).

[4] Archibald (1998; 306).

[5] Archibald (1998; 305).

[6] Archibald (1998; 306).

[7] I use 'prejudice' here in its Gadamerian sense (1993).

that in the Thrace of the Early Iron Age, contrary to what the Hellenisation thesis proposes, 'the first contacts with Greeks must be seen in the context of new elites seeking other status symbols of similar power and meaning to that which iron had held'.[1] She also analyses how Helleno-centric paradigms, and especially the barbarian / civilised dichotomy perpetuate an event-based view of history (Greek colonisation as a moment in time), which is not supported by the archaeological evidence.[2] In other words, Kyriakides' hypothesis of 'Komotinians of Hellenic descent' is not exemplary of an incidental and superficial historical appropriation of archaeology by a folklorist, but is symptomatic of the skewed view of ancient colonisation in terms of modern, European colonialism.

This perhaps explains why even in non-nationalist accounts, the employment of one or other standpoint cannot escape the reification of ethnicity. Offering 'a perspective on the ethnogenesis of the contemporary Greek people in opposition to the one that for decades now has been taught by the Greek educational system,' Nakratzas, a teacher in Thessaloniki's medical faculty, published in 1988 a book examining 'The ethnic relatedness between contemporary Greeks, Bulgars, and Turks'.[3] The objective of the author is 'the development of an ideology in opposition to the incipient nationalism' presented in ideas about an eternal and primordial Helleno-Christian nation.[4] The book's main thesis is that contemporary Greeks cannot be the direct descendants of the ancient ones because throughout the ages there has been considerable interaction with other peoples, which cannot be ignored — a claim dismissed as 'Fallmerayeran' (a word synonymous to treachery in Greece) and thus unacceptable by its critics. In support of this claim, the author traces the history of this interaction in Macedonia and Thrace and takes as his temporal focus for the latter the period between 480 B.C. (when references to 'Thracians' first appear in writing) and 1340 AD (when Thrace came under Ottoman rule). What is interesting about this account is that although origin points of pure Thracian-ness are clearly not sought, 'peoples' appear as bounded wholes, whether tribes or ethnic groups. Thus, different ethnic lines are thought to be discernible, even if these do not lead directly from ancient to present groups. Religious conversions are especially emphasised. For example, Thracians are thought to have completely Christianised by 396 AD, up to which point they were Hellenised, Latinised

---

[1] Owen (2000; 170).
[2] Owen (2000; 36).
[3] Nakratzas (1997; 11).
[4] Nakratzas (1997; 11-12).

or tribal.[1] As Goths, Slavs, proto-Bulgars (note the implication of origins here), Armenians and Syrians came, went, or settled, they left their ethnic traces in contemporary identities, which can now be read through family names.[2] In this sense, the past is transposed onto the present, in a definitely different way to that of nationalist accounts, but nevertheless in a way that still rests on the thesis of ethnic continuity even if this has been twisted in all kinds of directions in the process.

Thus, much like the narratives it refutes, this account also holds 'civilisational contact' to be a process whereby present identities can be lineally (even if zigzaggedly) extended into past ones. The problem lies in the fact that whereas racial purity is denied in the present, the same does not seem to hold for groups in the past. In this sense, attempts to accommodate the complexities of the past into any form of national accounts seem doomed to fail because they are articulated within a framework of pervasive nationalist ideas, based on paradigms of linear descent, racial homogeneity and oppositions between core and periphery and between barbarian and civilised peoples. Kyriakides' work is thus possibly most valuable for exposing rather than answering a question: how do twentieth-century peripheral identities in Greece fit into a scheme of pure descent, when this is held to originate in a centre that is not only geographically distant but also metaphorically situated on the wrong side of the civilisation / barbarianism dichotomy?

In the next section, I will examine how this problem is dealt with by some of my informants in Komotini, who belong to the Turkish minority. I consider their account significant less because it represents 'typical minority discourse' (in fact it quite overtly states it does not) than because it offers an alternative to the institutionalised concepts outlined above. And in this sense, it says just as much about their shortcomings, as about the way they are perceived.

*Mythology*

The ancient theatre of Maronya, near the coastal village of Rhodoppe bearing the same name, is currently being restored through an archaeological project.

---

[1] Nakratzas (1997; 10-11). My translation.
[2] Nakratzas (1997; 212-232).

It is also the central theme of a mixed Komotinian group supporting this restoration called 'The friends of the Maronya theatre'. But it is the Maronya cave, a few miles beyond, which is held to be the site of *Polífimos*' residence (the Cyclops mentioned in Homer's Odyssey),[1] that attracts most interest in discussions about the area and its sites. The mythological significance of the Cave is widely known and locals, as well as my *Gümülcineli*[2] friends often articulated it as an introductory statement on local history. Yet, this seemingly simple articulation ('this is where Homer placed *Polífimos*') implies the same problematic location of 'Greek-ness' described for historical / archaeological accounts. For if the Odyssean Cyclops was a creature on some distant barbaric shore, how can such a location claim Hellenic heritage?[3] This problematic seemed of no concern to my minority friends. Instead, the cave's mythology was no more than an insert to its other qualities. The cave offers exciting opportunities for exploration hikes to the few locals who are willing to take them.

Thus, despite the amount of nationalism it is loaded with (in terms of archaeology, history as well as mythology), this area is appropriated by some Gümülcinelis in very interesting ways. On a hot, humid noon in 1999, Celal (a single man in his thirties) appeared in his black T-shirt and complained about the unbearable heat. I wondered why he had never changed into another colour all through the summer, to which he smiled meaningfully and replied it was not just a colour. "It's about freedom", he said. He then went on to explain about the Maronya group, all the members of which own the same type of T-shirt, emphasising that he was one of the very few minority people to be part of it. The Greeks in it he knew very well, they are people that he appreciates and who are not chauvinists –they are his friends. They all care for this site, which is slowly eroding instead of being restored into a wonderful theatre featuring modern and classical plays.

He then went on to describe the area in general. He knew it in detail because he had hiked through it on several occasions. "This is what the group is about. We are good friends, we arrange excursions and we get to know nature." He also talked about the cave, the danger of getting lost in it, the beauty of the moist, trickle-sculptured rocks inside and the bats whose

---

[1] 'Cyclops' is the generic name for giant creatures possessing a single eye in the middle of the forehead. This particular Cyclops' name is usually transliterated as Polyphemus in the relevant literature.

[2] *Gümülcineli* is the Turkish word describing inhabitants of Komotini.

[3] Other suggested locations appear less problematic, as they are located outside modern Greece's borders, e.g. Sicily [Salmeri, personal communication].

excrement is highly allergic. "It's pure freedom. You just arrive there, and all you do is look at things. You do whatever you like- sing, drink, talk, sleep underneath the stars, no constraints and no plan to follow. It's only a matter of what you want to do."

I was at first a bit puzzled by what appeared to be a glorification of the ancient / mythological past, especially since Celal is not exceptional in his disapproval of Greek nationalism. Indeed, the reason why he is one of only a few Turks who have joined this group seems to be a suggestion of the dangers other minority members see in this logic. Celal is aware of this and is in fact very careful not to suggest that Thrace is Greek because of its ancient past. He is well versed in Greek mythology, like many Komotinians of various ages and ethnic backgrounds. It is indicative that he calls himself a 'Dionysian' (*Dionisiel*) person as opposed to an 'Apollonian' (*Apoloniel*) one, interestingly enough explaining the terms without reference to Nietzsche.[1] This indicates, I would argue, irrespective of its source, an engagement with mythology in a very personal way.

At the same time, it provides clues as to how this discourse relates to the Greek academic nationalism I have examined. The two focal sites of Celal's local history belong to two different genres –the Maronya theatre to archaeology and the Cyclops' Cave to mythology. His own direct identification with a Dionysian character drawn from the latter gives mythology precedence over archaeology. Furthermore, his own appropriation of archaeology, i.e. the use into which he puts both sites, retains few of the connections they have to contemporary Hellenic identity. Walking through the remains of antiquity is about freedom rather than connecting to the ancestors, and the theatre should be restored to stage a variety of events rather than re-enact its days of Hellenic glory.

The preference of the Cyclops' Cave over the theatre as a site around which this subversive classicism is appropriated is particularly suitable because the two instances of cyclopic appearance in ancient Greek literature are jocular, in opposition to the stereotypical view of classical works as sombre in atmosphere and momentous in significance. Euripides' 'Cyclops' is the satirical final part of a tragic trilogy, while the Odyssey is generally considered to be the feminine-stature accompaniment to the more serious, 'male' Iliad [Tony Nuttall, personal communication]. In this sense, Celal's reference to the Cyclops is important both as a reference and as just a reference, quickly

---

[1] For the latter's discussion of these concepts see Nietzsche (1999) and Paglia (1990; 72-98).

overpowered by the description of experiencing the cave in the present. For it exposes, even if unintentionally, the Helleno-centricity of deconstructionist accounts that employ, in their very critique or Orientalism, the language of ancient Greek myth as the arch-signifier. Such an account is Grosrichard's, who, despite his attack on Enlightenment ideas about Oriental despotism in *The Sultan's Court*,[1] employs Polyphemus, 'the Cyclops leaving his lair with the stake in his eye to accuse Nobody' as the ultimate signifier for the Unconscious '[b]ecause it is ultimately the gaze and the phallus [that become] enigmatic and all-powerful signifiers, since, from the family to the State, from the love of the couple to the love of the despot, they rule the world'.[2] Celal's radical take on the local past is only hinted at by the mention of the Cyclops –what sustains it is the emphasis on the dangerous creatures of the present.

In a sense, Celal brushes over antiquity in his own historiography, passing from Greek mythology to a concept of history that is substantially different to what we have already seen. In his discourse, history begins much later. He told me this story by the seaside one evening, while cooking freshly caught fish. Parts of it I had also heard from other minority members, some I had read in various minority publications, and other parts are corroborated by academic studies – I therefore use Celal on this occasion as the mouthpiece of several viewpoints.[3]

> Thrace was incorporated into the Ottoman Empire in 1363. Turkic tribes arrived from the East –you know, Asia Minor was actually called that because it reminded tribal Turks of the steppes deep in Asia that once used to be their home. Their entry into Europe followed two routes, parallel to the Black Sea coast. One was from the North, through Russia and down into the Balkans. The second one was from the South, through the Caucasus and current Turkey. At the point when this movement happened, the *Bizans* (Byzantine) kingdom was concentrated around İstanbul, Selanik, and the Morea. The Balkans, including Thrace and South-Eastern Europe largely belonged to the Serb kingdom. Thrace was conquered by the great-great grandfather of Fatih Sultan Mehmet (conqueror of İstanbul). At that time, the only Muslim tribes in the area were the Peçenek. The subsequent spread of Islam to the area was primarily related to the fact that under Ottoman law, Muslim subjects paid less tax than non-Muslims. In fact, religion had much

---

[1] Grosrichard (1998a).

[2] Grosrichard (1998b; 146).

[3] What follows is a reconstruction of the story from notes I took on the night and expanded on the following morning, as it has not been possible to tape-record, and hence transcribe precisely. I have instead tried to check and complete my notes using subsequent accounts of the same story by both Celal and other members of the group. It is notable that although I have found myself adding onto the story after such recounting, I have never come across diversions or discrepancies. This is why I have bestowed upon Celal the role of voicing the group.

less significance for these early Ottomans than it did for Christians. Just think that the reason Turkey is now almost completely Sunni is that Sunnism was the religion of the bureaucracy. Until the great rise of the Ottoman Empire, most of its subjects were Alevis,[1] who were only later given incentives to adopt more orthodox (Muslim) practices.

[In a softer, more serious tone:] Also, something that you won't find in books, and it is obvious why Turkish historians would not want to talk about it, is this: Ever since the split of the Roman and Byzantine churches, Christians were trying to unify under one Empire. With the conquest of İstanbul that hope was shattered. However, when *Kânuni* Sultan Süleyman (the Magnificent) tried to expand westwards into Italy, the *Bizans* approached him and made a deal. They offered their assistance in the campaign, if Süleyman would be baptised and conquer Rome as a Christian. This would unite the Eastern and Western churches under one Christian Empire. Süleyman in fact agreed, but unfortunately died before the campaign was over and Rome was never conquered. He did, however, conquer an Italian fortress, which is evidence enough for the existence of the scheme. Why else would he have gone up there? And why would Ottoman Greeks call themselves *Rum* and nothing else? They considered themselves Romans.

These events loosely correspond to the war with Venice (1537-40), which was preceded by the siege of Vienna (1529).[2] Furthermore, their narration seems to echo what İnalcık calls 'the other side of the story', speaking of the Eastern/Ottoman version of events in opposition to Western/Italian historical accounts.[3] Thus, although Süleyman's decision to be christened may indeed not get any mention, İnalcık leaves no doubt as to Byzantium's rather tense relations with Venice and its friendly disposition towards Mehmet II who 'doubtless received tacit acquiescence from the Greeks, Armenians, Bulgars and Tatars'.[4] Similarly, instead of reporting a Christian vision of uniting the Eastern and Western Roman Empires, İnalcık speaks of Mehmet the Conqueror's 'idea of reviving the Eastern Roman Empire under his sceptre... [by restoring and thus uniting] political and economic control of the Aegean and Black Sea; thus he preferred the titles 'the sultan of the two lands' (Asia Minor and the Balkans) and 'the khakhan of the two seas' (the Aegean and the Black Sea)'[5]. Celal's story seems in this sense, to refer as much to these events as it does to the Greek historiography of Thrace, where the latter in its entirety is treated as part of the Greece of 'the two continents and five seas', which is the backbone of the *Megáli Idéa* (Great Idea) of Greek irredentism. I should note here that this Idea was in fact far removed from the first

---

[1] I should perhaps make explicit here that Celal is not himself Alevi.
[2] İnalcık (1997; xvi, 271-274), Lewis (1996; 274-278).
[3] İnalcık (1997; 271).
[4] İnalcık (1997; 271).
[5] İnalcık (1997; 273-4).

idealisations of a Hellenic state, as a Greek-speaking state where all Balkan peoples were bound through a sense of civic nationalism[1].

In relation to this historiography, it is thus significant that Celal chooses a particular part of Ottoman history to narrate, and that he gives just as much background as is needed to get his point across. Similarly, he chooses a specific part of Greek mythology to comment on and to internalise. In both these choices, he is making particular statements about himself in as far as he seeks to locate himself in both grand narratives –which is, after all, the ultimate objective of any (national) history. In the Greek story there is an overarching conflict between Greek and Hellenic identification, which Celal explicitly emphasises in his explanation about the meaning of Rum.

Although not his main point, there is in his question (why do Anatolian/Istanbul Greeks call themselves *Rum*?) an implication of questioning authority. This because the single most debatable issue regarding the minority in Greece is whether it should be called 'Turkish' or 'Muslim'. The first term is the one insisted upon, by both the Turkish authorities and the minority itself, the second equally strongly insisted upon by the Greek authorities and Greek nationalists. In calling the them *Rum* and not *Éllines* (the common word for 'Greeks', bearing allusions to Hellas), Celal is thus deciding their identity for them, even if he is presenting it de facto as their choice — in the same way that (nationalist) Greeks decide his Muslim identity for him.[2] I should mention here, that Celal is in fact strongly opposed to the notion of religion being a determinant of identity, especially when applied to him individually –he often stressed to me that he is an atheist and not a Muslim (*Müslüman*).

At the same time, he is transposing the *Rum/Yunan* distinction in Turkish (between the Greeks living on Turkish soil and those living in Greece) onto the *Éllines/Romyí* distinction in Greek (between ancient and Byzantine forms of Greek-ness). In this way, by choosing to describe 'Greeks' as 'Rum' he is deciding that the thing uniting all Greeks is their religion and hence the Greek absurd (to him and expectedly to me as well in light of our knowledge of subsequent events) aspirations of conquering Rome. The proposition to Süleyman is meant to be seen not only as cunning, but also

---

[1] It was in fact Cannini, an Italian, who first imagined a Hellenic Balkan Empire, including the Danubian Principalities, Montenegro, Serbia and Greece, to replace the Ottoman against the Russian.

[2] Note that this conversation (as most I had with him and his group), took place in Greek, which makes the use of a Turkish word (*Rum*) to denote Greeks, even more interesting.

naive. Thus, 'Rum' comes to denote Byzantine, Christian Greeks with a rather silent implication that they were eventually conquered by the Ottomans. Furthermore, by maintaining that the Greek ideal is a Christian Empire, he is de-emphasising the Hellenic component of Greek identity (ancient heritage). This is precisely where he locates himself when he professes his love for the Maronya theatre, and Greek mythology. He thus becomes heir of a great civilisation long extinct, but without becoming Greek because Greek-ness is equated with Byzantine Christianity. I would in fact argue that the precedence of mythology over ancient history described above, is reinforced through the undermining of the temporal split between them — Celal considers the heritage of both his, and the civilization that gave rise to them extinct.

His location in the Turkish story is similarly affected. He identifies the problem of religion as the underlying dichotomy of Turkish identification and he stresses the unimportant character of religion in early Ottoman times. While questioning the faith in Islam of Süleyman the Magnificent and portraying him as 'almost a Christian', he is merging the Islamic and Christian worlds along ethnic lines, which allows his own ancestral past to claim presence in both ancient Greek and early Ottoman worlds –at other points he would emphasise that a lot of Sultans' mothers were actually Greek. He never questions the fact that he is a Turk, but he does question whether a good Turk is a religious Turk.

*Folklore*

In short, Celal integrates in this way Greek and Turkish official rhetoric about national pasts into a personally meaningful discourse about the minority's specific location in these pasts. This discourse articulates ideas about roots and continuity (in its factual approach to the past and its reflection into the present) but does so concurrently with a critical theorisation of the various official positions (in the analysis of the latters' factually flawed content and their unwillingness to incorporate different facts). In fact, it is the discordance between what is implied but left unmentioned when the two official accounts are put together that Celal's own historical narrative is based on. And it is in this dual position as alternative and as critique that the importance of Celal's individual discourse lies. While the national accounts appear to present an academic, high class, official standpoint, Celal's account defies classification into the other side of the story, as lay, marginal, and representative of the minority. For even though it is founded on a concept of the group, its representation of 'minority discourse' (in the singular) is not evident. By contrast, the academic publications with which I have compared it lay claim to exactly such representation of a reified Greek-ness. And yet, reification of identities does not seem to constitute a point for criticism for Celal. It rather forms the basis on which the story is told.

The question thus is where to place Celal's discourse as an alternative to formal accounts. Celal belongs to a relatively small group of youngsters made up of men and women from the minority, the local Greek and the student community, who share above all an understanding of entertainment (eating and drinking inside Komotini and at countryside locations). He sees the make-up of this group as a political statement against Greek and Turkish nationalist (locals and otherwise) and against conservative members of the minority who dislike inter-communal socialisation and especially sexual relationships. Celal and his group are thus marginal, but also subversive individuals, whose activities are often criticised by (usually older) Greeks and Turks alike.

With this in mind, one way to approach the question above would be to relate his story to 'folk' accounts –the most relevant of which appears to be the eighth story of Dede Korkut. This folk tale is set sometime during the move of Turkic tribes (one of which are the Oğuz Turks) from central Asia into current Turkey (that Celal describes above). The two main characters are *Tepegöz*, the child of a fairy raped by a shepherd, who grows into a man-eating creature, and Basat, his eventual killer, who is the son of the clan's leader, lost in the forest at infancy during an expedition and found years later, after having been mothered by a lioness. *Tepegöz* (literally translated as 'head-eye') is a Cyclops that terrorises the transhumant Oğuz upsetting their grazing cycle, before he is outwitted, blinded and killed by Basat. The story seemed remarkable to many literary theorists in the 19th century and up to the 1950s because of the resemblance of *Tepegöz* to *Polífimos*, as well as of the struggle between the former and Basat to that between the latter and Ulysses. There are, of course, other parts in the story that seem to resonate with folktales ranging, in the words of one scholar, 'from Scotland to Turkistan'.[1] During a period of protracted 'ink spilling' on this issue[2], and having viewed *Polífimos* as a post-*Tepegöz* insertion into the Odyssey, or alternatively as the base on which *Tepegöz* stories developed, analyses converged on the assessment that *Tepegöz*'s origins are much more diverse than at first appears. Thus, the

---

[1] Mundy (1956; 280).
[2] Lewis (1974; 15).

academic question seems to have been: was the *Tepegöz* story based on the Odyssean event, was *Tepegöz* a later insertion into an 'originally' shorter tale or was the Polyphemus incident borrowed from a proto-Oğuzian tale and inserted into the Odyssey? Needless to say, the question provides a perfect cue for questioning 'originality'. In a Turkish literary study of the Dede Korkut stories, this question is by-passed and their significance is found to lie in their expression of 'original' Turkish literature, although resemblances to Homer, such as dream-divination, are mentioned[1]. Their quality as prototypic examples thus lies not in any unquestionably 'Turkish origin' they may have had as literary works, but in their reflection of the Turkish spirit of 'hard work and vitality' and of the 'Turkish intelligent sense of humour and plasticity of language'.[2] What is remarkable in the specific context is that Celal does not invoke *Tepegöz* but only *Polífimos* in his description of the Maronya Cave. The importance of this omission is twofold. First, the relatedness of the two Cyclops is an element that could further catalyse the merging of Greek and Turkish pasts that Celal is at pains to achieve. Secondly, Dede Korkut's temporal setting, which functions as an 'origin of Turkish-ness', is also the starting point in Celal's story. In short, whereas Celal could have employed the connection to show that Greeks and Turks share not only genealogies but folk traditions as well, he does not –in fact, in all probability, given the widespread popularity of Dede Korkut stories, chooses not to.

Whichever the case, it is worth considering the fact that other (and usually older) minority individuals did point out a connection between Homer and the Turkish name Ömer. This suggestion is a polyvalent one, as it can imply commonalities between Turks and Greeks, but at the same time pose questions as to who (and which 'culture') came first, and how it was passed on. In other words, it is a suggestion that throws up the problems that the *Tepegöz — Polífimos* connection might raise as soon as it is mentioned. However, the Homer — Ömer connection, when I mentioned it to Celal, seemed neither particularly interesting nor very tenable. Judging by my (admittedly little) experience of its circulation in Turkey, I would suggest that it probably seemed trite above all. But in light of the political debate that ownership of national symbols, such as the sun/star of Macedonia/Vergina[3] has previously stirred between Greece and its neighbours, the possibility that

---

[1] Defne (1988; xvi, 61).

[2] In the original from which I summarised these phrases appear as "*Türk ruhu... bize durmak dinlemek bilmeyen bit hayatın en canlı ifadelerini vermektedir*" (Defne 1988; 66) and "*Türk'ün ince zekâsıyla espri kabiliyeti...*", "*Türk dilinin ... ifadedeki elâstikî ve yatkın değerini gösterir*" (Defne 1988; 101).

[3] See Brown in Cowan (2000).

both connections could have been treated as significant does not seem far removed. Yet, this possible claim on a Hellenic figure has interestingly never been voiced by people who drew this link. Instead, it was mentioned almost as a strange coincidence that could at best point to the futility of the search of origins. Indeed, the idea that Greeks and Turks have so many things in common that it is futile to search for 'originals' is one that permeated many discussions (on politics as well as other subjects) I had in Komotini. Perhaps this might be one reason for avoiding to trace (or simple disinterest in tracing) the genealogy of *Tepegöz*. Perhaps more simply, the *Tepegöz* story (at least in its current written presentations) is so imbued with nationalist connotations in terms of Turkish origins that its invocation seems futile. In either case, the significance of its non-articulation is for me to be found in the implication that Greek mythology appears more malleable than its Turkish counterpart. I would further argue that this is precisely because the latter has institutionally taken on the task of presenting Turkish origins, a task that in Greece is performed by archaeology rather than mythology.

*Conclusion*

It is in this paradox between different origins, different lines of continuity and the refusal to accept them that I locate Celal's story. In effect, Celal's history is as linear as that of Kyriakides', and influenced by the author's present just as much. And it is in this sense that they can be placed in a dialogic relationship –because even though they both employ disconnections to make the story coherent (Kyriakides between antiquity and Byzantium, Celal between mythological antiquity and the Ottomans) they, to a surprising extent use similar terminology. One key idea that is shared in both accounts is that of descent –and related to that, ethnicity. For both of them, Turks and Greeks seem to have existed in a primordial past and they seem to have developed into modern Turks and Greeks. However, Celal's story allows for ethnic mixing in a rather unproblematic way (Sultans did it, why not commoners?) while Kyriakides' and later Vakalopoulos' story is inflexible to any such possibility (hence concern with the descendants of Thracian races). In short, the past seems to be assimilated into the present in different ways –because, expectedly, there are different presents.

What is even more crucial, however, is that these presents are much more diverse than nationalist classifications might indicate. They are not simply 'Greek' and 'Turkish', but as Celal shows, individual as well. And it is from this individuality that Celal's account gains its value –not as an account of a 'typical minority member', but as an account situated in a personal experience of being a minority individual. The difference between Celal's one and the narratives I have reviewed is that despite their sharing of ideas about origin and descent lines into the present, the former allows for the merging of these lines to occur in a hazy past. More specifically, in national narratives no merging is allowed for at all. Alternative narratives like Nakratzas' have tried to refute this view by locating this merging and following it through to the present –however, such views leave the idea of discernible ethnic lines linking peoples of the past to those of the present intact. The Dede Korkut stories allow for some merging on one hand (but this is only in terms of literary borrowing and thus more symbolic than actual), and on the other hand, provide a pristine location for 'original' Turkish-ness that goes against any thesis of merging that might be posed on the literary level. For Celal, there are multiple origin points that converge. But exactly how this convergence happens is not important. What is important is that in the present, there are separate identity locations that on the official level relate to each other oppositionally. Celal locates himself quite unproblematically within this framework in a Turkish identity position, but refutes the nature of the relationship between Greek-ness and Turkish-ness. In other words, the constructedness of modern Greek-ness and Turkish-ness is acknowledged, and so is their difference; but their mutual exclusivity is, for him, far from evident.

Celal's present as an identity is, in this sense, both a Greek and Turkish one –and it is towards this present that the past gets assimilated. The past as an identity becomes, in other words, the combination of mythological heritage, Turkish lineage, ancient achievement and religious irreverence / profanity. It includes, in comparison, many of the elements that Kyriakides is at pains to ignore. Moreover, it fuses these elements together in the idea that these glorious pasts are now gone forever. No matter to what extent ancient Greeks and Ottoman Turks can be considered ancestors, they are both extinct and Celal's current Turkish-ness is more of heir than descendant to them. And it is in this sense that Celal's answer is valuable: because half a century after Kyriakides' answer to the riddle of how to merge a multi-culturalist reality with a nation-state ideology, he seems to me to have managed a counter-answer. It is an answer that aims specifically at the possibility of being Turkish in Greece, while acknowledging the inconsistencies of both Greek and Turkish identities. And it shows how an individualized form of collective memory can successfully account for cultural interaction.

REFERENCES

1985. *Η Ιστορική, Αρχαιολογική Λαογραφική Ερευνα για τη Θράκη Συμπόσιο - Ξάνθη, Κομοτηνή, Αλεξανδρούπολη, 5-9 Δεκεμβρίου 1985 · Πρακτικά. ΙΜΧΑ: Ινστιτούτο Μελετών Χερσονήσου του Αίμου* (Papers from a seminar on Historical, Archaeological and Folklore studies on Thrace, held in Xanthi, Komotini and Alexandroupoli 5-9 December 1985. Institute of Balkan Studies)

Anderson, B. 1991 *Imagined Communities*, London; Verso.

Archibald, Z. 1998 *The Odrysian Kingdom of Thrace: Orpheus Unmasked*, (Oxford Monographs on Classical Archaeology) Oxford; Clarendon Press.

Chondrogiannes, P. 1997 *Εργογραφία, Ήτοι, Δείκτες Εργασιών του Καθηγητού Αποστόλου Βακαλόπουλου. Εθνική Βιβλιοθήκη: Δημοσιεύματα. Εταιρεία Μακεδονικών Σπουδών.* (An index of the works of the Professor A. Vakalopoulos. Society of Macedonian Studies)

Cowan, J. (ed.) 2000 *Macedonia: The Politics of Identity and Difference*, London; Pluto Press.

Dakin, D. 1972 *The Unification of Greece 1770-1923*. New York; St Martin's Press.

Defne, Z. 1988 *Dede Korkut Hikayeleri Üzerinde Edebî Sanatlar Bakımından Bir Araştırma* (Türk Dil Kurumu Yayınları 548), Ankara; Atatürk Kültür, Dil ve Tarih Yüksek Kurumu.

Faroqhi, S., B. McGowan, Q. Donald & P. Şevket. 1997 *An Economic and Social History of the Ottoman Empire 1600-1914* (2), Cambridge; Cambridge University Press.

Gadamer, H. 1993 *Truth and Method*, New York; Continuum.

Grosrichard, A. 1998a *The Sultan's Court: European Fantasies of the East*. London; Verso.

Grosrichard, A. 1998b The Case of Polyphemus, or, a Monster and Its Mother in Žižek, S. (ed) *Cogito and the Unconscious*. USA; Duke University Press.

Herzfeld, M. 1987 *Anthropology through the looking glass: Critical Ethnography in the margins of Europe*, Cambridge; Cambridge University Press.

İnalcık, H. 1997 *An Economic and Social History of the Ottoman Empire 1300-1600*1), Cambridge; Cambridge University Press.

Kondis, B. & Manda, E. 1994 *The Greek minority in Albania: a documentary record 1921 - 1993* (IMXA: 258), Thessaloniki; *Ίδρυμα Μελετών Χερσονήσου του Αίμου.*

Kyriakides, S. 1928 *Ο καπουκινός Robert de Dreux στη Θράκη στα 1666. Θρακικόν Κέντρον.*

Kyriakides, S. 1940 *Η Θράκη κατά τους Βυζαντινούς Χρόνους. Θρακικά Χρονικά.* (Thrace during Byzantine times)

Kyriakides, S. 1993 *Περί την Ιστορίαν της Θράκης.* Thessaloniki: IMXA. (On the History of Thrace).

Lewis, G. 1974 *The Book of Dede Korkut*, Bucks: Penguin Books.

Lewis, B. 1996 (1995) *The Middle East: 2000 Years of History from the Rise of Christianity to the Present Day*, London; Weidenfeld & Nicolson.

Mundy, C. 1956 Polyphemus and *Tepegöz*, in *Bulletin of the School of Oriental and African Studies* XVIII, 278 - 302.

Nakratzas, G. 1997 (1988). *Η Στενή Εθνολογική Ευγγένεια των Σημερινών Ελλήνων, Βουλγάρων και Τούρκων: Μακεδονία⁻ Θράκη* Thessaloniki: *Εκδόσεις Μπατάβια.* (The Proximal Ethnic Relatedness of Today's Greeks, Bulgarians and Turks: Macedonia — Thrace).

Nietzsche, F. 1999 *The Birth of Tragedy and Other Writings*, (*Cambridge Texts in the History of Philosophy*), Cambridge; Cambridge University Press.

Onurkan, S. 1988 *Doğu Trakya Tümülüsleri Maden Eserleri: İstanbul Arkeoloji Müzelerindeki Trakya Toplu Buluntuları. Türk Tarih Kurumu Yayınları VI. Dizi — Sa. 26.* Ankara; Türk Tarih Kurumu Basimevi.

Owen, S. 2000 A theory of Greek colonisation: EIA and initial Greek contacts. Ph. D.: Cambridge.

Paglia, C. 1990 *Sexual Personae: Art and Decadence from Nefertiti to Emily Dickinson*, New York; Vintage Books

Sümer, F., Uysal, A. & Walker, W. 1972 *The Book of Dede Korkut: A Turkish Epic*, Austin; University of Texas Press.

Vakalopoulos, A. 1976 *The Greek Nation 1453-1669: The Cultural and Economic Background*

Vakalopoulos, A. 1985 *Ο Μακεδονικός Αγώνας 1904-1908· ως κορυφαία φάση των αγώνων των Ελλήνων για τη Μακεδοία. IMXA: 208.* Thessaloniki: *Ίδρυμα Μελετών Χερσονήσου του Αίμου.* (The Macedonian Struggle 1904-1908: as a major phase of the struggles of the Greeks for Macedonia).

Vakalopoulos, A. 1986 *Σύγχρονα Βαλκανικά Εθνολογικά Προβλήματα* (*Μακεδονική Βιβλιοθήκη*). Thessaloniki: *Εταιρεία Μακεδονικών Σπουδών* (Current Balkan Ethnological Problems).

Vakalopoulos, A. 1987 *Νέα Ελληνική Ιστορία.* Thessaloniki: *Εκδόσεις Βάνιας.* (History of Modern Greece).

Vakalopoulos, K. 1983 *Ο Βόρειος Ελληνισμός κατά την Πρώϊμη Φάση του Μακεδονικού Αγώνα (1878-1894)* (IMXA: 196). Thessaloniki: *Μελετών Χερσονήσου του Αίμου.* (Northern Hellenism during the initial phase of the Macedonian Struggle).

Vakalopoulos, K. 1987 *Μακεδονικός Αγώνας (1904-1908): Η Ένοπλη Φάση.* Thessaloniki: *Βαρβουννάκης.* (The Macedonian Struggle, 1904-1908: the Armed Phase).

Vakalopoulos, K. 1988 *Νεότερη Ιστορία της Μακεδονίας 1830-1912.* Thessaloniki: *Βαρβουννάκης.* (Modern History of Macedonia 1830-1912)

Vakalopoulos, K. 1990a *Ιστορία του Βορείου Ελληνισμού: Θράκη.* Thessaloniki: *Εκδοτικός Οίκος Αδελφών Κυριακίδη.* (History of Northern Hellenism: Thrace)

Vakalopoulos, K. 1990b *Κείμενα Εθνικής Αυτογνωσίας.* Thessaloniki: *Εκδοτικός Οίκος Αδελφών Κυριακίδη.* (Essays on National Self-recognition)

Vakalopoulos, K. 1998 *Διωγμοί και Γενοκτονία του Θρακικού Ελληνισμού: Ο πρώτος Ξεριζωμός (1908-1917) (Εθνικά Ζητήματα).* Athens: *Ηρόδοτος.* (Expulsions and Genocide of the Thracian Greeks: the First Uprooting, 1908-1917).

# 37. CHRONOLOGIES OF DESIRE AND THE USES OF MONUMENTS: EFLATUNPINAR TO ÇATALHÖYÜK AND BEYOND

## Lucia NIXON

The first of my two major themes is subsumed in the phrase 'chronologies of desire', which I have adapted from Lynn Meskell's phrase 'archaeology of desire'.[1] I am suggesting that time and dating are often very much what we make of them, particularly when we think we are being most objective. Chronologies of desire are always linked with an intention to control people's views of time: as Geary puts it, 'Those who could control the past could direct the future'.[2] Chronologies of desire also involve selection. Some events or aspects of a period are selected for remembrance; others are selected for suppression and oblivion.

There are perhaps two main types of chronologies of desire: those that seek to encompass the whole of history in one chronological system ('all-encompassing'); and those that insist on an important threshold, before or after which everything was fundamentally different, either incomparably better or immeasurably worse. In both types of chronology, there can also be subdivisions, the number and length of the chronological periods varying according to the agenda of those making them. In some cases, two different groups can regard the same landscape in very different chronological terms, depending on their perspective. One group may hold a dominant view; the other group's view may be muted or submerged.

The second major theme of this paper has to do with monuments and how people use them. Monuments constitute the locus of public memory and public forgetting, both of which are important in making chronologies of desire visible and material. The construction of monuments and their subsequent treatment can reflect very directly the successive chronologies of desire involved at each stage of the monument's life. By looking at a monument and the landscape of which it is a part, it is possible to read the particular chronology of desire which created it, and then maintained or destroyed it.

---

[1] Meskell (1998; 60).
[2] Geary (1994; 6) in discussing early mediaeval Europe; also quoted in Alcock (2001; 325).

The selection of events for remembering and forgetting can have very specific affects on monuments. Alcock has used the phrase 'memory theatres' to describe the manipulation of existing monumental landscapes, in relation to the Roman treatment of the Agora at Athens.[1] I have added a similar phrase, 'theatres of oblivion', as a way of describing the destruction, total or partial, of monuments, such as the Buddhas at Bamiyan.

Control of monuments is thus tantamount to control of the past, and therefore of time itself. Many monuments manipulated in this way are sacred structures, or were when they were built, and changing them therefore has a direct effect on the sacred landscape of a particular period.[2] But all the monuments used in the ways I describe here have one thing in common, whether they are sacred or otherwise: they resonate with powerful symbolic meaning. It is not an accident that that when powerful people reshape their chronologies of desire, they soon make changes to monuments, and in so doing manipulate their symbolic power. For example, the Old Bridge at Mostar, which linked the two banks of the River Neretva, is a poignant example of a conspicuous structure which was destroyed because its ability to connect people symbolically as well as literally was no longer desired. It was built by the Ottoman Turks in 1566, and destroyed by Christians in 1993, who wanted to obliterate the Muslim heritage of Bosnia.[3]

In this paper I will be talking about how and why groups of people, including academic research teams, ethnic groups, and states construct chronologies of desire, and in some cases, apply them directly to powerfully symbolic monuments. My aim is not to criticise, but rather to show what it is that people are doing when they construct their desired chronologies. As a Canadian I come from a country that once worked very hard to forget that native people arrived in Canada long before Europeans arrived, and to remember only the British and the French: a very particular chronology of desire.[4] Instead my goal is to draw attention to the constant construction and

---

[1] Alcock (2001; 334ff). I will discuss the definition and application of this phrase in greater detail below when discussing the Parthenon.

[2] Alcock (2001; 333).

[3] Blakstad (2002; 154-91). The symbolic importance of the Old Bridge is obvious in this quotation: 'I cried when my husband died and I cried when my children died in the war, but the day I cried the most was the day that the Old Bridge came down' (p. 157); and see now Ignatieff (2003).

[4] Histories of Canada used to begin with the arrival of explorers such as John Cabot and Jacques Cartier, as a way of suggesting that time began in Canada only with the arrival of Europeans. More recently, the *Historical Atlas of Canada* has made it clear that the story of what we call Canada began much earlier (18,000 to 10,000 BC); Cole Harris and Matthews (1987).

revision of chronologies of desire, in which all of us have been complicit at one time or another - the understandable wish to pick and choose what we remember and what we forget.

I will begin with a discussion of Hasluck's study of a monument on one side of the Konya Plain in south west Turkey, and end with an archaeological site on the other side, with detours to Athens and to Afghanistan along the way. Eflatunpınar, studied by Hasluck, provides an example of an all-encompassing chronology of desire, and includes a monument. The Parthenon at Athens is an excellent example of a memory theatre; the Buddhas at Bamiyan exemplify a theatre of oblivion. Çatalhöyük is an archaeological site which also constitutes a monument, though of a somewhat different kind. Four different views of the site are discussed here. All of them belong to the threshold kind of desired chronology, and all of them are different.

Before moving to the four examples, I present Table 1, which shows four different ways of reckoning time. Three belong to the religions of the book (Judaism, Christianity, and Islam); the other belongs to Greek religion which was literate, but did not organize and codify time in quite the same way. Two (Greek religion and Judaism) are chronological systems which begin with the creation of the world and move seamlessly through time thereafter; the other two, Christianity and Islam, begin with an important event, the birth of Christ and the journey (Hijrah) of Mohammed from Mecca to Medina.

In each of these two cases, time begins with the important event. There remains the problem of what to do with the time before the important event. Both Christianity and Islam have been at best ambivalent about it. Both make use of the Old Testament, but repudiate any possible influence of pagan ignorance. Indeed, the Muslim name for the time before Islam is Jahiliyya, which means the Time of Ignorance. In both cases, it is extremely clear, and extraordinarily interesting, that the names of the months retain the obvious imprint of the repudiated 'time before': Roman names for the Christian calendar, and pre-Islamic Arabic names for the Islamic calendar.[1]

---

[1] For the Jahiliyya see Lewis and Schlacht (1965), under Djahilyya and Fatra. Cf. (Ali 2002; 27, 62).

## Table 1. Four Different Time Systems[1]

| | Classical Greek religion | Judaism | Christianity | Islam |
|---|---|---|---|---|
| **Creation** | World created (Hesiod, *Theogony*) | World created (*Genesis*) | World created (*Genesis*) | World created, (*Genesis*) |
| **Continuous or threshold with time before?** | Continuous (but see below) | Continuous | Threshold. Time before divided into two: useful Judaic heritage; pagan (Greek and Roman etc) idolatry to be repudiated | Threshold. Time before seen as mono-lithically Jahiliyya (time of ignorance). |
| **Calendar** | 12 months (names varied from city to city) plus use of eponymous years, again variable Seleucid calendar used 312/ 311 BC as year 1; Olympiads used only from 3rd c. BC | 12 months  Time counted from 3761 BC | 12 months.  Jesus' birth is starting point of Christian chronology., hence AD, 'in the year of our Lord.'  B C added later to keep track of 'time before'. | 12 months.  The Hijrah of Mohammed in AD 622 is starting point, hence AH Before that the Seleucid calendar. |
| **Names of the month** | Greek | Hebrew | Roman, including two names referring to 'pagan' Roman emperors (Julius Caesar and Augustus). | Pre-Islamic Arabic. |
| **2002 equivalent** | None | 5763 | 2002 | 1380 |

---

[1] References for Table 1 on chronological systems: Blackburn and Holford-Strevens (1999: Greek;. 712f.; Jewish, 722f.; Christian, 766f.; Muslim, 731f). Other sources: Hesiod, and the book of Genesis. I have deliberately not used BCE/CE terminology in this paper. I am aware that some people think that it is somehow more neutral than BC/AD, but it still seems to me to be a concealed way of maintaining a dating system based on Christianity.

## Table 2. Eflatunpınar[1]

|  | Eflatunpınar |
|---|---|
| **Construction** | Mound with evidence for settlement (Late Chalcolithic, Early Bronze II and III, Middle Bronze, Late Bronze, Iron Age, Classical; Hittite sanctuary with pool, late 13th c. BC). |
| **Afterlife** | Ruined village, ?date.<br>17th c. AD Haji Khalfa refers to Plato as preventer of floods in the Konya Plain.<br>Church with spring of Plato in Konya.<br>Eflatunpınar referred to as 'ancient' (1842); 'Hittite' (1886).<br>Hasluck studies folklore of site.<br>Atatürk encourages Turks to think of Hittites as 'ancestral'.<br>Mellaart investigates site. |
| **Current** | Turkish excavations take place at Hittite sanctuary. |

*Eflatunpınar*

At Eflatunpınar (Plato's Spring), near Beyşehir at the western edge of the Konya Plain, stands a monument with sculptured figures in human form. By Hasluck's time, the monument was already known to the scholarly world as a Hittite structure, therefore dating to the Bronze Age. It was also known that Hittite was an Indo-European language. In his article 'Plato in the Folklore of the Konia Plain', originally published in 1913, Hasluck explored the connection between a Hittite monument and an ancient Greek philosopher. Using local accounts and texts, Hasluck showed that both in Konya and in the surrounding plain, Plato was seen, at least by some people, as a magician-philosopher-engineer who prevented floods in the area, and then set 'talismans' (the monument at Eflatunpınar) to guard the spring. Plato in these Turkish traditions was a benignly Islamicised sage, and the Hittite monument he established 'long ago' was apparently totally unproblematic in Hasluck's own time, despite its anthropomorphic reliefs.

---

[1] References for Table 2 on Eflatunpınar: previous archaeological work includes Hamilton 1842 (Vol. II; 350-1), who identified the monument as 'ancient'; Ward (1886, fig. 1), as Hittite; Mellaart (1962) for a description of the Hittite monument as it then was, and a summary of the material of other periods, including a mention of the ruined village, with sketch plan on p. 112, plus references to other archaeological studies; Özenir (2001) on the current excavations, with numerous plans. Hasluck (1929a) on the stories of Plato associated with the site. It is important to note that we do not know how many people in the area of Konya held the view of Eflatunpınar recorded by Hasluck. Delaney 1991: 289 mentions the official Turkish view of the Hittites as 'ancestral', citing only Gurney's book on the Hittites (1954) with no page number. I have been unable to find additional references on this subject, but see Özdoğan (1988; 116-117) and note also that Hittite emblems appear frequently on a variety of items, from Turkish museum tickets to modern Turkish textiles.

As stated above, the local views of Eflatunpınar, as recorded by
Hasluck in the early twentieth century, are a good example of an 'all-
encompassing' chronology of desire. There is nothing that cannot be
accommodated here. A second millennium BC Hittite monument; a fourth
century BC Greek philosopher; Christianity, a new religion unsure of the
value of pagan writers; Islam, a new religion beginning in the seventh century
AD, whose practitioners were responsible for the translation and survival of
many ancient Greek texts; worries about floods and how to prevent them; a
plain preserving the name of a classical city (Iconium): all these elements are
combined, sometimes in very deep disguise, in the story of Plato's Spring as
analysed by Hasluck. The dates of the individual elements are compressed into
one long period, the time since Plato stopped the floods forever. When exactly
that was does not matter; what does matter is the eternal present since he did
stop them.

The Hittite monument at Eflatunpınar was a pre-existing structure
which could have been ignored or destroyed by people living near Beyşehir in
the Ottoman period. Instead it was neither: it was incorporated, seemingly
without question, into a narrative that suited the people living in the locality.
The 'no questions asked' strategy is in itself a chronology of desire; the
questions aren't asked because the answers might disturb the chronological
narrative already constructed.

Archaeological work has now established that the Hittite monument at
Eflatunpınar is a spring sanctuary dating the thirteenth century BC, and
currently excavations are being conducted at the site. At this point, national
(Turkish) points of view come to the forefront. Since the time of Atatürk,
Turks have been taught that the Hittites, who lived in Anatolia from the
second millennium BC, and spoke a form of Indo-European, were their
ancestors. Thus it is possible for Turkish officialdom not only to tolerate pre-
Islamic anthropomorphic representations but also actively to excavate and
preserve them. Eflatunpınar is now part of an official Turkish chronology of
desire which stresses the Hittite phase of the monument's life, and de-
emphasises any others.

## Table 3: The Parthenon[1]

| | Parthenon |
|---|---|
| Construction | Temple to Athene, city goddess of Athens,447-432 BC. |
| Afterlife | Attalids erect sculptural monument at very steps of temple |
| | part of second c. AD Roman memory theatre (see text). |
| | 3$^{rd}$ c. AD fire; and disappearance of cult statue? |
| | 5$^{th}$ or 6$^{th}$ c. church, with mutilation of sculptures and apse built at east end, new entrance at west. |
| | 12$^{th}$ c. cathedral of Virgin Mary |
| | western church |
| | 15$^{th}$ c. mosque 1 (simple conversion of church with minaret added) |
| | 1687: mosque 1 used as refuge and powder magazine by Turks; bombarded and ruined by Venetian general Morosini. |
| | Mosque 2 (small structure built inside ruins, on different axis) |
| | 1805: Lord Elgin removes the marbles |
| | 1821: rallying point in Greek War in Independence |
| | restoration of Akropolis to 5$^{th}$ c. BC state begins in 1842; mosque 2 dismantled 1844. |
| | Major restoration of Parthenon under Balanos after earthquake begun 1895, continues until 1933. |
| | New restoration under Korres since 1980s. |
| Current | Symbol of 'grown-up' Greek state, able to ask UK for return of Parthenon marbles as member state to member state of EU. |

*Memory Theatres: The Parthenon at Athens*

Eflatunpınar, though interesting, is problematic because there are many gaps in the story of the monument, for example from its last phase of Hittite use to the Ottoman period. In the case of the Parthenon, we can track how people have used it ever since it was constructed. The complicated history of the building is summarised in Table 3 above. Here I show how the Parthenon has

---

[1] References for Table 3 on the Parthenon: Travlos (1971), Andrews (1979), Yalouri (2001; 27ff.), Beard (2002). Travlos (1971; 44) gives the history of the Parthenon site before its construction; see also 52-71 for the Akropolis. Note also Ferrari (2001), who discusses the role of the Parthenon's predecessor in the choreography of memory on the Akropolis at Athens. Plans and photographs: Parthenon: Travlos (1971; 446), Church: Travlos (1971; 456), Mango (1995), Price (1999; 166, n. 82). Cathedral: Beard (2002; 53), Mosque 1: Beard (2002; 79 = Parthenon being blown up by Venetians), Mosque 2: plan, Travlos (1971; 457); photograph, Beard (2002; 84 - taken in 1839; the earliest photograph of the Parthenon). Later stories connected with Parthenon: Yalouri (2001; 18 and 142). Note the seventeenth century Turkish traveller Evliya Çelebi's description of 'the divine philosopher Plato' giving counsel in the Parthenon (Beard 2002; 76 and Andrews 1979; 71) – another example of Muslim regard for 'Eflatun'.

been the focus of successive chronologies of desire for some two and a half millennia, by focussing on a selection of crucial episodes in the afterlife of the Parthenon.

The temple to the goddess Athene Parthenos known as the Parthenon was already controversial when it was built on the Akropolis at Athens in the fifth century BC Built entirely of marble, lavishly adorned with architectural sculpture, and housing a cult statue of gold and ivory, the temple was expensive. It was also immediately conspicuous: in antiquity it could be seen for miles around, and even today it is visible for some distance. As soon as it was constructed, it became a powerful symbol of Athenian supremacy, both military and cultural. Since then, nearly all those with power over Athens and its territory have proclaimed their conquest by doing something in or near or to the Parthenon.

Like the Hittite monument at Eflatunpınar, the Parthenon was a pre-existing structure. But there is an important difference between the two monuments: neither the Parthenon's original date of construction, nor the cultural milieu which it so conspicuously represents were ever lost from public understanding. Indeed, the Parthenon stood and still stands for something so important, and so desirable, that it has had to be incorporated in all later chronologies relating to Athens — even though incorporating it reminds everyone of a non-Roman, non-Christian, non-Ottoman, non-western European, non-modern Greek time, which existed before all these periods. Some of these later groups have attempted to destroy the Parthenon; others have tried to preserve it. The degree of mutilation and destruction of the Parthenon on the one hand, and conspicuous care and reverence on the other, is a direct reflection of the feelings, negative and positive, toward the time and culture represented by the temple. I want to look now closely at three of the episodes listed in Table 3. The first is the Roman period, which is of exceptional interest here.

Alcock in discussing the reconfiguration of memory in the eastern empire introduces the concept of 'memory theatres': 'spaces which conjured up specific and controlled memories of the past through the use of monuments, images and symbols, spaces which served to remind communities at large of just who they were by drawing on who they had been'. During the Roman period, classical buildings and other architectural elements were moved to the Agora, and new structures were built; indeed the new Odeion of Agrippa was constructed in the formerly open centre of the Agora. Alcock suggests that in the second century AD the Agora at Athens was a memory theatre; entering it then was to 'confront a space newly configured and charged with monuments, statues and structures, all carrying with them a burden of memory.'[1]

To Alcock's memory theatre I would add the Akropolis, including the Roman additions to it. Alcock's reconstructed view of the Agora includes the Sacred Way leading up to the Akropolis. Soon after 27 BC the Romans made their presence felt on the Akropolis by building a temple or altar to Roma and Augustus east of the Parthenon and on axis with it. This new Roman structure affected the Akropolis in two ways: first, you could no longer enter the Parthenon without seeing this visible reminder of Roman power. Second, a new view of the Akropolis - the great Parthenon punctuated by the small, new Roman temple/altar - could be seen from the Agora. This new architectural combination would have been an early part of Alcock's memory theatre, and part, too, of what she sees as an attempt to avoid 'severe disjunctures between past and present'. [2]

The Christian approach to the Parthenon was more violent. When Christians converted the temple into a church, probably around the end of the sixth century AD, they destroyed most of the sculptures in the eastern pediment by building an apse. Christians irrevocably opposed to the pagan subjects depicted in the sculptures mutilated the metopes on the west, north, and east sides, sparing only N32 because the figures in it resemble those of an Annunciation scene. Clearly the intention of the Christians was to make use of the temple but also simultaneously to distance themselves from its pre-Christian past by destroying anything conspicuously connected with pagan worship. This kind of destruction, when done on a grander scale, is part of the

---

[1] Alcock (2001; 334-338); first quotation is p. 335; second quotation is p. 337; reconstructed view of the Agora in the second century AD with Akropolis and Parthenon in the background (336).
[2] Roman changes to the Akropolis: temples/altar to Roma and Augustus, Travlos (1971; 71, 494-7); possible identification as altar rather than temple, Camp (2001; 188). Travlos mentions Roman refurbishment of structures on the slopes of the Akropolis (1971; 54, 70-1). In the last quarter of the first century BC, a statue of Agrippa was erected on a base which had previously displayed statues of Hellenistic kings of Pergamon, and then of Antony and Cleopatra. The base and any statue on it were visible in front of the Propylaia (monumental gateway of the Akropolis) to people going up to the Akropolis; Travlos (1971; 70-1, 487, 493); Camp (2001; 189). The Odeion of Herodes Atticus was built between 160-170 AD on the south slope of the Akropolis; Travlos (1971; 70-71, 378-86); Camp (2001; 215-7). Picture of Agora and Akropolis model (with Parthenon and Roma and Augustus), Camp (2001; 258). The Roman buildings on the Akropolis and in the Agora are not the only Roman structures in Athens, but they are the most significant in the construction of the Roman memory theatre there; for more information see Camp (2001; ch. 6, Roman Athens).

construction of theatres of oblivion, to be discussed in the next section on Bamiyan.[1]

The third episode which I wish to examine is the construction of the second mosque after Morosini's bombardment of 1687. The first mosque had been a simple conversion of the more or less complete temple-turned-church. After the bombardment there was enough room on the Akropolis to build a new mosque elsewhere, yet this option was not pursued. Instead, the second mosque, a completely self-contained structure which was effectively free-standing, was set inside the bombed-out Parthenon. The one major difference was that the second mosque was placed on a different axis, presumably to align it more accurately with Mecca. The Parthenon, even in ruins, remains so symbolically powerful that no one in charge of it has ever been able to let it alone.

The citizens of the new modern Greek state who removed the second mosque had their own chronology of desire, which did not include visible monuments of the Tourkokratia, and which did include the restoration of the Parthenon as a conspicuously Greek building. Between the construction of the mosque in the seventeenth century and its dismantling in the nineteenth, another chronology of desire had affected the Parthenon: that of imperial Britain, in the form of Lord Elgin. Depending on whose chronology of desire you follow, either Lord Elgin rescued the sculptures of the Parthenon for the benefit of world civilisation from the ignorant inhabitants of Athens - so ignorant that they were burning fifth century BC marble sculptures for lime; or he stole a vital part of the cultural heritage that links ancient and modern Greece, by distorting the terms of a permit which was issued by an occupying power, i.e. the Ottoman Turks. It is of course relevant that Britain at the time was emerging as a major world power, and that many people in Britain wished to establish a close link between that most respectable of all ancient pasts, the classical world, and their own culture. The sculptures displayed in the British Museum were called the Elgin Marbles after the person who brought them to England. In the twentieth and twenty-first centuries the Greek government (like its nineteenth century predecessor) has continued to pour huge sums into the restoration of the Parthenon, and to ask for the return of the Parthenon

---

[1] For details of the Christian mutilation of the Parthenon, see Parthenon metopes (including those on the east and west sides mutilated by Christians), Boardman (1991; 96-105, and figs 85-91). Many temples were turned into churches; see for example the Temple of Aphrodite at Aphrodisias (Aphrodite's city) in western Turkey, renamed Stavroupolis (city of the cross) as part of an aggressive programme of Christianisation discussed by Cormack (1990) and Smith (1993). For the Romanisation of Greek Aphrodisias before that, see now Alcock (2001; 338-342).

Marbles. In the meantime the Louvre is keeping very quiet about the section of Parthenon frieze on display in Paris.[1]

The story of the Parthenon is thus one that involves many chronologies of desire. Outsiders with power over Athens always desire to incorporate all or part of the temple into their own histories (Roman temples, Christian church, mosque, museum collections) — and in some cases to eliminate histories that are considered unsuitable. Similarly, the now Orthodox Greeks seem to deny that there have been any changes to the temple since its construction in the fifth century BC, by removing all traces of any other subsequent period (the churchly adaptations as well as the second mosque), possibly as a way of forgetting that Greece was ever subjugated by anyone. In this case the pagan-ness of the Parthenon can be overlooked, because establishing and maintaining a connection to the 'free' classical past is more important for national identity than denying the existence of all pre-Christian religions. In all cases the Parthenon has served as a focus for a series of chronological agendas, each one made visible by changes to the temple or its setting.

## Table 4. Bamiyan[2]

|  | Bamiyan |
|---|---|
| **Construction** | Buddhas constructed in 5th-6th c. AD plus other Buddhist structures and paintings. |
| **Afterlife** | 7th c. Chinese pilgrim Hiuen-Tsang records visit. 7th-8th c. arrival of Islam. 12th-13th c. Islamic city of Shahr-i-Gholghola built. 19th c. stories about Buddhas recorded: 1. Islamic ruler (Aurangzeb or Nadir Shah) ordered shots at larger Buddha but when statue's leg bled and he had bad dreams, shots called off. 2. local Hindus, Buddhists, and Muslims all have different identifications of the statues and their origins; e.g. they were built by Christian infidels. Late 20th c. Buddhas part of official Afghan gov't site under Minstère de l'Information et de la Culture. March 2001. Buddhas blown up by Taliban. |
| **Current** | Theatre of oblivion |

---

[1] The Parthenon East Frieze slab VII in the Louvre is illustrated in Boardman (1991; fig. 96.15).

[2] References for Table 4 on Bamiyan: MacDowell and Taddei (1978); Wilford (1799, also quoted in Godard et al. 1928; 85-6), Burnes (1833), Baker and Allchin (1991, 1-21).

*Theatres of Oblivion: Bamiyan, Buddhism, and the Taliban*

Buddhism came to Afghanistan in the third century BC. The Buddha statues and other Buddhist structures, such as cave monasteries and a stupa, were constructed at Bamiyan in the fifth or sixth centuries AD. Together they constituted one part of an extensive Buddhist landscape in what is now Afghanistan. Other Buddhist monuments are known from many other parts of the country.[1]

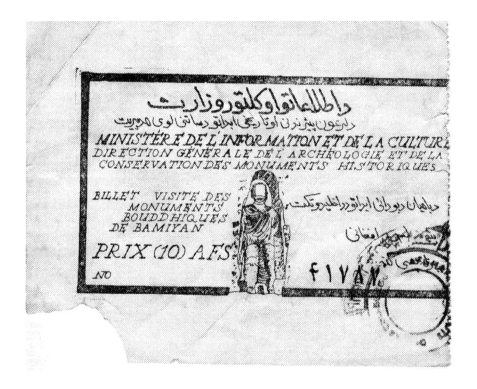

Figure 1: Entry ticket to Bamiyan

At Bamiyan, there was a later Islamic city, which included the palace of a Muslim governor. These structures lay opposite the great cliff into which the Buddha statues were cut. The statues were therefore visible from the later settlement. By the eighteenth century the statues had already been mutilated by the then Islamic inhabitants - mutilated but not destroyed. There were also a

---

[1] The partially preserved inscription in Greek and Prakrit found at Kandahar, recording the Edict of Asoka, constitutes part of the evidence for the early phase of Afghan Buddhism; MacDowell and Taddei (1978; 192-3, 195-6).

number of legends about the statues which enjoined Muslims to refrain from destruction. The Buddha statues and other Buddhist remains which more or less surrounded the Islamic settlement at Bamiyan could then be tolerated as part of the landscape.

By the late 1970s when I went to Bamiyan, the site had become one of several tourist destinations for those passing through Afghanistan. These destinations included Islamic monuments such as the Great Mosque at Herat, which I also visited. The ticket receipts for these two sites were large pieces of paper printed with a picture of the monument with text in Dari and English (Herat), or in Dari and French (Bamiyan, Fig. 1). In other words, in 1978 the Afghan Ministry of Information and Culture was happy to charge people for the privilege of visiting a broad range of monuments, even when those monuments were clearly anthropomorphic in nature. It was still possible for the then government of Afghanistan to acknowledge the existence of other cultures before the coming of Islam.

Less than 25 years later, the Taliban decided to destroy the Buddha statues of Bamiyan. I interpret this act as an attempt to 'forget' Buddhism in Afghanistan, indeed to deny the existence of any kind of pre-Islamic time. The destruction of the Buddhas was thus part of a Taliban chronology of desire, through the creation of a very conspicuous theatre of oblivion. But what was it that the Taliban wanted to forget, in destroying the Buddhas? After all, Buddhism has not been a serious threat to Islam in Afghanistan for a millennium. The Buddhas were selected, I suggest, precisely because they constituted a conspicuous monument of a non-Islamic kind, and because people would notice if they were destroyed. The ideological target is more likely to be any and all non-Islamic belief systems, including Buddhism, but also including the far greater threat of western (particularly American) values which can be made religious by calling them Christian.

Afghanistan of course had and has many Buddhist monuments, including the cave monasteries at Bamiyan itself. The landscape of Afghanistan still retains the imprint of local Buddhism, just as the Christian and Muslim calendars retain the imprint of the 'ignorant' paganism so conspicuously repudiated by the authorities. The Taliban have failed to obliterate all vestiges of the Buddhist past, but they have certainly succeeded in making their chronology of desire very clear: there never was a time before Islam, and if there was, we want to forget all about it.[1]

### Çatalhöyük: Local and Archaeological Views

It may seem unusual, even perverse to call an excavation a monument. But the physical process of digging makes visible what was previously covered, and the metaphysical process of interpretation can, in cases like that of Çatalhöyük, monumentalise the significance of what is found. Çatalhöyük is clearly of particular archaeological interest because it has been excavated by two different archaeologists and their teams within the space of 30-odd years.

Table 5 opposite summarises how four different groups of people see the site of Çatalhöyük.[2] The first three seem to agree that the Neolithic Period, the floruit of Çatalhöyük, is a crucial threshold after which things have been either much better, or much worse. The fourth group focusses on a different threshold altogether, the Exchange of Populations mandated by the Treaty of Lausanne in 1928. What interests us here is how and when these two crucial thresholds were constructed, and what they mean for the chronologies of desire that led to their construction.

The first three groups see the Neolithic as the important chronological threshold. Mellaart thought that the Neolithic was the time when important cultural resources were transmitted from Anatolia to Europe, and that Çatalhöyük was the place where this transmission occurred. The second two groups, women participating in Goddess worship (mainly from the U.S.) and contemporary archaeologists (mainly but not exclusively western), think that the Neolithic was the time when two pivotal changes occurred. The first of these was a change in subsistence from a mobile economy based on gathering

---

[1] There is more than one way of 'forgetting' the destruction of the Buddhas of Bamiyan. Tariq Ali in his recent book *The Clash of Fundamentalisms* (2002) simply omits any mention of it, despite much excellent discussion of Afghan history and politics, particularly in ch. 17, Afghanistan: Between Hammer and Anvil.

[2] References for Table 5 on Çatalhöyük: Mellaart (1967; 11, 52-3); Hodder (1990; 3-11, 16-18, 69, 97, and Hodder 1996); Shankland (1996; 35 and 1999; 145, 153); Meskell (1998; 47-8, 52-55, 60); Eller (2000; 142-147). Again, the villagers' view of Çatalhöyük as recorded by Shankland (and which I use here) is only one view, not necessarily a dominant one, as he points out.

**Table 5. Çatalhöyük: Four Views of the Site**

| Çatalhöyük | Archaeo-logical Sequence | Mellaart, 1960s | Goddess Worshippers | Contemp-orary Archaeo-logists | People from Villages |
|---|---|---|---|---|---|
| **Constructon** | Settled ca 6500 BC; deserted 5600 | Art, economy, goddess religion of site all exported to form foundations of western civilisation via Greece; site is monument to this important threshold. | Site represents acme of peaceful matrilineal culture -- harmonious and artistic. The Goddess embodies the sacred earth; site is monument to this important threshold. | During the Neolithic, major domesticati ons of plants and animals. Possibly also of women by men; site is monument to this important threshold. | Pre-Islamic site with anthro-pomorphic wall-paintings. |
| **Afterlife** | Çatalhöyük West abandoned ca 4900 BC<br><br>BC<br>------------<br>AD<br><br>Turkey Islamicised<br><br>1928 Treaty of Lausanne and the Population Echange<br><br>1961-63 Mellaart's excavations. | Hittites in second millennium BC = another major Anatolian civilisation (and they are speakers of Indo-European).<br><br><br><br><br><br><br><br>It's all getting better and better. | Decline into nasty and brutish (and very long) patriarchy; only bright spot since Neolithic is the peaceful matrilineal civilisation of Minoan Crete.<br><br><br>It's all getting worse and worse. | Finally! Men in more or less complete charge of economy, and women relegated to the house<br><br><br><br><br>It's all getting better and better | Descend-ants of site's original inhabitants were the local Rum (infidel Greeks), now gone because of Population Exchange; a formerly mixed population is now more safely pure.<br><br>It's mostly getting better and better |
| **Current** | 1993 - Hodder's excavations | Site is memory theatre for origins of western civilization. | Site is memory theatre for matriarchal utopia. | Site is memory theatre for threshold of domesti-cation. | Site is a theatre of ambiva-lence; should this alien time be remem-bered or forgotten? |

and hunting, to a sedentary, agricultural way of life. There is also a view that men domesticated women as well as plants and animals, so the second change has to do with a major change in the relative status of women and men - for the worse if you are a Goddess worshipper, for the better if you are a contemporary archaeologist. The views of the Goddess worshippers and contemporary archaeologists are mirror images of each other, with the Neolithic acting as the chronological pivot. These two groups see Çatalhöyük as one of the places where these two changes may have taken place.[1]

The fourth group consists of at least some of the people who live in the local village of Küçükköy. Their crucial chronological threshold, the Treaty of Lausanne in 1928, is completely different in time, place, and consequences. The main result of the Treaty was the Exchange of Populations, which meant that Christian Greeks left Turkey forever; ever since, the area of Çumra, once dangerously mixed, has been safely Islamic. It was the ancestors of the Greeks who lived at Çatalhöyük, and it was they who created the non-Islamic anthropomorphic wall-paintings there, some of which may represent women. The Treaty of Lausanne is the threshold that made an important difference to the villagers' own lives, but the most important threshold of all is the conversion of what is now Turkey to Islam. In contrast to the Eflatunpınar accounts analysed by Hasluck, these narratives of the late twentieth century AD/late fifteenth century AH reveal a new preoccupation with the categories Islamic, and pre- or non-Islamic.

It is easy to dismiss the views of Mellaart, the Goddess Worshippers, and the villagers as unfashionable or unscientific, and to privilege the more or less dominant view of contemporary archaeologists: easy, but wrong, because it means that the views of these archaeologists are not properly scrutinised by comparing them with other ways of looking at the site.[2] While the Neolithic does seem to be the time when some people did domesticate some plants and animals in this part of the world, we do not know whether women or men (or a combination of both) did the domestication, nor do we know what effect domestication had on their relative status. Indeed we will never know what, if any, gender transformations happened in the Neolithic, or any other period, until we develop the methodologies for finding out, instead of assuming that we already know.

---

[1] I discuss another set of mirror images connected with Minoans and Mycenaeans in Nixon (1994; 8-13).
[2] Hasluck was certainly aware of local views of foreign visitors; see his article, 'Western Travellers through Eastern Eyes' (1929b).

In the meantime, the archaeological site of Çatalhöyük, itself a construct, has become a monument in various debates about time. Neolithic Çatalhöyük reflects the chronologies of desire of the two groups of archaeologists and of the Goddess worshippers, just as the non-Islamic site of 'Greek' Çatalhöyük reflects some villagers' chronology of desire.[1] The two main groups, archaeologists and goddess worshippers on the one hand, and villagers on the other, home in on the chronological thresholds and periods which are most relevant to their agenda. The archaeologists think that they are being 'objective' when in fact their chronological focus reveals their very subjective concerns, just as the stories told by the villagers reveal theirs. It is all the more important that archaeologists like Hodder and his team continue their search for more appropriate ways of determining archaeological agendas, and excavating and interpreting archaeological data.[2]

*Conclusions*

In this paper I have looked at four monuments, Çatalhöyük, Eflatunpınar, the Parthenon, and the Buddhas at Bamiyan, to list them in the order in which they were built. The construction of monuments is the result of complex human decisions, and so is everything that happens to them later on. Sometimes a monument remains significant throughout its entire history (the Parthenon); sometimes a monument becomes significant only millennia after it came into being (Çatalhöyük). The events of 11 September 2001 AD/ 22 Jumada al-thani 1422 AH show that monuments need not be old to be suddenly and crucially significant in ways that their builders and users never intended. It is also important to notice that the aim of the al-Qa'ida bombers was precisely the destruction of monuments, in this case the World Trade

---

[1] It is important to note that two of these narratives have formal parallels with other chronologies of desire. The contemporary archaeological view has much in common with the accounts in Hesiod and Genesis (both roughly Eighth century BC, linking the origins of agriculture with the status of women and men. The narrators of both ancient texts narrators were convinced that things had once been much better, when Adam and Eve lived in the Garden of Eden (Genesis), and when men (literally only men) co-existed with the gods (Hesiod). Both narrators thought that human life since then had become much worse. But both texts, Genesis and Hesiod, blame specific women (Eve and Pandora), for the separation of people from the divine sphere, and for the difficulty of making a living through agriculture. This story is clearly a very old one with contemporary archaeologists narrating the most recent version. I have discussed these similarities in my lectures on 'Archaeology and Gender: the Power of Narrative' given at Oxford University, and will be producing a written version in due course. The story at the village that Çatalhöyük and its problematic images were created by Christians who have now left the area, is remarkably similar to local stories about the Buddhas at Bamiyan, noted above in Table 4. Both narratives assign responsibility for a problematic monument to another religious group which has now disappeared from the local landscape.

[2] Hodder (1997). See also Nixon (2001) for an earlier discussion of some of these issues.

Center in New York City, and the Pentagon in Washington D.C.[1] They could
have killed many more people than they did, *if* wholesale murder had been
their aim. I have no wish to trivialise the tragic deaths of several thousand
people, but rather to emphasise the symbolic content of the two attacks that
caused them.[2] The World Trade Center was a powerful symbol of international
commerce dominated by the U.S.; the Pentagon symbolises American
military might. Attacking these two conspicuous monuments was a way of
attacking American dominance in two crucial areas of modern life. Thus the
al-Qa'ida bombers were people with a symbolic purpose: to insist on their
own chronology of desire, where the very existence of non-Muslim time and
culture could be denied, by creating theatres of oblivion where infidel
monuments once stood.

Like the destruction of the Old Bridge at Mostar and the Buddhas at
Bamiyan, the events of 11 September confirm that using monuments to make
new chronologies of desire visible is not something that happened only in the
past. People are still constructing chronologies of desire to suit their own
agendas, and no doubt will continue to use monuments in the ways I have
described.

In this paper, then, I hope to have shown that chronologies of desire
exist in a wide variety of periods and places. Chronologies of desire and the
use of monuments are linked by a desire to control the present and the future
by manipulating the past. Some chronologies of desire are to do with
remembering, other with forgetting. Most are connected with monuments and
their manipulations. All are human artefacts.

There is often a direct link between chronologies of desire and the
monuments selected as their focus. In considering the relationship between
changing chronologies of desire and their effect on monuments, it is useful for

---

[1] World Trade Center: http://www.GreatBuildings.com/ buildings.World_Trade_Center.html;
The Pentagon:http://www.GreatBuildings.com/buildings/The_Pentagon.html. There is no space
here to describe the place of these two monuments in their respective landscapes; I will simply
note that the WTC was intervisible with its predecessor, the Empire State Building, and that the
Pentagon lies directly across the Potomac River from the Washington Monument. Yamasaki, the
architect of the WTC, was certainly aware of its symbolic significance: 'I feel this way about it.
World trade means world peace and consequently the World Trade Center buildings in New
York ... had a bigger purpose than just to provide room for tenants. The World Trade Center is
a living symbol of man's dedication to world peace ... beyond the compelling need to make this
a monument to world peace, the World Trade Center should, because of its importance,
become a representation of man's belief in humanity, his need for individual dignity, his beliefs
in the co-operation of men, and through co-operation, his ability to find greatness.' (Yamasaki
quotation from Paul Heyer, *Architects on Architecture: New Directions in America*, p. 186, cited
on WTC section of Great Buildings website as given above.)

[2] Consider, for example, Arthus-Bertrand's aerial photograph of the city of Priapat in the
Ukraine (1999; 348-9, caption 332). Priapat (former population 50,000) was abandoned when
the nuclear reactor at Chernobyl exploded in 1986, as a result of which many people died, and
several million people were affected by cancers and immune deficiencies. People left Priapat
for horrific reasons, but their disappearance is invisible -- the buildings of their city still stand in
the snow.

researchers to consider *all* episodes or stages in the history of a monument. It can be very revealing to consider not only the time of a monument's construction, but also its entire Nachleben or afterlife. In a number of cases, monuments and how they are treated make chronologies of desire conspicuous and visible, both when the monuments are built, and in their Nachleben. Indeed in some cases, the fate of a monument constitutes the first public declaration that the dominant chronology of desire is changing.

The same monument can be used in different ways at different times. As Alcock remarks, 'reworking of the past is most pronounced in periods of dramatic social transformation'.[1] Monuments can be used to create memory theatres, or destroyed to make theatres of oblivion. Memory theatres arise from a desire to integrate the past and the present; theatres of oblivion arise from a desire to separate them, often through fear of future dominance by a past or present power. By looking at monuments, then, politicians and archaeologists alike can monitor changes in the agendas of powerful groups, and distinguish between integrative memory and destructive forgetting

Monuments receiving this kind of desirous attention need not be religious in origin, but they do have to be conspicuous, and to command instant recognition. Monuments are commonly used by people who are motivated by their own belief system, sometimes regardless of the religious focus of the monument. In the case of Çatalhöyük, the site has *become* religious for at least one of the groups discussed above. It is important to remember that more than one view of a monument is possible during the same period. Again, Çatalhöyük reveals that a heterogeneous community will produce a heterogeneous response. Alcock discusses different strands of Greek memory and identity in second century AD Athens - panhellenic, inter-city, intra-city, and subject to Roman power. [2] It is when one group insists that their memories and their chronology of desire are the right ones, and that all others must be suppressed that problems arise. One example of such a situation is the metamorphosis of multiple views and agendas in NW India during the second millennium AD into a fiercely binary view, brilliantly dissected by Thapar. It should come as no surprise that the focus of all these views — recorded in Turco-Persian and Jaina texts, Sanskrit inscriptions, nineteenth century debates in the House of Commons in London, and modern nationalist readings — is a raid on a temple, in Somanatha (Gujarat), in which its idol was broken or stolen. Out of a highly complex mixture of identities

---

[1] Alcock (2001; 325).

[2] Alcock (2001; 345-6).

and agendas has come a dichotomous twentieth century Hindu-Muslim view, which repudiates complexity, and insists that there is only way of thinking about the original event.[1]

The desire to create special chronologies of desire and the wish to monumentalise them by projecting them onto conspicuous structures is not necessarily bad. But acting on these desires and wishes without being aware that this is what we are doing can be extremely dangerous. The reduction of multiple issues into sharply polarised views (that was then, this is now; that was them, and this is us) is not always an appropriate way of considering a complicated reality. It can result in a bid for control by one group insisting that their view is dominant, as though to reach some pluralistic accommodation both in belief systems and in monumental space were impossibly dangerous. The real danger may lie in not doing so.

One of the worst effects of applying unexamined chronologies of desire to monuments is that it closes off interesting lines of enquiry. What will happen to Hittite monuments, nearly all of which are anthropomorphic, if Islamic fundamentalists in Turkey choose to construct a chronology of desire which insists that they ought never to have existed, that there never was a time when people in Turkey could conceivably have thought that such monuments were a good thing? Why did the newly created modern Greek state see post-fifth century BC monuments and structures on the Akropolis as separators rather than links between it and the Parthenon? Why did the Taliban think that destroying the Buddhas would make people forget them, instead of bringing worldwide attention to the former presence of Buddhism in Afghanistan? Why, exactly, may people living near Çatalhöyük become bothered by the notion that their local past is a mixture of non-Islamic and Islamic? Why do educated, urban women from the West find religious consolation in wall-paintings interpreted by a male archaeologist at a Stone Age village site? Why does the agenda of many archaeologists focus so tightly on issues such as human exploitation of the environment, changes in gender relations and the division of labour, and elaborate symbolism and the processes of social control, with similarly tight insistence that these changes took place at Neolithic Çatalhöyük? These are only some of the questions that one might pose in connection with the chronologies of desire discussed here.

---

[1] Thapar (2000; 24-50).

My final point is to repeat that all of us create chronologies of desire, archaeologists as well as imperialists and fundamentalists of every kind and belief. The problem stems not from the construction of chronologies of desire, but from a lack of awareness that this is what we are doing. Chronologies of desire are precisely that, and they exclude all questions that do not contribute to the desired view of a particular past. Our goal should be to recognise them for what they are, and to be aware of their dangers. Achieving this goal would be a suitable commemorative monument to Hasluck and his work.

*Acknowledgements*

My first acknowledgement must be to Hasluck himself. In his own work he set a shining example of the importance of taking notice of what you see before you, even if it isn't what you thought you were investigating to begin with, or what you were 'officially' meant to be looking at. As assistant director and librarian of the Canadian Archaeological Institute at Athens in 1983-85, I enjoyed thinking of Hasluck (who occupied a similar post at the British School at Athens) as an illustrious predecessor. Since 1987 I have co-directed, with Jennifer Moody, an interdisciplinary diachronic survey in Sphakia, SW Crete; information about the Sphakia Survey can be found on our website (Nixon and Moody et al. 2000). I have always hoped that this is the sort of project that Hasluck himself would have liked. I am also grateful to David Shankland for organising the Hasluck conference in November 2001, which enabled me to think longer and harder about these issues. The papers given by Keith Hopwood and Charles Stewart were particularly relevant. Before the conference, the events of 11 September 2001 focussed the world's attention on the fate of people and monuments when ideologies are in conflict. I organised a discussion at Magdalen College, Oxford on these events on 11 October, which brought together specialists who spoke about terrorism, international law, Islam, and humanitarian aid; I spoke briefly about the use of monuments to make statements about time and ideology. Some of this material is incorporated here, in particular the discussion of Bamiyan.

At the Hasluck conference David Barchard told me about the Islamic concept of the Jahiliyya. Later Clive Holes and Christopher Melchert (Oriental Institute, Oxford) helped me to follow up on this information. Simon Price (Lady Margaret Hall, Oxford) directed me to references on the Christianisation of time. Robin Osborne (King's College, Cambridge) and John Bennet (Institute of Archaeology, Oxford) also provided useful comments and references. I thank all of them for their help. I thank also my students, chiefly in Archaeology and Anthropology, who have heard and commented on some of this material in tutorials. I am grateful, as always, to helpful members of staff in several libraries in Oxford: the Sackler (classical archaeology, including Afghanistan); the Oriental Institute (Buddhist monuments); the Indian Institute; the Modern History Faculty; Magdalen College. As readers will see, I learnt a great deal from Alcock's article (2001); her 2002 book (Archaeologies of the Greek Past. Landscape, Monuments, and Memories, Cambridge University Press) appeared too late for me to benefit further from her work. The faults that undoubtedly remain in this article are my own.

## REFERENCES

Alcock, S. 2001 'The Reconfiguration of Memory in the Eastern Roman Empire', in Alcock, D'Altroy, Morrison, and Sinopoli 2001 (eds), pp. 323-350.

Alcock, S., D'Altroy,T., Morrison, K. and Sinopoli, C. (eds) 2001 *Empires. Perspectives from Archaeology and History*, Cambridge; Cambridge University Press.

Ali, T. 2002 *The Clash of Fundamentalisms, Crusades, Jihads and Modernity*, London; Verso.

Allchin, F. and Hammond, N. (eds) 1978 *The Archaeology of Afghanistan from earliest times to the Timurid period*, London; Academic Press.

Andrews, K. 1979 *Athens Alive*, Athens; Hermes Publications.

Arthus-Bertrand, Y. 1999 *The Earth from the Air* , transl. from the French by David Baker, London; Thames and Hudson.

Baker, P. and Allchin, F. 1991 *Shahr-i Zohak and the History of the Bamiyan Valley, Afghanistan*, Ancient India and Iran Trust Series No. 1, British Archaeological Reports International Series 570, Oxford; Tempus Reparatum.

Beard, M. 2002 *The Parthenon*, London; Profile Books.

Blackburn, B. and Holford-Strevens, L. 1999 *The Oxford Companion to the Year. An Exploration of Calendar Customs and Time-Reckoning*, Oxford; Oxford University Press.

Blakstad, L. 2002 *Bridge. The Architecture of Connection*, Basel; Birkhäuser.

Boardman, J. 1991 *Greek Sculpture. The Classical Period*, London; Thames and Hudson.

Burnes, A. 1833 'On the Colossal Idol of Bamian' [sic], *Journal of the Asiatic Society (Bengal)*, Vol. 2; 560-4.

Camp, J. 2001 *The Archaeology of Athens*, New Haven; Yale University Press.

Cole Harris, R. and Matthews, G., (eds) 1987 *Historical Atlas of Canada* vol. I. *From the Beginning to 1800*, Toronto; University of Toronto Press.

Cormack, R. 1990 'Byzantine Aphrodisias: Changing the Symbolic Map of a City', *Proceedings of the Cambridge Philological Society* 36; 26-41.

Delaney, C. 1991 *The Seed and the Soil: Gender and Cosmology in Turkish Village Society*, Berkeley and Oxford; University of California Press.

Eller, C. 2000 *The Myth of Matriarchal Prehistory. Why an Invented Past Won't Give Women a Future*, Boston; Beacon Press.

Ferrari, G. 2002 'The Ancient Temple on the Acropolis at Athens', *AJA* Vol. 106; 11-35.

Geary, P. 1994 *Phantoms of remembrance: memory and oblivion at the end of the first millennium*, Princeton; Princeton University Press.

Godard, A., Godard, Y. and Hackin, J. 1928 *Les Antiquités Bouddhiques de Bamiyan*, Mémoires de la Délégation Française d'Archéologie en Afghanistan II.

Goodison, L. and Morris, C. (eds) 1998 *Ancient Goddesses. The Myths and the Evidence*, London; British Museum Press.

*The Great Buildings Collection* 1997-2002 http://www. GreatBuildings.com/gbc.html (2 August 2002).

Gurney, O. 1954 *The Hittites*, second edition with later revisions, Harmondsworth; Penguin.

Hamilton, W. 1842 *Researches in Asia Minor, Pontus, and Armenia; with Some Account of their Antiquities and Geology*, London; John Murray.

Hasluck, F. 1929 *Christianity and Islam under the Sultans*, edited by M. Hasluck, 2 Vols, Oxford; Clarendon.

Hasluck, F. 1929a 'Plato in the Folk-lore of the Konia Plain.' In Hasluck 1929; 363-9.

Hasluck, F. 1929b 'Western Travellers through Eastern Eyes', In Hasluck, 1929; 641-5.

Hesiod 1959 [8th c. BC], *The Works and Days, Theogony [The Begetting of the Gods], and The Shield of Herakles*, translated from Greek by Richmond Lattimore, Ann Arbor, MI; University of Michigan Press.

Hodder, I. 1990 *The Domestication of Europe. Structure and Contingency in Neolithic Societies*, Oxford; Basil Blackwell.

Hodder, I. (ed.) 1996 *Archaeology on the Surface; Çatalhöyük 1993-95*. Cambridge and London; The Çatalhöyük Research Trust, Çatalhöyük Project Vol. 1.

Hodder, I. 1997 'Always Momentary, Fluid and Flexible: Towards a Reflexive Excavation Methodology.' *Antiquity* Vol. 71; 691-700.

Hodder, I. 27 June 2002 *Çatalhöyük. Excavations of a Neolithic Anatolian Höyük* http://catal.arch.cam.ac.uk/catal/catal.html (2 August 2002).

Ignatieff, M. 2003 'The Bridge Builder', in *Empire Lite. Nation-Building in Bosnia, Kosovo and Afghanistan*, London; Vintage, 27-43.

Lewis, B., Pellat, C. and Schlacht, J. (eds) 1965 *Encyclopaedia of Islam*, vol. II (s.v. Djahiliyya, Fatra).

MacDowell, D. and Taddei M. 1978 'Chapter 4. Early Period. Achaemenids and Greeks', in Allchin and Hammond; 170– 231.

MacDowell, D.W. and Taddei, M. 1978 'Chapter 5. The Pre-Muslim Period. Achaemenids and Greeks,' in Allchin and Hammond; 233-99.

Mango, C. 1995 'The Conversion of the Parthenon into a Church: the Tübingen Theosophy,' *Deltion tis Khristianikis Arkhaiologikis Etaireias (Bulletin of the Society for Christian Archaeology)* Delta' Tomos IH; 201-203.

Mellaart, J. 1962 'The Late Bronze Age Monuments of Eflatun Pınar and Fasıllar near Beyşehir,' *Anatolian Studies* Vol. 12; 111-17.

Mellaart, J. 1967 *Çatal Hüyük. A Neolithic Town in Ancient Anatolia*, London; Thames and Hudson.

Meskell, L. 1998 'Twin Peaks: the Archaeologies of Çatalhöyük', in Goodison and Morris (eds), 36-62.

Nixon, L. 1994 'Gender Bias in Archaeology', in Archer, L. Fischler, S. and Wyke, M. (eds), *An Illusion of the Night: Women in Antiquity*, London; Macmillan; 1-23.

Nixon, L., Moody, J. Price, S. and Rackham, O. 2000 *The Sphakia Survey: Internet Edition*, http://sphakia.classics.ox.ac.uk.

Nixon, Lucia 2001 'Seeing Voices: Filming an Archaeological Survey', *American Journal of Archaeology*, 105; 77-97.

Özdoğan, M. 1998 'Ideology and Archaeology in Turkey', in *Archaeology under Fire*, edited by L. Meskell, London; Routledge, 111-123.

Özenir, A. 2001 'Eflatunpınar. Kutsal Anıt — Havuz (1966-2000)', 2000 Yılı Anadolu Medeniyetleri Müzesi Konferansları, Ankara; Türkiye Cumhuriyeti Kültür Bakanlığı, Anadolu Medeniyetleri Müzesi; 35-66.

Price, S. 1999 *Religions of the Ancient Greeks*, Cambridge; Cambridge University Press.

Shankland, D. 1995 'An Anthropology of Archaeology?' *Anatolian Archaeology*, 1; 20.

Shankland, D. 1996 'Çatalhöyük: the Anthropology of an Archaeological Presence,' in Hodder 1996; 349-57.

Shankland, D. 1999 'Integrating the Past. Folklore, Mounds and People at Çatalhöyük.' In *Archaeology and Folklore*, edited by Gazin-Schwartz, A. and Holtorf, C. London; Routledge; 139-157.

Smith, R. 1995 'Aphrodisias 1993'. in *Kazı Sonuçları Toplantısı* 16: 191-206, esp. 193-4 (article in English).

Thapar, R. 2000 *Narratives and the Making of History. Two Lectures* , New Delhi; Oxford University Press.

Travlos, John 1971 *Pictorial Dictionary of Ancient Athens*, New York; Praeger

Yalouri, E. 2001 *The Acropolis. Global Fame, Local Claim* , Oxford; Berghahn

Ward, W. 1886 'Unpublished or imperfectly published Hittite Monuments I. The Façade at Eflatun-Bunar. *American Journal of Archaeology* Vol. 2; 49-51.

Wilford, F. 1799 'On Mount Caucasus', *Asiatick Researches* Vol. VI; 455-536.

# 38. DORIAN ARCHAEOLOGY, HISTORY AND LOCAL FOLKLORE IN DATÇA

Begümşen ERGENEKON[1]

The Datça (Dadya/Knidia) peninsula is situated in southwest Turkey, where the Aegean meets the Mediterranean. The remains we see there today are witness to a brilliant past in the first millenium BC. Today, the Datça and Bozburun (Loryma) peninsulas are declared sites of national heritage and protected by law by virtue of their natural beauty, local architecture and number of archaeological sites. The peninsula is inhabited by 11,458 people in one town centre and nine villages. The town is divided into three districts (İskele, Eski Datça/Dadya and Reşadiye *Mahallesi*). The villages fall into two groups, with Emecik, Hızırşah, Karaköy and Kızlan in the Datça area and Yaka, Mesudiye, Sındı, Cumalı-Çeşme and Yazı Villages in the Betçe area.

Knidia has been the home of many civilizations, the oldest of which that has been investigated until now being the 'Dorian Hexapolis'. The traces of many settlements and antique routes may still be seen on the surface in and around the villages, fields, and orchards, on the hills and the mountains, in spite of earthquakes, volcanic eruptions on the near-by island of Sanotrini and the plunder of pirates and occupants. The inhabitants relate to these remains with strories, legends and have found new meanings and functions for ancient objects and sites. In this paper, I shall consider initially some of the historical developments that have led to the unique cultural assemblage that is today's Datça, offer a note on the population, and then move on to a description of the way that the villagers today interact with the archaeological heritage in which they live.

---

[1] The data presented here are part of my Datça Ethno-archaeological research project, which started in 1998. Data collection methods include participant observation, interviewing, archival and literature research, and photography.

*History*

The Dor colonization of the Datça peninsula dates back to the eleventh century BC. Knidos (which today falls within the territory of Yazı village in Datça), Halikarnasos (modern Bodrum), Kos (today the Greek island of Chios) and the three cities of Ialysos, Lindos and Rodos on Rhodes formed a political trade hexapolis, which became a pentapolis after Halicarnassos was excommunicated. Various settlements of importance existed on Datça (Knidia), the most striking of which were Dadya and Knidos.[1]

The peninsula was occupied by the Persian commander Harpagos in 546 BC after the fall of Kharun, the Lydian King of Sardes. At that point, the Knidians tried to detach the peninsula from the mainland, attempting to dig a five hundred metre channel between the bays of Bencik and Balıkaşıran (also known as Kayıkaşıran) where the neck of land is at its narrowest.[2] However it appears that Zeus was not pleased with this endeavour and the diggers either got sick or died of some disease. Zeus claimed through the oracle Phythia at Delphoi (where the Knidians had donated funds toward the decoration of a splendid hall) that he wished there to be neither an island nor a channel, and he could have done this himself if he had so wanted.[3]

Between 468-411 BC Knidos became a member of the Delos Sea League.[4] Around 396 BC, Knida changed hands between Athens, Rhodes and Sparta. But Spartan naval domination was brought to an end in front of the so-called 'Lioned Cape' near Knidos, named after the sculpted lion that looked out over the sea there.[5] After 321 BC, in the 50 years following the death of Alexander the Great, the King of Pergamon Attalos Kaunos led several unsucsessful military campaigns against Knidos and Rodos. In the years 297/6 BC Knidos came under the domination of the Eygptian Kingdom of Seleukos, one of Alexander's generals, and paid taxes to him.

When the war (192-190 BC) between Syria and Rome ended with Roman victory, Knidos was awarded with independence. This did not last long because they were attacked by the Pontus armies of Mithridates in 88 BC as

---

[1] See Demand (1989).

[2] See Demand (1989). Also Herodotes (I.144, 174; II. 178; III.138; IV. 164). On the topography of the peninsular at this point see, *Datça İlçesi Brifing Dosyası*, Mart 1999, Datça Kaymakamlığı, 1.

[3] Demand, N. (1989; Footnote 3).

[4] Sönmez (1998).

[5] This lion (c. 350-200 BC) is today displayed at the entrance of the British Museum right behind the information desk, taken there by Sir Charles Newton.

well as plundered by Mediterranean pirates. In the summer of 48 BC Ceasar paid a visit to Ephesos and Knidos. Nobleman Gaius Julius Theopompus managed to secure another treaty of independence, alliance with Rome and tax exemption. Augustus also approved this independence. From 'Acta Apostola' we know that St Paul tried to visit Knidos but could not manage to because of the famous north wind.

During Christian times, Knidia belonged to the Aphrodisian denomination. The city and the peninsula then seem to have lost their importance and faded away during the late Roman era, becoming the target of Arabian raids of the seventh century. Knidia was under Byzantian rule when the Seljukian Sultan Kılıç Aslan conquered Knidos in 1095. Between 1282-1304 Karia and Doria were ruled by the Turkish Menteşe Beyliği (principality) until the peninsula became part of the Ottoman Empire in 1392.[1] In the following centuries the Datça coasts became a pirate base, as indeed did other southern coastals settlements such as Alanya and Kuşadası. The locals say that the villages were founded by their Yörük ancestors (nomadic Turks from Asia) five hundred years ago, on hill-sides well hidden from but with a good view of the sea as a defense against pirate raids. Before 1923 a township of the Ottoman Province of Rodos, after the foundation of the Turkish Republic Datça became a township of the province of Aydın, then later Muğla.

During the Byzantian period, Dorian, Ionian and Roman works of art at Knidos, the Knidian peninsula and the islands around were plundered and the graves were robbed. The temples in Knidos were knocked down and replaced by churches. Chapels and monastries were built on almost every rock on the Aegean. The destruction continued under the Moslem Arabs, who knocked down the churches and other riches of Knidos during their raids in the seventh and eighth centuries. The story does not end even then. The stones, statues and the inscriptions of the great amphitheatre were taken to Cairo by the Ottoman Governor in Egypt, Kavalalı Mehmet Ali Paşa, and used in the construction of his palaces and government buildings there. Later, the same theatre also provided stones for the construction of Dolmabahçe Palace in İstanbul.[2]

The Datça (Knidian) peninsula became important once again when interest rose in archaeology and ancient ruins. The site of Knidos was first described by Lord Charlemont, an Irishman followed by the excavations of Admiral F. Beaufort in 1753; the Italian Dilettanti Foundation in 1760; C.H.

---

[1] Sönmez, O. (1998; 35-47).
[2] Sönmez, O. (1998; 46-51).

Texier in 1811; Colonel W. Leake in 1812; and Sir Charles Newton in 1857-58.[1] While Mehmet Ali Ağa provided food for Newton, Newton's team provided him with stones to build the Ulucami (Great Mosque) at Reşadiye today.[2] The lion of Knidos, the statue of seated Demeter, fragments from temples and other statues (as well as finds from the rest of Karia and Kos/Chios) Newton carried to England, and they are today displayed at the British Museum in London. Other excavations and surveys of Knidos and the peninsula were carried out by Merchant Polemikos of Simi in 1907; by G. E.Bean[3] and J. M. Cook[4] between the end of 1940s and the begining of the 1960s; by Iris Love[5] between 1967-1973; by N.Tuna between 1980-86,[6] and J. Empereur[7] between 1988-92. Ongoing excavations and research on the peninsula continue. Prof. Dr. Numan Tuna has been excavating at Burgaz since 1992, the ceramics of which are studied by B. Özer.[8] The Marmaris museum has an excavation at the ancient harbour of Datça (Dadya) town and also at the Emecik Temple since 1998. Prof. Dr. Ramazan Özgan has been directing excavations at Knidos since 1988 and my own project on Knidian Ethnoarchaeology has also been running since 1998.[9]

## The people of Datcha today

The Datçians today reside on and near ancient settlements all over the peninsula. The local *Rums* (Anatolian Greek) population emmigrated to the surrounding islands of the Aegean during the Turkish War of Independence. As already been noted, the majority of the remaining population claim to have roots in nomadic groups who have come from outside and settled in the area. Nevertheless, other residents may identify with a very varied past; Dadians, Rodians, Aegean islanders, Cretan Turks, Rumeli Turks (that is, Turks from the Balkans), Arabs, Egyptians, Sudanese, Ethiopians, Çerkez (Circassians), Jews, Armenians, Tahtacı Alevis, Spanish Gypsies, Berbers from the Magreb, Indians and Crimean Tartars.[10]

---

[1] Aydal and Bruns-Özgan (nd), also Sönmez (1998).
[2] See Newton's account (1963).
[3] Bean (1987).
[4] Bean and Cook (1952; 175-176).
[5] See Love (1972, 1973, 1978).
[6] Tuna (1987).
[7] Tuna and Empereur (1993).
[8] Özer (1998).
[9] Ergenekon (1998, 2000, 2001).
[10] Ergenekon (1998).

The Berbers from the Magreb claim to be descendents of original Datçians, taken there by Admiral Barbaros and Turgut Reis in the sixteenth century. They married local women in North Africa but did not forget that they were Turks and remigrated to Datça. The story of Spanish gypsies is also particularly interesting: they were expelled from Spain after the Catholic invasion of Andalucia. Those who had leprosy were left on an island just in front of Sarı Limanı ('Yellow Port'), in front of the temple of Emecik. In low tide a shallow passage way appears between the land and the island. In time, the gypsies settled on the peninsula, populating the village of Emecik. It is said that they were healed by the abundant herbs of Datça, and that they therefore brought healthy children to life. The most recent immigrants are Kurds who migrated from the troubles in east and southeast Turkey after the 1980s. There are also summer migrants, mostly city people who occupy summer houses at Aktur, Özil and Özbel and so on, and go back to work in Ankara, İzmir and İstanbul when their vacations are over.

The Datçians are reserved people and feel themselves almost as islanders because of their topography, difficult internal communications, distance from the city of Muğla, and their relative economic self sufficiency. However their previous cultural and naval ties with neigbouring islands are severed because of national borders. Today there is taking place a transformation. The Datçians' relations with the ancient settlements under or around their houses, fields, gardens, orchards as well as the surrounding hills and mountains are gradually changing from relative indifference to one of interest because of the artefacts that emerge, and the wages excavations and tourism may provide. On the other hand these sites may be an object of dislike for those who own parcels of land, houses or other property which becomes declared as protected as primary, secondary or third degree archaeological heritage.

*Folklore*

In spite of the seeming indifference to the archaeological remains, the legends and the stories told indicate that the distant past does play a part in the villagers' self-conception and identity. The locals try to explain why the peninsula is divided into two geographically and culturally distinct districts (Datça in the northeast and Betçe in the southwest) with a legend, 'Dadya and Petya'. According to this, the Knidian King had a daughter and a son. He divided his estate between the two before he died, giving his daughter Petya the southwest, therefore the name Betçe, and his son the northeast half, therefore the name Datça. The Datça area is less hilly and has valleys while the Betçe area is mountainous and without valleys. Although people speak a uniform dialect that can be identified as unique to Datça, there are still linguistic differences between Datça and Betçe.

Sacred structures such as temples, churches and mosques, graves and sites of natural beauty have attained sacredness in the eyes of the locals, and they may still be visited for spiritual reasons. Some of the legends or stories are about these places. Aşlama is such a site, part of the antique road to Mesudiye and Knidos, and geologically speaking a fault line (Datça peninsula is a primary earthquake area and often shakes like a cradle). A story told by lawyer Ziya Gökalp's father's mother is as follows:

> A shepherd has a son and a daughter. When his wife dies he remarries. One day the children lose the geese they are herding. When the stepmother hears this she wants their father to punish them. He shuts them in a cave at Aşlama, but hangs two [dried] water pumpkins at the entrance so that people who hear their clatter should come and save them. The son and the daughter of the King of Knidos hear of this and order their soldiers to set the captives free. The shepherd's children tell their story. Their parents are found and punished. The children are then taken to the Knidos palace and raised by the King. When they grow up the shepherd's daughter marries the King's son.

Local villagers attribute certain functions and meanings to natural and archaeological sites. The caves on the side of Mt. Karadağ function as gigantic sun dials for the Hızırşah villagers. At Aşlama, certain sign on rocks are interpreted as traces of the Prophet Muhammed's horse's shoes. Graves are considered sacred because they belong to beloved ones. There are stories about the terrible fate that comes to people who have stolen tomb stones and other archaeological objects. The popular *Eskicami* (old mosque) originally a temple, near by Hızırşah has always been the target of treasure hunters. They believe that *Rum*s buried their gold and other valuables there before they fled to the islands of Simi and Kos upon the retreat of the Greek forces at the end of the Turkish War of Independence. During the restoration of *Eskicami* in 1992, a tomb and forty graves in Cemal Bey's uncle's and aunt's lot to the east of the mosque were removed with an excavator from their resting places. He reports

> After I returned home from Canada I saw a small tombstone at Eski Datça Mahallesi (Dadya). It was brought there by a tractor driver who removed the debris of the graves but wanted to return the tombstone to its owners

because of nightmares. A few days later the driver died under his own tractor. Two years later another driver died the same way. I wonder if he also was a grave thief. Unless they bring back the tombstones of my great grandfather and relatives they won't rest in peace. I filed a complaint to the public prosecutor but it was in vain. There are some local and foreign grave thieves here. It is a lucrative but illegal business.

## Beliefs

The Hacetevi mountain[1] which constitutes the southeast border of Hızırşah village is a low but steep mountain with a good view of the Körmen Bay in the Aegean, of the antique harbour of Datça-Burgaz on the Mediterranean, of the Kızlan and Datça plains and of Emecik Mountain (704 m.) to the north and Bozdağ (1174 m.) to the south. A gigantic heap of large stones like big eggs form the peak. It reminds one of a stone tumulus. It is hard to climb up when it is hot. The air is heavy. It is difficult to come down before one eats, drinks and takes a good rest. One feels drowsy, taking a nap is easy. The villagers believe that there is an entombed saint buried at Hacetevi in the tumulus-like structures, a supposition which is perhaps encouraged by virtue of the fact that such imposing remains customarily represent the graves of important people.

The peak is not described archaeologically, so there is yet no information about the nature and period of the remains. However graves, and especially the tombs of religous or important people in Turkey are visited by people, especially women, who have certain expectations and hopes. People believe that pilgrimage to such places may make their prayers come true. Nurel Batırlı from Hızırşah said:

> Those who have wishes and would like to plead for them to come true to Allah, climb this mountain by sunrise. When they reach the top they perform and recite their prayers (*namaz*). Some tie a rag on branches of the only bush there. Then they sit down and take a short nap. They recite their wish in the form of a daydream and then fall asleep. And what they have dreamt of comes true.[2]

Mrs. Özalp from Reşadiye made such a trip, wishing for a good future for her eldest son. She then dreamt of her son in a white uniform by a tent. The same month the news came home that her son had managed to enter the naval

---

[1] Hülagü (2000).

[2] On the practice of incubation (sleeping at the site of a shrine), see Stewart's chapter in this volume.

academy in İstanbul. When she and her husband took him to the academy they were welcomed into a huge tent at the garden of the school by officers dressed in white uniforms. As further examples we can mention the pyramid grave visited in Çeşme (Selimiye) and another one at Kumburnu, in Palamut Bükü (Bay).[1] People from all over the peninsula come and tie rags on the bushes around these graves and make wishes such as to be married, to have children, to buy a house or to make wishes as to the well-being of their family. Subsequently, they return to offer their thanks and may offer gifts of money, food or clothes to the poor.

Mountain tops, dreams and dead people are widely believed to be the medium with which humans communicate with gods.[2] Moses was revealed the ten commandments at Mt. Sinai, Soloman spent time on mountain tops, the Hitite King sanctified Mt. Daha (Kerkenes in Yozgat-Turkey),[3] the neo-Babylonian King Key Kavus (Kay Kawus, Nabunaid) had moon temples, zigurats and observatories built to contact heavenly gods,[4] the Prophet Muhammed received the revelations from Allah in his sleep at Mt. Hira. These practices in Datça can be identified as nature worshipping realized through ataism, mountain, stone and tree cults mixed with the heavenly religion of Islam.

*Cultural Heritage*

Finds from excavations are officially considered objects of cultural heritage and protected by law. A representative of the Ministry of Culture is present at every excavation site. After finds are cleaned, archived, and whenever possible, conserved, they are stored. An old church with frescoes by the ancient site of pottery kilns on the Hızırşah road is used to store finds from Datça-Burgaz. However the Hızırşah villagers want this church back in order to open it to visitors. The finds from Knidos are sent to Bodrum and Marmaris Museums. The Yazıköy villagers, who view Knidos as common village property, are conscious of the value and meaning of this site and its artefacts. They would like therefore a local museum in Knidos and Datça to display finds at the site where they have been discovered. A group of local intellectuals and professionals have made attempts to retrieve the lion, Demeter and other

---

[1] Kabaağaçlı (1988).

[2] Lewy (1949). See also Ergenekon (1999a, 1999b, 1999c, 2002 In press).

[3] Gurney (1995). Ergenekon (1998b).

[4] Lewy (1949).

objects of Knidos currently displayed at the British Museum. In 1999 Yazıköy villagers attempted to claim a lorry carrying archaeological finds from Knidos to Bodrum Museum. They were unsuccessful.

Fragments from archaeological objects found on peoples own property have to be returned to museums. They can legally be kept only if the museum is notified, the item registered and a certain fee paid for it. They have to be available for inspection each year. Such items then can be used as decorations in homes. The columns, marble tombs of various sizes, millstones, etc. left here and there in public areas are registered and cannot be removed. More recent artifacts such as wheels of horse carts, wooden doors, cupboards, beams of old houses; local kilims known as 'Alasılı', textiles of cotton called *bez* and silk called *bürümcük* recirculate as decorations in the houses of new Datçians from other places in Turkey, Europe and USA.

Stones, bricks and blocks from sites have also been used in making the walls of the traditional stone houses of by-gone Datça.[1] This was before the laws concerning the protection of archaeological materials were so widespread. Reliefs are used in garden walls and as interior and exterior decorations in houses, and as window beams. Tomb stones are used as door beams.[2] Larger blocks are used as bricks in corners of houses, as pedestals in *a la turca* toilets, as barriers against floods. Water troughs are used as drains on roofs, columns were cut in smaller sizes and used to press flat roofs, or as mortars to grind coffee or crush the wheat of the wedding food 'keşkek';[3] mouth pieces from ancient wells are used for the same purposes elsewhere; flat stones are used as floors of houses or gardens; pieces of ancient pottery were mixed with wall plasters to avoid humidity inside the houses. Buildings having such secondary use of material are registered by the Office of Monuments and Antiquities of Turkish Ministry of Culture and cannot be torn down. Such reuse is an old and widely employed custom. In excavations, the foundations and walls unearthed are sometimes also discovered to be made of stone bricks from different periods.

---

[1] These houses are rectangular, one or two storied, have a height of not more than six metres, and generally dimensions of 4.5 by 10 metres.

[2] One such Roman tombstone has inscriptions on it written by a Latin-speaking people who did not master the old Greek well, resulting in a kind of Greekified Latin. For this reason it is not clear whether there are some spelling mistakes because of the use of round Sigma and lunate Sigma in the same inscription. However, the tomb stone belongs to a lady called 'Julias of Liyidos'. Then comes the name 'Ti. Fla. Sotiros' (savior) (who is the husband), 'Titus Flavius' (the father) daughter is 'buried' (here). 'Worth commemorating is also her husband (or brother) who paid for/had this grave made for his (Titus Flavius') daughter and here is to the life/health of the same man'. (Read and interpreted by Stavros Yolcoğlu, Dept. of Greek Language and Literature, University of Ankara, 2001, to whom I offer my thanks).

[3] On 'keşkek' see Uslu (2001), also Ünal and Aksoy (2001).

Old houses, wind and water-mills, old-style olive oil factories are bought and restored by Turks and foreigners as a hobby. However getting permission for this requires long and painstaking procedures and disobeying any restrictions during restorations may result in prosecution. On the other hand there are quite a few abandoned stone houses on the peninsula, neither restored nor sold because they have many heirs. Beautiful houses and buildings get slowly demolished, like Mehmet Ali Ağa's mansion in Reşadiye. Others include Selimiye's (now called Çeşme köyü) Governor's building, the mansion of Ömer İhsan Bey of Bosnia (built in the 1800s by masons from Rodos) in Çeşme, the Church of Belen at Yazıköy (which later was a mosque and now has Muslim graves in its vicinity), the water cistern at Aşlama, the houses of Emecik, the wind and water mills everywhere, traditional oil factories here and there. These are all part of Datça's recent history yet variously need further restoration or repair.

*Conclusion*

Not much is yet known about the possibility of earlier remains than those discussed here, such as those of the Neolithic and Paleolithic ages, although the locals point out to places which seem to be older than the Dorian colonization of the peninsula. Nevertheless, legends and stories about various events, Paganism, Polytheism, Judaism, Christianity and Bektaşi Islam have been amongst the identifiable religious beliefs found throughout its history. Each new religion has destroyed, plundered or reinterpreted the traces of former beliefs. At the same time old construction materials are used for a second or third time through recycling while some are deliberately carried away to be displayed at local or foreign museums. All this shows how archaeology and living cultures interact in forming historical consciousness, creating legends, adapting ancient material culture and finding new uses for them, shaping a cultural identity through socialization based on local honour and pride, and yet potentially turning all of these into economic profits.

*REFERENCES*

Aydal S. and Bruns-Özgan C. (nd) *Knidos Brochure*, translated by C. Lightfoot, Antalya.
Bean G. 1987 *Karia*, Istanbul; Gümüş Basımevi.
Bean, G. and Cook, J (1952) *The Cnidia*, London; British School of Athens.

Demand N. 1989 'Did Knidos Really Move? The Literary and Epygraphical Evidence', in *Classical Antiquity*, Vol. 8, No.2, October.

Ergenekon, B. 1998a 'Dadya Yarımadası Kültürü', Halk Bilimi, *ODTÜ Türk Halk Bilimleri Topluluğu Dergisi*, 25-29.

Ergenekon, B. 1998b 'Keykavus ve Kerkenes Efsaneleri', *Sıla*, Yıl 2, Sayı 6, Yozgurt; Doğuş Matbaası.

Ergenekon, B. 1999a 'Keykavus-Kerkenes Efsaneleri ve Şahmurat (1)', *ODTÜ Türk Halk Bilimleri Topluluğu Dergisi*, Ankara; pp.5;

Ergenekon, B. 1999b 'Keykavus-Kerkenes Efsaneleri ve Şahmurat (2)', *ODTÜ Türk Halk Bilimleri Topluluğu Dergisi*, Ankara.

Ergenekon, B 1999c, 'Ethnoarchaeology in Şahmuratlı Village by Kerkenes Excavations in Turkey', in *Caesaraugusta*, 73, Zaragoza-Sapin, 169-175.

Ergenekon, B. 2000 'The Role of Ethnoarchaeology in Archaeometry with examples from Çatalhöyük (1998), Kerkenes (1995-97), Datça-Burgaz Excavations and Cnidian (Datça) Ethnoarchaeology (1998-99)'.

Ergenekon, B. 2001 'Knidia Etnoarkeolojisi 2000 Raporu', in *19. Araştırma Sonuçları Toplantısı*, T.C. Kültür Bakanlığı, Anıtlar ve Müzeler Genel Müdürlüğü, Ankara.

Ergenekon, B 2002 (in press) 'An Ethnoarchaeological Comparison: The Kerkenes Archaeological Survey, the Legend of the Kerkenes City and the Keykavus Castle', Proceedings of the 31st International Symposium of Archaeometry in Budapest, Hungary, April 1998; BAR/Archaeolingua.

Gurney O. 1995 'The Hitite Names of Kerkenes Dağ and Kuşaklı Höyük', Reprinted from *Anatolian Studies*, in *The Implications of Ethnography for Archaeology*, New York; Columbia University Press.

Hülagü, F. 2000, 'Datça'dan Yudum Yudum', *ODTÜ Türk Halk Bilimleri Dergisi*, pp.68-9, Güz 13, Ankara.

Kabaağaçlı, C. (The Fisherman of Halicarnus) 1988 *Uluç Reis*, Istanbul; Bilgi Yayınevi.

Lewy, H. 1949 'The Babylonian Background of the Key Kaus Legend', in *Orientalia* Vol. XVII, 28-108.

Love, I. 1972 'A Preliminary Report of the Excavations at Knidos 1971' in *American Journal of Archaeology*, Vol. 76.

Love, I. 1973 'A Preliminary Report of the Excavations at Knidos 1972', *American Journal of Archaeology*, Vol. 77.

Love. I. 1978 'A Brief Summary of Excavations at Knidos 1967-1973', *The Proceedings of the Xth International Congress of Classical Archaeology*, Ankara.

Newton, C. 1963 *A History of Discoveries at Halicarnassus, Cnidus and Branchiadae II*, London.

Özer, B. 1998 'Datça-Burgaz Kazılarında Ele Geçen Arkaik Dönem Bezemeli Seramikleri', Ege Üniversitesi, Klasik Arkeoloji Bölümü (Unpublished Master's Thesis).

Sönmez, O. 1998 *Knidos: Mavide Uyuyan Güzel*, Istanbul; Ege Yayınları.

Tuna, N. 1987 'Ionia ve Datça Yarımadası Arkeolojik Yüzey Araştırmaları', 1985-86, V. *Araştırma Sonuçları Toplantısı I*, Ankara; Directorate of Museums and Antiquities, Ministry of Culture.

Tuna, N. and Empereur, J. 1993 'Datça/Reşadiye Knidos Seramik Atölyeleri Kazısı', *Kazı Sonuçları Toplantısı II*, Ankara; Directorate of Museums and Antiquities, Ministry of Culture.

Türkeş, Ü. 1973 *Kurtuluş Savaşında Muğla*, Vols. 1 and 2.1, İstanbul; Baskı Yelken Matbaası.

Ünal A. and Aksoy, P. 2001 'Datça'da Asker Uğurlaması', *Halk Bilimi, ODTÜ Türk Halk Bilimi Topluluğu dergisi*; Ankara, 85.

Uslu, Ö. 2001 'Datça'daki Toplumsal Olaylarda Yemek', *Halk Bilimi, ODTÜ Türk Halk Bilimi Topluluğu Dergisi*, Güz, Ankara, 80-82.

# 39. THE LOCAL AND THE UNIVERSAL AT ÇATALHÖYÜK, TURKEY

## David SHANKLAND

### Introduction

Paradoxically for a discipline whose practice is still largely predicated upon researching alone, anthropology in Great Britain has long been haunted by its supposed links with other bodies. We have debated our part in the now defunct colonial encounter. Though uncertain of the legitimacy of this activity, we are often consultants for multi-nationals, governmental agencies and diverse legal teams. The role of 'commitment' in anthropology is becoming increasingly part of our agenda in public gatherings. This running thread of self-awareness intrudes too on our discussion of 'indigenous knowledge', one of the most lively and interesting topics that we at present debate.[1] Indeed, we are hardly able to consider any substantive research field without at the same time re-evaluating and re-assessing our diverse role within the accelerating processes of development and globalisation.

Here, I suggest that one particular aspect of this wider process deserves to be taken into account within anthropology more explicitly than it is at present: that is, the international archaeological endeavour and our relationship with it. It seems to me that the uneasy separation that, by and large, has obtained between archaeology and anthropology in this country means that we have been tempted to overlook archaeology's significance in a number of overlapping ways.[2] Archaeologists are, literally, the cutting edge of history. Almost as soon as it is unearthed, sometimes even within hours, the material that they produce from their excavations begins to take on a defined place in international scholarship, one quite divorced from its local context. The secular, rational, parceled chronological vision of history that (even taking into account their individual diversity) archaeologists support and extend is an integral part of an increasingly dominant scientific 'knowledge' tradition. Indeed, archaeology's ever-increasing pursuit of near and distant human history

---

[1] See, for instance, the edited volume by Bicker, Sillitoe and Pottier (2004).
[2] There are exceptions, of course, notably new undergraduate degrees in Archaeology and Anthropology, and the accompanying literature eg. Gosden (1999).

is a corollary of science's equally expanding understanding of the natural world. It is no surprise, therefore, that archaeological discoveries are featured at both the American, and the British Associations for the Advancement of Science, and given equal weight in their reported publicity, alongside the latest discoveries in medicine, biology and physics.[1]

Moving from global science to the local, the actual context of this process of archaeological discovery is equally potentially of interest. Excavations often take place in rural areas. Their methodology, however, is different from that of social anthropology in that whereas we try, sometimes unavailingly admittedly, to live among the people concerned, archaeologists often build a dig-house that constitutes a type of ghetto: largely cut off from the language and culture of the people who actually live in the area. At present, we have little idea of the extent that the archaeological investigations influence these indigenous peoples, materially or culturally. Certainly, however, archaeology's local activities at once provide a potential laboratory through which encounters with indigenous peoples and diverse cognitive interpretations of the world can be directly witnessed, and also (from the local's point of view) a possible source of disruption that is potentially highly significant.

These two extremes of the local and the global are connected and mediated in a host of different ways by the different interest groups that interact with any excavation and the artifacts that it uncovers. Part at least of this variation, however complex the situation may become when looked at in detail, is dependent on the respective nation-state in which any particular dig takes place. As illustrated so well by Özdoğan in this volume, nation-states invariably teach a particular version of human history, one of varying plausibility and content, but one that draws on a specific vision or visions of the past. The international archaeological endeavour often finds itself supporting the nationalist tradition in which the excavation is physically situated, even if only passively through a form of symbiosis whereby permission is given to dig in return for their results being used as 'history'. Thus archaeology is internationally, nationally, and locally significant. It complements, and to some extent overlaps with our own pre-occupations with development, industrialisation and economic dominance, but is at the same time distinct in its emphasis in extracting knowledge that may have no resemblance whatsoever to the existing cultural context in which it is found.

---

[1] It is also perhaps worthy of note that, in the years that I have been part of the Archaeology and Anthropology Section at the BAAS (1997-2004), audiences have usually been greater for archaeological talks than for anthropological.

It might be argued that these points are hardly novel: in North America, where archaeology and anthropology have traditionally been taught together, the links between the disciplines have not been overlooked, whilst the increasing consciousness of minority rights in this same region means the relationship between archaeology and indigenous cultures is in any case becoming increasingly problematic and contested.[1] This is true indeed, but in reply I would stress in turn that this process of greater interaction has not been universal. Throughout south-east Europe, the area that I know best, there is a growing, even a rapidly accelerating endeavour of international archaeological scholarship that operates at different levels simultaneously: it feeds directly into that almost seamless process of globalisation wherein science and history appear to be inextricably intertwined, and simultaneously acts as a support for the respective historical foundations of the nation state. Thus, the often violent seemingly parochial nationalisms in the Middle East and the Balkans are in fact not purely local: archaeologists from Britain, the USA, and other European countries are feeding into these debates through their results, whilst the actual work itself is being conducted through a direct, face-to-face encounter with indigenous peoples who may have not the slightest interest or even share the views being explored. I maintain that this encounter between archaeologists and these indigenous peoples is potentially as fascinating as the wider process of cultural globalisation that the team from outside are helping to expand, and that we have not, as yet, systematically explored its consequences.[2]

*Archaeology, nationalism and the local in Turkey*

Turkey, the country in which I have conducted much of my research, is a case in point. Under the Ottoman Empire, the foundations of the state were established through conquest and reinforced through a combination of right of dynastic rule, theological exegesis and administrative lore that owed little, if anything to archaeological investigation or indeed, systematic investigation of the multiplicity of Anatolia's past. Archaeology became noticed only right at the end of the Empire, and (as described by Eldem in this work) became established through the pioneer efforts of a distinguished museumologist, Hamdi Bey. Under his supervision, excavations were conducted in Iraq (then a province of the Ottoman Empire) and the renowned sarcophagi exhibited in

---

[1] Among many others, see Tunbridge and Ashworth (1996).
[2] From within archaeology, however, these issues are being explored actively, see for example Diaz-Andreu and Champion (1996), also Meskell (1998).

Istanbul today result from finds having been taken from Iraq to Istanbul, the Imperial capital.[1] Yet, in spite of his efforts, the archaeology, and the cultural exploration of Anatolia, remained mainly the province of foreigners, mostly European.

Indeed, just how significant this foreign exploration has been is easy to overlook. Anatolia was not just part of a grand tour, used for self-learning or publicity by wealthy individuals, but the results obtained from such investigations have been incorporated into our collective self-image in many different ways. One impulse was religious exploration of some of the birth-places of Christianity, resulting in volumes with titles such as *The Seven Churches of Asia Minor* even as early as the seventeenth century,[2] but individual sites too have achieved striking fame, such as Troy, Ephesus, Aphrodisias, Side and Sardis. Earlier peoples, such as the Hittites, feature large too in Western visions of the development of culture and literacy.

This programme by the West to investigate Turkish soil manifestly expanded in the great expeditions of the nineteenth century, but the drive to survey and dig continued throughout the twentieth century, if anything intensifying. There are today more than a hundred foreign archaeological research teams coming to Turkey each year: the majority of these are North American but there are others from Japan, Germany, Holland, Austria, Italy, France and Britain. These teams are not organised entirely from outside, but also have significant permanent representation within the country through foreign 'schools', all (accept in the American case), funded by their respective governments.

Whilst they differ from one another, collectively these schools represent a major source of influence on our interpretation and understanding of Anatolia's past. Thus there is a large German Institute in Istanbul that runs three major excavations, oversees three more on behalf of German universities, and has the largest archaeological library in Turkey. The British Institute lies in Ankara. Founded just after the Second World War, it also has an important library, certainly the most extensive such collection in Turkey outside Istanbul. Particularly in the field of pre-history, the Institute has made a massive contribution to world archaeology, a contribution that is dominated by Çatalhöyük, the site where I have researched, but has other important sites

---

[1]See Cezar (1987).
[2]Eg. Smith (1678).

to its name too, such as Hacılar, Beycisultan, and Can Hasan.[1] There are further institutes, run by the Dutch, French, Swedes and Japanese respectively.

It is sometimes held that these schools are relics of a colonial past. This is not quite true, not just because of the simple fact that Turkey has never been colonised, but rather because they are present as a result of arrangement and negotiation, indeed they have been encouraged. This may be explained partly in that, within Turkey, archaeology changed from being peripheral to becoming absolutely central after Atatürk founded the Turkish Republic in the years after the First World War. In his programme, which was aimed to produce a state that was both modern and secular, Atatürk stressed not the Islamic but the pre-historical roots of Anatolia. Under his patronage, there was founded a Museum of Anatolian Civilisations in Ankara, the new capital. He encouraged the excavation of early sites, and founded university departments of archaeological research, which also often specialised in pre-history. Several promising Turkish students were sent abroad, particularly to Germany, in order to study. The most well-known of these, Tahsin Özgüç, directed Kültepe, one of the richest sites in the whole Middle East, which is still yielding thousands of tablets.

Today, both local and foreign archaeological excavations are co-ordinated by the General-Directorate of Museums and Antiquities in Ankara. Nominally, the same rules apply to both, and there is often a close working relationship, particularly through rescue archaeology, for which permits are issued in the name of local institutions, but the finance for the dig provided by foreign teams. The results of both Turkish and foreign excavations are placed on permanent display in museums administered by the Directorate. These form part of the official civil service in most provincial centres in Turkey, and their displays within them are shown to school children regularly. The school system too teaches the complexities of Anatolia's past in history lessons, and material from major excavations conducted by foreign teams features strongly. In this way, Turkey has become a clear and highly significant example of the way that archaeology may be used to support a particular nationalist ideology. This local need for archaeological research to provide an intellectual foundation for the transformation from Empire to Republic underpins the symbiotic relationship between western academia and the Turkish state. Both require material, albeit for different purposes, and this common need helps the two to work together.

---

[1] See the autobiography of the institute's founder, Seton Lloyd (1986).

*The practice of archaeology*

In spite of this striking and extensive programme of international and national scholarship, until now almost nothing has been said on the circumstances in which archaeology is practised. Dig reports, even when they have run through many seasons and diverse volumes, contain nothing at all about the way work has taken place, the negotiations, the financial constraints, the economic effect that they may have had on the local community, the role of the tourism that they have attracted to the site, or the political contexts into which their work has been pressed. They are simply expunged from the record. This is not to attack the often outstanding, brilliant work that is being done, it is to claim, however, that the process of the creation of knowledge is being presented in as if it took place in a neutral, sanitised environment with no political, ideological or economic pressures.

Not just is the material or intellectual effect of this digging programme overlooked, there has also been no general attempt to look at the indigenous interpretation of the distant past. In effect, the volumes published by successive excavation teams present a cosmology imposed on an existing, and perhaps complex indigenous understanding of the place of the remnants of the past within their community, but one that they make no attempt to research or explore.

This neglect of the asymmetrical relationship with the indigenous people is at once both surprising and comprehensible. It is comprehensible when the overall circumstances of archaeology within Turkey are taken into account. Archaeology, whether local or foreign, can only take place after a long procedure through which permission to excavate is obtained. Such permissions are considered not just by the Ministry of Culture, but also by the Ministry of the Interior, and, if permission to excavate a new site is sought, it must be granted and approved by the full Council of Ministers. After permission has been granted, all work is conducted within a specified framework, and under the supervision of a government representative and only after all people on the permit have been individually cleared.

This emphasis on control and supervision is paralleled on the ground through a particular approach by the state to archaeological remains. A significant site, before it is dug, is listed as being protected, and often the ground expropriated by the state. If it is felt in danger, then a watchman is hired, and a fence built around the area. The watchman is regarded a civil servant, and a pole with the Turkish national flag planted by the watchman's hut or cubicle. All finds located through an official excavation, of whatever age or potential value are regarded as being the property of the state. All this means that, whilst there is a clear and close relationship between the investigating team and the state, the local people are excluded from participation except as workmen at the site, because the area in question has been so clearly removed from their immediate responsibility.

This administrative separation is matched by an equal hierarchy in authority between the state and the villagers. Whilst the archaeology has not yet been considered by anthropologists working in Turkey, relations between citizens and the state have been examined, and much of the research that has been done in this area is applicable here. The state is at once the co-ordinator and the fount of authority vis a vis its citizens in way that is much sharper and distinct than it would be, for example, in Britain.[1] Its boundaries are not closed, in that it is comparatively easy to become a civil servant, *memur*, but there is a clear conceptional divide between something which is the business of the state, *devlet*, and which is not.

The Republican state is held to be secular, and the pursuit of science for its own sake not so much the individual prerogative of every member of society, but rather something that is co-ordinated, led and maintained by the organised activity that the state pursues through its different institutions. The state's presence at the site, therefore, evokes a setting in which decisions and motives are decided and implemented largely outside village life. After the land has been appropriated, the archaeology ceases to be of direct interest, not just in terms of the record that is being explored but also in terms of their understanding of the state's activity.

*The villagers and the state*

Whilst it is hardly possible to make sensible generalisations about the practice of religion, very roughly it is legitimate to affirm that the theoretically secular basis of the state and the activity that it supports contrasts with the village communities' clearer acceptance of their Islamic heritage. Whilst such a sharp division may not stand up to sustained theoretical scrutiny, this means that it is possible for individuals to contrast their own personal commitment to Islam (albeit expressed in many different ways), with that of the state, and its

---

[1]See, for example, the work of Delaney (1992, 1993).

pursuit of the pre-historic remains of Anatolia.[1] That there should be an excavation taking place within a village community, therefore, raises the possibility of a number of sharp contrasts; a distinction between state and citizen, foreigner and local, secular versus personal piety, as well as the more obvious possible conflict in historical interpretation between indigenous and external interpretations that the activity itself may entail. The mediated separation between local community and international excavation that is an inherent part of the archaeological research permission in Turkey explains why, perhaps, this interaction has not been made more explicit by the archaeologists involved, but it nevertheless provides potentially a most fruitful field of investigation when considering the relationship between authority, knowledge, power and global understandings of history that is, even today, neglected.

*Çatalhöyük*

The re-opening of Çatalhöyük, and the way that the present-day project has been put together, has provided an ideal opportunity to begin to consider these issues afresh. First dug in the 1960s by Jimmy Mellaard, Çatalhöyük is known today for a number of reasons. The site is exceptionally well-preserved, enabling systematic research into early agriculture including the domestication of various animals and crops. It is the site of some of the earliest known domestic wall-painting in the world. Further, perhaps most tantalising of all, it has yielded a number of women figurines, often corpulent, and sometimes depicted in the act of giving birth. Famously (albeit controversially) these have sometimes held to be illustrative of an early 'fertile Goddess' religion that has preceded the later dominating patriarchal, monotheistic religions. All this means that Çatalhöyük has long been the focus not just of academic archaeology, but also popular mythology, alternative religious organisations and feminist groups, both within Turkey and further afield.[2]

My own interest in the site stemmed from being the Assistant, and then the Acting Director of the British Institute of Archaeology at Ankara just at the point at which it was being re-opened. Whilst engaged in administration I was anxious also to explore the ways in which a practising social

---

[1]There is a parallel here with the Tappers' work in Eğridir, where the inhabitants made a distinction between pious individuality and a secular state (Tapper and Taper 1987). Curiously, the gradual re-Islamification of the state since 1950 means that such a characterisation is empirically inaccurate, though it is still made, see Shankland (1999a, Chapter 1).

[2]Mellaart (1967). See also Nixon's contribution in this volume.

anthropologist might be able to contribute toward the archaeological endeavour. Professor Hodder kindly welcomed this approach, and gave me permission to work at the site. Funded largely by the ESRC, the project that stemmed from this desire is now drawing to a close. It concentrates largely on the way that the indigenous people understand the diverse heritage of the past in their landscape. However, at the project's outset, Professor Hodder also asked me to look at the site's long-term influence on the village community. Then, when I asked, the seemingly routine question, "How have you been influenced by the presence of the site?", the answer was repeatedly and laconically, "Hiç yok!" which can be translated loosely as "Not in the slightest!". Of course, it is always possible to argue that such simple answers are always slightly inaccurate: that my fieldwork had just begun, that the villagers were not prepared to waste time on such a question and so on. In spite of all these possibilities, it nevertheless appears to be the case that an excavation, nationally and internationally famous for more than two decades, had had remarkably little discernable influence on the community within whose fields it lies.

This, then, was the response that I was given in 1995.[1] Since then, there has been nearly a decade of intense digging, and the reopening continues to attract diverse attention from figures all over Turkey, from local administrators, civil servants in Ankara, politicians, Istanbul sponsors, international companies and academics from a host of countries. It is no longer the case, even if this answer was initially absolutely correct, that there has been no influence at all: there is a steady, if comparatively small drip of funds into the community through the wages paid by the excavation to those from the village who work there. The researchers at the excavation, many of whom have been associated with the project from its outset are gradually forming friendships with the local people, and it is hardly likely, even though tourism is still comparatively underdeveloped at the present moment, that it will remain so for ever. Indeed, there are some signs that the local sub-province centre, acutely sensitive to the place of the town in Turkey and its growing economy as a whole, is taking steps to appropriate any tourism revenues that may accrue from the site.[2]

Nevertheless, there remains a niggling kernel of truth in that first response. In many respects there really does appear to have been very little overlap between the villagers' and the archaeologists' interpretation of the

---

[1]The project's initial season is discussed in Shankland (1997).
[2]See Shankland (1999b), Hodder (1999: 165-169).

past. The relationship between local people and scientific teams working in their communities is often delicate, and potentially difficult to research in a situation such as that at Çatalhöyük, where it is difficult to avoid the hierarchy inherent within the relationship between villagers and researcher.[1] Nevertheless, summing up here only the most clear difference between the two approaches, it appears that the dominant mode of interpretation amongst the villagers who actually live among the remains of the past is quite different from the archaeologists' axiomatic assumption of a clear chronology. Indeed, the villagers appear to react toward the remains of the past in a way that predominantly does not call for its temporal periodicisation.

In Küçükköy ('Little Village'), the village in which Çatalhöyük lies, these remains consist largely of very substantial mounds of varying periods, and some classical debris: worked stone, and tiles, within otherwise largely flat fields. The villagers regard the mounds as potential field boundary markers, as depots for waterproof mud to put on their roofs to keep out the rain, and as repositories of hidden treasure. If a mound impedes the possibility of working a field, and they believe that they will not be restrained or caught by the authorities, they may simply flatten the mound with a tractor. They use some of the classical worked stone pieces as rubbing strakes positioned just at the corners of their houses, so that cattle scratch their backs on these, rather than their walls.[2]

Whilst they regard the material remains of the past with functional, piecemeal utility, the villagers also attach spiritual and religious significance to the human bones that are often found within them. They do not distinguish sharply between Muslim and non-Muslim graves or skeletons: any resting place may be protected by the soul of the departed person, and therefore may inflict damage on he or she who disturbs them. The residents have provided me with an abundance of accounts and descriptions that testify to this fear: a man was unable to open a mound because he was blown flat by a wind whistled up by a talisman placed there by the dead owner before they died. Two men tried to rob a mound but disturbed the grave of a beautiful woman who had long, blond hair. They died after a long debilitating illness. Another man was unable to sleep, dreaming himself strangled by the owner of the bones he had disturbed when collecting earth from a mound for his roof. He

---

[1] Contrast this with the work of Bravo on the Inuit and the scientific work that takes place in their community (1996).

[2] On this reuse of material, see also Ergenekon's contribution in this volume.

was able to rest again only when he had reburied the bones with a proper ceremony with an *imam* (prayer leader).[1]

According to the villagers, the souls of the departed are not just the protectors of their bones, but they may also influence the lives of living humans in diverse ways. If a deceased person is particularly holy, then praying, sacrificing or undergoing a vow at their burial place may lead to a cure, or an intercession with God to assure an auspicious outcome to their worries. If thus holy, their souls may be seen as little lights, wandering between the mounds at night at around shoulder height, visiting each other in their resting places. Contrariwise, resting places may be regarded as places where evil, and the devil is particularly likely to lurk. There are many accounts wherein the devil has appeared to people just as they pass by a certain mound and they may regard ploughing their fields there as inauspicious or even impossible.

The relationship between the mounds and the cosmology of the local people is therefore subtle and complex, both utterly pragmatic and spiritual at the same time. It is not, however, their dominant approach to divide up the heritage in their midst between periods, nor do they question whether a skeleton is Christian, Pagan or Muslim when it comes to the possibility of it being protected by its soul.[2] All burial places are potentially dangerous (or auspicious), and are treated so.

*Indigenous knowledge and boundaries*

Whilst there are a number of different ways that this noticeably tolerant interpretation of the past might be analysed, I would like to flag up two issues in particular for further thought and speculation, the first regarding locality, the second what might be termed the ideological division of labour.

Whilst I am not aware that a technical definition exists, it would seem indisputably appropriate to permit the Küçükköy villagers' interpretation of the past to fall into that general rubric that we now call 'indigenous knowledge'. However, then we immediately come across a problem. Whilst a

---

[1] These accounts are given in full in Shankland (1999b).

[2] My emphasis here, thus, is slightly different from Nixon in her most interesting chapter in his volume. The villagers are naturally aware that the mounds come from different periods, and that some of them may be Christian, or pre-Christian, but it seems to me that their predominant mode of interaction with these remains does not press them into a chronological sequence.

local view in the sense that the people in a specific locality, Küçükköy, embrace it, it is by no means purely local. Over the years that I have researched at the mound, I have slowly come to realise that the desire to view monuments of the past in general as being potential repositories of human souls shows surprising geographical extent in the region. It is prevalent in the village and in the immediate settlements around it, but extends also to the city. Konya, for example, which is one of the most modern centres in Turkey possesses an established shrine in the form of the Mausoleum of the Mevlana (the head of the Mevlevi dervishes), and there are a host of lesser shrines, which are regarded as efficacious in terms of the protection that is given by praying at them, and remain popular. These are the most acknowledged shrines, but (as Hasluck insisted) the whole process of awarding sanctity is always in flux. These beliefs in turn, may easily spread to the classical masonry that is found all around the area, and give rise in turn to the rise of a new saint's cult, for example, when a bulldozer turns up a new piece of sculpture.

Similar instances can be noted for Ankara, as well even as for Istanbul. This is in spite of the scepticism with which such ideas are regarded both by the secular Kemalist tradition, and indeed by various of the Islamist reformist groups such as the Nakşibendi brotherhood, or the increasingly resurgent Islamist political movement. Whilst there is little space here for such a diversion, this in turn might take us into an analysis of the way these seemingly heterogeneous beliefs can be grafted on to a more mainstream belief in Islam, and even perhaps, as suggested in a recent article by Stringer, back to consideration of Tyler and the possibility that human beings may possess an innate animism that they will express whatever other ideological transformation that they are forced to live through.[1]

If this is the case, then much of the 'indigenous' very quickly becomes global. If we then attempt to get round this by restricting only those instances where 'indigenous' appears to be 'local', then we may find ourselves in precisely the same problem that beset social anthropology after Malinowski, whereby by concentrating on diversity we failed to take into account just how much of human behaviour appears to be universal and therefore not culturally specific at all. This last chain of thought is admittedly speculation, but it does reinforce the point that it is highly unlikely that 'indigenous' can be equated purely with the local.

---

[1] Stringer (1999). The diverse essays in the recent volumes edited by Gazin-Swartz and Holtorf (1999) are also highly relevant in this connection.

*The local and the global*

The second, and related, point that I would like to raise for discussion is this. The particular model of the interaction and incorporation of the past within the village community that I have insisted upon in this paper, when set alongside that of the archaeologists' vision, leads to a counter-intuitive conclusion. Whilst the archaeologist's endeavour is international, it is nevertheless much more diverse, splintered and ultimately perhaps even more local than that of the villagers. It relies on Çatalhöyük being a unique, not a general phenomenon. Every piece of material from the excavation that is incorporated into the archaeological record from the site is presumed so because it is in some way discernibly different from the rest of the landscape. Indeed, the plethora of scientific analysis at the site might be characterised, I think not unfairly, by suggesting that it is continuously searching for new ways to differentiate finds from each other in ever more minute ways.

This contrasts sharply with the local view, which is much more universal in its simple assumption of equality, both pragmatically and spiritually, that all people who may rest in the archaeological remains in the landscape may protect their bones, whatever culture they may stem from and which provides a philosophy which is immensely easy to expand and generalise. It relies on an endless, simple repeated motif in which many of the characteristics crucial for the archaeologists matter not at all. Thus, it is the indigenous incorporation of the remains of the past at Çatalhöyük that is characterised by its universality, not the scientists. This contrast recalls, perhaps, Durkheim's categories of the division of labour: whereby, albeit at an ideological level, the 'mechanical' village philosophy is based on ever repeated elements, whilst the 'organic' or complex division of labour is pursued by the archaeologists at the site. Perhaps this is too simple a contrast, but it does give some idea of the differences that appear to be emerging between the two approaches.

*Conclusions*

In this paper, I have concentrated largely on three broad conceptional spheres; the international, national and local. These are only three of the surely many different ways that there are to evaluate the relationship between archaeology and the societies within which it is practiced. It seems clear though that many of my opening suppositions are supported: international archaeology has played a quite crucial role in the founding of a new, and specifically Turkish nationalism. From Çatalhöyük it feeds too, rapidly into the process that is changing our global understanding of humanity's past. Part of this encounter does consist of an interaction with local people whose indigenous way of looking at these things is both resilient, and bears no obvious resemblance to that of the archaeologists at the site.

Nevertheless, not all the consequences of the investigation seem so straightforward. At Çatalhöyük, it is clear that indigenous need not mean local, global may not mean universal. On the contrary the indigenous approach appears the more universal, and the global the more specific. I have only offered a very limited example, of this I am aware, but if this thought bears further examination, it means perhaps that we should be guarded if we attempt to think of indigenous knowledge as a thing in itself, something that can be captured within specific cultural boundaries. Rather, we should perhaps conceive of competing frameworks of human understanding that are inherently cross-cultural. That seemingly useful phrase 'glocalisation', then, that is so often used to refer to the contemporary process of reaffirmation of community or group identity may therefore be profoundly misleading. It is perhaps the scientific side of the great modernist project that may lead to the establishment of such local knowledge, whereas it is (at least on occasion) the indigenous that may be the less variegated.

My desire in this paper has been to reaffirm the importance of archaeology for anthropology in our study of the changing world, and the indigenous peoples that inhabit it. More generally though, at the conclusion of not just my contribution, but also of these volumes as a whole, I cannot but reflect that even if the separation between archaeology and anthropology was inevitable it has had profoundly deleterious as well as beneficial consequences. It is surely possible now that this division can be put to one side.

*REFERENCES*

Bicker, A., Sillitoe, P. and Pottier J. (eds.) 2004 *Development and local knowledge: new approaches to issues in natural resources management, conservation, and agriculture,* London; Routledge.

Bravo, M. 1996 *The Accuracy of Ethnoscience: a Study of Inuit Cartography and Cross-Cultural Commensurability,* Manchester; Papers in Social Anthropology, No. 2.

Cezar, M. 1987 *Müzeci ve Ressam Osman Hamdi Bey*, Istanbul; Turk Kültürune Hizmet Vakfı.

Delaney, C. 1992 *The Seed and the Soil: Gender and Cosmology in Turkish Village Society*, Berkeley; University of California Press.

Delaney, C. 1993 'Traditional Modes of Authority and Co-operation' in P. Stirling, (ed.) *Culture and Economy: Changes in Turkish Villages*, Huntingdon; Eothen Press, 140-145.

Diaz-Andreu, M. and Champion, T. (eds.) 1996 *Nationalism and Archaeology in Europe*, London; University College London Press.

Gazin-Schwartz, A. and Holtorf, C. (eds.) 1999 *Archaeology and Folklore*, London; Routledge.

Gosden, C. 1999 *Anthropology and Archaeology: a Changing Relationship*, London; Routledge.

Hodder, I. 1997 (ed.) *On the Surface: the re-opening of Çatalhöyük*, Cambridge; MacDonald Institute, and London: British Institute of Archaeology at Ankara.

Hodder, I. 1999 *The Archaeological Process: an introduction*, Oxford; Blackwells.

Mellaart, J. 1967 *Catal Huyuk, a Neolithic Town in Anatolia*, London; Thames & Hudson.

Meskell, L. (ed) 1998 *Archaeology Under Fire: Nationalism, Politics and Heritage in the Eastern Mediterranean and Middle East*, London; Routledge.

Lloyd, S. 1986 *The Interval: a Life in Near Eastern Archaeology*, Faringdon; Lloyd Collon.

Shankland, D. 1997 'The Anthropology of an Archaeological Presence' in Hodder I. (ed.), pages 218-226.

Shankland, D. 1999a *Religion and Society in Turkey*, Huntingdon, Eothen Press.

Shankland, D. 1999b 'Integrating the past: folklore, mounds and people at Çatalhöyük' in Gazin-Schwartz, A. and Holtorf, C. (eds.), pages 139-157.

Smith, T. 1678 *Remarks upon the Manners, Religion and Government of the Turks. Together with a Survey of the Seven Churches of Asia, as they now Lye in their Ruines: and a Brief Description of Constantinople*, London; Moses Pitt.

Stringer, M. 1999 'Rethinking Animism: thoughts from the infancy of our discipline' in *Journal of the Royal Anthropological Institute*, Vol. 5; 541-556.

Tapper, N. and Tapper R. 1987 'Thank God We're Secular! Aspects of Fundamentalism in a Turkish Town' in Caplan, L. (ed.) *Aspects of Religious Fundamentalism*, London; Croom Helm.

Tunbridge, J. and Ashworth, G. 1996 *Dissonant Heritage: the Management of the Past as a Resource in Conflict*, London; Wiley.

# APPENDIX 1

# AN OUTLINE CHRONOLOGY OF THE LIFE OF F.W. HASLUCK

## David SHANKLAND

**1878**     16 February; born in Bytham Lodge, Southgate, Middlesex, father Percy Pedley Hasluck. Educated at the Leys School, Cambridge.

**1896**     2 December; elected to an honorary scholarship in classics, King's College, Cambridge

**1897**     12 October; admitted to King's College

**1901**     Graduates BA with a First in the Classics Tripos, also 1901 wins the Sir William Brown Medal for Latin Eprigram.

**1904**     12 March; top in fellowship election at King's, with 15 nominations. His fellowship dissertation is based upon his work at Cyzicus.

**1904**     Becomes Librarian and Assistant Director (1906) in turn at the British School at Athens.

**1911**     Becomes Acting Director whilst Dawkins takes long leave for domestic reasons.

**1912**     24 May Announces engagement to Miss M. M. Hardie.

**1913**     Passed over for the Directorship in favour of A. Wace.

**1914**     War service as counter-intelligence office in Athens.

**1915**     22 June; Hasluck is dismissed from his post by the Managing Committee in London. Remains in Athens growing ever more sick until:

**1916**     Leaves Greece for France, and then to Switzerland to seek a cure.

**1920**     22 February; dies in Switzerland, at the Beau Revill sanatorium, Leysin.

Much of his work in preparation or published in article form is subsequently collected by Mrs F. W. Hasluck.

# APPENDIX 2

## AN OUTLINE CHRONOLOGY OF THE LIFE OF M.M. HARDIE (Mrs F. W. HASLUCK)

Roderick BAILEY

| | |
|---|---|
| **18 June 1885** | Born Margaret Masson Hardie at Chapelton, Drumblade, near Elgin, Scotland, eldest of the nine children of John Hardie, a farmer, and his wife, Margaret (nee Leslie). Early years spent in Moray-shire, partly in the care of her grandparents. Educated at Elgin Academy. |
| **1907** | Graduates BA (First Class Honours) in Classics from Aberdeen University. To Newnham College, Cambridge, on a Fullerton Scholarship. |
| **1910** | First woman to be nominated for a studentship at the British School at Athens (BSA). |
| **1911** | Leaves Cambridge with a First in Classical Tripos. Joins a dig in Anatolia under Sir William Ramsay. Meets Frederick William Hasluck. |
| **26 Sept 1912** | Marries F.W.H. at the United Free Church, Pluscarden, Elgin, Scotland. |
| **1913** | Visits Konia with F.W.H. |
| **1915-16** | Works for British intelligence in Athens, with F.W.H., and in London. |
| **1916-20** | Moves to Switzerland with F.W.H. |
| **22 Feb 1920** | Widowed. Moves to London where she assembles and edits her late husband's notes for publication. |
| **1921** | Begins ethnographic fieldwork in Macedonia and Albania. Funded by first of two Wilson travelling fellowships from Aberdeen University (1921-23 and 1926-28). |
| **1923-39** | In Albania. |

**1935**          Settles in the town of Elbasan.

**April 1939**    Leaves Albania apparently expelled by King Zog. Settles in Athens.

**1939-41**       In Athens, working in the Press Office of the British Legation.

**April 1941**    Evacuated from Athens to Alexandria. Subsequently moves to Cairo.

**Feb 1942**      Recruited by Britain's Special Operations Executive (SOE).

**1942-44**       Living and working for SOE in Istanbul, Palestine and Cairo.

**Feb 1944**      Resigns from SOE.

**Early 1944**    Diagnosed with advanced leukemia.

**Sept 1944**     Gazetted MBE (recommended in June) for her work with SOE.

**1944**          Returns to England.

**1945-47**       Living in London and Scotland and on health grounds in Switzerland and Cyprus, preparing what became *The Unwritten Law in Albania*.

**1947**          Moves to Dublin.

**18 Oct 1948**   Dies in Dublin of leukemia. Subsequently buried beside her parents in St Michael's churchyard, Dallas, Scotland.

**1954**          Publication of *The Unwritten Law in Albania*.

## Published sources used in the preparation of this Chronology

Marc Clark, 'Margaret Masson Hasluck' in John B. Allcock and Antonia Young (eds) *Black Lambs and Grey Falcons: Women Travellers in the Balkans* (Bradford: Berghahn Books, revised edition 2000). Clark's study includes a comprehensive list of Hasluck's known publications.

Richard Dawkins, 'Margaret Masson Hardie' (Obituary), *Folklore* Vol. 60, No. 2 (June 1949)

Preface by J.E. Alderson in M. Hasluck, *The Unwritten Law in Albania* (Cambridge: CUP 1954)

# APPENDIX 3

# A PRELIMINARY BIBLIOGRAPHY OF THE WORKS OF F. W. HASLUCK AND Mrs F. W. HASLUCK (M. M. HARDIE)

David GILL

## Obituaries

F. Babinger, 'F. W. Hasluck. An Obituary Notice', *Mitteilungen zur Osmanischen Geschichte*, II, Wien, 1923-1926; 321-325.

Richard M. Dawkins, 'Obituary: Margaret Masson Hasluck', *Folklore* 60 (1949) 291-92.

W.R. Halliday, 'Obituary: F.W. Hasluck', *Folklore* 31 (1920) 336-38.

## Publications

'Sculptures from Cyzicus', *Annual of the British School at Athens* 8 (1901/02) 190-96.

'An inscribed basis from Czyicus', *Journal of Hellenic Studies* 22 (1902) 126-34.

'Inscriptions from Cyzicus', *Journal of Hellenic Studies* 23 (1903) 75-91.

'Unpublished inscriptions from the Cyzicus neighbourhood', *Journal of Hellenic Studies* 24 (1904) 20-40.

(and Arthur E. Henderson) 'On the topography of Cyzicus', *Journal of Hellenic Studies* 24 (1904) 135-43.

'Dr. Covel's notes on Galata', *Annual of the British School at Athens* 11 (1904/05) 50-62.

(and Alan J.B. Wace) 'Laconia I. Excavations near Angelona', *Annual of the British School at Athens* 11 (1904/05) 81-90.

(and Alan J.B. Wace) 'Laconia II. Geraki. 1. Excavations', *Annual of the British School at Athens* 11 (1904/05) 91-99.

'Notes on the Lion group from Cyzicus', *Annual of the British School at Athens* 11 (1904/05) 151-52.

'Inscriptions from the Cyzicene district, 1904', *Journal of Hellenic Studies* 25 (1905) 56-64.

(and Richard M. Dawkins) 'Inscriptions from Bizye', *Annual of the British School at Athens* 12 (1905/06) 175-83.

'Roman Bridge on the Aesepus', *Annual of the British School at Athens* 12 (1905/06) 184-89.

'Notes on MSS. in the British Museum relating to Levant geography and travel', *Annual of the British School at Athens* 12 (1905/06) 196-215.

'Notes on coin-collecting in Mysia', *Numismatic Chronicle* 6 (fourth series) (1906) 26-36.

'Poemanenum', *Journal of Hellenic Studies* 26 (1906) 23-31.

'Bithynica', *Annual of the British School at Athens* 13 (1906/07) 285-308.

'Supplementary notes on British Museum MSS. relating to Levantine geography', *Annual of the British School at Athens* 13 (1906/07) 339-47.

'Inscriptions from the Cyzicus district, 1906', *Journal of Hellenic Studies* 27 (1907) 61-67.

(and Alan J.B. Wace) 'Laconia II. Topography. South-eastern Laconia', *Annual of the British School at Athens* 14 (1907/08) 161-82.

(and Alan J.B. Wace) 'Laconia II. Topography. East-central Laconia', *Annual of the British School at Athens* 15 (1908/09) 158-76.

'Albanian settlements in the Aegean islands', *Annual of the British School at Athens* 15 (1908/09) 223-28.

'Monuments of the Gattelusi', *Annual of the British School at Athens* 15 (1908/09) 248-69.

'Frankish remains at Adalia', *Annual of the British School at Athens* 15 (1908/09) 270-73.

'The Marmara Islands', *Journal of Hellenic Studies* 29 (1909) 6-18.

'Note on the inscription of the mausoleum frieze', *Journal of Hellenic Studies* 29 (1909) 366-67.

'The Latin monuments of Chios', *Annual of the British School at Athens* 16 (1909/10) 137-84.

'A French inscription at Adalia', *Annual of the British School at Athens* 16 (1909/10) 185-86.

'Terra Lemnia', *Annual of the British School at Athens* 16 (1909/10) 220-31.

*Cyzicus: being some account of the history and antiquities of that city, and of the district adjacent to it: with the towns of Apollonia ad Rhyndoveum, Miletupolis, Hadrianutherae, Priapus, Zeleia, etc.* Cambridge archaeological and ethnological series. Cambridge: Cambridge University Press, 1910.

'Tholos tomb at Kirk Kilisse', *Annual of the British School at Athens* 17 (1910/11) 76-79.

'The first English traveller's account of Athos', *Annual of the British School at Athens* 17 (1910/11) 103-31.

'Genoese heraldry and inscriptions at Amastra', *Annual of the British School at Athens* 17 (1910/11) 132-44.

'Heraldry of the Rhodian knights, formerly in Smyrna Castle', *Annual of the British School at Athens* 17 (1910/11) 145-50.

'Depopulation in the Aegean islands and the Turkish conquest', *Annual of the British School at Athens* 17 (1910/11) 151-81.

'Genoese lintel-reliefs in Chios', *Burlington Magazine* 18 (96) (1911) 329-30.

'Datcha - Stadia – Halikarnassos', *Annual of the British School at Athens* 18 (1911/12) 211-16.

'On imitations of the Venetian sequin struck for the Levant', *Annual of the British School at Athens* 18 (1911/12) 261-64.

'Plato in the folk-lore of the Konia plain', *Annual of the British School at Athens* 18 (1911/12) 265-69.

'Topographical drawings in the British Museum illustrating classical sites and remains in Greece and Turkey', *Annual of the British School at Athens* 18 (1911/12) 270-81.

'Archaeology in Greece 1911-1912', *Journal of Hellenic Studies* 32 (1912) 385-90.

'Contributions to the history of Levant currencies', *Annual of the British School at Athens* 19 (1912/13) 174-81.

'Graves of the Arabs in Asia Minor', *Annual of the British School at Athens* 19 (1912/13) 182-90.

'Christianity and Islam under the Sultans of Konia', *Annual of the British School at Athens* 19 (1912/13) 191-97.

'Studies in Turkish history and folk-legend', *Annual of the British School at Athens* 19 (1912/13) 198-220.

' "The Forty" ', *Annual of the British School at Athens* 19 (1912/13) 221-28.

'Constantinata', in *Essays and studies presented to William Ridgeway on his sixtieth birthday, 6 August 1913*. Cambridge: Cambridge University Press, 1913: 1-4.

'Thevet's Grand Insulaire and his travels in the Levant', *Annual of the British School at Athens* 20 (1913/14) 59-69.

'Dieudonne de Gozon and the dragon of Rhodes', *Annual of the British School at Athens* 20 (1913/14) 70-79.

'The tomb of S. Polycarp and the topography of Ancient Smyrna', *Annual of the British School at Athens* 20 (1913/14) 80-93.

'Ambiguous sanctuaries and Bektashi propaganda', *Annual of the British School at Athens* 20 (1913/14) 94-122.

'Stone cults and venerated stones in the Graeco-Turkish area', *Annual of the British School at Athens* 21 (1914/15, 1915/16) 62-83.

'Geographical distribution of the Bektashi', *Annual of the British School at Athens* 21 (1914/15, 1915/16) 84-124.

'Mosques of the Arabs in Constantinople', *Annual of the British School at Athens* 22 (1916/17, 1917/18) 157-74.

'Rise of modern Smyrna', *Annual of the British School at Athens* 23 (1918/19) 139-47.

'Prentice Pillars: the architect and his pupil', *Folklore* 30 (4) (1919) 134-35.

(and Harry Herbert Jewell) *The church of Our Lady of the hundred gates: (Panagia Hekatontapyliani) in Paros*. London: Macmillan and Co., 1920.

'Columns of ordeal', *Annual of the British School at Athens* 24 (1919/20, 1920/21) 68-77.

'The crypto-Christians of Trebizond', *Journal of Hellenic Studies* 41 (1921) 199-202.

'The Levantine coinage', *Numismatic Chronicle* 1 (fifth series) (1921) 39-91.

'The caliph Mamoun and the prophet Daniel', *Journal of Hellenic Studies* 42 (1922) 99-103.

'Heterodox tribes of Asia Minor', *Journal of the Royal Anthropological Institute of Great Britain and Ireland* 51 (1922) 310-42.

'Constantinopolitana', *Journal of Hellenic Studies* 43 (1923) 162-67.

'The multiplication of tombs in Turkey',*Journal of Hellenic Studies* 43 (1923) 168-69.

(and Margaret Masson Hardie Hasluck) *Athos and its monasteries*. London; New York: K. Paul, Trench, Trubner & Co. Ltd : E.P. Dutton & Co., 1924.

(and Margaret Masson Hardie Hasluck and Richard M. Dawkins) *Letters on religion and folklore*. London: Luzac & Co., 1926.

(and Margaret Masson Hardie Hasluck) *Christianity and Islam under the sultans*. Oxford: Clarendon Press, 1929.

## M.M. Hardie (Hasluck)

'The shrine of Mên Askaenos at Pisidian Antioch', *Journal of Hellenic Studies* 32 (1912) 111-50.

'Dionysos at Smyrna', *Annual of the British School at Athens* 19 (1912/13) 89-94.

*Kendime Englisht-Shqip or Albanian-English Reader.* Cambridge; Cambridge University Press, 1932.

*The Unwritten Law in Albania,* Cambridge; Cambridge University Press, 1954.

# CONTRIBUTORS

Marc BAER is Assistant Professor of History at University of California, Irvine. He has published in *Comparative Studies in Society* and *History*, *Gender & History*, and *IJMES*. Currently Dr. Baer is working on a monograph concerning radical changes in the Ottoman Empire in the late seventeenth century.

Roderick BAILEY graduated MA in History from the University of Edinburgh and MPhil in Historical Studies from the University of Cambridge. He returned to Edinburgh for his PhD, to research the wartime activities in Albania and Kosovo of the Special Operations Executive (SOE). He was the Alistair Horne Fellow at St Antony's College, Oxford, for 2000-01.

Ömür BAKIRER received his BA from the University of Ankara (1962), MA from Chicago (1964), and PhD from Ankara (1969). He continued post-doc studies in the US at New York University Conservation Centre and Columbia University. (1970-71). Since 1965, he has been a teaching member of the Middle East Technical University, Department of Architecture/Restoration.

Michel BALIVET is Professor of Byzantine and Turkish History at the University of Province. He has worked and researched in universities in Greece and Turkey, as well as at the French School in Istanbul. Amongst his publications are *Konya, la ville des Derviches tourneurs: un centre mystique à travers les ages* (CNRS, 2001), and *Romanie byzantine et pays de Rûm turc* (Isis, Istanbul, 1994)

David BARCHARD is a specialist on Turkey, and a former member of the Council of the British Institute of Archaeology at Ankara. In 1995 he rediscovered the late Roman village of Sykeon with Professor Peter Brown. He is currently researching Ottoman Crete and attitudes to Turkey in nineteenth century Europe.

Olga DEMETRIOU is currently Democracy 2500 Research Fellow in Aegean Studies at St Peter's College, Oxford. Her doctoral work (LSE, 2002) in social anthropology examined the politicisation of identity among the Turkish minority in the town of Komotini, northern Greece. She is currently working on questions of coexistence in Cyprus.

Edhem ELDEM is Professor of History at Boğaziçi University, Istanbul, and has worked on the Levant trade in the eighteenth century, the history of the Imperial Ottoman Bank, Ottoman funerary epigraphy, the bourgeoisie of Istanbul in the late-nineteenth and early-twentieth centuries, and Ottoman biographies of the late-nineteenth century.

George ELLINGTON is a professor of English at Salt Lake Community College and an adjunct instructor in history at the University of Utah. He has also taught in Japan, where he published two English language textbooks, and in Turkey, where he continues to conduct research on Turkish and Alevi cultures.

Matthew ELLIOT holds a PhD in history from SOAS. His book *Independent Iraq: The Monarchy and British Influence 1941–58* was published by Tauris in 1996. He runs the Kenyon Institute (formerly the British School of Archaeology) in Jerusalem, Council for British Research in the Levant.

Begümşen ERGENEKON is a social anthropologist interested in migration, urban, rural studies and ethnoarchaoelogy teaching currently at METU. She has conducted research in Norway and villages near archaeological sites at Yozgat, Çatalhöyük and Datça in Turkey. She has various publications and is currently writing a book on the Datça Peninsula (Muğla).

Alice FORBESS is currently finishing her PhD at the London School of Economics. Next year, she will be a lecturer at Goldsmiths College (London). Her research examines processes of democratisation in post-socialist Romania, focusing on the relations between the Orthodox Church, political elites and ordinary people.

David GILL is Senior Lecturer in Ancient History and Sub-Dean at the University of Wales Swansea. He is a former Rome Scholar at the British School at Rome. He was involved with the Liverpool University and British School at Athens survey of the Methana peninsula in Greece, and is currently involved with the publication of the Greek city of Euesperides in Cyrenaica.

Renée HIRSCHON is based at Oxford University, having been Professor of Social Anthropology at the University of the Aegean, Lesbos. Her major work is *Heirs Of The Greek Catastrophe* (1989: Turkish edition 2000; Tarih Vakfı). She recently edited the multi-disciplinary book *Crossing the Aegean* (2004, Berghahn) on the 1920s population exchange.

Keith HOPWOOD is Lecturer in Classics at the University of Wales Lampeter. He is interested in Classical and Byzantine Asia Minor and early Ottoman Turkey, particularly questions of piracy, law and order. He has conducted extensive field-research in Anatolia, and written widely on inter-cultural interaction during the Turkish conquest.

Amalia KAKISSIS received her BA in Classical Civilisations and Anthropology from Minnesota in 1995 and her MA in Public History/Archive Management from North Carolina State in 2000. She worked with the Heinrich Schliemann Collection at the American School of Classical Studies at Athens before becoming Archivist at the BSA in 2000.

Aphrodite KAMARA studied at Athens University and conducted postgraduate studies in Manchester and Oxford, focusing on Asia Minor and Syria in Late Antiquity. Since 1999 she has worked as a researcher at the Hellenic World Foundation. In 2002 she founded TIME Heritage, a private company working on cultural heritage management.

Ayfer KARAKAYA-STUMP is a PhD candidate in History/Middle Eastern Studies at Harvard University. She received her MA in Islamic History from The Ohio State University, and her BA in political science from Bilkent University. Her areas of interest include social and cultural history of the Ottoman Empire in the late medieval and early modern eras, with an emphasis on women and sufi orders.

Hans-Lukas KIESER is Lecturer in Modern History, particularly Near Eastern History at the Universities of Zurich, Fribourg and Geneva. His two most recent works are *Der verpasste Friede. Mission, Ethnie und Staat in den Ostprovinzen der Türkei* (Zurich 2000, Turkish translation Istanbul: İletişim forthcoming); and *Der Völkermord an den Armeniern und die Shoah* (Zurich 2002, second ed. 2003).

Michael MEEKER is Professor Emeritus at the University of California, San Diego. He received his PhD in Anthropology from the University of Chicago (1970). He has written books on poetry, society, and religion among pastoral peoples as well as on social structure, local elites, nationalism, and religion in provincial Turkey.

Irène MELIKOFF is Emeritus Professor at Strasbourg University, France. She has worked for many years in the field of early Muslim Anatolia, and in particular the Alevi-Bektashis. Amongst her published works are Hadji Bektach: *un mythe et ses avatars* (Leiden; Brill, 1998), and *Au banquet des quarante* (Istanbul; Isis, 2001).

Lucia NIXON teaches archaeology at Oxford, mainly for the Archaeology and Anthropology degree; she also lectures on archaeology and gender. Having excavated in Italy, Turkey and Greece, she currently co-directs the Sphakia Survey, an interdisciplinary project investigating landscape/human interaction in Crete from circa 3000 BC to AD 1900.

Harry NORRIS is Emeritus Professor of Arabic and Islamic Studies at London University, and has carried out his research principally in the fields of Arabic literature. More recently, he has extended his researches to Eastern Europe. Amongst his recent published work is *Popular Sufism of Eastern Europe* (RoutledgeCurzon 2003).

Birgit OLSEN has taught Modern Greek and Latin at Copenhagen University and Greek Literature and Folklore at Arkansas University. She has held visiting fellowships at Lucy Cavindish and Churchill Colleges, Cambridge, and written on Greek chapbooks and Greek folktales. She is co-translator (into Danish) of Alki Zei's novel *Achilles' Fiancée*.

Bülent ÖZDEMIR currently teaches at Balıkesir University (Turkey). He is a graduate of Marmara University, Istanbul, and holds a Master's degree from California State University (1997) and a PhD from the University of Birmingham (2000). His published work includes the monograph *Ottoman Reforms and Social Life: Reflections from Salonica, 1830-1850*.

Mehmet ÖZDOĞAN is Professor of Archaeology at the Institute of Pre-History, Istanbul University, Turkey. For many years, he has been an active excavator in Thrace and eastern Turkey, including co-directorship of the early site Çayönü. Amongst his many publications is *The Neolithic in Turkey: the cradle of civilization* (1999).

Giovanni SALMERI is Professor of Latin Epigraphy and History of Ancient Historiography at the University of Pisa. His many publications concentrate on the history of the Greek world under the Roman empire and the history of classical scholarship.

David SHANKLAND is Senior Lecturer in Social Anthropology at Bristol University. He has conducted extensive fieldwork in Anatolia, and was Assistant/Acting Director of the British Institute of Archaeology at Ankara, 1992-1995. Currently working on Turkish migration to Germany, he was Humboldt Fellow at the University of Bamberg in 2002-3.

Rustam SHUKUROV teaches at Moscow State University. His books include *A Personal History of a Bukharan Intellectual, Sadr-i Ziya's Diary* (Leiden; Brill, 2004), *The Grand Komnenoi and the Orient (1204-1461)*, (St. Petersburg; Aletheia 2001, in Russian), and, in collaboration with Dr. Sharif M. Shukurov, *Peuples d'Asie Centrale* (Paris; Syros, 1994).

Hovann SIMONIAN is a PhD candidate in the Department of Political Science at the University of Southern California. He is the co-author, with Professor Dekmejian, of *Troubled Waters: The Geopolitics of the Caspian Region* (London; I.B. Tauris) and the editor of *The Hemshin* which will be published by RoutledgeCurzon.

Charles STEWART is Reader in Anthropology at University College London. He has conducted extensive field research in Greece into topics of local religion, perceptions of the past, and dreaming. His publications include: *Demons and the Devil: Moral Imagination in Modern Greek Culture* and *Syncretism/Anti-Syncretism: The Politics of Religious Synthesis.*

Frank TROMBLEY is Reader in Religious Studies at Cardiff University. He is author of *Hellenic Religion and Christianization* (Leiden, 1993-94) and (with John W. Watt) *The Chronicle of Pseudo-Joshua the Stylite* (Liverpool, 2000). His research has dealt with the problem of religious experience in early Christian and Byzantine literature.

Fotini TSIBIRIDOU is Assistant Professor at the University of Macedonia (Thessaloniki-Greece), and author of the book *Les Pomak dans la Thrace grecque* (Paris; L'Harmattan, 2000), and many articles in Greek, French and English. Presently she is working in the Middle East exploring local perceptions of consumerism and globalization 'from below'.

Galia VALTCHINOVA graduated in history from Sofia University, and took her PhD in History 1988. Currently research fellow senior at the Bulgarian Academy of Sciences, she has taught at Sofia University and at the New Bulgarian University (Sofia), and published extensively on religion and identity in Orthodox societies in the Balkans.

Malcolm WAGSTAFF is Professor Emeritus in the University of Southampton and Visiting Professor in its School of Geography. He is chairman of the Association for the Study of Travel in Egypt and the Near East (ASTENE) and has research interests in Greece and Turkey. He is writing a biography of Colonel Leake.

Tom WINNIFRITH was Senior Lecturer in the Department of English and Comparative Literature at the University of Warwick from 1976 to 1998. As well as books on English literature he has written *The Vlachs* (1987), *Balkan Fragments* (1995) and *Badlands, Borderlands: A History of Southern Albania* (2002), all published by Duckworths.

İpek YOSMAOĞLU is a doctoral candidate at Princeton University, finishing her dissertation 'Peasants, Rebels and Soldiers: A Social History of Ethnic Conflict in Macedonia, 1897-1912'. She was fellow of the American School of Classical Studies at Athens in 2000-2002. Her publications include articles on press censorship in the Ottoman Empire.